Counseling Theory and Practice

FIRST EDITION

EDWARD NEUKRUG
Old Dominion University

BROOKS/COLE
CENGAGE Learning™

Australia • Brazil • Japan • Korea • Mexico • Singapore • Spain • United Kingdom • United States

BROOKS/COLE
CENGAGE Learning™

Counseling Theory and Practice
Edward Neukrug

Acquisitions Editor: Seth Dobrin

Developmental Editor: Art Pomponio

Assistant Editor: Nicolas Albert

Editorial Assistant: Rachel McDonald

Media Editor: Dennis Fitzgerald

Senior Marketing Manager: Trent Whatcott

Marketing Coordinator: Darlene Macanan

Marketing Communications Manager: Tami Strang

Content Project Manager: Rita Jaramillo

Creative Director: Rob Hugel

Art Director: Caryl Gorska

Print Buyer: Linda Hsu

Rights Acquisitions Account Manager, Text: Bob Kauser

Rights Acquisitions Account Manager, Image: Leitha Ethridge-Sims

Production Service: PrePressPMG

Photo Researcher: Bill Smith Group

Copy Editor: Deborah Freeland

Cover Designer: Lisa Langhoff

Cover Image Photographer: Momoko Takeda

Compositor: PrePressPMG

For product information and technology assistance, contact us at **Cengage Learning Customer & Sales Support, 1-800-354-9706.**

For permission to use material from this text or product, submit all requests online at **cengage.com/permissions.** Further permissions questions can be emailed to **permissionrequest@cengage.com.**

Library of Congress Control Number: 2009942949

Student Edition:

ISBN-13: 978-0-495-00884-2

ISBN-10: 0-495-00884-2

Brooks/Cole
20 Davis Drive
Belmont, CA 94002-3098
USA

Cengage Learning is a leading provider of customized learning solutions with office locations around the globe, including Singapore, the United Kingdom, Australia, Mexico, Brazil, and Japan. Locate your local office at **www.cengage.com/global.**

Cengage Learning products are represented in Canada by Nelson Education, Ltd.

To learn more about Brooks/Cole, visit **www.cengage.com/brookscole**
Purchase any of our products at your local college store or at our preferred online store **www.CengageBrain.com.**

Printed in the United States of America
1 2 3 4 5 6 7 13 12 11 10

Brief Contents

Contents

SECTION IV   Post-Modern Approaches   381

Chapter 12   Narrative Therapy   383

Preface

PURPOSE OF THE BOOK

A helper's theory of counseling and psychotherapy is the driving force behind how the professional practices, whether the helper is a human service professional, counselor, social worker, or psychologist. Thus, it is critical that counselors and psychotherapists are solidly grounded in the theories that have most impacted the helping professions. Because theories are the bedrock of the helping relationship, it is essential that you begin to develop your own theory of counseling and psychotherapy. Reading *Counseling Theory and Practice* will be an important step toward that goal.

With the above in mind, this book will provide you with (1) an understanding of what it means to be an effective helper, (2) the opportunity to learn the classic theories of counseling and psychotherapy, (3) the ability for you to review some recent, popular theories of counseling and psychotherapy, (4) a brief overview of extensions, adaptations, and spinoffs of the major theories, and (5) the opportunity for you to reflect on your own approach to conducting counseling and psychotherapy.

ORGANIZATION OF THE BOOK

Chapter 1, Becoming an Effective Counselor and Psychotherapist, will help orient you to the text. The beginning of the chapter examines research on the effectiveness of counseling and psychotherapy, provides a discussion about the difference between counseling and psychotherapy, and then explores the importance of a theorist's view of human nature. Here you will have the opportunity to develop your own view of human nature. To facilitate this process, you will be referred to a Web site (http://www.odu.edu/~eneukrug/therapists/survey.html), or to Appendix A, where you can take a 20-minute instrument that will help you define your view of human nature, the theories with which you most identify, and the conceptual orientation that is most like your own. The theories and the conceptual orientations highlighted in this survey go hand-in-hand with the theories and conceptual orientations you will find in Sections 1, 2, 3, and 4 (Chapters 2 through 13) of the text.

Chapter 1 examines the importance of developing your own theory and the stages of development you are likely to pass through as you develop your own integrative (formerly called "eclectic") approach to counseling and psychotherapy. Intimately related to doing effective counseling is being ethical in the manner in which you practice and being effective when working with diverse clients. Thus, this chapter also examines ethics, ethical decision-making, and competent cross-cultural counseling. The chapter concludes with an overview of the text that allows you to understand how the theories you will read are organized into different conceptual orientations.

Sections 1, 2, 3, 4, and 5 (Chapters 2 through 15) of the text describe the theories. Section 1 (Chapters 2 through 4) houses the conceptual approaches that are "psychodynamic" in nature. This section begins with a brief explanation of what it means to be psychodynamic followed by three psychodynamic theories: psychoanalysis, analytical psychology, and individual psychology. Section 2 (Chapters 5 through 7) houses the conceptual approaches that are "existential–humanistic" in their focus. This section begins with a brief explanation of what it means to be existential–humanistic and is followed by three theories: existential therapy, Gestalt therapy, and person-centered counseling. Section 3 (Chapters 8 through 11) describes cognitive–behavioral approaches, begins with a definition of this conceptual orientation, and then goes on to examine four approaches: behavior therapy, rational emotive behavior therapy, cognitive therapy, and reality therapy. Section 4 (Chapters 12 and 13) begins with a description of post-modern theories, and then goes on to describe two theories of this relatively new conceptual approach: narrative therapy and solution-focused brief therapy (SFBT). The last section of the book, Section 5, describes extensions, adaptations, and spinoffs to the theories already described. Chapter 14 briefly describes a number of individual approaches to counseling and psychotherapy, and Chapter 15 describes a number of couples and family therapy approaches. With hundreds of theories to choose from, it was challenging to decide which theories most deserve to be in those last two chapters.

To a large degree, the book is historical in nature, in that it starts with the oldest of the theories (psychoanalysis) in Section 1 and loosely works its way, chronologically, to the most recent and modern approaches later in the book. Time period and context greatly affected the development of each theory, and it is for this reason that there are extensive biographies of the theorist most associated with each of the theories in Chapters 2 through 13. Background, history, and context are also offered in Chapters 14 and 15. I encourage you to examine how history and context affected the development of each theory, its efficacy, and its impact on diverse clients. To help understand context, you are periodically referred to a Web site I have been developing called "Stories of the Great Therapists" (http://www.odu.edu/sgt). Here, I am collecting interesting, sometimes profound, and once in a while funny oral stories about some of the theorists you will read about in the book. I hope you enjoy this different type of learning.

Within Chapters 2 through 13 you will find background information on the theorist or theorists most associated with each theory; the view of human nature that drives each theory; key concepts and important techniques of every theory; the therapeutic process related to each theory; social; cultural; and spiritual issues related to the theory being examined; and research on the efficacy of each theory. Since Chapters 14 and 15 provide information about multiple theories, these chapters are set up somewhat differently, but similar information can be found within them.

In addition to the electronic survey (hard copy found in Appendix A) that helps you define your theoretical orientation and the "Stories of the Great Therapists" Web site, which offers additional background information about each theory, a number of other tools can be found to help you understand the theories in this text. For instance, after reading the theories presented in Chapters 2 through 13, you are encouraged to turn to Appendix B, where you can observe how one member of the Miller family has grown from his or her experience in the therapy that you just read about. Similarly, after reading Chapter 15, you will have an opportunity to examine how the whole family experiences family counseling. Also, throughout the text, you will find boxes, figures, and experiential exercises that will help to highlight a point, elucidate an idea, and provide additional learning tools, sometimes in a very personal manner. Key words and important names at the end of every chapter offer a summary of the important aspects learned in the chapter and highlight important figures discussed.

Finally, a DVD has been developed to help you understand each of the theories presented in Chapters 2 through 13. Your instructor has access to this DVD and may show it in class. The DVD includes a brief description of each of the theories, a short role-play between a therapist and a client that elucidates some aspect of the theory (generally, these "role-plays" are "real" situations), and a post role-play discussion between me and the individual who played the therapist. In the three role-plays in which I am the therapist, my colleague, Garrett McAuliffe, has a discussion with me regarding my role-plays. I think you'll find the DVD interesting and thought-provoking. If you do not view the DVD in class, you can find verbatim transcripts of the role-plays by clicking "student downloads" at: www.cengage.com/counseling/neukrug/CTP1e.

SPECIAL AIDS AND UNIQUE TOOLS TO HELP
YOU LEARN THE THEORIES

Some of unique aids and tools that will help you learn the theories in this text include the following

1. *Discussion about theory*: Chapter 1 allows you to examine the efficacy of counseling and psychotherapy, as well as the difference between counseling

and psychotherapy, and helps you on your journey toward building your own theory.

2. *Electronic survey to assess your theoretical orientation*: In Chapter 1, you will be referred to a survey that can help you identify your view of human nature and the theory with which you are mostly aligned (see www.odu.edu/~eneukrug/therapists/survey.html) (hard copy can be found in Appendix A).

3. *Oral histories of some of the theorists*: At different points throughout the text, you will be referred to an oral history Web site ("Stories of the Great Therapists"), where you can hear stories about some of the theorists discussed in the text (http://www.odu.edu/sgt).

4. *The Miller family*: Referred to throughout the text and found in Appendix B, you will find descriptions of different members of the Miller family participating in most of the therapies described the book.

5. *Role-plays in DVD format*: Your instructor has access to a DVD that describes each of the major theories, offers a role-play that demonstrates one or more aspects of the theory, and provides a discussion about the role-play (verbatim transcripts are also available by clicking "student downloads" at: www.cengage.com/counseling/neukrug/CTP1e).

6. *Biographies.* In most chapters, you will find extensive biographies about the major theorist described in the chapter and which provides the historical context in which the theory was formed.

7. *Boxes, figures, and experiential exercises*: Throughout the text, you will find boxes, figures, and experiential exercises that help to highlight a point, elucidate an idea, and provide additional learning tools.

8. *View of human nature, key concepts, important techniques, and the therapeutic process*: These essential elements are described for all of the theories in Chapters 2 through 13 as well many of the theories in Chapters 14 and 15.

9. *Social, cultural, and spiritual issues*: Each of these areas is discussed at the end of most chapters.

10. *Efficacy*: Evidence that supports or contradicts the theory's use is offered at the end of most chapters.

11. *Key words and important names*: Words and names highlighted during the chapters are summarized at the end of each chapter.

12. *Ethics*: The use of ethical codes and the ethical decision-making process is discussed in the text, particularly in Chapter 1. (URLs of the codes of ethics of a wide variety of professional association can be accessed by clicking "student downloads" or "instructor resources" at: www.cengage.com/counseling/neukrug/CTP1e).

ANCILLARIES TO THE TEXT

For the instructor, there are a number of ancillaries to assist in assuring student learning. These include the following:

1. *Text Bank*: An extensive text bank is available by clicking "instructor resources" at: www.cengage.com/counseling/neukrug/CTP1e.

2. *Teaching Tips*: These suggestions, found by clicking "instructor resources" at: www.cengage.com/counseling/neukrug/CTP1e, are based on the way I teach a theories course and may provide the instructor with possible pedagogical suggestions as he or she navigates through the chapters.

3. *Sample Syllabus*: A sample syllabus is available by clicking "instructor resources" at: www.cengage.com/counseling/neukrug/CTP1e.

4. *Electronic Survey To Help Student's Assess Their Theoretical Orientation*: As previously noted, in Chapter 1 students are referred to a survey that can help them identify their view of human nature and the theory with which they are mostly aligned. I urge you to have you students take this important survey (www.odu.edu/~eneukrug/therapists/survey.html) (hard copy can be found in Appendix A)?

5. *Oral Histories of Some of the Theorists*: Throughout the text students will be referred to an oral history website (Stories of the Great Therapists) where they can hear stories about some of the theorists discussed in the text (www.odu.edu/sgt). If you have any stories, please contact me!

6. *The Miller Family*: At different points throughout the text students will be referred to a case study about one member of the Miller family participating in the therapy described in the chapter they are reading. In Chapter 15, they can read about the whole family participating in family counseling. These case studies can be found in Appendix B.

7. *DVD Role-Plays*: Included with the instructor's desk copy of the text is a DVD that describes each of the major theories, offers a role-play that demonstrates one or more aspects of the theory, and provides a discussion about the role play (verbatim transcripts are also available by clicking "student downloads" or "instructor resources" at: www.cengage.com/counseling/neukrug/CTP1e). This DVD can be shown during the lecture that coincides with the role-play. If the instructor has not received a copy of the DVD, he or she should contact his or her Brooks/Cole representative.

8. The URLs of the ethics codes of a wide variety of professional associations can be accessed by clicking "student downloads" or "instructor resources" at: www.cengage.com/counseling/neukrug/CTP1e.

ACKNOWLEDGMENTS

Many people were a great help to me as I wrote this book. First, Art Pomponio, my developmental editor, challenged me in helpful ways and supported me throughout this process. His ideas were great, and his knowledge deep. I gratefully thank him for his ongoing effort toward the successful completion of this book. Also, Cheree Hammond spent endless hours developing the case studies for the Miller Family. Her beautiful writing, thoughtful ideas, and ongoing support are especially appreciated. Cheree also helped write two sections in Chapter 14.

In addition to Art's and Cheree's help, a number of well-known experts on specific theories reviewed targeted chapters of the text. Their critical feedback made each of these chapters better. Their names and the chapters they reviewed are listed on page xxiii. Also, a number of educators who teach theories courses reviewed this text and gave me valuable feedback. They include Mary S. Adamek, University of Iowa; Mary Jo Blazek, University of Maine at Augusta; Normajean Cefarelli, Southern Connecticut State University; Steven Cockerham, Eastern Tennessee State University; Dolores McCarthy, John Jay College; Mary McGlamery, Angelo State University; Paul Niemiec, Duquense University; Elizabeth R. O'Brien, University of Tennessee at Chattanooga; Lois C. Pasapane, Palm Beach Community College; Ken Oliver, Quincy University; Lesley Travers, Casper College; Antony R. White, University of North Dakota; and Skip Dine Young, Hanover College. A special thanks goes to Nancy Nolan and her students from Vanderbilt University, who used and reviewed some early chapters of the text.

From Brooks/Cole and affiliated companies, I am indebted to a number of people. First, Seth Dobrin, Acquisitions Editor for Brooks/Cole, has done a great job in helping me think things through as I wrote this book and in offering me ideas for the book. He also was a great support in moving me toward finishing the book. And, a special thanks to my former acquisitions editors, Marquita Flemming and Lisa Gebo, without whom this book would never have been written. Others of critical assistance from Brooks/Cole include: Rita Jaramillo, Project Manager for the book; Nic Albert, Assistant Editor, who helped with the ancillaries; Rachel McDonald, Editorial Assistant who helped out in numerous ways; Bob Kauser who assisted with permissions, Sarah Bonner who assisted with graphics and pictures. Also, a special thanks to Preetha Sreekanth from PrePressPMG and Deborah Freeland (the freelance copyeditor), who were instrumental in copy editing and in assuring that the book was ready for production.

Others also helped me. For instance, Julia Forman and Suzan Thompson were critical in their contributions by writing two sections of Chapter 14. Many students assisted me in multiple ways, and the book could not have been finished without them. They include Betty Davis, Africa Costa, Scott Jaeschke, Sarah Joyce, Jesse Mitchel, and Sherry Todd. Some others who assisted me include: Susanna Chamberlain, Jeff Moe, Howard Kirschenbaum, John Lanci, Garrett McAuliffe, and Henry T. Stein, and Bob Daniel.

And finally, thank you to Emma, Hannah, and Kristina for your thoughtful ideas and in helping me choose the cover. I love you all.

Chapter	Reviewer*
Chapter 1: Becoming an Effective Counselor and Psychotherapist	Ted Remley, Old Dominion University. ACA Fellow.
Chapter 2: Psychoanalysis	Allen Bishop, Pacifica Graduate Institute. Certified Psychoanalyst.
Chapter 3: Analytical Therapy	Thomas Elsner, Pacifica Graduate Institute. President, C.G. Jung Study Center of Southern California.
Chapter 4: Individual Psychology (Adlerian Therapy)	Richard E. Watts, Sam Houston University. Director: Center for Research & Doctoral Studies in Counselor Education. Diplomate in Adlerian Psychology.
Chapter 5: Existential Therapy	Cheree Hammond, James Madison University. Crossroads Counseling Center.
Chapter 6: Gestalt Therapy	Paula Justice, Old Dominion University. Certified Gestalt Therapist.
Chapter 7: Person-Centered Counseling	Howard Kirschenbaum, University of Rochester. Professor Emeritus. Carl Rogers's Biographer.
Chapter 8: Behavior Therapy	Bryan Porter, Old Dominion University. Behavioral Researcher.
Chapter 9: Rational Emotive Behavior Therapy	Korrie Allen, Eastern Virginia Medical School. Certified REBT Therapist.
Chapter 10: Cognitive Therapy	Garrett McAuliffe, Old Dominion University.
Chapter 11: Reality Therapy/ Choice Therapy	Bob Wubbolding. Director, Center for Reality Therapy.
Chapter 12: Narrative Therapy	John Winslade, California State University, San Bernadino. Garrett McAuliffe, Old Dominion University.
Chapter 13: Solution-Focused Behavior Therapy	Richard E. Watts. Director: Center for Research & Doctoral Studies in Counselor Education.
Chapter 14: Adaptations, Spinoffs, and New Directions	Julia Forman, Sherry Todd, Garrett McAuliffe, Suzan Thompson, Old Dominion University. Cheree Hammond, James Madison University; Crossroads Counseling Center.
Chapter 15: Couples and Family Therapy	Jack Grimes. Family Solutions, Inc.

*A special thanks to Art Pomponio for his feedback and suggestions throughout the text.

About the Author

Born and raised in New York City, Dr. Ed Neukrug obtained his B.A. in psychology from SUNY Binghamton, his M.S. in counseling from Miami University of Ohio, and his doctorate in counselor education from the University of Cincinnati.

After directing a counseling program at Notre Dame College in New Hampshire, he accepted a position at Old Dominion University, in Norfolk, Virginia, where he currently is a professor of counseling and human services. Dr. Neukrug has worked as a crisis and substance abuse counselor, a mental health center therapist, an associate school psychologist, a school counselor, and as a psychologist and licensed professional counselor in private practice. He has also held a variety of positions in professional associations and has published numerous articles and received a number of grants over the years. Dr. Neukrug He has taught for close to thirty years and has received numerous awards for his teaching and writing.

In recent years, Dr. Neukrug has developed a series of DVDs that demonstrate therapeutic practice ("Skills and Tools" and "Theories in Action"). Also, he has developed the *Stories of the Great Therapists* Web site, where one can listen to short stories that illuminate the lives of famous counseling and psychology theorists, such as Carl Rogers and B. F. Skinner (http://www.odu.edu/sgt). Another Web site offers a survey where individuals can determine their theoretical orientation. These, and other links, can be found at his homepage at http://www.odu.edu/~eneukrug.

Books he has written include *Counseling Theory and Practice; The World of the Counselor; Experiencing the World of the Counselor; Theory, Practice, and Trends in Human Services: An Introduction; Skills and Techniques for Human Service Professionals; Skills and Tools for Today's Counselors and Psychotherapists;* and *Essentials of Testing and Assessment for Counselors, Social Workers, and Psychologists.* For information about his books and DVDs, go to http://www.brookscole.com.

Dr. Neukrug is married to Kristina Williams Neukrug and has two children, Hannah and Emma.

Chapter 1

Becoming an Effective Counselor and Psychotherapist

An Introduction to the Text

Learning Goals

- To briefly review the efficacy of counseling and psychotherapy and identify attributes that appear to be important to its effectiveness.
- To discuss the difference between counseling and psychotherapy.
- To stress the importance of theory when practicing counseling and psychotherapy.
- To define "view of human nature" and to examine your view of human nature.
- To understand the relationship between theory and the development of an integrative approach to counseling and psychotherapy.
- To identify a number of stages you are likely to pass through as you develop your approach to counseling, including chaos, coalescence, theoretical multiplicity, and metatheory.
- To review the historical background and purpose of ethical codes.
- To identify a number of major ethical topics found in most ethical codes that are relevant to the counseling relationship.
- To learn about models of ethical decision-making, including problem-solving models, moral models, and developmental models.
- To highlight a number of best-practice tools to lessen the likelihood of an ethical violation or malpractice suit.
- To contrast culturally incompetent counseling with culturally competent counseling.
- To learn about the Multicultural Counseling Competencies and the RESPECTFUL model of counseling, and to provide a method of ensuring helpers are addressing the needs of those who have been traditionally disenfranchised in counseling.
- To offer an overview of the text that allows you to understand how the theories you will read about are organized into different conceptual orientations.

I certainly am a better counselor and psychotherapist than I used to be! When I first started doing counseling, I didn't have a well-formed theory. I struggled with ethical decisions, and I didn't attend to cross-cultural differences as much as I could have. My clients caught the brunt of my ignorance and naivety. I hope that I was still helpful, but perhaps I was not as helpful as I could have been or as I eventually became. As I became more seasoned, I developed a clearer theory that guided my practice, and I became more knowledgeable about my ethical code and more able to make ethical decisions. My knowledge of cross-cultural counseling increased and, I believe, my skills at working with diverse clients became enhanced. Also, knowledge of my own cultural biases became sharper. Some of my early "mistakes" were caused by lack of knowledge, but time in the helping professions added to my ability to think in more complex ways and helped refine the way that I did counseling and psychotherapy. It takes a combination of knowledge, skills, and self-awareness to become a master therapist. I'm not saying I'm there yet, but I hope I am taking steps to move in that direction.

This chapter will examine some important issues that enhance one's ability to be an effective counselor or psychotherapist, but first, we will start by answering the question: Do counseling and psychotherapy work? After all, it doesn't make sense to do any of this if what we're doing doesn't work! Then, we will examine the difference between counseling and psychotherapy; the importance of theory, including the development of your view of human nature and how one's theory changes over time; ethical issues and ethical decision-making; and important cross-cultural concerns that we all must address. The chapter will conclude with a brief introduction to the layout of the text. Enjoy.

DO COUNSELING AND PSYCHOTHERAPY WORK?

In 1952, Eysenck examined 24 uncontrolled studies that looked at the effectiveness of psychotherapy on treatment outcomes and found that "roughly two-thirds of a group of neurotic patients will recover or improve to a marked extent within about two years of the onset of their illness, *whether they are treated by means of psychotherapy or not*" (p. 322). Although Eysenck's research was found to have serious methodological flaws, it did lead to debate concerning the effectiveness of counseling and resulted in hundreds of studies that examined its usefulness. Years later, analyses of many studies revealed something very different than what Eysenck had found:

> When counseling effectiveness is calculated by determining the number of clients who improved, the results are amazingly similar across various studies. On the basis of both client and counselor ratings, approximately

22% of clients made significant gains, 43% made moderate changes, while 27% made some improvement ... (Sexton, 1993, p. 82)

But what is it that makes counseling effective? In recent years, it has become increasingly evident that certain kinds of treatment methodologies work more effectively with certain kinds of presenting problems. Called "evidenced-based practice" (Norcross, Beutler, & Levant, 2006; Stout & Hayes, 2005), or using "treatment methodologies for which there is scientifically collected evidence that the treatment works" (Hayes, 2005, p. 1), this practice is quickly becoming commonplace. In addition, it has also become clear that some qualities of the therapist seem to show efficacy regardless of the approach being employed. For instance, the ability to show empathy, the capacity to build a therapeutic alliance, and adherence to a theoretical approach (regardless of the approach) all seem to be critical factors in positive client outcomes (Beutler et al., 2004; Lambert & Ogles, 2004; Sexton, 1999; Wampold, 2001). Finally, as you might expect, the personal resources that the client brings with him or her is critical to successful outcomes. So, it seems that counseling and psychotherapy are effective, but what is actually the difference between the two? Let's take a look.

THE DIFFERENCE BETWEEN COUNSELING AND PSYCHOTHERAPY

In the training of helpers today, the words *counseling* and *psychotherapy* are generally used interchangeably in textbooks. In fact, most counseling and psychotherapy texts do not make a distinction between these words. Despite this lack of distinction, a differentiation between counseling and psychotherapy is often made by the average person, frequently made by students, and commonly made by professors. Acknowledging this common usage distinction, one can represent these differences by placing counseling and psychotherapy on opposite ends of a continuum when looking at a number of attributes typically associated with therapy (see Figure 1.1).

Although such distinctions are commonly made by the lay public, students, and even professors, they are generally not highlighted by theorists or theory texts. The theory is the same whether one is practicing counseling or psychotherapy. However, whether one ends up practicing counseling or psychotherapy, as defined above, is probably dependent on a number of factors, including:

- The expectations of the client.
- Whether the setting in which the helper works supports counseling or psychotherapy.
- Whether the specific approach the helper practices lends itself more to counseling or to psychotherapy.
- How comfortable the helper is in guiding the client toward psychotherapy.

Counseling		Psychotherapy
short-term	>>>>>>>>>>>>>>>>	long-term
surface issues	>>>>>>>>>>>>>>>>	deep-seated issues
"massaging" personality	>>>>>>>>>>>>>>>>	personality reconstruction
here and now	>>>>>>>>>>>>>>>>	there and then
conscious	>>>>>>>>>>>>>>>>	unconscious
moderate client revelations	>>>>>>>>>>>>>>>>	deep client revelations
uncomfortable	>>>>>>>>>>>>>>>>	painful
focused issues	>>>>>>>>>>>>>>>>	life stories

F I G U R E   1.1   The Differences between Counseling and Psychotherapy

- How much time the helper and client will have to work together (psychotherapy takes longer).
- Whether there is a fit between the client and helper that would allow the helper to practice psychotherapy if the client wanted to go that way.
- Whether the helper has worked through his or her own issues that will allow the in-depth work that is necessary in psychotherapy.
- The belief of the helper in the efficacy of practicing counseling or practicing psychotherapy (the belief that one approach might work better than another).

Based on the distinction made in Figure 1.1, some of the theories discussed in this book are clearly leaning more toward counseling, while others lean heavily toward psychotherapy. For instance, solution-focused brief therapy (SFBT) tends to lean toward the side of counseling. In fact, many SFBT therapists would argue that psychotherapy is not needed by most clients. In contrast, psychoanalysis is heavily oriented toward the psychotherapy end of the continuum. Psychoanalysts would argue that real healing can only occur with psychotherapy. Many of the theories, on the other hand, could easily fit on either end of the continuum. So, as you read the text, consider the following:

- How comfortable are you with doing counseling or psychotherapy?
- What would you prefer to do: counseling or psychotherapy?
- Which theories lend themselves more toward counseling versus psychotherapy?
- Taking the last item into consideration, which theories would you likely include in the manner in which you do counseling?

Finally, in this book, my approach will be to use the words *counseling* and *psychotherapy* interchangeably. This does not necessarily endorse the notion that they are the same, but makes it much easier for me not to have to discern whether one approach is "counseling" while another one is "psychotherapy." So, you be the decider as to which is counseling or psychotherapy when you read the chapters.

THEORY

Theory—what is it, and why is it important? This section will answer that by examining the importance of theory in the delivery of counseling and psychotherapy as well as the process that one uses in developing one's theory, which generally includes knowing one's view of human nature and examining how an integrative approach to counseling develops over the span of one's career.

Why Have a Theory of Counseling and Psychotherapy?

Superstring theory: The universe is composed, not of subatomic particles … but of tiny strings tied together at the ends to form loops. These strings exist in a ten-dimensional universe, which some time before the Big Bang cracked into two pieces, a four-dimensional universe (ours; that's three dimensions plus time) and a six-dimensional universe that [is] so small we haven't been able to see it. What physicists have been thinking of as subatomic particles are actually vibrations of the strings, like notes played on a violin. (Jones & Wilson, 2006, p. 508)

Do you remember learning about the atom and how it is composed of a nucleus with electrons floating around it like a solar system? And, we were told, all matter is made up of these atoms. What if this is not the case? What if this theory—which seems to fit our way of understanding the world—is incorrect? Today, some say the atom, and its relationship to matter, may not be what it appeared to be. Instead, they say that the atom is actually a series of strings that lead into other, parallel universes, and what we call the "atom" is simply the vibration of these strings. Whether superstring theory will be "proven" to define the intricacies of the universe (and other universes!) is a mystery we will have to live with for a while. However, the idea that theories evolve as our understanding of the world evolves is a known fact. The development of new knowledge periodically leads to **paradigm shifts** where a marked change in the perception of our world takes place. So it was with the discovery that the earth was round and with Einstein's theory of relativity, and so it will be when a cure for AIDS is found or a new counseling theory is developed. New knowledge is based on sound scientific hunches, connected to all of what has come before, and only later corroborated by scientific evidence.

In the arena of counseling and psychotherapy theories, in the late 1800s, Freud put forth the first comprehensive theory of psychotherapy and created a shift in thinking in the Western world. His ideas about the unconscious, intrapsychic forces, and sexuality greatly changed the way the Western world perceived human nature—and still does until this day. However, his theory was not developed in a vacuum; it evolved because others before him had pondered similar questions. Over the years, we have learned that we can discard some of Freud's theory, accept other aspects, and continue to examine the rest. Whether it's psychoanalysis or New Age therapy, theory offers us a framework from which to work by providing us with a comprehensive system of conceptualizing our clients' problems, applying techniques, and predicting client change (Neukrug & Schwitzer, 2006). Having a theory tells the world that we are not haphazard in the way in which we apply knowledge, because to "function without theory is to operate without placing events in some order and thus to function meaninglessly" (Hansen, Rossberg, & Cramer, 1994, p. 9). In addition, theories are **heuristic**; that is, they are researchable and testable and ultimately allow us to discard those aspects shown to be ineffective and build on those aspects that seem to work best. With regard to becoming a helper, as new knowledge in the helping professions is created, the helper will have at his or her disposal new and more effective ways of mastering the helping relationship. And one thing I can guarantee: As you embrace new knowledge and new theories, whatever theory you start out practicing will look different than the theory you employ when you retire.

Developing Your Theory, Part 1: Your View of Human Nature

Probably the most important aspect of any theory is its *view of human nature*, which is critical to the formation of the theory's template. Typically, the view of human nature held by each theorist takes into account the effects that biology, genetics, and environment have on the personality development of the individual. So, if I believe that an individual's behavior is determined by genetics, my theory will reflect this notion. On the other hand, if I believe that the environment holds the key to personality formation, then my theory will reflect this belief. If you complete the exercise in Box 1.1, you can begin to get a sense of your view of human nature.

In this text, there are 12 individual approaches to therapy highlighted, each of which is based on a unique view of human nature. If you go to http://www.odu.edu/~eneukrug/therapists/survey.html or Appendix A of this text, you can take an instrument to examine which theory is most like your view of human nature, and you will also be able to discover with which therapeutic school you are most aligned (psychodynamic, existential–humanistic, cognitive–behavioral, or post-modern). (Note: The online version is much more "user-friendly.")

Please take the instrument in Appendix A
or
Online at: http://www.odu.edu/~eneukrug/therapists/survey.html

---

B o x 1.1   Understanding Your View of Human Nature

For each of the following four statements, circle *all* items that best describe your beliefs. Then, using your responses as a guide, develop a paragraph describing your view of human nature. Feel free to add other items.

1. At birth, I believe people are born:
    a. good
    b. bad
    c. neutral
    d. with original sin
    e. restricted by their genetics
    → f. with a growth force that allows them to change throughout life
    g. capable of being anything they want to be
    h. with sexual drives that consciously and unconsciously affects their lives
    i. with aggressive drives that consciously and unconsciously affect their lives
    j. with social drives that consciously and unconsciously affect their lives
    k. with other attributes: _____

2. Personality development is most influenced by:
    a. genetics
    b. learning
    c. early child-rearing patterns
    d. drives
    e. values that we are taught
    → f. environment
    g. relationships with others
    h. biology
    i. instincts
    j. modeling the behavior of others
    k. cultural influences
    l. developmental issues (e.g., puberty)
    m. conscious decisions
    n. the unconscious
    o. language

    p. feelings of inferiority
    q. primordial images
    r. other _____

3. As people grow older, I believe they are:
    a. capable of major changes in their personalities
    b. capable of moderate changes in their personalities
    c. capable of minor changes in their personalities
    d. incapable of change in their personalities
    e. determined by their early childhood experiences
    f. determined by their genetics
    g. determined by how they were conditioned and reinforced
    h. determined by unconscious motivations
    i. able to transcend or go beyond early childhood experiences

4. Change is likely to be most facilitated by a focus on:
    a. the conscious mind
    b. the unconscious mind
    c. thoughts
    d. behaviors
    e. feelings
    f. early experiences
    g. the past
    h. the present
    i. the future
    j. the use of medications
    k. unfinished business
    l. repressed memories
    m. biology
    n. language
    o. memories
    p. one's "real" self
    q. other: _____

Developing Your Theory, Part 2: Integrative Counseling and Psychotherapy

The idea that a helper might be able to combine varying theoretical approaches into his or her own way of working with clients is not new (Gold & Stricker, 2006; O'Leary, 2006). In fact, today, about one-fourth of mental health professionals identify themselves as using a purely integrative approach

(Norcross, Bike, & Evans, 2009). In many ways, as most of us mature as professionals, we take on a more integrative approach as our adherence to one theoretical orientation becomes less rigid and we incorporate other ideas into our way of doing counseling and psychotherapy.

Formerly called **eclecticism**, an **integrative approach** is when the helper develops a core theory by integrating elements from different theories into his or her approach. Unfortunately, a therapist who uses an integrative approach is sometimes practicing a mishmash of techniques that have little or no underlying theoretical basis. This type of atheoretical eclecticism is counterintuitive and is considered by many to be "shooting-from-the-hip" therapy. Integration of this kind is not based on systematic research and is detrimental to the goals of our profession and, more important, to the successful treatment of clients. Effective helpers, on the other hand, know that an integrative approach involves a deliberate effort at integrating techniques into the helper's repertoire. Although different models attempt to explain this process (cf. Brooks-Harris, 2008; O'Leary & Murphy, 2006; Stricker & Gold, 2006; O'Leary, 2006), most of these models address some common elements that lead me to view an integrative approach as a developmental process that starts with chaos and ends with a commitment to a metatheory (see Figure 1.2).

*Stage 1: **Chaos**:* This initial stage of developing an eclectic approach is based on a limited knowledge of theory and involves moment-to-moment subjective

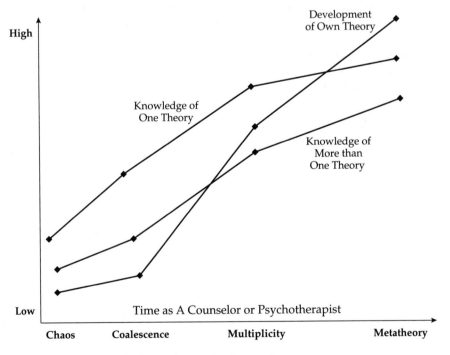

FIGURE 1.2 Developing an Integrative Approach

judgments of the helper. Often practiced while students are still in training programs, this approach is the helper's first attempt to pull together different theoretical orientations, and if used with clients is likely to be of limited help.

*Stage 2: **Coalescence***: As theory is learned, most helpers begin to drift toward adherence to one approach. Although they mostly ascribe to one theory, they are beginning to use some techniques from other approaches when they believe it would be helpful to clients.

*Stage 3: **Multiplicity***: During this stage, helpers have thoroughly learned one theory and are beginning to gain a solid knowledge of one or more other theories. They are also now beginning to realize that any of the theories may be equally effective for many clients. This knowledge presents a dilemma for the counselor: What theoretical perspective should I adhere to, and how might I combine, or use at different times, two or more theoretical perspectives so that I could offer the most effective treatment (Spruill & Benshoff, 2000)? Ultimately, this helper is able to feel facile with different approaches and is willing to sometimes integrate other approaches into his or her main approach.

*Stage 4: **Metatheory***: At this point, the helper has become a master therapist and has settled into a theoretical orientation based on his or her work with clients and the gathering of knowledge about theories over the years. This master therapist has a metatheory that drives what he or she does. This metatheory is a thought-through approach that defines the theoretical nature of the therapist's work (e.g., psychodynamic, humanistic, cognitive–behavioral, post-modern, systems, etc.), and usually incorporates a number of different elements from many theories into the helper's way of doing counseling and therapy. However, the elements chosen from other approaches have a "flavor" that reflects the helper's unique style of helping. For instance, the "humanist" will use behavioral techniques but use them from the framework of the humanistic perspective. This ability to assimilate techniques from varying theoretical perspective takes knowledge, time, and finesse.

If you are just beginning your journey as a counselor, you should expect to eventually pass through these four stages as you begin to sort through the various theoretical approaches and develop your own unique style of counseling.

ETHICS IN THE COUNSELING RELATIONSHIP

Regardless of the theoretical approach you take in your journey as a counselor or psychotherapist, you will face some thorny ethical issues. It is therefore critical that you have a strong background in ethics, that you are facile with your ethical code, and that you are able to effectively make ethical decisions. Therefore, this section of the chapter highlights the background and purpose of ethical codes, spotlights ethical issues related to the counseling relationship, provides ethical decision-making models which can be applied when faced with ethical dilemmas, and offers some pointers for providing best practices so that you are less likely to provide unethical services or be sued.

Background and Purpose

The establishment of ethical guidelines in the helping professions began during the midpoint of the twentieth century, when, in 1953, the **American Psychological Association** (APA) published its first **code of ethics**. Not long after, in 1960, the **National Association of Social Workers** (NASW) adopted its code, and in 1961, the **American Counseling Association** (ACA) developed its ethical code. More recently, the **National Organization of Human Services** (NOHS) developed its ethical code (NOHS, 1996). The associations' guidelines have undergone a number of major revisions over the years to reflect society's ever-changing values as well as the changing values of the associations (see ACA, 2005; APA, 2003, NASW, 2008). Today, the **ethical codes** of the professional associations are remarkably similar and serve the same general purposes (Corey, Corey, & Callanan, 2011; Dolgoff, Loewenberg, & Harrington, 2009; Ponton & Duba, 2009; Remley & Herlihy, 2010):

- They protect consumers and further the professional standing of the organization.
- They are a statement about the maturity and professional identity of a profession.
- They guide professionals toward certain types of behaviors that reflect the underlying values considered to be desirable in the profession.
- They offer a framework in the sometimes difficult ethical decision-making process.
- They can be offered as one measure of defense if the professional is sued for malpractice.

Although ethical guidelines can be of considerable assistance in a professional's ethical decision-making process, there are limitations to the use of such a code:

- Codes do not address some issues and offer no clear way of responding to other issues.
- There are sometimes conflicts within the same code, between related codes, between the code and the law, and between the code and a helper's value system.
- It is sometimes difficult to enforce ethical violations in the codes.
- The public is often not involved in the code construction process, and the public interests are not always taken into account.
- Codes do not always address "cutting-edge" issues.

Counseling Relationship Issues Addressed in Ethical Codes

Although ethical codes cover a wide variety of possible counseling and consulting relationships, there are certain topics related to the helping relationship which are "**ethical hot spots**" and particularly important when counseling clients. These topics are repeatedly addressed in research on ethics and tend to be highlighted in most ethical codes. Summarizing some of these, we find the following are most often addressed in the literature and are generally the most frequent areas with which helpers find themselves struggling (APA, 2008; Glosoff & Freeman, 2007; Neukrug, Milliken, & Walden, 2001). (To see the websites of the professional associations and their affiliated ethics codes, click "student downloads" at: www.cengage.com/counseling/neukrug/CTP1e).

- *Promoting the welfare of the client:* Helpers should consider the ways in which they are helping their clients, make efforts to promote their clients' well-being, and avoid harming their clients.

- *Obtaining informed consent:* Prior to treatment, clients should be provided with information regarding the nature of the helping relationship (e.g., a *professional disclosure statement*), and helpers should obtain informed consent for treatment.

- *Transmission of values:* Helpers should avoid imposing their own values onto clients.

- *Multiple relationships:* Helpers should avoid relationships with a client when he or she already has an existing relationship with the client (e.g., your client is your child's teacher) and when the **dual relationship** will likely make the counseling relationship difficult.

- *Banning of sexual relationships:* Knowing that a sexual relationship with a client will cause damage to the client, sexual relationships with current or former clients are deemed unethical (some associations state the number of years since the counseling relationship ended to be considered a "former" client).

- *Confidentiality:* Helpers should protect the confidentiality of clients, except when there may be impending harm to the client or to others, when one is required by law to break confidentiality, or in other compelling situations in which the breaking of confidentiality would be necessary (see Box 1.2).

- *Technology:* In the age of the Internet and other new technologies, helpers should know how to use technology effectively and ethically (e.g., counseling on the Internet).

- *Counseling for end-of-life decisions:* Based on legal limits and the helper's level of comfort, helpers can counsel terminally ill clients who are facing end-of-life decisions by discussing their options with them.

- *Termination and referral:* Helpers should know when it is in the client's best interest to terminate a client or refer a client to another helper.

- *Fee for services:* Helpers should know the potential problems associated with fee payments and should ensure that clients are informed about the rules and issues related to fees for services (e.g., bartering, co-payments, insurance issues, etc.).

B o x 1.2   The Tarasoff Case and Duty to Warn

A precedent-setting case, the Tarasoff case offers us a window into the thinking of the courts, values in our society, and the current ethical issue of breaking confidentiality by helpers. After you read about this decision, discuss your feelings about your obligation to break confidentiality if a client is in danger of harming himself or herself.

This case involved a client named Prosenjit Poddar. Poddar, who was being seen at the counseling center at the University of California at Berkeley, told his psychologist that as a result of his girlfriend's recent threats to break up with him and date other men, he intended to kill her. As a result, his psychologist informed

his supervisor and the campus police of his client's threat, at which point the campus police detained him. The supervisor reprimanded the psychologist for breaking confidentiality; finding no reason to further detain Mr. Poddar, the campus police released him. Two months later, he killed his girlfriend, Tatiana Tarasoff. Ms. Tarasoff's parents sued the university, the therapist, the supervisor, and the police, and won their suit against all but the police. The decision, which was seen as a model for "duty to warn," now sometimes called "foreseeable harm," was interpreted by courts nationally to mean that a therapist must make all efforts to prevent danger to another or to the client.

- *Impaired work:* Helpers should refer clients to others when their own problems interfere with their ability to effectively help others (e.g., fatigue, substance abuse, countertransference).

- *Limits of competence:* Helpers should gain additional knowledge and/or supervision, or refer the client if the helper does not have expertise in the client's presenting problem.

- *Safety and confidentiality of records:* Based on laws and ethical guidelines, helpers should ensure the safety and confidentiality of client records.

- *Misrepresentation of credentials:* Helpers should ensure that credentials are adequate for treating specific client problems and that such credentials are made clear to the client.

- *Reporting abuse:* Based on legal requirements and ethical guidelines, helpers should know when, how, and to whom to report abuse (e.g., child abuse, elder abuse, spousal abuse).

- *Social and cultural issues:* Helpers should have the knowledge, skills, and attitudes that would allow them to work effectively with diverse clients.

Resolving Ethical Dilemmas: Models of Ethical Decision-Making

Although ethical codes provide us with guidelines regarding how to make decisions, ultimately, it is the helper who is the decision-maker. Making thorny ethical decisions can be difficult, and decision-making models have been developed to help us in this process. Three such models include **problem-solving models**, **moral models**, and **developmental models**.

Problem-Solving Models.   Problem-solving models provide the clinician with a step-by-step approach to making ethical decisions. They are practical, hands-on approaches that are particularly useful for the beginning clinician. One such model, developed by Corey et al. (2011), is an eight-step approach that consists of: (1) identifying the problem or dilemma, (2) identifying the potential issues involved, (3) reviewing the relevant ethical guidelines, (4) knowing the applicable laws and regulations, (5) obtaining consultation, (6) considering possible and probable courses of action, (7) enumerating the consequences of various decisions, and (8) deciding on the best course of action. This and other similar models can be great aids to the clinician in the sometime difficult ethical decision-making process.

Moral Models. Because ethical codes are guidelines, it is important that practitioners rely on more than the codes when making ethical decisions. For instance, based on the research of Kitchener (1984, 1986), Remley and Herlihy (2010) have suggested a moral model of decision-making that identifies six moral principles important in making thorny ethical decisions. They include **autonomy**, which has to do with respecting the client's right of self-determination and freedom of choice; **nonmaleficence**, or ensuring that you "do no harm"; **beneficence**, which is promoting the well-being of others and of society; **justice**, such as providing equal and fair treatment to all people and being nondiscriminatory; **fidelity**, which has to do with being loyal and faithful to your commitments in the helping relationship; and **veracity**, which means that you will deal honestly with the client. The clinician who employs this model will not reject the use of codes but will refer to the codes while using these moral principles in his or her decision-making process.

Another moral model by Rest (1984) suggests that the helper follow a critical decision-making path that includes making an interpretation about the situation, gauging and selecting the moral principles that underlie the decision to be made (e.g., a person should not murder), and acting on the basis of the selected moral principle(s). At each stage in the model, Rest has pinpointed potential helper difficulties that include: (1) the helper may misinterpret or fail to see the need for moral action; (2) the helper may be incapable of making a principled moral judgment in the face of a complex dilemma; (3) the helper may be unable to plan a course of action; and (4) the helper may lack the will to act.

Developmental Models. Regardless of the approach one takes in ethical decision-making, the ability to make wise ethical decisions is likely influenced by the clinician's level of ethical, moral, and cognitive development (Foster & Black, 2007; McAuliffe & Eriksen, 2002; Neukrug, Lovell, & Parker, 1996). In most developmental models, lower-level thought characteristically tends toward black-and-white thinking, concreteness, rigidity, oversimplification, stereotyping, self-protectiveness, and authoritarianism, while higher-level thinking is more flexible, complex, nondogmatic, and sensitive to the context in which a decision is being made. Thus, the individual who is at lower levels of development is likely making decisions based on a set of "musts" and "should," and will more rigidly adhere to perceived dictates in ethical codes, regardless of whether they actually exist.

B o x 1.3   Making Ethical Decisions

Your instructor will distribute one of the ethical topics highlighted earlier on pp. 11–12 to small groups of three to four students. Then, each group will develop an ethical dilemma based on that issue.

Discuss in your group how you resolved the ethical dilemma. In making your decision, don't forget to use one or more of the ethical decision-making models just discussed.

Final Thoughts on Resolving Ethical Dilemmas.   So who makes the best ethical decisions? Likely, it is the helper who knows his or her ethical codes, understands and reflects on the moral questions involved, deliberately consider the kinds of problem-solving stages that Corey et al. (2011) suggest, and is developmentally mature—that is, is a reflective, thoughtful, complex decision-maker. As you read the various theories presented in this text and learn about the various theorists, consider if they always made the best ethical and moral decisions in their professional lives. Then, consider how flawed we all are and how sometimes, even when we're equipped with all the tools, we falter when working with clients (see Box 1.3).

Best Practice: Avoiding Ethical Violations and Malpractice Suits

As one can see from the discussion on ethics, making ethical decisions can be an arduous and potentially career-threatening process. It is therefore essential that clinicians are equipped with the clinical knowledge and tools necessary to make the best decisions when working with clients. Gerald Corey and his colleagues (2011) give additional ways in which a clinician can ensure that he or she has been following best practices. Some of the more salient items follow.

- Keep good records.
- Know relevant laws.
- Report cases of abuse.
- Keep your appointments.
- Ensure security of records.
- Stay professional with clients.
- Document treatment progress.
- Preserve appropriate confidentiality.
- Treat only within your area of competence.
- Know the danger signs of suicide and volatility.
- Obtain written permission when working with minors.
- Refer when it is in the best interest of your client to do so.
- Be attentive to your clients' needs and treat them with respect.

- Inform clients of their right to terminate counseling at any point.

- Have a clear definition of fees and know about billing regulations.

- Do not engage in sexual relationships with current or former clients.

- Provide a professional disclosure statement and obtain informed consent regarding course of treatment.

- Have a sound theoretical approach and a clear understanding of why one uses certain techniques.

- Whenever possible, obtain permission from a client to consult with others.

- Consult and seek feedback concerning any potential conflicts if considering a dual relationship or multiple relationships.

MULTICULTURAL COUNSELING AND THE COUNSELING RELATIONSHIP

Multicultural counseling has been a paradigm shift in the counseling profession, with some identifying it as the **"fourth force"** in the helping professions (Pederson, 2005), the first three forces being psychoanalysis, behaviorism, and humanistic psychology, respectively. Changing the ways in which we understand the counseling relationship and the manner in which we do counseling (Locke & Faubert, 2003; Pedersen, Draguns, Lonner, & Trimble, 2002), this force has come about partially because a substantial number of the theories of counseling and psychotherapy, including many you will read in this book, have been biased toward nondominant groups in society. Thus, these approaches have had to be adapted and sometimes not used with certain clients. As you read the book, consider how each theory might work with a wide range of clients and reflect on how each theory could be adapted and sometimes may need to be discarded by a cross-culturally astute helper. Within each chapter, you will find discussion about the social, cultural, and spiritual issues relative to the chapter content. Bias in theories is not the only reason problems arise when working with diverse clients. Sometimes, the problem is helper incompetence. Thus, the next sections will examine culturally incompetent counseling and culturally competent counseling.

Culturally *Incompetent* Counseling

If you were distrustful of therapists, confused about the counseling process, or felt worlds apart from your helper, would you want to go to or continue in counseling? Assuredly not. Unfortunately, this is the state of affairs for many diverse clients. In fact, it is now assumed that when clients from nondominant groups work with majority helpers, there is a possibility that the helper will (1) minimize the impact of social forces on the client, (2) interpret cultural differences as psychopathological issues, and/or (3) misdiagnose the client (Buckley & Franklin-Jackson, 2005; Constantine & Sue, 2005). Perhaps this is why a large body of evidence shows that diverse (nonwhite) clients are frequently misunderstood, often misdiagnosed, find counseling and therapy less helpful than their majority counterparts, attend counseling and therapy at lower rates than majority clients, and tend to terminate from counseling more quickly than whites (Evans, Delphin, Simmons, Omar, & Tebes, 2005; Sewell, 2009; U. S. Department of Health and Human Services, 2001). In addition, many people of color who seek counseling appear to feel more satisfied when seeing a helper of their own cultural background. Why is counseling not working for a good segment of our population? Often, it is helper incompetence; the helper holds one or more of the following viewpoints (Buckley & Franklin-Jackson, 2005; Constantine & Sue, 2005; McAuliffe, Gomez, & Grothaus, 2008; Suzuki, Kugler, & Aguiar, 2005):

- *Believing in the "melting pot" myth.* Some believe this country is a "melting pot" of cultural diversity. However, this is not the experience of many diverse clients who find themselves on the fringe of American culture, view themselves as different from the mainstream, and cannot relate to many of the values and beliefs held by the majority. In truth, most cultures want to maintain their uniqueness and are resistant to giving up their special traditions. Thus, the helper who assumes the client should conform to the values of the majority culture may turn off some clients. Called **multiculturalism**, viewing America as society with a myriad of diverse values and customs, or a *cultural mosaic*, more accurately represents the essence of diversity that we find today.

- *Having incongruent expectations about counseling.* The Western, particularly American, approach to counseling and psychotherapy tends to contain a number of assumptions, including presuming that the counseling process should emphasize the individual; stressing the expression of feelings; encouraging self-disclosure, open-mindedness, and insight; and showing cause and effect. In addition, most helpers are not bilingual, approach counseling from a nonreligious perspective, and view the mind and body as separate. These beliefs and behaviors create barriers that result in diverse clients' entering helping relationships with trepidation, feelings of disappointment, and sometimes clients' being harmed by techniques that should not be used with them. For example, the Asian client who is proud of her ability to restrict her emotions may leave counseling feeling as if she disappointed her helper, who has been pushing her to express feelings.

- *De-emphasizing social forces.* Although helpers may be effective at attending to clients' *feelings* concerning how they have been discriminated against, abused, or affected by other "external" factors, the same helpers will often de-emphasize the actual influence these social forces have on clients. Helpers often assume that most, if not all, negative feelings are created by the individual, and they often have difficulty understanding the power of social influences. The helper's negation of social forces results in an inability to build a successful relationship with a client who has been considerably harmed by external factors. For instance, the client who has been illegally denied jobs due to his disability may be discouraged when a helper says, "What have you done to prevent yourself from obtaining the job?"

- *Holding an ethnocentric worldview.* Ethnocentric helpers, or helpers who see the world only through their own lenses, tend to falsely assume that their clients view the world in a similar manner as they do or believe that when their clients present a differing view of the world, they are emotionally disturbed, culturally brainwashed, or wrong. Although the importance of understanding a client's unique worldview is always crucial to an effective helping relationship, it becomes particularly significant when working with diverse clients whose experience of the world may be particularly foreign to the helper's. For instance, a helper may inadvertently turn off a client who is a Muslim by saying, "Have a wonderful Christmas."

- *Ignorance of one's own racist attitudes and prejudices.* Of course, the helper who is not in touch with his or her prejudices and racist attitudes cannot work effectively with diverse clients, and will often cause harm to those clients. Understanding our own stereotypes and prejudices takes a particularly vigilant effort, as many of our biases are unconscious. For instance, the heterosexual helper who unconsciously believes that being gay or lesbian is a disorder but consciously states that he is accepting of all sexual orientations may subtly treat a gay or lesbian client as if there is something wrong with him or her.

- *Misunderstanding cultural differences in the expression of symptomatology.* What may be seen as "abnormal" in the United States may be considered quite usual and customary in another culture. The helper's lack of knowledge about cultural differences as they relate to the expression of symptoms can seriously damage a counseling relationship and result in misdiagnosis, mistreatment, and early termination of culturally diverse clients from counseling. For instance, whereas many individuals from Anglo-European cultures would show grief through depression, agitation, and feelings of helplessness, a Hispanic might present with somatic complaints.

- *Misjudging the accuracy of assessment and research procedures.* Over the years, assessment and research procedures have notoriously been culturally biased. Although advances have been made, one can still readily find tests that have cultural bias and research that does not control adequately for cultural differences. One common problem in the use of assessment instruments is that individuals from other cultures may inadvertently be answering questions in a manner that would be considered abnormal by American standards when indeed they do not have an emotional disorder. For example, when an item on a test asks if a person "hears voices," a religious Hispanic client might answer "yes," thinking that she "talks to God"—a normal response in her culture. Although acculturated Americans might also "talk to God," they have learned to deny that they "hear voices" because that implies psychopathology in traditional American culture.

- *Ignorance of institutional racism.* Because institutional racism is embedded in society, and some would argue, even within the helping professional organizations, it is likely that materials used by helpers will be biased and helpers will unknowingly have a skewed understanding of culturally different clients. Examples are plentiful. For instance, some diagnoses that have been listed in the *Diagnostic and Statistical Manual IV* (Text Revision, *DSM-IV-TR*) have been shown to be culturally biased; some counseling approaches given precedence in the professional journals have been shown to be practically useless when working with clients from some cultures; and training programs have, until recently, not stressed multicultural issues. No doubt there are culturally biased statements in this text of which I am not aware.

Culturally *Competent* Counseling

In recent years, there has been a push toward culturally competent counseling in training programs. Led by research, books, and standards, this thrust has resulted in helpers who have had more training than helpers in the past in how to successfully work with nondominant groups. The following describes the **Multicultural Counseling Competencies**, which have been used as a model in the training of helpers; the **RESPECTFUL model** of counseling, another method of ensuring helpers are addressing the needs of the traditionally disenfranchised in counseling; and some additional suggestions on how to work with clients from nondominant groups.

Multicultural Counseling Competencies.   To guide helpers during their training, we have seen the development of the Multicultural Counseling Competencies (Roysircar, Arredondo, Fuertes, Ponterotto, & Toporek, 2003). These competencies, which represent minimum standards needed by helpers if they are to work effectively with diverse clients, focus on increasing helper competency in three areas: (1) awareness of the helper's **attitudes and beliefs** that might negatively impact the cross-cultural helping relationship, (2) **knowledge** to be able to understand the worldviews of diverse clients, and (3) **skills** and intervention techniques that can be applied to clients from nondominant groups. Let's examine each of these areas.

Attitudes and beliefs: The effective cross-cultural helper has an awareness of his or her own cultural background and has actively pursued gaining awareness of his or her own biases, stereotypes, and values. Although the effective cross-cultural helper may not hold the same belief system as his or her client, he or she can accept differing worldviews as presented by the client. And perhaps most important, differences are not seen as pathological (Sue & Sue, 2008). Being sensitive to differences and tuned into his or her own cultural biases allows the cross-cultural helper to refer a client from a diverse background to a helper of the client's own culture when a referral will benefit the client.

Knowledge: The effective cross-cultural helper has knowledge of the group from which the client comes and does not jump to conclusions about the client's ways of being. In addition, he or she shows a willingness to gain greater depth of knowledge of various cultural groups. This helper is also aware of how sociopolitical issues such as racism, sexism, and heterosexism can negatively affect clients. In addition, this helper knows how different theories of counseling carry values that may be detrimental for some clients in the counseling relationship. This helper understands how institutional barriers can affect the willingness of clients from diverse groups to use mental health services.

Skills: The cross-culturally effective helper is able to apply, when appropriate, generic interviewing and counseling skills, and also has knowledge of and is able to employ specialized skills and interventions that might be effective with clients from nondominant groups. This helper also understands the verbal and nonverbal language of the client and can communicate effectively with the client. In addition, the culturally skilled helper understands the importance of having a systemic perspective, such as understanding the impact that family, culture, and society have on clients; being able to work collaboratively with community leaders, indigenous healers, and other professionals; and advocating for clients when necessary.

A helper who has a clear understanding of self, especially his or her own cultural identity, is able to develop healthy attitudes and beliefs and is able to gain the needed knowledge base to work with diverse clients. In addition, the competent cross-cultural counselor knows which skills to use for clients who are culturally different.

RESPECTFUL Counseling. If counseling and psychotherapy is to be an equal-opportunity profession, helpers must graduate from training programs with more than a desire to help all people. As a profession, we will have achieved competence in counseling diverse clients when graduates from all training programs have learned counseling strategies that work for a wide range of clients, have worked with clients from diverse backgrounds, and leave their programs with an appreciation for diversity and identities that include a multicultural perspective (Bobby, 2005; D'Andrea, 2005). In addition to the Multicultural Counseling Competencies just noted, D'Andrea and Daniels (2005, p. 37) suggest that all helpers should adopt the RESPECTFUL counseling model, which highlights 10 factors to which helpers should attend in their relationships with clients:

R – Religious/spiritual identity

E – Economic class background

S – Sexual identity

P – Psychological development

E – Ethnic/racial identity

C – Chronological disposition

T – Trauma and other threats to personal well-being
F – Family history
U – Unique physical characteristics
L – Language and location of residence, which may affect the helping process

Ideally, as you go through your training program, you will attain an appreciation of these factors in yourself and learn how to attend to them in your clients.

Counseling Individuals from Different Cultures. Integrating the Multi-cultural Counseling Competencies with the RESPECTFUL model, and adding a few other items critical to being a culturally competent helper, the following offers a list of suggestions you might want to use when working with diverse clients. After you have read the following list, reflect on the ethical vignettes in Box 1.4.

- *Have the right attitudes and beliefs, gain knowledge, and learn skills.* Be prepared to work with clients with varying cultural heritages by embracing the appropriate knowledge, skills, and beliefs prior to meeting with them.

- *Be RESPECTFUL.* Address the areas that D'Andrea and Daniels suggest in the RESPECTFUL model.

- *Encourage clients to speak their own language.* Make an effort to know meaningful expressions of the client's language. When language becomes a significant barrier, refer to a helper who speaks the client's language.

- *Check the accuracy of your interpretation of the client's nonverbals.* Don't assume that nonverbal communication is consistent across cultures. Ask the client about his or her nonverbals when in doubt.

- *Make use of alternate modes of communication.* Use appropriate alternative modes of communication, such as acting, drawing, music, storytelling, collage-making, and so forth, to draw out clients who are reticent to talk or have communication problems.

- *Assess the impact of sociopolitical issues on the client.* Examine how social and political issues affect your client and make a decision about whether advocating for the client can be helpful in alleviating the client's problems.

- *Encourage clients to bring in culturally significant and personally relevant items.* Have clients bring in items to help you better understand them and their culture (e.g., books, photographs, articles of significance, culturally meaningful items, and the like).

- *Vary the helping environment.* When appropriate, explore alternative helping environments to ease the client into the helping relationship (e.g., take a walk, have a cup of coffee at a quiet restaurant, initially meet your client at his or her home, and so forth).

B o x 1.4 Ethical and Professional Issues Related to Cross-Cultural Concerns

The following ethical and professional issues will allow you to use your ethical code and decision-making models while you focus on some cross-cultural concerns. You can do them on your own or in small groups in class.

1. Because of cross-cultural differences, you believe that your work with an Asian client has not been successful. Rather than referring the client to another counselor, you decide to read more about your client's culture in order to gain a better understanding of him. Is this ethical? Is this professional?
2. A colleague of yours consistently makes misogynistic (dislike of women) statements when referring to clients. What should you do?
3. A colleague of yours identifies herself as a feminist counselor. You know that when she works with some women, she actively encourages them to leave their husbands when she discovers the husband is verbally or physically abusive. Is she acting ethically? Should you do anything?
4. You discover that a colleague of yours is telling a homosexual client that he is acting immorally. Is this ethical? Professional? Legal? What should you do?
5. A friend of yours advertises that she is a Christian counselor. You discover that when clients come to see her, she encourages reading parts of the Bible during sessions and tells clients they need to ask repentance for their sins. Is this ethical? Is this professional?
6. An African-American counselor in private practice who has expertise in a specific mental health problem decides he should only work with African-American clients. A white client, who has this problem, has heard that this counselor is quite effective and calls him for an appointment. The counselor refers him to someone else and tells the client he works only with African Americans. Does the African-American counselor have a responsibility to see this client? Is he acting ethically? Professionally? Legally?
7. When working with an Asian client who is not expressive of her feelings, a counselor you know pressures the client to express feelings. The counselor tells the client, "You can only get better if you express yourself." Is this counselor acting ethically? Professionally? Do you have any responsibility in this case?
8. When offering a parenting workshop to individuals who are poor, some of the participants challenge you when you say "hitting a child is never okay." They tell you that you are crazy, and that sometimes a good spanking is the only thing that will get the child's attention. Do they have a point? What should you do?
9. A counselor who is seeing a client who is HIV-positive discovers that his client is having sex with others without revealing his HIV status. The counselor tells him that he has a responsibility to report him to the police. Would this be ethical? Professional? Legal?
10. A colleague of yours is working with a Hispanic client who states there is little hope for happiness in her marriage. The client states that her husband's attitude toward her is constantly demeaning, but that there is little she can do. After all, she tells you that it is "out of her control" and in God's hands. Your colleague tells you that she is helping the client gain autonomy and that she is helping the client give up the notion of "fatilismo," that fate controls one's life—a common value held by many Hispanics. Is your colleague acting appropriately? Is there a better way for the colleague to respond?

LAYOUT OF THE BOOK

Today, it is generally agreed that there are hundreds of different kinds of psychotherapies, each with its own unique view of human nature, techniques, and process (Gabbard, 1995; O'Leary, 2006; List of psychotherapies, 2009). However, based on their views of human nature, most of these theories can be categorized into four conceptual orientations: psychodynamic, existential–humanistic, cognitive–behavioral, and post-modern (Norcross et al., 2009). This text is organized around these four orientations and offers an overview of some of the more popular theories within each of them (see Table 1.1). However, it must be emphasized that some of the theories do not always neatly fit into a particularly section, as their views of human nature may have leanings toward a second, or even third, orientation. Thus, we find theories like *individual psychology* in the psychodynamic section, although many believe it was the first humanistic theory, and rational emotive behavior therapy (REBT) in the cognitive–behavioral section, although the founder of this approach argued it was also post-modern. Finally, we have *reality therapy*—a theory that in some ways has no home, as its view of human nature seems a blend of cognitive–behavioral, post-modern, and existential–humanistic. Because of its focus on "doing" (thinking and behaving), I have (somewhat arbitrarily) placed it in the cognitive-behavioral section. So, as you read about these theories, keep in mind that in some cases, they can fit into more than one conceptual orientation. The last section of the book offers extensions, adaptations, and spinoffs to the conceptual orientations and theories already discussed (Chapter 14) as well as a chapter on family therapy (Chapter 15) (see Table 1.1).

Each chapter within the first four sections of the text is ordered in the same fashion. I first offer biographical information on the major theorist(s) who developed the theory. Next you will find the theory's view of human nature, key concepts, techniques, and therapeutic process. This is followed by a section on social, cultural, and spiritual issues, and the chapter is concluded with a section on the efficacy of the approach. Key words and names are identified near the end of each chapter, and a short summary concludes each chapter. Also, within each chapter is a reference to a DVD that can be used in conjunction with this text. The DVD will allow you to see, firsthand, a short clip of how the particular theory is practiced. In many of the chapters, there is also a reference to a Web site I have created that has oral stories about some of these famous theorists (http://www.odu.edu/sgt). These stories are of actual encounters individuals had with the famous theorist discussed in the chapter and are, at varying times, sad, interesting, funny, and informative. If you have a chance, listen to some of them. Also, near the end of each of these chapters will be a reference to one or more members of the Miller family. Each member of this fictitious family participates in one or more of the therapies being described. You can read about each of their therapeutic journeys in Appendix B. You also will have an opportunity to see what it's like for the Millers to participate in family therapy. Finally, the fifth section of the text describes a number of individual and family approaches without some of the bells and whistles found in the earlier chapters.

T A B L E 1.1 An Overview of the Text

Sections	Chapters		
Section I Psychodynamic Theories	**Chapter 2** Psychoanalysis (Freud)	**Chapter 3** Analytical Psychology (Jung)	**Chapter 4** Individual Psychology (Adler)
Section II Existential–Humanistic Theories	**Chapter 5** Existential Therapy (Frankl and others)	**Chapter 6** Gestalt Therapy (Perls)	**Chapter 7** Person-Centered Counseling (Rogers)
Section III Cognitive and Behavioral Theories	**Chapter 8** Behavior Therapy (Skinner and Others)	**Chapter 9** Rational Emotive Behavior Therapy (Ellis)	**Chapter 10** Cognitive and Cognitive–Behavioral Therapy (Beck)
			Chapter 11 Reality Therapy (Glasser)
Section IV Post-Modern Approaches	**Chapter 12** Narrative Therapy (White)	**Chapter 13** Solution-Focused Therapy (Berg and de Shazer)	
Section V Extensions, Adaptations, and Spinoffs	**Chapter 14:** Individual Approaches Psychodynamic Approaches Erickson's Stages of Psychosocial Development Object Relations Kohut's Self Psychology Relational and Intersubjectivity Cognitive–Behavioral Lazarus's Multimodal Therapy Dialectical Behavior Therapy Acceptance and Commitment Therapy ("ACT") Mahoney's Constructivist Approach Based on A Variety of Approaches Eye Movement Desensitization and Reprocessing (EMDR) Motivational Interviewing Gender Aware Counseling (Feminist Therapy and Counseling Men) Positive Psychology Complementary, Alternative, and Integrative Approaches	**Chapter 15:** Couples and Family Counseling Human Validation Process Model (Satir) Structural Family Therapy (Minuchin) Strategic Family (Haley, Madanes, and the Milan Group) Multigenerational Approaches (Boszormenyi-Nagy; Bowen) Experiential Family Therapy (Whitaker) Psychodynamic Family Therapy (Ackerman and Skynner) Behavioral and Cognitive–Behavioral Narrative Family Therapy (White and Epston) Solution-Focused Therapy (Berg, de Shazer, O'Hanlon, others)	

SUMMARY

This chapter first examined the efficacy of counseling and psychotherapy, and came to the conclusion that they are effective. The importance of **evidence-based** practice was discussed and certain qualities deemed important in the helping relationship were examined, including the use of empathy, the ability to build a therapeutic alliance, adherence to a theoretical approach, and the resources brought by the client. Next, we examined the differences between counseling and psychotherapy, and noted that most theories of counseling and psychotherapy do not make a distinction between these words, while many individuals do. Some terms associated with each were examined and reasons why a helper might end up doing counseling or psychotherapy were highlighted.

The chapter then moved on to a discussion of the importance of theory. Here it was noted that theories provide a framework from which the helper can work, and it was stressed that to operate without theory is chaotic. We also noted that theories are heuristic, or researchable and testable. Part of constructing a theory, we noted, was the development of a view of human nature. We identified a number of attributes that are often important in the development of one's view of human nature and offered an exercise and a survey to help identify your view of human nature and with which theoretical school you are likely most affiliated. We next noted that the development of your own theoretical approach will likely occur in stages as you, over time, increasingly begin to integrate different approaches into your way of helping. The stages identified included chaos, coalescence, multiplicity, and metatheory.

The chapter next focused on ethics in the counseling relationship. We first offered some background on the development of ethical codes and addressed the purpose of ethical codes. A number of ethical "hot spots" related to the counseling relationship, discussed in research, and often identified in codes were then highlighted. One precedent-setting case relevant to **duty to warn** (now often called, "**foreseeable harm**"), the **Tarasoff case**, was presented. Next, a discussion on ethical decision-making ensued, including a description of problem-solving models, moral models, and developmental models when making thorny ethical decisions. This section concluded by identifying a number of tools for "best practices" that will assist the helper in avoiding ethical violations and malpractice suits.

As the chapter continued, there was a discussion of the "fourth force" in counseling, otherwise known as *multicultural counseling*. We first noted that counseling has not been effective for many clients from nondominant groups and then identified eight reasons why helpers are sometimes incompetent. We next identified ways of developing cultural competence, including using the Multicultural Counseling Competencies and the RESPECTFUL model. An additional model that integrated and expanded upon the competencies and the RESPECTFUL model was offered. The chapter concluded by providing an overview of the text that allows you to understand how the theories you will read about are organized into different conceptual orientations, with a warning that not all of the theories fit neatly into any one conceptual orientation.

KEY WORDS

American Counseling Association

American Psychological Association

attitudes and beliefs

autonomy

banning of sexual relationships

believing in the "melting pot" myth

beneficence

chaos

coalescence

code of ethics

confidentiality

counseling for end-of-life decisions

culturally competent counseling

culturally incompetent counseling

de-emphasizing social forces

developmental models

dual relationship

duty to warn

eclecticism

ethical codes

ethical hot spots

evidence-based

Eysenck

fee for services

fidelity

foreseeable harm

fourth force

Freud

having incongruent expectations about counseling

heuristic

holding an ethnocentric worldview

ignorance of institutional racism

Ignorance of one's own racist attitudes and prejudices

impaired work

integrative approach

justice

knowledge

limits of competence

metatheory

misjudging the accuracy of assessment and research procedures

misrepresentation of credentials

misunderstanding cross-cultural differences in the expression of symptomatology

models of ethical decision-making

moral models

Multicultural Counseling Competencies

multiculturalism

multiple relationships

multiplicity

National Association of Social Workers

National Organization of Human Services

nonmaleficence

obtaining informed consent

paradigm shifts

problem-solving models

professional disclosure statement

promoting the welfare of the client

reporting abuse

RESPECTFUL model

safety and confidentiality of records

skills

social and cultural issues

Tarasoff case

technology (counseling over the Internet)

termination and referral

transmission of values

veracity

view of human nature

KEY NAMES

Eysenck, Hans

Freud, Simund

REFERENCES

American Counseling Association. (2005). *Code of ethics*. Retrieved from http://www. counseling.org/Resources/CodeOfEthics/TP/Home/CT2.aspx

American Psychological Association. (2003). *Ethical principles of psychologists and code of conduct*. Retrieved from http://www.apa.org/ethics/code2002.html

American Psychological Association. (2008). Report on the ethics committee, 2007. *American Psychologist, 63*(5), 452–459.

Beutler, L. E., Malik, M., Alimohamed, S., Harwood, T. M., Talebi, H., Noble, S., & Wong, E. (2004). Therapist variables. In M. J. Lambert (Ed.), *Bergin and Garfield's handbook of psychotherapy and behavior change* (5th ed., pp. 227–306). New York: Wiley.

Bobby, C. (2005, September). A letter from CACREP to ACA governing council. *Counseling Today, 4*, 26.

Brooks-Harris, J. E. (2008). *Integrative multitheoretical psychotherapy*. Boston: Houghton Mifflin.

Buckley, T. R., & Franklin-Jackson, C. F. (2005). Diagnosis in racial-cultural practice. In R. T. Carter (Ed.), *Handbook of racial-cultural psychology and counseling: Theory and research* (vol. 2, pp. 286–296). Hoboken, NJ: John Wiley.

Constantine, M. C., & Sue, D. W. (2005). *Strategies for building multicultural competence in mental health and educational settings*. Hoboken, NJ: John Wiley.

Corey, G., Corey, M. S., & Callanan, P. (2011). *Issues and ethics in the helping professions* (8th ed.). Belmont, CA: Brooks/Cole.

D'Andrea, M. (2005, August). Multicultural counseling competencies and CACREP. *Counseling Today, 34–36.*

D'Andrea, M., & Daniels, J. (2005, July). A socially responsible approach to counseling, mental health care. *Counseling Today, 36–38.*

Dolgoff, R., Loewenberg, F. M., & Harrington, D. (2009). *Ethical decisions for social work practice* (8th ed.). Belmont, CA: Brooks/Cole.

Evans, A. C., Delphin, M., Simmons, R., Omar, G., & Tebes, J. (2005). Developing a framework for culturally competent systems care. In R. T. Carter (Ed.), *Handbook of racial-cultural psychology and counseling: Theory and research* (vol. 2, pp. 492–513). Hoboken, NJ: John Wiley.

Eysenck, H. J. (1952). The effects of psychotherapy: An evaluation. *Journal of Consulting Psychology, 16*, 319–324.

Foster, D., & Black, T. G. (2007). An integral approach to counseling ethics. *Counseling and Values, 51*, 221–234.

Gabbard, G. O. (1995). Are all psychotherapies equally effective? *The Menninger Letter, 3*(1), 1–2.

Glosoff, H., & Freeman, L. T. (2007). Report of the ACA ethics committee: 2005–2006. *Journal of Counseling and Development, 85*, 251–254.

Gold, J., & Stricker, G. (2006). Introduction: An overview of psychotherapy integration. In G. Stricker & J. Gold (Eds.), *A casebook of psychotherapy integration* (pp. 3–16). Washington, D.C.: American Psychological Association.

Hansen, J. C., Rossberg, R. H., Cramer, S. H. (1994). *Counseling: Theory and process* (5th ed.). Boston: Allyn & Bacon.

Hayes, R. A. (2005). Introduction to evidenced-based practice. In C. E. Stout & R. A. Hayes (Eds.), *The evidenced-based practice: Methods, models, and tools for mental health professionals* (pp. 1–9). Hoboken, NJ: Wiley.

Jones, J., & Wilson, W. (2006). *An incomplete education* (3rd ed.). New York: Ballantine Books.

Kitchener, K. S. (1984). Intuition, critical evaluation and ethical principles: The foundation for ethical decisions in counseling psychology. *The Counseling Psychologist, 12*(3), 43–45.

Kitchener, K. S. (1986). Teaching applied ethics in counselor education: An integration of psychological processes and philosophical analysis. *Journal of Counseling and Development, 64*(5), 306–311.

Lambert, M. J., & Ogles, B. (2004). The efficacy and effectiveness of psychotherapy. In M. J. Lambert (Ed.), *Bergin and Garfield's handbook of psychotherapy and behavior change* (5th ed., pp. 139–193). New York: Wiley.

List of psychotherapies. (2009). The Wikipedia free encyclopedia. Retrieved from http://en.wikipedia.org/wiki/List_of_psychotherapies

Locke, D., & Faubert, M. (2003). Cultural considerations in counselor training and supervision. In F. D. Harper & J. McFadden (Eds.), *Culture and counseling: New approaches* (pp. 324–448). Boston: Allyn & Bacon.

McAuliffe, G., & Eriksen, K. (Eds.). (2002). *Teaching strategies for constructivist and developmental counselor education.* Westport, CT: Bergin & Garvey.

McAuliffe, G., Gomez, E., & Grothaus, T. (2008). Race. In G. McAuliffe (Ed.), *Culturally alert counseling: A comprehensive introduction* (pp. 105–145). Los Angeles, CA: Sage Publications.

National Association of Social Workers. (2008). Code of ethics. Retrieved from http://www.socialworkers.org/pubs/code/code.asp

National Organization of Human Services. (1996). *Ethical standards of human service professionals.* Retrieved from http://www.nationalhumanservices.org/mc/page.do?sitePageId=89927&orgId=nohs

Neukrug, E., Lovell, C., & Parker, R. (1996). Employing ethical codes and decision-making models: A developmental process. *Counseling and Values, 40,* 98–106.

Neukrug, E., Milliken, T., & Walden, S. (2001). Ethical practices of credentialed counselors: An updated survey of state licensing boards. *Counselor Education and Supervision, 41*(1), 57–70.

Neukrug, E., & Schwitzer, A. M. (2006). *Skills and tools for today's counselors and psychotherapists: From natural helping to professional counseling.* Pacific Grove, CA: Brooks/Cole.

Norcross, J. C., Beutler, L. E., & Levant, R. (2006). *Evidenced-based practices in mental health: Dialogue on the fundamental questions.* Washington, D.C.: American Psychological Association.

Norcross, J. C., Bike, H., & Evans, K. L. (2009). The therapist's therapist: A replication and extension 20 years later. *Psychotherapy Theory, Research, Practice, Training, 46*(1), 32–41.

O'Leary, E. (2006). The need for integration. In E. O'Leary & M. Murphy (Eds.), *New approaches to integration in psychotherapy* (pp. 3–12). New York: Routledge.

O'Leary, E., & Murphy, M. (2006). *New approaches to integration in psychotherapy.* New York: Routledge.

Pedersen, P. (2005). The importance of cultural psychology theory for multicultural counselors. In R. T. Carter (Ed.), *Handbook of racial-cultural psychology and counseling: Theory and research* (vol. 1, pp. 3–16). Hoboken, NJ: John Wiley.

Pedersen, P. B., Draguns, J. G., Lonner, W. J., & Trimble, J. E. (2008). *Counseling across cultures* (6th ed.). Thousand Oaks, CA: Sage.

Ponton, R. R., & Duba, J. D. (2009). The ACA Code of Ethics: Articulating counseling's professional covenant. *Journal of Counseling and Development, 87,* 117–121.

Remley, T. P., & Herlihy, B. (2010). *Ethical and professional issues in counseling* (3rd ed.). Upper Saddle River, NJ: Merrill.

Rest, J. R. (1984). Research on moral development: Implications for training counseling psychologists. *The Counseling Psychologist, 12,* 19–29.

Roysircar, G., Arredondo, P., Fuertes, J. N., Ponterotto, J. G., & Toporek, R. L. (Eds.). (2003). *Multicultural counseling competencies 2003: Association for Multicultural Counseling and Development.* Alexandria, VA: Association for Multicultural Counseling and Development.

Sewell, H. (2009). *Working with ethnicity, race and culture in mental health.* Philadelphia, PA: Jessica Kingsley Publishers.

Sexton, T. (1993). A review of the counseling outcome research. In G. R. Walz & J. C. Bleuer (Eds.), *Counselor efficacy: Assessing and using counseling outcomes research* (Report No. ISBN-1-56109-056-5). Ann Arbor, MI: ERIC Clearinghouse on Counseling and Personnel Services (ERIC Document Reproduction Service No. ED362 821).

Sexton, T. L. (1999). *Evidence-based counseling: Implications for counseling practice, preparation, and professionalism* (No ED435948). Greensboro, NC: Eric Clearinghouse on Counseling and Student Services (ERIC Document Reproduction Service No. ED99CO0014).

Spruill, D. A., & Benshoff, J. M. (2000). Developing a personal theory of counseling: A theory building model for counselor trainees. *Counselor Education and Supervision, 40,* 70–80.

Stout, C. E., & Hayes, R. A. (Eds.). (2005). *The evidenced-based practice: Methods, models, and tools for mental health professionals.* Hoboken, NJ: Wiley.

Stricker, G., & Gold, J. (2006). *A casebook of psychotherapy integration.* Washington, D.C.: American Psychological Association.

Sue, D. W, & Sue, D. (2008). *Counseling the culturally different: Theory and practice* (5th ed.). New York: Wiley.

Suzuki, L. A., Kugler, J. F., & Aguiar, L. J. (2005). Assessment practices in racial-cultural psychology. In R. T. Carter (Ed.), *Handbook of racial-cultural psychology and counseling: Theory and research* (vol. 2, pp. 297–315). Hoboken, NJ: John Wiley.

U.S. Department of Health and Human Services. (2001). *Mental health: Culture, race, and ethnicity: A supplement to mental health: A report to the Surgeon General.* Retrieved from http://www.surgeongeneral.gov/library/mentalhealth/cre/sma-01-3613.pdf

Wampold, B. E. (2001). *The great psychotherapy debate: Models, methods, and findings.* Mahwah, NJ: Erlbaum.

SECTION I

Psychodynamic Approaches

This first section of the book will examine three classic and prominent psychodynamic approaches to counseling and psychotherapy: psychoanalysis (Freudian therapy), analytical (Jungian) therapy, and individual psychology (Adlerian therapy). Developed near the beginning of the twentieth century but maintaining widespread popularity today, psychodynamic approaches vary considerably but contain some common elements. For instance, they all suggest that an unconscious and a conscious affect the functioning of the person in some deeply personal and "dynamic" ways. They all look at early child-rearing practices as being important in the development of personality. They all believe that examining the past, and the dynamic interaction of the past with conscious and unconscious factors, are important in the therapeutic process. Although these approaches have tended to be long-term, in recent years, some have been adapted and used in relatively brief treatment modality formats.

Chapter 2

Psychoanalysis

Learning Goals

- To gain an understanding of the originator of psychoanalysis, Sigmund Freud.
- To understand the historical context in which Freud created his theory.
- To understand the roles that instincts, drives, personality development, and the unconscious play in the development of one's psychic reality and in Freud's view of human nature.
- To learn about key concepts that are the basis for psychoanalytic theory, including consciousness and unconsciousness, drives and instincts, the structure of personality (id, ego, superego), anxiety (realistic, moral, neurotic), defense mechanisms, psychosexual stages of development (oral, anal, phallic, latency, genital), and transference and countertransference.
- To review some of the major techniques used in psychoanalysis, including ways of creating a trusting atmosphere, analytic neutrality, free association, interpretation of resistance, dream analysis, interpretation of parapraxes, and interpretation of the transference relationship.
- To examine the therapeutic process and highlight those techniques most useful at different stages of that process.
- To review important social, cultural, and spiritual issues related to psychoanalysis, including how Freud's cultural upbringing affected his theory, Western-based values inherent in the theory, feminist criticism and feminist acceptance of psychoanalysis, the past and present push for low-cost and free analysis, and past and current psychoanalytic views on religion.
- To review studies that have shown the effectiveness of psychoanalysis, to identify which populations seem to most profit from this approach, and to examine recent research which supports some of Freud's original ideas.
- To see how psychoanalysis is applied through vignettes, DVDs, and case study.

Today, historians rank Freud's scientific contributions with those of Planck and Einstein. He appears on most lists of the greatest physicians in history. He was recently on the cover of *Time* (with Albert Einstein) for an issue dedicated to the greatest scientific minds of the century, and was ranked sixth in a book on the hundred most influential scientists. Yet if Freud's fame and influence have continued to grow since his death more than 60 years ago, so have the criticism and the controversy surrounding him. He persists in spite of it all. Freud's photo graces Austrian currency. His ideas remain permanently embedded in our culture and our language.

We use terms such as *ego, repression, complex, projection, inhibition, neurosis, psychosis, resistance, sibling rivalry,* and *Freudian slip* without even realizing their source. Freud's model of the mind is still perhaps the most developed of all. Of the more than 100 forms of psychotherapy, many continue to use one or another of Freud's concepts. Perhaps most important of all, his theories influence how we interpret human behavior, not only in biography, literary criticism, sociology, medicine, history, education, and ethics, but also in law. We now take for granted the basic psychoanalytic concept that our early life experiences strongly influence how we think, feel, and behave as adults. Because of the unmistakable impact of his thought, some scholars refer to the twentieth century as the "century of Freud." (Nicholi, 2002, p. 2)

After reading this excerpt, perhaps you're wondering—who was this man, and how did he manage to influence the world in such a remarkable way? Let's take a look at Sigmund Freud.

Key Color - Photolibrary

Sigmund Freud

SIGMUND FREUD

On May 5, 1856, Sigmund Freud was born in what is today the Czech Republic. When he was four years old, Freud's family moved to Vienna for a better life. A Jewish wool merchant, Freud's father was a widower, and his second wife, Amalia, was 20 years younger than him. Freud had two half-brothers from his father's first marriage and was the oldest and favorite of his mother's eight children. His half-brothers were about the same age as his mother, and "Sigi," as his mother liked to call him, was only slightly younger than one of his nephews. This interesting family constellation might have been one of the reasons Freud was so fascinated by how family dynamics affected childhood development. Sensitive and brilliant as a child, it is not surprising that he went to the University of Vienna, where he studied neurology and psychiatry. Eventually, Freud became well-known in the field of neurology

—the science and study of nerves and nervous disorders. Although Freud would make a lateral move to the field of psychiatry, he continually assumed that there was a large neurobiological component to the development of personality, a component that only in recent years has to some degree been validated (Leichsenring, 2005; Stein, Solms, & van Honk, 2006).

In 1885, Freud went to Paris to study with Jean-Martin Charcot, who found that when persons with **hysteria** (e.g., anxiety disorders, fainting, muscle spasms, paralysis, dissociation, and a variety of other symptoms) were placed under deep hypnosis, their symptoms would often be relieved. Hysteria was particularly common in women during those times, and seen as an organic (physical) disease that was associated with sexual frustration (Maines, 2001):

> … [I]t has been speculated that many of these women may have been suffering from extreme sexual frustration—a theory lent credence by the fact that a goodly number of these women gained temporary relief from their symptoms by visiting the physician for clitoral "massage." (NNDB, 2007, para. 5)

Although Freud viewed sexual drives as a major factor underlying mental disorders, the fact that he viewed hysteria as a psychological disorder and eventually treated such symptoms with "talk therapy" was seen as revolutionary and changed the manner in which disorders would be treated (Bankart, 1997; Maines, 2001).

After returning to Vienna in 1886, Freud married Martha Bernays. The couple had six children, his youngest, Anna, becoming a well-known child psychoanalyst. During the late 1880s, Freud set up his own private practice using hypnotic suggestion as his primary technique. At the time, the use of hypnosis was all the rage, and many saw it as having the ability to cure a large range of diseases from constipation to deafness to mental illness (Weltmer, 1900).

> … [T]he world at large should understand the nature, as well as the power, of suggestion, and should know how to use it, for with such knowledge man would be free; he would no longer be a creature of circumstances, but would be the master instead of the slave of disease. (Weltmer, 1900, preface)

In 1887, Freud befriended Wilhem Fliess, an ear, nose, and throat specialist who believed that due to similarities between nasal and genital tissue, nose surgery could treat a number of disorders that were believed to be fueled by sexual frustration (Breger, 2000). Although beginning to develop his own approach to clients[1], Freud was fascinated by Fliess's theory of "nasal reflex neuroses," and particularly interested in the possible relationships among the nose, sexuality, and hysterical symptoms. As a result, Freud started to refer some

---

1. Freud and other psychoanalysts of his time used the word *patients*, and some contemporary analysts still do. However, the word has come under disfavor in recent years due to its association with the medical field and its air of aloofness. For convenience, this chapter will use the word *clients*.

of his own patients to Fliess to have surgery on the nose to help cure them of their hysterical symptoms.

> … Like many "hysterical" or "neurasthenic" patients of the era, she came to Freud with vague complaints, including stomach aches and menstrual problems. He deduced that she suffered from excessive masturbation that could be cured by operating on her nose. He prevailed on his best friend, Wilhelm Fliess, to perform the operation. (Pendergrast, 1995, pp. 407)

Freud and Fliess became particularly close (Breger, 2000). Fliess was the person to whom Freud opened up—his confidant—and the two soon were sharing esoteric ideas about the nature of being. Fliess was also a proponent of the use of cocaine to cure a host of diseases. Due in large part to Fliess's influence, Freud experimented with the drug and eventually had to struggle to break free of a cocaine addiction he developed. However, as Freud's ideas about the origins of symptoms and their relationship to sexuality changed, so did his relationship with Fliess, and their friendship would eventually end.

From 1893 through 1896, Freud worked on documenting case histories with his colleague Josef Breuer (1842–1925), who, like Charcot and Fliess, was trying to understand the development of hysterical symptoms in patients. One patient in particular, a 21-year-old named Anna O., intrigued the two curious physicians. Anna had come to Breuer with hysterical symptoms, including paralysis of limbs, unusual eye movements, problems with vision, difficulty maintaining her head in a suitable position, nausea, difficulty drinking despite being thirsty, problems with speech, confusion, and delirium (Freud, 1910/1965). Having been treated unsuccessfully by a number of doctors, many of whom believed she was faking her symptoms, Breuer treated Anna with humaneness from1880 to 1882. Through hypnosis and early attempts at **free association**, Anna was encouraged to talk about a number of underlying issues, which, Breuer hypothesized, were partially causing her symptoms. Eventually, Breuer believed that Anna blamed herself for the death of her father, whom she had cared for, and that she unconsciously caused her paralysis as a form of punishment. Anna's "talk therapy," as *she* called it, allowed her to release emotionally blocked aspects of herself. The importance of experiencing this **"catharsis"** or **"abreaction"** eventually became a critical tenet of many subsequent therapies, including psychoanalysis. Breuer worked tirelessly with Anna, often seeing her twice daily and putting 1,000 hours into her treatment (Gilhooley, 2002). However as Breuer continued to see Anna, he realized that she had become addicted to his presence and her mental health seemed correlated with his being there for her. Initially, this meticulous and dedicated physician was captivated by Anna, but he later became overwhelmed by her. In fact, some suggest that Breuer eventually became so distraught over her ongoing symptoms and insatiable needs that he turned to giving her psychotropic drugs in an effort to reduce her dependency (Gilhooley, 2002). Eventually, partly out of frustration, Breuer transferred her to a sanatorium. Although controversy about this case continues, most people suggest that it shows the power of client **transference** of past issues onto the therapist and of

countertransference, or the therapist's transference of past issues onto the client (to be discussed in more detail later). Despite treatment problems, it is likely that Breuer's therapy was a first step toward Anna's mental health, as Anna, later revealed to be Bertha Pappenheim, became a writer and early feminist, and is often identified as one of the first social workers in Germany. As a result of the work with Anna, in 1895, Freud and Breuer published *Studies in Hysteria* (1895/1974). Charcot, Fliess, and Breuer all influenced Freud's developing theory, but Freud alone had the genius to synthesize their ideas with ideas of his own and develop a comprehensive theory of counseling and psychotherapy. Some of the pieces of Freud's theory that grew out of these early consultations included such concepts as **neurosis**, the **unconscious**, **free association**, **defense mechanisms**, **transference** and **countertransference**, **resistance**, and **dream analysis**. But even then, his journey to a comprehensive theory had just begun to take shape.

As Freud continued to experiment with different techniques, he eventually decided to discontinue the use of hypnosis, as he found that some patients could not be hypnotized and that "cures" were often only temporary (Bankart, 1997). And, as he increasingly became interested in the relationship between sexuality and symptoms, he tried a new technique where he would "press" clients to uncover memories of early sexual trauma by pushing on their foreheads and encouraging them to reveal repressed memories.

> I have invented a strange therapy of my own: I search for sensitive areas, press on them, and thus provoke fits of shaking which free [the patient] … (Masson, 1985, p. 120)

Freud found that his push to get clients to talk usually resulted in the revelation that they had been molested at a young age by their fathers. Apparently, as a function of the unconscious influence Freud placed on these patients to come up with such memories led to the development of his "**seduction theory**," which suggested that early childhood sexual trauma was the cause of many of the symptoms exhibited by his patients. However, Freud eventually abandoned this theory for one in which childhood sexuality would play a major role and memories of early sexual trauma were seen as fantasy, often in an effort to repress memories of early masturbation. Freud's abandonment of the seduction theory has been criticized by some who say molestation of children was, and in many places still is, tolerated and ignored (Masson, 2003). Today, this issue remains controversial (Pendergrast, 1995), but what is not at question is Freud's ability to continually question his own theory. In fact, Freud's later version of psychoanalysis would seem far different than his earlier version.

In 1895, Freud published *The Interpretation of Dreams* (Freud, 1899/1976a), in which he first suggested that dreams represent underlying unresolved concerns and desires. Although this book would initially have modest sales, his career would soon take off on the basis of this and other publications. For instance, his 1901 book *The Psychopathology of Everyday Life* began to gain much popularity and some notoriety due to its compilation of "slips of the tongues," which could be quite funny at times. Then, after a number of delays probably related to anti-Semitism in Vienna, in 1902, Freud was appointed as associate professor at the University of Vienna. This was followed in 1905 with *Three Essays on the Theory of Sexuality*, which described the **psychosexual stages** of development, including the **oral**, **anal**, **phallic**, **latency**, and **genital stages**, and an explanation of what was to be commonly known as the **Oedipus complex** (Freud, 1905/1976b). In 1908, Freud was responsible for founding the ***Viennese Association of Psychoanalysis***, a predecessor to the many psychoanalytic societies found throughout the world today. As the years continued, Freud influenced and mentored dozens of early psychoanalysts, many of whom became well-known psychoanalysts and some of whom, like Carl Jung, Alfred Adler, and Otto Rank, eventually became disillusioned with Freud and went on to develop their own well-respected theories. Over the years, Freud wrote a number of other works that expanded on his theory, such as *Totem and Taboo* (1913/1950), *Introductory Lectures on Psychoanalysis* (1917/1973), *Beyond the Pleasure Principle* (1920/1961a), *The Future of an Illusion* (1927/1961b), and *Civilization and Its Discontents* (1930/2005).

As Freud continued to develop his ideas, he increasingly used the word "neurosis" to describe nervous symptoms that had no obvious organic basis. Believing such symptoms to be the manifestation of unconscious, unresolved psychosexual issues, Freud was not immune to the neuroses he talked about (Breger, 2000; Gay, 1988). No doubt his own struggles and neuroses fueled his desire to develop psychoanalytic theory. For instance, Freud struggled with anxiety, depression, a number of psychosomatic illnesses, a fear of trains and traveling, superstitious beliefs about numbers (e.g., the year he might die), and generalized fears of dying. Through his own self-analysis, he explored his memories and dreams, and came to recall sexual feelings toward his mother as well as feelings of anger and hostility toward his father. These memories, and his own sexual repression, likely led to the development of his famous Oedipus complex, which formed the basis for his ideas on childhood sexuality and an understanding of the superego. He was for a short time addicted to cocaine. He twice destroyed his personal papers, as he felt they were not particularly worthwhile, and he would often go into tirades when colleagues disagreed with him (Library of Congress, 2001). Finally, it was recently reported that Freud likely had an affair with his wife's sister, Minna Bernays, who lived with the Freuds (Blumenthal, 2006). No, Freud was not free from his own struggles; however, in his defense, he would have said that none of us are, and that we all have our own unique neuroses. In fact, it was his belief that the unconscious—the hidden, secretive, part of ourselves—hides our desires, fantasies, and wishes, which are the causes for all of our neuroses.

In 1938, with anti-Semitism growing in Austria and Europe, and following the Nazi invasion of Austria, Freud fled to London. In 1939, following a 15-year battle with cancer of the jaw, Freud asked a physician friend to assist him in suicide.

> On the following day, September 21, while I was sitting at his bedside, Freud took my hand and said to me: ... "My dear Schur, you certainly remember our first talk. You promised me then not to forsake me when my time comes. Now it's nothing but torture and makes no sense any

more." ... I indicated that I had not forgotten my promise.... When he was again in agony, I gave him a hypodermic of two centigrams of morphine. He soon felt relief and fell into a peaceful sleep. I repeated this dose after about twelve hours. Freud was obviously so close to the end of his reserves that he lapsed into a coma and did not wake up again. He died at 3:00 A.M. on September, 23, 1939. (Schur, 1972, p. 529)

Undoubtedly, Freud was a brilliant man of great complexity who changed the way people came to understand their existence (cf. Makari, 2008). Clearly, Freud was a man who struggled in his own life with unconscious desires and the demons associated with them. Assuredly, Freud was a person who changed the understanding and treatment of mental disorders and who brought us a new paradigm of understanding the individual.

VIEW OF HUMAN NATURE

Developing his theory at the turn of the twentieth century, Freud was immersed in the world of modernism (Brenkman, 2004). This world rejected traditionalism and the notion that the divine was the explanation for everything from the solar system to our reason for being. Instead, science and objectivity took precedence, as well as a search for new knowledge and truth. It is not surprising that at this point in time, Charcot and Breuer were found experimenting with hypnotism, and Fliess was developing his theory of nasal reflex neurosis, as they attempted to uncover reasons for individuals' neuroses. Freud, too, was experimenting, and his attempts at understanding the self would lead to a new model that continues to affect how we view our selves today. Radically challenging all of what had come before, Freud's model would evolve over time. In fact, what will be presented as Freudian theory in this text should be viewed as one of many iterations of Freud's ever-changing model. Don't for a minute think that what you read in this book is what Freud always believed, or that all psychoanalysts embraced every aspects of Freudian therapy—then or today. Freud and others of his day were experimenting—examining new ways of understanding self, new models to make sense of those aspects of *Homo sapiens* which could not at the time be measured in any objective scientific manner. No doubt, if Freud were alive today, he would continually be reshaping his theory to make it fit with current science and contemporary ways of understanding the psyche. So let us drift into the past and view a moment in time of Freudian theory and why it so affected the world we live in today.

Freud believed that humans are motivated by **instincts**, sometimes called **drives**. This innate **psychic energy** comprises what is called the **id** and steers behavior toward the satisfaction of unmet needs (e.g., hunger, thirst, survival, sex). However, because instincts are indiscriminate about the attainment of those needs, Freud postulated that restraints must be placed on the individual through the development of higher-order cognitive processes, which he called the **ego** and **superego**. Otherwise, individuals would respond in animalistic ways and the world would be chaotic, at best.

Finding acceptable ways of satisfying our instincts or resolving the tension of conflicting instincts are mostly unconscious processes; thus, we rarely experience the instinctual drives directly. However, Freud stated that their essence could be detected through our dreams, by slips of tongues, by understanding how our defense mechanisms manage the instincts, and by understanding how our neuroses and psychoses, manifested through symptoms, are representative of our unsuccessful attempts at redirecting instincts. Because the majority of time we spend unconsciously struggling to satisfy our unmet needs, Freud believed that happiness was an elusive feeling experienced infrequently and that we were destined to often be discontent:

> … One feels inclined to say that the intention that many should be 'happy' is not included in the plan of 'Creation'. What we call happiness in the strictest sense comes from the (preferably sudden) satisfaction of needs which have been dammed up to a high degree, and it is from its nature on possible as an episodic phenomenon. … Thus our possibilities of happiness are already restricted by our constitution. Unhappiness is much less difficult to experience. (Freud, 1930/2005, p. 53)

Freud said that our understanding of the world is based on how our psychological processes, unconscious and conscious, create what is called our **psychic reality**, or a person's subjective understanding of the world (Barratt, 1984; Meissner, 2001). This reality should be distinguished from objective reality, which is external to the person yet difficult to "know," as each person is operating from his or her own psychic reality. Freud believed that through psychoanalysis, one could gain a slightly greater understanding of one's motivations, and perhaps operate a little more from a stance that knows objective reality. However, even with analysis, Freud believed that many of our motives would remain unconscious. Using the "tip-of-the-iceberg" analogy, we all have the capability of understanding small pieces of behavior, and through therapy, see a slightly larger piece of ourselves, but our motivations, Freud believed, will still largely remain hidden (see Figure 2.1). Although our conscious wants to believe it's in charge, it is really those animalistic, instinctual, drives that underlie everything we do.

The paradox of Freud's theory is that society (which humans create) places restraints on behaviors, and the more restraints placed, the more likely we can live in peaceful coexistence. However, since we are inherently driven to satisfy our needs, placing restraints is unnatural and will inevitably lead to neurotic and even psychotic behavior as the individual attempts to control his or her urges through the use of **defense mechanisms**.

Freud hypothesized that from birth, instincts impinge on the person, and early child-rearing practices mold the manner in which individuals ultimately manage those instincts. This process occurs in often subtle and complex ways, and the management of those instincts becomes largely unconscious. Clearly, poor parenting results in behaviors that are not particularly effective in the management of instincts and leads to neurotic and psychotic behaviors. Since the template for

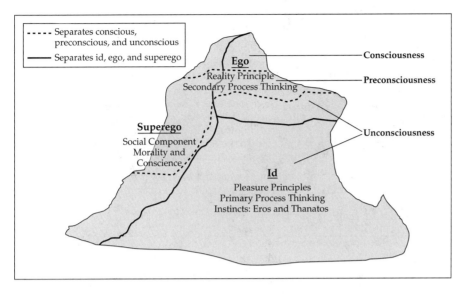

FIGURE 2.1 The "Tip of the Iceberg"

personality is developed at a very young age and is largely unconscious, making personality changes later in life is a monumental task. That is why his theory is often considered to be **deterministic**—our personalities are framed for us at very young ages and are quite difficult to change. However, there is some hope, as we can gain an increased understanding of our behaviors through therapy and self-analysis.

KEY CONCEPTS

Consciousness and Unconsciousness

Consciousness, or all of our feelings, thoughts, fantasies, and behaviors of which we are aware, is a small part of what Freud believed motivates the individual. The **unconscious** and more primitive mind, however, is the true motivator of our underlying desires and wants. The unconscious is driven by our id energy, which is comprised of our instincts. Again using the tip-of-the-iceberg analogy, consciousness represents a small portion of self, while unconsciousness represents the vast portion of all that motivates behavior (see Figure 2.1). In addition, being the storehouse of drives, the unconscious also houses repressed material and memories that hold a strong negative emotional charge and have been pushed out of consciousness to protect the individual. In contrast, those parts of ourselves that are relatively close to consciousness but not in awareness, Freud believed, were in the **preconscious**. The preconscious houses all memory that has been lost to consciousness but can be accessed and

---

B o x 2.1   Eros, Thanatos, and "Bug Chasers"

In recent years, there has been an increase in the number of gay men who seem driven to contract the HIV virus (Freeman, 2007). These "bug chasers" actively seek out HIV-positive men, known as "gift givers," in an effort to be "initiated or brought into the brotherhood" (Freeman, 2007, para. 5). How can this behavior be explained? Schoenewolf (2008) gives the following explanation:

> ... [P]sychiatrist ... Antoine Douaihy ... says that confusion, depression and mental illness contribute to what he considers self-destructive behavior. "They [bug chasers] are reaching out for some

kind of intimacy. They want to feel accepted and a part of something. It's a distorted way of exploring how you can become intimate with someone else." The distortion to which Douaihy is probably referring is the bug chaser's association of intimacy with disease and death; bug chasing would seem to be an ultimate demonstration of a death wish among some gay men. (para. 5)

In light of what you have learned about Eros and Thanatos, how might you explain the behavior of "bug chasers?"

---

remembered with relative ease (Freud, 1917/1973). The goal of psychoanalysis is to make a greater part of the unconscious conscious. This would enable the individual to gain increased understanding and more control over primitive urges and desires.

Drives and Instincts

Freud suggested that we are born with coexisting instincts: our **life instinct (Eros)**, and our **death instinct (Thanatos)**. The life instinct operates to meet our basic need for love and intimacy, sex, and survival of the individual and the species. It is associated with cooperation, collaboration, and harmony with others. The death instinct is a drive that seeks our own demise and dissolution. Freud believed that "the aim of life is death" (Freud, 1920/1961a, p. 32) and that fear, hate, self-destructive behaviors, and aggression toward others (death instinct projected outward) is a reflection of this instinct. Freud called all of the psychic energy that drove the life and death instincts the "**libido**," although the word has often been associated solely with the sex drive.

By their very nature, instincts are raw, have no conscience, and are largely unconscious. Consequently, we must find ways to restrain them if we are to live in a civilized world. This is accomplished through the development of higher cognitive functions, such as the formation of the ego and superego. It is the ego that helps us find outlets for our libido, such as working in order to make money to buy food and shelter, love to satisfy our need for intimacy and sex, the watching of and participating in sports events to manage our aggressive and self-destructive tendencies, and the finding of creative outlets to channel our psychic energy (e.g., an artist's painting of erotic symbolism). It is the superego that causes us to feel shame and guilt over our impulses and redirects us toward our ego to find acceptable outlets for those impulses. Problems with ego and superego development can sometimes lead to self-destructive behaviors (see Box 2.1).

B o x 2.2 Polymorphous Perversion

Freud strongly believed that our sexual instincts are raw and directionless at birth, and that early parenting roles shaped the emerging ego and superego, which would redirect the psychic energy from the sexual instincts. Thus, at birth, our sexuality could be expressed in any manner that would be pleasurable. Those individuals who did not successfully manage their sexual instincts, Freud stated, would end up with one of five perversions:

> First and foremost, it is an untenable error to deny that children have a sexual life and to suppose that sexuality only begins at puberty with the maturation of the genitals. On the contrary, from the very first children have a copious sexual life, which differs at many points from what is later regarded as normal. What in the adult life is

described as 'perverse' differs from the normal in these respects: first, by disregarding the barrier of species (the gulf between men and animals), secondly, by overstepping the barrier against disgust, thirdly that against incest (the prohibition against seeking sexual satisfaction from near blood-relations), fourthly that against members of one's own sex and fifthly the transferring of the part played by the genitals to other organs and areas of the body. (Freud, 1973/1917, p. 245)

Although we still hold to sexual prohibitions on bestiality and incest, homosexuality, bisexuality, and sexual stimulation of different parts of the body are today seen as some of the varied and normal responses to human sexuality.

Structure of Personality

Considered one of the early proponents of a theory of child development, Freud suggested that personality is powerfully affected by how early parental influences manage the development of three structures: the id, ego, and superego.

The Id. All of the psychic energy from our life and death instincts comprise the id—or more literally, "the it." We are born all id, and Freud believed that the id, sometimes called the **primitive mind**, unconsciously motivates almost all of our behaviors (see Figure 2.1). The id operates from raw, irrational impulses called **primary process**, and is fueled by the **pleasure principle**, whose aim is to reduce tension through the simplest means possible. Although tension reduction is sometimes achieved through the acquisition of the need-satisfying object (e.g., breast, food, person with whom to have sex), oftentimes the object is not immediately available—thus the development of the ego and superego, which help the psyche find alternative mechanisms for dealing with this tension. Imagine what kind of world we would live in if we had no mechanism for curbing our id (see Box 2.2).

The Ego. By default, the ego owes its development to the id, because without an id, the ego has no function. Called the "I" by Freud, the ego develops sometime after the infant is born as the child begins to wrestle with the external world of reality. Partly conscious, but also operating out of the preconscious and unconscious (see Figure 2.1), the manner in which the ego functions is often called **secondary process** (created secondarily after the id has formed). The main function of the ego is to temper the id by finding socially acceptable ways of meeting the needs of the demanding id. Thus, the ego is often said to be operating from the **reality principle**. The ego's functioning can be complex, because while it initially deals solely with the demands of the id, it soon also has to respond to the demands of the superego, which are generally in conflict with the id's instinctual desires. How an individual resolves the conflict between the id's desire for immediate gratification and the superego's press for moral behavior is said to be a reflection of the individual's **character**.

The Superego. Freud postulated that the superego, developed in the first few years of life, was the internalization of the moral imperatives of our parents and other significant others, and led to the development of a personal conscience. Freud believed that the superego emerged from the individual's Oedipal struggle. In this struggle, the individual is desirous of the parent of the opposite sex and wanting to eliminate the same-sexed parent. Realizing that this is not a possibility, the individual comes to grips with the fact that instincts must be constrained. How are they constrained? Through our moral imperatives—which are housed in our superego. "Thou shall renounce incestual desires and thou shall not kill!" says the superego. Clearly, without a conscience, we would be all id, living in a chaotic and animalistic world run by our instincts as we attempted to stake out our territory and satisfy our needs (Freud, 1961c/1927). Operating largely out of the unconscious and preconscious, it is often said that the major function of the superego is to "control the beast within" (see Figure 2.1). Consider the largely unconscious struggles a person goes through as he or she is driven to meet his or her needs (the id), is periodically reprimanded for having such needs (the superego), and struggles to find socially acceptable ways of satisfying those needs (the ego). At the same time, consider the importance of an id in helping us have fun, be creative, and be spontaneous (letting loose!); of the superego in assisting us in laying a foundation for living in a moral world; and of the ego in helping to balance these two contrasting aspects of ourselves. In the end, a healthy ego will step in to mitigate the harshness of the superego and manage the energy of the id as the individual learns how to live in a relatively civilized world despite the many internal conflicts that exist (see Box 2.3).

Anxiety

Freud realized that the complexities inherent in the development of the id, ego, and superego, as the individual tries to master living in the world, naturally lead to a life that is burdened with some amount of anxiety. More specifically, he identified three kinds of anxiety:

Realistic Anxiety. Ever walk down a dark street, alone, at night, in a part of town noted for its crime? Get nervous? Well, you should. You could get mugged, or worse. This is **realistic anxiety**, and Freud said that it is important for our ego to experience this kind of anxiety in order to take action—make it go away.

Moral Anxiety. Ever get caught masturbating? Ever do something that was "wrong" and get nervous about it? Ever think about doing something illegal or immoral? Did you get anxious? This is **moral anxiety**. Moral anxiety is an

---

Box 2.3 "Why War"

Freud believed that our intellect was a mechanism for individuals to control their animalistic urges and forge a world of peaceful coexistence. Although he undoubtedly felt this would be a difficult process, you can see his limited hopefulness concerning peace in the world in his reply to Albert Einstein who, as a member of the Society of Art and Letters of the League of Nations (the precursor to the United Nations), was asked to develop correspondence with other intellectuals around a topic of his choice. Einstein chose Freud—the topic, "Why War" (Freud, 1931–1932, as cited in Nathan & Norden, 1960):

> I now can comment on another of your statements. You are amazed that it is so easy to infect men with the war fever, and you surmise that man has in him an active instinct for hatred and destruction, amenable to such stimulations. I entirely agree with you. I believe in the existence of this instinct and have been recently at pains to study its manifestations.... (pp. 196–197)

> ... On the psychological side two of the most important phenomena of culture are, firstly, a

strengthening of the intellect, which tends to master our instinctive life, and, secondly, an introversion of the aggressive impulse, with all its consequent benefits and perils. Now war runs most emphatically counter to the psychic disposition imposed on us by the growth of culture; we are therefore bound to resent war, to find it utterly intolerable. With pacifists like us it is not merely an intellectual and affective repulsion, but a constitutional intolerance, an idiosyncrasy in its most drastic form....

How long have we to wait before the rest of men turn pacifist? Impossible to say, and yet perhaps our hope that these two factors—man's cultural disposition and a well-founded dread of the form that future wars will take—may serve to put an end to war in the near future, is not chimerical. But by what ways or byways this will come about, we cannot guess. Meanwhile we may rest on the assurance that whatever makes for cultural development is working also against war. (pp. 201–202)

---

important message about how we are living in the world. Clearly originating from the superego, it tells our ego that we are having thoughts that are unacceptable to our developed conscience.

Neurotic Anxiety.   It was a hot summer; I was in college, and I was staying in one of the residence halls with my girlfriend. We were the only ones there, and we hadn't been getting along. I woke up in the middle of the night, in a sweat, nervous that I was going to harm her in some way. I started walking around campus as I attempted to calm myself down. I was afraid I was going crazy. My "anxiety" had gotten the better of me. This **neurotic anxiety** was related to my id—in this case, my fear that my naturally aggressive drives would somehow take control of me and cause me to harm someone else. Neurotic anxiety is an important message to one's ego that the individual needs to take steps to ensure that the id doesn't take over.

Defense Mechanisms

The ego is in a difficult position as it attempts to fend off anxiety caused by strong urges from the id, demands from the superego, and real and perceived fears that we harbor. In order to protect the ego from anxiety, Freud, and later his daughter Anna Freud (1936/1966), identified a number of defense mechanisms that unconsciously help the individual cope with anxiety. Defense mechanisms are healthy when they

---

B o x 2.4   Examples of Some Defense Mechanisms

Asceticism: The repudiation of needs in an effort to deny urges and desires. *Example*: The anorexic is not only denying himself or herself food, but also his or her sexual impulses.

Compensation: The replacement of a perceived weak behavior by a perceived strong behavior. *Example*: A man becomes a bodybuilder because he feels inadequate as a conversationalist with women.

Denial: Not admitting that something has occurred. *Example*: The parent who refuses to admit that his child was molested.

Displacement: Redirecting an unacceptable impulse to a more acceptable object or person. *Examples*: An individual who has sexual urges toward a sibling becomes involved with computer sex. Or, murderous feelings toward one's parent become enraged feelings toward a political figure (e.g., the president).

Dissociation: The removal of oneself from feelings in order to delay experiencing those feelings. *Example*: A rape victim dissociates during the violent act in order to separate self from the fear and rage within.

Humor: Using comic relief to defer feelings. *Example*: After hearing that she needs a mastectomy for advanced breast cancer, the woman says to her friend,

"Well, at least I won't be viewed as a sex object any longer!"

Idealization: Overstating and overestimating the value of an object or a person to deny negative feelings toward that person. *Example*: A husband who is often criticized by his wife states, "My wife—she is the best person ever—she's bright, gorgeous, kind, and just perfect!"

Identification: Associating with certain individuals or groups in order to affiliate with specific values and deflect underlying feelings. *Example*: An individual becomes caught up with the "Virgin Vow Ministries," which professes the importance of remaining a virgin until marriage.

Intellectualization: Concentrating on the intellectual components of a situation in an effort to distance oneself from the anxiety-provoking emotions associated with the situation. *Example*: A person who has just been diagnosed with a virulent form of cancer wants to know all about the science of the disease.

Introjection: Identifying with an idea so completely that you accept it with little question. *Example*: The religious zealot who never questions her parents' or church's views on religion. This has the result of not

---

assist the individual in functioning in adaptive ways in society; however, they become pathological when they are overused and result in behaviors that impair everyday living. Consider the young child who skips along the sidewalk trying not to step on the lines, singing, "step on the crack and break your back." This child is binding his or her anxiety as he or she is beginning to realize that life is filled with some real fears. However, what if these fears continue into adulthood? The adult who feverishly tries to stop himself or herself from stepping on the cracks may have some serious psychosocial problems. Many adults will find other ways to bind their anxiety about living. Box 2.4 offers a partial list of some of the more well-known defense mechanisms. As you read through this list, think about what drives may be impinging on the person to create the defense mechanism, and to what anxiety the defense mechanism is responding. In what ways can the following defense mechanisms be adaptive or maladaptive?

Psychosexual Stages of Development

Freud had a unique and complex theory of how a child's libido is dispersed through specific stages of development. He postulated that as the child grows, having to fear certain of life's ambiguities or uncertainties (e.g., death).

Projection: Attributing unacceptable qualities in others that the individual actually has. *Example*: An individual calling a co-worker "judgmental and bossy," when the individual actually acts in that manner and has urges to tell others how to act.

Rationalization: The cognitive distorting of events to make them more acceptable with the implications being that there are good reasons for some unacceptable actions. *Example*: A parishioner says, "Our minister didn't harm anyone; he just had an affair—so what if she was married? The way he was treated after his wife died, you can understand why he would have an affair with someone who was putting herself out there."

Reaction formation: The replacing or conversion of an unacceptable impulse into an acceptable one. *Example*: An individual who has strong attractions to the same sex becomes virulently anti-gay and protests same-sex marriage.

Regression: Reverting to behavior from an earlier stage of development. *Examples*: A 10-year-old suddenly starts to wet his bed after he discovers his parents are getting divorced. Or, after losing his job, a 50-year-old becomes overly dependent on his wife.

Repression: Pushing out of consciousness threatening or painful thoughts. *Example*: The individual who does not allow herself to remember being molested.

Somatization: Converting strong feelings or impulses into physical symptoms. *Example*: An individual's fear of his sexuality is converted into hypochondriacal symptoms.

Splitting: Viewing people or objects as "all bad" or "all good." *Example*: "Guns are horrible killing machines," or "My co-worker is evil—she is just out for herself."

Sublimation: The channeling or refocusing of unacceptable impulses into socially accepted forms of behavior. *Example*: A person struggling with extreme anger becomes a butcher or boxer, or a person's sexual energy is channeled into creative and artistic endeavors.

Suppression: The act of pushing conscious thoughts into the preconscious because they are too anxiety-evoking. *Example*: The "good wife" who has thoughts of having an affair with a neighbor's husband pushes those thoughts out of consciousness.

Undoing: Performing a ritualistic or magical gestures to undo a behavior for which one is feeling guilty. *Examples*: Following a woman's passionate lovemaking, she always has to clean the house. Or, after spanking his children, a father takes them out for ice cream.

---

his or her psychic energy becomes focused on differing **erogenous zones** that correspond to the unfolding biological development of the child. First, the child receives pleasure through the mouth, then the anus, and finally the genitals. As the child develops, the manner in which his or her needs are met relative to the erogenous zone being focused upon will affect later personality development. When a child is overindulged or frustrated during a stage, his or her libido becomes locked or **fixated** at that stage. In other words, the child will have unfinished psychological issues related to that stage and resort to childlike behaviors that are reflective of the unresolved stage. In contrast, the child whose libido is properly dispersed through a stage will continue on to the next stage with less difficulty. The five stages as identified by Freud include the oral, anal, phallic, latency, and genital stages.

1. *Oral stage.* Between birth and 18 months of age, the infant's erogenous zone is the mouth, and pleasure is found through sucking, eating, and biting. Problems with early feeding through neglect and abuse can lead to adults who seek to complete their missing oral gratification. They may do this by becoming dependent on others, by smoking or drinking too much, by

overeating, by overtalking, and so on. On the other hand, children who have been overindulged may become needy, demanding, and upset as they constantly expect their needs to be coddled—as they were during their oral stage. Still others may develop an *oral aggressive* personality as a result of problems during teething. These individuals may become verbally aggressive, argumentative, dogmatic, sarcastic, and so forth.

2. *Anal stage.* Obtaining control over bowel movements is a major task of this stage, which occurs between ages 18 months and 3 years. The inherent conflict in this stage arises due to tension between the child's desire to obtain pleasure through the expulsion of feces and the child's need to please parents who are trying to teach the child how to control this important bodily function. The conflict between wanting to recklessly expel feces and learning how to appropriately go to the bathroom can have far-reaching implications. Parents who are particularly lenient may raise children who have an **anal expulsive** personality, and tend to be messy, cruel, sloppy, disorganized, reckless, careless, defiant, and perhaps overly generous. However, parents who are particularly strict and use punishment and humiliation in potty training will have children who have an **anal retentive personality**. These children tend to be stubborn, perfectionistic, neat, precise, orderly, careful, stingy, withholding, obstinate, meticulous, and passive-aggressive. As you might well imagine, this stage also has implications for how individuals deal with issues of authority and control, both as children and adults.

3. *Phallic stage.* Experiencing pleasurable genital sensations is a major focus during this stage, which occurs between ages 3 years and 5 or 6 years. Children in this stage will self-stimulate (masturbate) and have a fascination with bodily functions. They can be particularly influenced by the moral imperatives of their parents. As children begin to have sexual feelings, Freud posited that there is an unconscious desire to possess the parent of the opposite sex and eliminate or kill the parent of the same sex. Keep in mind that the libido is unconscious and has no conscience. It simply wants, and is impinging on the individual in an effort to be expressed. For most boys, who have generally been parented by mothers at this early stage, their natural sexual drive will lead them to desire their mothers. Since dad is the obvious obstacle to mom, a boy's natural aggressive instincts will want to get rid of dad. Thus, we see Freud's development of the **Oedipus complex,** or desire to sleep with or possess one's mother and kill one's father, as in the Greek story of king Oedipus, who unknowingly killed his father and married his mother.

With a boy's realization that some people don't have a penis (e.g., his mother!), he develops an unconscious fearful fantasy that his father will castrate him in an effort to rid him of his sexual desires for his mother (and make him like his mother). This fear has become known as **castration anxiety**. Resolution of this stage occurs through the son's repression of his feelings for his mother as he realizes he is no match for his father. It is also at this point that the son will begin to identify with the aggressor, his father, and displace the sexual feelings he has toward his mother, to girls, and later to women. As he identifies with his father, he internalizes male sex roles behaviors and joins the "club" of men. Although Freud was much more vague on a similar process for women, he did talk of a "female oedipal complex" (Scott, 2005). However, his disciple, Carl Jung, used the term *Electra complex*, and this term seemed to take hold, despite Freud's dislike of the phrase. The **Electra complex** in women is characterized by the girl's realization that she lacks a penis and her unconscious belief that she must have been castrated. She sees her genitals as wounded and inferior. She subsequently desires a penis of her own and, when she realizes she will not have a penis, her **penis envy** is eroticized through a desire for her father and the wish for a child by him. In essence, she wants to "take in" his penis so she has one of her own. Feeling rebuffed by her father, eventually, the young woman identifies with her mother and replaces her erotic desire for her father for other, more appropriate men—still hoping to have a child to substitute for the missing penis. However, Freud believed that women must go through life feeling lacking, which manifests itself in passive role-taking and feelings of competitiveness with men. Today, Freud is believed to have had a culturally encapsulated view of men and women (consider the role women had at that time in history!) and has been largely and justifiably criticized by feminists and others for his belief that women can never fully resolve their inherent conflicts. Consequently, Freud's understanding of women's development has been challenged by many, and this aspect of his theory is no longer seen as viable (Breger, 2000) (see Box 2.5).

Freud believed that phallic stage fixation can lead to a variety of conflicts, including issues related to the sex role identity. For instance, the boy who is overly attended to by his mother and whose father is relatively uninvolved may exhibit traditional feminine characteristics *or* may become "macho" as he attempts to compensate for his lack of identification with his father. Or consider "daddy's little girl," whose mother is seen as subservient. This girl may become particularly self-centered and narcissistic as she expects to be treated particularly well by all men in her life.

4. *Latency stage.* Strictly speaking not a psychosexual stage, the latency stage occurs between the ages of 5 or 6 years and puberty. Here, there is repression of the libido, and during this holding pattern, the child focuses on peer relationships and other age-appropriate activities, such as athletics and school. However, the repression of one's sexuality soon ends with movement into the genital stage.

5. *Genital stage.* Occurring around the onset of puberty, there is a resurgence of one's sexuality. It is during this stage that resulting patterns of behavior from passage through the earlier stages become expressed. Fixation at these earlier stages will yield neurotic and psychotic behaviors, said Freud.

Although Freud has been criticized over the years for what some have been described as his extreme focus on the erogenous zones and their effect on personality development, many today view Freud's theory from a broader perspective. These individuals tend to focus more on a global view of the growing

---

B o x 2.5 Penis Envy or Womb Envy?

"I worked with Freud in Vienna. We broke over the concept of penis envy. Freud felt that it should be limited to women." (Woody Allen in *Zelig*)

Even before the feminist revolution of the 1960s, a number of early feminists and psychoanalysts took issue with Freud's conceptualization of female sexuality (cf. Horney, 1967). For instance, renowned psychoanalyst Karen Horney took umbrage with Freud's notion of penis envy as early as the 1930s. During the 1960s, Horney took exception to Freud's contention that women are inherently inferior to men due to their "penis envy":

> When one begins, as I did, to analyze men only after a fairly long experience analyzing women, one receives a most surprising impression of the intensity of this envy of pregnancy, childbirth, and motherhood, as well as of the breasts and of the act of suckling." (Horney, 1967, pp. 60–61)

Almost 30 years later, Gloria Steinem (1994) takes a much stronger stance against Freud's ideas in her satirical essay, "*What If* Freud *Were Phyllis*?":

> … All life begins as female, in the womb as elsewhere (the only explanation for men's residual nipples), and penile tissue had its origin in the

same genital nub, and thus retained a comparable number of nerve endings as the clitoris. But somewhere along the evolutionary line, the penis had acquired a double function: excretion of urine *and* sperm delivery. Indeed, during the male's feminine, masturbatory, clitoral stage of development—before young boys had seen female genitals and realized that their penises were endangered and grotesque compared to the compact, well-protected aesthetically perfect clitoris—it had a third, albeit immature, function of masturbatory pleasure.

> It was almost as if Father Nature himself had paid "less careful attention" to the male. (pp. 50–51)

> Even designing their own clothes could be left to men only at the risk of repetitive results. When allowed to dress themselves, they seldom could get beyond an envy of wombs and female genitals which restricted them to an endless success of female sexual symbols. Thus, the open button-to-neck "V" of men's jackets was a well-known recapitulation of the "V" of female genitalia; the knot in men's ties replicated the clitoris, while the long ends of the tie were clearly meant to represent the labia. As for men's bow ties, they were the clitoris *erecta* in all its glory. All these were, to use Phyllis Freud's technical term, "representations." (p. 34)

---

individual at early stages of development and how parenting skills affect the developing child (see Box 2.6).

Transference and Countertransference

Indira was a 32-year-old woman who complained of difficulties in her relationships with men. Indira said that she perceives most men as untrustworthy, rarely allowed herself to get close to a man, and then invariably experienced some form of betrayal or hurt. During her first session, she gave a detailed description of a difficult childhood. Her father had a severe drinking problem—when sober, he would be loving and kind; when drunk, he would often be physically or verbally abusive to her mother and herself. In her second session, Indira stated that she had come to see her psychiatrist because of his excellent reputation, but that she was upset that some of his comments at their initial encounter seemed inappropriately critical of her and was unwilling to continue the therapy.

B o x 2.6   A Modern-Day Look at the Psychosexual Stages

Freud has been justifiably criticized for his extreme focus on the erogenous zones of the developing child as well as his assumptions about the psychosexual development of girls resulting in a whole gender that is inferior. However, many have argued that if one were to take a more generalized view of the affects of parenting on early child development, Freud undoubtedly had much to offer. In fact, in reviewing those aspects of Freudian theory that seem to have been supported by research, Westen (1998) notes that one area that appears to have stood the test of time is that "stable personality patterns begin to form in childhood, and childhood experiences play an important role in personality development, particularly in shaping the ways people form later social relationships" (p. 334).

For instance, the infant who is under two years of age is mostly concerned with sustenance, being nurtured, early motor development, and beginning language development. Almost all would agree that these very young children are dealing with the beginning development of trust and feeling safe in the world. Imagine a parent who rarely holds his or her infant, lets the child go hungry, or slaps his or her baby

when the baby cries out from hunger or not being held. This child will clearly form different attachments early in life and will undoubtedly develop a very different "character" or personality style than the child who is lovingly held and fed when hungry.

Or think about the child in the anal stage who is just learning how to use the "potty" and gain independence. The parent who yells at this child's unsuccessful attempts to go to the bathroom or ridicules this child's early attempts at exploring the world is clearly raising a different child than the parent who is accepting of this child's early but unsuccessful attempts at toilet training or the parent who praises a child's attempts at exploration.

Finally, consider parents who create shame and guilt by chiding a child who is exploring his or her body versus parents who teach the child that his or her body should be honored and special. And even more globally at this stage, think about the kind of moral imperatives children at this age (3 to 6 years) are hearing from their parents and the manner in which they are hearing them (e.g., for a child's misbehaving: "you're going to hell" versus "let's see if we can find a different way of doing that.")

Over the next several sessions, she alternated between indicating a sense of attachment to and reliance on her therapist and feeling let down by his words or actions. (Stein et al., 2006, p. 580)

Early on in Freud's work, he realized that clients were projecting feelings, thoughts, and attitudes onto the therapist as if the therapist were someone else. This "**false connection**," as Freud referred to it, suggested that—much like Indira in the vignette you just read—clients were not really relating to the therapist, but to a past image of an important person in the client's life (Freud & Breuer, 1895/1974). Calling this **transference**, Freud realized that these projections could play an important role in uncovering the impact that significant relationships had on the client's life. If the client were indeed responding to the therapist as if he or she were someone else, helping the client to understand this process could be the door to opening important insights for the client. For instance, on a very basic level, if I am seeing my therapist as aloof and emotionless, and if these are projections on my part, it could be that this was my experience of my father (or mother) and I am transferring these feelings onto my therapist, ultimately believing that this is indeed how my therapist is. Helping me understand this could free me from creating a "false connection" with the therapist or indeed with other significant people in my life. Thus, one of the goals of psychoanalysis is to assist the client in seeing the **transference relationship** the client has created so that the client can relate more honestly with the analyst and with others:

> The patients, too, gradually learnt to realize that in these transferences on to the figure of the physician it was a question of a compulsion and an illusion which melted away with the conclusion of the analysis. (Freud & Breuer, 1895/1974, p. 392)

A corollary to transference is **countertransference**, or the unconscious transferring of thoughts, feelings, and attitudes onto the client by the therapist. Imagine what havoc such countertransference can cause in a therapeutic relationship. If the therapist sees the client as someone other than who he or she is, the therapist is working with an imaginary client—one who was manufactured by the therapist's own projections. Countertransference can be devastating to the therapeutic relationship, and since the process is unconscious, the only way to ensure that countertransference is not occurring is for the therapist to have undergone his or her own therapy to minimize unresolved issues that may cause such projections, and for the therapist to participate in supervision so that an objective third person can assess this relationship. Now, what if the supervisor has countertransference to the therapist or to the client and the therapist has countertransference to the client? What a mess! (See Figure 2.2).

THERAPEUTIC TECHNIQUES

Psychoanalysts believe that all children are faced with the inherent struggles that each of the psychosexual stages pose, although effective parenting will help ease these struggles and is one factor critical to the development of healthy functioning. The end result of passage through these stages is the development of defense mechanisms, and the purpose of classical psychoanalysis is to help the client understand how he or she has come to use defenses in an attempt to mediate psychic energy. Defenses are healthy if they can effectively route psychic energy toward acceptable behaviors. However, they become dysfunctional when they lead to behaviors that cause problems in living, as manifested in neuroses or psychoses. Thus, clients are encouraged to uncover the true meaning of their behaviors, which are a reflection of the diversion of psychic energy, and the therapist can help interpret early childhood patterns that result in such behaviors. This can clearly be a labor-intensive process and can take years. A number of techniques have evolved to help the analyst facilitate deeper understanding by clients, including **creating a trusting atmosphere**, **free association**, **interpretation of resistance**, **dream analysis**, **interpretation of parapraxes**, and **interpretation of the transference relationship** (Ursano, Sonnenberg, & Lazar, 2004).

Creating a Trusting Atmosphere

If clients are to feel free enough to share feelings, thoughts, and behaviors that can be deeply embarrassing and shameful, the analyst must create an

FIGURE 2.2 Countertransference Gone Awry

environment safe enough to encourage such revelations. In classical analysis, the analyst would use **analytic neutrality**, which was accomplished by having the client lie on a couch with the analyst sitting in a chair off to the side, listening carefully and responding empathically. Encouraging the client to share his or her deepest thoughts, the analyst would respond in a nonjudgmental manner to any client revelations. Although you still find some analysts practicing in this manner, today, most have given up the aloofness of the couch and have a more engaging style where periodic self-disclosure might even be seen as appropriate in an effort to build the relationship and explore the inner thoughts of the clients. In either case, many of the basic precepts of classical psychoanalysis are adhered to. For instance, it is core to all analytical approaches to examine the **transference relationship**. As noted earlier, such a relationship mimics early patterns between the client and significant others, often parents. Here, the client projects onto the therapist and begins to see the analyst as embodying qualities of these significant people from the client's past. At appropriate times, the therapist can then interpret these projections for the client and show how they are related to early child-rearing issues (see "Interpretation of the Transference Relationship").

Free Association

Free association is the shedding of cognitive restraints such that the client feels "free" to "associate" to any thought available without editing or suppression of what the client might otherwise consider irrelevant, unimportant, or too distressing to talk about publicly. Free association assumes that the psyche does its best to try and protect itself from exposing repressed parts of oneself in an effort to maintain the current manner of functioning and one's ego defenses. Exposure to repressed parts through free association can reveal our true thoughts, feelings, wishes, and desires, and can only occur in a trusting, facilitative environment.

Interpretation of Resistance

Resistance is anything that impedes the work of analysis or prevents the analyst from gaining access to the client's unconscious. It is particularly manifest when it impedes the process of free association, but can occur throughout the relationship. Client resistance is a signal that the client is close to dealing with an unconscious issue. Some examples of client resistance are showing up late or missing appointments, getting upset and angry at the analyst, or retreating or regressing in therapy. Analysts will interpret such resistance to help clients deal directly with the threatening issue inherent in the resistance.

Dream Analysis

The interpretation of dreams is the royal road to a knowledge of the unconscious activities of the mind. (Freud, 1899/1976a, p. 769)

Freud believed that dreams are a projection of our unconscious and represent symbolic images of our desires and wishes. These images, said Freud, have **manifest** and **latent meanings**. The manifest meaning is the obvious, more conscious meaning of the dream. However, even in our dreams, our wishes are repressed, and thus dreams are believed to have underlying or latent meanings that can be discovered through analysis. Although a client often feels more comfortable sharing the manifest meaning of a dream, he or she will also feel comfortable delving into the latent meaning if the therapeutic environment is trusting enough to allow such in-depth work (see Box 2.7).

Interpretation of Parapraxes

He that has eyes to see and ears to hear may convince himself that no mortal can keep a secret. If his lips are silent, he chatters with his fingertips; betrayal oozes out of him at every pore. (Freud, 1905/1953, pp. 77–78)

B o x 2.7   Jeannie's Unresolved Father Issues

Read and/or watch Dr. Paula Justice help Jeannie understand some of the unresolved issues she had regarding the death of her father and how this is related to current issues with her husband, who acquired a disability, as well as how her death wish impacts her.

You can read this session by going to www.cengage.com/counseling/neukrug. Then click on "companion site" of this book and go to "student downloads." Or your instructor may show this session in class with the DVD that accompanies his or her copy of the text.

So, a client walks into his analyst's office, chuckling to himself, and says: "How many therapists does it take to change a light bulb?" Going along with this "joke," the therapist says, "How many? Tell me." The client says, "Just one, but the light bulb has to really want to change." The analyst then looks at the client and says, "Are you telling me that maybe *you* don't really want to change, and I'm going to have to work really hard to help you change?" The client, who thought he was just "telling a joke," suddenly realizes that maybe there was something else behind this "joke."

Jokes are a type of **parapraxes**, or errors of speech, slips of the tongue, "misspeaks," or subtle behaviors that reveal unconscious meanings that are symbolic of repressed wishes and desires (Freud, 1905/1976c). Of all parapraxes, perhaps the best known is the "**Freudian slip**." Interpretation of such slips in a timely fashion could help the client understand the hidden meanings behind such a slip. In addition to jokes and Freudian slips, Freud felt that such things as satire, nonverbal behaviors, atypical behaviors, misspelled words, forgetting words, bungling actions, and so forth could be symbolic of hidden desires and conflicts (Freud, 1901/1989) (see Box 2.8). On the other hand, when a student asked the icon who smoked cigars incessantly what the symbolic meaning of a cigar might be, Freud reportedly said, "Sometimes a cigar is just a cigar."

Interpretation of the Transference Relationship

As noted earlier, a cornerstone of the relationship with the analyst is the development of the **transference relationship**, in which the client projects or "transfers" onto the analyst unacceptable thoughts, feelings, fantasies, and patterns of behavior which were experienced as a child toward another, usually a parent, but were repressed due to the client's unique personality structure that was developed as a result of early child-rearing practices. These unconscious thoughts, feelings, fantasies, and behaviors are now projected onto the therapist (and others). For instance, consider what the client might be saying about himself or herself when he or she sees his or her therapist as lewd, disengaged, critical, or angry. The therapist can now interpret these projections and help the client examine their origins and how they affect all of the client's relationships. For instance, the client who calls his or her therapist "stingy" might be reflecting repressed childhood feelings of being

---

B o x 2.8   What Did He Really Mean?

See, in my line of work you got to keep repeating things over and over and over again for the truth to sink in, to kind of catapult the propaganda.

(former President George W. Bush, Greece, New York, May 24, 2005)

---

unloved by his or her parents (stingy with love) that led to the adult client's feeling a sense of emptiness. This need for love is likely experienced with many people in the client's life but seen, by the client, as an inability of others to show love. Thus, timely therapeutic revelations not only can help the client resolve the transference relationship that occurs in therapy, but also can help to resolve similar "transference relationships" with other important people in the client's life. In a sense, Freud and others were suggesting that our relationships are not real; in actuality, we are experiencing ourselves through our projections. Life is an illusion!

THE THERAPEUTIC PROCESS

Psychoanalysis is a long-term, in-depth process in which the client may meet with a therapist three or more times a week for five or more years. In an effort to build the transference relationship, the analyst remains relatively quiet vis-à-vis the client. Empathy and listening skills are crucial at the beginning of therapy to help build the alliance but are also used throughout to help anchor the client in the relationship. At the beginning of the relationship, resistance is explained, and throughout the relationship it is pointed out as clients attempt to avoid discussing difficult topics through a wide range of resistant behaviors (coming late, not paying, missing appointments, seeing the analyst as incompetent, etc.). As therapy continues, interpretation and analysis become key techniques. Over time, and as issues are resolved, the therapist will begin to be seen by the client in a more objective and realistic manner. Late in the therapeutic process, as anonymity becomes less important, the therapist may feel free to reveal small aspects of himself or herself. Ultimately, the relationship ends when the client has gained increased knowledge and awareness of underlying dynamics and how these dynamics are expressed through his or her patterns and symptoms, and when the client has made some changes based on these insights. It should be noted, however, that since so much of our behavior is mitigated by our unconscious desires and needs, therapy can only unravel a portion of why we do what we do. However, increased understanding of our psyche and the forces that shape our behaviors can lead to a kind of limited freedom as we increasingly understand ourselves. In addition, now that we have a model of our psyche and an understanding of why we do the things we do, after analysis is finished, clients have the means to explore and understand themselves.

SOCIAL, CULTURAL, AND SPIRITUAL ISSUES

A number of cultural considerations should be taken into account in regard to psychoanalysis. First, one should consider the context in which psychoanalysis was formed. As a member of a Western, male-dominated society, Freud viewed his approach through the eyes of white, European, mostly well-off males. Second, as a Jew faced with rampant anti-Semitism, Freud undoubtedly was impacted by the cultural norms of his religion and the ongoing prejudice that he faced. Also, Vienna—and Europe in general—was seen as a modern yet sexually repressed society. Finally, keep in mind that much of Freud's theory grew out of Freud's own self-analysis and his work with patients, not from empirically proven studies. Thus, here we have a Jewish man who sees the world through a misogynistic lens, understands the family from the perspective of the Jewish culture that stresses internal locus of control, is repressed sexually himself, and lives in a sexually repressed culture. However, despite the fact that Freud was embedded with these cultural values, it is evident that he was a revolutionary, radically challenging the then-understanding of the mind. From acknowledging childhood sexuality to defining an unconscious to describing the conflictual psychic forces, Freud challenged the established way of understanding motivation and personality and was one of the first persons willing to explore new frontiers and hypothesize about novel ways of understanding the mind. In fact, much of the language commonly used today to describe the Western world's understanding of the psyche can be credited to Freud. So, given this historical context, does psychoanalysis offer much to clients in today's world? Undoubtedly, yes; however, it clearly would depend on what the client is looking for and the kind of diagnosis being presented. Those looking for "quick cures" or sharply focused treatment would likely not do well with this approach. Those who are not comfortable or even deny the presence of intrapsychic processes might be better off seeking treatment elsewhere. However, understanding how internal conflicts and early parenting issues may have played a role in the development of one's psyche is not solely the ilk of the developed Western world. Clearly, others can find some common ground in an approach like this.

Relative to women, some feminists have challenged Freud's view of women, suggesting he saw them as second-class citizens who were somehow "lacking" as compared to their male counterparts. Others suggest that by giving up his seduction theory, which suggested that sexual abuse of children was rampant, he may have capitulated to the forces of the prevailing zeitgeist of the times, which was afraid to look at this potentially explosive issue (Pendergrast, 1995). Still others believe that he at least acknowledged the power of sexuality and the potential for its abuse. At the very least, given the time period, Freud should be hailed for acknowledging that women had an internal world that affected their way of being and which must be addressed:

> The cultural influence of feminist *denunciation* of Freud (like that of
> Rush—for falsifying women's experience) has been shadowed by an

equally powerful feminist emphasis on the necessity of *returning* to Freud to understand women's psychic life. (Segal, 1996, p. 290)

Although most would be hard-pressed to call Freud a social justice advocate, he clearly saw the importance that the external world placed on the development of the psyche. While on one hand, Freud believed in the importance of the development of the autonomous ego, on the other hand, he recognized the interdependence among ego development and family and societal values and dictates (Danto, 2005). Believing that peace and relative contentment could only come if people understood themselves *and* if societies made decisions for the betterment of all their citizens, perhaps it's not surprising that Freud suggested the establishment of free clinics to help the poor have the opportunity to understand their inner world:

In 1918, just two months before the Armistice, Freud had rallied the psychoanalysts assembled in Budapest for their fifth international congress to start these "institutions or out-patient clinics … where treatment shall be free. The poor man should have just as much right to assistance for his mind as he now has to the life-saving help offered by surgery," he affirmed. (Danto, 2005, pp. 1–2)

Freud's appeal was heard, and up to one-fifth of the work of first- and second-generation psychoanalysts of the time was made available to individuals who could not normally afford such treatment (Danto, 2005). In addition, in a number of cities across Europe, free clinics run by sympathetic psychoanalysts who believed they were in the middle of a revolution that could help free individuals from their neurotic constraints began to arise.

Although psychoanalysis is certainly not as popular as it was early in the twentieth century, it still has quite a following. And although it is true that money and time can afford a person the ability to undergo in-depth analysis, it is also true that many analysts today see clients for free or at a reduced cost, and that the traditional method of analysis has often been adapted based on new knowledge and the current needs of society. So, it is not unusual to see many analysts practicing a modified psychoanalytical approach in which a client is seen once a week. Although not a short-term approach, such a modified approach can have wide appeal. And what might the world look like if we all underwent some version of psychoanalysis? Well, it is likely we would have much greater understanding of our motivations and increasingly make intentional choices that would less likely harm others and more likely bring peace to the world.

A word about religion. Although an atheist, Freud had a complex view of religion. Belief in God, said Freud, was partly leftover remnants of projections from early tribes. He believed that early tribes needed to "find" an external force that would control primal urges and thus prevent the tribe from killing themselves off. Thus, they manufactured "gods" to pray to, and gave these external authorities the power to control their internal drives. He also believed that God was a projection from an internalized image of our father as a result of the Oedipal complex. As the child comes to grips with the fact that he or she is not more powerful than the father, the father becomes revered and internalized as an all-powerful figure. This **imago**, or idealized image of the loved father, then becomes projected onto the world in the form of God. Freud had respect for those who reflected on the complexity of religion but also believed that most people were caught up in their projections and could not see how they live in what he considered to be a fantasy world:

> ... [I]t is painful to think that the great majority of mortals will never be able to rise above this view of life. It is still more humiliating to discover how large a number of people living to-day, who cannot but see that this religion is not tenable, nevertheless try to defend it piece by piece in a series of pitiful rearguard actions. (Freud, 1930/2005, pp. 49–50)

Freud suggested that religion was used to avoid one's ultimate fears concerning living and dying. However, others have taken a kinder view of psychoanalysis and religion. For instance, MacIsaac (1974) suggests that original sin is an important concept with which we all must come to grips and is very similar to Freud's concept of unconscious instinctual drives:

> ... This book is rooted in the conviction that the kind of sinful reality referred to by the terms *peccatum originale originatum* [original sin] and the sin of the world bears primarily on man as unconscious. (p. 4)

Today, Freud's views on religion are seen as just his voice. Although many analysts might still agree that most people's gods are a projection from their unconscious, they do not eliminate the concept of God in its totality. The idea that there is something "more" than our own humanness is a "leap of faith" embraced by many psychoanalysts (and others). Today, religion, spirituality, and the acceptance of God are choices that each analyst makes on his or her own and are not seen as avoidance of deeper life-and-death issues.

> With greater awareness of the meaning and function of its own rituals, psychoanalysis can now appreciate religious ritual in a way more differentiated than was possible in Freud's early formulations. (Kakar, 1991, p. 67)

EFFICACY OF PSYCHOANALYSIS

> The critique that empirical research cannot capture the wealth of unconscious processes evolving in patient and analyst, and that, characteristically, empirical research misses the deeper aspects of oedipal and pre-oedipal, sexual and aggressive fantasy life and conflicts, seems correct. (Kernberg, 2006, p. 920)

In examining the efficacy of psychoanalysis, the problem is: How does one measure changes in the unconscious? Indeed, the unconscious, by its very nature, is unknown, so how do you measure the unknown? At best, one can measure some nebulous subjective changes that an individual might say he or she is experiencing. So, if it's difficult or impossible to measure, can one make statements that progress has been made? Some can argue that you can measure outcomes related to treatment (e.g., fewer sick days from work, higher self-esteem, a better relationship with a loved one), but are such changes really the result of changes due to greater consciousness and a reintegration of self? Perhaps they are simply the result of being with a therapist who is modeling more effective behaviors, or due to growing older. Keeping in mind that researching such constructs as the unconscious and internal conflicts is, at best, difficult to measure (Leuzinger-Bohleber & Target, 2002), and knowing that due to its length there are many who do not participate in psychoanalysis, you can see why research on the effectiveness of psychoanalysis is complex. Nevertheless, dozens of studies have been completed that look at the efficacy of psychoanalysis (cf. Carhart-Harris, Mayberg, Malizia, & Nutt, 2008; Gabbard, Gunderson, & Fonagy, 2002; Galatzer-Levy, Bachrach, Skolnikoff, & Waldron, 2000; Fonagy, 2000; Fonagy, 2002; Frey, 2006; Leichsenring, 2005; Stein et al., 2006). Summarizing these studies, we find the following:

- From numerous clinical studies involving hundreds of clients who "were selected as suitable for psychoanalysis," 60 to 90 percent show significant improvement (Galatzer-Levy et al., 2000, p. 123).

- Although psychoanalysis is today practiced around the world, it likely has its best outcomes with individuals who are comfortable with traditional Western values.

- Building a therapeutic alliance, so key to the psychoanalytic process, has been shown to be one of the most important qualities in successful outcomes of therapy.

- Many who enter psychoanalysis have a keen sense of what they are about to experience, and since meeting client expectations of what will happen in therapy has been shown to be related to successful outcomes, it makes sense that one would find a high satisfaction rate with psychoanalysis.

- In dozens of studies, psychoanalysis has been found to be effective when working with individuals who are seeking such treatment and are not in dire straits.

- Some specific disorders in which psychoanalysis has shown efficacy include depressive disorders, anxiety disorders, disorders based on neurotic conflicts, relationship problems, post-traumatic stress disorder, somatoform disorder, bulimia, anorexia, borderline personality disorder, substance-related disorders, and Cluster C personality disorders (avoidant, dependent, and obsessive–compulsive).

- Although psychoanalysis may be helpful for people who are experiencing serious disorders, it has not been shown to be helpful with clients who have a long history of unsuccessful treatment attempts and when psychoanalysis is seen as a last effort to help the person.

B o x 2.9   Jake Meets with a Psychoanalyst

Please review the Miller family's background, which can be found in Appendix B, and then read about

Jake's encounter with a psychoanalyst, which can also be found in Appendix B.

- Although not as efficacious as full-term psychoanalysis, there is some evidence that brief psychoanalysis (e.g., once a week), can be as effective as or more effective than other treatment modes.

- Psychoanalysis is less likely to be helpful for those disorders that typically can be treated in brief therapy mode, such as phobias and other disorders in which problems are focused and goal-setting can be accomplished in relatively short amount of time.

- Recent advances in brain imagery appears to indicate that there are aspects of the brain which respond to emotion without conscious awareness and specific areas of the brain that seem to be associated with unwanted memories, thus giving some credence to the theory of an "unconscious" part of the brain. In addition, other research appears to indicate that a mechanism to repress difficult materials may be inherent in our brains. (See Box 2.9.)

SUMMARY

This chapter began by offering biographical information about Sigmund Freud, the originator of psychoanalytic therapy. This information placed a historical reference point for this important theory, which has influenced how many in the world view the development of personality. Some of the major points covered in this part of the chapter included a description of Freud's family; information about individuals who influenced Freud's early work, such as Charcot, Fliess, and Breuer; his early work with hypnosis; his abandonment of the seduction theory; and how his early work influenced the development of such concepts as neurosis, the unconscious, free association, defense mechanisms, transference and countertransference, resistance, and dream analysis. The chapter next examined the psychoanalytic view of human nature, and we particularly looked at the roles that instincts, drives, and the unconscious play in the development of personality. Using the "tip-of-the-iceberg" analogy, we examined the relationships among the id, ego, superego, consciousness, and unconsciousness. We also discussed the importance of defense mechanisms in managing the id, ego, and superego. We pointed out that through psychoanalysis, we can gain a greater understanding of our behavior, but that a large portion of our selves will remain hidden and unconscious. We noted that Freud believed that our understanding of the world was based on how our psychological processes, unconscious and conscious, create what is called our psychic reality. We stated that sometimes psychoanalysis is considered deterministic in the sense that our personalities are believed to be framed for us at very young ages and are quite difficult to change. However, we noted that therapy affords some hope, as we can gain an increased understanding of ourselves.

The next part of the chapter provided some detail about a number of key concepts central to psychoanalytic theory. Thus, we learned about the preconscious, the conscious, and the unconscious and we noted that the goal of psychoanalysis is to make more of the unconscious conscious. We also discussed drives and instincts, including our life instinct (Eros) and our death instinct (Thanatos), which together comprise the psychic energy that form the libido. We outlined the structure of personality, including the id, which is fueled by the pleasure principle and whose impulses are called primary process; the ego, which operates from the reality principles and is often called secondary process; and the superego, which is the internalization of moral imperatives. We then discussed three types of anxiety, realistic, moral, and neurotic, and their relationships to the id, ego, and superego. The chapter next described a number of defense mechanisms that the individual creates to deal with the various kinds of anxieties.

Looking next at the psychosexual stages of development, we discussed in some detail the oral, anal, phallic, latency, and genital stages. We pointed out that the development of personality occurs through a dynamic interchange between the id, ego, and superego, and the developmental issues that are faced throughout these stages. We stated that as the child grows, his or her psychic energy becomes focused on different erogenous zones as a function of these stages. We discussed what might happen if a child's libido becomes locked or fixated at a particular stage and highlighted Freud's ideas about the Oedipal and Electra complexes. We also discussed the importance of examining the transference relationship in analysis and avoiding countertransference when working with clients.

We next went on to examine some of the major techniques of psychoanalytic therapy, including the importance of creating a trusting atmosphere, analytic neutrality, free association, interpretation of resistance, dream analysis, interpretation of parapraxes, and interpretation of the transference relationship. We also looked at how these different techniques are used throughout the helping relationships in an effort to assist the individual in examining his or her unconscious and in understanding how early parenting issues affect personality development.

As the chapter continued, we examined some social, cultural, and spiritual issues related to psychoanalysis, including how Freud's cultural upbringing affected his theory, Western-based values inherent in the theory, feminist criticism and feminist acceptance of psychoanalysis, the past and present push for low-cost and free analysis, and past and current psychoanalytic views on religion.

The chapter concluded by examining the efficacy of psychoanalysis, and we pointed out that psychoanalysis seems effective for those seeking such treatment; it is likely most effective with those who are comfortable with traditional Western values; it stresses the therapeutic alliance, which has been shown to be a critical factor in therapeutic outcomes; it has better efficacy for some specific populations, which we highlighted; brief psychoanalysis may be as effective as longer-term analysis; and recent brain research seems to be validating some of Freud's original ideas.

KEY WORDS

abreaction
anal expulsive
anal retentive
    personality
anal stage
analytic neutrality
anxiety
asceticism
castration anxiety
catharsis
character
compensation
consciousness
countertransference
creating a trusting
    atmosphere
death instinct
defense mechanisms
denial
deterministic
displacement
dissociation
dream analysis
drives
ego
Electra complex
erogenous zones
Eros
false connection
fixated
free association

Freudian slip
genital stage
humor
hysteria
id
idealization
identification
imago
instincts
intellectualization
interpretation of
    parapraxes
interpretation of
    resistance
interpretation of the
    transference
    relationship
introjection
latency stage
latent meanings
libido
life instinct
manifest meanings
moral anxiety
nasal reflex neurosis
neurosis
neurotic anxiety
Oedipus complex
oral stage
parapraxes
penis envy

phallic stage
pleasure principle
preconscious
primary process
primitive mind
projection
psychic energy
psychic reality
psychosexual stages
rationalization
reaction formation
realistic anxiety
reality principle
regression
repression
resistance
secondary process
seduction theory
somatization
splitting
sublimation
superego
suppression
Thanatos
transference
transference relationship
unconscious
undoing
Viennese Association of
    Psychoanalysis

KEY NAMES

Adler, Alfred
Anna O.

Bernays, Martha
Bernays, Minna

Breuer, Joseph
Charcot, Jean Martin

Fliess, Wilhem

Freud, Amalia

Freud, Anna

Horney, Karen

Jung, Carl

Pappenheim, Bertha

Rank, Otto

Steinem, Gloria

REFERENCES

Bankart, C. P. (1997). *Talking cures: A history of Western and Eastern psychotherapies.* Belmont, CA: Brooks/Cole.

Barratt, 1984. *Psychic reality and psychoanalytic knowing.* Hillsdale, NJ: Analytic Press.

Blumenthal, R. (2006, December 24). Hotel log hints at illicit desire that Dr. Freud didn't repress. *New York Times.* Retrieved from http://www.nytimes.com/2006/12/24/world/europe/24freud.html

Breger, L. (2000). *Freud: Darkness in the midst of vision.* New York: John Wiley & Sons.

Brenkman, J. (2004). Freud the modernist. In M. S. Micale (Ed.), *The mind of modernism: Medicine, psychology, and the cultural arts in Europe and America, 1880–1940* (pp. 172–196). Stanford, CA: Stanford University Press.

Carhart-Harris, R., Mayberg, H. S., Malizia, A. L., & Nutt, D. (2008). Mourning and melancholia revisited: Correspondences between principles of Freudian metapsychology and empirical findings in neuropsychiatry. *Annals of General Psychiatry,* 7 (special section), 1–23. Retrieved from http://www.pubmedcentral.nih.gov/articlerender.fcgi?artid=2515304

Danto, E. A. (2005). *Freud's free clinics: Psychoanalysis and social justice, 1918–1938.* New York: Columbia University Press.

Fonagy, P. (2000). The outcome of psychoanalysis: The hope for a future. *The Psychologist, 13*(12), 620–623.

Fonagy, P. (Ed.). (2002). *An open door review of outcome studies in psychoanalysis* (2nd rev. ed.). London: International Psychoanalytic Association.

Freeman, G. A. (2007). In search of death. *Rolling Stone Magazine.* Retrieved from http://www.rollingstone.com/news/story/5939950/bug_chasers

Freud, S. (1950). *Totem and taboo: Some points of agreement between the mental lives of savages and neurotics.* (J. Strachey, Trans.). New York: W. W. Norton. (Original work published 1913)

Freud, S. (1953). "The first dream," fragment of an analysis of a case of hysteria. In J. Strachey & A. Freud (Eds.), *Complete Works of Freud* (vol. 7). (Original work published 1905)

Freud, S. (1961a). *Beyond the pleasure principle.* (J. Strachey, Trans.). New York: W. W. Norton. (Original work published 1920)

Freud, S. (1961b). *The future of an illusion.* (J. Strachey, Trans.). New York: W. W. Norton. (Original work published 1927)

Freud, S. (1961c). *The ego and the id.* (J. Strachey, Trans.). New York: W. W. Norton. (Original work published 1927)

Freud, S. (1965). *The origin and development of psychoanalysis.* Henry Regnery Company. (Original work published 1910)

Freud, A. (1966). *The ego and the mechanisms of defense*. New York: International Universities Press. (Original work published 1936)

Freud, S. (1973). *Introductory lectures on psychoanalysis*. (J. Strachey, Trans.). New York: Pelican Books. (Original work published 1917)

Freud, S. (1976a). *The interpretation of dreams*. (J. Strachey, Trans.). New York: Penguin Books. (Original work published 1899)

Freud, S. (1976b). *Three essays on the theory of sexuality* (J. Strachey, Trans.). New York: Basic Books. (Original work published 1905)

Freud, S. (1976c). *Jokes and their relation to the unconscious*. (J. Strachey, Trans.). New York: Penguin Books. (Original work published 1905)

Freud, S. (1989). *The psychopathology of everyday life*. (J. Strachey, Trans.). New York: W. W. Norton. (Original work published 1901)

Freud, S. (2005). *Civilization and its discontents*. (J. Strachey, Trans.). New York: W. W. Norton. (Original work published 1930)

Freud, S., & Breuer, J. (1974). *3 studies in hysteria*. (J. Strachey, Trans.). New York: Penguin Books. (Original work published 1895)

Frey, R. J. (2006). *Psychoanalysis*. Retrieved from http://www.lifesteps.com/gm/Atoz/ency/psychoanalysis.jsp

Gabbard, G. O., Gunderson, J. G., & Fonagy, P. (2002). *The place of psychoanalytic treatments within psychiatry*. Archives of General Psychiatry, *59*(6), 505–510.

Galatzer-Levy, R. M., Bachrach, H., Skolnikoff, A., & Waldron, S. (2000). *Does psychoanalysis work?* New Haven, CT: Yale University Press.

Gay, P. (1988). *Freud: A life for our time*. New York: W. W. Norton.

Gilhooley, D. (2002). Misrepresentation and misreading in the case of Anna O. *Modern Psychoanalysis*, *27*(1), 75–100.

Horney, K. (1967). *Feminine psychology*. New York: W. W. Norton.

Kakar, S. (1991). *The analyst and the mystic*. Chicago, IL: The University of Chicago Press.

Kernberg, O. F. (2006). The pressing need to increase research in and on psychoanalysis. *International Journal of Psychoanalysis*, *87*, 919–926.

Leichsenring, F. (2005). Are psychodynamic and psychoanalytic therapies effective?: A review of empirical data. *International Journal of Psychoanalysis*, *36*(3), 841–868.

Leuzinger-Bohleber, M., & Target, M. (2002). Introductory remarks. In M. Leuzinger-Bohleber & M. Target (Eds.), *Outcomes of psychoanalytic treatment: Perspectives for therapists and researchers* (pp. 1–15). New York: Brunner-Routledge.

Library of Congress (2001). Freud: Conflict and culture (Section 3: From the individual to society). Retrieved from http://www.loc.gov/exhibits/freud/freud03.html

MacIsaac, S. (1974). *Freud and original sin*. New York: Paulist Press.

Maines, R. P. (2001). *The technology of orgasm*. Baltimore, MD: The Johns Hopkins University Press.

Makari, G. (2008). *Revolution in mind*. New York: HarperCollins.

Masson, J. M. (Ed.). (1985). *The complete letters of Sigmund Freud to Wilhelm Fliess: 1887–1904*. (J. M. Masson, Trans.). Cambridge, MA: Belknap Press of Harvard University Press.

Masson, J. M. (2003). *The assault on truth: Freud's suppression of the seduction theory*. New York: Ballantine Books.

Meissner, W. W. (2001). Psychic reality in the psychoanalytic process. *Journal of the American Psychoanalytic Association, 49,* 855–890.

Nathan, O., & Norden, H. (1960). *Einstein on peace.* New York: Simon and Schuster.

Nicholi, A. M. (2002). *The question of God: C.S. Lewis and Sigmund Freud debate God, love, sex, and the meaning of life.* New York: Free Press

NNDB (2007). *Sigmund Freud.* Retrieved from http://www.nndb.com/people/736/000029649/

Pendergrast, M. (1995). *Victims of memory: Incest accusations and shattered lives.* Hinesburg, VT: Upper Access, Inc.

Schoenewolf, G. (2008). A psychoanalyst's perspective: AIDS and the death wish. *National Association for Research and Therapy of Homosexuality.* Retrieved from http://www.narth.com/docs/deathwish.html

Schur, M. (1972). *Freud: Living and dying.* New York: International Universities Press.

Scott, J. (2005). Electra after Freud: Myth and culture. Ithaca, NY: Cornell University Press.

Segal, L. (1996). IV. Freud and feminism: A century of contradiction. *Journal of the American Psychoanalytic Association, 6,* 290–297.

Stein, D. J., Solms, M., & van Honk, J. (2006, August). The cognitive-affective neuroscience of the unconscious. *CNS Spectrums, 11*(8), 580–583.

Steinem, G. (1994). *Moving beyond words.* New York: Simon and Schuster.

Ursano, R. J., Sonnenberg, S. M., & Lazar, S. G. (2004). *Concise guide to psychodynamic psychotherapy: Principles and techniques of brief, intermittent, and long-term psychodynamic psychotherapy* (3rd ed.). Washington, D.C.: American Psychiatric Publishing.

Weltmer, A. A. (1900). *Suggestion simplified.* Nevada, MO: American School of Magnetic Healing.

Westen, D. (1998). The scientific legacy of Sigmund Freud: Toward a psychodynamically informed psychological science. *Psychological Bulletin, 124*(3), 333–371.

Chapter 3

Analytical Therapy

Learning Goals

- To gain a biographical understanding of the originator of analytical therapy, Carl Jung.
- To understand the historical context in which Jung created his theory.
- To understand the roles that instincts, the conscious, the personal unconscious, and the collective unconscious (including archetypes), as well as attitudes and mental functions, play in the development of Jung's view of human nature.
- To learn about the following key concepts of analytical therapy:
  - Psychological types, including the attitudes of extraversion and introversion and the mental functions of thinking, feeling, intuiting, and sensing
  - The psyche, including consciousness and the ego; the personal unconscious and complexes which it houses; and the collective unconscious, with archetypes such as the persona, the shadow, anima and animus, and the Self
  - Individuation
  - Symbols
  - Synchronicity
- To review the major techniques of analytical therapy, including being dialectical, active imagination, dream analysis, use of creative techniques, amplification, transference/countertransference, and interpretation.
- To examine the therapeutic process of analytical therapy, especially in light of clients' developmental readiness to examine issues related to the personal and collective unconscious.
- To review important social, cultural, and spiritual issues relative to analytical therapy, including critics and supporters of Jung's approach relative to women's issues, cross-cultural adaptability, and his symbolic notions on religion.
- To examine the efficacy of analytical therapy and to examine what factors might show its effectiveness given that much of the theory is elusive and therefore difficult to measure.
- To see how analytical therapy is applied through vignettes, DVDs, and case study.

Carl Jung lit his farts on camping trips, danced with tribal people in Africa, built a stone tower with his own hands, socialized with his patients, and installed his mistress in his house (breaking his wife's heart). He was unafraid to delve psychologically into mysticism, the occult, alchemy—anywhere he thought he could find truths. Without him, there'd have been no Joseph Campbell or the legions of myth-minded, spiritual authors whose ideas have found their way into many aspects of contemporary psychotherapy. Some think of him as the first manifestation of the therapist-as-rock-star because he had groupies and often seemed more like a guru than a therapist. But Jung originated the basic form of psychotherapy still practiced today in most fields: unlike Freud, he faced his patients, talking, consoling, taking their ideas seriously as they sat across a table. "I realized," he wrote, "that one gets nowhere unless one talks to people about the things they know."

It was Jung who first argued that we possess male and female aspects (animus and anima), as well as an unacknowledged, forbidding region, which he called the Shadow. He introduced the concepts of "introvert," "extravert," "synchronicity," and "the complex." ("The top 10," 2007, Section 8: Carl Jung, para. 1–2)

One of the most interesting and influential psychotherapists of all times, there is little doubt that Carl Jung's personal struggles and history had a large impact on his beliefs. Fascinated by the metaphysical world, he was also a man deeply interested in empirical and scientific facts. Perhaps this is why he has been so readily embraced by both those fascinated by the mystical as well as more traditional therapists who believe he developed a theory that can, at times, offer a reasonable explanation for that which is not known. But let's take a closer look at the background of this unusual yet thoughtful and innovative man.

Photo by Hulton Archive/Getty Images

Carl Gustav Jung

CARL JUNG

Born in a small Swiss village on July 26, 1875, the environment in which Carl Gustav Jung grew up might be considered unusual by today's standards, but was not uncommon in rural Switzerland years ago. Surrounded by eight uncles and a father who were pastors, a mother who spoke with spirits, and a rural community that leaned heavily on a mixture of religion, magic, and spells, it's not surprising that as a child, Jung sometimes had trouble deciphering fantasy from reality (Hayman, 2001). Jung was the second of three children born to Paul and Emilie, although their first child died only a few days after birth. However, this death would make Paul and Emilie particularly nervous about young Carl's development.

Paul and Emilie Jung slept in separate bedrooms, and it was clear even to the very young Carl that his parents were not in a "loving" relationship. Jung describes his mother in contrasting ways (Jung & Jaffé, 1961). On one hand, he saw her as sickly, often overcome by physical and emotional problems, obsessed with the paranormal, a critical parent, and a parent who was emotionally absent and even physically gone due to months spent in a mental hospital. On the other hand, he states that she was warm, fun, a good listener, strong, humorous, and pleasant. Although Jung felt close to his father, he described him as reliable but meek, irritable, depressed by his wife's emotional condition, and filled with faltering religious beliefs as a result of the ill-tempered atmosphere in the home. The images of his parents would have a lifelong effect on Jung, and he even attributes a case of severe eczema, at the age of 6 years, as well as a knee-jerk negative reaction to the word "love," to the emotional environment in the home. Jung believed that the household mood was at least partially responsible for his growing introversion and secretiveness.

Jung's home life was one in which he would encounter ominous-looking priests dressed in black, heard people weeping at the cemetery near his house, heard strange noises at night in his home, saw his mother trying to communicate with spirits, and had ongoing thoughts and daydreams about the nature of good and evil and Satan and Jesus. Between the ages of 6 and 10 years, Jung proved to be a somewhat unusual child, showing an odd curiosity in such things as corpses from a flood, setting fires, and a fascination with watching the slaughtering of pigs. At the same time, he was drawn to intellectual pursuits, and would often visit museums, was intrigued by the arts, and learned Latin at a very young age. The unusual and murky home atmosphere, along with a series of illnesses, such as croup, was at least partly responsible for periodic psychotic-like visions:

> One night I saw coming from her [mother's] door a faintly luminous, indefinite figure whose head detached itself from the neck and floated along in front of it … (Jung & Jaffé, 1961, p. 18)

Jung's school life was not much better than his home life. Having trouble relating to his peers, he increasingly alienated himself by daydreaming, playing with fire, and making towers out of blocks (Hayman, 2001; McLynn, 1996). Interestingly, it's Jung's depressive childhood that led him to one of his greatest discoveries. One day, while experiencing the negative home atmosphere, Jung decided to carve a manikin out of wood. This manikin would become his secret doll to which he would write messages and from which he felt comforted. Later in Jung's life, he realized that this manikin was shaped like many figures carved in ancient civilizations. Jung came to believe that such images arose from what he called the **collective unconscious**, or a depository of ancient images which we all hold in common. This term was to be a cornerstone of Jung's theory.

When Jung was 11, he was sent to a boarding school, where he realized how little he had compared to his wealthy peers. The stress of a new boarding school, the emotional burden he carried from his gloomy home life, and a possible sexual assault perpetuated on him at some point in adolescence made it difficult for Jung to maintain any close friendships. Increasingly, he became solitary, often wandering into elaborate daydreams, fantasies, and deep contemplation about religion, God, and the meaning of life (Hayman, 2001). One day while away at school, Jung was pushed by a boy and fell, landing on his head. This injury sent him home, and he soon began to develop fainting spells when asked to go to school or to do homework. This "illness" convinced his parents to keep him home from school—for six months! However, after overhearing a conversation between his father and a friend who suggested that the young Carl might have epilepsy, Jung decided it was time to work hard on ridding himself of his illness. In reflecting on his fainting spells, Jung remarks, "That was when I learned what a neurosis is" (Jung & Jaffé, 1961, p. 32).

Back at boarding school, Jung increasingly seemed to live in two worlds. In fact, he came to believe he had two personalities; an unremarkable schoolboy who was inferior in dress and status who managed the daily routine of life, and a strong, authoritarian, and noteworthy man of the eighteenth century who would raise his voice periodically (Hayman, 2001). In some ways, Jung seemed to think that he was channeling this eighteenth-century personality or that it was a reincarnated soul. This tendency to differentiate aspects of the person would later become a part of his theory as represented in what he eventually called **archetypes**. Although struggling within himself, Jung excelled in school, despite hating competition and purposefully underachieving in an effort to avoid being at the top of his class.

After boarding school, Jung attended the University of Basel and decided to pursue a career in medicine. In addition to his interest in medicine, Jung was fascinated by religion, philosophy, spirituality, séances, and psychic phenomenon (Jaffé, 1971), no doubt a combination of his family's focus on religion and his mother's interest in spirits. In fact, Jung relates a number of experiences such as a wooden table splitting in half and a knife exploding into four pieces that he attributed to psychic phenomenon (Adler, 1973; Jung & Jaffé, 1961; Jung & von Franz, 1964). Thus, when he was finally asked to find a focus for his medical studies, he went into psychiatry:

> Here alone the two currents of my interest could flow together and in a
> united stream dig their own bed. Here was the empirical field common
> to biological and spiritual facts, which I had everywhere sought and
> nowhere found. Here at last was the place where the collision of nature
> and spirit became a reality. (Jung & Jaffé, 1961 p. 109)

Interest in science, spirits, and spirituality were common at the time, as society moved from the more traditional world that had relied on the church's providing answers to life's questions to the modernist interest in science's holding truth. With an interest in both science and the occult, Jung eventually wrote his dissertation on the psychology of the occult based on the experiences he had with a 15-year-old medium.

In 1902, Jung accepted a position at **Burghölzli**, a renowned psychiatric hospital in Zurich run by the well-known psychiatrist Eugen Bleuler. In 1903,

Jung married Emma Rauschenbach, a young woman from a well-to-do family with whom he would have four daughters and one son. It was during this same year that Jung saw his first patient, Sabina Spielrein. A Jewish intellectual from a wealthy Russian family, Sabina was sent to Burghölzli for what was diagnosed as hysteria:

> … [P]atient laughs and cries in a strangely mixed, compulsive manner. Masses of tics, rotating head, sticks out her tongue, legs twitching. (Hoffler, 2001, p. 120)

For Jung, analysis of Sabina relied heavily on the new psychoanalytic technique of free association (Hoffler, 2001). However, he would eventually become dissatisfied with its use, believing it promoted a focus on the dark and pessimistic aspects of the individual as opposed to other possible explanations of symptoms. Jung ended up having a brief affair with Sabina, and after correspondence and intervention from Freud, the affair ended (Felixson & Marton, 2002). Interestingly, this affair helped Freud to coalesce his thoughts on countertransference and the importance of having boundaries with clients. Sabina became one of the first child psychoanalysts and became well-known in her own right. Though she married and had two daughters, she never really got over her feelings for Jung. In the early 1940s, she and her two daughters were shot and killed by the Nazis during their invasion of Russia.

At Burghölzli, most of Jung's patients were schizophrenics, and Jung was fascinated by the different aspects of their personalities (Jung, 1918/1969a). It was during this time that Jung developed one of the first word-association tests, in which he examined the responses of individuals to a list of stimulus words. Eventually, he came up with the word **complex** to describe unusual and delayed responses that individuals had to groups of words that seemed to point to a problematic or neurotic area in a person's life (Storr, 1973). Jung came to believe that individuals could have one or more of an indefinite number of complexes (e.g., mother complex, father complex, inferiority complex, etc.). Each complex, said Jung, could cause the person to act in distinctive ways, almost as if they were separate personalities. Eventually, Jung stressed that one important aspect of therapy was to **integrate** the different complexes into consciousness through a process called **individuation** (Jung, 1969b).

The early part of the twentieth century saw Jung beginning to develop his own ideas about analysis as he collaborated from a distance with Freud who was in Vienna. Seen as a "father figure" by Jung, Freud talked of Jung as his "prized pupil" (Storr, 1973; Young-Eisendrath & Dawson, 2008). From the beginning, Jung disagreed with many of Freud's ideas; however, he also had clearly learned much after reading Freud's early work. Wanting to be the "good son," he did not actively refute Freud on some points. In 1907, the two met for the first time. For Freud, who lived in Vienna, which was increasingly becoming anti-Semitic, it was good to have a non-Jew supporting his ideas, as most of his inner circle was Jewish. For Jung, Freud offered a distant mentorship and support for an approach which was still widely criticized in Europe. In 1911, Jung became president of the **International Psychoanalytic Association**.

During this time, Jung's private practice expanded, and he eventually left Burghölzli. As Jung's writings and thoughts became increasingly different from Freud's, he founded the **Society for Psychoanalytic Endeavors**, which was one of the first forums that examined Jung's own "take" on psychoanalysis. As Jung developed his theory, he knew that with the eventual publication of his book, *Psychology of the Unconscious* (1916), his differences with Freud would be accentuated. The two would part their ways in 1913, which was devastating for both. It is not surprising that at this juncture, Jung resigned as president of the International Psychoanalytic Association.

At around the same time that Freud and Jung split, Jung began to have dreams and visions about world destruction, which he initially believed were psychotic in nature. At the time, Jung believed he was on the verge of an acute schizophrenic episode; however, he later came to view such visions as reflective of the state of the world and believed that he had a special ability to be able to access this deep material. As Storr (1973) so aptly states, "The borderline between being regarded as an inspired prophet and being regarded as mentally ill is often a narrow one" (p. 16). Jung himself came to believe that schizophrenics had the unique gift of being able to release unconscious aspects of self which we all harbor (the collective unconscious), but only some, like himself, could do this while maintaining a sense of reality.

At the time when Jung was struggling with his inner world, he befriended and eventually had an affair with Toni Wolf, a former patient who had a strong interest in Eastern philosophy (Hayman, 2001; McLynn, 1996; Young-Eisendrath & Dawson, 2008). This would not be Jung's only affair, but probably the one that would most impact him and the development of his theory. In fact, Wolf is often seen as the person who kept Jung grounded during these trying years. Jung's wife, Emma, eventually found out about the affair and tried to make him end it. However, the affair lasted for years, and Jung would even have Toni over for dinner with his wife, and would meet her on a regular basis at his summer house at Bollingen.

Bollingen was a getaway for Jung, but was also symbolic of his continued interest in spirits and the unconscious. There, he had recurring dreams about death, experienced visions, had what he described as "hauntings," and would hear strange sounds at the house (McLynn, 1996). Another time, at Bollingen, his eldest daughter, who was described by Jung as having psychic powers, told his father she sensed corpses on the grounds. Later, a skeleton of a French soldier was found on the property, and Jung arranged to have a "proper burial" for the soldier's remains. These experiences were fodder for the development of his theory, especially his notions of the psychological meaning of **symbols** and their relationship to the collective unconscious.

As Jung continued to refine his theory, he became fascinated by common elements found in people's dreams, myths, fables, religious writings, and cultural artifacts and symbols. He also showed interest in **Gnosticism**, a pre- and early-Christian religious belief that examined the development of the psyche as it relates to the transcendence of the soul; **astrology**, the relative position of celestial bodies in understanding human nature; and **alchemy**, the conversion of basic metals to precious metals (e.g., gold or silver) as well as the belief that there was a liquid mixture that could extend life indefinitely. Jung was fascinated by the psychology of the human psyche and how we come to make sense out of such experiences. And, he saw in these beliefs the human species' projection of a deep-seated need to change and complete ourselves—to undergo a metamorphosis from one form of consciousness to a newer, expanded consciousness and **wholeness**. As Jung increasingly pieced together his theory, he originally called it **complex psychology**, then **hermeneutical psychology**, but eventually ended up with the name **analytical psychology**.

Over the years, Jung continued to refine his theory and slowly became internationally recognized. As he reached his mid-forties, he increasingly became interested in other cultures and traveled worldwide to better understand the collective experiences of people. His travels deepened his interest in Eastern philosophies and religions and his belief in an unconscious, common collective experience that all people inherit. A prolific writer and worldwide lecturer, many of his ideas would eventually become well-known.

At the height of Jung's popularity, the Nazis took hold in Europe, and in Germany, Jews lost their jobs and professional posts. The German chapter of the **Society for Psychotherapy** threw out their Jewish members, and Jung took on the presidency of the newly formed **International Society** in an effort to allow Jews to have membership in what would be considered the umbrella association (Ellenberger, 1970). However, at that time and continuing into today, Jung's response to Nazi Germany has been a bone of contention for some. For instance, some have argued that Jung held unconscious anger toward Freud and other Jewish psychoanalytic leaders, and that the Nazis' suppression of psychoanalysis provided Jung the opportunity to have analytical psychology become the prominent form of analysis (Hayman, 2001; Rowland, 2002). Others believed that Jung's lack of response to the Nazis was because he waited to see if some good would come out of the Nazi regime, as all archetypes contain "good and evil" (Rowland, 2002). On the other hand, many Jewish analysts, including many of whom were close friends of Jung, insist that he wholeheartedly supported the Jews as best he could during this horrible time (Clarke, 1992; Ellenberger, 1970; Jaffé, 1971).

Although Jung retired in 1946, he continued to give talks and travel the world, and was particularly interested in visiting tribal cultures in his effort to better understand symbols and the collective unconscious. In his later years, he became increasingly interested in the relationship between the psyche and such things as the paranormal, psychic phenomenon, and UFOs, often suggesting that such experiences were unconscious projections but sometimes alluding to the possibility that they were real (McLynn, 1996). After his wife died in 1955, he became increasingly reclusive. He died in 1961 in his home in Switzerland. During his life, he authored hundreds of papers and books, most of which are documented in the 21 volumes of the Bollingen Series of the *Collected Works of Jung* published by Princeton University Press. His most famous books include *Psychology and Religion* (1938), *The Undiscovered Self* (1957), *Man and his Symbols* (Jung & von Franz, 1964), and his autobiography, *Memories, Dreams, Reflections* (Jung & Jaffé, 1961).

VIEW OF HUMAN NATURE

Jung did not believe we are born a blank slate (*tabula rasa*) as did the early behaviorists, or that we are capable of free choices, as the existentialists suggested (Clarke, 1992). He also did not believe we are determined by or victims of our biology, or of our past. He did believe that childhood influences affect our psychological makeup and that symptoms represent a desire to regain lost parts of self, including parts that have been repressed as well as parts that have never been revealed to consciousness. By expanding our consciousness (revealing unconscious material to consciousness) the individual is able to integrate parts of self that have been pushed into the unconscious as well as primordial parts of self that have never been revealed to consciousness, and become a more fully functioning, "whole" person.

Although Jung believed that sex could be a powerful motivator, in contrast to Freud, he insisted that it was no more powerful, and sometimes less so, than many other drives, including the power drive, ambition, envy, fanaticism, revenge, hunger, creativity, self-reflection, activity, and spirituality (Jung, 1969b). Also in contrast to Freud, Jung believed that sexuality and other instincts could play a significant symbolic nature in people's lives, such as the importance of the incest taboo in religious writings.

> Usually incest has a highly religious aspect, for which reason the incest theme plays a decisive part in almost all cosmogonies and in numerous myths. But Freud clung to the literal interpretation of it and could not grasp the spiritual significance of incest as a symbol. I knew that he would never be able to accept any of my ideas on the subject. (Jung & Jaffé, 1961, p. 167)

Splitting from many of his contemporaries, Jung suggested that the psyche consists not only of what is in **consciousness**, which represents all of which we are aware; and our **personal unconscious**, which represents all of our thoughts and behaviors that we have experienced but don't remember; but also a **collective unconscious**, which contains **primordial images** called **archetypes**. Archetypes were hypothesized by Jung to be inherited by all people and to provide the psyche with its tendency to perceive the world in certain ways that we identify as "human." Evidence for archetypes, said Jung, can be found in similar behaviors, myths, symbols, and artwork that is found in all cultures.

Jung stated that consciousness develops soon after birth and is related to how each of us uses the **mental functions** of **sensation**, **thinking**, **feeling**, and **intuition**. In addition to the mental functions, Jung suggested we are born with the **attitudes** of **extraversion** and **introversion**, although there is an innate tendency to favor one (Jung, 1971). Jung also suggested that as children, we develop an **ego** which manages our mental functions and attitudes and allows continuity of our basic personality structure with the possibility that change can occur relatively slowly over time. Based on which mental functions are favored, the ego sorts experiences into those that will be maintained in consciousness and those which will be diverted to the personal unconscious. How one's mental functions and attitudes divert experiences into

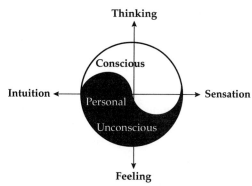

Figure A: *Tai-chi-tu* ("Yin Yang") Symbol

Figure B: Inverted *Tai-chi-tu* showing mental functions and psyche relationships. In this example, "thinking" is in consciousness.

F I G U R E 3.1 Using the "Yin Yang" Symbol: The Relationship between Mental Functions and the Psyche for an Individual Whose Primary Mental Function Is "Thinking"

consciousness or the personal unconscious Jung called the individual's **character** or personality (Ekstrom, 1988).

Jung often used the Chinese symbol for **Tai-chi-tu**, or **"yin yang"** (female/male) to convey his ideas about the mental functions (Figure 3.1A) (Jung, 1976; Pascal, 1992). The symbol suggests that the only constant in the universe is change, and that we must learn to be in harmony with change. The symbol also suggests that opposing forces in the universe complement one another and merge over time (e.g., female merges with male, and male with female). Inverting the symbol, with the top part representing consciousness and the bottom representing the personal unconscious, Figure 3.1B shows how the mental functions might be configured if the "thinking" mental function was primary (favored), the "feeling" function was inferior (secondary and mostly unconscious), and intuition and sensation hovered somewhere between consciousness and unconsciousness.

Jung suggested that archetypes are constantly impinging on us in mysterious and unconscious ways, and provide energy for what he named "complexes." For example, a "father complex" could evolve within an individual who has been physically abused by his father. The abuse, which is repressed, still "lives" in the personal unconscious and becomes attached to the archetypal image of the father, becoming a complex. This complex then impinges on the waking life of the individual; perhaps, the individual becomes angry toward all male authority (father) figures.

Jung believed that the person is born whole, with all of the ingredients necessary to embody a fully functioning human being. However, because there is a tendency for one or more mental functions to take priority, because we build complexes, and because we repress traumatic experiences, an individual's psyche will often become damaged or split, and develop unconscious personalities that act almost like separate functioning individuals. The goal of therapy, said Jung, is to become whole by discovering parts of self that have never been experienced, aspects of self that have become repressed, and portions of self that have been split off. Thus, if I am more of a thinking type, it would be important for me to become in touch with my "feeling" side. And, if I'm more of an extravert, I should try to find the introvert part of me. If I have repressed memories and complexes, I should attempt to get in touch with them. Jung called the development of consciousness about our mental functions, attitudes, complexes, and repressed parts of self, **individuation**. He suggested that the individuation process was developmental, critical if we are to live in a civilized world that thrives on healthy relationships, and likely to occur if we are afforded the atmosphere that nurtures such growth (Jung, 1971; Papadopoulos, 1992; Storr, 1973).

KEY CONCEPTS

Psychological Types

After years of self-reflection, Jung wrote a book called *Psychological Types* (1921/1964a), which was based on his belief that that there were two **attitudes** and four **mental functions** that described an individual's major ways of processing information and making sense of the world. The attitudes, which included extraversion and introversion, oriented one to the outside objective world *or* to the internal subjective world. The functions are the ways in which we operate in our outer or inner world and include **thinking, feeling, sensing,** and **intuiting**. Jung believed that one is inherently **extraverted** or **introverted**; thus, crossing extraversion or introversion with the four functions produces eight possible combinations or "types."

By the way, if this is sounding familiar, it's probably because you have come across the test known as the **Myers-Briggs Type Indicator (MBTI)**. After reading *Psychological Types*, Katharine Briggs and her daughter, Isabel Briggs Myers, became fascinated with Jung's typology of people. They ultimately added a fourth dimension to Jung's factors, which they called **judging** *versus* **perceiving**, and developed this very popular instrument often used in personality assessment and career counseling (Quenk, 2000). The following examines the original two attitudes and four functions that Jung identified.

The Attitudes (Introversion and Extraversion).   Are you self-reflective, an observer, more withdrawn than interactive, and think a fair amount about life's meaning and how you fit into the world? If that is the case, you are probably an introvert. On the other hand, if you tend to be social, outgoing, and more interested in objects and people than you are in internal thoughts and feelings, then you are likely an extravert. Jung suggested that one is born with a tendency to be one or the other, although over a lifetime, one's attitude can change. He also suggested that people tend to be conscious of their predominant attitude, and that the opposite attitude largely operates out of one's unconscious. So, the individual who is a social butterfly and concerned about the outside world will unconsciously focus upon internal aspects, which will be evidenced in the kinds of dreams the person has and other symbols in the person's life (e.g., the kinds of movies a person might like, pieces of art one might pick, etc.).

The Mental Functions (Thinking, Feeling, Intuiting, and Sensing). Jung identified four mental functions, which he tended to group in two pairs. The thinking and feeling functions were considered **rational functions** because people use them to make decisions on evidence gathered. The thinking type evaluates or judges information from a detached perspective and uses logic, reason, and the examination of data and causal relationships in this process (consider the stereotypic scientist or behaviorist). Feeling types make decisions by evaluating or judging situations through the use of empathy, by understanding relationships, and by considering the needs of people (think of the humanistically oriented counselor stereotype). Feeling types should not be confused with individuals who make decisions based on feelings or affect.

Contrast the thinking and feeling types with the **irrational functions** of the sensing and intuiting types. In these cases, information is gathered and understood through one's perceptions. Sensing involves making sense of information that is derived from the five senses: hearing, seeing, smelling, touching, and tasting. Intuition involves making sense of abstract information that is derived from the "gut" and unconscious (e.g., sensing type: "I can smell your lover's perfume," versus intuitive type: "I just know that you're having an affair—I just have that gut feeling.").

In the two pairs of functions just noted (thinking–feeling, intuiting–sensing), people tend to favor one of the four functions, called the **primary function**. Whatever one's primary function is, its complementary function in the pair is called the **inferior function**, which resides mostly in the unconscious (see Figure 3.1B). Thus, if my primary function is feeling, my inferior function is thinking. The inferior function longs to be "heard," and can provide great information about an individual's unconscious. The second pair, which does not contain the primary or inferior functions, comprises the secondary functions. Of these, one is generally favored, because one cannot think and feel or intuit and sense at the same time. The secondary functions hover between consciousness and unconsciousness (see Figure 3.1B).

The Eight Types. Pairing each of the two attitudes with the four possible combinations of mental functions leaves one with eight possible psychological types. Figure 3.2 shows the four possible combinations of mental functions, each of which could be matched with an extraverted or introverted attitude—yielding the eight types. Remember, Jung hypothesized that whatever your predominate type is, the complementary type resides in your unconscious and longs to have its voice and become developed. As a person becomes more individuated, he or she can bring all eight types into consciousness and can use all types at different times.

Thinking Type

Feeling Type

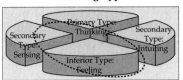

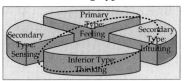

Sensing Type

Intuiting Type

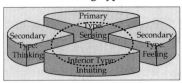

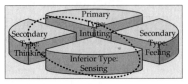

F I G U R E 3.2 The Four Types of Mental Functions*

*Inside the elliptical figure represents unconsciousness, and the outside, consciousness. These are hypothetical examples of how much of each type is in consciousness or is unconscious. The first example, in the top left corner, shows a "thinking type" person whose consciousness is largely (but not totally) of a thinking type, and minimally of a feeling type. The intuitive and sensing types in this example is largely in consciousness, with "intuiting" being more present in consciousness.

The Psyche

For Jung, the psyche represented all of our psychological processes and contained all which is in consciousness, the personal unconscious, and the collective unconscious. Like Freud, Jung believed consciousness to be the tip of the iceberg, representing only a small piece of the psyche. However, unlike Freud, Jung had a very different view of the unconscious, which he said consisted of both a personal unconscious and a collective unconscious. Jung also suggested that archetypes, one aspect of the collective unconscious, can seep into our personal unconscious and affect many aspects of our day-to-day behaviors.

Consciousness.   Jung defined consciousness as all of what we are aware—all of what we know. So, consciousness is when the individual can identify a feeling, recognize an experience, consider a fact, or reflect on self. Consciousness, said Jung, is created from unconsciousness, as we are hard-wired to develop a sense of "I" at birth, perhaps even before birth, when the infant has his or her very first encounters with and recognition of objects outside of self. For instance, right after the birth of my first child, I watched my newborn daughter seek out her mother's breast—clearly an instinctual act, yet the very early beginning of consciousness, as awareness of her **Self** starts to become developed. The ego, which is sometimes used to describe the self-conscious "I," mediates what will come into consciousness, and is part of the larger Self.

The ego: Jung saw the ego as the center of consciousness and described it as having four functions: sensing, intuiting, thinking, and feeling. By age eight or nine, the ego is largely intact and acts as filter to experience, allowing only that which matches the individual's psychological type to remain in consciousness. As the child grows into adulthood, the ego can be expanded as other psychological types (e.g., inferior, secondary) are experimented with and as unconscious aspects of Self are integrated into consciousness. Expansion of ego consciousness and psychological maturity was called **individuation** by Jung.

What causes the ego to allow only certain information to remain in consciousness? Probably a combination of genetics that tends to orient us toward a certain way of acting (e.g., extraversion or introversion) and environmental factors, such as parents, who reinforce certain ways of living in the world (stressing the importance of one mental function over another). For instance, a child born with a genetic tendency toward introversion might also have parents who reinforce the "feeling" and "intuitive" mental functions. This results in an introverted child who is a "feeling type" with a secondary intuitive function.

At the same time that the ego is the filter to experiences from the outer world, the ego is also being affected by the inner world from the unconscious. Thus, the ego can be invaded, possessed, and taken over by complexes that have been formed in the personal unconscious (Hollis as cited by Bridle & Edelstein, 2000). That is why what we are conscious of may not always match how we act, such as the jealous lover who has little awareness of her passive–aggressive behaviors. When asked about her feelings toward her lover, she describes her lover as "the love of my life" and denies other motivations to her behavior. This is why Jung (1966a) said, "Generally speaking, therefore, an unconscious secret is more injurious than a conscious one" (p. 53).

As we grow, the ego makes us who we are—for good or bad. For instance, a friend of mine once accused me of a rather shameful behavior. I said to him, "I'm not aware that my motivation was underhanded." He responded by saying, "Great, so you're unconscious about why you did that—that even makes it worse." I retorted: "But, if I'm unconscious about my reasons, don't I get a pass?" He said, "No, make yourself more conscious." So, the bad news is that I was unconscious of my shameful behavior. The good news is that with a good amount of effort, I can make myself more conscious.

Jung believed that over time, especially in the second half of our lives, the ego could expand and allow additional information to flow into consciousness, thus allowing ourselves to experience the various ideas, feelings, memories, and perceptions that have not been allowed into consciousness or have been repressed. For instance, feeling types can increasingly allow their thinking counterpart to enter consciousness, and intuitive types can allow their sensing parts to enter consciousness. However, even when you expand your ego, there will always be more hidden areas. Stand on the top of the Empire State Building, and you can see a lot more than you could when you were standing on the street; however, if you didn't know better, you might think that all of what you see is all there is.

What the ego comprehends is perhaps the smallest part of what a complete consciousness would have to comprehend. (Jung, 1969b, p. 324)

The Personal Unconscious.   The personal unconscious houses all material from an individual's unique experiences that have been filtered out of consciousness and repressed into unconsciousness. In contrast, inherited universal unconscious material can be found in the collective unconscious (discussed in the next section). Believing that all of life's experiences are remembered or have the potential to be remembered, Jung asserted experiences incongruent with an individual's psychological type are diverted to the personal unconscious—in a sense, waiting to be discovered if afforded the opportunity. For example, unconsciously, the feeling type person's ego diverts the thinking part of self to the personal unconscious, the intuiting person's ego diverts the sensing parts of self to the personal unconscious, and so forth. In addition, traumatic experiences may be repressed and housed in the personal unconscious. However, through self-discovery, such as that which occurs in therapy, all of our diverted and repressed parts of self can be rediscovered.

> The total material that is added to consciousness causes a considerable widening of the horizon, a deepened self knowledge which, more than anything else, one would think, is calculated to humanize a man and make him modest. (Jung & Campbell, 1928/1971, p. 80)

In considering the proposition that all can be remembered, I often think of individuals who have had a near-death experience, and, in a fleeting moment, are said to remember all aspects of their lives as it flashes by them. It's as if their personal unconscious, in that moment, floods consciousness. So, all of those experiences, along with complexes associated with them (which will be expanded upon later), are held in the personal unconscious and impinge on our conscious behaviors. Thus, a major goal of therapy is to assist the individual in becoming more aware of the personal unconscious and to integrate the various split-off parts of self into consciousness. This, said Jung, is one piece of what leads us toward becoming whole. However, Jung also believed there was much more unknown that was housed in what he called the **collective unconscious**.

The Collective Unconscious and Archetypes.   Perhaps the most interesting aspect of Jung's theory was his belief in a collective unconscious, sometimes called the **impersonal unconscious** (Bennet, 1961). Although the concept of an unconscious had been around with Freud and others (Hall & Nordby, 1973/1999), it had always been associated with repressed material that was the result of actions that occurred after birth (e.g., a traumatic event). Jung, however, suggested that such repressed material was housed in the personal unconscious and that in addition there was a collective unconscious. A product of the evolutionary process, Jung believed the collective unconscious is inherited, identical in all of us, and contains the archetypes, which provide the psyche with its tendency to perceive the world in certain ways that we identify as "human." Evidence for archetypes, said Jung, can only be inferred and is found in the similar behaviors, artwork, images, and myths that are recognized in all cultures.

> My thesis, then, is as follows: In addition to our immediate conscious-
> ness, which is of a thoroughly personal nature and which we believe
> to be the only empirical psyche (even if we tack on the personal un-
> conscious as an appendix), there exists a second psychic system of a
> collective, universal, and impersonal nature which is identical in all
> individuals. This collective unconscious does not develop individually,
> but is inherited. It consists of pre-existent forms, the archetypes, which
> can only become conscious secondarily and which give definite form to
> certain psychic contents. (Jung, 1968a, p. 43)

The scope of potential behaviors reflected by the archetypes is wide and depends
on the psychological type of the person and the kinds of repressed events that
have impinged on the individual. For instance, the "mothering" archetype is the
innate energy that *all* of us have toward nurturing and caring for children. How
that gets actualized in each of us will vary, as a function of our psychological
type as well as important events that have affected us. Jung believed that all
humans have the same archetypes that impinge on us in unconscious and
mysterious ways, unless, that is, we can become conscious of their influence
through the process of integration and individuation.

In traveling the world, Jung found an array of similar myths, symbols,
behaviors, and artwork that reinforced his belief in archetypes. Archetypes
provide the form for our understanding and images related to birth, rebirth,
death, power, magic, the hero, the child, the trickster, God, the demon, the
wise old man, and the Earth Mother, to name just a few. From culture to
culture, we see similar stories, myths, and artwork that explain these concepts,
said Jung. For instance, the Romans projected their power and fear by creating
Jupiter, their sensuality through the formation of Venus, and their suspicions
about the unknown by creating Neptune (the unconscious?). Today, we still
project our archetypes, representing our hidden parts of selves, onto such things
as the heroes we invent in our movies (e.g., Superman), the "evil-doers" we
identify in the world, the football games we cheer for, or the people we idolize
(e.g., Mother Theresa). In actuality, the hero, evil, our competitive parts, and
our nurturing parts may all be hidden parts of ourselves, having their origins in
our archetypes and resting comfortably in our personal unconscious, if not
acknowledged in consciousness (see Box 3.1).

Although there are a limitless number of archetypes, there are four that have
become particularly well-known and important to the makeup of the individual.
In order of their embeddedness to the unconscious (or closeness to consciousness),
they include: the **persona**, the **shadow**, the **animus** and **anima**, and the **Self**.

The Persona.   A number of years ago, I took a five-day workshop with Sid
Simon, one of the founders of the values clarification movement. At that
workshop, we were asked not to reveal our occupation or the degrees we held.
Working on my doctorate, I quickly realized how much of my identity was
based on presenting myself as a potential "Dr." in the field of counseling. This
very humbling experience helped me see the importance that the masks we

---

B o x 3.1   The Hero Within

I remember when there was a plane crash in Washington, D.C., during the winter. A man who saw the plane go down rushed to a bridge right near the crash and jumped into icy waters to save some of the passengers. *What a hero*, I thought. But what made this man, who had never done anything particularly heroic, suddenly do this at that moment? Jung would say, it is the hero within, and that we all have this. Like the time when I was just married and on a pier with my wife. Suddenly, I saw a pelican with hook and line hanging from his beak. I reached out, held his razor-sharp beak, and cut off the line to save the bird's life. Or like the time I suddenly performed the Heimlich maneuver on my then seven-year-old daughter, who was choking. The hero is within us all, and at times, it can show itself. As we grow and mature, we can nurture it and have it become more prominent.

---

wear plays in defining who we are in our conscious lives. That mask, said Jung, is the persona.

The persona is our façade—the mask that hides aspects of ourselves from others and sometimes even from ourselves. It helps us get along with one another, and indeed, we probably would be a pretty chaotic society without it. We may even present a different persona throughout the day. For instance, I wake up and have my "father" persona on; a little later, I wear my "work" persona; and at some points in my day, I likely wear my "social" and my "spousal" persona. Some people get so caught up in their persona, they lose track of who they are underneath their mask. Jung believed that the part of you being hidden by the persona yearns to be realized, and will be shown to you in your dreams and in other symbolic ways in your life. Relatively easy to gain consciousness of, it is not surprising that in both individual and group counseling, one of the first things that clients gain awareness of is how they are "fake" in different parts of their lives and the various personas they wear to "get through" the day. Although the persona can be an aspect of our "fake" selves, it also represents the amount of Self we want to reveal to others. Keep in mind that there are many people in our lives we wisely choose not to reveal intimate details of ourselves to.

The Shadow.   The shadow reaches out of the collective unconscious and attaches to all of the aspects ourselves that we do not want to claim. It has the power to encapsulate our hidden parts and keep them safely walled off from consciousness. It is all of what we are not in our conscious lives. If I'm extraverted, then my introverted self is part of my shadow. If I am a thinking type, then my feeling type is part of my shadow. If I am male, it is my female part of self. If I am loving, the hating side is part of my shadow, and, if I am hating, the loving side is part of my shadow. It may include what many might view as a pleasant side of humanity (e.g., the male who is afraid to show his sensitive side), and it often will hold our darkest secrets, our shameful behaviors, our murderous thoughts, and our most devilish selves. We are alive because of it, for without a shadow, we cannot be fully human. The shadow is Adam and Eve after the fall, and it can give us pleasure—pleasure perhaps that we dare not admit to ourselves.

The Anima/Animus.   We all have an inner gender-opposite that calls us. As a male, my inner opposite is my anima; my wife's is her animus. For me, my anima is that part of me that loves musicals, adores colorful clothing, and feels at home with (other) women discussing whatever. It's always been there—since I was a child—and has gained more prominence as I've aged. For my wife, it is the part of her that is competitive, strong, and loves to take charge—a part she has increasingly become more comfortable with. My anima, or the female part of myself, reaches out and tries to define me in ways that are opposed to its male animus counterpart, and vice versa for my wife. This can create a state of tension as one tries to stay within one's gender-specific identity role. However, to be fully human means that one allows oneself to be in touch with and accept the opposite within.

The Self.   Symbolic of "the God within us," the Self represents the unity of consciousness and unconsciousness. Since consciousness expands as we age, the Self is always changing as we integrate different parts of ourselves into consciousness. The Self has to do with what we are becoming and is closely related to the process of individuation. In a young person, the Self is egocentric, focused mostly on consciousness. As we age, and as increasingly allow ourselves to grow and deepen, we begin to see the parts of ourselves that have been split off. First, our shadow becomes our partner, then our anima or animus becomes known and embraced. The Self changes and includes parts of ourselves that were formerly unconsciousness. The Self does not seek to be "better" or to be "perfect"—it seeks to be complete, integrated, and whole.

Jung found that as clients moved toward wholeness by integrating unconscious aspects into consciousness, they often would draw increasingly complex representations of art that approximated the Hindu or Buddhist **mandala** (see Figure 3.3). A concentric diagram that was used centuries ago to represent the divine, God, wholeness, and existence, the mandala is still used today as a source of meditation, peace, and harmony, and to indicate one's search for completeness. Each person's mandala is, of course, unique, and symbolic of his or her own path toward wholeness.

FIGURE 3.3 A Mandala

Complexes.

> [A complex] has a sort of body, a certain amount of its own physiology. It can upset the stomach. It upsets the breathing, it disturbs the heart—in short, it behaves like a partial personality. (Jung, 1976, p. 72)

Imagine if you were not "you," but instead were a number of "yous." This idea was basic to Jung's theory and brings us to his concept of complexes. If you remember from earlier in the chapter, Jung found evidence for complexes in the reactions that individuals had to a word-association test. He found delayed or unusual responses (e.g., a tic) to certain words usually meant that those words seemed to fit into a logical grouping, which he called a "complex." For instance, imagine how one might respond to the following words if verbally and physically abused by a mother or father: *hand, voice, eyes, hit, mother, parent, father.*

Jung believed that an indeterminate number of complexes are formed out of repressed material and fueled by our archetypes. What gets repressed? Well, any experience that is not congruent with one's psychological type, as well as material that we want to forget (abuse, shame, intensely negative feelings, traumatic events). Repressed material of a similar nature gets clumped together, said Jung, and becomes a complex which gets its energy from an archetype of a similar nature.

One can have many "complexes," although some may become prominent (Jung, 1976), and complexes are not necessarily pathological, such as the mother complex formed out of many traditionally positive women's instincts. However, in some cases, complexes become walled-off and create a separate personality that does not serve the person well, such as when a woman's maternal instincts are focused exclusively on childbirth to the exclusion of relationships. (And, in actuality, the persona, anima and animus, shadow, and Self are complexes—but that's for the next book). Finally, sometimes complexes can be fueled by more than one archetype. For instance, the "bully," might get its psychic energy from the trickster and power archetypes (see Box 3.2).

Organization of the Psyche. Figure 3.4 shows the relationship between the collective unconscious with archetypal energy, the personal unconscious with its complexes (including archetypes), and consciousness. The four most popular archetypes of the Self, anima or animus, shadow, and persona are noted, as well as the ego, which is considered by some to also be an archetype.

Individuation

Individuation is the lifelong process of becoming conscious of the many separate parts of ourselves, with the goal of integrating the various parts into the whole person. It is not inevitable but can flourish if the individual is in an environment that is safe and encouraging of self-reflection. It includes the integration of all that is conscious with all that is unconscious, and is closely

---

B o x 3.2   The Bully Complex

Imagine the young child who is verbally intimidated and physically abused by his or her parents. As a function of the child's psychological type, certain feelings of anger, shame, rage, revenge, and hurt, as well as the memories of being brutally physically abused, may become repressed. Ultimately, such feelings and remembrances linger in unconsciousness and become attached to one or more archetypes, creating a complex. What archetype might become attached to such feelings?—perhaps the "trickster," and "power" archetypes. These archetypes served a survival mechanism thousands of years ago when being manipulative and powerful might have been critical to physical survival. Today, they become "bound" in a personality style, called the "bully complex." This complex allows the bully to get through the day without experiencing those horrible feelings and remembrances. However, it comes with a price, for it prevents closeness and can wreak havoc on people the bully knows and even on society. However, there is hope for the bully. Through self-examination, the bully can begin to understand the repressed parts of self and how they became associated with the trickster and power archetypes. But this is not an easy task, for it means bearing witness to some difficult and shameful memories. However, if the child and growing adult does not examine these aspects of Self, the child will grow into an adult who will likely continue to bully and may become a "gangster." Gangsters treat their children like they were treated—and the cycle continues.

---

aligned with an increasing awareness of Self and movement toward wholeness and completeness. In other words, as we grow, and if given the opportunity to broaden our consciousness, we can begin to understand our unique psychological types, our complexes, and the archetypes that make up who we are. Who are those who are most individuated? Jung suggested Buddha and Jesus. I might add Gandhi, Eleanor Roosevelt, and Martin Luther King.

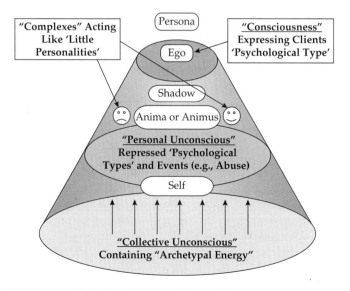

F I G U R E 3.4   Organization of the Psyche

Symbols

> What we call a symbol is a term, a name, or even a picture that may be familiar in daily life, yet that possesses specific connotations in addition to its conventional and obvious meaning. It implies something vague, unknown, or hidden from us. (Jung, 1964b, p. 20)

To Jung, symbols represented projections of archetypes from the unconscious, and because the unconscious could not be seen directly, Jung postulated its existence by noting similarities among symbols in different cultures (Jaffé, 1964). For instance, the symbol of the circle appears in early mandalas drawn by Tibetan monks, on cathedral floors in the middle ages, on Native American petroglyphs (rock carvings), in primitive artwork representing sun worshipping, and in ancient architectural plans of cities. These drawings often had concentric circles leading to the middle and seemed to represent the desire for wholeness as one works toward finding one's center. And just about all primitive and modern-day religions have used live animals, drawings and figures of animals, or stories about animals as symbolic messages of the instinctual (animalistic) nature of people that is generally split off from the more conscious aspects of the soul (psyche):

> ... [T]he relationship of these two aspects of man is beautifully symbolized in the Christmas picture of the birth of Christ, in a stable among animals. (Jaffé, 1964, p. 238)

In contrast to Freud, Jung did not believe that symbols were the manifestation of how the person has learned in early childhood to contain and manage instincts (e.g., men create phallic symbols in an effort to divert themselves away from their sexual drive). Instead, Jung saw symbols as a method that the Self uses to make unconscious psychic energy conscious (e.g., becoming fascinated by animal motifs is symbolic of our unconscious animal instincts). Jung believed that symbols have their origins in archetypes, are transformed by the person's unique psyche, and represent an important part of self that needs to be acknowledged and integrated on our way toward wholeness. Therefore, they can hold different meanings for different people, yet due to their relationship to the archetypes, often bear resemblance to symbols found in antiquity:

> Jung told the story of a schizophrenic patient who spoke to him one day in 1906 in a Zurich hospital. The patient said that if he looked up at the sun and moved his head from side to side, he would be able to see the sun's penis wagging to and fro, producing all the winds on our planet. Four years later Jung happened to read a newly discovered two-thousand-year old Greek text describing a ritual and initiation into the worship of Mithras, the Sun-god of ancient Persia. According to the text, the initiate was to move his head from side to side to observe the sun's phallus producing the east and west winds on earth. The schizophrenic Jung spoke with could not have consulted this newly unearthed ancient text before recounting his own version of its content to Jung. (Pascal, 1992, p. 94)

Symbols are continually found in our lives, and as we become more conscious, we can make sense out of them. They are in the artifacts and stories of our religions, in the types of jobs we pursue, in the languages we speak, in the cars we buy, in aspects of the dreams we have, and on and on. In the end, much of our life is a symbolic life, and the more we can become conscious of our symbols, the more complete we will become.

Synchronicity

Jung often walked a fine line between his belief in modern-day science's focus on external reality and the idea that the world only made sense if one suspended left-brain (logical) thinking (Lawrence, 2000). When it came to the concept of synchronicity, this line was as thin as ever. Jung saw synchronicity as a reflection of a psychic event happening at the same time that a physical event occurred, the two events having some meaningful relationship to one another and there being no causal relationship between the two. This meaningful coincidence provides fodder for a person understanding his or her Self more deeply.

As an example of synchronicity, Jung tells a story about a client with whom he was making little progress. During a session with a woman who was staunchly based in rational thought and not allowing herself to delve into the unconscious, she started to talk about a dream in which a piece of jewelry, in the shape of a golden scarab, was given to her. At that very moment, Jung heard something tapping on his window, looked over and saw a scarab beetle, which he let fly into his office. He caught the beetle, which looked remarkably like the one in her dream, and handed it to the client, while saying: "Here is your scarab." (Jung, 1969b, p. 526). The scarab, which represents a rebirth symbol, was used by Jung to help point the client toward a new rebirth of Self, a rebirth in which she could now visit the irrational and the unconscious. With this event, says Jung, treatment then took off. Although not a "technique" that one uses in therapy, or something that happens on a regular basis, synchronicity provides additional material that can help a client understand the Self (see Box 3.3).

THERAPEUTIC TECHNIQUES

Although Jung wrote volumes on his theory, he never pulled it together into one, succinct approach, and for this, he has been much criticized (Frager & Fadiman, 2005). However, it was clear that whatever technique was used, the purpose was to engage the unconscious in order to understand and become aware of split-off and fragmented parts of Self, and to integrate those parts into consciousness; otherwise, said Jung, the unconscious could wreak havoc:

> … [M]any patients, who as a result of difficult circumstances that might well have driven weaker natures to suicide, sometimes developed a

B o x 3.3   Symbols and Synchronicity

I've always wanted to find a shark's tooth. Every summer I go to the beach and spend a week or two walking on the sand looking through all the shells to find my elusive tooth. Then, one summer, I'm sitting on the beach and my wife says, "What's that under your chair?" I look down and see a 1½" × 1" shark's tooth. I'm ecstatic, finally finding my artifact. I carry it around with me constantly. A week later, she comes up to me and says, "I have something I need to tell you; I bought that shark's tooth and put it under your chair." I was shattered and realized my quest had to continue.

A few weeks after the shark's tooth incident, I'm preparing my lecture on analytical psychology and reviewing the section on symbols, when a colleague walks in and sees my shark's tooth on my desk. He blurts out, "What's that symbolic of?" I immediately tell him the whole story and he says, "Well, what's important is not finding a shark's tooth, but what it symbolizes." "Oh yeah," I say to him and to myself, as I reflect on that important statement. Meanwhile, I look at him and I tell him: "That's synchronicitous. I was just reviewing my section on symbols."

So I go to class with my shark's tooth, and the first thing I do is to hold it up proudly. I show the class my "symbol" and talk about the importance of symbols in our lives and how they are projections of inner parts of our selves. A few days later, one of my students sends me this e-mail:

I went on a walk with my wife at the beach. We always look for shells, sea glass, and sharks' teeth. My wife is a sixth-grade science teacher, so she brings them into her class to use as examples while doing lessons. Of course, it's really much more common to find good shells and sea glass specimens and, like you, I haven't been able to find a shark's tooth in any of my beach-walk searches. Now for the synchronicity: I was telling my wife your story about your shark tooth obsession, and how you had not been able to obtain one in all of your searches, either. At exactly the same time I was telling her the part of how you were at the beach and you looked under your chair to find your first shark tooth, I looked down and thought I was looking at yet another deceivingly shark-tooth-shaped rock. I bent down to pick it up, only to realize that I was wrong. It was a shark's tooth! Me and my wife both looked at each other and confessed goose bumps. After some thought, I realized my folly. I should have substituted the word "shark's tooth" for "one million dollars." I retold her the story with the substitution, but the universe didn't bite.

This true story shows a meaningful coincidence and provides me (and my student) with something to think about. I guess I better think some more about what that shark tooth means to me.

---

suicidal tendency but, because of their inherent reasonableness, prevented it from becoming conscious and in this way generated an unconscious suicide-complex. This unconscious urge to suicide then engineered all kinds of dangerous accidents—as, for instance, a sudden attack of giddiness on some exposed place, hesitation in front of a motor-car, mistaking corrosive sublimate for cough mixture, a sudden zest for dangerous acrobatics, and so forth. When it was possible to make the suicidal leaning conscious … [the patients could] avoid the situations that tempted them to self-destruction. (Jung, 1966a, p. 57)

With the above in mind, it is not surprising that all techniques in analytical therapy attempt to construct an atmosphere that allows the client to access the unconscious. The following represents a brief review of a few of the more commonly used techniques, including **the dialectical method, active imagination, dream analysis, use of creative techniques, amplification, transference/countertransference,** and **interpretation.**

Dialectical Method

Differing from the psychoanalytic approach, in which the analyst is empathic but a bit removed from the client, Jung believed it was critical to create a meaningful dialogue between the client and the therapist. Such a dialogue, said Jung, would foster the "mutual commitment and care that occurs between healer and the healed" as the client explores unknown parts of self in his or her attempt to heal the soul (Hopcke, 1989, p. 55). This was done mostly by showing acceptance, encouraging dialogue, and gently stressing the importance of introspection (Dry, 1961; Jung, 1966a).

Jung also recognized that both the therapist and the client had unconscious forces that would interplay within the relationship, and that could sabotage client movement toward increased consciousness, especially if the therapist had not made movement toward his or her own individuation. Believing that clients would intuit a therapist's lack of psychological development, he suggested that therapists should attend to their own psyche, especially issues of counter-transference.

> In any such discussion the question of whether the doctor has as much insight into his own psychic processes as he expects from his patient naturally counts for a very great deal, particularly in regard to the "rapport," or relationship of mutual confidence, on which the therapeutic success ultimately depends. (Jung, 1966a, p. 116)

Active Imagination

Active imagination offers one method that analytical therapists use to access repressed material. Differing from simply imagining a scene, active imagination is the process of allowing one's unconscious mind to drift while the conscious mind acts as a nonjudgmental observer. Active imagination is different from hypnosis or dreaming, which is involved solely with the unconscious mind, or daydreaming or active directing of fantasies, which are driven by conscious thought.

In doing active imagination, an individual usually starts with a significant piece of a dream, thought, or fantasy that seems to have an important "message" to the person. Then, the individual allows the unconscious mind to take the visualization to wherever it needs to go in order to conjure up the deepest recesses of the mind. In fact, trying to move one's thoughts in a particular direction will often have the result of moving the person away from important repressed parts of self as the unconscious attempts to protect the individual from painful material. As the process continues, it is always important for the individual to have an active conversation between the conscious mind and the unconscious mind, in which the conscious mind sets up a conversation with the images, and asks such questions such as: "Why are you important to me?" "What purpose do you serve for me?" and "What part of my Self is being awakened by you?"

As an individual allows himself or herself to access deeper parts of self, aspects of the persona and then the shadow usually will first be accessed. This is because these archetypes are closer to consciousness and safer to access (see Figure 3.4). However, as one allows oneself to become more deeply involved in the active imagination process, aspects of the anima or animus will emerge, and eventually, the individual will even be able to access the Self. Ultimately, the purpose of active imagination is to uncover repressed and split-off parts of oneself and integrate those parts into the fully functioning person.

Dream Analysis

For Jung, dreams were a mirror that reflected unconscious parts of self to the ego. Dreams bring our unconscious to us, but it is the conscious mind that does the remembering and relating of the dream. The therapist's role is to help the individual allow his or her dream to rise from the unconscious, rather than directing the individual toward a therapist-centered interpretation of the dream. Whereas Freud believed that dreams provide distorted images of unconscious aspects of self which one has to uncover to understand the repressed, hidden latent meanings of the dream, Jung believed that dreams hold personal and symbolic meanings that can be understood by encouraging a person to freely associate to the dream and amplify the many aspects of the dream (McLynn, 1996) (see amplification in later section). You might say that with Freud, you're trying to tear down the dream to get to hidden parts of self, whereas with Jung, you're trying to expand upon the dream to understand its symbolic meaning (Ellenberger, 1970).

In analytical therapy, clients are encouraged to remember their dreams by actively making an effort, such as waking up and saying to oneself, "What did I dream last night?" or by keeping a dream journal in which one writes down his or her dreams. In addition, in therapy, clients would be encouraged to associate to or brainstorm aspects of a dream and to amplify aspects of a dream (to be discussed in a later section). Jung generally discouraged interpretation about dreams (e.g., dreams of falling means giving in to sexual desire), believing that individual meanings could vary for each person and that each person could reveal for himself or herself the often unique meaning that a dream held. However, he was not opposed to offering his thoughts about a dream (McLynn, 1996) and would invite discussion about a dream if he believed it might help the client come to a realization about self:

> Further, I present him with my ideas and opinions. If, in so doing, I open the door to "suggestion," I see no occasion for regret; for it is well known that we are susceptible only to those suggestions with which we are already secretly in accord. (Jung, 1966a, pp. 44–45)

Discussions about dream associations and amplifications with the therapist leads to insight about the dream from many sources, including the individual's unique personal understanding of the dream that may be related to the personal unconscious and symbolic meanings of the dream that are rooted in archetypes

---

B o x 3.4   Dr. Justice Works with Carin's Dream

Read or watch Dr. Paula Justice's work with Carin. Examine how Dr. Justice uses Carin's dream to help her get in touch with the Shadow side of her self. Consider how ready Carin is to make changes in her life and to accept her Shadow side. Jung, after all, stated that transcendent change did not take place until the second half of one's life. What do you think?

You can read this session by going to www. cengage.com/counseling/neukrug/CTP1e and click "student downloads." Or your instructor may show this session in class with the DVD that accompanies his or her copy of the text.

---

that form the collective unconscious. Recapturing parts of self through such dream analysis is the goal of analytical therapy and is why Jungian analysis is generally seen as holistic, not reductionistic (see Box 3.4).

Use of Creative Techniques

Whenever the creative force predominates, life is ruled and shaped by the unconscious rather than by the conscious will, and the ego is swept along on an underground current, becoming nothing more than a helpless observer of events. (Jung, 1966b, p. 103)

Jung believed that we constantly project our unconscious onto the world. Thus, he suggested that finding creative outlets for projections could help a client realize his or her inner unconscious voice. Whether through poetry, prose, use of clay, drawing, painting, or other creative endeavors, if done in a manner that was spontaneous, the unconscious would have an outlet. The results of a creative piece could then be looked at, analyzed, understood as a projection of the client's personal and collective unconscious, and ultimately integrated into consciousness.

From a Jungian perspective, the key to doing creative work is allowing the unconscious to emerge spontaneously. In fact, directing the client could have the effect of stifling the creative process and not allowing the unconscious to emerge. Instead, like active imagination, clients are encouraged to let themselves "go" and allow their creative selves to emerge. There is a scene in the movie *Close Encounters of the Third Kind* in which some people have an uncontrollable urge to create a mountain—out of mashed potatoes, out of dirt, out of whatever is around. Ultimately, the mountain they are creating is in the same shape as the mountain where aliens will land. Symbolically, the mountain they are creating represents an escape fantasy. Climb the mountain and escape from the day-to-day constraints placed on us by our ego. And ultimately, we can be whisked away on a spaceship into the universe and discover the unknown—our unconscious. As you can see, understanding the metaphoric and symbolic meaning of creative expressions by releasing the inner self, examining what is there, and integrating unconscious aspects into consciousness is the key to this technique.

Amplification

Jung believed that it was important for clients to amplify symbols found in their lives in order to have the client go beyond the personal meanings they held. For instance, parts of a dream could hold multiple meanings for a person, and Jung believed the therapist should try to encourage all of the symbolic meanings of each part of a dream. In this process, the therapist is trying to uncover what meaning symbols hold relative to material that is held in the personal unconscious and the collective unconscious (e.g., meanings derived from archetype). To help facilitate the process of amplification, Jung recommended using "suggestion, good advice, understanding, sympathy, encouragement" (Jung, 1966a, p. 173), and other techniques that could gently help the client examine the multiple meanings of dreams or other symbols found in the client's life (e.g., artwork, daydreams, fantasies, etc.).

For instance, as a child, I had a recurring dream that I was walking on a concrete path parallel to the ocean. As I walked, I saw piers with skulls hanging on wooden entranceways. The dreams followed heart disease I had between the ages of 8 and 13. Table 3.1 shows just a small sample of some of the multiple meanings I might find by amplifying this dream.

T A B L E 3.1   Amplification of a Dream

Symbol	Association	Possible Meaning
Self walking	Ego. The conscious me.	My ego has a glimpse at my personal and collective unconscious as represented by the pier, skull, and ocean.
Concrete path	Solid and grounded.	I am strong, as long as I remain on this solid path.
Concrete path	Father archetype (the concrete representing my father, who had a construction company).	My father is with me. I am my father and can draw strength from my animus.
Skulls	Impending death.	Annihilation of Self. Fear of my being not existing. Dying literally or figuratively. Can I face my fears?
Skulls	Repressed anger toward parents and God for impending doom and annihilation.	Shadow self. The "not-nice" boy. Being the other part of me. Being free to be angry.
Ocean	The unconscious.	All that is unknown to the ego. I wonder and fear unknown parts of myself.
Wooden pier	Soft wood—shaky, not grounded.	The entranceway to my unconscious mind is shaky and scary.
Long pier	Long walk to the unconscious guarded by the skulls.	The skulls sit at the beginning of the pier warning me to not go toward my unconscious.

B o x   3.5   A Dream Highlighting Transference (and a little synchronicity)

In the midst of writing about transference, I had a "blowup" with my daughter, which ended up highlighting the concept of transference (perhaps this "blowup" was also an example of synchronicity). It was the evening, and I got angry with my daughter because of the time she spends on the Internet. Angry back, her last words to me that evening were, "I'm going to sleep!" as she stomped upstairs to her room. When she awoke in the morning, she asked if I would drive her to school (she woke up late, and usually takes the bus). At first, on the way to school, there was silence. Then she says to me, "I had a dream last night." I asked her to tell me about it. She relayed a dream about the lead singer of her favorite rock band. (One of the band members is her computer wallpaper, looks like me when I was younger, and is Jewish—like me). In the dream, she is at a concert, and the lead singer comes up to her, and they go back to our house. While at the house, he calls her best friend and is nasty to her. She then realizes that he is balding (I am balding) and he becomes very short (he and I are tall in real life). She then says, "but it's okay, the drummer was really nice." I ask my daughter how she felt in the dream, and she says "disappointed."

My interpretation: The lead singer is me, and my daughter is disappointed in me. To my daughter, I am the projection of the archetypal father hero, and my anger at her last night brought me down a notch as she begins to deal with her father not being perfect. She unconsciously reveals this to me by asking me to drive her to school and telling me about the dream. On a more human level, I have much more empathy for my daughter when I realize how disappointed she is in me—and I said "I love you" as I dropped her off at school. Now, if I were to have a dialogue with my daughter, who knows?—maybe she would come up with a totally different interpretation! After all, it was *her* dream.

Transference/Countertransference

Jung believed that material from the unconscious is projected onto others and deeply affects all relationships (Ulanov, 1982). Because our parents form with us our first, most important relationships, these projections often first occur with them. For instance, the archetype of the "hero" may be first projected onto our parents, and this projection will affect our interactions with our parents (see Box 3.5). In therapy, similar projections can occur, and one role of the analytical therapist is to assist the client in understanding these projections through the dialectical process. This can be one additional method of helping to make the unconscious conscious. Finally, Jung saw transference as a normal part of all relationships, although from a developmental perspective, as one ages, one is more likely to understand and become increasingly conscious of his or her transference.

As an example of transference, imagine that a male client who is seeing a female therapist has a dream that they suddenly switch roles during the session, and he is now the therapist. In this role, he sees himself being understanding, sensitive, and respectful of his client's needs. He does not try to problem-solve with her, which would have been his usual method of responding to people's problems, but instead shows empathy. As the dream is explored with the therapist, the therapist helps the client see how this is actually a part of him. His anima had been awakened through his dream, and he can now integrate this "feminine" side into his life. Consider how different he might now be, and how his ego has expanded to make room for this new, formerly repressed part of self.

Similar to transference were Jung's thoughts on countertransference. In this case, the therapist's unconscious becomes projected onto the client. Jung believed it is impossible to avoid countertransference totally, and suggested that all therapists go through their own analysis in an effort to minimize its effects. (Machtiger, 1982). Sometimes, if one understands his or her countertransference, it could be discussed with the client in an effort to elucidate this important principle and to act as a model for how to understand relationships in general.

Interpretation

Because Jungians believe it is important for clients to uncover their own unconscious content, they do not rely heavily on interpretation. However, they will suggest how certain aspects of behavior may be indicative of the unconscious. Thus, at moments in therapy when the therapist believes the client is ready to hear feedback, the therapist might suggest such things as how complexes are formed; point out how opposites hide in the unconscious (e.g., the anima for a male client); explain what psychological type the client seems to fit (e.g., thinking type) and how the inferior type is hidden in the unconscious; suggest how some of the more common archetypes might affect the client's behavior; and note how dreams and symbols in the client's life may be indicative of the unconscious. Although some analytical therapists will become more directive and offer more specific interpretations, others rely on helping the client self-direct the therapeutic process. This is mostly a function of the therapist's unique personality style.

THE THERAPEUTIC PROCESS

Jungian analysis is usually long-term and has the aim of helping a client become increasingly aware of his or her unconscious, which often means being open to parts of self that are "less rational, more ambiguous, and often mysterious" (Stein, 1982, p. 33). Meeting one to two times a week, a client sits face-to-face with the therapist, who encourages dialogue while gently directing the client toward examining the unconscious content of his or her life. As the client increasingly feels comfortable sharing in this dialogue, the therapist will begin to incorporate techniques that might encourage exploration of the unconscious. Thus, the therapist might use dream work, active imagination, creative techniques, amplification, interpretation, and so forth.

As you might expect, therapy moves from the external to the internal, as clients feel increasingly comfortable sharing deeper parts of themselves and looking more critically at what is present in consciousness and hidden in their personal and collective unconscious. Using Figure 2.4 as a model, let's take a look at how therapy moves from issues that are apparent only in consciousness, to awareness and identification of how the personal unconscious affects the individual, and finally to an understanding of how the collective unconscious affects behavior.

Consciousness: Generally, the client who first seeks counseling is only aware of a small part of his or her total psyche. Consciousness is limited at this point, and early on in therapy, the client is processing life in a mostly nonreflective manner as opposed to examining his or her internal processes. With the help of the therapist, the client slowly begins to identify his or her "psychological type" as well as the persona he or she presents to the world. This beginning awareness brings with it a very early intuitive sense that "if this is what I am in the conscious world, I wonder what else is lurking in my unconscious world." Although at this point the client's ego-consciousness is limited, soon it will be expanding as the ego begins to tap into the personal unconscious.

Personal unconscious: As the client continues in therapy, he or she becomes more self-reflective. This occurs for a number of reasons. First, the client is feeling increasingly safe with the therapist, who is using a dialectical process to gently nudge the client to examine other parts of self. Soon, the therapist encourages the use of some of the various techniques described earlier and also might suggest that other aspects of self exist. The client then realizes that there is likely repressed material that can be brought to the surface. The first of this material is generally repressed traumatic events (e.g., abuse) or the opposing psychological types (e.g., mental functions and attitude not in consciousness).

Success with understanding these other parts of self slowly yields to the adaptation of new behaviors that are based on the client's newfound awareness. Thus, other "psychological types" can now be tried out, and new behaviors can be adapted as catharsis occurs over the remembrance of traumatic events. Now, the client is willing to go further, and is ready to look at his or her shadow and then anima or animus. Looking at the "dark side" of one's self is not easy, but the client has gained experience with the therapist and is increasingly more trusting of the self-reflective process. Over time, the client is willing to integrate aspects of the shadow and anima or animus. Slowly, these aspects of self are accepted and become part of an expanded ego-consciousness. Eventually, the client is also willing to look at complexes that have taken over and "invaded" the client's way of being in the world. Complexes can now be deconstructed, understood, and redefined in ways that are productive for the client. It is critical that the personal unconscious has been examined first, for as Jung (1968b) noted, "otherwise the gateway to the collective unconscious cannot be opened" (p. 62).

Collective unconscious: Having examined the personal unconscious, the client is now primed to go further and look at the deepest and most hidden parts of self in the collective unconscious. The collective unconscious, filled with its archetypes, affects the person in subtle yet profound ways. Understanding aspects of the collective unconscious generally occurs through the awareness of projections in the client's dreams and symbols. Slowly, over time, the client can come to understand how archetypes affect the total psyche. Eventually, there is increased ego-consciousness and a deepening sense of the Self archetype and how it operates to unite all aspects of the individual.

Not all clients are ready to go through the full process of Jungian analysis, and generally, the depth of the work for the client, and the willingness of the therapist to gently "push" the client, will depend on the client's stage of life. Clients in their first half of the life (by age 40 psychologically) are dealing more with external issues, such as, "How do I define myself in terms of work?" "How do people see me?" "What is my role as mother, father, partner to my lover?" and so forth (Jung, 1966a; McCurdy, 1982). These clients are more likely to discuss obvious issues of which they are conscious, perhaps look at their personas, maybe begin to examine some basic issues from their personal unconscious, and are less inclined to examine in-depth, unconscious content. This is highlighted in the role-play between Dr. Justice and Carin that you may have read or viewed earlier (see Box 3.4). Carin, who is in her early twenties, is still mostly involved with external appearances (how she looks) and is just beginning to look at internal processes. This is normal, functional, expected, and healthy for Carin as she attempts to build a career and work on issues of intimacy in her early life.

The work of clients like Carin can be contrasted with clients in the second half of life, who are more likely to want to build an ongoing bridge or openness between their ego and their unconscious, particularly their collective unconscious, so that information can freely flow between consciousness and unconsciousness. For "older" clients, acceptance of aspects of the unconscious which have been repressed, and acceptance of self, even the "dark side" of self, is the ultimate goal of Jungian analysis and leads to completeness and individuation.

SOCIAL, CULTURAL, AND SPIRITUAL ISSUES

Relative to cross-cultural counseling, analytical therapy is unique because it assumes that health is not a function of whatever the majority culture says is "usual," but a function of one's ability to embrace all aspects of one's being, even those aspects that may not be common or even acceptable to the majority culture. However, Carl Jung and Jungian therapy is by no means free from criticism. For instance, some have charged Jung and his theory with racism, anti-Semitism, sexism, and being anti-religious. Interestingly, others have sung Jung's praise, saying he developed one of the most accepting theories relative to different cultural groups. Let's take a look at some of these disparate views.

In relation to gender development, some have criticized Jung's concept of male and female development, saying it tends to be an outgrowth of Jung's own male way of understanding the world (Goldenberg, 1990; Rybak, Russell-Chapin, & Moser, 2000). In fact, some feminists take issue with the Jungian notion that women need to integrate their "maleness" (their animus). What real evidence, after all, is there that an animus and anima even exist? However, more recently, there has been a growing acceptance that Jung, the man, was imperfect, but his ideas may have some merit (Rowland, 2002). This is particularly true relative to his thoughts that men have a tendency to develop a "male" consciousness and women a "female" consciousness, and that both can learn from their **contrasexual** (their other internal gender; their anima or animus) as they move to a more androgynous way of being.

Men must identify and claim their feminine archetypes as well as their familiar, and often culture-based, male archetypes.... Women must

claim their feminine archetypes, and they must make a conscious decision to break with established images of the feminine and to begin the
traditional hero's journey in quest of their masculine archetypes. (Rybak
et al., 2000, p. 60)

From this perspective, Jungian therapy can be particularly helpful for those
struggling with gender-identity issues by normalizing what the culture has had
a tendency to make abnormal (e.g., effeminate behavior in men, masculine
behaviors in women, being transgendered, etc.) (Fraser, 2005).

As you might expect, Jung's views on God and religion were as profound as his
views on personality and gender development. Seeing himself as a Christian, he
believed that the values put forth in Christianity and the other major religions of the
world were critical to how the psyche was organized (Homans, 1990). The nature
of the psyche, argued Jung, includes our ego, which embraces values from our
learned religions, but also includes our God-image archetype, which we come to
know later in life. Jung suggested that as our search for self-understanding deepens
with age, we must come to grips with the God that we learned about and the God-
image archetype that we slowly come to know. As a person who was individuated,
it is therefore not surprising that, when asked on a BBC broadcast if he believed in
God, Jung said, "I do not need to believe in God; I know" (Jung, as cited by
Bennet, 1967, p. 167). What did he know? Assuming Jung understood his own
religious upbringing and had come to know his God-image archetype, then he had
settled into his own truth. This "I know" is a personal truth, not a universal truth, as
each individual attempts to make sense and integrate his or her early ego God with
the later God-image archetype. Finally, although Jung may have "known" for
himself what God is, Jung's truth has been seen as challenging to some of the more
traditional notions of God and religion. Ultimately, as a Jungian therapist, one must
come to grips with one's own religious values, the God-archetype, understand the
religious orientation of the client, and then make a decision how to best work with
the client.

In reference to cross-cultural differences, one must ask if any of Jung's work
is based on some real notion of the psyche, or if it is all just an elaborate,
fictionalized system. For instance, does an unconscious exist? Are there really such
things as archetypes, psychological types, and a collective unconscious? Or, are
these concepts based on anything other than the collective imaginations of
a number of highly educated, Western-based philosophers, psychologists, and
psychiatrists? In some ways, Jung himself would probably say it doesn't matter
whether his theory is based in "reality"—what matters is our psychic or subjective
reality, because even if these structures do not exist, their symbolic meaning can
help us make some sense of who we are.

Although Jung might question the "reality" of his own theory, he did believe
in its cross-cultural universality. However, it is likely that many from non-
Western cultures would have a difficult time accepting a significant portion of
Jung's concepts (Gross, 2000). In fact, Jung's belief that some cultures are
"primitive" compared to the evolved consciousness of Western civilization is
seen as patronizing and even racist by many. Others accuse Jung of being

embedded in European values to the point that he brought into his theory negative stereotypes of some cultures, including Jews and blacks, and that his theory actually ended up propagating a white supremacist approach to counseling:

> And Jung claims to have found in uncivilized peoples the same psychic structure that his diagram portrays. Personally, I think that Jung has deceived himself. Moreover, all the peoples that he has known—whether the Pueblo Indians of Arizona or the Negroes of Kenya in British East Africa—have had more or less traumatic contacts with the white man. (Fanon, 2008, p. 187)

On a more positive note, from Jung's perspective, we are all so different, and yet we are all the same. Outwardly, we may have different values, jobs, looks, ways of interacting, but in the end, we are all connected. We're connected to one another through the common archetypes which we all hold and we are connected to the universe and timelessness through unknown and yet vital psychic forces. From this inner perspective, we could always understand the "other."

EFFICACY OF ANALYTICAL PSYCHOLOGY

> … [T]he master therapist, informed by psychological knowledge and theory and guided by experience, produces an artistry that assists clients to move ahead in their lives with meaning and health. (Wampold, p. 2001, 225)

In terms of outcome research, it is clear that some therapies are more easily researchable than others. Jungian analysis is not one of them. After all, how does one measure changes in consciousness? And not many researches want to spend years before examining their results—the time it takes for many Jungian clients to reap benefits. However, the spattering of studies examining psychodynamic approaches have generally shown them to be effective for many mental health issues, with the possible exception of substance abuse treatment, probably because these clients need an approach that can help them to stop abusing immediately (cf. Freeman & Power, 2007; Heather, 2007; Roth & Fonagy, 2005; Wampold, 2001). But even here there is the possibility that psychodynamic therapy following recovery could be beneficial.

With hundreds of studies demonstrating the usefulness of approaches that are easily adaptable to experimental methods, such as cognitive and behavioral treatments, Wampold (2001) warns us not to get too caught up in a numbers game when looking at efficacy. He suggests that the more compelling aspect of the efficacy research shows that it is not the approach that is important, but specific factors that seem critical in ensuring positive client outcomes. These include building a working alliance, allegiance to the client, and competence of the therapist. With this in mind, he says the vast preponderance of approaches would be effective if the following exists: there is a well-defined paradigm, the

B o x 3.6   **Angela's Experience with a Jungian Therapist**

Please review the Miller family's background, which can be found in Appendix B, and then read about

Angela's encounter with a Jungian therapist, which can also be found in Appendix B.

therapist is committed, the therapist is well-trained, and the therapist can connect with his or her clients. Clearly, Jungian analysis fits this mold. It is well-defined, clinicians are almost always well-trained in it, the importance of commitment is highlighted, and there is an emphasis, through the dialectical process, to building a relationship. Although additional long-term studies would be helpful in highlighting its effectiveness, as a classic approach that has a solid theoretical grounding, analytical therapy likely has efficacy for a large array of mental health concerns. (see Box 3.6)

SUMMARY

This chapter began with a biography of Carl Jung, the developer of analytical therapy. Born in Switzerland, Jung's childhood was difficult, and his struggles early in life can be directly linked to his later theoretical formulations, including his ideas about universal symbols, archetypes, and the personal and collective unconscious. In Jung's early professional life, he was a psychoanalyst, but as he began to do his own research and examine Freud's theory more fully, he went in a different direction.

Jung did not believe we are determined by or victims of our biology, or of our past. He did believe that childhood influences affect our psychological makeup and that symptoms represent a desire to regain lost parts of self—parts that have been repressed as a function of one's psychological makeup. By expanding our consciousness (revealing unconscious material to consciousness), the individual is able to integrate parts of self that have been pushed into the unconscious as well as primordial parts of self that have never been revealed to consciousness, and become a more fully functioning "whole" person.

Jung stated that awareness of our conscious world develops soon after birth and is partly related to how we develop our mental functions of sensation, thinking, feeling, and intuition. In addition to the mental functions, Jung suggested we are born favoring one of two attitudes: extraversion and introversion. The mental functions and attitudes make up what Jung called our character. The ego, Jung believed, manages our mental functions and attitudes, and allows continuity of our basic personality structure.

Splitting from many of his contemporaries, Jung suggested that the psyche consists of the conscious mind, which represents all of what we are aware, the personal unconscious, which represents repressed memories as well as experiences incongruent with our psychological type, and the collective unconscious, which houses our primordial images, called archetypes. Some of the more typical archetypes that Jung identified included the persona, the shadow, the anima and animus, and the Self. Jung also stated that certain complexes are formed in the personal unconscious and that these complexes obtain their energy from these and other archetypes. Jung stressed the importance of reclaiming and understanding all that is repressed if one is to be whole. He also noted that symbols in our life, and the sometimes-mysterious synchronistic events that happen to us, can be indicative of unconscious material important to our understanding of self.

Jung was a prolific writer, although he never comprehensively described his theory in an orderly fashion. However, a number of techniques commonly used by Jungian analysts include the dialectical method, active imagination, dream analysis, use of creative techniques, amplification, transference/countertransference, and interpretation. These techniques are all used to help the client get in touch with the unconscious in an effort to illuminate repressed parts of self, integrate those parts, and move toward completeness and wholeness—a process Jung called individuation.

From a multicultural perspective, analytical therapy has its critics and supporters. For instance, Jung's thoughts about the anima and animus has raised the ire of some feminists, who reject Jung's notion of each woman having a male counterpart, but have been embraced by other feminists, who see his ideas as moving us toward a type of androgyny. His ideas about "primitive" culture have been criticized by some who have called him racist and have been praised by others who say he has identified common factors in all cultures. And his ideas about God have been seen as universal by some and a challenge to existing religions by others.

Finally, although analytical therapy is not a theory that is particularly amenable to research, due to its elusive concepts and because it is a long-term therapeutic approach, it seems to embody many of the requirements that would make it an efficacious approach, including a theory to which people could ascribe, a commitment to the client, and stressing the importance of the therapeutic relationship.

KEY WORDS

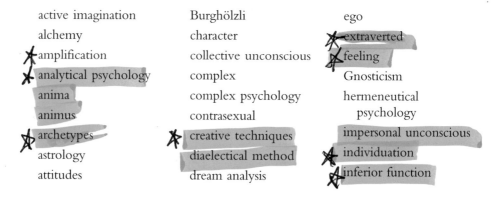

active imagination
alchemy
amplification
analytical psychology
anima
animus
archetypes
astrology
attitudes

Burghölzli
character
collective unconscious
complex
complex psychology
contrasexual
creative techniques
diaelectical method
dream analysis

ego
extraverted
feeling
Gnosticism
hermeneutical
  psychology
impersonal unconscious
individuation
inferior function

integrate
International Psychoanalytic Association
International Society
interpretation
introverted
intuiting
irrational functions
judging
mandala
mental functions

Myers-Briggs Type Indicator (MBTI)
perceiving
persona
personal unconscious
primary function
primordial images
psyche
rational functions
Self
sensing
shadow

Society for Psychoanalytic Endeavors
Society for Psychotherapy
symbols
synchronicity *Finding coincidences*
Tai-chi-tu
thinking
transference/ countertransference
wholeness
yin yang

KEY NAMES

Bleuler, Eugen
Briggs, Katherine
Freud, Sigmund
Jung, Emilie

Jung, Paul
Myers, Isabel Briggs
Rauschenbach, Emma

Simon, Sid
Spielrein, Sabina
Wolf, Toni

REFERENCES

Adler, G. (Ed.). (1973). *C. G. Jung Letters: 1906–1950* (vol. 1). Princeton, NJ: Princeton University Press.

Bennet, E. A. (1961). *C. G. Jung*. London: Barrie and Rockliff.

Bennet, E. A. (1967). *What Jung really said*. New York: Schocken.

Bridle, S., & Edelstein, A. (2000, Spring/Summer). Was ist "das ich"? *EnlightNext Magazine, 17,* 123–126, 174.

Clarke, J. J. (1992). *In search of Jung*. London: Routledge.

Dry, A. M. (1961). *The psychology of Jung: A critical interpretation*. New York: John Wiley & Sons.

Ekstrom, S. R. (1988). Jung's typology and DSM-III personality disorders: A comparison of two systems of classification. *Journal of Analytical Psychology, 33*(4), 329–344.

Ellenberger, H. F. (1970). *The discovery of the unconscious: The history and evolution of dynamic psychiatry*. New York: Basic Books.

Fanon, F. (2008. *Black skin, white masks* (1st ed., new ed.) New York: Grove Press. (Original work published in 1952).

Felixson, H. (Producer), & Marton, E. (Director). (2002). *My name was Sabina Spielrein* [Motion picture]. Stockholm, Sweden: Folkets Bio.

Frager, R., & Fadiman, J. (2005). *Personality and personal growth* (6th ed.). New York: Pearson.

Fraser, L. (2005, Summer). Therapy with transgender people across lifespan. *APA Division 44 Newsletter, 21*(3), 14–18.

Freeman, E., & Power, M. (Eds.). (2007). *Handbook of evidence-based psychotherapies: A guide of research and practice.* West Sussex, England: John Wiley & Sons.

Goldenberg, N. R. (1990). A feminist critique of Jung. In. R. Moore & D. J. Meckel (Eds.), *Jung and Christianity in dialogue: Faith, feminism, and hermeneutics* (pp. 104–111). Mahwah, NJ: Paulist Press.

Gross, S. (2000). Racism in the shadow of Jung. In E. Christopher & H. M. Solomon (Eds.), *Jungian thought in the modern world* (pp. 71–86). New York: Free Association Books.

Hall, C. S., & Nordby, V. J. (1999). *A primer of Jungian psychology.* New York: Meridian. (Original work published 1973).

Hayman, R. (2001). *A life of Jung.* New York: W. W. Norton & Company.

Heather, N. (2007). Alcohol problems. In C. Freeman & M. Power (Eds.), *Handbook of evidence-based psychotherapies: A guide of research and practice* (pp. 251–268). West Sussex, England: John Wiley & Sons.

Hoffler, A. (2001). Jung's analysis of Sabina Spielrein and his use of Freud's free association method. *Journal of Analytical Psychology, 46,* 117–128.

Hoffman, E. (Ed.). (2003). *The wisdom of Carl Jung.* New York: Kensington Publishing Company.

Homans, P. (1990). C. G. Jung: Christian or post-Christian psychologist? In. R. Moore & D. J. Meckel (Eds.), *Jung and Christianity in dialogue: Faith, feminism, and hermeneutics* (pp. 21–37). Mahwah, NJ: Paulist Press.

Hopcke, R. H. (1989). *A guided tour of the collected works of C. G. Jung.* Boston: Shambhala Publications.

Jaffé, A. (1964). Symbolism in the visual arts. In C. G. Jung, & M. L. von Franz (Eds.) *Man and his symbols* (pp. 230–271). Garden City, NY: Doubleday and Company.

Jaffé, A. (1971). *From the life and work of C. G. Jung.* New York: Harper & Row.

Jung, C. G. (1916). *Psychology of the unconscious: A study of the transformations and symbolisms of the libido, a contribution to the history of the evolution of thought* (B. Moses, Trans.). Princeton, NJ: Princeton University Press.

Jung, C. G. (1938). *Psychology and religion.* New Haven, CT: Yale University Press.

Jung, C. G. (1957). *The undiscovered self.* New York: Penguin Books.

Jung, C. G. (1964a). *Psychological types* (H.G. Baynes, Trans.). London: Pantheon. (Original work published 1921)

Jung, C. G. (1964b). Approaching the unconscious. In C. G. Jung & M. L. von Franz (Eds.), *Man and his symbols* (pp. 18–103). Garden City, NY: Doubleday and Company.

Jung, C. G. (1966a). *The collected works of C. G. Jung: The practice of psychotherapy* (vol. 16). (R. F. C. Hull, Trans.). Princeton, NJ: Princeton University Press.

Jung, C. G. (1966b). *The collected works of C. G. Jung: The spirit in man, art, and literature* (vol. 15). (R. F. C. Hull, Trans.). Princeton, NJ: Princeton University Press.

Jung, C. G. (1968a). *The collected works of C. G. Jung: The archetypes and the collective un-conscious.* (vol. 9, part 1). (R.F.C. Hull, Trans.). Princeton, NJ: Princeton University Press.

Jung, C. G. (1968b). *The collected works of C. G. Jung: Psychology and alchemy* (vol. 12) (R.F.C. Hull, Trans.). Princeton, NJ: Princeton University Press.

Jung, C. G. (1969a). *Studies in word-association: Experiments in the diagnosis of psychopatho-logical conditions carried out at the psychiatric clinic of the University of Zurich under the di-rection of C. G. Jung.* New York: Russell & Russell. (Original work published 1918)

Jung, C. G. (1969b). *The collected works of C. G. Jung: The structure and dynamics of the psyche* (vol. 8). (R.F.C. Hull, Trans.). Princeton, NJ: Princeton University Press.

Jung, C. G. (1971). *The collected works of C. G. Jung: Psychological types* (vol. 6). (H. G. Baynes, Trans.). Princeton, NJ: Princeton University Press.

Jung, C. G. (1976). *The collected works of C. G. Jung: The symbolic life: Miscellaneous writings* (vol. 18). (R. F. C. Hull, Trans.). Princeton, NJ: Princeton University Press.

Jung, C., G., & Campbell, J. (Eds.). (1971). *The portable Jung.* (R. F. C. Hull, Trans.). New York: Penguin Books. (Original work published 1928)

Jung, C. G., & von Franz, M. L. (Eds.). (1964). *Man and his symbols.* Garden City. NY: Doubleday and Company.

Jung, C. G., & Jaffé, A. (Eds.). (1961). *Memories, dreams, reflections.* (R. Winston & C. Winston, Trans.). New York: Pantheon Books.

Lawrence, G. (2000). Forward. In E. Christopher & H. M. Solomon (Eds.), *Jungian thought in the modern world* (pp. xii–xviii). New York: Free Association Books.

Machtiger, H. G. (1982). Countertransference/transference. In M. Stein (Ed.), *Jungian analysis* (pp. 86–110). La Salle, IL: Open Court Publishing Company.

McCurdy, A. (1982). Establishing and maintaining the analytical structure. In M. Stein (Ed.), *Jungian analysis* (pp. 47–67). La Salle, IL: Open Court Publishing Company.

McLynn, F. (1996). *Carl Gustav Jung.* New York: St. Martin's Press.

Papadopoulos, R. (1992). Commentary. In R. Papadopoulos (Ed.), *Carl Gustav Jung: Critical assessments* (vol. 2, pp. 97–103). New York: Routledge.

Pascal, E. (1992). *Jung to live by.* New York: Warner Books.

Quenk, N. (2000). *Essentials of Myers-Briggs Type Indicator assessment.* New York: John Wiley & Sons.

Roth, A., & Fonagy, P. (2005). *What works for whom? A critical review of psychotherapy research* (2nd ed.). New York: The Guilford Press.

Rowland, S. (2002). *Jung: A feminist revision.* Malden, MA: Blackwell Publisher.

Rybak, C., Russell-Chapin, L., & Moser, M. (2000). Jung and theories of gender development. *Journal of Humanistic Counseling, Education and Development, 38*(3), 152–161.

Stein, M. (1982). The aims and goal of Jungian analysis. In M. Stein (Ed.), *Jungian analysis* (pp. 27–46). La Salle, IL: Open Court Publishing Company.

Storr, A. (1973). *C. G. Jung.* New York: The Viking Press.

The top 10: The most influential therapists of the past quarter-century (2007, March/April). *Psychotherapy Networker.* Retrieved from http://www.psychotherapynetworker.org/index.php/magazine/populartopics/219-the-top-10

Ulanov, A. B. (1982). Transference/Countertransference: A Jungian perspective. In M. Stein (Ed.), *Jungian analysis* (pp. 68–85). La Salle, IL: Open Court Publishing Company.

Wampold, B. E. (2001). *The great psychotherapy debate: Models, methods, and findings.* Mahwah, NJ: Erlbaum.

Young-Eisendrath, P., & Dawson, T. (2008). *The Cambridge companion to Jung* (2nd ed.). New York: Cambridge University Press.

Chapter 4

Individual Psychology
(Adlerian Therapy)

Learning Goals

- To gain a biographical understanding of Alfred Adler, the creator of *individual psychology*.
- To understand the historical context in which Adler developed his theory.
- Two briefly highlight two additional theorists, Richard Dreikurs and Don Dinkmeyer, who have also influenced the popularity of individual psychology.
- To examine the Adlerian view of human nature in regard to how each child's unique capabilities and personality traits are affected by early experiences and how memories of those experiences drive the individual toward his or her unique final goal.
- To understand how feelings of inferiority are related to one's striving for perfection in light of the holistic and teleological framework of Adlerian therapy.
- To explore the psychodynamic, existential–humanistic, and constructivist leanings of individual psychology.
- To examine a number of key concepts of individual psychology, including: uniqueness of the individual, feelings of inferiority, private logic versus common sense, compensation, subjective final goal, style of life, striving for perfection, social interest, holism, schema of apperception, birth order, and courage.
- To describe a wide range of therapeutic techniques that can be used with adults and separate techniques that can be used with children.
- To examine how techniques geared for use with adults and children can be applied through four phases of therapy: building the therapeutic relationship; assessing and understanding the lifestyle; insight and interpretation; and reeducation and reorientation.
- To examine how individual psychology lends itself toward a deeper understanding of the roots of oppression and to social justice advocacy.
- To reflect on the Adlerian notion of God as an ideal image and see how such an image is used by individuals in their efforts to reach their goals.

- To review why it is difficult to measure client changes in Adlerian therapy, the evidence for its efficacy, and some of the qualities inherent in the approach that support the likelihood of good client outcomes.
- To see how individual psychology is applied through vignettes, DVDs, and case study.

"The fastest swimmer alive." "The greatest athlete of all time." "No one will ever outdo what he's done." These are the types of things that have been said today about Michael Phelps, the winner of 11 Olympic gold medals. But it wasn't always that way. Earlier in his life, Michael was mocked by his peers for his large ears, told by teachers he would never amount to anything, and bullied at school for having ADHD. But he overcame it all, and in fact was driven to do well because he felt inadequate. And now he's the "best ever."

So what do Michael Phelps and Alfred Adler, the developer of **individual psychology**, have in common? Everything! A fragile boy, Adler saw in his own background how feelings of inferiority could drive a person, and he then based his theory on the importance that people place on overcoming their sense of inferiority. But let's take a closer look at how Adler came to be one of the most talked about theorists of the twentieth and twenty-first centuries.

ALFRED ADLER

"It is always easier to fight for one's principles than to live up to them" (Adler as cited in Bottome, 1957, p. 64).

© The Print Collector/Alamy

Alfred Adler

Born February 7, 1870, Alfred Adler was the second of seven children in a family of five boys and two girls (Furtmuller, 1964; Hoffman, 1994). The son of a Jewish grain merchant and his wife, like Freud, Adler spent his early years in Vienna, Austria. In his first few years of life, Adler struggled with rickets, a vitamin D deficiency which causes softness of the bones and potential fractures. Finally recovering, he almost died at the age of five of pneumonia. The memories of these illnesses and how they affected him were to have a profound effect on his understanding of what motivates people.

Despite his illnesses, Adler was a popular and outgoing child who did well in school but was not considered an outstanding student (Furtmuller, 1964). Closer to his father than to his mother, he would often try to outdo his "model" older brother, ironically named Sigmund, whom he believed his mother favored (during his career, Adler would often be compared to his older colleague, Sigmund Freud) (Bottome, 1957; Selesnick, 1966). A natural interest in science, a need to achieve, and his early illnesses led him in the direction of medicine, and in 1895, he received his medical degree from the University of Vienna.

Adler's young adulthood was spent in an Austria that was intrigued by Marxism, while at the same time saw the spreading of anti-Semitism. Although his parents were Jewish, Adler did not particularly relate to his cultural heritage. However, socialism was a "religion" of the time, and Adler had a philosophical interest in the aspect of socialism that stressed the importance of the common good. This common interest brought together Adler and his future wife, Raissa Timofeyewna Epstein. A strong woman and early feminist, she had come from Russia to study in Vienna. They married in 1897 and in 1898 had their first daughter, Valentine.

Although establishing himself initially as an ophthalmologist, Adler later went into general practice. Perhaps due to his sickly childhood, early in his career, Adler developed an interest in how feelings of inferiority could be motivating. This interest was piqued when he began to treat circus performers who worked at the amusement park across from his office. Realizing that many of these athletically superior performers had compensated for weaknesses in body and mind, he began to reflect on how a person responds to the sense of inferiority that resulted from such conditions.

Adler's interest in the psychological effects of **organ inferiority** eventually turned him to psychiatry. Although Adler had already begun to develop his own theory of the person, he soon found himself defending Freud's ideas, which were revolutionary at the time and being rebuked by the local intelligensia (Furtmuller, 1964). Adler respected the elder Freud and believed that his ideas needed to be examined scientifically. This is probably why, despite his independent views on psychiatry, in 1902, Adler accepted an invitation by Freud to join an informal discussion group on psychoanalysis. Although a member of Freud's inner circle, Adler never really saw himself as a psychoanalyst, and instead reveled in being an objective scientist who was interested in examining some of Freud's unique ideas (Ansbacher, 1962; Maslow, 1962).

The same year that Adler joined Freud's inner circle, Alexandra, his second daughter, was born. Like her father, she too was to become a psychiatrist and eventually would have a major role in interpreting much of what Adler had written. In 1905, Adler and his wife had their first son, Kurt, who would also follow in his father's footsteps and eventually extend some of his father's theories. Also that year, Adler converted to Protestantism, although his conversion seemed due to his sense that Judaism was too insular as well as the importance he placed on being part of a "group," and not due to any belief in God (Bottome, 1957; Selesnick, 1966). In fact, Kurt Adler, in an interview late in his life, insists that he and his family were all atheists, although they believed in the importance of society's striving for many values represented in religion (Kaiser, 1995). In either case, religion did not seem to play a major role in Adler's life, except for how it affected personality development, particularly the drive for wholeness and perfection (God being symbolic for the epitome of perfection) (Adler, 1933/1964a; Bottome, 1957). It was also around this time that we begin to see Adler's early focus on how social issues can affect the person with his publication, in 1904, of the article "Physician as Educator" (Adler, 1904/2002a).

Although Adler remained actively involved with Freud's psychoanalytic group, his thinking was often in stark contrast to Freud's, and he would quietly question some of the basic tenets of psychoanalysis, such as the sex drive's being the underlying basis of our behaviors (Selesnick, 1966). In fact, Adler's thinking was increasingly evolving toward the belief that individuals were predominately motivated by a desire to overcome **feelings of inferiority**, a **striving for wholeness**, and a **striving for perfection**. This eventually led to the writing of one of his first books, called *A Study of Organ Inferiority and Its Psychical Compensation: A Contribution to Clinical Medicine* (Adler, 1907/2002b).

In 1909, Adler and his wife had their fourth child, Cornelia (Nelly), and soon after, in 1910, he became president of the **Vienna Psychoanalytic Society**. Adler's ascendancy to the presidency is interesting in that his ideas increasingly differed from Freud's. For Adler, his weekly meetings with the Society were his opportunity to examine and challenge some of Freud's ideas in an attempt to more fully understand what motivates people and personality formation. However, Adler's continued belief that education, politics, gender roles, poverty, and other social issues played a critical role in the development of the person, as well as other views that questioned some of the basic tenets of psychoanalysis, could hardly be tolerated by its founder, Freud. It is not surprising that ongoing tensions between Freud and Adler led Adler and a number of likeminded colleagues to resign from the Psychoanalytic Society. Considered to be the first major schism of Freud's followers, a year later, in 1912, some of this group established the **Society for Individual Psychology**.

> Adler no doubt felt betrayed by Freud and remained deeply embittered toward him for the rest of his life. Adler, however, continued to acknowledge Freud's pioneering efforts in psychology but, neverthe-less, went out of his way to demonstrate the "superiority" of his views compared with those of Freud. Moreover, he insisted that he was never a pupil or disciple of Freud's and that Freud and his followers appropriated his ideas…. Freud, once he accomplished Adler's "excommunication," never forgave, and continued to heap abuse upon Adler for the "heresy" of rejecting the tenets of psychoanalysis. (Fiebert, 1997, pp. 263–264)

In 1912, Adler published *The Neurotic Character* (1912/2002c), which elucidated his views more clearly, and in 1914, Adler founded and became the first editor of the ***Journal for Individual Psychology***. Drafted during WWI by the Austrian army to work as a physician, Adler saw the ravages of war after being sent to the Russian front and later to a children's hospital. This considerably moved him, and he became convinced of the importance that education could play in eliminating war. After the war, he became particularly interested in educational issues and in the training of teachers. This was a natural fit, as he believed that external forces (e.g., teachers) could have a great influence over the lives of children (Adler, 1931/1992).

During the 1920s, Adler developed one of the first **child guidance clinics** (Bottome, 1957). Believing in the importance that social factors played in child development, he offered workshops at his clinic for teachers. On a voluntary basis, he also consulted with teachers and parents regarding any child who was having difficulty in school. His clinics were generally housed in a school, and it was not long before Adler became well-known for his ability at working with children and their families. Because he was one of the first to stress the importance of family members being present in order to fully understand the child, he is considered an important figure in the development of family therapy models (Goldenberg & Goldenberg, 2008; Sherman, 1999). In addition, Adler was also one of the first to stress the importance that groups could play in teaching people appropriate social behaviors, in helping the individual obtain feedback from others, and in gaining a sense of togetherness from others (Adler, 1931/1992; Ansbacher & Ansbacher, 1956; Buchheimer, 1959; Deutsch, 1958).

In his fifties and sixties, Adler gave a series of lectures throughout Europe and the United States. Writings that documented these talks revealed a person who was becoming increasingly holistic, future-oriented, humanistic, and socially focused (Carlson, Watts, & Maniacci, 2006). In 1926, he accepted a visiting professorship at Long Island College of Medicine, and in 1929, he became an adjunct professor at Columbia University. In 1930, he became *honoris causa*, or an honorary citizen of Vienna, for his achievements. Then, in 1932, despite his award and even though he had converted to Protestantism, most of his clinics in Vienna were closed due to his Jewish heritage. This led him to leave Europe and take a full-time professorship at Long Island College.

Throughout much of his adult life, Adler fought all forms of oppression and tried to show how feelings of inferiority led to abuse of power. In fact, Adler campaigned for women's rights and often spoke about the injustice to minorities (Carlson et al., 2006). Known as a peace activist, Adler was to personally suffer the ravages of war and abuse of power when his daughter, Vali, moved to Russia to escape the Nazis but was held captive by the Stalinist regime under false political charges. Missing her tremendously, in 1937, Adler wrote: "I cannot sleep and cannot eat. I do not know how much longer I can endure it" (Adler as cited by Alexandra Adler in Manaster, Painter, Deutsch, & Overholt, 1977, p. 20). Days later, while on a lecture tour in Scotland, he died on the street of a heart attack. In 1942, Vali died under very harsh conditions in a Siberian prison camp.

Over his lifetime, Adler wrote over 300 books and articles that tended to be more easily understood by laypersons than the writing of many of his contemporaries. Some of the more well-known books he wrote in his later years included *The Practice and Theory of Individual Psychology* (1925/1963a), *Understanding Human Nature* (1927), and *What Life Could Mean to You* (1931/1992).

Adler's influence over the years was widespread, with Rudolf Dreikurs (1897–1972) and Don Dinkmeyer (1924–2001) becoming particularly well-known for adapting individual psychology to their work with children. Like Adler, Dreikurs was an Austrian-born psychiatrist who immigrated to the United States. A student and colleague of Adler's, in 1952, he founded the **Adler School of Professional Psychology**. Don Dinkmeyer, an American psychologist, met Rudolf Dreikurs

B o x 4.1   Want to Hear a Story About Rudolf Dreikurs?

Click "Rudolf Dreikurs" at the
"Stories of the Great Therapists" Web site:
http://www.odu.edu/sgt

in 1958. Impressed by Dreikurs, Dinkmeyer would spend the rest of his life developing Adlerian methods for children. Eventually, Dinkmeyer would develop training programs based on Adlerian principles, such as DUSO (developing an understanding of self and others), which used hand puppets to facilitate communication with children, and the **systematic training for effective parenting (STEP)** program.

Dinkmeyer and Dreikurs (1963) believed that children have an inherent desire to belong and to feel part of their peer groups (similar to Adler's concept of "**social interest**"), but due to feelings of inferiority and maladaptive parenting, some exhibit maladaptive behaviors in an unsuccessful attempt to gain this sense of belonging. Typical behaviors such children exhibit include **attention-seeking** (e.g., interrupting), the **use of power** (e.g., bullying), **revenge-seeking** (e.g., playing nasty practical jokes), and **displaying inadequacy** (e.g., withdrawing). Dinkmeyer and Dreikurs believe that children can and must be taught new behaviors by significant others in their lives, such as parents, counselors, and teachers (Wolfgang, 2001). As the result of the influence of Adler, Dinkmeyer, Dreikurs, and others, individual psychology lives on with numerous associations and institutes around the world advocating this understanding of the development of the person. (See Box 4.1).

VIEW OF HUMAN NATURE

A thousand talents and capabilities arise from the stimulus of inadequacy. Now the situations of individual children are extraordinarily different. In the one case we are dealing with an environment which is hostile to the child and which gives him the impression that the whole world is an enemy country.... If his education does not forestall this fallacy, the soul of such a child may develop so that in later years he will act always *as if* the world really were an enemy country. (Adler, 1927, p. 35)

The above quote has major implications for Adler's view of human nature. Here Adler asserts that despite the fact that environmental influences can lead toward the development of a neurotic character, the child is not determined by it. In fact, Adler asserted that we are not determined by our environment, or our instincts, or our early child-rearing—we can change. The child, if afforded a corrective education, can change. And, if the child can change, so too can the adult!

Adler believed that every child is born with innate and unique capabilities and is inherently moving toward the future, not determined by the past. Using the word **teleology**, from the Greek "teleos," meaning "goal-directed process," Adler suggested that we move toward the future to makes ourselves whole and complete and to fulfill our one true drive, our **striving for perfection**. If un-impeded, this path would bring out our uniqueness and natural creativity, lead us toward connection and cooperation with others, and promote meaningfulness in life (Sweeney, 1998). Adler stated that all other drives, including our sexual or aggressive instincts, are subsumed by this drive. However, he also warned that if one's natural striving for completeness, wholeness, and perfection was diverted, the individual would develop neurotic or even psychotic behaviors.

Part of being human, said Adler, was dealing with inevitable feelings of inferiority. In attempting to overcome those feelings, Adler believed that we all develop unconscious beliefs, or **private logic**. This private logic leads to what Adler originally called a **fictional final goal**, but which was later referred to as a **subjective final goal** or **guiding self-ideal** to emphasize the subjective nature of this phenomenon (Watts & Holden, 1994). Adler stated that the child's experiences by age 5 years, and the subsequent memories of those experiences, were critical factors in the development of one's private logic and subjective final goal. He also asserted that the picture in one's mind of what the individual would like to be, which was shaped by the subjective final goal, can drive a person throughout his or her life. Thus, Adler said, all behavior is goal-directed and purposeful and is related to the drive to attain the image held in our subjective final goal.

Adler suggested that our drive toward our subjective final goal often results in the development of behaviors that compensate for our feelings of inferiority (a "100-pound weakling" becomes an obsessed bodybuilder). Ultimately, we believe that our subjective final goal will bring us a sense of mastery, superiority, and—eventually—perfection, completion, and wholeness. For instance, Adler's feelings of inferiority over his ailments as a young child led him to develop a subjec-tive final goal of conquering death, and thus, he was driven to become a doctor in this unconscious quest (Hoffman, 1994). Michael Phelps developed his own private logic about what it meant to be bullied and compensated for these feelings of in-feriority by putting his all into his natural ability at swimming. We can only imagine what his subjective final goal was considering his performance at the Olympics.

Whereas some private logic and subjective final goal leads toward behaviors that enhance a person's natural abilities and characteristics, other private logic and subjective final goal leads toward maladaptive, neurotic, or even psychotic behaviors. Children free of mistreatment by others and children who have learned through healthy parenting how to effectively manage feelings of inferiority create a private logic in line with their natural abilities and characteristics and form a subjective final goal that eventually includes cooperation with others and social consciousness (Adler, 1932/1964b; 1933/1964c). Imagine the situations faced and parenting received by children who becomes bullies or class clowns, and compare that to the situations and parenting likely encountered by children who strive to be cooperative members of the classroom. Finally, Adler suggested that the individual develops a **style of life** that is reflective of the person's movement toward his or her subjective final goal. Whether our subjective final goal results in a lifestyle that is reflected by healthy or maladaptive behaviors, it is deeply rooted in the past, affects our present, and leads us toward our future (see Figure 4.1).

Considered by some to be a psychodynamic theorist, Adler hypothesized that an individual's drive toward completion, wholeness, and perfection could best be understood through in-depth counseling. In such work, the therapist helps the client understand how early experiences, and the memories of those experiences, have led to private logic that affects the development of one's subjective final goal and is reflected in one's style of life. However, there are also clear existential and humanistic leanings in Adler's approach (Ansbacher, 1964; Ellenberger, 1970; Maslow, 1968; Stein, 2007). For instance, Adler stressed the importance

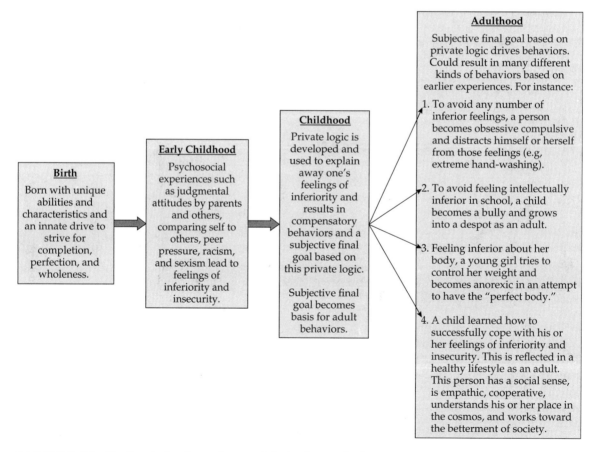

F I G U R E 4.1 The Developing Person from an Adlerian Perspective*

*At any point, through therapy and education, a person can come to understand his or her own private logic and compensatory behaviors and develop a subjective final goal in line with his or her innate characteristics and abilities.

of *Gemeinschaftsgefühl*, which loosely translated means "**social interest**." If unimpeded by feelings of inferiority, Adler believed that one would naturally move toward meaningful relationships, the best interest of others, the betterment of society, and an understanding of our place in the universe (Ansbacher & Ansbacher, 1956). Much like Maslow's self-actualized person, he believed in the individual's capability of becoming empathic, cooperative, social, and appreciative of the beauty of the world. Called one of the **first humanists** by some (Ansbacher, 1964), Adler believed that people can change, and his theory is seen as an optimistic and **anti-deterministic** approach that impacted the development of subsequent humanistic theories of counseling.

In recent years, Adler has been referred to as a **constructivist** (Carlson et al., 2006; Mahoney, 2003; Watts, 1999; Watts, 2003a). These individuals point to the fact that Adler was focused on the future (e.g., teleology), stressed the importance of social factors in the development of one's understanding of the world, and saw the individual as a person in process who is holistically "constructing" a new meaning-making system as he or she moves through life. Finally, Adlerian therapy has been described as an approach that should be tailored to the client and therefore may be long-term or brief. Indeed, Adlerian counseling is often used as a brief treatment modality in schools as well as in clinical and agency settings (Carlson et al., 2006; Dinkmeyer & Sperry, 2000). Many of Adler's ideas concerning his view of human nature are summarized by Ansbacher and Ansbacher's (1956) 12 propositions, which can be found in Box 4.2.

KEY CONCEPTS

Uniqueness of the Individual

From the perspective of individual psychology, each person is seen as unique, with innate abilities and personal characteristics that interact with and are affected by early childhood experiences and the memories of those experiences (Adler, 1935/1964d). When interacting with others, feelings of inferiority are inevitable, and some will respond to these feelings by developing private logic and compensatory behaviors that lead to maladaptive, neurotic, and dysfunctional ways of living, while others will develop private logic and compensatory behaviors that support their unique abilities and characteristics. As you might imagine, those who develop behaviors that support their abilities and characteristics—as compared to those who develop maladaptive, neurotic, and dysfunctional behaviors—are more likely to be empathic and are more likely to develop and work toward a sense of harmony with self, community with others, and unity with all of humankind.

Feelings of Inferiority

Every neurosis can be understood as an attempt to free oneself from a feeling of inferiority in order to gain a feeling of superiority. (Adler, 1925/1963a, p. 23)

B o x   4.2   Twelve Propositions of Adlerian Therapy[*]

1. **(Striving for perfection)** There is one basic dynamic force behind all human activity, a striving from a felt "minus" situation toward a "plus" situation, from a feeling of inferiority toward superiority, perfection, totality.

2. **(Uniqueness of the individual; Subjective final goal)** The striving receives its specific direction from an individually unique goal or self-ideal, which though influenced by biological and environmental factors is ultimately the creation of the individual. Because it is an ideal, the goal is a fiction.

3. **(Unconscious)** The goal is only "dimly envisaged" by the individual, which means that it is largely unknown and little understood to him/her. This is Adler's definition of the *unconscious*: the unknown part of the goal.

4. **(Teleology; Subjective final goal)** The goal becomes the final cause, the ultimate independent variable. To the extent that the goal provides the key for the understanding the individual, it is a working hypothesis on the part of the psychologist.

5. **(Style of life)** All psychological processes form a self-consistent organization from the point of view of the goal, like a drama that is constructed from the beginning with the finale in view. This self-consistent personality structure is what Adler calls the *style of life*. It becomes firmly established at an early age, from which time on behavior that is apparently contradictory is only the adaptation of different means to the same end.

6. **(Holism)** All apparent psychological categories, such as different drives or the contrast between conscious and unconscious, are only aspects of a *unified relational system* and do not represent discrete entities and quantities.

7. **(Subjective final goal)** All objectives determiners, such as biological factors and past history, become relative to the goal idea; they do not

function as direct causes but provide probabilities only. The individual uses all objective factors in accordance with his/her style of life.

8. **(Schema of apperceptions)** The individual's opinion of himself/herself and the world, his/her "apperceptive schema," his/her interpretations, all as aspects of the style of life, influence every psychological process.

9. **(Social interest)** The individual cannot be considered apart from his social situation. "Individual psychology regards and examines the individual as socially embedded. We refuse to recognize and examine an isolated human being."

10. **(Social interest)** All important life problems, including certain drive satisfactions become social problems. All values become social values.

11. **(Social interest)** The socialization of the individual is not achieved at the cost of repression, but is afforded through an innate human ability, which, however, needs to be developed. It is this ability that Adler calls *social feeling* or *social interest*. Because the individual is embedded in a social situation, social interest becomes crucial for his/her adjustment.

12. **(Private logic)** Maladjustment is characterized by increased inferiority feelings, underdeveloped social interest, and an exaggerated uncooperative goal of personal superiority. Accordingly, problems are solved in a self-centered "private sense" [private logic] rather than a task-centered "common sense" fashion.

(Adapted from Ansbacher & Ansbacher, 1956, pp. 2–3)

---

[*] Words bolded in parentheses are not in the original and are this author's attempt at associating the proposition with a key concept which has been or will be discussed in this chapter.

Key to Adlerian therapy is the belief that each of us will inevitably experience feelings of inferiority. **Primary feelings of inferiority** are universal, such as when the infant and young child struggle to overcome natural physical, cognitive, and psychological hurdles of life (e.g., the 10-month-old's attempt to walk, the toddler's attempt to comprehend basic knowledge) (Stein, 1999). Such feelings, suggested Adler, can be positive and motivating, leading the person to strive to overcome adversity. To some degree, we are all driven to overcome these basic and natural feelings of inferiority, and ultimately, we learn how to cooperate with others for the betterment of ourselves and society in an effort to reach our unique subjective final goal and state of perfection. Thus, primary feelings of inferiority can lead to growth, wholeness, and cooperation. However, feelings of inferiority can be also be debilitating. Called **secondary feelings of inferiority** (Stein, 1999), these feelings occur as a result of psychological struggles from poor parenting, child abuse and neglect, and cultural injustice (embedded racism in society). Such feelings can result in a person who retreats into self in an effort to avoid a sense of inferiority (e.g., becomes depressed and withdrawn), a person who tries to avoid feelings of inferiority by **striving for superiority** over others, or other maladaptive behaviors. Secondary feelings of inferiority lead to the development of private logic and compensatory behaviors, as a well as a subjective final goal that leads an individual on a path toward maladaptive behaviors, a neurotic existence, and narcissistic desires. By its very nature, secondary feelings of inferiority will cause discomfort and strife among people (see Figure 4.1). However, it should always be remembered that even these individuals are doing the best that they can to manage difficult experiences that resulted in feelings of inferiority, and they have the misguided belief (private logic) that attainment of their subjective final goal will make them whole and complete. An individual's level of neurosis is based on the degree to which secondary feelings of inferiority have impacted the development of one's private logic, subjective final goal, and associated maladaptive compensatory behaviors.

Private Logic versus Common Sense

> … [N]o matter how wacky the child's actions may seem to an adult, they are logical to the child if it is recognized that his own picture of the world around him governs his reactions. So the trick is to find out how he sees the world, how this makes him do what he does, and help him to feel secure. (Armour, 1953, p. 63)

As the above quote implies, **private logic** is one's inner voice, self-talk, or internal images that justifies one's style of life and fuels one's subjective final goal. Private logic can result in compensatory behaviors that divert the individual from feelings of inferiority. Each person's private logic makes sense to him or her. However, when others view another person's compensatory behaviors, they may not understand the private logic that drives those behaviors. This is when the other person is seen as "different," "crazy," or "mentally ill," and often given any of a host of diagnostic labels. If one were to truly listen to the inner world of the "different," "unusual," "crazy," or "mentally ill" person, one would find that it is logical—it makes sense within that person's inner world. Understand a person's private logic, and you will understand his or her subjective final goal, because that person's private logic is responsible for its development.

Whereas private logic will sometimes work at keeping us illogical and insane, **common sense** suggests that we must put effort into developing attitudes, beliefs, and behaviors that benefit the common good. Common sense tells us that despite the fact that we all have our own private logic, to live together peaceably and constructively, we must find the common ground that allows us to get along with one another. Common sense reminds us that relationships take work because we each have our own unique private logic and subjective final goals. And common sense reminds us that we need to take responsibility for our actions and not blame others if we are to live in a world that is reasonable. Finally, common sense tells us we must work with others and within our communities to build a better life for all.

Compensation

> If a person is a show-off it is only because he feels inferior, because he does not feel strong enough to compete with others on the useful side of life. (Adler, 1929, p. 83)

In varying degrees, individuals attempt to rid themselves of feelings of inferiority through a process called **compensation**. Individuals can overcome their feelings of inferiority in healthy and socially promoting ways (Michael Phelps, the Olympic swimmer) or by developing a set of behaviors that will eventually cause them harm and does little to promote the good of society. Healthy compensation is a response to primary feelings of inferiority, is in line with the individual's natural abilities and talents, and does not divert the individual from the development of social interest. Individuals such as these are able to show empathy, be cooperative, and work toward the betterment of society. Unhealthy compensation (e.g., undereating, overworking, overspeaking, drinking too much) is based on secondary feelings of inferiority and leads toward the development of maladaptive, neurotic, and narcissistic behaviors, which negatively impacts the self, others, and the world.

Consider how two peace activists with the same goal—"peace on earth"—might approach this goal in different ways depending on whether the individual is compensating for primary as compared to secondary feelings of inferiority. The first peace activist has all people's interest in mind, is empathic, and can hear different points of view. This person tries to form cooperative and collaborative relationships that lead to common goals. The second peace activist is not concerned about other people's feelings and will develop behaviors, such as being argumentative, spiteful, and malicious, that will turn people off to his or her cause, and may even harm people.

Subjective Final Goal

> You can transverse the country in a Volkswagen bus looking for "the answer," but you still have to bring yourself with you.

The above quote from my college philosophy teacher describes the essence of one's subjective final goal. Developed out of one's private logic and compensatory behaviors, an individual's subjective final goal is the person's unique image of what he or she wants to be, and the person imagines that attainment of this image will lead to a sense of completion and wholeness. Adler believed that we spend our lives moving consciously and unconsciously toward attainment of our subjective final goal in order to complete ourselves. To understand one's subjective final goal, one of the first questions Adlerian therapists often ask is, "Toward where is this person moving?" Like the person driving the VW bus, "the answer" is not found by looking at where the VW bus stops, but where it is going, because where it is going is based on the driver's image of where he or she wants to be—the individual's subjective final goal.

Private logic that has been markedly affected by secondary feelings of inferiority results in a subjective final goal that diverts the person away from the path in life he or she would have taken if such feelings had not existed. These individuals develop maladaptive, neurotic, and narcissistic behaviors that do not help themselves, the common good, the larger community, or society (Ansbacher & Ansbacher, 1956). Like the woman seeking thinness, the greedy man seeking money at anyone's expense, or the despot seeking power, they have lost their way, but they're still in the driver's seat thinking they are on the right path.

To uncover a subjective final goal, the Adlerian therapist must get to know the inner world of the client. By listening to the client's private logic, by examining compensatory behaviors, and by exploring early experiences, the therapist can understand the underlying insecurities and feelings of inferiority that led to the individual's subjective final goal.

> The child imagines some time in the future when they will grow up, when they will be strong, when they will overcome insecurity or any-thing else that bothers them. So if they feel that they are ugly, they will be beautiful. If they feel that they're stupid, they will be brilliant. If they feel that they're weak, they'll be strong. If they're at the bottom, they'll be at the top. (Stein as cited in Bridle & Edelstein, 2000, p. 128)

Style of Life

> The style of life of a tree is the individuality of a tree expressing itself and moulding itself in an environment. (Adler, 1929, p. 98)

As we strive to attain completion, wholeness, and perfection, we develop a unique repertoire of behaviors, cognitions, and values that Adler called our **style of life**. Each person's style of life is unique and is reflective of how that person responded to early feelings of inferiority, the individual's private logic, the compensatory behaviors that were developed, and the individual's movement toward his or her subjective final goal. Our style of life is represented in all of our waking actions and is also reflected in our dreams. It can be seen in all of what we do, and it gives us hints about where we want to be (see Box 4.3).

B o x 4.3   Dr. Gilchrist Examines "Shannon's" Style of Life

Read or watch Dr. Gilchrist's work with Shannon and consider how Shannon's style of life supports her subjective final goal of being perfectly successful academically and in many aspects of her life.

You can read this session by going to www. cengage.com/counseling/neukrug/CTP1e and click "student downloads." Or your instructor may show this session in class with the DVD that accompanies his or her copy of the text.

Striving for Perfection

Adler originally posited that we are born with an inherent aggressive drive, but later modified this as a **striving for superiority**, and lastly as a **striving for perfection** (Adler, 1933/1964e). Despite its name change, the emphasis pretty much stayed the same: Adler believed that there was one innate motivating force that is positive, pushes us toward reaching our subjective final goal, and lends direction toward our future as we strive for fulfillment, wholeness, and completion. Individuals who are not marred by secondary feelings of inferiority will develop private logic and subjective final goals based on their innate abilities and characteristics, and will exhibit qualities similar to individuals in Maslow's higher stages (e.g., the self-actualized person). For instance, this person is altruistic, empathic, loving, and has concern for family, community, and society foremost in mind (see Figure 4.1). For many people, God represents a metaphor for the ideal self for which we strive but never actually become (Bottome, 1957). In contrast, individuals who are affected by secondary feelings of inferiority will develop misguided private logic and associated dysfunctional behaviors that result in subjective final goals that cause personal or psychological harm to self and to others (e.g., becoming anorexic, becoming a greedy, power–hungry politician) (see Figure 4.1). Although still striving for perfection, these individuals have the misguided belief that if they obtain their subjective final goals, they will be fulfilled, whole, and complete. Unfortunately, their paths in life have been diverted by their responses to secondary feelings of inferiority.

Social Interest

We need the conscious preparation and advancement of a mighty social interest and the complete demolition of greed and power in the individual and in peoples. What we all lack and for which we struggle relentlessly are new methods to raise the social sense... (Adler, 1928/ 1966, p. 171)

Derived from the German word **Gemeinschaftsgefühl**, Adler believed that **social interest**, sometimes called **community feeling** or **social concern**, is an innate/evolutionary desire to relate to one another and to build a sense of belonging and community with others. In its ideal form, it means a uniting of all humankind for eternity (Adler, 1933/1964e). However, Adler also believed that there is a learned component to social interest and that the compensatory process that emerges from feelings of inferiority could prevent a person from developing his or her social interest fully. Thus, children who feel badly about themselves due to strong feelings of inferiority develop poor empathy skills and do not fully develop their social interest. These children become adults who compensate for their feelings of inferiority and develop subjective final goals that are not in the interest of the common good. Contrast this with children who have not been burdened heavily by such feelings. These children become adults who build love and work relationships marked by empathy, caring, acceptance, and concern for the common good as they strive to reach their goals in life (Watts, 2007). Not unlike individuals who are self-actualized, such individuals have a sense of meaning in life, treasure the interconnectedness of relationships, work toward the betterment of society, are naturally esteemed by others, and feel valued and worthwhile. As you might imagine, one of the goals of therapy is to help the client regain his or her natural social interest by helping him or her see how it has been thwarted by feelings of inferiority, misguided private logic, and compensatory behaviors.

Holism

In contrast to some other forms of psychodynamic therapy that see the individual composed of internal structures or forces that may at times be in conflict with one another (e.g., id, ego, superego), the Adlerian views the individual as a holistic entity that is attempting to move toward the completion of self and perfection. Even when such movement leads toward problematic behavior, Adler believed it is the individual's misguided attempt to strive for completion and perfection (Adler, 1929). Adler even viewed the conscious and the unconscious as working together toward a single goal, although the goal was sometimes not a healthy one. In fact, the name "individual psychology" is actually a poor translation from Adler's actual title, "*Individuum*," which in Latin means "holistic." (Watts, personal communication, May 1, 2009).

Schema of Apperception

Produced by our imaginations, our **schemas of apperception** are the cognitive rules (our schema) we have developed in our assimilation of our experiences (our apperception). In other words, it is how we come to understand and make sense of the experiences in our lives. Developed within the first five years of life, the schemas are often based on distortions of memory and are developed to direct us away from our feelings of inferiority. For instance, rigid, dualistic, black-and-white thinking is often the result of a schema that needs to view parts of the world as good and other parts as evil. Such thinking is antithetical to the building of peaceful, loving relationships. Ultimately, our schemas impact the development of our private logic and are reflected in our style of life. When an individual is not capable of building healthy relationships and concomitantly has a subjective final goal that results in a dysfunctional style of life, he or she is sometimes said to have an **antithetical schema of apperception**.

Birth Order

Realizing that birth order can greatly affect how one feels about oneself, Adler became one of the first theorists to focus on its importance. For instance, with first-born children, parents are generally anxious about being good parents, are very concerned with how the child is growing and learning, are extremely focused on the needs of the child, and place more demands on this child as compared to later-born children. Is it surprising that this child is often a high achiever and perfectionist? In a similar vein, second-born children often experience not being the "first love" and are often attempting to catch up or dethrone the first-born. And, as you might expect, the middle child often feels "squeezed" and ends up being the "mediator" or "negotiator" of the family. Based on knowledge like this, Adler and others began to identify typical behaviors of children that were a function of their birth order (see Figure 4.2). However, Adler was also quick to note that psychological order was probably a more significant factor than biological order. Thus, other factors could also play an important role in how a person ultimately perceives himself or herself. In addition, Adler also said that birth order was not only about physical or psychological order, but also about psychological disorder. Clearly, the effects of birth order on feelings of inferiority have great implications for Adlerian therapy. For instance, the first-born who is being pressured to achieve in school and is not doing well may develop compensatory behaviors (e.g., become the class clown) in an effort to manage those feelings. Leman (1998) suggests a number of characteristics that one might hold based on birth order but also acknowledged Adler's notion of psychological order by identifying nine factors that can mediate the development of the child (see Figure 4.2). For instance, under some circumstances, a second-born might have the experience of being a first-born (e.g., a long-awaited male child is born and is given the attention the first-born usually receives).

Courage

Most clients who initially come in for counseling find ways to avoid responsibility and tend to blame others for their problems. Their private logic has resulted in a subjective final goal that is reflected in a style of life that is harmful to themselves and others. Courage, for these individuals, means being willing to take a look at how early feelings of inferiority fueled their private logic, led to compensatory behaviors, and were partially responsible for the development of their subjective final goals. These individuals must develop the courage to face life's difficulties and take responsibility for change. In later stages of therapy, individuals show courage when they decide to actively work toward cooperation in their love and work relationships and when they demonstrate social interest.

THERAPEUTIC TECHNIQUES

The following section is broken down into those techniques that are generally applied with adults and those techniques generally applied with children.

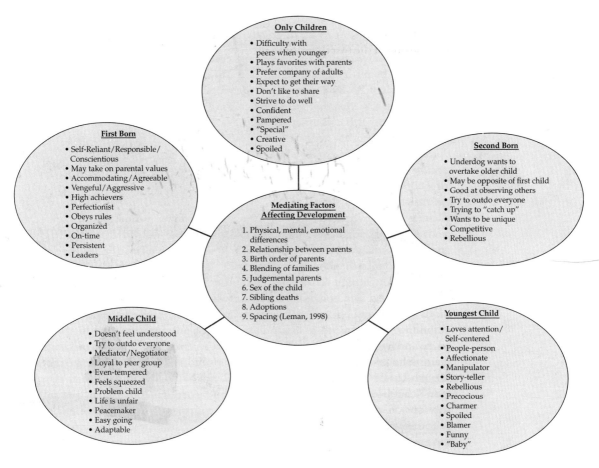

Only Children

- Difficulty with peers when younger
- Plays favorites with parents
- Prefer company of adults
- Expect to get their way
- Don't like to share
- Strive to do well
- Confident
- Pampered
- "Special"
- Creative
- Spoiled

First Born

- Self-Reliant/Responsible/Conscientious
- May take on parental values
- Accommodating/Agreeable
- Vengeful/Aggressive
- High achievers
- Perfectionist
- Obeys rules
- Organized
- On-time
- Persistent
- Leaders

Second Born

- Underdog wants to overtake older child
- May be opposite of first child
- Good at observing others
- Try to outdo everyone
- Trying to "catch up"
- Wants to be unique
- Competitive
- Rebellious

Mediating Factors Affecting Development

1. Physical, mental, emotional differences
2. Relationship between parents
3. Birth order of parents
4. Blending of families
5. Judgemental parents
6. Sex of the child
7. Sibling deaths
8. Adoptions
9. Spacing (Leman, 1998)

Middle Child

- Doesn't feel understood
- Try to outdo everyone
- Mediator/Negotiator
- Loyal to peer group
- Even-tempered
- Feels squeezed
- Problem child
- Life is unfair
- Peacemaker
- Easy going
- Adaptable

Youngest Child

- Loves attention/Self-centered
- People-person
- Affectionate
- Manipulator
- Story-teller
- Rebellious
- Precocious
- Charmer
- Spoiled
- Blamer
- Funny
- "Baby"

FIGURE 4.2 Effects of Birth Order Position

However, keep in mind that many of the techniques with adults can be used with children, especially older children, and most of the techniques with children can be applied to adults.

Techniques with Adults

Individual psychology relies on a number of techniques that encourage the client to become more aware of how early feelings of inferiority have been compensated for, as reflected in the subjective final goal and style of life, and how this lifestyle diverts the client's natural movement toward completion and holism. These techniques are used through four phases of therapy that will be examined in some detail in the next section of the chapter, "Therapeutic Process."

Building a Trusting Relationship.   Adler talked about the importance of building a trusting and egalitarian relationship with the client so the client could feel free to examine feelings of inferiority, private logic, compensatory behaviors, and a resulting dysfunctional style of life. This can often be accomplished by using basic attending skills, including the important skill of empathy. In addition, counselors will build the relationship by being respectful, being egalitarian, focusing on strengths, being optimistic, being nonjudgmental, and showing unconditional positive regard (Carlson et al., 2006; Dinkmeyer & Sperry, 2000).

Encouragement

> According to psychiatrist Rudolf Dreikurs, humans need encouragement much as plants need water. He believed that every person with whom one comes in contact feels better or worse based on how others behave toward him or her. (Dinkmeyer & Eckstein, 1996, p. 17)

Encouragement is one of the more important skills the Adlerian counselor uses and is important throughout the therapeutic relationship. From an Adlerian perspective, encouragement has to do with "helping clients become aware of their own worth" (Dinkmeyer & Sperry, 2000, p. 105). To facilitate a client's sense of self-worth, Watts and Pietrzak (2000) suggest a broad range of encouragement skills that include "demonstrating concern for clients through active listening and empathy; communicating respect for, and confidence in, clients; focusing on clients' strengths, assets, and resources; helping clients generate perceptual alternatives for discouraging fictional beliefs; focusing on efforts and progress; and helping clients see the humor in life experiences" (pp. 442–443).

Near the beginning of the relationship, encouragement takes the form of showing clients you value them by providing empathy, by being nonjudgmental, and through acceptance. As clients begin to examine their lifestyles, they are encouraged by the counselor's support of their willingness to take an in-depth look at themselves. Clients are also encouraged later in the relationship when counselors recognize the clients' courageousness as clients begin to make needed vital changes in their lives. For some clients, late in therapy, encouragement takes the form of the counselor's supporting their courageous efforts at working toward the common good and being cooperative with others in their love and work relationships.

Assessment.   Critical to understanding the client is conducting a thorough assessment of memories of early experiences, family relationships, work and love relationships, dreams and daydreams, and how the client has responded to important events and problems in his or her life. Conducted near the early phase of treatment, such an assessment helps the therapist understand how early feelings and experiences have led the client toward his or her current style of life and can provide clues concerning the client's subjective final goal. Assessments are often rather involved and could include checklists, open-ended questions, and responses to specific structured questions (see Eckstein & Kern, 2002, for a sample of different assessment instruments). Areas that are generally focused upon in an assessment may include the following:

- Description of symptoms and presenting problems.
- Early memories and recollections.
- How the client believes he or she would act differently if symptoms and problems did not exist.
- The family constellation of the family of origin.
- Information about the family dynamics of the family of origin.
- Significant events in the client's life and the client's response to them.
- Current love relationships and how they might look if they were better.
- Current work relationships and how they might look if they were better.
- Current friendships and how they might look if they were better.
- Times when the client believes he or she has been treated poorly.
- Times when the client believes he or she has been discriminated against (or experienced discrimination).
- Health issues and how the client responds to them.
- Use or abuse of substances.
- Addictions other than drug and alcohol.
- Physical well-being, or lack thereof.
- Emotional well-being, or lack thereof.
- Memorable dreams.
- Daydreams and fantasies.

Examining Early Recollections

> In the style of life formed at the age of four or five we find the connection between remembrances of the past and actions of the present. And so after many observations of this kind we can hold fast to the theory that in these old remembrances we can always find a real part of the patient's prototype. (Adler, 1929, p. 118)

Early recollections can be viewed as a projective test and can be seen as one of a number of ways to understand a client's style of life (Adler, 1931/1958; Clark, 2002). Such recollections may or may not be based on actual events, as clients may distort events, and they reflect the client's perceptions of past events and affect how the client currently perceives the world. Memories of early experiences also provide a window to a client's early feelings of inferiority and help a therapist understand why a protective compensatory process may have been developed. Therefore, helpers can glean much about a client by eliciting early memories.

Responses to simple questions can elicit information about earliest memories and can help counselors comprehend how clients understand the world. Asking clients to talk about early memories is also a way to build the relationship, as many clients find a sense of ease and comfort talking about such material and feel a sense of closeness with the interviewer (Clark, 2002). Later in therapy, questions regarding early recollections can be used to prod the client toward changing his or her private logic—private logic that has tended to maintain a dysfunctional style of life. The following offers a few examples of the types of questions that might be used:

- Can you tell me the first memory (or memories) that you have?
- What do you think that memory tells you about yourself?
- What message about your life does that memory provide?
- Has that memory been a metaphor or reflective in some manner of how you have lived your life?
- How has that memory mimicked some feelings and behaviors you have had later in life?
- If you could change the memory, what would it look like?
- If the changed memory would, in some way, affect the rest of your life, how would your life now look?

Exploring the Family Constellation.   Like early memories, one's placement in the family offers a glimpse into the development of the individual. Often, placement is indicative of certain personality styles, as noted earlier in Figure 4.2. However, mediating factors can greatly affect one's childhood experiences and can change what might be expected if one were only to examine biological birth order. Thus, the Adlerian therapist will often spend time collecting information about the family constellation as well as possible mediating events that would have affected the experience of the client when he or she was a child (see Box 4.4). In fact, many Adlerians will bring families into the sessions to explore their interactions and to better understand how placement in the family affected the client's style of life (Starr, 1973; Sweeney, 1998).

Dream Analysis

A dream is always a part of the style of life and we always find the prototype involved in it. (Adler, 1929, p. 155)

In contrast to Freud's interpretation of dreams as having sexual and aggressive underpinnings, the Adlerian perspective has to do with how the dream is representing the individual's style of life. Thus, dreams are generally seen as representative or metaphoric of a client's current lifestyle, and may sometimes bring up possibilities for the development of a more fulfilling style of life that includes greater social interest. This is why Adler stated that dreams were forward-looking and had problem-solving functions (Adler, 1929; Ansbacher & Ansbacher, 1956). As with psychoanalysis,

---

B o x 4.4   The Effects of Birth Order and Idiosyncratic Issues

I was the middle child, the second born in a family of two parents, a sister five years older, and a brother five years younger. Based on this information alone, you might expect me to have a mixture of some second born and middle child characteristics (see Figure 4.2). And indeed, I do have some of those qualities. However, my mother had been pregnant with another child that she sometimes said was "spontaneously aborted" and other times stated was a "stillbirth." Since this child came between my sister and myself, in some ways I can be considered a third-born. Also, I was overweight and sick with a heart disorder as a child.

These factors also left me with memories of being pampered and special—often being taken care of by my parents and being told to "take it easy." These early memories affected how I viewed myself and, ultimately, how I've interacted in the world. The feeling of being special and being taken care of (being pampered) has deeply affected my relationships and at times have left me with narcissistic tendencies which do not always do me well in intimate relationships. These tendencies I've had to fight in order to have some balance and realism in my love relationships.

Adler believed that dreams had manifest (obvious; on the surface) and latent (hidden) meanings, and that it was important to point out, or interpret to the client, how a dream could be a vehicle to help the client take a new and more courageous and meaningful path in life.

Socratic Questioning and Use of the Dialectical Method.   A centerpiece of Adlerian therapy is to build an equal relationship in which there is a give-and-take between the client and therapist (a "dialectic"). The ultimate aim of this dialogue is to encourage the client to seek the underlying reasons why the particular style of life has been developed. This back-and-forth dialogue is used to suggest to the client that he or she may have developed a style of life due to earlier feelings of inferiority. In this process, questions and gentle prodding are used by the therapist in an effort to dislodge the self-indulgent, narcissistic, and noncooperative tendencies that many clients have developed as a reaction to their early feelings of inferiority. In essence, clients are shown that their current style of life is not working for them and given reasons why this is the case. Questions such as, "Is this working for you?" or "Do you think *that* is the most effective way of acting?" or "What might be some other ways you could have responded?" can all be used to gently challenge the client to examine his or style of life. As the client accepts the possibility that his or her current style of life is not effective, he or she is gently prodded toward developing a new style of life unencumbered by maladaptive private logic and compensatory behaviors and one that includes empathy, cooperation, and social interest.

Teaching and Interpretation.   Throughout therapy, the client is taught how feelings of inferiority may have affected personality development, specifically, the development of private logic, the subjective final goal, and one's style of life. Although key Adlerian terms may or may not be voiced by the therapist, the basic ideas are presented to the client. For instance, the client is encouraged to examine how early recollections and placement in the family have affected current ways of living. When the therapist sees such parallels and the client does not, the therapist may interpret current behavior in light of past recollections and feelings of inferiority that have been voiced by the client.

Spitting in the Client's Soup. In their own inimitable ways, clients have crafted styles of life that seem correct, but are preventing them from reaching higher goals, ones that embrace empathic, loving, and cooperative relationships. In fact, clients are sometimes so stuck in their current ways of acting that they become blocked from seeing the essence of their styles of life. In these cases, therapists can use a variety of responses that attempt to "spit in the client's soup" or show them that their current ways of functioning are not healthy. For instance, satire can be used, such as in the following therapist–client dialogue:

CLIENT: Well, you know, I really feel like I deserve more respect from my wife. I work hard, earn lots, and I feel like she doesn't even give me the time of day. All she does is take care of the house, and now that the kids are older, she doesn't even have that responsibility. She just lives off of my money. She needs to listen to me more and respect what I say.

COUNSELOR: Well, I guess you are the king of this house! She should just listen to your every wish. Why, you shouldn't even have to make any effort at having a dialogue with her—should you?

Guided Imagery Exercises. As clients become increasingly aware of their maladaptive styles of life, they can begin the change process by imagining new ways of being. Therapists can help clients do this by providing guided imagery sessions in which clients mentally imagine new ways of acting and being with loved ones, in work relationships, and in social situations. Such guided imagery is often the first step prior to trying out new behaviors.

Role-Playing and Acting "As If" (Fake It Till You Make It). Realizing they could have a more highly functioning style of life, clients can begin to toy with the idea of what that life might look like. With the therapist's help, clients can first reflect on, and later role-play, new desired behaviors (cf. Watts, 2003b). When comfortable, the client can begin to act as if he or she *is* that new person. The therapist can encourage these new behaviors and can act as a "coach" as the client attempts to practice new, healthier ways of living. Groups, where trust has been built, can often be the first place a client can practice out a new behavior and receive feedback as to its effectiveness.

Catching Oneself. As clients become increasingly aware of the maladaptive behaviors they exhibit that are driven by their subjective final goals, counselors can suggest that they try to "catch" these behaviors prior to their happening (Dinkmeyer & Sperry, 2000). Catching a behavior often starts with listening to one's inner voice and being mindful that the behavior is about to occur. This takes thoughtful practice, and at first, clients will have difficulty catching their

---

B o x 4.5   Children Can "Catch Themselves" Too

Catching oneself is not just a technique for adults. A funny but poignant example is from my daughters. My wife noticed that my 9-year-old, when having a disagreement with her 14-year-old sister, would say things to her like, "You are *always* mean to me" and sometimes follow up with an attempt to hit her. My wife suggested to my 9-year-old that she "catch" the word "always" and change it to "sometimes," and, of course, not hit her sister. This was a more realistic response, as most of the time the girls actually got along. It would also help to create a more ongoing caring relationship as the two would be less likely to dig into their different "camps" that suggested each were "evil." I watched my younger daughter practice this change. At first, she would blurt out: "You *always—sometimes*—are really nasty to me." Over time, however, she was able to move to a more consistent statement of: "You sometimes are really nasty to me," and this would not be followed up by an attempt to hit her. This was a small but significant change.

---

thoughts and subsequent behaviors. However, with practice, clients will be successful (see Box 4.5).

Task-Setting.   Tasks are used to help the client develop a new style of life more compatible with the individual's unique personality style than their current maladaptive one. (Dinkmeyer & Sperry, 2000). After gaining insight about their styles of life and deciding to make changes, new ways of being can be identified, and clients can develop specific steps they can take in the change process. Tasks should be client-initiated, although they can be counselor-enhanced. In addition, they should be time-limited so clients do not feel they will have to struggle with the task for life. Finally, they should be attainable, measurable, and realistic so that each session, the client and counselor can discuss the progress made toward the goal.

Techniques with Children

More than most other therapies, basic Adlerian principles have been adopted for children. This has been a natural progression for a number of reasons:

- Adler believed that feelings of inferiority experienced in childhood are the main causes for maladaptive behavior. Prevent early feelings of inferiority, and you prevent maladaptive behaviors.

- There is no clear separation between the unconscious and conscious; thus, one can work directly with children's current knowledge base and not have to "break through" to some mysterious unconscious.

- Adlerian therapy is optimistic and anti-deterministic, and change can occur (or start) at any point in a person's life.

- Adler stressed the importance that external changes and interventions can make in inducing change. Thus, effective parenting and teaching can all impact a child's mental health.

- Adlerian principles can be easily understood, thus making them easy to use by laypersons and by children.

The following offers a brief overview of a few of the major techniques that have been suggested for use with children.

Building a Trusting Relationship. As with adults, building a trusting relationship with the child is crucial if you are going to garner accurate information from the child and be able to execute effective interventions. Counselors should be good relationship-builders by using attending and empathy skills, being nonjudgmental, being optimistic, focusing on strengths, asking questions in a nonthreatening manner, and fostering open discussion. In addition, they should be willing to "get on the floor" with children and do play activities, use art, and conduct play and creative therapies. These skills demonstrate interest toward the child, are ways of eliciting information from the child, and can be mechanisms for offering feedback to the child.

Encouragement. Those in positions of authority over children, such as parents, teachers, and therapists, play vital roles in the development of a child's sense of well-being and feelings of being worthwhile. One way they can assist children in developing a positive sense of self is by exhibiting behaviors that encourage children. Encouragement by a significant person helps the child feel uplifted and fosters the child's willingness to change behaviors. Dinkmeyer and Dreikurs (1963) suggested four ways that encouragement is shown: (1) valuing and accepting the child, (2) using words that build a child's sense of self, (3) believing in the child, and (4) planning experiences that ensure success.

Democratically Held Discussion Groups. Children who exhibit maladaptive behaviors in the classroom or in the family have generally not been exposed to discussions based on democratic principles. Counselors, teachers, and parents can lead democratically held discussion groups by ensuring that all individuals are given an opportunity to talk, that all individuals are heard, and that basic principles like consensus-taking or voting are applied when making decisions. Providing an atmosphere of acceptance while offering the structure that allows children to make decisions in a fair-minded way can help them develop increased social sensitivity and dissolve some of their past ineffective ways of behaving.

Assessment. As noted earlier, Dinkmeyer and Dreikurs (1963) identified four types of dysfunctional behavior in children: attention-seeking, the use of power, revenge-seeking, and displaying inadequacy. It is important for the therapist to identify a child's general style of behaving in order to assess his or her developing style of life and to match appropriate interventions to types of behaviors exhibited. As you might imagine, a child who is bullying (power-hungry) needs different kinds of interventions than one who is withdrawing (displaying inadequacy). Assessment can be conducted by asking a child to draw his or her place in the family and by drawing significant events in the child's life; by talking with and asking questions of the child in an attempt to try to assess the child's primary mode of acting; by observing the child in the home, classroom, and other important places in the child's life; and by asking others, such as teachers and parents, about the ways they see the child behaving. Children and significant adults can also be queried about birth order and significant events in the child's life.

Art, Play, and Creative Therapies.   As noted earlier, art, play, and creative therapies can be used to develop a trusting, safe relationship with children. In addition, such therapies can be used to uncover the style of life that the child has adopted (Gondor, 1954/1959). Since art, play, and creative therapies minimize verbal responses, they are often more amenable to children, especially younger ones. As the child draws or responds to objects, whether they are paintings, clay, or dolls, he or she is exhibiting his or her style of life. The child who is insecure will reflect this in his or her drawings and in how he or she plays with objects. The aggressive child will similarly reflect this in the art or play object, and so forth.

Today, play therapy has become one of the most popular approaches to working with children. Play therapy can actually be traced back to the early 1900s, when some psychoanalysts dabbled in its use. In 1919, the psychoanalyst Melanie Klein began to develop a more formal process of conducting play therapy using psychoanalytic techniques (Landreth, 2002). Adlerian play therapy, however, did not come about until the last quarter of the twentieth century. Developed by Terry Kottman (1995), Adlerian play therapy integrates Adlerian concepts and techniques into the play therapy process:

> Everything the child does or says in the session communicates information about how the child views himself or herself, the world, and others. The child's play and the child's verbalizations in play are metaphors representing the child's life-style and life situation. In Adlerian play therapy, the counselor's job is to observe the child in the play room, understand how the child's life-style and life situation are present in the play, and begin to articulate that understanding to the child. (Kottman, 1995, p. 25)

Ultimately, the goal of Adlerian play therapy is to help the child learn new attitudes and behaviors that can replace former, self-defeating ones that were based on the child's dysfunctional style of life.

Responding to Identified Behaviors.   Once behaviors are identified, interventions can be applied. For instance, Albert (2003) suggests dozens of responses that could be applied for the four maladaptive behaviors noted earlier. As an example, some responses to a child who repeatedly makes himself or herself the center of attention could include ignoring the behavior; giving an "I-message" ("I'm disappointed that you don't want to help out more."); making a lesson out of the behavior; doing the unexpected, such as turning out the lights or talking to the wall; lowering your voice; distracting the child by asking a direct question or by changing the activity; and moving the child to a "thinking chair."

Limit-Setting.   As children exhibit behaviors nonconducive to healthy functioning, limit-setting will sometimes be used to change the child's behaviors.

While keeping in mind that the child is exhibiting these behaviors in an effort to continue his or her current style of life, limit-setting involves the development of a set of rules established by the therapist (e.g., no hitting during a session). The therapist should encourage the child not to break limits as he or she gently prods the child toward new, healthier behaviors. If the rules continue to be broken, despite encouragement on the part of the therapist, then **natural** or **logical consequences** should be employed.

Natural Consequences.   Perhaps best explained as "letting nature take its course," natural consequences involves letting the results of an ill-advised behavior happen. For instance, a child who loses track of time because he's talking to friends misses getting to his favorite gym class on time. The door has already been locked and he is not allowed in. A child who doesn't eat her dinner is not given dinner later that evening. Or, the child who insists on not taking an umbrella gets rained on.

Logical Consequences.   Similar to natural consequences, logical consequences involves the intervention by another person, usually one who is in a position of authority, who places a "logical" or "commonsense" consequence to a behavior. So, the child who talks excessively during class is asked by the teacher to leave so she won't distract others. Later, this child is asked by the teacher to make up the work during recess, when the student can't distract others. Or, the child who acts aggressively toward the counselor loses "play time" with the toys in the counselor's office.

Catching Oneself.   The same technique as described in the adult section, catching oneself has to do with children learning how to "catch" thoughts and behaviors that are incompatible with a healthy style of life. Children are often not given credit for their ability to have insight and catch behaviors. However, they often are able to understand more than is generally acknowledged. As with adults, children can be taught how to catch their thoughts and behaviors and begin to make change (see Box 4.5).

Task-Setting.   As with "catching oneself," task-setting is a technique that can be applied to adults or to children. With children, counselors may be more proactive in suggesting tasks be completed, although such tasks should resonate with the change in the child's style of life. As with adults, such tasks should be time-limited, attainable, measurable, and realistic so that clients and counselors can discuss progress made toward the task during each session.

Commitment and Practice.   When working with a child, it is important that the counselor show that he or she is committed to that child. Constantly modeling healthy behaviors and giving the child the message that the therapist believes the child can change and take on responsible and socially minded behaviors is critical to the change process (Adler, 1930/1963b). Change is not easy, and children will need someone in their corner cheering them on if change is going to occur and be long-lasting.

THERAPEUTIC PROCESS

For children and adults, the purpose of the therapeutic relationship is to help clients gain insight into how their current style of life is not working for them and for the clients to develop new behaviors that will lead to healthier relationships that are highlighted by empathy, a sense of belonging, and cooperation (Carlson et al., 2006). For children and adults, Adlerian therapy can be viewed through a series of four phases: building the therapeutic relationship; assessing and understanding the lifestyle; insight and interpretation; and reeducation and reorientation (Mosak & Maniacci, 1999; Oberst & Stewart, 2003; Sweeney, 1998). As clients move through the phases, they are encouraged to give up their misguided private logic, dysfunctional subjective final goals, deleterious compensatory behaviors, and dysfunctional styles of life, and to adopt new values and behaviors that reflect a healthier style of life that increasingly focuses on the importance of others and the broader community.

In contrast to many other psychodynamic approaches, the Adlerian therapist is more collegial and friendly, and the approach tends to be much briefer and is more action-oriented (Carlson et al., 2006). As you read through the phases, review Table 4.1, which lists the techniques that tend to be used during each phase. Also, keep in mind that the Adlerian therapist feels free to use some of these techniques at varying phases if it will facilitate client growth. Finally, there are dozens of other techniques that Adlerians use through the phases that are not described in this text, and the well-trained Adlerian readily applies a variety of these with clients.

Building the Relationship

As in most therapeutic relationships, this first phase of therapy involves the development of a trusting relationship. The Adlerian therapist does this by using the relationship-building skills identified earlier as well as encouraging the client for beginning the therapeutic journey (see Table 4.1).

Assessing and Understanding Lifestyle

With knowledge that the client's values and behaviors are based on the client's unique schemas of apperceptions, and are therefore often filled with distortions, a thorough assessment is conducted to help clients begin to examine their current lifestyles and resulting dysfunctional behaviors. The Adlerian therapist uses a wide range of methods to uncover relevant information about the client's feelings of inferiority, misguided private logic, and compensatory behaviors, and to better understand the resulting lifestyle. Some of these include asking the client about early recollections, discussing birth order influences, asking the client to describe unique experiences, and gently asking probing questions regarding why the client exhibits certain behaviors (see Table 4.1).

T A B L E 4.1   Phases and Commonly Used Techniques in Adlerian Therapy

	Techniques Commonly Used with Children	Techniques Commonly Used with Adults
Phase I **Building the** **Therapeutic** **Relationship**	Building a trusting relationship ■ Attending skills ■ Empathy ■ Being optimistic ■ Being nonjudgmental ■ Asking questions in nonthreatening manner ■ "Getting on floor" with child ■ Art and other creative therapies ■ "Play" therapy ■ Fostering open discussion ■ Giving gentle feedback Encouragement ■ Value and accept child ■ Use words that build sense of self ■ Believe in child ■ Plan experience that ensure success	Building a trusting relationship ■ Attending skills ■ Empathy ■ Being optimistic ■ Being nonjudgmental ■ Being respectful ■ Being egalitarian ■ Focusing on strengths ■ Showing unconditional positive regard Encouragement ■ Showing clients you value them through: ■ Empathy ■ Being nonjudgmental ■ Acceptance Examining Early Recollections
Phase II **Assessing and** **Understanding** **the Lifestyle**	Assessment ■ Drawings of place in family ■ Drawings of significant events ■ Talking with and asking questions ■ Observation by therapist ■ Observation by others ■ Query child and significant others about significant events Encouragement	Assessment ■ Checklists ■ Open-ended questions ■ Responses to structured questions Examining early recollections Exploring the family constellation Dream analysis Encouragement
Phase III **Insight and** **Interpretation**	Empathy Feedback Democratically held discussion groups Open discussion Encouragement Limit-setting	Dream analysis Socratic questioning and use of dialectical method Teaching and interpretation Spitting in the client's soup Encouragement
Phase IV **Reeducation and** **Reorientation**	Responding to identified behaviors from assessment Limit-setting Applying natural consequences Applying logical consequences Democratically held discussion groups Encouragement Catching oneself Task-setting Commitment and practice	Socratic questioning and use of dialectical method Role-playing and acting "as if" Encouragement Catching oneself Task-setting

Insight and Interpretation

A thorough assessment can help clients and therapists become insightful regarding the reasons the client has developed a certain style of life. Through the use of Socratic questioning and by highlighting pieces of a client's dreams, daydreams, fantasies, early memories, patterns of behaviors, and issues related to birth order, the therapist shows the client how the evidence points toward the development of the client's misguided private logic and resulting dysfunctional style of life. It is also during this phase that the therapist can educate the client about how the client's styles of life has impacted him or her. As the client integrates and accepts this knowledge, he or she becomes ready to make significant change (see Table 4.1).

With younger children who have not fully developed the capacity for insight at deep levels, the counselor can be the vehicle for devising techniques based on his or her interpretation of the child's style of life. With children in particular, it is important to recognize that although insight often precedes change, it is not a prerequisite for change. Whether it is the counselor who has gained insight into the young child's behaviors, or the older client and counselor together who have jointly begun to understand the client's unique lifestyle, the stage is now set for the final phase of therapy—reeducation and reorientation (see Table 4.1).

Reeducation and Reorientation

The goal of this last phase of therapy is to have the client adopt a new style of life based on the insight that has been gained about the client's current lifestyle. Here, either the therapist devises a plan for change (as in the case of a young child), or the client, in consultation with the therapist, jointly discuss ways in which the client can change. Activities chosen at this phase can be practiced during sessions or outside of sessions and are selected to develop and embed a new lifestyle more congruent with the client's unique personality and driven by a subjective final goal that is not built on misguided private logic.

As the client continues in this phase, he or she increasingly experiments with new behaviors and new values, and the therapist gently encourages the client to let go of unproductive patterns while reinforcing and affirming the new, healthier patterns that include cooperation and the valuing of others. Increasingly, the client realizes the struggles inherent in living and the courage needed to make changes that will lead to cooperation and empathy toward others. At this point, therapy may end, although some clients may continue in what Stein and Edwards (1998) call the **meta-therapy phase**, where clients examine the nature and meaning of life (see Table 4.1 and Box 4.6).

B o x 4.6   Dr. Gilchrist Works with Shannon

Read or watch Dr. Gilchrist's work with Shannon and identify how she uses empathy to build the relationship and how she encourages Shannon to understand the relationship between her early recollections and her current way of viewing the world.

You can read this session by going to www. cengage.com/counseling/neukrug/CTP1e and click "student downloads." Or your instructor may show this session in class with the DVD that accompanies his or her copy of the text.

SOCIAL, CULTURAL, AND SPIRITUAL ISSUES

A person who clearly saw the importance of how external forces could deleteriously affect the person, Alfred Adler could be said to be one of the first therapists to focus on social justice issues and peace (Rudmin, 1991):

> The striving for personal power is a disastrous delusion and poisons man's living together. Whoever desires the human community must renounce the striving for power over others. (Adler, 1928/1966, p. 169)

Adler saw how power is misused by parents, in relationships, by men over women, by culture over culture, and by one country over another. For instance, he believed that the desire for power and the lost of social interest and social concern could be seen in men's subjugation of women:

> The subjugation of women came with the invention of war and the consequent rise in the importance attached to physical strength and endurance. The resulting mass attitude and movement was decidedly unfavorable to women.... The conflict resulting from the attempt to subjugate women has played great havoc both in private and social life. (Adler, 1937, p. 117)

And, in a similar vein, he saw the desire for power and superiority as being a root of class struggles and the oppression of minorities:

> Those who have traveled have found that people everywhere are approximately the same in that they are always inclined to find something by which to degrade others.... Until mankind consents to take a step forward in its degree of civilization, these hostile trends [prejudices] must be considered not as specific manifestations, but as the expression of a general and erroneous human attitude. (Adler as cited in Ansbacher & Ansbacher, 1956, p. 452)

As you might guess, he believed that the desire for power, which is always rooted in feelings of inferiority, resulted in the loss of social consciousness and the reason why wars are waged:

> To prevail through violence appears to many as an obvious thought. And we admit: the simplest way to attain everything that is good and promises happiness, or even only what is in the line of a continuous evolution seems to be by means of power. But where in the life of men or in the history of mankind has such an attempt ever succeeded? As far as we can see, even the use of mild violence awakens opposition everywhere, even where the welfare of the subjugated is obviously intended. (Adler, 1928/1966, p. 169)

In the end, however, Adler was an optimist, and his theory was one that invited change. He saw individual psychology as the mechanism to enlighten people about their need for power and how such power oppresses others.

He believed that people could understand that the very oppression that they experienced was the root of their feelings of inferiority and that those same feelings are the cause for a cycle of oppression that they could cause. Understanding this, thought Adler, would be the first step to change, as individuals could begin the process of rising above such feelings. He believed that through therapy and education, there could be an enlightenment that allowed individuals to seek what he believed was an inherent tendency in all people: to work together for the common good—to have a social sense.

In practical terms, to be an Adlerian means that you understand the roots of oppression. You can certainly understand and see it in those who have been historically oppressed, but you will also understand how all people are oppressed in some ways. You will understand why people are motivated to do awful things, as they are driven by misguided private logic and compensatory behaviors toward the subjective final goal. And, such an understanding will bring with it a responsibility to do something about oppression. You can do this by being a therapist, by being an educator, or by advocating for political change. Being an Adlerian means that you understand the importance of a social conscience, and you will have no choice but to advocate for the betterment of all.

From the perspective of minority clients, you might be asking what, if anything, does the Adlerian therapist do differently? Probably, most Adlerians would say that the key piece to working with minorities is being able to forge a successful therapeutic alliance. This critical element allows the counselor to build a cooperative and equal relationship that can help the client understand how his or her feelings of inferiority have led to his or her style of life. It is this understanding that can begin to set individuals free from their early shackles, and for those continuing to experience racism and discrimination, can set them free from their continued oppression as they learn how to effectively cope with such acts.

But what about the religious person; how would the Adlerian work with him or her? Well, as you have seen, to say Adler was *not* a religious man would be an understatement, yet Adler understood the nature and importance of religion. Believing that religions fashioned God to be the perfect image of what we all should strive for, Adler saw religion as serving an important purpose for people.

> God, as man's goal, is the harmonic complementation for the groping and erring movements on the path of life. (Adler as cited in Ansbacher & Ansbacher, 1956, p. 461)

Religions help us define the values for which we should strive, values that for the most part stress equality, cooperation, and love, many of the same values highlighted in Adlerian therapy (Watts, 2000; 2007). And, religions suggest that God symbolizes perfection and reflects an image of how to embody these values. Although some Adlerian therapists might not understand or even validate specific religious dogma, they are likely to reinforce the sense of importance that God brings to their clients and even encourage them to keep that image in their mind as something for which they could strive. No one can ever become God-like, but one can always strive to become loving, caring, and socially sensitive.

EFFICACY OF ADLERIAN THERAPY

Dynamically oriented psychotherapy has only infrequently been tested to demonstrate its effectiveness when compared with other kinds of therapeutic interventions. Of course, this does not mean that it lacks effectiveness; rather there has been reduced commitment to empirical testing probably owing to insufficient support from the therapeutic-analytic community. (Silverman, 2005, p. 306)

As with psychoanalysis, one of the problems with any dynamically oriented therapy (a therapy that explores intrapsychic issues) is that it's difficult to measure. For example, how does one measure how a dream is reflective of one's lifestyle? Today, many approaches focus on specific presenting problems, such as phobias, depression, sexual dysfunction, and so on. Since Adlerian therapy has a much broader focus, one must ask what should be measured to show the effectiveness of this approach. For instance, would it be reasonable or even possible to examine a changing subjective final goal? And, if yes, how would one measure such a vague construct?

So, where does that leave us? Carlson et al. (2006) suggest that there are some common elements to Adlerian therapy that are likely to make it a particularly effective form of therapy. First, they note that research has consistently shown that the ability to develop a relationship with the client is a critical factor in successful client outcomes. Clearly, the Adlerian focus on a trusting and egalitarian relationship would place such an approach in the forefront of counseling theories. Next, they point out that the research on counseling outcomes demonstrates the importance of client hope and expectations. Here, too, the Adlerian shines. With the emphasis on encouragement, and the anti-deterministic, positive approach of Adlerian therapy, it is likely to be one of the more effective approaches. Finally, they note that trends these days have moved to approaches being short-term, psychoeducationally oriented, and future-oriented. This matches nicely with the Adlerian approach. So, although empirical studies are lacking, it appears as if Adlerian therapy embodies many of the characteristics that would speak favorably for positive client outcomes.

Although there has been a paucity of controlled, outcome studies examining the efficacy of Adlerian therapy as compared to other approaches, a number of studies have examined specific elements of Adlerian therapy, such as the importance of birth order, early recollections, and social interest (Carlson et al., 2006; Watkins & Guarnaccia, 1999; Watts & Shulman, 2003). Given the positive results of these studies, along with the emphasis that Adlerian therapy places on the common elements noted earlier, Adlerian therapy probably has much to offer. However, more controlled studies clearly need to be completed. Finally, it should be noted that play therapy, which had its origins with Adlerian therapy, has been greatly researched and has been shown to be effective in numerous studies. Keeping in mind that play therapy is often based on an Adlerian model, this approach should be given careful consideration when working with children. (See Box 4.7.)

> **B o x 4.7 Jake's Experience with an Adlerian Therapist**
>
> Please review the Miller family's background, which can be found in Appendix B, and then read about Jake's encounter with an Adlerian therapist, which can also be found in Appendix B.

SUMMARY

Alfred Adler, the son of a Jewish grain merchant, grew up in Vienna, Austria, and developed a theory of counseling that focused on how a young child's responses to feelings of inferiority would direct the child, and later the adult, toward healthy or unhealthy behaviors, or what he called the "style of life." Adler, who was a sickly child until the age of 5 years and who had a "model" older brother, experienced firsthand what it was like to feel "less than" in life. Out of the memories of these experiences, Adler became driven to understand how such feelings could permeate and affect the lives of all individuals. At first becoming intrigued with some of Freud's notions, Adler later developed his own theory that stressed a holistic perspective. Considered a psychodynamic theorist by some, an existential–humanist by others, and more recently, a constructivist, Adler believed that the whole person was driven by one drive, a striving for perfection. This force subsumed all other instincts, but could be diverted from its natural path if the child had not learned how to effectively deal with feelings of inferiority.

Adler believed that based on one's schema of apperception and private logic, a person develops a subjective final goal that is an image of what the person wants to be. The subjective final goal is reflected in the individual's style of life. Adler contrasted private logic with common sense, noting that private logic is one's inner voice, self-talk, or internal images that justifies one's style of life and fuels one's subjective final goal, whereas common sense is the realization that we must put effort into developing attitudes, beliefs, and behaviors that benefit the common good.

Adler believed that each child is born with unique capabilities and personality characteristics, and develops ways of responding to feelings of inferiority. Primary feelings of inferiority lead to private logic and compensatory behaviors that enhance the person's natural abilities and characteristics, and lead to a subjective final goal that fosters cooperative love and work relationships, empathy toward others, and a desire to work toward the common good. Secondary feelings of inferiority, however, lead to private logic and a subjective final goal that yields maladaptive compensatory behaviors and neurotic ways of living.

In working with clients, Adler believed that early experiences, and the memories of those experiences, deeply affected the development of an individual's private logic and subjective final goal. Such things as birth order, major events in a person's life, and types of parenting could all affect the development of the child's private logic. Thus, it is important to do a thorough assessment of the individual in order to understand the development of an individual's private logic and subjective final goal, and resulting maladaptive and neurotic compensatory behaviors.

Today, most Adlerian therapists view therapy as occurring through four phases: building the therapeutic relationship; assessing and understanding the life style; insight and interpretation; and reeducation and reorientation. Techniques for adults include building a trusting relationship, encouragement, assessment, examining early recollections, exploring the family constellation, dream analysis, Socratic questioning and use of the dialectical method, teaching and interpretation, spitting in the client's soup, guided imagery exercises, role-playing and acting "as if," catching oneself, and task-setting. For children, they include building a trusting relationship; encouragement; democratically held discussion groups; assessment, art, play and creative therapies; responding to identified behaviors; limit-setting; natural consequences; logical consequences; catching oneself; task-setting; and commitment and practice. Courage to take responsibility and make change is encouraged by Adlerian therapists as clients work through the phases.

Adler's ideas have been often applied to children by such individuals as Rudolph Dreikurs and Don Dinkmeyer, who suggested styles that children tend to adopt to compensate for feelings of inferiority, and Terry Kottman, who developed Adlerian play therapy.

Relative to social and cultural uses, it was noted that Adler saw most oppression, such as child abuse, oppression of women, and oppression of minorities, as well as the need to go to war, as rooted in feelings of inferiority and the resulting private logic and subjective final goal. He suggested that through education and therapy, individuals can understand their misguided private logic and subjective final goals, and develop new goals more in line with their unique abilities and characteristics and which would lead toward the development of a person who is empathic, loving, cooperative, and self-knowing, and who works for the betterment of society. As for spiritual issues, Adler believed that God is an image that is important for individuals to model after in their quest for completion and wholeness.

Although research on individual psychology is limited, it was noted that many of the qualities inherent in the therapeutic relationship of those who practice individual psychology are qualities that have been shown to be important for effective outcomes in counseling.

KEY WORDS

acting "as if"
Adler School of Professional Psychology
anti-deterministic

antithetical schema of apperception
art therapy
assessment

assessing and understanding the lifestyle (phase II)
attention-seeking
birth order

building a trusting relationship

building the therapeutic relationship (phase I)

catching oneself

child guidance clinics

commitment and practice

common sense

community feeling

compensation

constructivist

courage

creative therapy

democratically held discussion groups

developing an understanding of self and others (DUSO)

dialectical method

displaying inadequacy

dream analysis

early recollections

encouragement

exploring the family constellation

examining early recollections

feelings of inferiority

fictional final goal

first humanist

Gemeinschaftsgefühl

guided imagery exercises

holism

honoris causa

individual psychology

insight and interpretation (phase III)

Journal for Individual Psychology

limit-setting

logical consequences

meta-therapy phase

natural consequences

organ inferiority

play therapy

primary feelings of inferiority

private logic

reeducation and reorientation (phase IV)

revenge-seeking

responding to identified behaviors

role-playing

schema of apperception

secondary feelings of inferiority

social concern

social interest

Society for Individual Psychology

Socratic questioning

spitting in the client's soup

striving for perfection

striving for superiority

striving for wholeness

style of life

subjective final goal

systematic training for effective parenting (STEP)

task setting

teaching and interpretation

teleology

unconscious

uniqueness of the individual

use of power

Vienna Psychoanalytic Society

KEY NAMES

Adler, Alexandra
Adler, Cornelia (Nelly)
Adler, Kurt
Adler, Sigmund

Adler, Valentine
Dinkmeyer, Don
Dreikurs, Rudolf

Epstein, Raissa Timofeyewna
Klein, Melanie
Kottman, Terry

REFERENCES

Adler, A. (1927). *Understanding human nature*. New York: Greenberg Publisher.

Adler, A. (1929). *The science of living*. New York: Greenberg Publisher.

Adler, A. (1937). Mass psychology. *International Journal of Individual Psychology, 3,* 111–120.

Adler, A. (1958). *What life should mean to you* (A. Porter, Ed.). New York: G. Putnam. (Original work published 1931)

Adler, A. (1963a). *The practice and theory of individual psychology* (P. Radin, Trans.). Patterson, NJ: Littlefield, Adams, & Co. (Original work published 1925)

Adler, A. (1963b). *The problem child: The life style of the difficult child as analyzed in specific cases*. New York: Capricorn. (Original work published 1930)

Adler, A. (1964a). Religion and individual psychology. In H. L. Ansbacher & R. R. Ansbacher (Eds.), *Superiority and social interest: A collection of later writings* (pp. 271–310). Evanston, IL: Northwestern University Press. (Original work published 1933)

Adler, A. (1964b). The structure of neurosis. In H. L. Ansbacher & R. R. Ansbacher (Eds.), *Superiority and social interest: A collection of later writings* (pp. 83–95). Evanston, IL: Northwestern University Press. (Original work published 1932)

Adler, A. (1964c). Advantages and disadvantages of the inferiority feeling. In H. L. Ansbacher & R. R. Ansbacher (Eds.), *Superiority and social interest: A collection of later writings* (pp. 50–58). Evanston, IL: Northwestern University Press. (Original work published 1933)

Adler, A. (1964d). Typology of meeting life problems. In H. L. Ansbacher & R. R. Ansbacher (Eds.), *Superiority and social interest: A collection of later writings* (pp. 66–70). Evanston, IL: Northwestern University Press. (Original work published 1935)

Adler, A. (1964e). Advantages and disadvantages of the inferiority feeling. In H. L. Ansbacher & R. R. Ansbacher (Eds.), *Superiority and social interest: A collection of later writings* (pp. 29–40). Evanston, IL: Northwestern University Press. (Original work published 1933)

Adler, A. (1966). The psychology of power. *Journal of Individual Psychology, 22,* 166–172. (Original work published 1928)

Adler, A. (1992). *What life could mean to you* (P. Radin, Trans.). Oxford, England: Oneworld. (Original work published 1931)

Adler, A. (2002a). Physician as educator. In H. T. Stein (Ed.), *The collected clinical works of Alfred Adler* (Vol. 2, pp. 32–38). (G. L. Liebenau, Trans.). Bellingham, WA: Alfred Adler Institute of Northwestern Washington. (Original work published 1904)

Adler, A. (2002b). A study of organ inferiority and its psychical compensation: A contribution to clinical medicine. In H. T. Stein (Ed.), *The collected clinical works of Alfred Adler* (Vol. 2, pp. 115–222). (G. L. Liebenau, Trans.). Bellingham, WA: Alfred Adler Institute of Northwestern Washington. (Original work published 1907)

Adler, A. (2002c). The neurotic character: Fundamentals of a comparative individual psychology and psychotherapy. In H. T. Stein (Ed.), *The collected clinical works of Alfred Adler* (Vol. 1). (C. Koen, Trans.). Bellingham, WA: Alfred Adler Institute of Northwestern Washington. (Original work published 1912)

Albert, L. (2003). *Cooperative discipline: A teacher's handbook.* Circle Pines, MN: American Guidance Service.

Ansbacher, H. L. (1962). Was Adler a disciple of Freud? A reply. *Journal of Individual Psychology, 18,* 126–135.

Ansbacher, H. L. (1964). The increasing recognition of Adler. In H. L. Ansbacher & R. R. Ansbacher (Eds.), *Superiority and social interest: A collection of later writings* (pp. 3–19). Evanston, IL: Northwestern University Press.

Ansbacher, H. L., & Ansbacher, R. R. (Eds.). (1956). *The individual psychology of Alfred Adler: A systematic presentation in selections from his writings.* New York: Basic Books.

Armour, R. (1953, February 16). A child's private logic. *Time Magazine, 63.*

Bottome, P. (1957). *Alfred Adler: A portrait from life.* New York: The Vanguard Press.

Bridle, S., & Edelstein, A. (2000, Spring/Summer). Was ist "das Ich"? *EnlightNext Magazine, 17,* 126–129, 176–177.

Buchheimer, A. (1959). From group to "Gemeinschaft." In K. A. Adler & D. Deutsch (Eds.), *Essays in individual psychology: Contemporary applications of Alfred Adler's theories* (pp. 242–246). New York: Grove Press.

Carlson, J., Watts, R. E., & Maniacci, M. (2006). *Adlerian therapy: Theory and practice.* Washington, D.C.: American Psychological Association.

Clark, A. J. (2002). *Early recollections: Theory and practice in counseling and psychotherapy.* New York: Brunner-Routledge.

Deutsch, D. (1958). Didactic group discussions with mothers in a child guidance setting—A theoretical statement. *Group Psychotherapy, XI*(1), 52–56.

Dinkmeyer, D., & Dreikurs, R. (1963). *Encouraging children to learn: The encouragement process.* Englewood Cliffs, NJ: Prentice Hall.

Dinkmeyer, D., & Eckstein, D. (1996). *Leadership by encouragement.* Delray Beach, FL: Saint Lucie Press.

Dinkmeyer, D., & Sperry, L. (2000). *Counseling and psychotherapy: An integrated, individual psychology approach.* Columbus, OH: Merrill.

Eckstein, D., & Kern, R. (2002). *Psychological fingerprints: Lifestyle assessments and interventions.* Dubuque, IA: Kendall/Hunt Publishing.

Ellenberger, H. F. (1970). *The discovery of the unconscious: The history and evolution of dynamic psychiatry.* New York: Basic Books.

Fiebert, M. S. (1997). In and out of Freud's shadow: A chronology of Adler's relationship with Freud. *Individual psychology, 53*(3), 241–269.

Furtmuller, C. (1964). Alfred Adler: A biographical essay. In H. L. Ansbacher & R. R. Ansbacher (Eds.), *Superiority and social interest: A collection of later writings* (pp. 311–393). Evanston, IL: Northwestern University Press.

Goldenberg, H., & Goldenberg, I. (2008). *Family therapy: An overview* (7th ed.). Belmont, CA: Brooks/Cole.

Gondor, E. I. (1959). Art and play therapy. In K. A. Adler & D. Deutsch (Eds.), *Essays in individual psychology: Contemporary applications of Alfred Adler's theories* (pp. 206–215). New York: Grove Press. (Original work published 1954)

Hoffman, E. (1994). *The drive for self: Alfred Adler and the founding of individual psychology.* New York: Addison-Wesley.

Kaiser, C. (1995). *An interview with Kurt Adler on his 90th birthday.* Retrieved from http://home.att.net/~Adlerian/kurt-90.htm

Kottman, T. (1995). *Partners in play: An Adlerian approach to play therapy.* Alexandria, VA: American Counseling Association.

Landreth, G. L. (2002). *Play therapy: The art of the relationship* (2nd ed.). New York: Brunner-Routledge.

Leman, K. (1998). *The birth order book: Why you are the way you are.* Grand Rapids, MI: Revell.

Mahoney, M. J. (2003). *Constructivist psychotherapy: A practical guide.* New York: Guilford.

Manaster, G. J., Painter, G., Deutsch, D., & Overholt, B. J. (Eds.). (1977). *Alfred Adler: As we remember him.* Chicago: North American Society of Adlerian Psychology.

Maslow, A. H. (1962). Was Adler a disciple of Freud: A note. *Journal of Individual Psychology, 18,* 125.

Maslow, A. H. (1968). *Toward a psychology of being.* Princeton, NJ: D. Van Nostrand.

Mosak, H. H., & Maniacci, M. P. (1999). *A primer of Adlerian psychology: The analytic-behavioral-cognitive psychology of Alfred Adler.* Philadelphia: Brunner/Mazel.

Oberst, U. E., & Stewart, A. E. (2003). *Adlerian psychotherapy: An advanced approach to individual psychology:* New York: Brunner-Routledge.

Rudmin, F. (1991). Seventeen early peace psychologists. *Journal of Humanistic Psychology, 31*(2), 12–43.

Selesnick, S. T. (1966). Alfred Adler: The psychology of the inferiority complex. In F. Alexander, S. Eisenstein, & M. Grotjahn (Eds.), *Psychoanalytic pioneers* (pp. 78–86). New York: Basic Books.

Sherman, R. (1999). Family therapy: The art of integration. In R. E. Watts (Ed.), *Intervention and strategies in counseling and psychotherapy* (pp. 101–134). Philadelphia: Taylor and Francis.

Silverman, D. (2005) What works in psychotherapy and how do we know? What evidence-based practice has to offer. *Psychoanalytic Psychology, 22*(2), 306–312.

Starr, A. (1973). Sociometry of the family. In H. H. Mosak (Ed.), *Alfred Adler: His influence on psychology today.* Park Ridge, NJ: Noyes Press.

Stein, H. T. (1999). *Classical Adlerian quotes. Feeling of inferiority.* Retrieved from http://home.att.net/~Adlerian/qu-infer.htm

Stein, H. T. (2007). *Adler's legacy: Past, present, and future.* Retrieved from http://home.att.net/~Adlerian/adlers-legacy.htm

Stein, H. T., & Edwards, M. E. (1998). Alfred Adler: Classical theory and practice. In P. Marcus & A. Rosenberg (Eds.), *Psychoanalytic versions of the human condition: Philosophies of life and their impact on practice* (pp. 64–93). New York: New York University Press.

Sweeney, T. (1998). *Adlerian counseling: A practitioner's approach* (4th ed.). Philadelphia: Accelerated Development.

Watkins, C. E., & Guarnaccia, C. A. (1999). The scientific study of Adlerian theory. In R. E. Watts (Ed.), *Intervention and strategies in counseling and psychotherapy* (pp. 207–230). Philadelphia: Taylor and Francis.

Watts, R. E. (1999). The vision of Adler. In R. E. Watts (Ed.), *Intervention and strategies in counseling and psychotherapy* (pp. 1–13). Philadelphia: Taylor and Francis.

Watts, R. E. (2000). Biblically based Christian spiritual and Adlerian psychotherapy. *Journal of Individual Psychology, 56*(3), 316–328.

Watts, R. E. (2003a). Reflecting "As If": An integrative process in couples counseling. *The Family Journal, 11*(1), 73–75.

Watts, R. E. (Ed.). (2003b). *Adlerian, cognitive, and constructivist therapies: An integrative dialogue.* New York: Spring Publishing Company.

Watts, R. E. (2007). Counseling conservative Christian couples: A spiritually sensitive perspective. In O. J. Morgan (Ed.), *Counseling & Spirituality: Views from the Profession.* Boston: Lahaska/Houghton Mifflin.

Watts, R. E., & Holden, J. M. (1994). Why continue to use "fictional finalism?" *Individual Psychology, 50,* 161–163.

Watts, R. E., & Pietrzak, D. (2000). Adlerian "encouragement" and the therapeutic process of solution-focused brief therapy. *Journal of Counseling and Development, 78,* 442–447.

Watts, R. E., & Shulman, B. H. (2003). Integrating Adlerian and constructive therapies: An Adlerian perspective. In R. E. Watts (Ed.), *Adlerian, cognitive, and constructivist therapies: An integrative dialogue* (pp. 9–38). New York: Spring Publishing Company.

Wolfgang, C. H. (2001). *Solving discipline and classroom management problems: Methods and models for today's teachers* (5th ed.). New York: John Wiley & Sons.

SECTION II

Existential–Humanistic
Approaches

Section II offers an overview of three important existential–humanistic approaches to counseling and psychotherapy: existential therapy, Gestalt therapy, and person-centered counseling. Loosely based on the philosophies of existentialism and phenomenology, these approaches were particularly prevalent during the latter part of the twentieth century but continue to be widely used today. Existentialism examines the kinds of choices one makes to develop meaning and purpose in life, and from a psychotherapeutic perspective, suggests that people can choose new ways of living at any point in their lives. Phenomenology is the belief that each person's reality is unique and that to understand the person, you must hear how that person has come to make sense of his or her world. These approaches tend to focus on the "here and now" and gently challenge clients to make new choices in their lives. Although generally shorter-term than the psychodynamic approaches examined in Section I, these therapies tend to be longer-term than the cognitive–behavioral approaches you will explore in the next section of the book.

Chapter 5

Existential Therapy

Learning Goals

- To gain a biographical understanding of Viktor Frankl, one major contributor to the existential therapy approach to counseling.
- To understand the historical context in which Frankl created his theory.
- To become familiar with some of the main tenets of a number of existential therapists in addition to Viktor Frankl.
- To understand the roles existential philosophy and phenomenology play in the development of existential therapy's anti-deterministic view of human nature.
- To learn about key concepts that are the basis for existential therapy, including phenomenology; death and non-being; freedom; responsibility; meaninglessness; existential and neurotic anxiety; neurotic or moral guilt, and existential guilt; will to meaning; and authenticity.
- To review some of the major techniques used in existential therapy, including the dialectical method; educating the client about existential therapy philosophy; developing the authentic relationship; applying a phenomenological perspective by listening, showing empathy, being nonjudgmental, and inquiring; acceptance; confrontation; encouragement; paradoxical intention; and de-reflection.
- To examine the therapeutic process through a series of eight phases that include contact, understanding, education and integration, awareness, self-acceptance, responsibility, choice and freedom, and separation.
- To review important social, cultural, and spiritual issues related to existential therapy, especially in reference to the notion of "Mitwelt," or the social world, and to examine the role the therapist has in helping a client examine his or her spiritual life.
- To identify those client concerns where existential therapy might be most helpful, to highlight the factors that support the efficacy of existential therapy, and to acknowledge the difficulty in measuring outcomes of this approach.
- To see how existential therapy is applied through vignettes, DVDs, and case study.

I t was 1941, and the Nazis occupied Austria. Viktor Frankl, a prominent physician at a hospital in Vienna, is suddenly handed a visa that would allow only him to leave his beloved Austria. His parents would have to stay. Few Jews were afforded this opportunity, and many were already being sent to concentration camps, although the extent of the atrocities was not known at that time. Suddenly, Frankl had to decide between leaving his parents and the country he loved, and staying and hoping that his status at the hospital would continue to afford some protection for him and his parents, protection that was becoming less and less likely. He agonized about what to do as he walked home. Upon entering his house, he saw a piece of marble from the Ten Commandment tablet of his family's synagogue, which had been destroyed:

> If Frankl were to look closely, his father pointed out, he would recognize which commandment it came from. At that moment, Frankl's father began to recite in Hebrew the fourth commandment: "honour your father and your mother, that your days maybe be prolonged in the land which the Lord your God gives you!" (Exodus 20:12). Frankl felt as though he had been hit by lightning and knew instantaneously what his decision had to be. This was no sheer coincidence but a real "hint of heaven" for him. Frankl allowed the visa to expire and, 9 months later, the hospital he worked at was closed. He and his family (this included Frankl's first wife) were soon deported to the concentration camps. Only his sister managed to immigrate [*sic*] to Australia. (Längle & Sykes, 2006, p. 39)

Only 1 in 40 survived the concentration camps, and ironically, Frankl's time in the camps would become a mechanism for him to live the counseling theory which he had begun to write prior to being sent to the camps. Ultimately, his theory and its hypotheses about human nature would become known throughout the world.

Viktor Frankl is just one of many therapists who, over the years, were instrumental in the development of the school of therapy known as existential therapy. In fact, many would place Carl Rogers and Fritz Perls, also highlighted in this text, in this general school. These therapists all use some of the basic tenets of existential philosophy in their approach, although the manner in which they practice varies considerably. This chapter will present a generic approach to existential therapy, as opposed to Frankl's specific approach, which he called **logotherapy** ("meaning therapy"). At the beginning of this chapter, I have chosen to highlight Frankl because his life story is so compelling and brings forth many of the philosophical issues basic to existential therapy. In addition, Frankl was one of the first therapists to popularize this approach.

VIKTOR FRANKL

A middle child with an older brother, Walter, and a younger sister, Stella, Viktor Frankl was born in Vienna, Austria, on March 26, 1905, to Elsa and Gabriel Frankl (Frankl, 1943/2004a). Frankl described his family as being close and remembers feeling safe while growing up despite having been brought up during a time of world wars and rampant anti-Semitism. He remembers his parents as having a deep sense of faith and describes his father as being fair, principled, stoic, and determined, and his mother as being kindhearted, pious, and warm (Frankl, 1997). He loved her dearly.

Viktor Frankl

> In Auschwitz I thought very often of mother. Each time I fantasized how it would be when I would see her again. Naturally, I imagined that the only thing for me to do would be to kneel down and, as the expression goes, kiss the hem of her dress. (Frankl, 1997, p. 22)

As a child, Frankl had lofty expectations of himself, and even at the very young age of three, remembers wanting to become a physician (Frankl, 1997). As he grew into his teen years he discovered psychology, and at the age of 19 he wrote and subsequently sent an article on mimicry to Freud. At Freud's urging, it was published in the *Journal of Psychoanalysis*. After high school, Frankl went on to study medicine at the University of Vienna and eventually specialized in neurology and psychiatry with a focus on depression and suicide. This was an exciting time in Vienna. Freud, who was Viennese, had taken the world by surprise with his theory of psychoanalysis, and soon after, Alfred Adler, also Viennese, was to become almost as popular. To live in Vienna, become a physician, and have a keen interest in psychology meant you would encounter and work closely with some of the icons in the history of psychodynamic therapy.

Although initially intrigued with psychoanalysis, Frankl's allegiance to the Freudian approach was short-lived, and by his early twenties he was questioning the psychoanalytic emphasis on childhood sexuality. He soon discovered the Adlerian approach of individual psychology, which was much more optimistic and future-oriented. However, after a short affiliation with this group, he was to develop his own theory and open counseling centers for youth. His centers were quite successful, and despite still being a medical student, he was allowed to work as a therapist at the **University of Vienna Psychiatric Clinic**.

In 1930, Frankl received his medical degree, and two years later, at the young age of 27, he became head of the **Steinhof Psychiatric Hospital**, where he worked with suicidal women. Here, he began to wonder why some of the women were particularly set on killing themselves, while others seemed to be able to prevent themselves from this action. It was then that his ideas about why certain individuals can maintain a sense of meaning in their lives, and thus ward off deeply painful feelings, began to coalesce in his counseling theory, which he would eventually call logotherapy. This approach would later be called the "**third wave**" **of Viennese psychology**, and followed Sigmund Freud's psychoanalytic approach and the individual psychology of Alfred Adler (Frankl, 1943/2004a).

In 1938, the Nazis overran Austria, and in the next few years, Frankl would be faced with some difficult decisions regarding his own life and the lives of members of his family. In 1940 he became chief of neurology at the Rothschild hospital, which was one of the only hospitals still employing Jews. Here, Frankl would often purposefully misdiagnose patients in an effort to prevent them from being euthanized. Thus, schizophrenics became "aphasics" (loss of speech functions) and major depressions became "high fevers with deliriums." As highlighted at the introduction of this chapter, in 1941, Frankl turned down a visa in order to stay with his parents and attempted to offer them a bit of protection from the Nazis. Later in that year, he married Mathilde "Tilly" Grosser. However, in 1942, he, his pregnant wife, and his parents were sent to a concentration camp. Here, his mother would be gassed and his father would die of starvation and pneumonia. Frankl, who had managed to smuggle a vial of morphine into the camp, helped spare his father the horrors of his last moments:

> I asked him:
>   "Do you still have pain?"
>   "No."
>   "Do you have any wish?"
>   "No."
>   "Do you want to tell me anything?"
>   "No."
> I kissed him and left. I knew I would not see him alive again. But I had the most wonderful feeling one can imagine. I had done what I could. I had stayed in Vienna because of my parents, and now I had accompanied father to the threshold and spared him the unnecessary agony of death. (Frankl, 1997, p. 26)

His wife, Tilly, would be forced to have an abortion and eventually died in Auschwitz. His brother, Walter, who had fled to Italy, was captured and would also die in a concentration camp. Only he, and his sister Stella who had managed to emigrate to Australia, would survive.

When sent to the concentration camps, Frankl had hidden his initial manuscript for his theory in the lining of his coat. However, the coat was confiscated, and for the next few years, while in four different concentration camps, he began to rewrite his manuscript on scraps of paper using a blunt pencil given to him by a fellow inmate as a birthday gift. This book, in some ways, was a motivation for Frankl to keep living (Frankl, 1997).

While in the camps, Frankl watched how his fellow inmates would survive, or lose hope and die. Here, he began to recognize that unless they had meaning in their lives and some sense of hope for their future, their psychological lives would cease and oftentimes they would soon die. Meaning, he believed, came from a will to take responsibility for oneself and to choose to live a life of dignity with purpose, despite one's predicament. Even when being taken to the death chambers, Frankl could distinguish those who would find some larger meaning and stand erect from those who had given up.

From his experiences in the concentration camps, Frankl relayed a number of poignant memories that he believed highlighted the importance of having a sense of meaning in one's life. For instance, he tells the story of a time when a fellow inmate had told him that he knew that they would be liberated on March 30. Then, when this day came and no liberation was in sight, this inmate suddenly became ill and died the next day. Other times, he would watch inmates put aside a cigarette, waiting for the moment when they were liberated to smoke it. Periodically, an inmate would lose hope, cease having any sense of purpose in life, and smoke the cigarette. Invariably, that person would soon die of illness or commit suicide. Frankl and others tried to do their best to prevent inmates from moving into despair—their first step toward death. He could often be found trying to reassure them that their lives had meaning, even in such a place. Many of these stories, as well as Frankl's outline of his theory, were written in his best-selling book, *Man's Search for Meaning* (1946/2006), which Frankl dictated to his publisher in nine days. Listed as one of the 10 most influential books for Americans by the Library of Congress, the book has sold millions of copies and has been translated into dozens of languages. His next book, *The Doctor and the Soul*, published directly after *Man's Search for Meaning*, was the product of the scraps of paper he wrote on while in the concentration camps (Frankl, 1946/2004b).

Frankl believed strongly that each person was responsible for his or her actions, and as an example of this, refused to generalize anger, or what he called "collective guilt," toward "all Germans as many were doing after the war" (Lukas & Hirsch, 2002).

> In 1946, I lectured in the French occupation zone of Austria. I spoke against collective guilt in the presence of the commanding general of the French forces. The next day a university professor came to me, himself a former SS officer, with tears in his eyes. He asked how I could find the courage to take an open stand against collective guilt. "*You* can't do it," I told him. "You would be speaking out of self-interest. But *I* am the former inmate number 119104 and I *can* do it. Therefore I *must*." (Frankl, 1997, p. 103)

Frankl's philosophy regarding collective guilt explains one of the reasons he decided to return to Vienna following the war, despite the fact that Austrian resistance against the Nazis was minimal. After returning to Vienna, Frankl was given the post of director of the **Vienna Neurological Polyclinic** and remained at the clinic until his death. In 1947, he met Elenore "Elly" Schwindt, with whom he would fall in love and have one child, Gabriele.

Over the years, Frankl would become involved in dozens of humanistically oriented professional associations, hold visiting and honorary professorships at such places like Harvard and Stanford Universities, write 32 books and numerous articles that were translated into dozens of languages, and win dozens of awards for his writings and lectures (Viktor Frankl Institute, 2005). He became an avid

---

B o x 5.1   A Conversation with Viktor Frankl

Listen to Drs. Allen and Mary Ivey and Dr. Jeffrey Zeig discuss conversations they had with Viktor Frankl by   clicking on the Frankl link at the "Stories of the Great Therapists" Web site: http://www.odu.edu/sgt

---

mountain climber and, in his late sixties, learned how to fly planes. He died at the age of 92 of heart failure (see Box 5.1).

In the early 1990s, Viktor Frankl's daughter, Dr. Gabriele Frankl-Viseley, organized and helped to found the **Viktor Frankl Institute**, whose purpose is "to foster the lifetime work of Viktor Frankl and to provide access to authentic information about logotherapy and existential analysis" (Viktor Frankl Institute, n.d.; personal communication, Franz Viseley, March 21, 2008). Currently, Viktor Frankl's granddaughter is president of the Institute.

Viktor Frankl was undoubtedly influenced by a number of existential philosophers, theologians, and phenomenologists who came before or were his contemporaries. Some of these included Soren Kierkegaard (1813–1855), Friedrick Nietzsche (1844–1900), Edmund Husserl (1859–1938), Martin Buber (1878–1965), Paul Tillich (1886–1965), Martin Heidegger (1889–1976), and Jean-Paul Sartre (1905–1980). These individuals put forth some of the following ideas that would impact on Frankl's theory: the world is an absurd place into which we're thrust against our will, anxiety is a natural part of living, self-awareness and consciousness should not be assumed, reality is a self-created subjective experience, relationships are critical to who we are and who we become, and the choices we make affect who we are (existence precedes essence). He was also likely affected by Ludwig Binswanger (1881–1966), whom many see as the first existential therapist (Cain, 2002). Binswanger incorporated many of the ideas from his predecessors into one of the first approaches to working with clients and suggested that we can understand the person in three areas: the physical and biological (**Umwelt**), the interpersonal and social (**Mitwelt**), and the psychological, or world of the self (**Eigenwelt**). It was individuals like Binswanger and Frankl who took the esoteric writings of the existentialists and offered a new paradigm that was more optimistic and suggested possibilities for client change (Arbuckle, 1975). In addition, it was these theorists who reacted to the reductionism and determinism of the analytical and later behavioral approaches by offering an approach which was considered **anti-deterministic** (Blocher, 2000).

As Frankl was influenced by others, he too influenced many, including such famous Existential therapists as Rollo May (1909–1994) (May, Angel, & Ellenberger, 1958), James Bugental (1976), and Irvin Yalom (1980). May is often considered the father of American existential therapy, while Yalom is often looked at as the person who popularized the existential approach to therapy, partly because of his bestselling novels, *Love's Executioner* and *When Nietzsche Wept* (this book was also turned into a movie). These modern-day existential therapists looked at the importance of the relationship in defining who we are and viewed the change process in therapy as a joint journey between therapist and client in which both are deeply affected. In their view, therapist openness and therapist self-disclosure is critical and likely to lead to the same on the part of the client as the two work together, dialectically, in their mutual journey. In addition, the influence of Frankl and the existentialists can be seen in the views of human nature of most humanistic therapists, such as Carl Rogers and Fritz Perls. This chapter integrates the philosophies of many of the more well-known existential therapists.

VIEW OF HUMAN NATURE

Existential therapists believe that people are born into a world which likely has no inherent meaning or purpose. They are not born good or bad; they are just thrust into the cosmos. Whether there is broader meaning to existence (e.g., God; a "larger purpose" to life) one will never know, and although some may choose to have faith in something "more," such beliefs are unfathomable constructs which cannot be proven. Since life has no inherent meaning, each of us is charged with the responsibility of making it meaningful through the **choices** we make. Although not discussed in detail, most existential therapists agree that the ability to face life's struggles and bring meaning into one's life is at least partially related to the kind of parenting one receives. However, in existential therapy, one need not unravel years of early childhood issues to uncover core concerns that affect one's ability to do this. In fact, existentialist therapists reject the notion that we are determined by early childhood development, instincts, or intrapsychic forces, although talking about the past is not avoided if the client believes it would help him or her understand self in a more meaningful way.

Central to existential therapists' beliefs is the notion that, consciously or unconsciously, people struggle *throughout their lives* with basic questions related to what it is to be human. Some of this struggle has to do with a few core issues, such as the fact that we are born alone, will die alone, and except for periodic moments when we encounter another person deeply, we live alone; death constantly looms over us and reminds us of the relatively brief amount of time we have; we alone are responsible for making our lives meaningful; and meaningfulness, as well as a limited sense of freedom, comes through consciousness and the choices we make (Yalom, 1980).

Existential therapists believe that most people live a life of limited self-reflection as they put energy into avoiding the core issues related to their humanness. Such avoidance is the result of trying to maneuver around the anxiety and dread we *will* feel if we examine these issues head-on. After all, it is not easy to accept one's aloneness in the world, it can be frightful to be cognizant of one's ultimate demise (death), it can be humbling to examine whether one is living a meaningful existence, and it takes focused self-discipline to change the way one has been living. And, the result of living with limited self-awareness and steering clear of the inherent struggles of living is the development of neuroses and psychopathology, which from the existential perspective is the development of symptoms and anxiety from living inauthentically. In essence, we can live authentically, with a life that sometimes includes anxiety and dread, if we face these core issues squarely, but are doomed to an inauthentic, neurotic existence if we do not. Existential therapists suggest that in dialogue with others, people can gain a greater awareness of the choices they have made and can begin to direct their lives toward a more personally meaningful and authentic existence by making new choices that involve facing life's struggles honestly and directly. With this awareness, however, comes a great sense of responsibility, as we come to realize that every choice we make affects ourselves, those close to us, and to some degree, all people on the planet, as each decision we make has a ripple effect throughout the world.

As you might imagine, existential therapists believe that uncomfortable feelings or neurotic symptoms are important messages regarding the maneuvering in which one engages to avoid the ultimate questions of living. Sometimes, the behaviors people develop in this process can be quite odd, yet are in response to the same issues haunting each of us. In fact, in some ways, there is little difference between the obsessive–compulsive, germ-phobic neurotic who walks the streets with his pet goldfish around his neck (such as in the movie *What About Bob*), and the executive who is obsessively driven by her work and puts in an 80-hour workweek. They both have developed ways of avoiding facing the basic questions of life and in encountering others in an authentic manner. And there is really little difference between you and the next homeless person you pass on the street. Each of you has created your own ways of avoiding the ultimate questions of life and, perhaps, avoiding the humanness that each of you can recognize in each other through dialogue. Interestingly, years ago, Frankl (1968) was particularly concerned with how social influences impact our ability to relate to each other and warned of how industrialization had damaged the ability of people to interact in an authentic way. Imagine what Frankl might have to say about how computers and other technologies have been used to prevent us from having a "real" encounter with another person.

Many of the humanistic approaches to counseling share much in common with the existential approaches, and this is why you often see these approaches subsumed under the category of "existential-humanistic" approaches to counseling. For instance, both the existential and humanistic approaches are anti-deterministic, believe in the power of choice in redefining who the person is, view the relationship between the client and therapist as critical, and are optimistic about the individual's ability to change (Cain, 2002). In addition, like many of the humanistic therapies (e.g., person-centered, gestalt), existential therapy does not assert that the individual can be examined in a reductionistic manner. Instead, the whole is greater than its parts. People cannot be explained by attempting to reduce them into component parts (see parable, Box 5.2).

B o x 5.2   Reductionism and the Cat

This ancient parable has been told by Irvin Yalom (1980) and Viktor Frankl (1984) when talking about the false conclusions to which people may come when trying to reduce the human condition to smaller, component parts:

> Two neighbors asked a wise old person to arbitrate a dispute they were having. One neighbor said, "My neighbor's cat ate my butter." The other

neighbor responded: "My cat doesn't even like butter." So, the wise old person looked at the two of them and said, "How much butter was eaten, and how much does the cat weigh?" They both responded: "Five pounds." The wise old man then took the cat and placed it on a scale. It weighed exactly five pounds. The wise old man looked at the two of them and said: "Okay, now we have the butter, where is the cat?"

B o x 5.3   Summary of Core Beliefs of Existential Therapy

1. We are born into a world that has little inherent meaning.
2. We are born alone and we will die alone.
3. We alone make our lives meaningful.
4. We bring meaningfulness into our lives through the choices that we make.
5. Meaningful choices only occur if we are conscious of our aloneness and our limited time on earth.
6. Anxiety, feelings of dread, and having struggles are a natural part of living and are important messages about how we live and relate to others.
7. Limited freedom is experienced through the realization that we choose our existence.
8. With recognition that we choose our existence comes responsibility to choose wisely for ourselves and to recognize how those choices affect those close to us and all people.

What, then, are the differences between the humanistic and existential therapies? First, the existential therapies tend to focus their approach on "existential issues," so you will often see existential therapists talking directly about the following: how individuals make sense of their lives and their ultimate deaths, the fact that we are alone in the world and how we deal with our aloneness, how we make meaning in our lives, how we deal with the anxiety of living (and dying), and whether the choices we are making in our lives are working for us. The humanistic approaches, however, tend to have the client guide the session in the direction he or she wants to take it. Second, the humanistic therapist tends to believe that there is some type of growth force present within the person that, if allowed to be accessed, will lead the person toward a state of self-actualization whereby the person will be in harmony with self. This rather optimistic belief upon the parts of the humanistic therapies set them somewhat apart from the existential therapies, which tend to focus more on the absurdity of life and the fact that we must deal with the struggles of living and make conscious choices that will bring about a meaningful existence (Cain, 2002; van Deurzen, 2002). Some of the core beliefs of Existential Therapy are summarized in Box 5.3.

KEY CONCEPTS

Phenomenology

Phenomenology is a branch of philosophy concerned with the nature of reality, and emphasizes subjective experience as a way of approaching and understanding truth. Intertwined with most existential therapists' ways of understanding clients is the idea that from moment to moment, each thought, reflection, and experience that a person has should be understood as meaningful and provide a window into that person's understanding of truth. This way of understanding a person is contradictory to trying to understand a client by applying an external model or frame of reference, as do many other therapeutic approaches (van Deurzen & Kenward, 2005). It is also the basis for being nonjudgmental, for a therapist cannot judge another's experience if the therapist believes that the truth of each client's subjective experience lies only within that client. This philosophy, when applied in the therapeutic environment, is critical if the existential therapist is going to encourage clients to be self-reflective in their process of examining how they make meaning in their lives. Those who have a phenomenological perspective do not assume there are no truths; after all, if I let go of a ball, gravity pulls it to the ground. However, individuals who take an existential perspective do assume that one's experience of self is unique, real to that person, and ever-changing as the individual lives in the world and interacts with others (see Box 5.4)

Death and Non-Being

Cowards die many times before their deaths; the valiant never taste of death but once. (William Shakespeare, *Julius Caesar*, Act II, Scene 2)

With life comes death. We burst into the cosmos and eventually must face our ultimate demise. And facing death and non-being is not an easy task, for if we have no illusions to prevent us from accepting our death, we assuredly would become full of anxiety. However, we tend to find ways of avoiding this anxiety, ways of dodging the reality of our demise. These mechanisms also prevent us from dealing with the reality that our time is limited (May, 1967).

For some, the same methods that are used to avoid awareness that the Grim Reaper is at the door allow them to live relatively calm lives and work with one another peacefully. For instance, some may blindly embrace beliefs in religion, God, a hereafter, or values that put their minds at ease about death. Others may take a hedonistic view of life. These individuals only see value in self-enjoyment as they constantly try to have their needs met in an effort to momentarily take them away from worrying about death and non-being. Both types of individuals have found ways of avoiding the anxiety of death and non-being, and have not made conscious choices about their beliefs or behaviors.

Ultimately, one of the goals of existential therapy is to help the client see how he or she has avoided the anxiety of the knowledge of death and non-being;

B o x 5.4   Did He Really See That Eagle?

The phenomenological perspective can be seen in this incident of Billy Mills, an Olympic runner who "saw" something no one else saw. Read the following, and see if you believe that Billy saw the eagle:

> When Billy Mills was eight, his mother died. His father, a member of the Lakota nation in South Dakota, stroked the boy's arms and told him, "You have broken wings." He used a stick to draw a circle in the dirt. "Step inside your soul," he said. "It is the pursuit of the dream that will heal you."
>
> He encouraged his son to find his dream in sports, which were providing the Indians with a new way to compete against the white man after centuries of slaughter and treacherous treaties…. In the grueling 10,000-meter race during the 1964 Summer Olympics in Tokyo, 26-year-old Billy Mills, with his dark complexion and crew cut, was near the head of the pack. He was a virtual unknown, but he managed to stay neck-and-neck with the world record-holder from Australia. After the last lap bell, the Australian made his move, nudging Mills's elbow so he could break ahead.

Caught off guard, Mills staggered and drifted to an outer lane.

> Spotting an eagle on the jersey of another runner, he heard his deceased father's voice, "You will have the wings of an eagle." In the final stretch, the race for the gold was down to the Australian and a top-ranked Tunisian. Then, out of nowhere, Mills came charging with the long, easy strides of a sprinter. The television announcer could hardly believe what he was seeing. "Look at Mills!" he cried. "Look at Mills!" As the American crossed the finish line first, the announcer, witness to one of the greatest upsets in Olympic history, just screamed in a wordless spasm of shock and glee, "Aaahhh!"
>
> After the race, Mills realized that the eagle he had seen on the jersey hadn't actually been there at all. But the idea of it had been enough to propel him. He became the first American to win the gold in the 10,000-meter race. No one from the Western Hemisphere has done that since. (Swidey, 2008)

B o x 5.5   My Death Anxiety

I remember being 16 years old and sitting on the window seat in my room looking out at the stars. Suddenly, the immensity of the universe hit me and the reality of my limited time on earth came to bear. My heart started to beat as I began to have a panic attack. "I must stop this," I said to myself. "But how?" I wondered. I had started to experience my death anxiety and wasn't sure how to "turn it off."

---

that is, to assist the client in understanding what mechanism he or she has used to avoid knowledge of his or her demise. And, knowledge of avoidance mechanisms brings the client face-to-face with his or her death anxiety. Faced head-on, this reality allows the client to move forward, for it is only through such self-knowledge that one can decide whether to embrace one's former tactics for avoiding the knowledge of death and non-being or to choose a new way of being in the world, a way that is honest in its acceptance of one's ultimate fate and allows one to decide a new path toward a personally meaningful existence (see Box 5.5). And this new path does not necessarily mean that one gives up one's past values (e.g., religious values), but it does mean that the individual now chooses those values with consciousness and is aware of how those choices affect self and others.

Ultimately, we must all ask ourselves what beliefs and/or behaviors we have adopted to stop ourselves from experiencing the anxiety that results from facing the knowledge of our death and non-being. Then, we must see if we are brave enough to embrace this anxiety and decide whether we wish to keep our former avoidance mechanisms or to make choices that may lead us to a more meaningful existence.

Freedom

> ... [E]verything can be taken from a man but one thing: the last of the human freedoms—to choose one's attitude in any given set of circumstances, to choose one's own way. (Frankl, 1946/2006, p. 104)

One can reflect about freedom on multiple levels. Those who are enslaved by others have little freedom to do and act as they wish. Those who are oppressed by others have their social freedom limited. Those who are poor have their economic freedom limited. And, those who build psychological fences prevent themselves from choosing ways of being that would bring dignity and purpose to their lives, dignity and purpose that would be the road to their psychological freedom.

Sometimes individuals are oppressed by external factors, such as slavery, poverty, war, and disasters. In contrast, choosing dignity and purpose and its resulting psychological freedom is an internal creation. Thus, a group can fight against an external oppressor for years, decades, and even centuries, but when freedom finally comes may still be enslaved because they have not found inner freedom. In fact, finding freedom internally can be as much of a battle as fighting for freedom from external constraints. One is enslaved unless the external *and* internal constraints can be overcome. In fact, aspects of external enslavement can often be overcome psychologically as we can choose inner dignity and sense of purpose under the most horrible of conditions (see Figure 5.1).

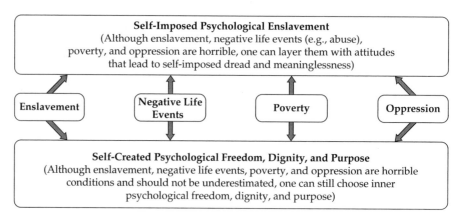

FIGURE 5.1   Enslavement versus Freedom

Once one comes to recognize that freedom is as much of an internal process as an external one, then one can begin to take steps toward ultimate freedom—freedom from self-created internal constraints. It is only at this point that one can gain mastery over the thoughts and feelings that we have and the actions that we take. And mastery can and will lead to a sense of dignity as one purposefully makes choices that result in a dignified way of life. Any other choice would be foolish, as it would lead to existential guilt, or what some have called the "wronging of self" (Yalom, 1980).

In the end, freedom is not found in the possession of material goods or attainment of physical pleasures, and freedom can sometimes come with a price. One need only look at some of the great figures of history to consider what freedom is. For instance, in many ways, were not Jesus, Gandhi, Mother Theresa, Martin Luther King, Nelson Mandela, and Viktor Frankl free? All of these individuals were enslaved, oppressed, or chose to have limited access to material goods, yet all somehow chose to live with dignity and felt a sense of purposefulness in life. This is true freedom.

Responsibility

Responsibility can be understood on two levels: responsibility toward self and responsibility toward others. Responsibility toward self is intimately associated with one's awareness that freedom is internally created. With this knowledge, every choice made then becomes one which is directly related to living a dignified life with purpose. Having such consciousness weighs on a person, for how can a person choose not to be responsible if the consequences of one's choices are self-evident?

In 1972, meteorologist Edward Lorenz gave a talk in which he presented evidence that the flapping of a seagull's wing in Brazil could cause a tornado in Texas. Somehow, this later became known as the "Butterfly Effect" and changed to how the wings of a butterfly could affect the weather in the United States (Hilbon, 2000). In either case, the point was that the smallest action in a part of the world could affect others in another part of the world. Having consciousness that every action we take will affect those around us, and likely impact the world in some fashion, is a monumental weight that carries with it a humbling responsibility. However, it is only by embracing this concept that we can have true peace and harmony in the world. It is only when each of us come to believe in the Butterfly Effect that we can realize the effects of our actions on others. And when we do realize this, we will be responsible to others.

When doing counseling and therapy, a critical point arrives when the client realizes that, to a large degree, freedom is internally constructed, and that one can choose to live responsibly by making choices that positively affect one's personhood as well as the personhood of others. Typically, however, clients have spent years finding ways of avoiding consciousness around responsibility. In fact, Yalom (1980) identified a number of mechanisms that clients use to avoid responsibility. Similar to the psychoanalytic concept of defense mechanisms, they include **compulsivity, displacement, playing the victim, losing control, avoiding autonomy, willing-denial**, and **physical disease**. In addition, you can probably come up with other ways one avoids taking responsibility. The following briefly defines Yalom's mechanisms:

Compulsivity. This is the quality of becoming so consumed with an activity that a person avoids examining his or her life. The "activity" overwhelms the person. These days, we see compulsive behaviors all around us, such as compulsive eating, computer sex, working unreasonably long hours, and so on. The underlying question that therapists want to ask their clients, and clients need to eventually ask themselves, is: "What is being avoided by these behaviors, and how is this avoidance keeping you from freedom?"

Displacement. This is the process of placing one's problems or issues onto others or other things so that one does not have to take responsibility for examining them. Displacement happens in numerous ways, such as projecting one's issues onto others, having a psychosomatic illness in an effort to avoid one's issues, blaming others for one's problems (if only my therapist was better at this!), or blaming events for one's problems (e.g., if it wasn't for that hurricane, I'd be happy).

Playing the victim. "I was raped." "My boss is a racist." "My parents emotionally abused me." "My lover left me." Yes, all of these events are horrible and can devastate a person. However, why is it that some people can move on from these events while others continue to wallow in the pain of the past, sometimes for years after the events occurred? Ultimately, if one is to live a life with purpose and meaning, one has to make good choices despite these unfortunate or even traumatic events.

Losing control. Ever know someone who just "lost it" for a while? Whether they "lost their minds" and literally went crazy for a while, became enraged and lost their temper, or simply "lost their way" in life, these are mechanisms some will use to avoid taking responsibility for their current state of affairs.

Avoiding autonomy. Some people know exactly what they need to do, but don't do it. They feel too tired, too stuck, too unwilling to move forward in their lives. Try to motivate these individuals, and they always have some reason for not moving ahead. This static existence is a way of avoiding making choices.

Willing-denial. There are numerous ways to deny oneself the possible choices that exist in one's life. One of the simplest is to deaden oneself to the world. For instance, if I numb myself to my existence, I am not allowing myself to be open to the possibilities that exist. I am willing myself into the denial of my experience. Or, if I live in a fantasy world, I am not facing my choices. Instead, I am willing myself into a world where reality and choices are askew.

> Jill is married to Jack. She does not want to be married to Jack. She is frightened to leave Jack. So she stays with Jack but imagines she is not married to him. Eventually she does not feel married to Jack. So she has to imagine she is. "I have to remind myself that he is my husband."
> (Laing, 1969, p. 47)

Although individuals rarely experience themselves as being willing participants to these neurotic styles of living, existentialist therapists believe this is exactly what they are doing. Bringing consciousness to this kind of resistance is critical to the change process.

Physical disease.   Although you would be hard-pressed to find a person who believes we create *all* the diseases we get, there is enough evidence to suggest that many diseases are an outgrowth of the behaviors that we manifest. Heart disease, some forms of cancer, colds from a lowered immune system due to stress, and many other illnesses have been shown to be related to the kinds of choices that one makes (Neukrug, 2001). Sometimes, having a disease may seem easier than taking responsibility for one's life.

Isolation

One can be isolated from others, isolated from self, or experience what is called **existential isolation**. Isolation from others is related to the aloneness one might feel if there is no one to relate to. Such isolation can be self-imposed (e.g., a monk taking a vow of silence, a neurotic who's fearful of people, etc.), or other-imposed, such as when a person in a position of authority mandates isolation (e.g., a warden placing an inmate in "isolation," a parent sending a child to his or her room).

Isolation from oneself occurs when a person ignores a part of self to the point that he or she is no longer aware of that part. To some degree, we have all done this, such as times when we may have ignored a particularly abusive remark. Some, however, deny major parts of themselves in an effort to separate themselves from a particularly painful event or trauma (e.g., sexual abuse). Such separation from oneself results in an inauthentic way of being as the individual unconsciously avoids the part that has been denied. For instance, the child who was molested may deny his or her sexuality, and then, when older, become incapable of enjoying sex. This part of self needs to be acknowledged and integrated back into the individual's personality, which in this case would include the recovery of the painful memories that resulted in the original separation from self. Almost all theories of counseling acknowledge isolation from self, although most use terms like *splitting*, *dissociation*, or *repression*.

The last kind of isolation, existential isolation, is the realization that we are born alone, will die alone, and ultimately live in the world alone, although we will have important moments when we "encounter" others. Humans are expert at avoiding existential aloneness, because to continually experience such isolation would undoubtedly prevent us from functioning in life. However, never facing or rarely becoming conscious of one's existential isolation has a price to pay—the development of unhealthy and destructive behaviors (see Table 5.1).

Avoidance of our existential isolation is generally an unconscious process whereby we prevent ourselves from experiencing the knowledge and associated panic of our aloneness in the world. Ultimately, to live a life of meaning that includes relationships that can periodically take us away from our sense of isolation, we must acknowledge our aloneness in the world. Only through such acknowledgement can we make conscious and clear choices about how we will find meaning in our lives.

T A B L E 5.1   Ways of Avoiding Existential Aloneness

The following lists some ways that people tend to avoid experiencing their existential aloneness. Can you add others that you might use and share them in class?

overeating	overthinking	angering	_____
undereating	overplaying	joking	_____
overdrugging	fantasizing	hating	_____
oversleeping	psychoticizing	forgetting	_____
overworking	panicking	depressing	_____
oversexing	obsessing	neuroticizing	_____
compulsing	cutting	drinking	_____

Meaninglessness

> The deeper the experience of an absence of meaning—in other words, of absurdity—the more energetically meaning is sought (Havel, 1990, p. 201)

Why do some people wholeheartedly give themselves over to a belief system, seek power, endlessly seek pleasure, or become obsessed with some inane work-related behavior? Existential therapists believe they do this to fill their void—their **existential vacuum**—the awareness that existence is an absurd joke and meaningless. But if existence is meaningless, what is meaningful? (see the drawing below)

At some point... We all have on existential crisis

Unless we have given ourselves permission to step into the abyss of meaninglessness, we cannot know what is meaningful. Taking a step into meaninglessness is

---

B o x   5.6   Some Thoughts About Meaninglessness and Meaningfulness

As you read the excerpt below on meaninglessness and meaningfulness, reflect on your own life and consider how you avoid your existential vacuum.

> I sometimes wake up in the morning, look at my two beautiful daughters, and wonder, what purpose does any of this have? Why did my wife bear them, if ultimately, like me, they face their final demise? Death is at their doorstep, likely to first find me, then soon to find them. And why does any of this matter? I knew my parents and my grandparents. My great-grandparents I knew not. And what if I did? What if I knew them, and their parents, and their parents' parents? So what? Ultimately, they have taken up so little space in the billions upon billions of years that the universe has existed and in the billions upon billions of

planets that stretch out forever. Why would they matter at all? They are nothing and they mean nothing in this vast expanse. Ultimately, I must ask myself, "How can I go on, knowing that I, my children, and all those that have come before me are an infinitesimal speck in time and space? What mark will they leave, and what purpose do they serve? In the end, I am left realizing that I alone make meaning out of my life. And, I also realize that every time I choose, I also affect the lives of my children, others close to me, and the world. There is a kind of exhilaration and joy with this knowledge—a freedom in knowing that I can choose my attitudes, my behaviors, and even my feelings, as I go through life. I am the captain of my ship.

B o x   5.7   Betty and Ed's Existential Journey

Read or watch Dr. Ed Neukrug's work with Betty, and consider how Betty is struggling with issues of meaninglessness in her life.

You can read this session by going to www.cengage.com/counseling/neukrug/CTP1e and click

"student downloads." Or your instructor may show this session in class with the DVD that accompanies his or her copy of the text.

---

often profoundly threatening, because it implies that we must first give up that which we have come to know. However, it can also be profoundly liberating. Initially, it means letting go of our values, faith, and beliefs, and being once again the naked infant willing to experience the absurdity of a world that has no meaning. Once we can touch this place within, we can reestablish contact with ourselves and begin to make new choices that will bring meaning and joy to our lives. And there is a kind of exhilaration we can experience in this knowledge—joy that we are in charge of our destiny. Ultimately, these choices may look eerily similar to how we were living before, but they are different, because they have been chosen—not swallowed whole without reflection. This is true meaningfulness (see Box 5.6 then Box 5.7).

Anxiety

Most existential therapists identify two types of anxiety: **existential anxiety** and **neurotic anxiety**. Existential anxiety ("**angst**") is the anxiety that is experienced when there is a realization of one's aloneness, the meaninglessness of life, and the knowledge of one's death. It is natural and normal to experience anxiety that results from our realization that we are ultimately alone, that we must be the ones to make our lives meaningful, and that we will have to face our non-being. Neurotic anxiety occurs as a product of the mechanisms that are developed to avoid facing the essential existential issues of life and the existential anxiety associated with it. How these mechanisms are developed is not as critical as the fact that they are used to avoid an individual's angst. The mechanisms noted earlier to avoid responsibility (compulsivity, displacement, playing the victim, losing control, avoiding autonomy, willing-denial, and physical disease) are generally also those used in the development of such neurotic anxiety.

Guilt

Existential therapists identify two types of guilt: neurotic guilt, sometimes called moral guilt, and existential guilt. **Neurotic** or **moral guilt** is the remorseful feelings one has from having behaved in a manner that is damaging to self or to others. Like the sex addict who continually goes back to his computer porn, the alcoholic who has to take another drink, or the abusive lover who becomes enraged, these individuals have developed a set of neurotic behaviors that prevent them from reflecting on the meaning of their existence. Such guilt is the result of a split within a person between how that person "knows" he or she should be acting, and how that person actually *does* act (see Box 5.8).

In contrast, **existential guilt** is experienced when the individual realizes he or she has not lived to his or her fullest potential because the individual has avoided dealing with core life issues and its associated existential anxiety. It is the guilt that the abuser would experience if that person did not get angry and could reflect on how he or she has not made his or her life more meaningful. And it is the guilt the computer sex addict or alcoholic would feel if instead of sitting at the computer or taking a drink, those persons could quietly sit with self and reflect on how they have not made better choices in life. It is the guilt that one can and should ultimately experience in therapy if the client is courageous

---

B o x 5.8   Moral or Neurotic Guilt

Make a list of how the following behaviors may be damaging to self or to others. In addition, identify behaviors you might list for yourself that are damaging to you or to others. Do you feel moral or neurotic guilt as a result?

Behaviors	Damaging to Self?	Damaging to Others?
Addictive computer sex	_____	_____
Alcoholism	_____	_____
Verbally abusive behaviors	_____	_____
Other _____	_____	_____
Other _____	_____	_____
Other _____	_____	_____

T A B L E 5.2   **Major Differences Between Moral/or Neurotic Guilt and Existential Guilt**

Moral or Neurotic Guilt	Existential Guilt
1. Remorse for misdeeds, omissions.	1. Free-floating and nonspecific.
2. Caused by the discrepancy between our behavior and standards.	2. A natural state of being that is the result of the difference between what we have achieved and our potential.
3. Temporary and passes with time.	3. Ongoing. One becomes increasingly conscious of this guilt with greater self-reflection and willingness to examine irresponsible behaviors.
4. Focused only on the area of the behavior that has caused remorse.	4. Pervasive and possesses our entire being.
5. We can relieve the tension by changing our behavior or standards.	5. We cannot overcome existential guilt; it is a natural part of our being.

(Adapted from Park, 2008, Section V: Section)

enough to embrace how he or she has avoided consciousness and, as a result, has made irresponsible choices (see Table 5.2).

Will to Meaning

The will to meaning, one's search for meaning, is the original concern (Frankl, 1972).

Frankl and other existential therapists believe that meaningfulness only comes with a deliberate effort on the part of the individual. This "will to meaning" is an active process in which each person chooses to participate in life as he or she defines his or her sense of purpose. And this will to meaning can only be developed after the individual has sorted through his or her neurotic lifestyle and neurotic guilt, faced his or her existential anxiety and existential guilt, and become increasingly aware of his or her true inner core. The person who has chosen not to take this journey is forever participating in behaviors that are self-destructive and destructive to others.

> … [O]nly a man who has been frustrated in this basic will to meaning then resorts either to power seeking or to pleasure seeking … [I]t is the very pursuit of pleasure, of happiness, that thwarts happiness, because happiness is a … side effect of finding and fulfilling a meaning or loving another being, another human being. (Frankl, 1972)

Those who have the courage to face their existential existences can move forward living meaningfully. And, despite the fact that a sense of purpose can evolve for such persons, meaningfulness does not bring with it ongoing happiness or the foregoing of existential anxiety, because it is this very anxiety that fuels the search for meaning. However, it does bring a limited sense of freedom, momentary joy in the realization that the individual alone decides his or her own destiny, and the humbling knowledge that each person alone is responsible for the choices he or she makes and how those choices affect others.

Authenticity

Living "authentically" means acceptance of many of the basic existential struggles already mentioned and that we have taken responsibility for our lives. It also means we have chosen to be honest with ourselves and open with others. In contrast, avoiding responsibility leads to a life of inauthenticity, neurotic anxiety, and moral guilt as the individual avoids taking an honest look at self and avoids authentic interactions with others. One of the goals of psychotherapy is to move the client toward a more authentic way of living in the world. (See Figure 5.2 for a summary of key concepts.)

THERAPEUTIC TECHNIQUES

Although existential psychotherapists are dismissive of any formal "technique," it must be acknowledged that attempts to educate clients directly about the formal properties and principles of existential phenomenology is as much a "technique" as is the assigning of homework or the training of clients to regulate their breathing. (Spinelli, 2007, p. 63)

The essence of existential therapy is the relationship between the therapist and the client, not the use of any specific techniques. However, within this relational context, existential therapists tend to respond in certain ways to clients, and some will even apply what might be perceived as techniques. And, as the above quote states, even an "approach" to the client can be seen as a type of technique. In either case, the following provides you with the manner in which most existential therapists approach the counseling relationship.

Dialectical Method

As with some of the other approaches in this text, the dialectical method of working with clients is core to building an effective and equal relationship between the client and the therapist. From an existential therapy perspective, this method of discussion and reasoning includes showing respect for the client, encouraging an open dialogue between the client and therapist, and providing an accepting atmosphere that allows for philosophical discourse about the meaning of life.

Educating the Client about Existential Therapy Philosophy

Since the existential approach to counseling is based on a philosophy of being in the world, any clients who attend such therapy need to become aware of the basic philosophy underlying the approach. Existential therapists do this in different ways. Some may simply talk to their clients about the basic philosophical structures inherent in the approach, such as death and non-being, the origins of

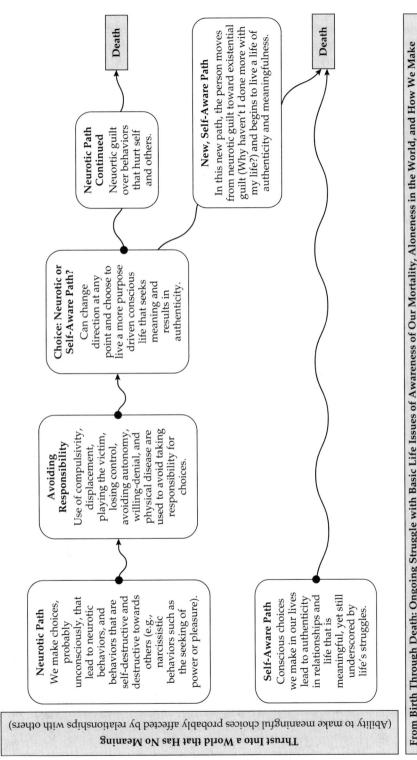

Thrust Into a World that Has No Meaning

(Ability to make meaningful choices probably affected by relationships with others)

Neurotic Path
We make choices, probably unconsciously, that lead to neurotic behaviors, and behaviors that are self-destructive and destructive towards others (e.g., narcissistic behaviors such as the seeking of power or pleasure).

Avoiding Responsibility
Use of compulsivity, displacement, playing the victim, losing control, avoiding autonomy, willing-denial, and physical disease are used to avoid taking responsibility for choices.

Choice: Neurotic or Self-Aware Path?
Can change direction at any point and choose to live a more purpose driven conscious life that seeks meaning and results in authenticity.

Neurotic Path Continued
Neurotic guilt over behaviors that hurt self and others.

Death

New, Self-Aware Path
In this new path, the person moves from neurotic guilt toward existential guilt (Why haven't I done more with my life?) and begins to live a life of authenticity and meaningfulness.

Death

Self-Aware Path
Conscious choices we make in our lives lead to authenticity in relationships and life that is meaningful, yet still underscored by life's struggles.

From Birth Through Death: Ongoing Struggle with Basic Life Issues of Awareness of Our Mortality, Aloneness in the World, and How We Make Our Lives Meaningful.

F I G U R E   5.2   Summary of Key Concepts of Existential Therapy existential anxiety and existential guilt, the importance of finding meaning in life, our aloneness in the world, the power and responsibility we have to make choices that can better ourselves and others, and the importance of being authentic. Other existential therapists might encourage clients to read books, listen to songs, or view movies that relate to this approach (e.g., books such as *Love's Executioner* by May, *Man's Search for Meaning* by Frankl; songs such as "While My Guitar Gently Weeps" by Harrison, "Oh No" by Gogol Bordello; movies such as *I Heart Huckabees, The Matrix*), and still others may choose to educate clients through modeling. Whatever educational approach therapists take, they have the same goal in mind—help the client learn about what it means to be human and to live the conscious life.

Developing an Authentic Relationship

Key to helping a client understand himself or herself is the therapist's ability to develop an authentic therapeutic relationship that is similar to what Buber (1958) called the **I–Thou relationship**. This relationship is highlighted by give-and-take between the client and therapist where the conversation is free-flowing, devoid of façades, and marked by authenticity and realness. This contrasts with an **I–It relationship**, where the client is objectified, as is the case with a therapist who would diagnose the client, be emotionally removed from the client, and use techniques "on" the client. Keep in mind, however, that every relationship has its share of I–Thou and I–It encounters; one cannot constantly maintain an I–Thou relationship:

> In the rhythm of participation in a union in a dual being and the eventual separation into individual autonomy are contained the two necessary poles of human existence itself … (May, 1969, p. 112)

Even though the therapist is real, open, and even self-disclosing at times, it is important to not confuse this relationship with one that a person might have with a close friend or lover. The therapeutic relationship is purposeful, with its goal being to help the client learn about self. In such a relationship, it would not make sense for the therapist to be overly self-disclosing or to engage in self-serving behaviors (e.g., becoming romantically involved with the client). Within this authentic therapeutic relationship, the therapist recognizes that boundaries exist and are necessary to foster the client's search for meaning.

Listening, Empathy, Being Nonjudgmental, and Inquiring: A Phenomenological Perspective

Using what's called a **phenomenological perspective** to gain a deep understanding of the client's subjective experience of the world, the therapist will listen intensely, use empathy to ensure deep understanding of the client, and ask questions that inquire about the client's perspective without judging the client. Some existential therapists believe it's important to understand four aspects of a client's world to understand the person fully (Binswanger, 1963; van Deurzen, 2002): **Umwelt**, a German term for the way the client interacts with the physical world, including such things as instincts, biology, and items one can touch and feel; **Mitwelt**, the manner in which the client comes to make sense of his or her interpersonal and social world, such as family, community, culture, society, and the therapeutic relationship itself; **Eigenwelt**, the way the client comes to understand his or her inner world, or self; and **Uberwelt**, or the manner in which we relate to the spiritual aspect of ourselves, or to the unknown.

Acceptance

As clients increasingly examine their worldviews, they will undoubtedly begin to challenge how they have been living their lives, will feel moral and existential guilt, and become self-critical. Often, deeply embedded ways of behaving that have been harmful to self and others will be unearthed. It is important that at these junctures, the therapist is not critical of the client and allows the client to continue to discuss his or her former ways of being as he or she embarks on a new journey toward a new way of being in the world.

Confrontation

Confrontation can occur in many forms and, depending on the style of the particular existential therapist, the level of confrontation can vary dramatically. For most existential therapists, confrontation involves gently challenging the client about the kinds of choices the client has made in his or her life. Generally, this would be done through the use of questions that focus on helping the client examine those choices and how they may have prevented the client from developing a sense of purpose and meaning in his or her life. Some examples might include the following:

- What aspects of your life do you feel good about?
- What aspects of your life do you feel bad about?
- Is what you are doing working for you?
- What kinds of behaviors have been helpful for you?
- What kinds of behaviors have been harmful to you?
- What brings you a sense of purpose and meaning in your life?
- How might you want to change your life?
- If you were to give up certain ways of being, what would you give up?
- If you were to adopt new ways of being in the world, how would that look?
- How do you avoid taking responsibility in your life for how you think, feel, and act?

Encouragement

Throughout the therapeutic process, clients are encouraged to self-reflect, consider the choices they have made, and work on the continual struggles of living. They are reminded that life is not trouble-free, and that although it sometimes seems easier to avoid life's difficulties than to face them head-on, ultimately, there is a price to pay for such an unconscious existence. They are praised for their ability to face their struggles squarely.

Paradoxical Intention

> Happiness must ensue. It cannot be pursued. It is the very pursuit of happiness that thwarts happiness. (Frankl, 1975, p. 85)

Paradoxes are strange phenomena. Sometimes, we seek out happiness, only to find misery, and when we find pleasure, it doesn't feel like enough. We seek power but want more when we get it. Frankl understood the complexity and elusiveness of the paradox and, relative to satisfaction and meaningfulness, believed happiness to be a by-product of living a meaningful life. Relative to symptoms, there is a paradox also, in that often the more we try to eliminate a symptom, the more it perseveres (Pattakos, 2004). Thus, Frankl, suggested why not do the opposite? Instead of trying to eliminate a symptom, try to have it occur more. Thus, the person who is germ-phobic and washes his or her hands frequently during the day is told to wash his or her hands more. Or, the person who is fearful of driving across a bridge is asked to drive across many bridges. Similar to this concept is what many therapists now call "prescribing the symptom." For some reason, and it's not perfectly clear why, prescription of a symptom seems to sometimes reduce the symptom. This may be because the client suddenly realizes the absurdity of the symptom, or that by doing it more, the client comes to see that he or she can actually control the symptom. In either case, paradoxical intention seems to help clients reduce their symptoms.

De-reflection

All too often, we begin to focus on those aspects of our behaviors that prevent us from developing meaning and purpose in our lives. In fact, sometimes, we end up exaggerating our symptoms because we become so fixated on them. The depressed person becomes more depressed because she is depressed. The phobic becomes more reclusive for fear of a panic attack. This never-ending cycle prevents the individual from examining underlying core issues related to how one creates meaning in life and the underlying **existential void** that exists in us all. In order to prevent this kind of obsessive focus, de-reflection, sometimes simply called **"refocusing,"** can assist the individual in developing a more meaningful existence (Pattakos, 2004). Frankl was particularly adept at the use of de-reflection when, instead of focusing on his probable impending doom while in the concentration camps, he focused his attention toward the hope of seeing his wife again or toward finishing his book.

THE THERAPEUTIC PROCESS

Talking about the therapeutic process of existential therapy reminds me of the movie *Forrest Gump*, when Bubba says there are "pineapple shrimp, lemon shrimp, coconut shrimp, pepper shrimp," and on and on and on. With existential therapy, there are so many ways of approaching the client that it's difficult to define a "one-size-fits-all" approach. After all, there are analytical existential therapists, humanistic existential therapists, Gestalt existential therapists, client-centered existential therapists, even REBT existential therapists, and more. Given this state of affairs, the following offers eight phases through which most existential therapists will pass as they work with their clients, although how they deliver this process can vary considerably.

Phase I, Contact: This is an initial contact phase whereby the counselor and client meet one another and there is an acknowledgement of different world-views. Initial education about existential principles may begin at this point.

Phase II, Understanding: In this phase, there is an attempt by the existential therapist to clearly understand the worldview of the client.

Phase III, Education and Integration: This phase occurs when the therapist continues to educate the client about the existential worldview and dialogues with the client about differences between their two world-views. Sometimes, it is in this phase that the therapist gently challenges the client to embrace the therapist's alternate worldview that is based on the underlying philosophy of existential therapy.

Phase IV, Awareness: Now that the client understands the basic philosophy of Existential Therapy, the client can begin the process of becoming conscious of how he or she has avoided existential angst and guilt and has instead developed neurotic ways of living that have harmed self and others and are a direct result of not taking responsibility for the choices made in his or her life.

Phase V, Self-Acceptance: Awareness of how one has avoided existential angst and guilt eventually leads to acceptance of the kinds of harmful neurotic behaviors that the client has embraced. The client now understands that, from this moment forward, he or she can choose differently. The client also realizes that "the unexamined life is not worth living" and that with self-reflection comes the ability to choose differently.

Phase VI, Responsibility: Acceptance of the importance of an examined life brings with it the recognition that, from moment to moment, the client chooses his or her attitudes, thoughts, and behaviors. The client now realizes that neurotic behaviors are self-imposed and that he or she is solely responsible for bringing meaning, dignity, love, and joy to his or her life.

Phase VII, Choice and Freedom: Realizing that we alone are responsible for our lives, the client can now begin to make conscious choices that free the client from his or her self-imposed neurotic constraints. The client now realizes that, from moment to moment, he or she is metaphorically choosing to live free (with all the inherent struggles of living) or die, and makes appropriate decisions based on this realization (see Box 5.9).

Phase VIII, Separation: As the client begins to live a more responsible life in which he or she freely chooses with consciousness the behaviors that will impact self and others, the client no longer needs the therapist

---

B o x 5.9   Live Free or Die

I don't want to achieve immortality through my work. I want to achieve it through not dying. (Woody Allen)

My first job as a college professor was in New Hampshire. I'll never forget driving to the "Granite

State" and suddenly seeing the license plates with their slogan on them: "Live Free or Die." I immediately became excited, thinking I was moving to a state where the legislators all must live the examined life. How disappointed (and naïve) was I when I realized that they were literal in their slogan!

---

and can separate from him or her. The client now also realizes that he or she can choose to be with, or separate from, other important people in his or her life as he or she constantly tries to live a life of meaning with authenticity.

Techniques and relational skills that the existential therapist uses to help the client move through these phases can vary dramatically. However, Table 5.3 shows how some of the techniques and relational skills that might be used throughout the phases just discussed. After you review Table 5.3, see Box 5.10.

T A B L E 5.3   Techniques and Relational Skills as a Function of Phase

Phase	Possible Techniques/Relational Skills
I: Contact	dialectical method encouraging open dialogue; showing acceptance; showing respect; encouraging philosophical discourse about the meaning of life; presenting and educating client about basic philosophical concepts of existential therapy; authenticity (give-and-take, no façades, sense of openness, realness, self-disclosure—all within boundaries of therapeutic relationship)
II: Understanding	phenomenological perspective: listening, empathy, inquiring, and being nonjudgmental; exploring client's Umwelt, Mitwelt, Eigenwelt, and Uberwelt; authenticity
III: Education and Integration	continue educating about philosophy; confrontation: asking questions that focus on helping client examine self; encourage client to adopt new philosophy; authenticity
IV: Awareness	empathy; acceptance; authenticity; encouragement
V: Self-Acceptance	empathy; acceptance; authenticity; encouragement
VI: Responsibility	dialectical method; acceptance; authenticity; encouraging clients to take responsibility for the choices they make; paradoxical intention; de-reflection
VII: Choice and Freedom	dialectical method; empathy; acceptance; authenticity
VIII: Separation	dialectical method; empathy; acceptance; authenticity

---

B o x 5.10   Betty and Ed's Existential Journey

At this point, you may want to again read or watch Dr. Ed. Neukrug's work with Betty. As you view the DVD or read the transcript, try to determine what techniques Dr. Neukrug is using with Betty and on which of the phases the two of them are working.

You can read this session by going to www.cengage.com/counseling/neukrug/CTP1e and click "student downloads." Or your instructor may show this session in class with the DVD that accompanies his or her copy of the text.

SOCIAL, CULTURAL, AND SPIRITUAL ISSUES

Existential therapy has a long history of attending to the social and cultural world of the client. If you remember back to earlier in the chapter, Binswanger and others highlighted the Mitwelt, or interpersonal and social world of the client, as one of four spheres that were critical to understanding the person. From the existential therapist's perspective, how the client makes sense of the world is at least partly a function of how the individual is embedded in his or her "social, political, and cultural environment" (van Deurzen, 2002, p. 69). Thus, an individual's sense of self is at least partly formed from the messages that were received relative to his or her ethnicity, cultural background, and sociological practices, as well as the political atmosphere of the times.

The role of the existential therapist is to try to understand the worldview of the client and ultimately help him or her comprehend the inherent struggles that may be faced as a function of this "Mitwelt." For instance, awareness of pervasive discrimination, sexism, and racism helps the client manage how to respond to such attitudes and behaviors. Ultimately, it allows the client to choose how to come to grips with such realities once he or she understands their influences.

Counselors who embrace the notion that culture is one aspect of what helps to develop client identity must be able to understand the client in his or her differentness (Ibrahim, 2003). As counselors come to know their clients, they can use the dialectical method to discuss differences in the worldviews between the two of them. It is only through this honest and authentic sharing of differences that trust can be developed. And when trust is developed, counselors and their clients can work on developing a shared worldview.

Differences, however, can sometimes be great. For instance, what if a client has the belief that the Devil is literally here on earth and that Armageddon is close at hand? Some existential therapists may see such thoughts as a projection of our fears of dying. Such beliefs, they think, may be the individual's way of trying to avoid the reality of death (Park, 2006). Trying to share one's differences in a dialectical conversation when such differences are great, as in this example, could be difficult for some existential therapists. Luckily, such differences are generally not quite that large, although some areas, like the spiritual dimension of the client ("Uberwelt"), raise some special concerns for existential therapists.

Although the spiritual dimension of the client has become an important focus of existential therapy, today it is broadly defined and includes such areas as one's religious beliefs, how one finds meaning, values held, the ability to love, and the way one gives to society (Gardner & Stevens, 1992; van Deurzen & Kenward, 2005). From an existential therapy perspective, a client's spirituality is directly related to that person's ability to reflect on these important areas of life and to make conscious choices regarding how those areas are addressed. So, the Catholic, Jew, Protestant, Moslem, New Age adherent, and atheist all show their spiritual essence by how they have effectively reflected on these areas. This self-reflective soul makes choices that lead to the betterment of society, because he or she remembers that every choice one makes affects every other person. The nonreflective person, on the other hand, has difficulty seeing that he or she is making choices or how his or her choices affect self and others. Like so much else that the existential therapist does, the therapist's role relative to the client's spirituality is to help the client examine this part of his or her life and assist the client in becoming more conscious of the kinds of choices he or she has made relative to his or her spiritual life.

EFFICACY OF EXISTENTIAL THERAPY

Because existential therapy does not focus on symptom reduction or "cures" as much as it tries to make sense of the meaning a symptom might hold in a person's life, client outcomes are difficult to measure. Also, since the goals of existential therapy include elusive concepts like helping clients live consciously and choose wisely, having clients recognize that life is filled with struggles, and assisting clients in finding what is personally meaningful, it is difficult to identify specific outcome measures to research (Walsh & McElwain, 2002; Wampold, 2001). This difficulty is not helped by the fact that many clients in existential therapy may be replacing a neurotic symptom with a more authentic way of living that sometimes looks very much like the neurotic symptom, such as when neurotic anxiety and neurotic guilt is replaced by existential anxiety and existential guilt. Although existential therapists would see this replacement as "progress," measuring such changes would be nearly impossible (Walsh & McElwain, 2002). Although client outcomes are difficult to measure using this approach, examining whether existential therapy may be successful due to the way it is conducted has turned up some interesting results, including the following (Walsh & McElwain, 2002; Wampold, 2001):

- The aspect of being authentic, open, and willing to examine self seems to be an important aspect of the change process.
- The therapeutic alliance has been consistently shown to be the most important feature of successful therapeutic outcomes. Such an alliance is strongly suggested through the importance of the I–Thou relationship in existential therapy.
- Empathy, one important skill and relationship variable in existential therapy, has consistently been shown to be a crucial element to successful outcomes in therapy.

B o x 5.11   Jake Meets with an Existential Therapist

Please review the Miller family's background, which can be found in Appendix B, and then read about

Jake's encounter with an existential therapist, which can also be found in Appendix B.

- "Liberation," which is similar to freeing oneself from past constraints and the ability to make choices, has been shown to be an important aspect of effective therapy.

- Existential therapy seems to provide an environment that helps a client understand his or her anxiety and guilt, and such self-examination is likely transformative for clients' understanding of self.

In addition to the above, humanistic therapies, with which existential therapy is sometimes lumped together, shows positive outcomes for individuals with relationship issues, anxiety disorders, depressive disorders, trauma, anger-related problems, schizophrenia, severe personality disorders, and health problems (Winter, 2007). Although there is clear evidence that some aspects of existential therapy are likely to be helpful, research on the effectiveness of existential therapy has been sparse, and more research that examines its efficacy should be completed (see Box 5.11).

SUMMARY

Existential therapy is a form of counseling based on the philosophical assumptions of existentialism and phenomenology. Although Viktor Frankl was one of the first to pull together these philosophies into a therapeutic form, others also influenced its development, such as Ludwig Binswanger, Irvin Yalom, and Rollo May. Frankl's biography was highlighted at the beginning of this chapter because his life, especially the time he spent in the concentration camps, is particularly compelling and greatly impacted his theory.

The view of human nature of existential therapists includes many of the basic ideas from the existential and phenomenological philosophers who came before them. Thus, most existential therapists believe that people are not born bad or good, but simply thrust into this absurd world. They view meaning as self-created and believe that there is no evidence that there is anything more to our existence than what we create (e.g., God, larger purpose). They go on to suggest that many, perhaps most, people are limited in their amount of self-reflection and do not realize that they have created their way of being. However, the approach is optimistic in the sense that they believe that through dialogue with others, individuals can gain a larger understanding of how their choices affect who they are and how they affect others. Understanding is the first step to making new choices that can lead to a life that is more meaningful and purposeful.

Most existential therapists agree that the ability to face life's struggles is at least partially related to the kind of parenting that occurs. However, existential therapists do not see their role as unraveling repressed childhood memories. Instead, existential therapists believe that consciously or unconsciously people struggle throughout their lives with basic questions related to what it is to be human.

Many humanistic approaches to counseling share much in common with the existential approaches, including the fact that they are anti-deterministic, believe in the power of choice in redefining who the person is, take a holistic perspective of the person, and are basically optimistic about the individual's ability to change. However, where the humanists believe there is a basic goodness to the person and that the therapist can facilitate clients in directing themselves toward becoming self-actualized, the existential therapist is more directive and educative, not quite as optimistic, and believes that the choices a person makes can help that person live an authentic life, with all of its inherent problems, anxiety, and joy.

In understanding existential therapy, a number of key ideas and concepts stand out. These include phenomenology; death and non-being; freedom; responsibility and avoidance of responsibility, through such means as compulsivity, displacement, playing the victim, losing control, avoiding autonomy, willing-denial, and physical disease; isolation (existential aloneness); meaninglessness; existential and neurotic anxiety; neurotic or moral guilt and existential guilt; will to meaning; and authenticity and inauthenticity.

The essence of existential therapy is the relationship between the therapist and the client, rather than the use of any specific techniques. However, within this context, some existential therapists embrace the following ways of working with clients: the dialectical method; educating the client about the existential therapy philosophy; developing an authentic relationship; applying a phenomenological perspective by listening, showing empathy, being nonjudgmental, and inquiring; acceptance; confrontation; encouragement; paradoxical intention; and de-reflection. The therapeutic relationship applies these relationship skills through what can be described as a series of eight phases that include contact, understanding, education and integration, awareness, self-acceptance, responsibility, choice and freedom, and separation.

Existential therapy has a long history of being sensitive to cross-cultural issues, especially in light of its historical focus on Mitwelt, or the social world, as one of the four client spheres important to focus upon. Such a focus helps the client understand how political, social, and cultural background affects the person and emphasizes the importance of how raising the client's awareness of these factors can impact the kinds of choices the client makes. Understanding the client's world and having an honest sharing of worldview differences between the client and therapist leads to trust and a joint journey of mutual understanding. Lastly, relative to spiritual issues, existential therapists define spirituality broadly and include such things as religious beliefs, how one finds meaning, values held, the ability to love, and the way one gives to society. The role of the existential therapist relative to a client's spirituality is to help the client examine this part of his or her life and assist the client in becoming more conscious of the kinds of choices he or she has made relative to his or her spiritual life (see Box 5.12).

B o x 5.12   Want More?

You can hear stories about some of the leaders of the existential humanistic movement by going to the "Stories of the Great Therapists" Web site at

http://www.odu.edu/sgt and clicking on "Leaders of Humanistic Psychology."

Finally, relative to the efficacy of existential therapy, it was noted that because this approach does not focus on symptom reduction or cures, it is difficult to measure client outcomes as compared to some of the more reductionistic approaches. Despite this, some research has shown that at least some of the key elements of the process of existential therapy have been borne out by research, such as the importance of empathy, being authentic, having a viable therapeutic alliance, and the importance of liberating oneself from past constraints (e.g., freedom to choose). More specifically, existential therapy has been shown to be helpful with relationship issues, anxiety disorders, depressive disorders, trauma, anger-related problems, schizophrenia, severe personality disorders, and health problems.

KEY WORDS

acceptance
Steinhof Psychiatric Hospital
angst
anti-deterministic
anxiety
authenticity
avoiding autonomy
being nonjudgmental
choice
compulsivity
confrontation
death and non-being
de-reflection
developing an authentic relationship
dialectical method
displacement

educating the client about existential therapy philosophy
Eigenwelt
empathy
encouragement
existential anxiety
existential guilt
existential isolation
existential vacuum
existential void
freedom
guilt
inquiring
isolation
I–Thou relationship
I–It relationship
listening
logotherapy

losing control
meaninglessness
Mitwelt
moral or neurotic guilt
neurotic anxiety
paradoxical intention
Phase I, Contact
Phase II, Understanding
Phase III, Education and Integration
Phase IV, Awareness
Phase V, Self-Acceptance
Phase VI, Responsibility
Phase VII, Choice and Freedom
Phase VIII, Separation
phenomenology

phenomenological
perspective

physical disease

playing the victim

refocusing

responsibility

third wave of Viennese
psychology

Uberwelt

Umwelt

University of Vienna
Psychiatric Clinic

Vienna Neurological
Polyclinic

Viktor Frankl Institute

will to meaning

willing-denial

KEY NAMES

Binswanger, Ludwig

Buber, Martin

Bugental, James

Frankl, Elenore (Elly)
Schwindt

Frankl, Elsa

Frankl, Gabriele

Frankl, Mathilde (Tilly)
Grosser

Frankl, Stella

Frankl, Viktor

Frankl, Walter

Frankl-Viseley, Gabriele

Heidegger, Martin

Husserl, Edmund

Kierkegaard, Soren

May, Rollo

Nietzsche, Friedrick

Perls, Fritz

Rogers, Carl

Rothschild Hospital

Sartre, Jean-Paul

Tillich, Paul

Yalom, Irvin

REFERENCES

Arbuckle, D. S. (1975). *Counseling and psychotherapy: An existential-humanistic view.* Boston: Allyn & Bacon.

Binswanger, L. (1963). *Being-in-the-world: Selected papers of Ludwig Binswanger.* New York: Basic Books.

Blocher, D. H. (2000). *The evolution of counseling psychology.* New York: Springer Publishing Company.

Buber, M. (1958). *I and thou* (2nd ed.) New York: Scribner.

Bugental, J. F. T. (1976). *The search for existential identity: Patient-therapist dialogues in humanistic psychotherapy.* San Francisco: Jossey-Bass.

Cain, D. J. (2002). Defining characteristics, history, and evolution of humanistic psychotherapies. In D. J. Cain (Ed.)., *Humanistic psychotherapies: Handbook of research and practice* (pp. 3–54). Washington, D.C.: American Psychological Association.

Fabry, J. B. (1980). *The pursuit of meaning* (rev. ed.). New York: Harper & Row.

Frankl, V. E. (1968). *Psychotherapy and existentialism.* New York: Simon & Schuster.

Frankl, V. E. (1972). *Viktor Frankl archive: Audio and videotapes: The will to meaning.* Retrieved from http://logotherapy.univie.ac.at/e/audioE.html

Frankl, V. E. (1975). *The unconscious God: Psychotherapy and theology.* New York: Simon & Schuster.

Frankl, V. E. (1997). *Viktor Frankl—Recollections: An autobiography.* (J. Fabry & J. Fabry, Trans.). New York: Insight Books.

Frankl, V. E. (1984). *Viktor Frankl archive: Audio and videotapes: On reductionism.* Retrieved from http://logotherapy.univie.ac.at/e/audioE.html

Frankl, V. E. (2004a). Yearly report, October 1942–October 1943. In E. Makarova, S. Makarov, & V. Kuperman (Eds.), *University over the abyss: The story behind 520 lectures and 2,430 lectures in KZ Theresienstadt 1942–1944* (pp. 249–252). Jerusalem: Verba Publishers. (Original work written in 1942–1943)

Frankl, V. E. (2004b). *The doctor and the soul: From psychotherapy to Logotherapy.* London: Souvenir. (Original work published 1946)

Frankl, V. E. (2006). *Man's search for meaning.* Boston: Beacon Press. (Original work published 1946)

Gardner, S., & Stevens, G. (1992). *Red Vienna and the golden age of psychology: 1918–1938.* New York: Praeger.

Havel, V. (1990). *Disturbing the peace: A conversation with Karel Hvizdala.* (P. Wilson, Trans.). New York: Alfred. A. Knopf.

Hilborn, R. C. (2000). Chaos and nonlinear dynamics: An introduction for scientists and engineers (2nd ed.). New York: Oxford University Press.

Ibrahim, F. A. (1999). Transcultural counseling: Existential worldview theory and cultural identity. In J. McFadden (Ed.), *Transcultural counseling* (2nd ed., pp. 3–22). Alexandria, VA: American Counseling Association.

Ibrahim, F. A. (2003). Existential worldview counseling theory: Inception to applications. In F. D. Harper & J. McFadden (Eds.), *Cultural and counseling: New approaches* (pp. 196–208). Boston: Allyn and Bacon.

Laing, R. D. (1969). *Self and others.* Baltimore: Pelican Books.

Längle, A., & Sykes, B. (2006). Viktor Frankl—Advocate for humanity: On his 100th birthday. *Journal of Humanistic Psychology, 46*(1), 36–47.

Lukas, E., & Hirsch, B. Z. (2002). Logotherapy. In F. W. Kaslow, R. F. Massey, & S. D. Massey (Eds.), *Comprehensive handbook of psychotherapy: Interpersonal/humanistic/existential* (vol. 3, pp. 333–356). New York: John Wiley & Sons.

May, R. (1967). *Psychology and the human dilemma.* New York: W. W. Norton.

May, R. (1969). *Love and will* (paperback ed.). New York: W. W. Norton.

May, R. (1980). *Psychology and the human dilemma.* New York: W. W. Norton.

May, R., Angel, E., & Ellenberg, H. F. (Eds.). (1958). *Existence: A new dimension in psychiatry and psychology.* New York: Basic Books.

Neukrug, E. (2001). Medical breakthroughs: Genetic research and genetic counseling, psychotropic medications, and the mind-body connection. In T. McClam & M. Woodside (Eds.), *Human service challenges in the 21st century* (pp. 115–132). Birmingham, AL: Ebsco Media.

Park, J. (2008). Existential guilt: Deeper than the pangs of conscience. Retrieved from http://www.tc.umn.edu/~parkx032/CY-GUILT.html

Park, J. L. (2006). *Our existential predicament: Loneliness, depression, anxiety, and death.* Minneapolis, MN: Existential Books.

Pattakos, A. (2004). *The prisoners of our thoughts: Viktor Frankl's principles at work.* San Francisco: Berret-Kohler.

Scully, M. (1995, April). Viktor Frankl at ninety: An interview by Matthew Scully. *The Journal of Religion, Culture, and Public Life*, 39–43.

Spinelli, E. (2007). *Practicing existential psychotherapy: The relational world*. Los Angeles: Sage Publications.

Swidey, N. (2008, March 20). The Jacoby factor. *The Boston Globe*. Retrieved from http://www.boston.com/bostonglobe/magazine/articles/2008/03/30/the_jacoby_factor/

van Deurzen, E. (2002). *Existential counseling and psychotherapy in practice* (2nd ed.). London: Sage Publications.

van Deurzen, E., & Kenward, R. (2005). *Dictionary of existential psychotherapy and counseling*. London: Sage Publications.

Viktor Frankl Institute. (n.d.). *The institute*. Retrieved from http://www.viktorfrankl.org/e/institutE.html

Viktor Frankl Institute. (2005). *Life and work*. Retrieved from http://logotherapy.univie.ac.at/e/lifeandwork.html

Walsh, R. A., & McElwain, B. (2002). Existential psychotherapies. In D. J. Cain (Ed.)., *Humanistic psychotherapies: Handbook of research and practice* (pp. 253–278). Washington, D.C.: American Psychological Association.

Wampold, B. E. (2001). *The great psychotherapy debate: Models, methods, and findings*. Mahwah, NJ: Erlbaum.

Winter, D. A. (2007). Constructivist and humanistic therapies. In E. Freeman & M. Power (Eds.), *Handbook of evidence-based psychotherapies: A guide of research and practice* (pp. 123–140). West Sussex, England: John Wiley & Sons.

Yalom, I. D. (1980). *Existential psychotherapy*. New York: Basic Books.

Chapter 6

Gestalt Therapy

Learning Goals

- To gain a biographical understanding of Fritz Perls, the creator of Gestalt therapy.
- To understand the historical context in which Perls created his theory.
- To understand the anti-deterministic, holistic, phenomenological, existentially based view of human nature upon which Gestalt therapy is based.
- To learn about key concepts that are the basis for the Gestalt approach, including holism, Gestalt psychology and Perls's expanded notion of "figure/ ground," polarities, contact, the need satisfaction cycle, unfinished business, closure, and resistances or blockages to experience.
- To review the commonly used techniques of empathy, being directive, being confrontational, avoiding intellectualizations, focusing on nonverbal behaviors, and experimentation.
- To examine the specialized techniques of using "now" language, I–Thou communication, I–It language, experiencing the present, not gossiping, making statements out of questions, the dialogue game and empty chair technique, "I take responsibility for that," playing the projection, the exaggeration technique, feeding the client a sentence, "I have a secret," making the rounds, dream work, and group work.
- To examine the structure of neurosis clients generally work through as they participate in Gestalt therapy including: (1) the cliché layer, (2) the role-playing or phony layer, (3) the impasse layer, (4) the implosive layer, and (5) the explosive/authentic layer.
- To understand how the strong phenomenological perspective of Gestalt therapy lends itself to supporters and to critics relative to cross-cultural counseling.
- To reflect on whether Gestalt therapy's Eastern view of spirituality is adaptable to different religions.
- To examine the efficacy of Gestalt therapy in light of the many elusive concepts it proposes.
- To see how Gestalt therapy is applied through vignettes, DVDs, and case study.

Fritz Perls's basic message was *be here now* and *be truly yourself*. This he taught by example as well as in therapeutic sessions. Laura Perls, his estranged wife, once referred to him as half prophet and half bum. Perls felt the description accurate and used it himself, proudly. The prophet in him, was fond of leading his psychological workshops in a reading of his *Gestalt prayer*:

I do my thing, and you do your thing.

I am not in this world to live up to your expectations

And you are not in this world to live up to mine.

You are you, and I am I,

And if by chance we find each other, it's beautiful.

If not, it can't be helped. (Shepard, 1975, p. 3)

Perls, the founder of Gestalt therapy, became an icon of the 1960s. As varying therapeutic modalities became increasingly popular, Perls offered something to his "followers" that others didn't: a sense that if you really "let it out," you would be free to be yourself. This fit in well with the "do your own thing" of the 1960s. A chain-smoker, overweight, and sometimes crass, he nevertheless became so popular that when he lay near death at a Chicago hospital, his friends asked the media not to let people know where he was, for fear that the crowd would become overwhelming (Shepard, 1975). They found out anyway and led a vigil outside of the hospital. He died on March 8, 1970. But where did this guru of the 1960s have his start?

FRITZ PERLS

Fritz Perls

Fritz Perls was born to Amelia Rund Perls and Nathan Perls in the Jewish ghetto of Berlin on July 8, 1893. Although his parents tried to assimilate into German society, they had little success partly due to the rampant anti-Semitism of the time (Shepard, 1975). Despite moving out of the ghetto to a fashionable neighborhood in Berlin when Fritz was only three, family life left much to be desired. Nathan, a philandering wine salesperson, could often be found in bitter fights with his wife over his absence from the home and suspected affairs. Amelia, angry at and bitter toward her husband, succeeded in causing Fritz and his two older sisters to turn against their father. Apparently, for Fritz, this was not difficult, as his father was authoritarian and stern and often referred to Fritz as a *stück scheiise* ("piece of shit"). In fact, Fritz's anger was so intense toward his father that it apparently led him to question whether Nathan actually was his father, thinking until the day that he died that his uncle may have been his actual biological father.

Fritz's problems were not solely with his father. In fact, his mother would often hit him with whips and carpet-beaters. It is interesting that, despite a clear lack of parental stability and trust, Fritz described his childhood as a "happy one" (Shepard, 1975). This was at least partly due to his relationship with his sister Grete, who was one and a half years older, with whom he was particularly close. He and Grete could often be found playing together, and Grete seemed to treat him like a younger "doll" baby whom she loved dearly. This was in stark contrast to his relationship with his other sister, Else, who was three years older, legally blind, and described as unattractive and clingy to his mother. Perls feared that he eventually would have to take care of her and even stated that he didn't mourn much when she died (Shepard, 1975).

At a relatively young age, Fritz showed a streak of rebelliousness underscored by behaviors that could sometimes be described as reckless. Probably originating from his parents' lack of a loving relationship, not having a stable male figure at home, the periodic violence he saw at home between his parents, and his mother's need to have him constantly sharing her vision that his father was no good, Fritz often found himself in trouble. In fact, despite having been the top student in his elementary school, at the young age of 13, Fritz was found stealing money from his parents, running away from home, causing problems at his new school, being truant from school, and engaging in early sexual experiences. It is not surprising that Fritz was eventually thrown out of his high school.

Eventually, finding another high school that offered a more humanistic approach to teaching adolescents, Fritz began to settle down. This school, whose positive approach to children was in stark contrast to the authoritarian approach of most German schools, was to be a second home for Fritz. During this time, he also stumbled across a theater group and became immensely interested in acting. Although admittedly not a great actor, his work in the theater allowed him to make some money and redirect some of his excess energy. It also was seen as a basis for many of the techniques he would eventually create that had a bit of the theatrical in them.

The varied and often negative early experiences of Fritz, says biographer Martin Shepard (1975), were at least partially responsible for the adult Perls having a lifelong difficulty sustaining a relationship, having a strong need to be affirmed, being obsessed with sex, and being outspoken. Shepard also hypothesized, that it was these very experiences that led to his greatness. For instance, Perls would likely have wanted his own past dealt with directly and quickly, as opposed to the ongoing scrutinizing that occurred in psychoanalysis. Thus, his childhood experiences were likely a primary force driving the part of his theory that encouraged experiencing the "**here and now**" and discouraged long, analytical examinations of the past.

As World War I loomed over the horizon, Fritz entered medical school. Having been particularly successful in math and science, becoming a physician seemed a natural fit for him. However, with the war beginning, he volunteered with the Red Cross and later, knowing he was to be drafted, enlisted in the German army. His involvement in World War I and the atrocities that he saw resulted in his somewhat pessimistic view of human nature, while at the same time made him passionate about trying to advocate for a more humanitarian world.

The 1920s were a decade of change for Perls. Attaining his medical degree and practicing as a neuropsychiatrist, Perls "concentrated on prescribing medical cures for a variety of psychological and neurological complaints" (Shepard, 1975, p. 29). Still living with his mother and his blind sister, Else, Perls had a poor self-image.

Increasingly, he began to spend time with the bohemians of the era: artists, poets, writers, and philosophers who were considered part of the counterculture of the time. He also became friendly with Sigmund Friedlander, a philosopher who forwarded the idea that opposites define the individual and that we all seek a "**zero point,**" or the point that brings us to **closure** or **homeostasis**. Friedlander suggested that when an organism expresses too much of one attribute, it becomes necessary for the organism to compensate by bringing in the opposite attribute in order to restore balance or equilibrium. Perls's friendship with Friedlander would greatly mold his view of the world and his eventual theory.

After a relatively brief but unfulfilling trip to America exploring possible work opportunities, Perls returned to Germany and would soon meet a distant relative, "Lucy." Perls was enamored by Lucy and she showed him a new world as they explored the outer limits of their sexuality. This charged relationship would "awaken" Fritz, but also cause him intense internal struggles, as he attempted to manage all of the intense feelings within. Thus, he decided to go into psychoanalytic treatment, the fad of the time. Perls found Karen Horney, a well-known psychoanalyst who eventually broke away from Freud and developed her own analytical theory. This forage into analysis would be the impetus for Perls to become an analyst himself and eventually to develop his own theory.

As the result of Perls's analysis with Horney, he decided to leave Lucy and move to Frankfurt, where many well-known **existentialists** like Martin Buber and Paul Tillich talked about and published their ideas. In addition, it was here that Kurt Goldstein, who was doing research on brain injury, proposed new hypotheses about how individuals perceive the world, which he called **Gestalt psychology**. Although it was a far cry from what would eventually become Gestalt therapy, Perls borrowed the name "Gestalt" for his theory. Frankfurt was also the place where Perls met Lore ("Laura") Posner, whom he would eventually wed. Despite being much younger than Perls, she had much to offer him. Being a graduate student of Gestalt psychology and having studied many of the famous existentialists and **phenomenologists**, she would influence some of Perls's ideas (Clarkson & Mackewn, 1993). However, coming from a refined family that found Fritz somewhat of a bohemian, her parents initially discouraged their relationship. Despite her family's misgivings, they married in 1929.

Meanwhile, Perls continued to undergo his own psychoanalysis, and eventually started to practice psychoanalysis under supervision. His psychoanalytic work helped him coalesce his ideas on how instincts impact the person, the meanings that dreams bring, the power of the unconscious, and the importance of what he called "**shouldisms**" in his life. Shouldism, in analytic terms, was related to the moralistic superego, and would later become an important part of Perls's concept of "**topdog**," where he believed a part of self splits off and tries to take charge of other parts of the self. Although some of his theory was influenced by psychoanalysis, Perls never really felt comfortable with this approach, and after years of practicing it, he drifted toward Wilhelm Reich, who was considered a radical psychoanalyst at the time. Reich taught Perls about "**body armor,**" or the process in which the body holds in feelings. This would greatly affect Perls's ideas about the importance of focusing on nonverbal behaviors in therapy.

During the early 1930s, Perls became active in the anti-Nazi movement in Germany. However, increasing anti-Semitism would leave Perls, his wife, and his new baby in desperate straits. Moving constantly to avoid the Nazis, Perls and his family eventually ended up in Holland, and then South Africa. There, with the help of the famous analyst Ernest Jones, Perls secured a position.

Relocating to South Africa proved to be a good move for Perls as he and Laura quickly established the country's first psychoanalytic training institute. The couple thrived monetarily. However, emotionally, this was not the case. The couple had two children, Renate and Steve, but Perls was only involved with the children in a cursory way. In addition, Perls's wandering eye left little passion for the marriage. Meanwhile, Perls began to read *Holism and Evolution* (Smuts, 1926), a book written by the then–prime minister of South Africa. This book would greatly influence Perls, and he began to incorporate holistic concepts into his own theory. Excited about his ideas and how they might affect analytical therapy, Perls went to Europe to present some of his thoughts to Freud and others at a psychoanalytic conference. However, at the conference, Perls was quickly dismissed for his radical ideas. Ironically, it was this very denunciation that led him to press forward and develop his own theory.

The early 1940s saw Perls publish his first book on this theory: *Ego, Hunger, and Aggression* (Perls, 1942/1947). This book challenged many of Freud's assumptions, and asserted such ideas as the importance of hunger as a motivating force and the de-emphasis of the sex drive; focusing on how the present carries unresolved conflicts in contrast to spending an endless amount of time dredging up the past; the importance of polarities or different parts of self in understanding the person; the importance of understanding how the body takes in and manifests experiences; de-emphasizing transference because it means having to understand the early origins of experiences rather than dealing in the "now" with their results; and creating a real relationship between therapist and client in order to break down delusions and myths that clients have about their therapists (in contrast to the "anonymity" in psychoanalysis).

During World War II, to support the war effort against the Nazis, Perls joined the English army as a medical officer. When the war ended, he became increasingly disgusted by the growing discrimination against the South African blacks. It was then that he decided to leave South Africa for New York City. Leaving his family, Perls left for New York and, with the help of the neo-Freudian Eric Fromm, established a practice with other well-known neo-Freudians. This professional group, and Perls in particular, was attempting to bridge the gap between the "therapist" and the "person." Increasingly, Perls tried to be the same "real" person in both settings. This led to Perls's experimenting with being blatantly honest with people, saying exactly what he thought, sometimes at inopportune times. It also led to increased sexual experimentation that ran the gamut from heterosexuality to bisexuality to homosexuality. In fact, Perls even challenged the taboo of having sexual encounters with clients, as he attempted to break the walls down between the client and patient. Although in today's world, Perls would have quickly lost his license, it was a different era, and Perls was on the cutting edge and experimenting with a new therapy.

As Perls increasingly settled into his own theory, he incorporated concepts from other ideas and philosophies, such as **psychodrama** (Clarkson & Mackewn, 1993). This therapeutic technique, developed by Jacob Moreno, had a client in a group setting describe his or her family dynamics and then had group participants role-play various family members. Psychodrama influenced Perls's ideas about the importance of role-playing aspects of oneself, others, and parts of one's dreams during a session. Around the same time, Perls began to show some interest in Eastern philosophy, especially **Zen Buddhism** and its concept of **mindfulness**, which to Perls seemed similar to the importance he placed on awareness of the now (Clarkson & Mackewn, 1993). Perls was also greatly influenced by Paul Goodman's ideas about the importance of breaking down traditional social mores and psychological assumptions, if a person is to truly reinvent oneself and establish a new kind of extended community. In fact, Perls, Goodman, and Ralph Hefferline would soon write *Gestalt Therapy*, one of the first definitive books on Perls's theory (Perls, Hefferline, & Goodman, 1951). Soon after the book was published, he and Laura opened the **Gestalt Institute of New York**.

Although the Gestalt Institute of New York did well, he and Laura were in an emotional tailspin. No longer could Laura take her husband's continued absence and sexual relationships with others. In the late 1950s, the two of them separated. Soon after their separation, having health problems, Perls left for the better weather in Miami to open a new practice. In this practice, Perls, who was in his mid-sixties, met a 32-year-old client named Marty Fromm. Over the next few years, the two of them would have a relationship of "realness" in which they would often be blatantly honest with one another, participate in sexual experimentation, and use "mind-expanding" drugs such as LSD. It was now the '60s, and Perls was continuing to experiment with new ways of doing therapy and breaking down boundaries. For instance, he continued to date Marty and treat her as a client in group therapy. It was in the group that Marty met and began to date Peter, another of Perls's clients. It was at this point that Perls decided to leave for California and asked Marty to choose between him and Peter. Marty stayed with the much younger Peter.

Perls had been offered a position as a long-term consultant to psychiatry residents at Mendocino State Hospital, and in some ways, his move to California was probably a relief from the intensity of his relationship with Marty. Although the drug scene had not fully erupted in California, it had for Perls, and he was taking LSD almost daily. Despite his drug use, health problems, and narcissistic tendencies, he managed himself fairly well. By this time, his reputation preceded him, with some viewing him as an aging narcissist and others seeing him as a seductive guru. As the 1960s rolled in, an increasing number of humanistically oriented therapies became more popular. The **Esalen Institute**, a retreat house on the coast of California, soon became known for its humanistically based workshops. Perls, who had become increasingly existentially/humanistically based, would find a home there. Perls moved to Esalen, where he spent most of his remaining years, although the last year of his life he spent developing the **Gestalt Institute of Canada**. At the Canadian institute, Perls is said to have found inner peace. In 1969, some of Perls's tape-recorded work with clients was

---

B o x 6.1   Stories of the Great Therapists

If you would like to hear some stories about Fritz Perls and Laura Perls, click on the link for "Fritz Perls" at the "Stories of the Great Therapists" Web site: http://www.odu.edu/sgt

---

edited and published in *Gestalt Therapy Verbatim* (Perls, 1969a). Also in this year, *In and Out of the Garbage Pail* was published, which, through Perls's poetry and prose, offered a candid view of Perls and others (Perls, 1969b).

Although in his later years Perls struggled with ongoing health problems, including heart irregularities, he nevertheless traveled much and conducted workshops. In 1970, while in Chicago to conduct one of his workshops, Perls became seriously ill with a high fever. While at the hospital, he reached out to Laura, who was in New York, and she came to his bedside. After exploratory abdominal surgery, Perls, as rambunctious as ever, had the following encounter with a nurse:

> At about nine o'clock that evening, he kind of half got up with all this paraphernalia attached. The nurse said, "Dr. Perls. You'll have to lie down." He sort of went back down and then almost sat up and swung his legs out a bit. Again she said, "You must lie down."
>
> He looked her right in the eye and he said, "Don't tell me what to do," fell back, and died. (Shepard, 1975, p. 192)

There is little question that Perls lived like he died: narcissistic, rambunctious, and honest to the end. Despite, or perhaps because of, Perls's willingness to experiment and stretch boundaries, he developed a new and vital therapy. Although today's Gestalt therapists are as careful about boundaries as all other therapists, the essence of Perls's theory and the many techniques conceived by him remain true to his original ideas (see Box 6.1).

VIEW OF HUMAN NATURE

Perls believed that the infant is **born neither good nor bad**, and with a capacity to embody an infinite number of personality dimensions. And he suggested that these dimensions come in pairs, each comprised of polar opposites. Where there is good, there is bad; the extrovert has an introverted side; and the angry person has a loving side. How these opposites are shown is one crucial piece of Gestalt's work, because if one aspect of the person is being expressed, its opposite is hiding somewhere, and if not expressed, the body is taking up energy trying to keep it out of awareness.

Grounded in the humanistic tradition of **existentialism** and **phenomenology**, Gestalt therapy posits that each individual's reality is based on his or her experience and that each person can make choices throughout life that can result in creating a new way of being in the world—a new reality. Humanistic psychologists are also steeped in **holism**. Thus, Perls, like many other humanistic psychologists, did not believe in the reductionistic theories of Freud, who dissected the person into the id, ego, and superego, or the micro lens of the experimental psychologists, who attempted to understand the individual relative to isolated aspects of behavior. Instead, he argued that the mind, body, and soul operate in unison; they cannot be separated. The evolving self is the result of how the whole being reacts to familial, social, and cultural influences. This is why Perls borrowed the term "gestalt" from the Gestalt psychologists, which means: "The properties of the whole are always different and more than the sum of its parts." Most likely, Perls would say that today's modern-day cognitive and behavioral therapists are misguided in their attempts to focus on minute aspects of behavior or cognitions.

Most Gestalt therapists believe that from the moment one is born, the individual is in a constant state of self-regulation through a process of need-identification and need-fulfillment. Some of the innumerable examples of this include the newborn infant who seeks to suckle the breast, the playful child who seeks attention, the budding adolescent who longs for peer relationships, and the adult who seeks out work and life fulfillment. An individual's pressing need dictates his or her perceptual field (what the person sees), or, as Gestalt therapists state, individual is only aware of the need that is in the "**foreground.**" Imagine watching a movie about your life. With some exceptions for "rest," each frame of the movie is reflective of a specific need that you are somehow trying to fulfill at that moment in your life. Because needs can vary dramatically, this theory contrasts with the psychoanalytic view, which suggests that a limited number of instincts drive behavior (e.g., hunger, thirst, survival, sex, aggression), or the Maslowian (humanistic) idea that basic needs (e.g., hunger, thirst) are addressed prior to higher-order needs (love and belonging, self-esteem).

> You can believe in two instincts … or you can believe in two million instincts, or unfinished situations, like I like to do. I believe that our organism is so complicated, that every time something happens to it, is experienced by it, we are thrown out of balance and at each moment we have to regain this balance. (Perls, 1978, p. 58)

For the Gestalt therapist, how the individual makes **contact** with his or her environment in an attempt to satisfy needs is reflective of the individual's way of being in the world and determines **the "self"** (Perls, Hefferline, & Goodman, 1951; Polster & Polster, 1973). The healthy individual has a semi-permeable boundary that allows the individual to maintain a sense of self, while also allowing material from the environment to be engulfed, "chewed," and taken in as it becomes assimilated (Yonteff, 1976). This person has a constant free-flowing exchange between self and "other" (all that is outside of self), and this exchange causes the self to be constantly changing; as needs are met, self changes. In fact, Perls viewed the changing self as synonymous with what he called the "**ego boundary;**" that is, as the self interacts with the environment and changes, so does the boundary that identifies who the person is and how the person sees himself or herself (Perls, 1969a). For instance, when "falling in love," the boundary extends out and includes the essence of the other person. At that moment, the person's sense of self, indeed the person's ego, has changed.

Satisfaction of needs is a natural process, and Gestalt therapists believe that individuals are driven to have their needs completed or finished. However, needs can be thwarted by such things as parental shoulds, social and cultural dictates, and peer norms. Such influences result in the development of mechanisms that resist the experience of that pressing need. These mechanisms yield individuals who are fake, incongruent, false to their nature, and "playing" at being a self-created image, all in an effort to avoid the experience of the need. Such false behaviors result in **impasses** or **blockages** that prevent experiencing and are revealed through dysfunctional and neurotic behaviors, which are called "**unfinished business**" by Gestalt therapists. Breaking free from these influences and the resulting impasses and dealing with one's unfinished business is one of the goals of Gestalt therapy. Successfully doing so allows individuals to live more congruent or authentic lives in which they are fully in touch with themselves and are able to have open and honest communication with others.

Because Gestalt theorists believe we can choose to experience ourselves fully and free ourselves from our impasses and blockages, the Gestalt approach is considered **anti-deterministic**. In fact, one of the greatest contributions of Gestalt therapy is that it circumvented the years of therapy that was needed in psychoanalysis to get to the raw, unconscious, hidden parts of self. Whereas psychoanalysts believed defense mechanisms should be dealt with gingerly because of their importance in maintaining ego integrity, Gestalt and related therapies viewed defenses as something which one should break free of in an effort to fully experience the present and become sane (Hart, Corriere, & Binder, 1975):

> … We feel that each person who is not completely feeling himself and sharing that level of feeling with those around him is reasonably insane. (p. 120) … Craziness or disorder allows a person to put up with almost anything—that was the original function of each disorder. But a sane person values his feelings and does not want even one moment of disorder to engulf him. (p. 375)

Gestalt therapists believe that the ultimate way of living is allowing oneself to access all of what is available to one's experience. Since unfinished business prevents a person from experiencing oneself fully, one goal of Gestalt therapy is to help the client once again experience the "now." And experiencing fully is the basis for seeing one's reality clearly. In fact, one of Perls's famous quotations is, "To me, nothing exists except the now. Now = experience = awareness = reality. The past is no more and the future not yet. Only the now exists" (Perls, 1970, p. 14).

Using a variety of techniques that help clients access all of their current feelings, thoughts, and experiences, clients increasingly experience the "now" and can quickly identify and understand their blockages, impasses, and work on their unfinished business. After specific unfinished business is worked through, it leaves the foreground and allows room for new issues to arise. This process is akin to the peeling-of-an-onion metaphor: "We can open one door at a time and peel off one layer of the onion at a time. Each layer is part of the neurosis …" (Perls, 1973, p. 84). For instance, a client who is angry at her spouse may avoid her rage by eating too much (stuffing down feelings), working excessively, staying away from home, extensively playing with her children, and so forth. As the therapist works toward helping the client experience her anger, she is likely to begin to have associations as to why she has avoided her anger (her unfinished business). For example, she may be avoiding anger because her parents told her that anger is not "ladylike." For her, the way to "act" has superseded the way she actually feels. From this example, one can see how the Gestalt therapist accentuates the present, but ends up examining issues from the past which will deeply affect how one makes choices in the future (Polster & Polster, 1999). In this sense, there is a kind of seamlessness between present, past, and future.

Developmentally, Gestalt therapists believe that people move from **environmental support** to **self-support** as they grow. Thus, the young child needs to rely on others to survive and feel whole. However, as the child grows, he or she increasingly relies on self to find ways of meeting his or her needs. Healthy people have learned how to be self-supportive, although not socially isolated, for relationships are basic to existence. An unhealthy person, however, relies and depends on others for his or her sense of self, and when things go wrong, will tend to blame others because his or her self is not seen as separate from others. It is never "I" who takes responsibility, because "I" is not separate from "them" or "it." And, like the spouse who evaded her anger, such individuals do not take ownership of their feelings. One can see why, for Gestalt therapists, examining whether a client is taking responsibility for his or her feelings and experiences is critical.

As you might guess from the view of human nature, the goal of Gestalt therapy is to help the client move from a state of little awareness of self, an inability to effectively respond to needs, and difficulty in taking responsibility to a healthy state where the individual is aware of his or her needs, is able to seamlessly respond to them in the moment, and can take responsibility for feelings, thoughts, and actions. Table 6.1 compares some of the qualities of the healthy and unhealthy person based on this understanding of the person.

KEY CONCEPTS

Holism

> From the Gestalt Therapy orientation, reductionistic approaches deny too much. They deny the physical in order to see the mental; they deny the internal to look at the external, the obvious to observe the hidden. (Van De Riet, Korb, & Gorrell, 1980, p. 10)

Although many humanistic psychologists have spoken about **holism**, Perls, more than most, highlighted holism as central to his theory. From Perls's point of view, holism means that all aspects of the individual are connected. And it also means that there is an intricate connection between the person and that which is outside of the person (family, community, world, and universe). Thus, the spiritual, mental, physiological, and psychological parts of the person are inseparable and also connected to external forces. There can be no split between the body and the mind, as so many modern-day therapists continue to suggest. Thus, when a person is hungry, he or she experiences the hunger, thinks about the hunger, has a bodily

T A B L E 6.1   **Gestalt View of the Healthy and Unhealthy Person**

Healthy Person	Unhealthy Person
1. Able to experience the "now."	1. Unable to experience the present.
2. Has clear perceptions about what needs are pressing and is able to differentiate those needs from all else that is in the background.	2. Unable to distinguish what needs are pressing on the person. Confused about what is "foreground" and "background."
3. Has clarity of bodily sensations and how they are related to the pressing needs at the moment.	3. Out of touch with bodily sensations that signal need-fulfillment.
4. Able to experience, state, and deal with needs as they arise; allows for the need with the next-highest demand to be addressed.	4. Unable to experience, express, and subsequently address needs.
5. Has a sense of openness and realness.	5. Closed off, fake, and phony.
6. Body language is congruent with how the individual responds to the world.	6. Body language does not match feelings and experiences.
7. Self-supportive and able to take responsibility for self and actions.	7. Uses environmental support and does not take responsibility for self and actions.
8. Has a sense of how one's actions affects others and the world.	8. Incapable of seeing how self affects others. Selfish and narcissistic.
9. Accepts and integrates all aspects of self, including polar opposites.	9. Denies aspects of self, particularly those that are seen as "bad" or "evil."
10. Accepts others in the world with their unique ways of understanding human nature.	10. Has a desire to have others see the world in the same manner that he/she sees the world.
11. Able to accept differences.	11. Unable to accept differences.

reaction to the hunger, and responds emotionally to the hunger. And perhaps the hunger of one person reverberates with those around him and her, and in the community, and in the world. And, in contrast to the causal thinking that has invaded the way many therapists conceptualize clients, Perls suggested that all parts of the person responds in unison. So, it is not irrational thoughts that cause negative consequences, or specific reinforcement contingencies that lead to dysfunctional behaviors, or the id that is impinging on the ego. Therapists who believe in this manner are artificially creating a wall between separate parts of the self, say Gestalt therapists.

Figure/Ground

Drawing from the school of Gestalt psychology, Perls molded part of his theory around their concept of **figure/ground**. The Gestalt psychologists, who had studied perception, had discovered that we tend to perceive what is in the **foreground** of experience, and conversely, tend not to recognize what is in the background.

FIGURE 6.1 Figure/Ground

Artist M. C. Escher played with figure/ground. Perceptions change whether looking at the light or dark figures.

They also noticed that one can learn how to "switch" or "flip" one's experience. For instance, in Figure 6.1, one can readily learn to flip either the white or the dark figure into the foreground. Perls extended this understanding to other kinds of human experience, stressing that when a need emerges, that need takes precedence over other needs, and moves into the foreground. As a need in the foreground becomes satisfied, it will move into the background and a new need will emerge. Perls went on to say that some needs become blocked and result in unfinished business in the sense that a blocked need prevents the individual from fully experiencing and results in individuals' living phony lives. For instance, an individual who is taught by his parents not to express his need for love develops ways of avoiding this need. The person's being puts energy into *not* experiencing this need. This energy is directed into the body and often finds its way out in nonverbal behaviors. The person unconsciously attempts to keep this unfinished business out of the foreground—to hide it in the background.

Polarities

Closely related to the concept of figure/ground are Perls's thoughts on **polarities** within the person. Perls believed that dimensions of self come in pairs and that we have an infinite number of dimensions (Polster & Polster, 1973, 1999). However, we often acknowledge and allow to come into the foreground the part of

---

B o x 6.2   Jill's Angry Side

Read or watch Dr. Neukrug's work with Jill and consider how much easier it is for Jill to accept her loving feelings for her mother and deny her angry feelings. Also reflect on how this very anger must be embraced if she is to work through her unfinished business with her mother.

You can read this session by going to www. cengage.com/counseling/neukrug/CTP1e and click "student downloads." Or your instructor may show this session in class with the DVD that accompanies his or her copy of the text.

---

ourselves with which we feel comfortable, while the opposite part hides away, out of awareness. Denying this hidden part is an unnecessary expenditure of pent-up energy, say the Gestaltists. For instance, if I know the "good" part of myself, and insist there is no "bad" part of me, I am expending energy keeping the "bad" part of me out of my awareness. One goal of therapy is to reach the hidden parts of self and to integrate those parts into one's personality style. Consider the implications this has for the "loving and nurturing" nunlike woman who denies her devilish side, or the "evil" rapist who has denied his empathy and goodness (see Box 6.2). From this perspective, you can see why Perls viewed people as neither good nor bad—they embody it all.

One pair of opposites that Perls popularized was the "topdog/underdog" polarity. The **topdog**, said Perls, is the part of self that is bossy and the "master," while the **underdog** is passive, slavelike, and inept. Perls would often have clients play out these two distinct aspects of self in an effort to show clients how one aspect has taken over and has created an imbalance within self as well as in the client's interpersonal relationships. Finding a balance between the two can make for more satisfying relationships with others where there is more of a give and take.

Contact

Contact defines the boundary between self and other, whether it be an object or a person. It is our lifeblood, as we cannot exist unless we make contact, and how we make contact determines how healthy we are. Contact with an object generally involves our sensory organs (e.g., I'm hungry; I touch some food and pick it up and eat it). With people, contact is a function of the ability to experience the other fully. It is, as Martin Buber (1958) noted, related to the **I–Thou** relationship.

Contact is directly related to what Perls called our **ego boundary**, or the constantly changing point where I "meet" other people and objects and discriminate me from "other" (Polster & Polster, 1973). When contacting a person or an object, I am identifying with it and it becomes part of my self. When I meet the "other" and experience little difference between myself and the other (e.g., when one is "in love"), it is called **confluence**. Contact disturbances occur when I must have "you" in "me" all the time (e.g., extreme confluence—the relentless lover whose boundaries are few), or when I am so blocked that I never want to experience "you" at all (extreme lack of contact—the narcissist who objectifies). One of the main functions of the Gestalt therapist is to help the person understand how his or her blockages (unfinished business) prevent need-satisfaction and result in an inability to meet another person fully.

Finally, Perls also believed that one may be able to transcend ego functioning and have no sense of self. Similar to certain Zen meditative states, transcending the ego is considered a spiritual state by those who believe that ego functioning binds us to a known reality. Some consider this to be the highest state of spiritual awakening.

Need-Satisfaction Cycle

Perls identified a number of stages that illuminate the process of satisfying a need (Clarkson, 2004; Perls et al., 1951). For instance, if we started at what Perls called the "**zero point**" or **withdrawal** stage, we would witness a person who is calm and experiencing is minimal. At some point after this restful period, the individual experiences a new **sensation** as a "figure" arises out of the background (e.g., as I'm walking down the street, I smell a pie cooking—this becomes my foreground). Next, the individual gains an increasing **awareness** of a need that is closely related to the sensation (I realize I'm hungry). The individual then moves into the **mobilization** phase, where plans are tentatively made to address the emerging need (I look around, find the bakery where the smell is coming from and realize I can go buy a pie). **Action** is the next step, where the individual takes steps to address the need (I walk over to the bakery). Then, through our sensory and motor functions (sensing, touching, moving, hearing, feeling) we make **contact** with the object that will meet our need (I buy the pie, hold it, and ready myself to eat it). After contact is made, **satisfaction** is found in taking in the object (Yes, that does taste yummy!). Finally, we find ourselves back in **withdrawal** (the zero point), where the individual moves back into a state of calm (see Figure 6.2). The body is at rest, and we no longer need to strive to attain something, whether it is food, sexual excitement, an intellectual pursuit, or so forth. In fact, Perls suggested that this zero point was similar to certain meditative states and that we should try to extend this zero point to experience what he called "the void." This tranquil and vacuous place is beyond need, and gives the individual a sense of nothingness and simultaneously a sense of connection to the universe.

Perls saw this cycle as being ongoing and seamless. For instance, consider the endless needs you have during the day, including such needs as hunger, sexual feelings, need to be close to a significant other, need to accomplish a work task, and on and on. There is an ongoing ocean of needs to which we attend and try to meet in some fashion. Not meeting a need leads one to feel unfinished. Not having met a significant need from the past yields significant unfinished business, which we carry around with us in the present and which affects our relationships in some manner.

Unfinished Business

Unfinished business is the negative impact of past unresolved issues on current day functioning. It is the result of the incompletion of a need attainment that leaves the individual feeling unresolved and desirous of having the gestalt completed

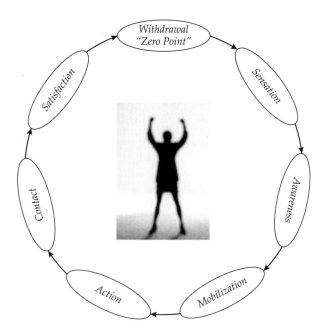

FIGURE 6.2 Need-Satisfaction Cycle

(the need met). Sometimes, the lack of completion is only temporary and can be resolved in a relatively short amount of time. For instance, I recently became quite upset about a statement a colleague of mine made about me in mixed company at work. I did not talk to her about my anger, but it remained in my awareness. A week later, I sat down with her and told her about my anger. We talked about it and resolved it.

Other times, the lack of completion of a need impinges on a person for long periods of time. In these cases, the individual uses one or more of a number of mechanisms to push the desire for need completion out of awareness. The resulting lack of awareness is the equivalent of what others have called "the unconscious" (Yonteff, 1976). When this occurs, the individual's whole being spends energy on ensuring that the need is not met, which results in a neurotic lifestyle. Such behavior is generally the result of parental shoulds or societal and cultural injunctions that are contrary to need-fulfillment. As an example, if a client was taught by his parents that he should "not cry" at the loss of a loved one, then when a significant loss occurs, this child's "whole" being goes into a non-crying mode. His thoughts tell him he should not cry, his emotions are cut off, his body tenses up to keep up the façade, and his tear ducts become blocked. His whole being is affected, and he does not allow himself to experience the grief. This manner of responding becomes his unfinished business and can be held in his body for years. And, when faced with similar situations in the future, he responds similarly. Years later, this individual may find himself in therapy, and as he peels away the layers of phoniness that are a product of his attempt to not experience his grief-associated sadness, he will again be faced with the experience of the early loss and have a renewed opportunity to experience it fully. This time, in the safety of the therapist's office, he can be real and work it through—complete the Gestalt. This resolution makes him whole again.

Closure

As with the concept of figure/ground discussed earlier, Perls also borrowed the idea of **closure** from researchers in the field of Gestalt psychology, who were studying how the brain has a tendency to want to complete (close) perceptions. As an example, look at the drawings in Figure 6.3. The Gestalt psychologists used such figures to show how there was a natural tendency for us to complete the figures. Most people have little or no trouble recognizing the top-left and bottom-right figures (Street, 1931). The bottom-left and top-right figures are more difficult to recognize—and yet we struggle to do so, to complete the figures. Similarly, think about how many hours of fun children have completing the "connect the dot" pictures—as if they inherently need to find out what the drawing is. Perls, however, extended the Gestalt psychology ideas by suggesting that the need for completion, or the desire to find wholeness, was inherent in other aspects of our being. Thus, whenever we have blockages that result in unfinished business and neurotic symptoms that prevent us from experiencing ourselves fully, the individual

F I G U R E 6.3 Gestalt Completion Test

Street, R. F. (1931). A *Gestalt completion test*. New York: Columbia University. pp. 43, 49, 55, 57.

B o x 6.3   Closure and Resolving Unfinished Business

Consider, for instance, the individual who at 10 years old lost his father to heart disease. Following his father's death, significant others told him he'd better take care of himself, otherwise he too might die an early death. Hearing these concerns, he "introjected" these values, or took them in whole, without processing them. As a result, throughout his life, he became obsessed with health, to the point where he rarely enjoyed himself. He obsessively washed his hands. He did not enjoy eating, as he was always watching what he took into his body and ate only "healthy" foods. He worked out compulsively and became an ultra-marathoner. Then, he went into therapy. His unfinished feelings about the loss of his father along with the introjected values from significant others had become directed toward a regime of health, yet he was unaware of this. As he continued in therapy, he realized the sadness that he still held about the loss of his father and also realized that he often listened to the introjected voices that told him to be healthy. He slowly began to realize that he did not listen to his own inner voice about how to address the needs of his body. Acknowledging this in therapy, his body responded by "letting go," and he slowly began to feel "free" again. Soon, he began to let go of his obsession to be healthy as he began to realizes that being healthy is "good" but being obsessed about health is not.

---

has an inherent need to once again become whole; that is, to take himself or herself back to a more normal state (see Box 6.3).

Resistances or Blockages to Experience

The introjector does as others would like him to do, the projector does unto others what he accuses others of doing to him, the man in pathological confluence doesn't know who is doing what to whom, and the retroflector does to himself what he would like to do to others. (Perls, 1973, pp. 40–41)

Perls believed that dictates or injunctions from significant others can result in individuals' responding in ways that are not natural or true to self and that prevent the individual from adequately meeting a need. Similar to the concept of defense mechanisms, Perls and others suggested that in response to these injunctions, an individual might develop a number of **resistances** or **blockages** to experiences that prevent that person from experiencing a need that he or she had been told to avoid (Enright, 1970; Latner, 1992; Perls, 1942/1947; Perls et al., 1951; Perls, 1973). For instance, the person who was brought up in a puritanical home might develop blockages to experiencing his or her sexual feelings. By understanding these resistances, the Gestalt therapist can actively focus on these mechanisms, knowing that they are being used to avoid unresolved issues (e.g., "do not feel sexual" injunction). Some of the more common resistances or blockages include: **introjection**, **projection**, **retroflection**, **desensitization**, **deflection**, **egotism**, and **confluence**.

Introjection involves the "swallowing whole" of the values of significant others without ever really examining whether one also holds those values. This process results in a person responding in ways congruent to the values one is being asked to adhere to, but incongruent to how one actually feels. Sometimes, the therapist can see the introjection of certain values through the client's nonverbal behaviors.

It's as if the client is saying one thing, but really believes in something else. In this case, the whole body responds in a restrictive manner to prevent awareness of the fact that the individual really does not believe what he or she is saying. Ask the person if he or she believes in that value, and the answer would be "yes." However, look at the person, and his or her body says "no." Try acting "as if" you believe in something you don't for one day, and see how much energy that takes.

> ... [T]he man who introjects never gets a chance to develop his own personality, because he is so busy holding down the foreign bodies lodged in his system. (Perls, 1973, p. 34)

Projection occurs when an individual sees attributes in others that are, in fact, his or her own. This "disowning" of a part of self allows the individual to delude himself or herself into believing that he or she does not have that quality. If I see others as being "lustful," and criticize them for it, I do not have to own up to my own sexual feelings. Such a process prevents me from owning a part of myself, and I end up living as a "phony," as Perls liked to say.

Retroflection, which is similar to repression and inhibition, is the holding back of an impulse intended toward others and substituting it with another one toward self. On the one hand, the impulse is attempting to show itself—on the other hand, it is held back by the body. Thus, when I encounter a "friend" with whom I have ongoing anger issues, my body tenses up as I try *not* to show the person my anger. Instead, my friend might see a tense jaw, or a clenched fist, or even a tic as I attempt to withhold the impulse. Or, as I listen to the sad news about my sibling's chronic illness, my eyes start to moisten, but I hold back my tears and my eyelids start to quiver because I am not "allowed" to cry.

Desensitization is the absolute dulling or numbing of one's senses in an effort not to experience, and can be contrasted with the letting out and then holding back found in retroflection. It is the friend you have who never seems to show emotion, or the calm boss you have who seems to be totally in control all the time.

Deflection is the psychological process of finding ways of avoiding contact with another person by redirecting the potential for contact. For instance, one may look away, laugh or talk a great deal, use intellectual language, be overly polite or overly rude, change topics frequently, and so forth. A technique which we all have used at times, deflection, allows us to avoid the reality of the moment. For instance, sometimes, when my wife notices that we are not getting along and wants to make contact with me, she might simply state, "I'm sensing that there's something going on with you because it doesn't seem like you're wanting to be close." Often, she is right, and rather than dealing directly with the real reasons, I change the subject, or state that things are really busy at work (when they're not—I'm being a "phony"), or state that "I'm tired and not getting enough sleep." All of these are ways that I've "deflected" her accurate observation.

Egotism is the overinvolvement with self that prevents real contact with others. With egotism, there is a meeting of two people; however, due to the self-absorbed attitude of one of the individuals, actual contact is never really achieved. You have certainly known of people who talk so much that they have "tuned you out." Start talking to them about a serious matter, and they endlessly talk about themselves, or they tell you their opinion without listening to your responses. It's as if they live in a world of their own. It seems that they do not have the ability to have a give-and-take with another person. Egotism protects the person from experiencing; and it is a way of preventing the person from truly meeting another. For instance, a woman who was molested as a child could take on an egotistic attitude around men because of her fear of making contact with men. In this case, a horrible event earlier in her life has resulted in the creation of a resistance toward contact with men.

Confluence is the blurring or dissolving of boundaries between people that results in a loss of identity and the inability to clearly define self. Although we are all born into a state of confluence (our selves are indistinguishable from our parents' selves), as we grow, we increasingly develop a sense of "I" as separate from "you." With confluence, certain words and phrases are used to suggest that others are included in one's experience or assumptions about the world. It is the boyfriend who states, "Come on, I know you'll love this movie," or the mother who refuses to see her teenage daughter's emerging sexuality, and says, "I'm glad you're not like some of those kids at you're school," or the colleague who states at a meeting, "I know there are others here who feel the same way that I do." Isadore From, a colleague of Perls, stated that when individuals make assumptions about what others "know," they are often avoiding taking personal ownership for a belief and are trying to pull others into their belief system. Such statements prevent individuals from experiencing their differences, differences that are an important aspect of identity development (Miller, 1996).

THERAPEUTIC TECHNIQUES

Depending on the therapist's personality style, there are a number of commonly used techniques that most Gestalt therapists employ, such as **empathy**, **being directive**, **being confrontational**, **avoiding intellectualizations**, **focusing on noverbal behaviors**, and **experimentation**. In addition, Gestalt therapy is known to use a wide range of specialized techniques to assist the client to increase his or her awareness and to understand the kinds of unfinished business that have impinged on the client's life and have prevented him or her from making contact with others. Some of the many specialized techniques identified over the years include **using "now" language, I–Thou communication, I–It language, experiencing the present, not gossiping, making statements out of questions, the dialogue game and empty chair technique, "I take responsibility for that," playing the projection, the exaggeration technique, feeding the client a sentence, "I have a secret," making the rounds, dream work**, and **group work** (Clarkson & Mackewn, 1993; Latner, 1992; Levitzky & Perls, 1970; Polster & Polster, 1973; Van De Riet et al., 1980).

Commonly Used Techniques

Empathy.   Because Gestalt therapy is based on existentialism and phenomenology, empathy is an important technique to use if the therapist wants to build a relationship

---

B o x 6.4   Gestalt Therapy Today

When watching Perls's work, there is little doubt that he was a masterful therapist much of the time. On the other hand, he could often be seen using heavy-handed confrontation and, as noted in his biography, even crossing boundaries with clients. Unfortunately, students sometimes assume that Gestalt therapy *is* the way that Perls practiced the approach. This is not the case, and an effective Gestalt therapist today is able to balance direction and confrontation in ways that gently push the client to greater awareness.

---

and begin to understand the client's perspective of the world. Thus, many Gestalt therapists will integrate the use of this technique into their repertoire of skills, especially when building the therapeutic alliance. However, most Gestalt therapists believe that in the long run, the nearly exclusive use of empathy, as proposed by person-centered therapists, tends to slow the therapeutic process down, and they will therefore employ more active and directive approaches as sessions continue.

Being Directive.   As Gestalt therapists feel increasingly comfortable with the client and as the relationship builds, they will embrace a more directive style. Direction generally is used by the therapist when picking a specialized technique and asking the client to participate in the proposed activity.

Being Confrontational.   Whereas being directive has to do with asking a client to participate in a specialized technique, confrontation is used when the therapist tells the client that he or she is preventing self from experiencing, being manipulative, or acting like a phony in some way. Perls was particularly adept at this, although some also saw this as his fatal flaw, as he would often tenaciously challenge clients by telling them they were hiding, acting like babies, being phony, and not being real (see Box 6.4). Therapists today are less likely to be this confrontational, although challenging a client is still an important tool for some therapists.

Avoiding Intellectualizations.   Many clients have an enormous capacity to intellectualize their lives away, and many of the Gestalt techniques are geared toward avoiding this pitfall. Thus, Perls warned against the use of "why questions" or other techniques that "produce only pat answers, defensiveness, rationalizations, excuses, and the delusion that an event can be explained by a single cause" (Perls, 1973, p. 76). Instead, Perls encouraged therapists to use "how" and "what" questions as they actively push the client toward experiencing themselves (e.g., "How does that feel?" or, "What are you experiencing now?"). Also, therapists are encouraged to direct clients to "show the therapist" how an experience might look by acting it out in the office or by demonstrating a conversation or interaction in the office. For instance, rather than the client's telling the therapist how sad it would be if a client broke up with his lover, the therapist might say, "Okay, have a conversation with your lover, right here, right now."

Focusing on Nonverbal Behaviors.   Influenced by the work of Wilhem Reich, Perls believed that our unfinished business is housed in our bodies. Thus, he suggested, our nonverbal behaviors hold the key to understanding issues that remain unresolved. By focusing on and having clients exaggerate nonverbal behaviors, he believed, the Gestalt therapist can bring out these unresolved conflicts. Thus, a woman who is constantly smiling is asked to smile more; as she does, she realizes she is smiling in an effort to always show the world a "happy face." She quickly realizes that she was taught by her parents to always show the good side of life and not express sadness. Thus, the smile helped to hide her deep sadness concerning failed relationships with her significant others in her life. Also, individuals are sometimes asked to "be" the nonverbal behavior. For instance, a person who is tapping his foot is asked to "be the foot" and to talk as if he is the foot. As he talks, he begins to say, "I'm trying to crush my father for the way he treated me."

Experimentation.   Although most, if not all, of the specialized techniques you are about to read are experiments in experiencing greater depths of self, Gestalt therapists generally feel free to create new techniques within the therapeutic setting with the emphasis being to help the client deepen his or her understanding of self and widening his or her awareness. In fact, for many Gestalt therapists, this is viewed as the creative aspect of Gestalt therapy, as they spontaneously develop new ways to confront the client's particular resistances.

Specialized Techniques

Using "Now" Language.   Clients can easily move away from their experience by using "then and there" language or by talking "about" something that occurred, and it is the job of the therapist to redirect their focus to the present. In fact, when clients would veer off into the ozone and prevent themselves from experiencing the present, Perls would sometimes accuse them of relaying "elephant shit," implying that what they were saying was a bunch of crap, and encouraging them to "get to work." Oftentimes, in an effort to have clients experience the present, therapists will ask such questions as, "What are you experiencing or feeling now?" And, when clients begin to talk about the past, they are generally asked to bring the past into the present. So, if I were to begin to talk about the death of my mother and how I wish I had been there when she had died, my Gestalt therapist might say something like, "Why don't you talk to your mother, now, and tell her how you feel about not being with her when she died?"

I–Thou Communication.   People become very adept at not encountering one another and avoiding the "I–Thou" relationship. And the language they use reflects this. For instance, a client comes in and says, "I'm so pissed off at the world." In this case, the Gestalt therapist might try to have the client focus upon exactly who the client is angry at by asking, "So who are you angry at?" Then, the therapist might encourage the client to have a discussion with that person, either in the office as a role-play or with the person directly. Another example is when a client comes in and says, "I wish I had a more loving relationship." In this case, the therapist might say, "Can you tell your (wife, lover, friend, etc.) that you want more love in your relationship?" In both these cases, the therapist is pushing the client toward having a real relationship with the person toward whom the client has these unresolved feelings.

I–It Language.   One mechanism that clients use to avoid experiencing fully is the use of the word "it" as opposed to "I." For most clients, saying "It just doesn't feel right," is not as powerful as saying "I just don't feel right." Similarly, a client's saying "The world sucks," is not nearly as powerful as saying "I suck," or "My life sucks." Here you can see how the simple change of the externalized "it" language to carefully choosing language that encourages ownership of feelings can move clients toward taking responsibility for their thoughts, feelings, and actions.

Experiencing the Present.   Helping clients get in touch with their moment-to-moment experience and bodily sensations is critical to helping them gain an awareness of their impasses and unfinished business. Therapists can accomplish this in many ways, such as simply saying to them, "Listen to your body," or "Experience whatever's there." When I underwent my own Gestalt therapy, my therapist had a very simple and effective technique of helping me experience the moment. Right after I would sit in my chair, he would ask me to close my eyes, take a few deep breaths, and tell him whatever I was feeling, sensing, or hearing. I was amazed at what blocks I could get in touch with, in a short amount of time.

Not Gossiping.   A particularly good technique for couples, family, or group work involves talking directly *to* an individual who is in the session as opposed to talking *about* that person. For instance, a husband in couples counseling might complain to the therapist that his wife sleeps too much and does not take good care of her health. In this case, the therapist might simply state, "Why don't you tell her that directly? She's right there."

Making Statements out of Questions

> The majority of questions the patient asks are seductions of the intellect …
> (Perls, 1973, p. 77)

While I was in Gestalt therapy, I had the opportunity to hear Albert Ellis talk. He was going on and on about how people should be allowed to do "whatever they want to" in life. I raised my hand and asked a question that went something like, "Well, you can't let anyone do whatever they want; for instance, what about when a person wants to rape someone?" Being a little phobic of public speaking and having asked my question in front of hundreds of people, I was quite proud of myself. A couple of days later, I went to see my Gestalt therapist for our scheduled session. I relayed my story. He looked at me and said, "Who do you want to rape?" Now, to this day, I don't believe I wanted to rape anyone, but my therapist's question did evoke some interesting responses. Gestalt therapists believe that all questions are actually statements about self. Next time you ask a question, think about what statement about yourself you might be making.

The Dialogue Game and Empty Chair Technique.   If you remember from earlier in the chapter, Gestalt therapists believe that our personality possesses a

---

B o x 6.5   The Empty Chair Technique

Read or watch Dr. Neukrug's work with Jill and see how he uses the empty chair to elicit unresolved feelings Jill has toward her mother. How effective do you think such a technique is when working with clients who have unresolved issues with individuals who are deceased or not available?

You can read this session by going to www. cengage.com/counseling/neukrug/CTP1e and click "student downloads." Or your instructor may show this session in class with the DVD that accompanies his or her copy of the text.

---

wide variety of polarities, and sometimes one is dominant over the other. Called a **split** in one's personality, such a dichotomy is generally the result of unfinished business that prevents the individual from being whole. Gestalt therapists believe it is important to acknowledge the nondominant part of the split and integrate it back into the individual's personality. This can sometimes be accomplished through the dialogue game. For instance, if there is a struggle between a part of me that wants to be "nice" to my friend and a part that is pissed off at him, I can play out the two parts. Or, if there is a part of me that is a show off, likely, there is also a shy part within. To emphasize such splits, a client can dialogue with an empty chair and have a conversation with the two parts of self. Often, the individual takes turn being each part, and actually switches chairs as he or she speaks to the other part of self in the opposing empty chair. Of course, it is important to pay particular attention to the nondominant side of self, as this side is often in hiding and has difficulty expressing itself. This technique is often employed when exploring topdog/underdog splits.

The empty chair technique is also used when there are unresolved issues with a person whom the client cannot contact directly (e.g., an estranged spouse, a deceased person). In this case, the client can imagine the person sitting in the empty chair and can be prompted by therapist statements like, "Tell _____ what you're feeling," "What is it like to talk with _____?" and "What do you need to say to _____?" More specific material can be added based on the situation (see Box 6.5).

"I Take Responsibility for That".   Since clients are often particularly adept at not taking responsibility for their actions, Gestalt therapists will often ask their clients to add a simple statement like "and I take responsibility for that." So, "My marriage is a shambles," becomes, "My marriage is a shambles, and I take responsibility for that." Or, "This job sucks," becomes, "My job sucks, and I'm responsible for that." (Notice how "this job" became "my job.") Or, "I'm horribly depressed," becomes, "I have created my horrible depression—I'm responsible for it" This technique is effective as it constantly pushes the client to take ownership of his or her feelings.

Playing the Projection.   Since Gestalt therapists see almost all questions and statements about the world as statements about self, clients are often asked to take ownership of phrases they use that may have far-reaching implications—implications of which the client is not aware. So, a client who constantly states, "This world is a scary place," is asked to role-play that projection. For instance, a therapist might suggest to the client, "Be scared and tell me what it's like to be scared." Or the client who states, "You can't trust anyone," might be asked to state, "I can't trust myself" or "No one should trust me; I'm untrustworthy." From these statements, which are projections of the inner world of the client, clients can begin to work on deep-seated unresolved issues that are lingering within and affecting everyday behavior. This technique is particularly useful in family and group settings where the client can look at each other person and make a statement about self to each member. For instance, a client might say to each person in the room, "I'm not trustworthy." This can often evoke deep emotions and help the client get in touch with unresolved issues. Members may or may not be given the opportunity to respond.

Exaggeration Technique.   One relatively easy method of helping clients get in touch with feelings is to ask them to emphasize or repeat a word, phrase, or sentence. Accenting in this manner, while asking them to be particularly tuned into their inner experience, can help them release the feeling they're protecting themselves from. For instance, imagine a client who feels ashamed of his body, and softly says, "I hate my body." Then, the client is asked to say the statement more loudly and then even more loudly. Soon, he is yelling it and realizes how he has desensitized himself and has few if any feelings about his body. His body has become split off from him. Saying the statement loudly makes him own his hated feelings toward his body and is the first step toward the polarity that he also feels—loving his body. In a similar way, read or watch how Dr. Neukrug asks Jill to repeat certain words in his effort to have her experience unresolved feelings she has toward her mother (see Box 6.5 to learn how to read or watch this session).

Feeding the Client a Sentence.   As clients work on core issues, their unfinished business is sometimes obvious to the therapist, but not to the client,. Based on the therapist's educated "hunch," he or she will create a sentence that seems to highlight a core issue and ask the client to repeat it. So, a client who is working on issues of closeness to women might be fed a statement like, "I am so scared that if I get close to a woman, I will lose my sense of self." Accurately feeding sentences to a client can hasten the progress of completing unfinished business.

"I Have a Secret".   Most people have a part of themselves that they feel guilty about or ashamed of. In an effort to take ownership of these feelings, a therapist will sometimes ask a client to make a statement about how the client thinks the therapist might respond if the secret was revealed. Or, in a group setting, the client might go to each group member and reveal how he or she imagines each member would feel if the secret was revealed. If trust has been built, clients might be asked to actually reveal the secret and then ask each member how they feel about the client. This allows the client to experience a disowned part of self and integrate it into his or her personality.

Making the Rounds.   This technique, generally used in group or family counseling, is when a client is asked to make a statement to every group member based on a theme on which he or she has been working. So, if a client is dealing with issues of trust, he or she might go to each person and say, "Joe, I am scared to trust you," "Georgette, I am scared to trust you," "Jamison, I'm scared to trust you," and so forth. The leader may or may not have each member reply. Sometimes, the leader will have the member go around twice; the first time, each member may not reply, but on the second round, members will be given opportunity to respond. Groups are notoriously good at assisting clients who are dealing with these core issues, and it is not unusual to have a group member reply with something like, "I care about you so much, and I hope you can come to trust me."

Dream Work.   Perls, like many Gestalt therapists, saw dreams as representing projections of different aspects of the self. In fact, Perls believed that what was not manifested consciously could often be accessed in dreams. The process of working with dreams generally follows the following framework: asking the client to describe a dream as if it is occurring in the present, asking the client to identify what stands out in the dream, having the client become aspects of the dream that stand out, and asking the client to have dialogues among the different aspects of the dream. In fact, Perls and current-day Gestalt therapists can often be found directing clients to have conversations with different parts of their bodies that stood out in a dream, objects that stood out in a dream, or people who popped up in a dream. Such experimentation, say Gestalt therapists, helps to bring out hidden aspects of the person that are reflective of unfinished business, with the goal of integrating split-off aspects of the person.

One interesting aspect of integrating parts of self is Perls's belief that we should embrace our nightmares. Nightmares have figures that represent unacknowledged parts of ourselves (e.g., the boogey man!). It is important that all aspects of self are embraced and integrated if we are to be whole, say Gestalt therapists. Dreams are also existential messages about our lives. If I have a dream about the world disintegrating, might that not mean that my life has no meaning and no direction? Finally, Perls felt strongly that therapists should not interpret dreams for clients, because that would lead to client intellectualization, which is the last thing you want clients to do in Gestalt therapy.

Finally, dream work is often conducted in a group setting, where clients are asked to bring a dream to the group and are able to "work it through" in a nonjudgmental and trusting atmosphere. In addition, others can help the "dreamer" act out parts of the dream. For instance, a client who has dreamt of being in a maze and not being able to get out might have the group members form a closed circle around her, as if she were trapped. Feelings that come up can then be processed by the client.

Group Work.   As we discussed the techniques, you probably noticed that many of them can be applied to group counseling. Gestalt therapy is particularly amenable to group work, as individuals will often project their experiences onto others, and it is these very projections that are fodder for the therapist. In fact, Gestalt therapists believe that almost every question asked, and most statements made about others within the group, are projections of self. Thus, the therapist can use many of the techniques already described to help clients see how they are really making statements about themselves through their seemingly "reasonable" questions and statements. For instance, within the group setting, a client might say to another group member, "Why do you bully people so much?" The astute therapist might say, "Make a statement about yourself out of that question," at which point the client says, "I have been so bullied and hurt in my life," and goes on to sob about the unfinished business of how she was put down by her first husband. Similarly, many of the other techniques already discussed can also be used in an effort to re-own parts of self. The group environment also offers an opportunity for clients to gain feedback from others about their behaviors and to experiment with a more honest way of interacting with others. As individuals take increased ownership of their unfinished business, they are better able to develop "real" relationships and can experiment with these new I–Thou encounters within the group setting.

THE THERAPEUTIC PROCESS

As you might expect from reading this chapter, the therapeutic journey of the Gestalt therapy client is like no other journey. Although Gestalt therapists apply their skills in different ways, the underlying assumption is that there will be movement toward greater acceptance of feelings, increased openness toward experience, greater honesty and realness, an increased sense of self-support, and the ability to engage with another person in open dialogue and mutual discussion without holding back, called by Martin Buber (1958) the "I–Thou" relationship. In helping clients move toward these goals, Gestalt therapists vary in how directive and confrontational they can be— from those like Fritz Perls, who tend to challenge clients, be provocative, and direct clients toward change, to those, like my work with Jill (see Box 6.5), where I gently push Jill and carefully challenge her to examine her unfinished business.

Whether the therapist is very directive and confrontational, or gently pushing the client toward greater experience, a general unraveling of the client's world occurs in a predictable fashion. In describing this process, Perls identified five layers of which the client increasingly becomes aware as the client continues in therapy. Called the **structure of neurosis**, the layers include, **(1) the cliché layer**, **(2) the role-playing or phony layer**, **(3) the impasse layer**, **(4) the implosive layer**, and **(5) the explosive/authentic layer** (see Figure 6.4) (Clarkson & Mackewn, 1993; Perls, 1969a; 1970).

The Cliché Layer

The cliché layer reflects typical ways that we act in our day-to-day existence when we're attempting to make small talk with others. It is the "socially acceptable" way to act with people as you pass them in the hallway at work, see them in the supermarket, or walk by them on the sidewalk. It is the "you" who is depressed but responds with "Great!" when someone asks you, in passing, "How are you doing?"

The Role-Playing or Phony Layer

One step below the cliché layer is the role-playing or phony layer, where we present a front to others in order to avoid actual contact. In this layer, we act

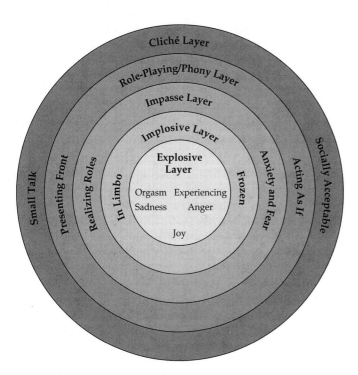

FIGURE 6.4 Structure of Neuroses

"as if" we are a certain type of person as opposed to acting as we actually are. We might act superior, like a "big shot," coquettish, incessantly respectful, or a thousand other roles, but it's all a front to avoid contact. Perls suggested that this layer includes the "topdog" and the "underdog," or the part of ourselves that acts righteous and is demanding versus the part of us that is subservient and unsure of ourselves. Some examples of a phony might be the individual who acts like the "cool professor" in an effort not to show his real self to students, or the business executive who is "in charge" all the time and uses his or her persona to seduce others to his point of view, or the psychologist who uses words in ways that suggest she's always analyzing others. All of these roles can seem real, but in the long run prevent the person from having a genuine encounter with another person. Just below this layer is a part of us that tries to resist who we really are.

The Impasse Layer

There is a Woody Allen movie called *Zelig* that describes a man who becomes whomever he is around. He is the ultimate "role-player." If he's around someone who is Chinese, he speaks fluent Chinese. If he is around someone who is obese, he becomes obese. If he's around a psychiatrist, he becomes a psychiatrist. During the movie, the psychiatrist treating him comes up with a novel intervention—she tells him that she is *not* a psychiatrist. If she is not a psychiatrist, then he must play the role of not being a psychiatrist—for after all, he always becomes the person he is around. When she tells him she is not a psychiatrist, he begins to respond with the same. Suddenly, he begins to have an anxiety attack as he realizes that if she is not a psychiatrist, neither is he. He starts to panic, saying something like, "Oh my God, if I'm not Zelig, the psychiatrist, *who am I*?" He has come face-to-face with the impasse, or the point where the individual realizes that he or she has been playing a role. This acknowledgement to self that one has been living a false existence catapults the individual into a state of anxiety as he or she contemplates, "If that person is not the real me, who am I?" Coming face-to-face with the impasse also raises the question, "Dare I move beyond it?

The Implosive Layer

As our fictitious Zelig hits the impasse, he must then decide who he really is. It is at this point that individuals often hit a wall and implode—or deaden themselves. They are fearful that if they were to really be themselves, they would not be loved. On the other hand, having knowledge that they have all along been playing a role, what should they do? It's hard to go back when one realizes that one has been fake. This is a place of limbo, and a place of waiting to decide what to do. It is a place where one feels frozen in time. Frozen, that is, until one is willing to risk everything and be oneself.

The Explosive/Authentic Layer

Ultimately, one has to decide—do I continue playing a role or do I risk being myself? When willing to risk, one experiences the final and ultimate layer. It is the layer where the person again feels. It is a place of orgasm, aliveness, anger, and sadness as the individual allows himself or herself to be truly alive, again. It is the place of experience.

Inevitably, one who has a successful experience in Gestalt therapy feels whole and renewed, and has a much stronger sense of self. This person is in touch with his or her moment-to-moment experience and is increasingly self-supportive and self-reliant. This person is real and able to communicate directly and honestly with others (see Box 6.6).

SOCIAL, CULTURAL, AND SPIRITUAL ISSUES

To read today's Gestalt theorists, you would think that Gestalt therapy is *the* approach most adaptable to a cross-cultural perspective. For instance, they talk about the importance of having a phenomenological perspective and understanding the client from his or her point of view. They highlight the importance of understanding the contextual field of the client, including the historical, cultural, and political influences that have affected the client. They talk about the importance of clients' becoming increasingly aware of their own experiences,

---

B o x 6.6   Jill's Layers

Read or watch Dr. Neukrug's work with Jill. As you review this session, try to identify the different techniques used by Dr. Neukrug and assess how many of the layers of neuroses Jill has worked on.

You can read this session by going to www. cengage.com/counseling/neukrug/CTP1e and click "student downloads." Or your instructor may show this session in class with the DVD that accompanies his or her copy of the text.

---

and that those experiences must only be defined by the client. They encourage all of us to experience the "void"—or the Zen notion of non-being so that we (both therapist and client) can sit with our inner selves and listen attentively to it. And, they highlight the importance of contact with others, so that our self can constantly change and transform (Crocker & Philippson, 2005; Ferbacher & Plummer, 2005; Gaffney, 2006; Kirchner, 2000).

Based on the above, the Gestalt approach does have much to offer to the therapist who wants to embrace a cross-cultural perspective. Yet there are some aspects of the Gestalt approach that can be questioned when working with diverse clients. For instance, despite its holistic nature, Gestalt therapy is clearly grounded in many Western values, such as the notion that clients need to increase their own sense of "self-support" and that responsibility for one's actions resides within the person, as opposed to within the family, community, or society. And, despite the fact that the "self" is constantly changing as it contacts others, there is a sense that the individual is primary. This may be contrary to the sense of self as defined in some cultures, which place greater emphasis on the importance of extended family and community.

In some cases, Gestalt therapy can be offensive to individuals from diverse cultures. For instance, even in its more passive forms, the Gestalt approach pushes the client to experience the "now" and stresses the importance of "awareness." Often, these gentle challenges to experience the now also encourages clients toward expression of feelings. For some clients, who are from cultures where expression of feelings is seen as inappropriate or misguided, such pressure to "be in touch" with their experience would feel unnatural and uncomfortable. In the end, the challenge for many Gestalt therapists when working with diverse clients is to find a balance between the therapist's need to delicately and perceptively understand the client and the importance of pushing the client toward the "now" experience.

> This is our work: to be fully present in our own fullness of person and culture, and to selectively and sensitively share our awareness with our environmental other, respectful both of our own cultural context and that of the other, and the interactional dynamics at the contact boundary between us. (Gaffney, 2006, p. 218)

Gestalt therapy has found a home with feminists. Many women who are Gestalt therapists believe that this approach, with its focus on reclaiming lost parts of self, can offer much to women, especially those aspects of women that have been traditionally oppressed by society.

> Gestalt therapy has confirmed and supported us in reclaiming our natural aggression, and in exploring the full range of our experience. (Caring et al., 2000, Conclusion, para. 1)

Despite its home with feminists, one must remember that many women and men do not buy into the concept of reclaiming a part of self. For some, the loss of self is not a loss—it never was. In fact, there are parts of self which some cultures insist do not belong in self. Ultimately, each of us has to struggle with our own definition of self and decide how we will apply it cross-culturally.

For religious people, Gestalt therapy has its challenges. For instance, the approach suggests that cultural and societal injunctions and "shoulds," which are often based on writings from the major religions of the world, are a prime source of unfinished business, and their usefulness should be questioned. Yet, it is these very injunctions and shoulds that many would argue are critical to living the moral and even spiritual life.

Relative to spirituality, if we mean Zen meditation and Buddhism, Gestalt therapy seems to hit the mark with its focus on holism, the "void," here-and-now awareness, and getting in touch with deeper aspects of ourselves (Ingersoll & O'Neill, 2005; Wolfert, 2000). In fact, many of the writings of Gestalt therapy fit nicely into the current trends in alternative therapies and mindfulness (see Chapter 14). This focus on present-centered consciousness suggests that people focus on acceptance of self and strive for a deeper sense of peace and happiness. For many people, however, spiritualism is not Zen meditation, Buddhism, or mindfulness, and many mainstream religious people who identify themselves as spiritual may not easily relate to many of the above concepts. For them, spiritualism may be defined quite differently.

In the long run, Gestalt therapy seems to be a mixed bag cross-culturally. On the one hand, those who embrace Gestalt theory seem to argue that the Gestalt approach is unique in its ability to see the client contextually and to understand the client within his or her unique understanding of the world. At the same time, the Gestalt approach has a firm footing in a view of human nature that stresses certain values—values that are not embraced by all cultures.

EFFICACY OF GESTALT THERAPY

As a therapeutic approach that examines the whole person, Gestalt therapy is one of the more difficult approaches to research. This is partly because it is easier to look at specific aspects of behavior rather than examining some indeterminate concept called "the whole person." And even if we were to try and measure some "aspects of the whole" like the ability to "experience the now" or "make contact with the environment," we run into some major methodological problems in deciding how we might measure such elusive concepts. Despite these inherent difficulties, some research, including some meta-analyses, found

---

B o x 6.7   Angela's Experience in Gestalt Therapy

Please review the Miller family's background, which can be found in Appendix B, and then read about

Angela's encounter with a Gestalt therapist, which can also be found in Appendix B.

---

that (Greenberg & Dompierre, 1981; Johnson & Smith, 1997; Kirchner, 2000; Paivio & Greenberg, 1995; Schoenberg, 2000; Wampold, 2001; Winter, 2007):

1. Gestalt therapy is an effective treatment overall, and certainly better than no treatment.

2. When measuring overall satisfaction, Gestalt therapy is as good as behavioral therapy or cognitive therapy.

3. Gestalt group therapy seems to be somewhat effective in reducing depression and anxiety.

4. The empty chair or two-chair technique seems to be effective in reducing anger, in the reduction of unfinished business, in improving decision-making, and in the treatment of simple phobias.

5. The empty chair technique may be more effective than empathic reflections when measuring depth of experiencing, shifts in awareness, and conflict resolution.

6. There is some preliminary evidence that Gestalt group therapy might be helpful when working with individuals with borderline personality disorder (BPD).

The research above is clearly limited, and more studies that examine the effectiveness of this approach with varying populations need to be undertaken. One hopeful sign is that the **Gestalt Research Consortium** (2003) was recently formed to bring together researchers and practitioners who are interested in expanding the research on Gestalt therapy (see Box 6.7).

SUMMARY

Gestalt therapy was developed by Fritz Perls during the twentieth century. Growing up in Germany, Perls eventually obtained his medical degree but had to flee Nazi Germany during the 1930s. Going to South Africa and later to the United States, Perls was influenced by many people and philosophies over the years, such as the anti-deterministic approach of the existentialists; the belief that each person's reality is unique and true for that person (phenomenology); the holistic notion that mind, body, and soul act in unison; and a number of ideas by the Gestalt psychologists, including the concepts of figure/ground and closure. His theory would become a novel approach to therapy and one of the first theories developed in the humanistic tradition. In line with this tradition, Perls suggested that people are born neither good nor bad, but with the capacity to embody many personality dimensions. He deplored the reductionistic approach of the Freudians and experimental psychologists, and suggested that the whole being cannot be broken down into separate parts.

Key to Perls's theory are the ways in which people have their needs met and make contact with their environment. Indicative of this process is a cycle that includes withdrawal (or rest—"zero point"), sensation, awareness, mobilization, action, contact, and satisfaction. For the Gestalt therapist, how the individual makes contact with his or her environment in an attempt to satisfy needs is reflective of the individual's way of being in the world and determines the "self." Parental injunctions as well as cultural and societal pressures could prevent the normal attainment of needs and be the impetus for the development of blockages and impasses in a person's life that create unfinished business. Perls and others have identified a number of resistances, or ways that individuals block themselves from experiencing, which ultimately create unfinished business, including introjection, projection, retroflection, desensitization, deflection, egotism, and confluence.

Gestalt therapists believe that the ultimate way of living is allowing oneself to access all of what is available to one's experience. Since unfinished business prevents fully experiencing, one goal of Gestalt therapy is to help the client once again experience the "now" that is the basis of the client's reality. In helping clients experience the "now," Gestalt therapists employ a number of commonly used techniques, including empathy, being directive, being confrontational, avoiding intellectualization, focusing on nonverbal behaviors, and experimentation. In addition, a number of specialized techniques have been developed including using "now" language, I–Thou communication, I–It language, experiencing the present, not gossiping, making statements out of questions, the dialogue game and empty chair technique, "I take responsibility for that," playing the projection, the exaggeration technique, feeding the client a sentence, "I have a secret," making the rounds, dream work, and group work. These techniques are used to help clients traverse the structure of neurosis, which Perls suggested included five layers: (1) the cliché layer, (2) the role-playing or phony layer, (3) the impasse layer, (4) the implosive layer, and (5) the explosive/authentic layer.

Cross-culturally, Gestalt therapy appears to be a mixed bag. On the one hand, it stresses many traditional Western values. On the other hand, the phenomenological perspective of Gestalt therapy urges us to understand clients from their unique cultural contexts. The contradiction continues when we look at women and at spiritual issues. For instance, many feminists find a home with the Gestalt idea of reclaiming parts of self (e.g., feelings of aggression). On the other hand, others might question whether such "lost parts" were ever really a part of self. Spiritually, those who adhere to Eastern philosophies may feel comfortable, as the Gestalt approach borrows much from them. However, traditionalists might see the Gestalt approach as somewhat odd and non-supportive of many of the values of mainstream religions.

For the relatively small number of research studies conducted on Gestalt therapy, it has been shown to be effective. However, with its emphasis on holism and other somewhat elusive concepts, methodologically, it offers a number of challenges to efficacy research.

KEY WORDS

action stage

anti-deterministic

avoiding intellectualizations

awareness stage

being confrontational

being directive

blockages

body armor

born neither good nor bad

cliché layer

closure

confluence

contact

contact stage

deflection

desensitization

dialogue game and empty chair technique

dream work

ego boundary

egotism

empathy

Esalen Institute

environmental support

exaggeration technique

existentialism

existentialists

experiencing the present

experimentation

explosive/authentic layer

feeding the client a sentence

figure/ground

focusing on nonverbal behaviors

foreground

Gestalt Institute of Canada

Gestalt Institute of New York

Gestalt prayer

Gestalt psychology

Gestalt Research Consortium

group work

here and now

holism

homeostasis

I-Thou

I–Thou communication

I-It language

"I have a secret"

"I take responsibility for that"

impasse layer

impasses

implosive layer

introjection

making statements out of questions

making the rounds

mindfulness

mobilization stage

need-satisfaction cycle

not gossiping

phenomenologists

phenomenology

playing the projection

polarities

projection

psychodrama

resistances

retroflection

role-playing or phony layer

satisfaction stage

self-support

sensation stage

shouldisms

split

structure of neurosis

the "self"

the implosive layer

topdog

underdog

unfinished business

using "now" language

withdrawal stage

Zen Buddhism

zero point

KEY NAMES

Buber, Martin

Friedlander, Sigmund

From, Isadore

Fromm, Eric

Fromm, Marty

Goldstein, Kurt

Goodman, Paul	Moreno, Jacob	Perls, Steve
Hefferline, Ralf	Perls, Amelia Rund	Posner, Lore ("Laura")
Horney, Karen	Perls, Grete	Reich, Wilhelm
Jones, Ernest	Perls, Nathan	Shepard, Martin
Lucy	Perls, Renate	Tillich, Paul

REFERENCES

Buber, M. (1958). *I and thou*. New York: Scribner.

Caring, M., Cook, C., Feinstein, G., Fodor, I., Friedman, Z., Gerstman, A., ... Wolfert, R. (1999). Adding women's voices: Feminism and Gestalt therapy. *Gestalt, 3*(1). Retrieved from http://www.g-gej.org/3-1/women.html

Clarkson, P. (2004). *Gestalt counseling in action* (3rd ed.). Thousand Oaks, CA: Sage Publications.

Clarkson, P., & Mackewn, J. (1993). *Fritz Perls*. Newbury Park, CA: Sage Publications.

Crocker, S. F., & Philippson, P. (2005). Phenomenology, existentialism, and Eastern thought in gestalt therapy. In A. L. Woldt & S. M. Toman (Eds.), *Gestalt therapy: History, theory, and practice* (pp. 65–80). Thousand Oaks, CA: Sage Publications.

Enright, J. B. (1970). An introduction to Gestalt techniques. In J. Fagan & I. L. Shepherd (Eds.), *Gestalt therapy now* (pp. 107–124). New York: Harper & Row.

Fernbacher, S., & Plummer, D. (2005). Cultural influences and considerations in Gestalt therapy. In A. L. Woldt & S. M. Toman (Eds.), *Gestalt therapy: History, theory, and practice* (pp. 117–132). Thousand Oaks, CA: Sage Publications.

Gaffney, S. (2006). Gestalt with groups: A cross-cultural perspective. *Gestalt Review, 10*(3), 205–219.

Gestalt Research Consortium (2003). The Gestalt Research Consortium. Retrieved from http://www.g-gej.org/grc/index.html

Greenberg, L. S., & Dompierre, L. M. (1981). Specific effects of Gestalt two-chair dialogue on intrapsychic conflict in counseling. *Journal of Counseling Psychology, 28*(4), 288–294.

Hart, J., Corriere, R., & Binder, J. (1975). *Going sane: An introduction to feeling therapy*. New York: Jason Aronson.

Ingersoll, R. E., & O'Neill, B. (2005). Gestalt therapy and spirituality. In A. L. Woldt & S. M. Toman (Eds.), *Gestalt therapy: History, theory, and practice*, (pp. 133–150). Thousand Oaks, CA: Sage Publications.

Johnson, W. R., & Smith, E. W. L. (1997). Gestalt empty-chair dialogue versus systematic desensitization in the treatment of phobia. *Gestalt Review, 1*(2), 150–162.

Kirchner, M. (2000). Overview of Gestalt therapy theory. *Gestalt, 4*(3). Retrieved from http://www.g-gej.org/4-3/theoryoverview.html

Latner, J. (1992). The theory of Gestalt therapy. In E. C. Nevis (Ed.), *Gestalt therapy: Perspectives and applications* (pp. 13–56). New York: Gardner Press.

Levitzky, A., & Perls, F. S. (1970). The rules and games of Gestalt therapy. In J. Fagan & I. L. Shepherd (Eds.), *Gestalt therapy now* (pp. 140–149). New York: Harper & Row.

Miller, M. V. (1996). Elegiac reflections on Isadore From. *The Gestalt Journal, 19*(1), 45–56.

Paivio, S. C., & Greenberg, S. (1995). Resolving "unfinished business": Efficacy of experiential therapy using empty-chair dialogue. *Journal of Consulting and Clinical Psychology, 63*(3), 419–425.

Perls, F. (1947). *Ego, hunger, and aggression: A revision of Freud's theory and method*. London: G. Allen and Unwin ltd. (Original work published 1942)

Perls, F. (1969a). *Gestalt therapy verbatim*. Moab, UT: Real People Press.

Perls, F. (1969b). *In and out of the garbage pail*. Moab, UT: Real People Press.

Perls, F. (1970). Four lectures. In J. Fagan & I. L. Shepherd (Eds.), *Gestalt therapy now* (pp. 14–46). New York: Harper & Row.

Perls, F. (1973). *The Gestalt approach and eyewitness to therapy*. Palo Alto: Science and Behavior Books.

Perls, F. (1978). Finding self through Gestalt therapy. *Gestalt Journal, 1*(1), 54–73.

Perls, F., Hefferline, R., & Goodman, P. (1951). *Gestalt therapy: Excitement and growth in human personality*. New York: Julian Press.

Polster, E., & Polster, M. (1973). *Gestalt therapy integrated: Contours of theory and practice*. New York: Brunner/Mazel.

Polster, E., & Polster, M. (1999). *From the radical center: The heart of Gestalt therapy*. Cleveland, Ohio: The Gestalt Institute of Cleveland Press.

Schoenberg, P. (2000). The impact of Gestalt group therapy on persons with borderline personality disorder (group therapy). Dissertation Abstracts International Section A: Humanities and Social Sciences, 60(7-A). (Order no.: EH9939729)

Shepard, M. (1975). *Fritz*. New York: Saturday Review Press, E. P. Dutton & Co.

Smuts, J. C. (1926). *Holism and evolution*. New York: Macmillan.

Street, R. F. (1931) *A Gestalt completion test: A study of a cross-section of intellect*. New York: Columbia University.

Van De Riet, V., Korb, M. P., & Gorrell, J. J. *Gestalt therapy: An introduction*. New York: Pergamon Press.

Wampold, B. E. (2001). *The great psychotherapy debate: Models, methods, and findings*. Mahwah, NJ: Erlbaum.

Winter, D. A. (2007). Constructivist and humanistic therapies. In E. Freeman & M. Power (Eds.), *Handbook of evidence-based psychotherapies: A guide of research and practice* (pp. 123–140). West Sussex, England: John Wiley & Sons.

Wolfert, R. (2000). The spiritual dimensions of Gestalt therapy. *Gestalt, 4*(3). Retrieved from http://www.g-gej.org/4-3/spiritual.html

Yonteff, G. M. (1976). Theory of Gestalt therapy. In C. Hatcher & P. Himelstein (Eds.), *The handbook of Gestalt therapy* (pp. 213–221). New York: Jason Aronson.

Chapter 7

Person-Centered Counseling

Learning Goals

- To gain a biographical understanding of Carl Rogers, one of the most influential therapists of all time and the developer of the person-centered counseling approach.
- To understand the historical context in which Rogers created his theory.
- To understand how each of the following play into the anti-deterministic, existential, and phenomenological perspective of Rogers's view of human nature: the organismic valuing process, the need for positive regard, conditions of worth, incongruence or nongenuineness, defense mechanisms and anxiety.
- To learn about key concepts which are the basis for person-centered counseling, including the actualizing tendency, the need for positive regard, conditions of worth, nongenuineness and incongruence, the organismic valuing process, choice and free will, self-determination, nondirective counseling, and the necessary and sufficient conditions.
- To understand the aversion to the word "techniques" by person-centered counselors and to examine the importance that person-centered counselors place on congruence or genuineness, unconditional positive regard, and empathy.
- To examine the importance of empathy, the various ways to make effective empathic responses, and to discuss scales, like the Carkhuff scale, that have been developed to assess how accurately one is making empathic responses.
- To examine the therapeutic process of person-centered counseling and particularly look at how the client moves from a more closed posture toward one in which there is expanding self-awareness, openness, and autonomy.
- To review important social, cultural, and spiritual issues related to person-centered counseling, especially in light of how it stresses the importance of understanding different value systems and how it can help bring a more loving and peaceful world.
- To examine Rogers's early research when he used the Q-sort technique, which looked at the difference between the client's self-concept and the client's ideal concept, to discuss the importance of empathy in therapeutic outcomes,

and to highlight when person-centered counseling is likely to be most beneficial.
- To see how person-centered therapy is applied through vignettes, DVDs, and case study.

> In the past few years, I have found myself opening up to much greater intimacy in relationships. I see this development as definitely the result of workshop experiences. I am more ready to touch and be touched, physically. I do more hugging and kissing of both men and women. I am more aware of the sensuous side of my life. I also realize how much I desire close psychological contact with others. I recognize how much I need to care deeply for another and to receive that kind of caring in return. I can say openly what I have always recognized dimly: that my deep involvement in psychotherapy was a cautious way of meeting this need for intimacy without risking too much of my person. Now I am more willing to be close in other relationships and to risk giving more of myself. I feel as though a whole new depth of capacity for intimacy has been discovered in me. This capacity has brought me much hurt, but an even greater share of joy.
>
> Carl Rogers, *A Way of Being* (1980, pp. 83–84)

Carl Rogers always impressed me. In fact, he was one of my idols as I entered the counseling profession. Today, many years since his death, his writings and the way he lived continue to be a model for me. As the above paragraph from his book *A Way of Being* exemplifies, even well into his late seventies, he continued to grow and change and willingly take the risks inherent in the development of deeper intimacy. He was a person who lived out his theory, a theory that he believed was not only a way of being with clients, but a way of being with people. I can only hope his impact on me is such that it makes me more of a risk-taker as well as a person who can increasingly love, care, and be real with others—qualities he repeatedly stated were critical elements to living in the world. But how did this man become one of the most important counselor and psychologist of the twentieth century? Let's take a look.

CARL ROGERS

Born on January 8, 1902, in a Chicago suburb, Carl Rogers was to eventually become recognized as the most influential psychologist of the twentieth century (Kirschenbaum & Henderson, 1989a; "The top 10," 2007). The fourth of six children, Rogers's civil engineer father and stay-at-home mother were to bring him up in a strict home with parents he described as uncompromisingly religious, controlling, and,

American psychologist Dr. Carl Rogers (1902–1987) holds a finger to his chin as he listens during a group therapy session, San Diego, California, 1966.

Photo by Michael Rougier/Time & Life Pictures/Getty Images

despite not being expressive with their affection, seemed to love and care for their children (Rogers, 1961; Kirschenbaum, 2009). A bright, sensitive, shy, and sickly child, Rogers developed a close relationship with his mother. His upbringing was to eventually yield a young person who was an independent thinker and self-disciplined.

At the age of 12, Rogers's family moved to a farm outside of Chicago, and perhaps it's not surprising that at 17, he left for the University of Wisconsin to major in agriculture. Given his mother's religiosity, it is also not surprising to find that he later switched majors to religion, thinking that he would eventually become a minister. Ironically, being chosen as one of a handful of students to go to the "World Student Christian Federation Conference" in Beijing would have the effect of widening his perspectives, which led to him to doubt many of his religious views.

Against his parents' wishes, at the age of 22, Rogers married Helen Elliott and soon moved to New York City to attend Union Theological Seminary. With doubt in his mind about whether he was pursuing the correct career path, and with the school encouraging students to actively reflect on why they were considering the ministry, in 1926, Rogers left the seminary to start his master's and then doctoral degree in psychology at Columbia University. After finishing all but his dissertation, he worked as a child psychologist at the **Rochester Society for the Prevention of Cruelty to Children** (RSPCC), and in 1929, he became the director of the clinic's Child Study Department. It was around this time that he and his wife had two children, David and Natalie, and he started his Ph.D. in Clinical Psychology at Columbia. In 1931, Rogers finished his dissertation: "Measuring Personality Adjustment in Children Nine to Thirteen Years of Age." He wrote his first book, *The Clinical Treatment of the Problem Child*, in 1939.

Although initially intrigued with the psychodynamic approach to treatment, while at RSPCC Rogers became increasingly fascinated with the work of Otto Rank, who had been one of Freud's favorite disciples, but split with Freud over differences concerning the Oedipal complex. Rank's approach had actually veered toward an **existential–humanistic** framework as he began to emphasize the importance of focusing on the present, free will, and having an egalitarian relationship with clients. Rank's work seemed to greatly influence Rogers and other humanists (Kramer, 1995; Rank, 1996). In fact, when being interviewed about influences in his life, Kirschenbaum (1979) quotes Rogers as saying: "I became infected with Rankian ideas and began to realize the possibilities of the individual being self-directing" (p. 95).

Rogers had other influences also, such as the educational philosopher and psychologist John Dewey (1859–1952), who stressed the importance of reflection and experience in learning, and existentialists such as Søren Kierkegaard (1813–1855), who wrote about how subjectivity affects the choices people make. He was probably also influenced by the philosophy of Jean Jacques Rousseau (1712–1778), who believed that people had a natural tendency to be kind, if governments could set up the environment for this to occur; Eastern philosophy and mystics; and even the modern-day views of scientists on the nature of the universe (Kirschenbaum & Henderson, 1989b). He was undoubtedly also influenced by his nondemonstrative and sometimes controlling parents. It is likely that his experience of his parents' judgmental attitudes and rigidity led him to the belief in the importance of communicating feelings openly and honestly and demonstrating a warm, caring relationship to others. Although Rogers was clearly influenced by others, he also repeatedly stated that he mostly relied on his own experiences with clients for the development of his theory: "Neither the Bible nor the prophets—neither Freud nor research—neither the revelations of God nor man—can take precedence over my own direct experience" (Rogers, 1961, p. 24).

In 1940, Rogers was offered a full professorship at Ohio State University, and in 1942, he wrote *Counseling and Psychotherapy*. It is here that we first see semblances of what became known as Rogers's nondirective approach to counseling—a theory that stood in stark contrast to the deterministic, authoritarian, interpretive position that Freud had taken when developing psychoanalysis:

> … *Effective counseling consists of a definitely structured permissive relationship which allows the client to gain an understanding of himself to a degree which enables him to take positive steps in the light of his new orientation.* This hypothesis has a natural corollary, that all the techniques used should aim toward developing this free and permissive relationship, this understanding of self in the counseling and other relationships, and this tendency toward positive, self-initiated action. (Rogers, 1942, p. 18)

In 1945, Rogers took a position at the **University of Chicago** to establish a counseling center, and during 1946–1947, he served as president of the American Psychological Association (APA). During the 1940s, while at the University of Chicago, Rogers and Thomas Gordon brought counselors together in a group setting so that they could discuss problems they might encounter in working with returning GIs from World War II (Kirschenbaum, 2009; Rogers, 1970). Applying his nondirective approach to this group format, he soon found that, for a good number of these therapists, self-disclosure within the group setting resulted in a deepening of expression of feeling and, in many instances, a deeper understanding of themselves. This is often seen as the precursor to the **encounter group movement** that became increasingly popular and flourished in the 1960s and 1970s.

In 1951, Rogers published a major work on his approach, *Client-Centered Therapy*. This title reflected Rogers's novel approach that trusted the client to direct his or her own session. In this work, Rogers increasingly focused on the attitudes of the therapist. It was now evident that Rogers believed the therapeutic relationship, not specific techniques, was the most critical factor in the change process (Kirschenbaum, 2009). In fact, Rogers began to avoid using the word "technique" when describing his approach. Instead, he argued that the most important therapeutic attributes necessary for clients to change was the ability of counselors to show acceptance and understanding toward their clients.

> … [T]o create a psychological climate in which the client feels that kind of warmth, understanding and freedom from attack in which he may

Client
vs.
patient

drop his defensiveness, and explore and reorganize his life style, is a far more subtle and delicate process than simply "reflecting feeling." (Rogers as cited in Kirschenbaum, 2009, p. 156)

As Rogers's ideas took hold, many quickly adopted his use of the word "client" instead of "patient," as the word "patient" was associated with the authoritarian approach found in the medical model (Kirschenbaum, 2009). It was also around this time that his theory became known as **client-centered counseling**. As Rogers's influence grew, therapists increasingly began to agree with Rogers's view of the person and began to trust their clients' ability to direct their own counseling sessions. This contrasted sharply with the authoritarian and interpretive approach used by psychoanalysts, or the directive and reductionistic perspective of the behaviorists:

I do not discover man to be well characterized in his basic nature by such terms as fundamentally hostile, antisocial, destructive, evil.

I do not discover man to be, in his basic nature, completely without a nature, a *tabula rasa* on which *anything* may be written nor malleable putty which can be shaped into *any* form.

I do not discover man to be essentially a perfect being, sadly warped and corrupted by society.

In my experience I have discovered man to have characteristics which seem inherent in his species, and the terms which have at different times seemed to me descriptive of these characteristics are such terms as positive, forward-moving, constructive, realistic, trustworthy. (Rogers, 1957a, p. 200)

Rogers believed in the importance of showing the effectiveness of his client-centered approach, so he became progressively more involved with finding ways of researching client change. As a result, in 1956, he shared, with two other researchers, the APA's first **Distinguished Scientific Contribution Award**. Also in 1956, and again in 1962, Rogers held debates with B. F. Skinner that pitted Rogers's humanistic philosophy with Skinner's behavioral approach. Although the tapes made from the second and longest debate were originally to be distributed to the public, Skinner would not allow transcripts of them to be released (Rogers, 1980). A quarter of a century later, the transcript was finally published in Kirschenbaum & Henderson's (1989d) book, *Carl Rogers: Dialogues*. Rogers viewed the debates as a discourse on how he and Skinner came to make sense of the world, and not as a discussion as to whether one of them held the "truth:" "I have come to realize that the basic difference between a behaviorist and a humanistic approach to human beings is a *philosophical* choice" (Rogers, 1980, p. 56). He went on to say, however, that choosing one approach over the other had consequences and, as you might guess, the consequences were better if one chose the humanistic approach.

In 1957, Rogers wrote a ground breaking article that described the **"necessary and sufficient conditions"** for counseling (Rogers, 1957b). As a result of this article and the books he had written, the client-centered approach became seen by some as the most important contribution to psychotherapy in the twentieth century (Kirschenbaum & Henderson, 1989a; "The top 10," 2007). It was during this same year that Rogers decided to return to teach at his alma mater, the University of Wisconsin. However, in 1964, after becoming disillusioned with some of the politics of higher education, he took a research position at the **Western Behavioral Studies Institute** (WBSI) in La Jolla, California. In this same year, he won the **Humanist of the Year award** by the American Humanist Association. In 1968, he left WBSI and started the **Center for the Studies of the Person**, which focused on humanistic educational, philosophy, and counseling. It was also during this year that the film *Journey into Self*, which showed Rogers facilitating an encounter group, won the Academy Award for feature-length documentary (Kirschenbaum, 2009).

In many ways, the 1970s was a decade of contrasts for Carl Rogers. Becoming internationally known for the documentary, his writings, and his lecturing, Rogers was idolized by many, especially those in the mental health fields. In 1972, he won the **Distinguished Contributions to Applied Psychology as a Professional Practice award** of APA. At the same time, Rogers was struggling with many of his own "human" issues. In a decade of "do your own thing" and experimentation with open relationships and sexuality, Rogers, too, was getting in touch with his sexuality. Sexual intimacy between Rogers and his wife had ceased, due in part to a number of ailments with which Helen was battling (Kirschenbaum, 2009). Rogers contemplated going outside of his marriage for intimacy. Meanwhile, Rogers was writing a book entitled *Becoming Partners* (1972), which spoke to the importance of open and honest communication with one's partner. Wanting to be "real," Rogers shared his desires with his wife as well as with others whom he trusted. This honesty would be very painful to Helen, and the couple struggled during much of this decade. In fact, while he was still married, Rogers fell in love with a woman much younger than himself and did have a few ongoing sexual relationships with other women, which Helen undoubtedly knew about. Despite their faltering marriage, Rogers loved Helen, as was apparent when she neared her death:

> When I went to the hospital as usual to feed her her supper, I found myself pouring out to her how much I had loved her, how much she had meant in my life, how many positive initiatives she had contributed to our long partnership. I felt I had told her all these things before, but that night they had an intensity and sincerity they had not had before. (Rogers as cited in Kirschenbaum, 2009, p. 465)

It was also during this decade that it became evident to his son and daughter, but not to others to whom Rogers was close, that he had a drinking problem (Kirschenbaum, 2009). Drinking heavily to help him sleep at night, Rogers initially denied that alcohol was a problem; however, he later admitted that he drank too much. Sadly, alcohol was a problem that plagued Rogers until he died, although it did not seem to affect his writing or ability to work with clients.

The last years of Rogers's life were spent traveling the world making speeches, providing counseling and therapy, writing, and addressing social justice issues. Always open to his approach's changing as he changed, it was

---

B o x 7.1   Stories of the Great Therapists

To hear some stories about Carl Rogers by Gay Swenson Barfield, co-founder with Carl Rogers and former Director of the Carl Rogers Peace Project;

Howard Kirschenbaum, biographer of Carl Rogers and author; and others, go to the following link and click on "Carl Rogers": http://www.odu.edu/sgt

---

during this time that his theory took a broader perspective and he began to call it "person-centered counseling." Believing that his approach was a philosophy of living, and that many of his concepts could be applied to all human relationships, it is not surprising that in 1980, we see Rogers publish one of his last books, *A Way of Being*. It was also during this decade that Rogers could be found facilitating encounter groups between Protestants and Catholics in Northern Ireland, trying to pull together blacks and whites in South Africa, and facilitating communication groups around the world, including what was then the Soviet Union. A different kind of peace activist, he believed that if individuals could have the opportunity to see the inner core of another person, they would realize the true essence of that person and come to understand why a person feels and acts the way he or she does. This understanding, believed Rogers, was critical to peaceful coexistence. Rogers had an uncanny ability to bring disparate people together and have them see one another in new and enlightened ways. A number of videotapes of Rogers's work with clients and groups clearly demonstrate how his quiet, empathic, peaceful manner would bring about healing within a person and among peoples (see http://www.nrogers.com).

> ... [T]his was, after all, the essence of Rogers's life's work—not only a theoretical belief in the ideal of better communication, but an ongoing search for realistic and effective ways of implementing that theory on the intrapersonal, interpersonal, intergroup, and, in the end, international levels of application. (Kirschenbaum & Henderson, 1989a, p. 435)

In January of 1987, Carl Rogers was nominated for the **Nobel Peace Prize**; in February of the same year, he died of heart failure following surgery for a broken hip. Over his lifetime, Rogers wrote dozens of books, chapters in books, and articles expanding on this theory, with his most well-known books being *Client-Centered Therapy* (1951), *On Becoming a Person* (1961), *Carl Rogers on Encounter Groups* (1970), *Becoming Partners: Marriage and Its Alternatives* (1972), *Carl Rogers on Personal Power* (1977), *Freedom to Learn* (1969), and *A Way of Being* (1980). In addition, two well-known books published by Kirschenbaum and Henderson (1989c, 1989d)—*Carl Rogers: Dialogues* and *The Carl Rogers Reader*— contain interesting essays that Rogers wrote and fascinating conversations that Rogers had with some of the leading intellectuals of the twentieth century. Finally, Natalie Rogers, Carl's daughter, continued in her father's tradition by becoming a well-known psychologist and by founding the **Person-Centered Expressive Therapy Institute** (see http://www.nrogers.com) (see Box 7.1).

VIEW OF HUMAN NATURE

> The only reality I can possibly know is the world as I perceive and ex-
> perience it at this moment. The only reality you can possibly know is
> the world as you perceive and experience it at this moment. And the
> only certainty is that those perceived realities are different. There are as
> many "real worlds" as there are people! (Rogers, 1980, p. 102)

Rogers had a **phenomenological perspective**, which means that he believed
that reality for each person is a function of that person's consciousness or
understanding of the world, and not something external to the person. Thus, he
trusted the subjective experience of the person and believed that no other
person could truly understand the experience of another. At the same time, he
believed that we could come close to sensing other people's unique inner worlds
(Rogers, 1957b, 1980). Like all living organisms, Rogers suggested that the
infant and growing child has what's called an **actualizing tendency**, which
lends directionality to lives as individuals seek to reach their unique and **full
potential** (Rogers, 1951). If unimpeded, this force leads to constructive growth
and healthy relationships.

As the child grows and interacts with others, Rogers stated that he or she
engages in what is called an **organismic valuing process**. In other words, the
person assesses whether the interaction is positive or negative to the actualizing
process. Generally, the person moves toward those experiences or interactions
that are positive to the actualizing process and away from those that are negative.
However, Rogers also believed that as a "**self**" emerges, an individual develops
a **need for positive regard**. Sometimes, said Rogers, this need was more
compelling than the push toward a positive actualizing experience. So, if a
significant other (e.g., a parent) gives the individual the message that he or she
would only be loved if certain qualities are shown, and if these qualities are
antithetical to the actualizing process, the individual will forego the actualizing
process and act in accordance to the wishes of the significant other. Rogers
believed that when these **conditions of worth** are placed on a person, they
thwart the natural growth process and result in the development of a nongenuine
or incongruent way of living in the world. These principles, some of which are
listed in Box 7.2, are highlighted in Rogers's (1951) book, *Client-Centered Therapy*.

Rogers believed that individuals sometimes do not perceive conditions of
worth being placed on them or the resulting incongruence, and he posited that
individuals develop a **process of defense** in which they **selectively perceive
situations**, **distort situations**, or **deny threats to self** in an effort to protect
themselves from a **state of anxiety** that is the result of this **incongruence**. The
ability to defend oneself, however, is not perfect, and anxiety and related
symptoms can be conceptualized as a signal to the individual that he or she is
acting in a nongenuine way and not living fully (see Box 7.3):

> When the individual has no awareness of such incongruence in
> himself, then he is merely vulnerable to the possibility of anxiety
> and disorganization.... If the individual dimly perceives such an

---

B o x 7.2   The Developing Self

I)   Every individual exists in a continually changing world of experience of which he is the center.

II)   The organism reacts to the field as if it is experienced and perceived. The perceptual field is, for the individual "reality."

IV) The organism has one basic tendency and striving—to actualize, maintain, and enhance the experiencing organism.

V)   Behavior is basically the goal-directed attempt of the organism to satisfy its needs as experienced, in the field as perceived.

VIII) A portion of the perceptual field gradually becomes differentiated as the self.

IX) As a result of interaction with the environment, and particularly as a result of evaluation interaction with others, the structure of self is formed—an organized fluid, but consistent conceptual pattern of perceptions of characteristics and relationships of the "I" or the "me," together with the values attached to these concepts. (Rogers as cited in Kirschenbaum 2009, p. 232)*

Note: A select list of Rogers's principles of the developing self.

B o x 7.3   The Story of Ellen West

This story, so eloquently told by Rogers (1961), describes the history of a famous psychotherapy client (a client Rogers knew about but never saw himself). Rogers described the estrangement of this person from her feelings—how she felt obligated to follow her father's wishes and not marry the man she loved, how she disengaged herself from her feelings by overeating, how a few years later, she again fell in love but instead married a distant cousin according to her parents' wishes. Following this marriage, she became anorexic, taking 60 laxative pills a day, again as an apparent attempt to divorce herself from her feelings. She saw numerous doctors, who gave her differing diagnoses, treated her dispassionately, and generally denied her humanness. Eventually, disenchanted with her life, Ellen West committed suicide.

This story, Rogers noted, gives a poignant view of what it is like to lose touch with self—to be incongruent. Because Ellen West felt she needed to gain the conditional love of her parents, she acted in ways not congruent with her self. Losing touch with self led to a life filled with self-hate and a sense of being out of touch. Eventually, therapists viewed her as being mentally ill, which Rogers implied might have added to her feelings of estrangement and her eventual suicide.

---

incongruence in himself, then a tension state occurs which is known as anxiety. (Rogers, 1957b, p. 97)

Rogers believed that when with a person (such as a client) is with a second person who demonstrates **genuineness** (or **congruence**), **empathy**, and **unconditional positive regard**, the first person will feel safe enough to experience his or her *self*, with all of its incongruities that may have been developed as a function of conditions of worth that had been placed on that person. Gaining awareness of the incongruent self is the first step clients take prior to making choices that will lead them toward a more congruent self (Rogers, 1959). Calling genuineness, empathy, and unconditional positive regard "**core conditions**," Rogers believed that these attributes, alone, are enough to facilitate change (Rogers, 1957b). And Rogers also believed that it is not only therapists that can embody these characteristics and help to induce change; any person has the potential of embodying these core conditions (Rogers, 1980).

As you can probably deduce, the person-centered approach is **anti-deterministic**, as highlighted by its belief that people can understand their defensiveness, make changes in their lives, and move forward as they actualize their full potential. This belief in choice and free will lends an **existential** flavor to the person-centered approach and stands in contrast to the deterministic leanings of the psychoanalytic approach, which says we are victims of our drives.

As Rogers believed his approach could be adopted by many and applied in different settings, he spent much time traveling the world and meeting with groups in conflict trying to facilitate greater understanding of one another. And he did this by embodying the qualities he so believed in (Kirschenbaum & Henderson, 1989e).

KEY CONCEPTS

Actualizing Tendency

Rogers believed that every individual is born with an actualizing tendency that motivates him or her to reach full potential if the individual is placed in an environment that supports this inherent process. This basic biological principal has its corollary in all living things. For instance, consider the flower that delightfully blooms if placed in an optimum environment but ends up wilting if not. This important assumption for person-centered counselors affects how they conceptualize their clients' concerns. Instead of seeing clients from an illness perspective, they believe their clients have the potential to change and grow if placed in a nurturing environment. Such counselors view client progress as occurring when clients become increasingly real and genuine and are able to make more effective choices for themselves and others.

Need for Positive Regard

In their development of self, children look to be positively regarded by significant others; that is, to feel loved, supported, and appreciated by those close to them. In fact, children will manifest behaviors they believe that those close to them want them to exhibit in their hopes that they will be positively regarded by those individuals, *even if those behaviors are antithetical to the individual's natural way of being.* In this case, the exhibition of such behaviors would create a false or nongenuine self. In cases such as these, there is a conflict between the individual's actualizing tendency and his or her need to be positively regarded and loved by significant others.

Conditions of Worth

Closely related to the need to be positively regarded are *conditions of worth* that occur when significant others, who have the power to withhold their love and regard for

FIGURE 7.1 A Mother's Conditions of Worth

another, place expectations on a person's way of responding. In this case, significant others are expecting an individual to respond in a certain manner, even if that type of response is not how the person wishes to respond. Love, or the promise of love, is withdrawn if the person does not respond in that manner, and love is given if the person does respond in that manner. Over time, the person learns to respond in the manner in which the significant other wants him or her to respond, *even if that response is not natural or true to self.* The dilemma for the child is whether to listen to their internal state, which tells them to respond in a certain manner, or to exhibit behaviors in an effort to gain the significant person's love and regard. Look at Figure 7.1 and consider the following:

1. When this child becomes an adult, how might she respond when confronted with similar situations (e.g., a controlling husband)?

2. In what other ways could the mother have responded?

Nongenuineness and Incongruence

Nongenuineness occurs as a result of conditions of worth being placed on the individual. The individual who is nongenuine is not in touch with his or her feelings, and is living out a life that is false. Alternatively, his or her thoughts, feelings, and behaviors are incongruent; that is, the individual's feelings are not in sync with the individual's thoughts and behaviors.

Organismic Valuing Process

The process of evaluating the environment and drifting toward those individuals who positively value one's natural tendencies or ways of being and drifting away

---

B o x 7.4 A Young Boy's Need for Regard and Development of Self

A young boy develops and exhibits what some might call traditional feminine behaviors. The parents of this young boy give verbal and nonverbal messages to the child that he should not act in this manner (conditions of worth). The parents withdraw their love from the child every time they perceive him acting in this manner. On the one hand, his actualizing tendency is telling him that his usual way of acting is natural and part of who he is. On the other hand, he has a great need to be regarded by these important people in his life. This need to be loved by his parents outweighs his actualizing tendency, and he ends up living a nongenuine life, exhibiting behaviors that seem unnatural to him. These unnatural behaviors, however, are slightly out of his experience (he is not fully aware that he is acting in this manner). As he grows into his teenage years, the internal tug that something is not right continues. He becomes older, expresses behaviors different from those that are truly who he is, and continues to feel some subtle generalized anxiety—a sign that something is not right. At some point, as he grows into adulthood and perhaps feels freer to be his true self, he may experience this tug, now in the form of anxiety, more fully. It is at this point that he might enter therapy or find significant others who demonstrate qualities that allow his true self to emerge. After years of living a false life, he slowly but surely becomes his true self—again!

---

from those who negatively value them is called the **organismic valuing process**. This process will naturally lead to a positive self-image, except when significant others place conditions of worth on the individual. In these cases, the client's need to be positively regarded by significant others can thwart the organismic valuing process, which results in the individual's acting in false or nongenuine ways in order to be positively regarded (see Box 7.4).

Choice and Free Will

Rogers had an interesting take on the concepts of **choice** and **free will**. As a phenomenologically based, existential theorist, Rogers believed that people are free to make choices in their lives based on their subjective view of reality. However, he also acknowledged that individuals are victims of their pasts, especially when they are living lives based on a false sense of self. In these cases, individuals make choices grounded in their defenses and distortions, and such choices are clearly not healthy ones. In contrast, individuals who are more fully functioning and congruent are burdened less by their defenses, determined little by their past, and have freedom of choice. These persons are in touch with and are aware of their feelings, thoughts, and behaviors. However, there's a paradox: Because these individuals are in touch with themselves, they have a clear sense of which choices are most growthful and healthy for them—almost as if there is no choice:

> Nevertheless it has meaning for me that the more the person is living the good life, the more he will experience a freedom of choice, and the more his choices will be effectively implemented in his behavior. (Rogers, 1961, p. 193)

So, if you are clouded by your past and make choices out of incongruence, you're likely to choose poorly. But, if you're in touch with yourself and congruent about who you are, the choices you need to make in your life will be clear, as if you "should" (and I say that very tentatively) act in a certain manner to respect who you are.

Self-Determination

In person-centered counseling, **self-determination** is the process of looking within to make choices about oneself as opposed to allowing others to direct one's life. As clients become increasingly in touch with themselves, they become clearer on which choices are better for them, and they become ever more self-determining. Because incongruent clients will often look for answers outside of themselves, Rogers stressed the importance of creating an environment that offers clients the ability to make their own choices as they continue on their journey to becoming fully functioning. In a sense, clients move from dependency to autonomy as they increasingly rely on their inner sense of what choices are best for them and as they gain an ever-increasing **internal locus of control**, or the sense that control over their destiny is in their own hands.

Nondirective Counseling

Rogers believed that the ingredients for discovering one's self are within each person. Thus, he viewed it as critical that counselors and therapists create an environment that facilitates client self-discovery, as opposed to one that is therapist-centered and has therapists directing, advising, or interpreting the sessions. By counselors embodying the characteristics of empathy, genuineness, and unconditional positive regard, clients are given the freedom to look inside themselves and discover their inner world. This nondirective approach allows clients to get in touch with themselves and allows them to make self-initiated positive and growthful choices. Directing the client would inhibit client self-determination and discourage self-exploration, said Rogers.

The Necessary and Sufficient Conditions

Rogers believed that personality change would occur if the therapeutic framework included six "**necessary and sufficient conditions**":

1.   Two persons are in psychological contact.
2.   The first, whom we shall term the *client*, is in a state of incongruence, being vulnerable or anxious.
3.   The second person, whom we shall term the *therapist*, is congruent or integrated in the relationship.
4.   The therapist experiences unconditional positive regard for the client.
5.   The therapist experiences an empathic understanding of the client's internal frame of reference and endeavors to communicate this experience to the client.

> **B o x 7.5   Rogers's Work with a Schizophrenic Man**
>
> I think of one man with whom I have spent many hours, including many hours of silence. There have been long stretches when I had no way of knowing whether the relationship had any meaning for him. He was uncommunicative, seemingly indifferent, withdrawn, inarticulate. I think of an hour when he felt completely worthless, hopeless, suicidal. He wanted to run away, wanted to do away with himself because, as he muttered in flat despair, "I just don't care." I responded, "I know you don't care about yourself, don't care at *all*, but I just want you to know that *I* care." And then, after a long pause, came a violent flood of deep, wracking, gasping sobs which continued for nearly half an hour. He had taken in the meaning of my feeling for him. It was dramatic evidence of what all of us have learned—that behind the curtains of silence, and hallucination, and strange talk, and hostility, and indifference, there is in each case a person, and that if we are skillful and fortunate we can *reach* that person, and can live, often for brief moments only, in a direct person-to-person relationship with him. To me that fact seems to say something about the nature of schizophrenia. It says something too about the nature of man and his craving for and fear of a deep human relationship. It seems to say that human beings are persons, whether we have labeled them as schizophrenic or whatever. And I know that these moments of real relationship with these persons have been the essential reward for all of us participating in the program. (Rogers, 1967, pp. 191–192)

6. The communication to the client of the therapist's empathic understanding and unconditional positive regard is to a minimal degree achieved. (Rogers, 1957b, p. 96)

These conditions were sufficient enough, said Rogers, to help clients feel free to understand their past pains and hurts that were caused by conditional relationships in their lives. In fact, such a therapeutic relationship would help clients change behaviors and assist them in their movement toward a more genuine way of living. But what about clients who are really difficult to reach? Admitting that some clients were certainly more difficult to connect with than others, Rogers believed that it was crucial for therapists to try and connect; otherwise, as noted in Step 6 above, the necessary and sufficient conditions would be for naught. Look at Box 7.5 to see how Rogers connected with a client who was schizophrenic.

Rogers believed that clients were likely to change and grow in counseling if the above six conditions were met, and he often would highlight some of the likely changes you might find when clients had participated in person-centered counseling. For instance, he suggested such clients would have the following (Rogers, 1959, 1961):

- an increased openness to experience
- a greater ability to be more objective and to have more realistic perceptions
- improved psychological adjustment
- more congruence, increased self-regard, movement from an external to an internal locus of control
- more acceptance of others
- being better problem solvers
- having a more accurate perception of others

THERAPEUTIC TECHNIQUES

Believing that the word "technique" detracted from the essence of the personal relationship that occurred within counseling, Rogers rarely used that word (Kirschenbaum, 2009). However, he often elaborated on three personal qualities that he thought counselors should embody if they were to be effective in the helping relationship: congruence, unconditional positive regard, and empathy.

Congruence or Genuineness

For Rogers, being congruent, genuine, or real, was the most important of the therapeutic qualities, as a relationship has no meaning if the counselor hides behind his or her own mask and is not willing to risk being himself or herself:

> … It is when the therapist is natural and spontaneous that he seems to be most effective. Probably this is a "trained humanness" as one of our therapists suggests, but in the moment it is the natural reaction of *this* person. Thus our sharply different therapists achieve good results in quite different ways. For one, an impatient, no-nonsense, let's-put-the-cards-on-the-table approach is most effective, because in such an approach he is most openly being himself. For another it may be much more gentle, and more obviously warm approach, because *this* is the way this therapist is. Our experience has deeply reinforced and extended my own view that the person who is able *openly* to be himself at that moment, as he is at the deepest levels he is able to be, is the effective therapist. Perhaps nothing else is of any importance. (Rogers, 1967, p. 186)

But what if a therapist has particularly strong negative or positive feeling toward a client, or feelings that are, as Rogers (1957b) described, mysterious, threatening, or frightening? At the very least, Rogers said, the counselor needs to be in touch with and aware of those feelings.

> It would take us too far afield to consider the puzzling matter as to the degree to which the therapist overtly communicates this reality in himself to the client. Certainly the aim is not for the therapist to express or talk out his own feelings, but primarily that he should not be deceiving the client as to himself. At times he may need to talk out some of his own feelings (either to the client, or to a colleague or supervisor) if they are standing in the way of the two following conditions [empathy and unconditional positive regard]. (Rogers, 1957b, pp. 97–98)

The level of self-disclosure that the therapist shows the client, however, may vary depending on the session and whether the feeling is persistent. Rogers noted that although one may have negative feelings toward a client during a session, these feelings will almost invariably dissipate as the client opens up and unravels his or her inner self. This is why he warned therapists against using excessive self-disclosure. Finding the balance between the counselor's awareness of his or her own feelings and the expression of those feelings in an effort to be real is one of the challenges facing the person-centered therapist (see Box 7.6).

B o x 7.6   Being Genuine and Timing Self-Disclosure

I remember working with a client who was in a very unhappy relationship. She described her partner as being periodically verbally abusive. She was very well-off and clearly could afford living on her own. Every week, she would come in and tell me how horrible her partner was. I began to feel frustrated, thinking, *Why isn't she leaving him if she feels so strongly about the situation*? Then, one day, after telling the same story for the umpteenth time, she

began to open up and describe how fragile she felt and how fearful she was to be on her own. She was afraid of her loneliness, afraid that she would start drinking heavily, and afraid that she might have a "nervous breakdown." It was soon after this disclosure that she had the courage to leave. Perhaps if I had pressured her into leaving, she would not have gotten in touch with her inner feelings that were so important for her to understand.

B o x 7.7   I Guess Nobody Is Perfect—Not Even Dr. Rogers

In the late 1970s, I went to hear Carl Rogers talk for my second time. I was excited—Rogers was my hero. There were thousands of people in the audience, and as he fielded questions, I shyly raised my hand. Suddenly, he was pointing to me. I stood up and blurted something out, at which point he asked me to repeat myself. I again tried to formulate my question, and he said something like, "I can't understand what you're talking about." He moved on to another

question. I was shattered, hurt, and felt like rolling up into a ball. And he—yes, Carl Rogers—had not been as caring as he could be to this young counselor. I then discovered that even our heroes are not perfect.

Hear this story (entitled "Oh My God, He Doesn't Like Me") and other stories about Carl Rogers by clicking "Carl Rogers" at the "Stories of the Great Therapists" Web site: http://www.odu.edu/sgt

---

Unconditional Positive Regard

Rogers believed that counseling relationships should be highlighted by a sense of acceptance, regardless of what feelings are expressed by the client. In other words, the counselor should not accept certain feelings and experiences of the client and deny others. This unconditional acceptance, or *responsible love*, as Leo Buscaglia (1972) called it, allows the client to feel safe within the relationship and to delve deeper into his or her self:

> Responsible love is accepting and understanding.... [L]ove helps us to accept the fact that the other individual is behaving only as he [or she] is able to behave at the moment. (p. 119)

As the client begins to take steps toward understanding this deepening self, he or she will understand those aspects of self that are false and those that are real. In other words, the client will begin to see how he or she is living out a false life as the result of past conditions of worth that were placed upon him or her. Although Rogers states that unconditional positive regard should be present for the totality of a session, he admits that this is the ideal and suggests that all therapists must continually strive to achieve this state of being (see Box 7.7).

Empathy

Perhaps the most researched and talked-about element of the counseling relationship, **empathy**, or deep understanding of the client, was Rogers's third crucial element in the helping relationship (cf. Bohart, Elliott, Greenberg, & Watson, 2002; Carkhuff, 2000; Elliott, Greenberg, & Lietaer, 2004; Luborsky, Crits-Christoph, Mintz, & Auerbach, 1988; Wampold, 2001). Such understanding can be shown in a number of ways, including accurately reflecting the meaning and affect of what the client expressed; using a metaphor, analogy, or visual image to show the client that he or she was accurately heard; or simply nodding one's head or gently touching the client during the client's deepest moments of pain. Such acknowledgment of the client's predicament tells the client that the therapist has experienced the inner world of the client:

> … To sense the client's private world as if it were your own, but without ever losing the "as if" quality—this is empathy, and this seems essential to therapy. To sense the client's anger, fear, or confusion as if it were your own, yet without your own anger, fear, or confusion getting bound up in it, is the condition we are endeavoring to describe. When the client's word is this clear to the therapist, and he moves about in it freely, then he can both communicate his understanding of what is clearly known to the client and can also voice meanings in the client's experience of which the client is scarcely aware. (Rogers, 1957b, p. 99)

Over the years, Rogers's explanation of empathic listening has been interpreted and often packaged into what many of us now call **reflection of feelings**, or parroting what the client said. In one of the last articles written by Carl Rogers, he voiced anger toward some of the ways in which his concept of empathic understanding had been interpreted. Noting in particular the use of the terms "reflection of feelings" and "parroting" of client statements, Rogers stated that he never meant the counselor to mimic what the client had said, but rather to use all possible avenues to show the client that the counselor understood the client's way of making meaning out of the world.

> From my point of view as therapist, I am not trying to "reflect feelings." I am trying to determine whether my understanding of the client's inner world is correct, whether I am seeing it as he or she is experiencing it at this moment…. Am I catching just the color and texture and flavor of the personal meaning you are experiencing right now? (Rogers, 1986, p. 376)

Rogers noted that the best empathic responses to a client are those in which the therapist is able to **"subceive"** feelings beyond those of which the client is aware (Rogers, Gendlin, Kiesler, & Truax, 1967). As opposed to interpreting feelings that the therapist thinks the client might be having, subceiving feelings means that the therapist is sensing deep feelings from the client, feelings of which the client may not be aware. Only when the client agrees that he or she is experiencing these feelings is the therapist "on target" with his or her response.

Applications of Empathic Responding.   The popularity of Rogers in the 1950s and 1960s naturally led to a number of operational definitions of empathy. For instance, Truax and Mitchell (1961) developed a nine-point rating scale to measure empathy, which was later revised by Carkhuff (1969) into a five-point scale. A scale to measure empathy had important implications. For the first time, researchers could measure the empathic ability of counselors and determine whether there was a relationship between good empathic responses and client outcomes in therapy. Indeed, numerous research studies indicated that good empathic ability was related to progress in therapy (Carkhuff, 2000; Carkhuff & Berenson, 1977; Elliott et al., 2004; Luborsky et al., 1988; Neukrug, 1980; Weaver, 2000).

Believing that scales like this focused too much on "technique" at the expense of focusing on how the professional brought himself or herself into the relationship, Rogers was ambivalent about the development of such instruments (Kirschenbaum, 2009). Despite Rogers's mixed feelings, the Carkhuff scale became a mainstay of counselor training during the 1970s and 1980s, and although it is no longer used as extensively, the scale set the stage for **micro-counseling skills training** methods in counseling programs (Baumgarten & Roffers, 2003; Egan, 2002; Gazda et al., 2006; Ivey & Ivey, 2003). The scale ranges from a low of 1.0 to a high of 5.0, with 0.5-point increments. Any responses below a 3.0 were considered **subtractive** or nonempathic, while responses of 3.0 or higher were considered empathic, with responses over 3.0 called "**additive**" responses (see Figure 7.2).

The original Carkhuff scale in its entirety is reproduced in Table 7.1. This "**Accurate Empathy Scale**" dramatically changed the education of helping professionals, as professors, students, and helpers could assess one another's ability to make an empathic response. As is obvious in Table 7.1, a Level 1 or Level 2 response in some ways detracts from what the person is saying (e.g., giving advice, not accurately reflecting feeling, not including content), with a Level 1 response being way off the mark and a Level 2 only slightly off. For instance, suppose a client said, "I've had it with my dad; he never does anything with me. He's always working, drinking, or playing with my little sister." A Level 1 response might be, "Well, why don't you do something to change the situation, like tell him what an idiot he is?" (advice-giving and being judgmental). A Level 2 response might be, "You seem to think your dad spends too much time with your sister." (does not reflect feeling and misses content). On the other hand, a Level 3 response, such as "Well, it sounds as though you're pretty upset at your dad for not spending time with you," accurately reflects the affect and meaning of the client.

1		2		3		4		5
	1.5		2.5		3.5		4.5	

F I G U R E 7.2 The Carkhuff Scale

T A B L E 7.1 Carkhuff's Accurate Empathy Scale

Level 1	The verbal and behavioral expressions of the first person either do not attend to or detract significantly from the verbal and behavioral expressions of the second person(s) in that they communicate significantly less of the second person's feelings than the second person has communicated himself.
Level 2	While the first person responds to the expressed feelings of the second person(s), he does so in such a way that he subtracts noticeable affect from the communications of the second person.
Level 3	The expressions of the first person in response to the expressed feelings of the second person(s) are essentially interchangeable with those of the second person in that they express essentially the same affect and meaning.
Level 4	The responses of the first person add noticeably to the expressions of the second person(s) in such a way as to express feelings a level deeper than the second person was able to express himself.
Level 5	The first person's responses add significantly to the feeling and meaning of the expressions of the second person(s) in such a way as to (1) accurately express feelings below what the person himself was able to express or (2) in the event of ongoing, deep self-exploration on the second person's part, to be fully with him in his deepest moments.

Source: Carkhuff, R. (1969). *Helping and human relations* (vol. 2). New York: Holt, Rinehart & Winston. p. 121.

Level 4 and Level 5 responses reflect feelings and meaning beyond what the person is outwardly saying and add to the meaning of the person's outward expression. For instance, in the above example, a Level 4 response might be, "It sounds as though you're pretty angry at your dad because he doesn't pay any attention to you." (expresses a new feeling, anger, which the client didn't outwardly state). Level 5 responses are usually made in long-term therapeutic relationships by expert therapists. They express to the helpee a deep understanding of the pain he or she feels as well as recognition of the complexity of the situation.

In the training of helpers, it is usually recommended that they attempt to make Level 3 responses, as a large body of evidence suggests that such responses can be learned in a relatively short amount of time and are beneficial to clients (Carkhuff, 2000; Neukrug, 1980, 1987; Schaefle, Smaby, Maddux, & Cates, 2005). Effective empathic responses not only accurately reflect content and feelings, but do so at a moment when the client can hear this reflection. For instance, you might sense a deep sadness or anger in a client and reflect this back to him or her. However, if the client is not ready to accept these feelings, then the timing is off and the response is considered subtractive.

Often, when first practicing empathic responding, it is suggested that beginning counselors first make what's called a "formula response," which generally starts with reflection of feeling followed by the paraphrasing of content. As beginning helpers become more comfortable with the formula response, they move to what some call a "natural response," which embodies all the components in the formula response (reflection of feelings and content) but does so in a manner that is natural to the helper. So, "I hear you feeling sad because you're not closer to your dad," becomes, "Boy, you really seem to be struggling with sadness about the distance you feel from your father." Finally, as therapists become more adept at making responses, they begin to include the use of analogies, metaphors, visual imagery, and self-disclosure in their attempts to show deep understanding to their clients (Neukrug, 1998). So, a client who reveals that she is really struggling and trying hard to make changes, but no matter what she does, things seem to be as bad as ever, could get a response like, "Sounds like you're rearranging deck chairs on the Titanic." Or, a client who is struggling with a hurtful and abusive spouse could get a response like, "You know, as you're talking, I feel like my stomach is twisting and turning; I wonder if you might be feeling similarly."

As you can see, making empathic responses can be as simple as reflecting feelings and content and as complicated as using metaphors. Learning how to do this effectively never ends and is part of the creative process of being an expert therapist.

THE THERAPEUTIC PROCESS

As might be expected, Rogers viewed the effective therapeutic relationship as one in which the counselor is able to embody and maintain the core conditions of empathy, genuineness, and unconditional positive regard. The ability of the counselor to do this is directly related to the client's experience of a caring, empathic relationship in which the client feels accepted. This experience enables the client to feel a sense of safety within the relationship as trust is slowly built. This conditions alone create what Rogers referred to as the necessary and sufficient conditions of therapy, which we discussed earlier.

With the core conditions being exhibited, over time, the client will feel safe enough to reveal deeper parts of self both to the therapist and to himself or herself. As the relationship deepens, the client realizes how he or she has lived in nongenuine and false ways, and generally realizes that conditions of worth had been placed on him or her to create this nongenuineness or incongruity. Rogers talked about the therapeutic process as occurring in a series of steps that "occur only approximately" in the following order (Rogers, 1942, pp. 30–45):

1. The client comes in for therapy, which is an important, responsible action the client takes in changing his or her life.
2. The helping relationship is defined by the counselor as one in which the counselor does not have the answer, but can offer the client a safe place where he or she can explore self and find solutions to his or her problems.
3. The counselor provides a space where the client feels free to express all feelings regarding the client's problems.
4. As the client experiences the sense that he or she is free to express all feelings, negative feelings that the client has been fearful of acknowledging will arise, are accepted by the counselor, and can be examined.

5. After the client has expressed and processed negative feelings, positive feelings will begin to arise. These feelings, which seemed almost hidden by the negative feelings, are sometimes a surprise for clients.

6. As with the earlier negative feelings, the positive feelings that arise will also be accepted, examined, and processed.

7. The exploration of all feelings within an accepting environment leads to an understanding and acceptance of self.

8. As counseling continues, increased insight is achieved and possible courses of action are decided.

9. The client begins to make small but important positive behavioral changes in his or her life.

10. Insight is expanded, and self-understanding becomes more complete and more accurate.

11. The client increasingly self-directs his or her life and becomes less fearful about making choices that will lead to more productive relationships and more effective behaviors.

12. The client becomes increasingly autonomous and gradually develops a sense that the therapist is no longer needed. Counseling winds down.

When originally developed, person-centered counseling was considered a short-term approach in comparison to the then–widely popular psychodynamic methods. This is likely because the approach did not place time limits on therapy, and clients were free to spend as little or as much time in counseling as they desired. In fact, the person-centered purist would be likely to allow the client to decide, session to session, whether to return, and clients who did not wish to return were not seen as "resisting" counseling, although a counselor who had a strong reaction to a client's ending counseling might be found self-disclosing so that the two of them could have a "real" sharing about the upcoming ending of counseling.

Whereas the expectation in many psychodynamic approaches was that the client needed to work on deep-seated issues and that it would take a considerable amount of time to do so, no such expectation was placed on clients who participated in the person-centered approach. In fact, in person-centered counseling, it was often just as usual to find some clients spending only a few sessions in counseling as it was to find clients spending years in counseling. Although the principles of person-centered counseling can be applied if you meet with a client one time or for five years, today, person-centered counseling generally lasts from a few sessions to a year or more. Probably the most important determining factors in the length of treatment are the level of incongruence in the client and the kinds of issues the client is bringing to treatment. Finally, it should be noted that many counselors today have integrated the core skills used in person-centered counseling with many of the brief techniques found in other approaches (see Box 7.8).

B o x 7.8   Applying the Person-Centered Approach

For an application of empathy and the person-centered counseling approach, read or watch Dr. Ed Neukrug's work with José.

You can read this session by going to www. cengage.com/counseling/neukrug/CTP1e and click

"student downloads." Or your instructor may show this session in class with the DVD that accompanies his or her copy of the text.

SOCIAL, CULTURAL, AND SPIRITUAL ISSUES

There's an old joke concerning a fictitious dialogue between Carl Rogers and a client that goes something like this:

CLIENT: "I'm feeling really depressed."

ROGERS: "So it sounds like you're feeling really depressed."

CLIENT: "I'm feeling so depressed that I think I might harm myself."

ROGERS: "I'm hearing you say that you're feeling so depressed that you think you might harm yourself."

CLIENT: "In fact, I'm feeling so awful, that I might just jump out that window over there."

ROGERS: "Hmmmm, you're feeling so awful you might just jump out that window."

CLIENT: "Yes, I'm walking over to the window now."

ROGERS: "I hear you; you're walking over to that window now."

CLIENT: "I'm on the ledge."

ROGERS: "Yes, I see you're on the ledge."

CLIENT: "I'm going to jump."

ROGERS: "You're going to jump."

CLIENT: "Ahhhhhhhhhhhhhhhhhhhhhhhhhhhhh!" (as he jumps)

ROGERS: "Ahhhhhhhhhhhhhhhhhhhhhhhhhhh."

Well, let's start with a strong statement that the person-centered counseling approach does not encourage the kind of parroting that is highlighted above. And as stated earlier, Rogers was outspoken about the fact that being with a client was much more than "reflection of feelings." However, as you probably are already thinking, person-centered counseling, even when it's done correctly, may not be for everyone. So, when does it work and when should one try something else? One should probably be wary of using a person-centered approach under the following circumstances (Gladstein, 1983; Kegan, 1982, 1994; Ridgway & Sharpley, 1990):

- When the client comes from a culture in which external references, such as religious scripture, moral truths, societal values, or parental dictates, are critical to the client's perception of reality and to the kinds of choices clients make.

- When acquiring an internal locus of control is not the chief aim of the therapeutic process. As in item one, in some cultures, being in touch with self and deriving a stronger sense of self are not critical factors. For instance, in cultures in which the extended family, such as grandparents, is revered, deferring to those individuals might take precedent over listening to self. In these cases, person-centered counseling could be in conflict with the values of the culture.

- When therapy needs to be brief and focused. Although many of the therapeutic qualities Rogers recommends can still be used in brief therapy, if movement toward closure is to occur quickly, a more directive and active approach sometimes needs to occur.

- When being in touch with feelings is frowned upon within the culture. Because empathy relies much on helping client access feelings, and because some cultures downplay the importance of the expression of feelings, the use of empathy too early can cause some clients to be frightened by the therapeutic experience.

- When the problem is not conducive to a person-centered approach. Some problems, such as depression, respond particularly well to the qualities Rogers highlights; other issues, such as working on phobias, might be helped more quickly through the use of other techniques.

- When the helper is not cognitively complex. Counselors who are not able to think in complex ways will have difficulty understanding the world of their client. On the other hand, counselors who can think in more complex ways and view the world from multiple perspectives are likely to work more effectively with all clients.

- When the counselor is not culturally competent. As with cognitive complexity, lack of cultural competence will prevent counselors from being fully with their clients and hinder the ability to show empathy.

A word about spirituality and person-centered counseling: The person-centered counselor only cares about religion and spirituality as it relates to how much the client cares about it. Religion and spirituality is seen as one of many values and beliefs which a client might embrace, struggle with, and churn over. The effective person-centered counselor would allow any individual, whether he or she is Muslim, Christian, Jew, Hindu, atheist, or agnostic, to struggle over his or her own meaning of religion and spirituality, and would allow that person to come to his or her own conclusion as to what it means in his or her life.

Finally, a word on the philosophy of the person-centered approach as it relates to a more peaceful world. In the later years of Carl Rogers's life, he increasingly became involved with projects that worked toward peace. As I increasingly have come to understand this approach, it seems inevitable that any individual who embodies the philosophy of this approach would come to the same conclusions as did Carl Rogers and also place his or her efforts toward creating a peaceful world. As one understands how incongruence and defensiveness is developed in a person, and that it is possible to help any individual unravel his or her inner core and find inner peace, harmony, and love, it seems natural that those who embrace this approach would work toward helping others reach this goal. The person-centered counselor believes that a person who has found inner peace can help spread global peace.

EFFICACY OF PERSON-CENTERED COUNSELING

During the 1940s and 1950s, Rogers became increasingly interested in showing the effectiveness of the client-centered approach. His interest led him to apply for and obtain a series of grants that would allow Rogers and his staff at the University of Chicago Counseling Center to be some of the first researchers to examine client change (Kirschenbaum, 1979, 2009). The researchers completed a series of experimental studies with control groups that included the use of what was called the **Q-sort technique**. Using this technique, the researchers examined a wide range of outcomes related to client-centered counseling, with the most important probably being whether clients who had gone through client-centered counseling had success at reducing the gap between how they actually saw themselves (their "**self-concept**") and how they wanted to be (their "**ideal concept**"). Although criticized as being methodologically weak by some, this research was seen as groundbreaking, as it was the first to use client self-report as well as client tapes and transcripts of sessions to examine client change. As you might suspect, the research did show that the clients were able to achieve an increased sense of congruence between their self-concepts and how they wanted to be, and also appeared to improve when rated by outside observers who used established instruments.

Recent research has also found some interesting results that relate to Rogers's theory. For instance, research on the relationship between the counselor and client suggests that, regardless of the background of the client, the most important quality for positive therapeutic outcomes is the therapeutic alliance, or the ability of the counselor to connect with the client (Beutler et al., 2004; Horvarth & Bedi, 2002; Norcross, 2001; Orlinsky, Rønnestad, & Willutzki, 2004; Safran & Muran, 2000; Sexton & Whiston, 1991; Vocisano et al., 2004; Wampold, 2001; Whiston & Coker, 2000). Such a relationship seems eerily similar to what Rogers described in the "necessary and sufficient conditions" when he spoke of the importance of the counselor's reaching the client through empathy and unconditional positive regard. In speaking to the importance of the therapeutic alliance, Gelso and Carter (1994) note that the alliance affects the counseling relationship from the moment the client starts his or her first session until the client terminates counseling, *regardless of whether it is acknowledged by the counselor and the client.* Thus, many of the personal qualities that Rogers suggested that counselors should embrace seem to have been demonstrated important in recent research and scholarship.

In addition to research on the therapeutic alliance, research that specifically focuses on the use of empathy has shown it to be one of the most critical factors for effective client outcomes (Bohart et al., 2002; Carkhuff, 2000; Elliott et al., 2004; Luborsky et al., 1988). However, the use of empathy may have some

---

B o x 7.9   Angela's Experience with a Person-Centered Counselor

---

Please review the Miller family's background, which can be found in Appendix B, and then read about

Angela's encounter with a person-centered counselor, which can also be found in Appendix B.

---

limitations, and its value may be contingent on (1) the stage of the counseling relationship (more important in relationship-building stages), (2) the kind of client problem (e.g., depression), (3) the ability of the clinician to be empathic, (4) the cognitive complexity of the clinician, and (5) the ability of the client to recognize empathy (e.g., a person who is psychotic may not have this capacity).

Person-centered counseling, especially when contrasted with psychoanalysis, used to be seen as a short-term approach to helping. However, in recent years, with the advent of some of the newer therapies, like cognitive–behavioral and the post-modern approaches, person-centered counseling is now considered a longer-term approach when compared to these briefer forms. Thus, in today's therapeutic climate, for problems that are focused and can be "fixed" within a short amount of time, person-centered counseling is generally not seen as the treatment of choice. However, for a wide range of other problems, person-centered counseling seems particularly suited. Clearly, for issues such as depression, embedded anxiety disorders, relationship concerns, and self-esteem issues, person-centered counseling would often be the treatment of choice (see Box 7.9).

SUMMARY

Growing up a shy boy outside of Chicago, Carl Rogers was to become the most influential therapist of the twentieth century. Being raised with parents who were strictly religious, early in his career, Rogers hoped to become a minister. However, after deciding that the ministry was not his calling, he pursued graduate degrees in psychology. Although initially intrigued with the psychodynamic approach to counseling, Rogers eventually became disenchanted with the deterministic and reductionistic flavor of that approach and took on a more existential–humanistic orientation. As he refined his approach and began to develop his theory, its name changed from nondirective counseling to client-centered counseling to *person-centered counseling*. Eventually, Rogers developed a type of therapy that would revolutionize how therapists work.

Rogers's view of human nature had an existential flavor in the sense that individuals can freely make new choices throughout their lives. In addition, he used a phenomenological approach to understanding his clients. This means that he believed that reality for each person is a function of that person's consciousness or understanding of the world, and not something external to the person. He also believed that each person is born with an actualizing tendency that, if unimpeded, would allow the person to reach his or her full potential. Rogers believed that each individual has an organismic valuing process that assesses whether a person should move toward or away from experiences based on whether those experiences match the individual's unique qualities. However, he also noted that people have a need for positive regard, and when conditions of worth are placed on a person by significant others, this need to be regarded could outweigh the valuing process. This would result, said Rogers, in the person's responding in nongenuine or incongruent ways as the individual attempts to act in ways that the person believes others want him or her to. How the person manages his or her organismic valuing process and the conditions of worth that are placed on the person results in the development of the individual's "self." Rogers also noted that defense mechanisms that involve selectively perceiving situations, distorting situations, or denying threats to the self are created in an effort to prevent oneself from experiencing incongruence, and that anxiety or symptoms are one sign that a person is living incongruently.

To help the reader understand person-centered counseling, a number of key concepts were explained in this chapter, including the actualizing tendency, the need for positive regard, conditions of worth, nongenuineness and incongruence, the organismic valuing process, choice and free will, self-determination, nondirective counseling, and the necessary and sufficient conditions.

Although Rogers and other person-centered counselors do not like to use the word "techniques," they have identified a number of ways in which counselors tend to bring themselves into the helping relationship. These include exhibiting the core conditions of congruence or genuineness, unconditional positive regard, and empathy. In reference to empathy, it is important to remember that it is much more than reflecting feelings or parroting. In addition, over the years, the Carkhuff scale and other related instruments have been developed to systematically evaluate a person's ability to empathically respond.

Relative to the therapeutic process, Rogers noted that over time, there is an evolving process that generally occurs if the counselor exhibits the necessary and sufficient conditions of therapy. This process sees the client feeling increasingly safe, slowly but consistently opening up over time, increasingly sharing his or her deepest feeling, achieving increased insight, changing behaviors to more effective ones, expanding self-understanding, and becoming more autonomous. It was also noted that today, person-centered counseling can last from a few sessions to a year or more, and that clients, not therapists, generally direct the amount of time they spend in counseling.

Although person-centered counseling has wide applications with many kinds of people, in this chapter, we identified the kinds of clients with whom this type of counseling is most likely to find a fit. We also noted that relative to religion and spirituality, the person-centered counseling view is that any value and belief can be heard within the context of the therapeutic relationship. In addition, we noted that Rogers believed that with his philosophy came a more peaceful world.

Rogers was one of the first to conduct research on therapy outcomes with his Q-sort technique, which looked at the difference between the client's self-concept and the client's ideal concept, among other things. It was also noted that empathy, so critical in person-centered counseling, has been shown to be a particularly important quality for any therapist to embrace. Finally, the kinds of disorders and problems person-centered counseling is likely to be most effective were highlighted.

KEY WORDS

Accurate Empathy Scale

actualizing tendency

additive

anti-deterministic

Center for the Studies of the Person

choice and free will

client-centered counseling

congruence

conditions of worth

core conditions

deny threats to self

Distinguished Contributions to Applied Psychology as a Profession Award

Distinguished Scientific Contribution Award

distort situations

empathy

encounter group movement

existential

existential–humanistic

full potential

genuineness

Humanist of the Year award

ideal concept

incongruence

internal locus of control

journey into self

microcounseling skills training

necessary and sufficient conditions

need for positive regard

Nobel Peace Prize

nondirective counseling

nongenuineness

organismic valuing process

Person-Centered Expressive Therapy Institute

phenomenological perspective

process of defense

Q-sort technique

reflection of feelings

Rochester Society for the Prevention of Cruelty to Children

selectively perceive situations

self

self-concept

self-determination

state of anxiety

subceive

subtractive

unconditional positive regard

University of Chicago

Western Behavioral Sciences Institute

KEY NAMES

Buscaglia, Leo

Carkhuff, Robert

Dewey, John

Elliot, Helen

Gordton, Thomas

Kierkegaard, Søren

Kirschenbaum, Howard

Rank, Otto

Rogers, David

Rogers, Natalie

Rousseau, Jean Jacques

Skinner, B. F.

Truax and Mitchell

West, Ellen

REFERENCES

Baumgarten, E., & Roffers, T. (2003). Implementing and expanding on Carkhuff's training technology. *Journal of Counseling and Development, 81*(3), 285–291.

Beutler, L. E., Malik, M., Alimohamed, S., Harwood, T. M., Talebi, H., Noble, S., & Wong, E. (2004). Therapist variables. In M. J. Lambert (Ed.), *Bergin and Garfield's handbook of psychotherapy and behavior change* (5th ed., 227–306). New York: Wiley.

Bohart, A. C., Elliott, R., Greenberg, L. S., & Watson, J. C. (2002). Empathy. In J. C. Norcross (Ed.), *Psychotherapy relationships that work: Therapist contributions and responsiveness to patients* (pp. 89–108). New York: Oxford University Press.

Buscaglia, L. (1972). *Love.* Thorofare, NJ: Slack.

Carkhuff, R. (1969). *Helping and human relations* (vol. 2). New York: Holt, Rinehart & Winston.

Carkhuff, R. (2000). *The art of helping in the twenty-first century* (8th ed.). Amherst, MA: Human Resource Development Press.

Carkhuff, R. R., & Berenson, B. G. (1977). *Beyond counseling and therapy* (8th ed.). New York: Holt, Rinehart & Winston.

Egan, G. (2002). *The skilled helper: A problem management and opportunity-development approach to helping* (7th ed.). Belmont, CA: Brooks/Cole.

Elliott, R., Greenberg, L. S., & Lietaer, G. (2004). Research on experiential psychotherapies. In M. J. Lambert (Ed.), *Bergin and Garfield's handbook of psychotherapy and behavior change* (5th ed., pp. 493–539). New York: Wiley.

Gazda, G. M., Balzer, F. J., Childers, W. C., Nealy, A., Phelps, R., & Walters, R. P. (2006). *Human relations development: A manual for educators* (7th ed.). Boston: Allyn & Bacon.

Gelso, C. J., & Carter, J. A. (1994). Components of the psychotherapy relationship: Their interaction and unfolding during treatment. *Journal of Counseling Psychology, 41*(3), 296–306.

Gladstein, G. (1983). Understanding empathy: Integrating counseling, developmental, and social psychology perspectives. *Journal of Counseling Psychology, 30*, 467–482.

Horvarth, A. O., & Bedi, R. P. (2002). The alliance. In J. C. Norcross (Ed.), *Psychotherapy relationships that work: Therapist contributions and responsiveness to patients* (pp. 37–61). New York: Oxford University Press.

Ivey, A. E., & Ivey, M. (2003). *Intentional interviewing and counseling: Facilitating client development in a multicultural society* (5th ed.). Pacific Grove, CA: Brooks/Cole.

Kegan, R. (1982). *The evolving self.* Cambridge, MA: Harvard University Press.

Kegan, R. (1994). *In over our heads.* Cambridge, MA: Harvard University Press.

Kirschenbaum, H. (1979). *On becoming Carl Rogers.* New York: Delacorte Press.

Kirschenbaum, H. (2009). *The life and work of Carl Rogers.* Alexandria, VA: American Counseling Association.

Kirschenbaum, H., & Henderson, V. (1989a). Introduction. In H. Kirschenbaum & V. Henderson (Eds.), *The Carl Rogers Reader* (pp. xi–xvi). Boston: Houghton Mifflin.

Kirschenbaum, H., & Henderson, V. (1989b). [Introduction to] A philosophy of persons. In H. Kirschenbaum & V. Henderson (Eds.), *The Carl Rogers Reader* (pp. 398–401). Boston: Houghton Mifflin.

Kirschenbaum, H., & Henderson, V. (Eds.). (1989c). *The Carl Rogers Reader*. Boston: Houghton Mifflin.

Kirschenbaum, H., & Henderson, V. (Eds.). (1989d). *Carl Rogers Dialogues*. Boston: Houghton Mifflin.

Kirschenbaum, H., & Henderson, V. (1989e). [Introduction to] A more human world. In H. Kirschenbaum & V. Henderson (Eds.), *The Carl Rogers Reader* (pp. 434–435). Boston: Houghton Mifflin.

Kramer, R. (1995). The birth of client-centered therapy: Carl Rogers, Otto Rank, and "the beyond." *Journal of Humanistic Psychology, 35*(4), 54–110.

Luborsky, L., Crits-Christoph, P., Mintz, J., & Auerbach, A. (1988). *Who will benefit from psychotherapy? Predicting therapeutic outcomes.* New York: Basic Books.

Neukrug, E. (1980). The effects of supervisory style and type of praise upon counselor trainees' level of empathy and perception of supervisor. (Doctoral dissertation, University of Cincinnati, 1980). *Dissertation Abstracts International, 41*(04A), 1496.

Neukrug, E. (1987). The brief training of paraprofessional counselors in empathic responding. *New Hampshire Journal for Counseling and Development, 15*(1), 15–19.

Neukrug, E. (1998). Support and challenge: Use of metaphor as a higher level empathic response. In H. Rosenthal (Ed.), *Favorite counseling and therapeutic techniques* (pp. 139–141). Washington, D.C.: Accelerated Development.

Norcross, J. C. (2001). Purposes, processes, and products of the Task Force on Empirically Supported Therapy Relationships. *Psychotherapy: Theory, Research, Practice, Training 38*, 345–356.

Orlinsky, D. E., Rønnestad, M. H., & Willutzki, U. (2004). Fifty years of psychotherapy process-outcome research: Continuity and change. In M. J. Lambert (Ed.), *Bergin and Garfield's handbook of psychotherapy and behavior change* (5th ed., 307–389). New York: Wiley.

Rank, O. (1996). A psychology of difference: *The American lectures*. Princeton, NJ: Princeton University Press.

Ridgway, I. R., & Sharpley, C. F. (1990). Empathic interactional sequences and counselor trainee effectiveness. *Counseling Psychology Quarterly, 3*(3), 257–265.

Rogers, C. R. (1931). *Measuring personality adjustment in children nine to thirteen years of age.* New York: Teachers College.

Rogers, C. R. (1939). *The clinical treatment of the problem child.* Boston: Houghton Mifflin.

Rogers, C. R. (1942). *Counseling and psychotherapy: New concepts in practice.* Boston: Houghton Mifflin.

Rogers, C. R. (1951). *Client-centered therapy: Its current practice, implications and theory.* Boston: Houghton Mifflin.

Rogers, C. R. (1957a). A note on the "nature of man." *Journal of Counseling Psychology, 4*(3), 199–203.

Rogers, C. R. (1957b). The necessary and sufficient conditions of therapeutic personality change. *Journal of Consulting Psychology, 21*, 95–103.

Rogers, C. R. (1959). A theory of therapy, personality and interpersonal relationships as developed in the client-centered framework. In S. Koch (Ed.), *Psychology: A study of science, Vol. 3, Formulations of the person and the social context* (pp. 184–256). New York: McGraw-Hill.

Rogers, C. R. (1961). *On becoming a person: A therapist's view of psychotherapy*. Boston: Houghton Mifflin.

Rogers, C. R. (1967). Some learnings from a study of psychotherapy with schizophrenics. In. C. R. Rogers & B. Stevens (Eds.), *Person to person: The problem of being human* (pp. 181–192). Moab, UT: Real People Press.

Rogers, C. R. (1969). *Freedom to learn: A view of what education might become*. Columbus, OH: Charles Merrill.

Rogers, C. R. (1970). *Carl Rogers on encounter groups*. New York: Harper and Row.

Rogers, C. R. (1972). *Becoming partners: Marriage and its alternatives*. New York: Delacorte Press.

Rogers, C. R. (1977). *Carl Rogers on personal power: Inner strength and its revolutionary impact*. New York: Delacorte Press.

Rogers, C. R. (1980). *A way of being*. Boston: Houghton Mifflin.

Rogers, C. R. (1986). Reflection of feelings. *Person-Centered Review, 1*(4), 375–377.

Rogers, C. R., Gendlin, E. T., Kiesler, D. J., & Truax, C. B. (1967). *The therapeutic relationship and its impact: A study of psychotherapy with schizophrenics*. Madison, WI: University of Wisconsin Press.

Safran, J. D., & Muran, J. C. (2000). *Negotiating the therapeutic alliance: A relational treatment guide*. New York: Guilford.

Schaefle, S., Smaby, M. H., Maddux, C. D., & Cates, J. (2005). Counseling skills attainment, retention, and transfer as measured by the Skilled Counseling Scale. *Counselor Education and Supervision, 44*, 280–292.

Sexton, T. L., & Whiston, S. C. (1991). A review of the empirical basis for counseling: Implications for practice and training. *Counselor Education and Supervision, 30*, 330–354.

The top 10: The most influential therapists of the past quarter-century. (2007, March/April). *Psychotherapy Networker*. Retrieved from http://www.psychotherapynetworker.org/index.php/magazine/populartopics/219-the-top-10.

Truax, C. B., & Mitchell, K. M. (1961). Research on certain therapist interpersonal skills in relation to process and outcome. In A. E. Bergin & S. L. Garfield (Eds.), *Handbook of psychotherapy and behavior change: An empirical analysis* (3rd ed.). New York: Wiley.

Vocisano, C., Klein, D. F., Arnow, B., Rivera, C., Blalack, J., Rothbaum, B., … Thase, M. E. (2004). Therapist variables that predict symptom change in psychotherapy with chronically depressed outpatients. *Psychotherapy: Theory, Research, Practice, Training, 41*, 255–265.

Wampold, B. E. (2001). *The great psychotherapy debate: Models, methods, and findings*. Mahwah, NJ: Erlbaum.

Weaver, K. M. (2000). The use of the California Psychological Inventory in identifying personal characteristics of effective beginning counselors. *Dissertation Abstracts International, 60*(12-A), 4334 (University Microfilms International 95011-031).

Whiston, S. C., & Coker, J. K. (2000). Reconstructing clinical training: Implications from research. *Counselor Education and Supervision, 39*, 228–253.

Cognitive–Behavioral
Approaches

The four approaches that constitute this area became popular during the latter part of the twentieth century and continue to have widespread appeal today. They include behavior therapy, rational emotive behavior therapy (REBT), cognitive therapy, and reality therapy. Cognitive–behavioral approaches look at how cognitions and/or behaviors affect personality development, behaviors, and emotional states. All of these approaches suggest that cognitions and/or behaviors have been learned and can be relearned. They tend to spend a limited amount of time examining the past, as they focus more on how present cognitions and behaviors affect the individual's feelings, thoughts, actions, and physiological responses. They all propose that after identifying problematic behaviors and/or cognitions, one can choose, replace, or reinforce new cognitions and behaviors that result in more effective functioning. These approaches tend to be shorter-term than the psychodynamic or existential–humanistic approaches.

Chapter 8

Behavior Therapy

Learning Goals

- To gain a biographical understanding of B. F. Skinner, the innovator of the operant conditioning form of behavior therapy.
- To understand the historical context in which Skinner created his theory.
- To briefly examine the history of the development of the classical conditioning approach of Pavlov and Watson, and the social learning (modeling) approach of Bandura.
- To examine the objective, deterministic, reductionistic, approach to counseling of the early radical behaviorists.
- To review today's collaborative, anti-deterministic, and sometimes humane approach to behavior therapy and cognitive–behavior therapy.
- To review key concepts related to classical conditioning, such as unconditioned stimulus, conditioned stimulus, conditioned response, unconditioned response, and related terms.
- To review key concepts related to operant conditioning, such as reinforcement, punishment, schedules of reinforcement, shaping, chaining, extinction, and related terms.
- To review key concepts related to social learning, otherwise called *modeling*.
- To review a wide range of techniques that today's behavior therapists use, including acceptance; relaxation exercises and systematic desensitization; modeling; token economy; flooding and implosion techniques; punishment to effect change in children's behavior, such as response cost, social reprimands, time-out, overcorrection, physical punishment, and contingent electric stimulation; aversive therapy; stimulus control; self-management techniques; and operant conditioning techniques.
- To understand the six stages of behavior therapy, including building the relationship, conducting a clinical assessment, focusing on problem areas and setting goals, choosing techniques and working on goals, assessing goal completion, and focusing on closure and follow-up.
- To consider how different cultural backgrounds would make clients more or less amenable to the directive, objectivist approach of the behaviorist and to examine changes in how current behavior therapists view religion and spirituality.

- To highlight the fact that behavior therapy has been particularly easy to research but may not be suitable for individuals who are looking for an insight-oriented, in-depth approach.
- To see how behavior therapy is applied through vignettes, DVDs, and case study.

> ... [D]ogs employed in the experiments are subjected to a preliminary minor operation, which consists in the transplantation of the opening of the salivary duct ... to the outside skin ... the saliva now flows to the outside, on to the cheek or chin of the animal.... (Pavlov, 1927, p. 18)

In 1906, Ivan Pavlov (1849–1936) was performing surgery on the mouths of dogs and connecting a device to their salivary glands to measure secretions. He found that pairing a bell with the sight of food would condition the dogs to eventually salivate to the bell alone. This Russian physiologist, who would eventually win the Nobel Prize, had discovered what was to eventually be called **classical conditioning**.

Some years later, John B. Watson (1878–1958), who was familiar with Pavlov's studies, was conducting his own experiments on conditioning in animals at Johns Hopkins University. Deciding to look at conditioning in people, he conducted an experiment in which he struck a steel bar near the head of an 11-month-old baby named Albert while Albert held a white rat. The loud noise created a fear response that generalized to a white rabbit, cotton, wool, a fur coat, a dog, a Santa Claus mask, and the experimenter's hair. Watson's discovery led to the behaviorist school of psychology. Although he believed that genetics was an important piece of development, he also concluded that behavioral conditioning could be very powerful:

> Give me a dozen healthy infants, well-formed, and my own specific world to bring them up in and I'll guarantee to take any one at random and train him to become any type of specialist I might select—a doctor, lawyer, artist, merchant-chief and, yes, even into a beggar-man and thief, regardless of his talents, penchants, tendencies, abilities, vocations and race of his ancestors. (Watson, 1925, p. 82)

And let's not forget Albert Bandura (b. 1925), who found that children who watched a model of adults aggressing toward a Bobo doll (a clownlike air-filled doll that rights itself after you hit it) became more aggressive than children who did not view the model (Bandura, Ross, & Ross, 1963). Bandura's research on **social learning** or **modeling** would soon become another major way of understanding how behavior is learned (Bandura, 1977).

Then we have B. F. Skinner, the developer of **operant conditioning**, and the man who many said brought his daughter up in a "**Skinner box**," where she was reinforced for exhibiting certain "appropriate" behaviors. But is this story true or just another urban myth? Skinner, Pavlov, Watson, and Bandura all greatly impacted what became known as behaviorism, but it is Skinner whom we most remember. Let's take a look at his life and discover why he became the most recognized name in the behavioral school and whether he actually did raise his daughter in a Skinner box.

BURRHUS FREDERIC (B. F.) SKINNER

Susquehanna County, a small rural part of northeast Pennsylvania, was the birthplace of Burrhus Frederic Skinner. "B. F.," the person who was to revolutionize the field of behaviorism, was born on March 20, 1904. Almost from the time he could walk, Skinner had a propensity to invent and build things—perpetual motion machines, farming inventions, a cabin in the woods, and more. An active and outgoing child, B. F. described his family as old-fashioned, warm, and stable.

Prof. B. F. Skinner

Skinner's family included his father, who was a lawyer, his mother, who was a housewife, and a younger brother who was to tragically die of a brain aneurysm at the age of 16. Skinner did particularly well in school, and in high school was mentored by his English teacher, to whom he would eventually dedicate his book, *The Technology of Teaching* (1968). Valedictorian of his high school class, he ended up becoming an English major at Hamilton College in New York State, wanting to become a writer. After graduating college, Skinner built himself a study in his parents' attic and tried his hand at writing; however, he was not very productive and subsequently called this period of his life his "dark year." Looking for something different, Skinner left his parents home for Greenwich Village, where he dabbled in writing newspaper articles and lived the life of a poor writer. He eventually took a job as a bookstore clerk and happened to read some books by Ivan Pavlov and John B. Watson. Perhaps it was then that his inventive self was sparked as he found in these books the experimental side of psychology. Intrigued, he soon enrolled in the psychology department at Harvard.

While at Harvard, Skinner's interest was piqued by the chair of the physiology department's interest in studying the whole animal, which contrasted greatly with the psychology department's focus on the "inside," or physiology of the animal. Soon, Skinner could be found experimenting in the lab and building new equipment that could help him measure responses of animals. Before long, Skinner was to discover that, in contrast to what Pavlov and Watson had hypothesized, the behavior of rats pressing a bar seemed to be influenced more by what happened *after* the animal pressed the bar than what preceded the response. Soon, Skinner named this new science that examined

reinforcement contingencies, "operant conditioning." In 1931, Skinner received his Ph.D. Obsessed with studying different **schedules of reinforcement**, he remained at Harvard doing research until 1936. In 1938, he published his first book based on his studies: *The Behavior of Organisms.*

Marrying Yvonne Blue and taking his first teaching job at the University of Minnesota were big life changes for Skinner in 1936. Not too long after, the couple had their first child, Julie, who was eventually to become a well-known educational researcher and academic. Today, Julie Skinner Vargas is President of the **B. F. Skinner Foundation** in Cambridge, Massachusetts. Continuing with his experiments, Skinner decided to put his talents to good use during World War II when he demonstrated that he could reinforce pigeons to steer gliders with explosives attached toward enemy targets—even when the gliders were bombarded with loud noises and on a fast, downward trajectory (Skinner, 1960). The invention of radar, however, made **Project Pigeon** moot.

In 1943, his wife again pregnant, Skinner invented a new kind of crib that was heated and enclosed in Plexiglas. Eventually, the crib, which Skinner called a **"baby-tender"** was written about in *Ladies' Home Journal* under the title **"Baby in a Box"** (Bjork, 1997). This article was the impetus for what was to become an urban myth. Many had come to believe that Skinner's younger daughter, Deborah, was brought up in a "Skinner box" (the name sometimes given to describe the box Skinner used when studying rats, pigeons, and other animals). The myth even went further: "She went psychotic" or "she committed suicide" because of "the box." This myth was to haunt Skinner for the rest of his life, as people would come up to him and ask how his poor daughter was doing. In reality, his daughter was doing great, was not brought up in a box, and today, Deborah Skinner Buzan is married and a successful artist in London. In fact, ask either of Skinner's daughters today, and they will describe a warm, caring father who was very much present in their lives.

Soon after World War II, Skinner wrote one of his best-known books, *Walden Two* (Skinner, 1948). This novel, which is largely based on behavioral principles, describes an experimental utopian community in which all behavior is oriented toward people living a fulfilled life through the use of reinforcement contingencies. In the novel, operant conditioning principles are applied within a communal setting to ensure the survival and contentment of the community. The book, which had its share of critics, was widely read, emulated in some communities, and made Skinner's name instantly known around the world.

The mid-1940s saw Skinner's career blossom as he became chair of the psychology department at the University of Indiana, helped to develop the **Society of the Experimental Analysis of Behavior**, and soon after joined the faculty at Harvard. As a culmination of some of the lectures he gave at Harvard, he published the book *Science and Human Behavior* in 1953.

The next 20 years saw Skinner continue to research his theory of operant conditioning and write dozens of articles and books on his theory. After visiting

---

B o x 8.1   Can a Behaviorist Be a Humanist?

During the defense of my doctoral dissertation, my advisor, who was a behaviorist, asked me if "a behaviorist can be a humanist." I went on to give what I thought was a rather esoteric response, noting that the basic orientations of the approaches were philosophically different and therefore incompatible with each other. A few years later, I had the opportunity to hear B. F. Skinner talk at a church in

New Hampshire. Following his talk, I went up to him and asked, "Can a behaviorist be a humanist?" Waiting a moment, he turned to me, and with a deeply reflective and austere look, he said, "Well, I don't know about that, but he can surely be humane."

You can hear this and other stories by clicking on "B. F. Skinner" at the "Stories of the Great Therapists" Web site: http://www.odu.edu/sgt

---

one of his daughter's elementary school classes and realizing that the teacher did not follow basic reinforcement concepts to help children learn, he decided to write about the proper use of reinforcement contingencies in teaching and then developed one of the first machines to do programmed learning. Out of his interest in education came two books: *The Analysis of Behavior: A Program for Self-instruction* (Holland & Skinner, 1961) and *The Technology of Teaching* (Skinner, 1968). In 1957, Skinner wrote a book entitled *Verbal Behavior* that theorized how the process of speaking, writing, and thinking follow operant conditioning principles. A conceptual book only, as opposed to much of his other research-based writing, it was widely criticized. Recently, however, it has gained some renewed attention (Sautter & LeBlanc, 2006).

During the 1960s and 1970s, and into the 1980s, Skinner became increasingly well-known and won a number of awards, including the **National Medal of Science** from President Lyndon B. Johnson in 1968, the **Gold Medal of the American Psychological Foundation** in 1971, and, one year later, the **Humanist of the Year award** of the American Humanist Association. During these decades, he wrote quite a bit on the moral and philosophical implications of operant conditioning to society. Thus, we saw the publication of such books as *Contingencies of Reinforcement* in 1969, *Beyond Freedom and Dignity* in 1971, *About Behaviorism* in 1974, and *Reflections on Behaviorism and Society* in 1978. He could also be frequently seen on television and at lectures discussing his philosophical point of view (see Box 8.1). Toward the end of his life, he remained very active professionally.

As Skinner aged, he wrote a number of books about his life, including *Particulars of My Life* (1976), *The Shaping of a Behaviorist* (1979), and *A Matter of Consequences* (1983). In these writings, he often highlighted how we all could benefit from the application of behavioral principles as we age (e.g., creating an environment that is user-friendly for our aging bodies). Eight days before his death, he received the **Citation for Outstanding Lifetime Contribution to Psychology** from the American Psychological Association. On August 18, 1990, ailing from leukemia, he finished a manuscript on a recent talk he had given at the American Psychological Association's annual conference. Later that day, he passed away.

VIEW OF HUMAN NATURE

Early Radical Behaviorists

> Skinner made no assumptions about behavior being caused by innate
> drives, nor did he believe that complex behaviors (for example, aggres-
> sion, sympathy, altruism, jealousy, and love) are adequately accounted
> for by referring to "human nature." (Nye, 2000, p. 134)

If you're a Freudian, you believe that the reasons for many of our behaviors
are known only to our unconscious, which is an aspect of some mysterious
underlying part of our selves. If you're a humanist, you are not likely to use the
word *unconscious*, but you probably believe in parts of our selves being "out of
awareness"—also as if there is some mysterious unknown part of self. But if
you're a **radical behaviorist**, none of these invented cognitive processes, often
called "**mentalistic concepts**" by Skinner, matter. In fact, radical behaviorists
believe that the unconscious, or idea that some things are just "out of awareness,"
are all concepts of which we have been conditioned to believe, and are figments of
our conditioned imaginations. In a Skinnerian world, there is no mention of these
kinds of mentalistic concepts—everything is related to how our behaviors have
been conditioned.

Genetics plays a very small role in operant conditioning. In fact, Skinner
believed that, with the exception of some reflexes, the infant is born a "**blank
slate**," or *tabula rasa*, and through conditioning, the growing child learns new
behaviors. Thus, the newborn may have an inborn suckling reflex, but through
conditioning, the infant learns other behaviors. Breast milk tastes good, so suckling is repeated. The mother smiles at the infant while the infant is suckling, and
the infant learns to smile back (suckling is associated with smiling), and so forth.

In the Skinnerian world, people are not born good or bad, happy or sad,
naturally jealous, inherently kind, or oriented toward some amorphous "growth
force." We are just born, perhaps with a pre-wired (genetic) tendency to orient
our being toward survival (e.g., the suckling instinct), but with little or no
inclination toward certain personality qualities or inward mental abilities. Our
conditioning history, as well as the present situation in which we find ourselves
(the reinforcers and punishments in our current environment), is what makes us
who we are. So, the behaviorist would say that if you find a person to be
kind, considerate, and insightful—you know, all those good qualities we tend to
like—look closely and you'll likely be able to identify how that person has been
conditioned to acquire those attributes. And if you want your client to become
kind, considerate, and insightful, you'd better make sure the environment is
arranged so the individual is likely to be reinforced to exhibit those behaviors.

So, take out those sticker charts, parents—those stickers can be very
powerful reinforcers for specific behaviors you want your children to exhibit.
But those sticker charts take work. You can't just leave them near the
refrigerator and hope that once in a while a sticker will appear on the chart.
Those stickers need to be applied at an optimal frequency and at the right
moment, and—this is a big "and"—your children need to experience them as

---

B o x 8.2   Rogers, Skinner, Free Will, and Making Healthy Choices

---

The concept of free will and choice is interesting and complex, and Carl Rogers and B. F. Skinner had different takes on it:

Rogers: Rogers suggested that persons who are self-actualized are in touch with themselves and reflect carefully about important decisions in their lives. Ultimately, when faced with important decisions, these persons have clarity about how to act, and alternative choices would not make much sense. He even said at one point that people who have such clarity are so clear on their choices, it's almost as if they don't have a choice. These individuals also understand the relationships among their choices and how such choices impact the world. So, choices they make would also be good ones for the world.

Skinner: Skinner believed that it is our past reinforcement histories that bring us to where we are now. Those individuals who have been reinforced for what we might call "healthy behaviors" will have a tendency to make choices that will continue those healthy behaviors. And, because what we call "healthy behaviors" are generally associated with getting along with others, the choices they make will likely have a positive impact on others and the world.

These are two disparate views; yet, in both cases, the path the "healthy" person takes is good for the person and good for the world. Perhaps these two roads lead to a similar place.

---

reinforcing. Maybe they would prefer some hugs or quarters instead. And perhaps more important, sticker charts are just a small piece of it all. Skinner suggested that reinforcement occurs in very subtle ways. It's the way you look at people (eyes warm and kind, or looking askance), it's the way you talk to them (rough tone, or sweet, or loving, etc.), it's the way that your body turns when you see them, it's your touch, or the removal of your touch, and it's your essence (if Skinner would allow me to use such a "New Age" term). It's how you place yourself in the environment of another person and how they experience you. Yes, sticker charts work, but reinforcers come in many sizes and shapes.

The Skinnerian is **deterministic** in the sense that he or she is a scientist who looks for causes that lead to effects. Thus, the behaviorist looks at how the environment impinges on the organism and determines (causes) specific behaviors (effects). In fact, Skinner did not believe we have **free choice**, because we are destined to act in certain ways based on our environmental histories (see Box 8.2). The distinction between acting in the here-and-now as a function of our past (cause and effect) histories versus *choosing* in the here-and-now is the crux of the difference between the concepts of determinism and free will. Skinner argued that we are never free to choose. Even people who think they are free believe that way because their behaviors have been reinforced in a manner that led them to think that way. Ultimately, these individuals will act in a predictable fashion based on their past reinforcement history. However, you can make changes in your environment so that you can live a more enjoyable life through a process of what Skinner called **self-management**. Is this a paradox in the Skinnerian position? Skinner would say not hardly, as our "choice" to change the environment is the result of our past reinforcement contingencies that brought us to a place where we are likely to make "choices" that bring us increased pleasure because we have been reinforced for making these types of choices in the past.

Modern-Day Cognitive–Behavioral Therapists

Today, it is rare to find a radical behavior therapist, because almost all therapists who believe in the importance of focusing on behaviors also believe that mental images and thoughts are conditioned. Thus, cognitive-behavioral therapists generally view their approach from a **learning theory** perspective because they believe that learning, through conditioning, is a central precept to both cognitive and behavioral therapy. So there is no longer the "**black box**" theory of behaviorism, or the belief that one should attend only to the box (outside of the person) and not to what's inside the box.

In addition to behaviors being conditioned, today's cognitive–behavioral therapists believe that deeply embedded cognitive structures, or illogical and irrational ways of thinking (see Chapters 9 and 10), or even beliefs about an unconscious, can be conditioned. Some cognitive–behavioral therapists even believe in a Freudian type of unconscious as they attempt to combine different schools of thought.

With recent advances in biology, virtually all cognitive–behaviorists realize the importance that genetics and other biological advances plays in a wide variety of mental disorders. And as you might guess, today's cognitive-behavioral therapists are **anti-deterministic**. They believe in the capacity of the person to change by identifying dysfunctional behaviors and irrational thinking, understanding how conditioning continues dysfunctional ways of living in the world, and devising methods of conditioning new behaviors and different cognitions. The modern-day cognitive–behavioral therapist usually agrees upon the following major factors that lead to healthy or abnormal development:

- The individual is born capable of developing a multitude of personality characteristics.

- Significant others and cultural influences play a particularly important role in how the individual is conditioned.

- Behaviors and cognitions are generally conditioned in very complex and subtle ways.

- The kinds of behaviors and cognitions that are conditioned play a central role in the development of normal and abnormal behavior.

- Genetics and other biological factors may play a significant role in who we become.

- By carefully analyzing how behaviors and cognitions are conditioned, one can understand why an individual exhibits his or her current behavioral and cognitive repertoire.

- By identifying what behaviors have been conditioned, one can eliminate undesirable behaviors and set goals to acquire more functional ways of behaving and thinking.

- By actively disputing dysfunctional thinking and through countercondi- tioning, change is possible in a relatively short amount of time.

KEY CONCEPTS

As you might expect, almost all of behavior therapy is based on the precepts of classical conditioning, social learning or modeling, and operant conditioning. The following are short descriptions of these three behavioral paradigms that collectively make up the key concepts of the behavioral approach.

Classical Conditioning

Classical conditioning, also called **associative learning**, is when an **unconditioned stimulus** becomes repeatedly paired with a **neutral stimulus**; eventually, the neutral stimulus evokes the same kind of response as does the unconditioned stimulus. The neutral stimulus has now become a **conditioned stimulus** and now yields a **conditioned response**. Thus, we saw with Pavlov's dogs the unconditioned stimulus (taste of the food) being paired with a neutral stimulus (the ringing of a bell); eventually, the bell became associated with the food and evoked the same response (salivating) as did the unconditioned stimulus (conditioned stimulus: the bell, yielded conditioned response: salivating). In the case of Baby Albert, a similar paradigm was operating in that a neutral stimulus (the white rat) was associated with an unconditioned stimulus (clashing of a steel bar) that yielded a fear response (unconditioned response). Eventually, the white rat alone (conditioned stimulus) evoked the fear response (conditioned response) (see Figure 8.1). After the conditioned response took hold, and through a process called **generalization**, this response was also evidenced when Baby Albert was exposed to other soft white items (e.g., Santa Claus beard, fur coat, cotton, etc.).

Soon after these early experiments established the basic conditioning paradigm, other related constructs were also discovered, such as **discrimination**, or the ability of a person to respond selectively to one stimulus but not a similar stimulus; and **spontaneous recovery**, or the tendency for responses to recur after a brief period of time after they have been extinguished.

Baby Albert, and similar experiments, showed how fear can be classically conditioned in humans. Over the years, a number of behavioral techniques (e.g., **aversion therapy**, **flooding**, and **systematic desensitization**) to extinguish such classically conditioned fear responses have been developed and will be discussed later.

Operant Conditioning

Operant conditioning, generally thought to be the most common type of conditioning, occurs when a behavior increases or decreases due to the consequences that occur *after* the emission of the behavior. In this paradigm, it is assumed that the organism is "operating" in the environment in some relatively random fashion, and behaviors periodically are reinforced, punished, or extinguished. The term "relatively random" is used because early behaviorists believed that individuals come into this world with little or no tendency to exhibit any specific behaviors. Thus, the infant's behaviors are random, and specific behaviors being emitted will

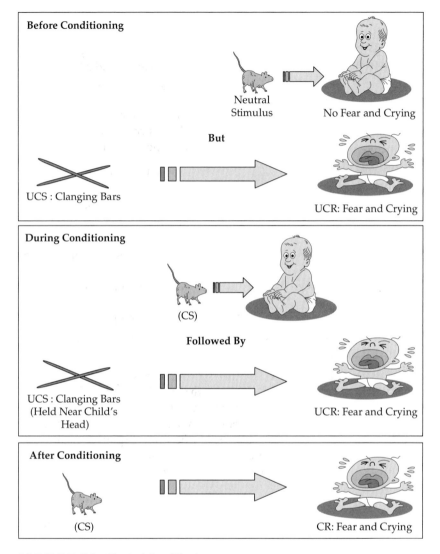

Before Conditioning

Neutral
Stimulus

No Fear and Crying

But

UCS : Clanging Bars

UCR: Fear and Crying

During Conditioning

(CS)

Followed By

UCS : Clanging Bars
(Held Near Child's
Head)

UCR: Fear and Crying

After Conditioning

(CS)

CR: Fear and Crying

F I G U R E 8.1 Classical Conditioning

either be reinforced and increase, be punished and decrease, or have no consequences and be extinguished. Skinner found that as the infant experiences the consequences of the relatively random behaviors he or she emits, some behaviors will have a tendency to repeat themselves through what Skinner called a process of **successive approximation** or **shaping**. As behaviors become shaped, they become less random. Parents can shape their children's behaviors deliberately or, as most parents do, behaviors can be shaped accidentally or inadvertently. Thus, one set of parents, ignorant of the power of operant conditioning, might unknowingly shape their child's behaviors in a manner that results in a sardonic and mischievous child, while another set of parents might deliberately shape their child's behavior so that the child acts in what most people would consider to be age-appropriate ways. There are many different ways to reinforce, punish, or extinguish behaviors, and understanding how to apply such concepts effectively can go a long way in shaping another's behaviors.

Over the years, through rigorous research, Skinner and others have delineated many principles of operant conditioning, each of which is crucial to the shaping of behaviors and the development of personality. A small portion follows:

1. **Reinforcement**: The addition or removal of a stimulus that leads to an *increase* in a specific behavior (see Table 8.1).

    a. **Positive reinforcement**: Any stimulus (usually considered favorable) that, when presented, increases the likelihood of a response. For instance, a child says "please," and a sticker is placed on her sticker chart.

    b. **Negative reinforcement**: Any stimulus (usually considered negative or aversive) that, when removed, increases the likelihood of a response. For instance, a child exhibits appropriate manners during a meal, and the child does not have to perform his or her usual task of cleaning the dinner table afterward (removal of the negative stimulus).

2. **Punishment**: The addition or removal of a stimulus that leads to a *decrease* in a specific behavior (see Table 8.1).

    a. **Positive punishment**: The addition of a noxious or aversive stimulus that leads to a decrease in a specific behavior. For instance, I grab my child and yell "no" to her after she runs into the street.

    b. **Negative punishment**: The removal of a pleasant stimulus that leads to a decrease in a specific behavior. For instance, a spouse/partner stops making dinners in response to the partner's coming home late. Or, a teacher removes recess as a response to a child's acting out during the day.

3. **Schedules of reinforcement**: The numerous ways in which a stimulus can be arranged to reinforce behavior; based on elapsed time and frequency of responses.

    a. **Ratio schedules**: Ratio schedules are when individuals are reinforced after a certain number of behaviors are exhibited. Ratio schedules can be fixed or variable. A **fixed ratio schedule** occurs when a reinforcer is given on an exact schedule (e.g., every time or every third time a person exhibits a behavior). For instance, first-grade students in a self-esteem

TABLE 8.1   Positive and Negative Reinforcement and Punishment

	Behavior will decrease	Behavior will increase
Stimulus presented	positive punishment	positive reinforcement
Stimulus removed	negative punishment	negative reinforcement

group are reinforced by their school counselor when he gives them a happy-face sticker every time they find something positive to say about themselves. In addition, for every third group meeting they attend, they get to have lunch with the school counselor. A **variable ratio schedule** means the behavior is not reinforced on a fixed schedule but is reinforced for an average number of times (e.g., on average, every tenth time). The reinforcement can come after the second time, twentieth time, third time, twenty-first time, etc., but averages every tenth time. A behavior learned through this type of schedule is particularly difficult to extinguish because the individual does not know when he or she will be reinforced but may "expect" the reinforcement at any time. For instance, a spouse may be continuing to exhibit specific behaviors in the anticipation that he or she will have sex or be loved. The expectation is that the love or sex will come eventually—after all, it has in the past. What kind of reinforcement do you think slot machines are based upon?

b. **Interval schedules**: Interval schedules are reinforcements that are based on periods of time instead of number of times. Like ratio schedules, interval schedules can be fixed or variable. If I reinforce my students every 2 minutes for paying attention in class, they are on a **fixed interval schedule**, but if I reinforce them, on average, every 2 minutes, but at a variable rate (after 1 minute, then after 5 minutes, then after 3 minutes, etc.), I am using a **variable interval schedule**.

4. **Shaping (successive approximations)**: Shaping involves systematically reinforcing certain behaviors in order to reach a specified end goal behavior. At the start of shaping, any behavior remotely similar to the target (end) behavior is reinforced, but as shaping continues, only behaviors increasingly similar to the target behavior are reinforced. For instance, Skinner spent a great deal of time shaping the responses of animals (e.g., pigeons) to the point where he was able to have them do some rather bizarre and incredible behaviors (e.g., consistently beat you at tic-tac-toe). Consider the kinds of behaviors parents could shape in their children if effort was placed on this kind of conditioning.

5. **Chaining**: Chaining involves reinforcing the last response or behavior in a series of responses so that each previous response is associated with the final reinforcer. For instance, if I want to teach a complex behavior to clients, I break it down into small pieces, with the final, end behavior being reinforced. Consider how teaching the behavioral skill of "slow eating," with the final behavior being swallowing, could be chained (e.g., picking up the fork, moving the fork to the food, stabbing the food with the fork, picking the fork up, moving the fork toward the mouth, etc.).

6. **Extinction**: Extinction involves the cessation of a behavior because it is not reinforced. For instance, rather than allowing our then-three-year-old to come into bed with us every night (which was reinforcing), we put a gate up at her door so she couldn't leave her room. After a few days (of extremely anguished crying), the behavior ceased and she slept through the night in her own bed.

Spontaneous recovery.

It's important to know that what reinforces one person may be punishing to another person. So, in order to be sure that something is reinforcing, you must pay attention to the target behavior. If the behavior is increasing, reinforcement is occurring. However, if the target behavior is decreasing, punishment is occurring. Generally, reinforcement and extinction are employed more frequently by therapists than punishment. In addition, reinforcement is usually considered to be more effective at making lasting change than punishment (Nye, 1992). This may be because reinforcement teaches a new behavior, whereas punishment does not—it simply works on stopping an old behavior. However, under some circumstances, punishment can be a powerful addition to the therapist's repertoire of behaviors (see the "Therapeutic Techniques" section).

Social Learning or Modeling

Social learning, which is often called **modeling**, is when a behavior is viewed and then repeated at a later time. Usually, the behavior has some intrinsic value and thus there is reason for the individual to maintain some mental image or model of the behavior so that it can be used later. Imagine a spouse who is verbally abused views a role-play on how to be assertive. The skills in the role-play are not needed immediately, but at the next opportunity, he or she can use them. If the assertive behavior is successful because there is reduction in the aversive stimulus of verbal abuse, the verbally abused spouse will be likely to repeat his or her assertive behavior in the future. Consider the kinds of behaviors that could be modeled for low-achieving elementary school students in an effort to increase their grades. Or, think about the potential effectiveness of a DVD that shows middle-school students how to respond to bullying behavior. And for adults, imagine an anger management group viewing a role-play on how to effectively express emotion. All of these new behaviors can be viewed, and subsequently implemented. Bandura (1977) talked about four conditions if a model is to be effective.

1. The client must be attentive to the model being offered.
2. The client must be able to remember the details of the model.
3. The client must have the ability to repeat the observed model.
4. The client must be motivated to repeat the model (there must be some payoff for repeating the model).

THERAPEUTIC TECHNIQUES

The number of behavioral techniques used today is huge, with one text on cognitive–behavioral approaches to counseling offering close to 70 techniques that could be applied for a wide range of mental health problems (O'Donohue, Fisher, & Hayes, 2003). Therefore, any short list of techniques would surely be limiting. However, over the years, some techniques have "stood the test of time" and have been consistently used by many, even those therapists who don't identify themselves as behaviorists. The following represents a few of these "tried-and-true" techniques.

As you examine the techniques that follow, keep in mind that there are few pure behaviorists these days, with most therapists who have this leaning identifying themselves as cognitive–behaviorists. This is because both behavioral therapy and cognitive therapy are based on learning theory, and both tend to promote a rather active, didactic style in working with clients. So in addition to the techniques listed below, you may want to review the chapters in this text that focus on cognitive therapy (Chapter 8 and Chapter 9) as many, if not most, of those techniques are often incorporated into the cognitive–behaviorist's repertoire of techniques.

Acceptance

Acceptance occurs at two levels: the therapist's acceptance of the client, and teaching the client how to accept himself or herself. Clients who feel unaccepted are unlikely to reveal hidden or shameful parts of themselves. Thus, the therapist must embody an attitude that is accepting of the client's feelings and shows understanding of the client, regardless of what the client shares. Such acceptance, however, does not imply validation of behaviors that are hurtful to self or others (Hayes & Pankey, 2003):

> … a pedophile might be encouraged to accept the presence of urges to
> molest children, but should not be encouraged to accept molesting
> behaviors; an abused spouse might be encouraged to accept angry reac-
> tions or feelings of shame, but should not be encouraged to accept
> abusive behavior or an abusive environment; a trichotillomanic might
> be encouraged to accept thoughts about pulling hair or the urge to do
> so, but should not be encouraged to accept hair pulling; a person with
> self-loathing thoughts would be encouraged to accept these thoughts as
> an ongoing process (e.g., "now I am having the thought that I am bad")
> but would not be encouraged to accept their literal content (e.g., "and
> in fact I am bad"). (p. 6)

If I were you, at this point, I would be asking myself why a humanistically oriented concept of acceptance is found in a chapter on behaviorism. Acceptance, as viewed from a behavioral perspective, is critical to the client's ability to identify problems accurately. If clients do not feel accepted, and if they do not accept their own feelings, they will not be able to identify or reveal those behaviors which they want to change. The pedophile who does not accept his urges to molest a child, and who does not feel accepted enough to talk about these urges, will not be able to identify the desired behavioral changes (not acting on these urges).

Acceptance from a behavioral perspective is an action—the therapist must take active steps to show his or her acceptance, and the client must actively try to accept his or her feelings and thoughts, even those that might result in such feelings as shame and guilt. How does the behaviorist actively show acceptance?—by showing with his or her body that the therapist is open to hearing from the client, by having good

---

B o x 8.3   Dr. Thompson's Work with Rayneer

Read or watch Dr. Thompson's work with Rayneer, and try to identify how Dr. Thompson shows acceptance to Rayneer.

You can read this session by going to www. cengage.com/counseling/neukrug/CTP1e and click

"student downloads." Or your instructor may show this session in class with the DVD that accompanies his or her copy of the text.

---

listening skills and being empathic, by telling the client that it is okay to discuss anything within a session, and by not being dismissive of the client through verbal and nonverbal cues. Similarly, the client can take certain actions to accept self, such as applying relaxation techniques in an effort to lessen stress so that he or she is more likely to be open to the thoughts and feelings being experienced.

As you might expect, acceptance of the client is a skill particularly important near the beginning of counseling as it is basic to trust-building. Having the client accept self, however, is an ongoing process that occurs throughout therapy (see Box 8.3).

Modeling

Clients can learn a wide variety of new behaviors by observing desired behaviors in others and later modeling these behaviors by practicing them on their own. Sometimes called **social learning**, **imitation**, or **behavioral rehearsal**, modeling can be a significant part of the change process as one imitates the behaviors of others and rehearses those behaviors one intends to integrate (Cooper, Heron, & Heward, 2007; Naugle & Maher, 2003).

Modeling can occur in a number of ways, such as (1) when a therapist decides to highlight certain clinical skills with hopes that the client will learn by example (e.g., expressing empathy, being nonjudgmental, being assertive), (2) through the use of role-playing during the session (e.g., the counselor might role-play job interviewing techniques for the client), and (3) by teaching the client about modeling and encouraging him or her to find models outside the session to emulate (e.g., a person who has a fear of speaking to a large group might choose a speaker he or she admires and view the specifics of how that person makes a speech).

With modeling, targeted behaviors that the client wishes to acquire must have a high probability for success (Bandura, 1977). Thus, as noted earlier, it is important to accurately identify desired behaviors to be changed, pick appropriate models from which one can emulate the identified behavior, ensure that the client can remember the model and has the ability to repeat what was observed, and make sure the client is motivated to practice the new behaviors within and outside of the session. For instance, an individual who has a fear of making speeches would first need to find a model to emulate. After observing this model, a hierarchy could be devised whereby the client would make a speech—first to the therapist, then to some trusting friends, then to a small group, and so forth—perhaps asking for feedback along the way in order to sharpen his or her performance.

Modeling has been used to help clients develop a wide range of new behaviors. Imagine how one might use modeling to help clients become more assertive, communicate more effectively, eat more slowly, or relax more efficiently. Finally, modeling occurs all of the time, even when one does not purposefully seek to model another person's behaviors. And the more perceived power the model holds, the more likely modeling will occur. As you might expect, counselors who are looked up to and sometimes even idealized by their clients can be very powerful models, even unintentionally (Brammer & MacDonald, 2003). Thus, regardless of the theoretical approach of the counselor, he or she should consider that the very skills being demonstrated during a session will likely be modeled to some degree by the client.

Relaxation Exercises and Systematic Desensitization

Since an individual cannot experience anxious and calm feelings simultaneously, **relaxation exercises** are often taught to clients who are experiencing anxiety, stress, and/or fear. This classical conditioning concept, called **reciprocal inhibition**, was first used by Jacobson (1938), who taught anxious clients how to progressively relax by focusing on each major muscle group in the body—tightening and then feeling the muscle relax, until the whole body was relaxed. Joseph Wolpe (1958, 1990), expanded this idea with the development of systematic desensitization. Wolpe suggested a three-step process in which the client (1) learns how to relax through the use of relaxation exercises, (2) in consultation with the therapist, develops a hierarchy of the anxiety-evoking situations, and (3) gradually is exposed to an image of the actual anxiety-seeking situation. Since the relaxed feeling is paired with the formerly anxiety-producing image or situation, over time, relaxation replaces anxiety. This method has been shown to be successful when used for anxiety disorders, particularly phobic behaviors, and obsessive–compulsive disorders (Head & Gross, 2003).

In working with clients using this technique, a hierarchy of fears is developed. For instance, imagine an individual who has a fear of elevators. A hierarchy might include (1) looking at an elevator, (2) standing in an elevator with the door held in the open position, (3) going up one flight in an elevator, (4) going up five flights in an elevator, (5) going up 20 flights in an elevator, (6) going up 50 flights in an elevator, (7) going up to the top of the Empire State Building. In the office, a counselor would start with the first level of the hierarchy by asking the client to close his or her eyes and then taking the client through the relaxation response. Next, the counselor would start at the bottom of the hierarchy, in this case, asking the client to imagine looking at the elevator. The client would be told to raise a finger as soon as he or she experienced any anxiety. When anxiety is felt, the counselor reestablishes the relaxing feeling and starts over. Often, therapists use the **subjective unit of discomfort** (SUD) scale in determining whether to move on to the next level of the hierarchy. Using this scale, 0 = the most relaxing experience imagined by a client and 100 = the most anxiety-evoking experience imagined by the client.

B o x 8.4   Dr. Thompson's Work with Rayneer

Read or watch Dr. Thompson's work with Rayneer to see how Rayneer uses relaxation techniques to help her deal with her anxiety about driving.

You can read this session by going to www. cengage.com/counseling/neukrug/CTP1e and click "student downloads." Or your instructor may show this session in class with the DVD that accompanies his or her copy of the text.

Clients can move up to the next level of the hierarchy when they experience a 10 or lower at the current level. Using this method, the counselor would repeat the process until the client is capable of imagining the whole hierarchy with little or no anxiety. This technique takes time, sometimes as many as four to six sessions, until the client is able to completely imagine the hierarchy without being anxious (Ferguson, 2003). After completing the hierarchy in the office, the client can practice in real life. Nowadays, many therapists will accompany clients while trying these behaviors (see Box 8.4).

Token Economy

The token economy has become one of the mostly widely recognized and used operant conditioning techniques. Originating in the 1960s, this approach has been mostly associated with individuals institutionalized for mental retardation or mental disorders (Ayllon & Azrin, 1965, 1968). However, a token economy can be used with a wide range of individuals in a variety of settings, including schools, homes, and work settings. The basis of this approach is that a token is given to an individual when an identified appropriate behavior is exhibited. After a certain number of tokens have been collected, and/or a specified amount of time has been passed, the individual can exchange the tokens for a reward. Although tokens on their own are not reinforcing, when associated with a powerful **backup reinforcer** for which they can be exchanged, they take on reinforcing properties (Cooper et al., 2007). Ghezzi, Wilson, Tarbox, & MacAleese (2003) suggest the following eight steps when setting up a token economy:

1. *Define the target behavior:* Clearly explain when an individual would obtain a token.

2. *Specify the setting:* Be specific concerning which settings are token-worthy. For instance, an individual who is institutionalized might receive a token for a specific behavior while at the institution but may not receive one for a similar behavior while on a home visit.

3. *Select tokens:* Choose tokens that are not easily counterfeited and are appealing to the clients.

4. *Identify backup reinforcers:* Clients should have a clear description of the kinds of rewards or backup reinforcers for which the tokens can be exchanged.

5. *Determine a schedule of reinforcement:* Clients should know how many tokens specific behaviors are worth and how often they can obtain such tokens.

6. *Establish the exchange rate:* The number of tokens that can be exchanged for various rewards or backup reinforcers should be unambiguous.

7. *Establish a place and time to exchange tokens:* When and where individuals can exchange their tokens should be made known.

8. *Keep records:* Records should be kept on the number of tokens each person has earned, which target behaviors earned the tokens, the number of tokens exchanged, and which rewards or backup reinforcers were purchased.

Flooding and Implosion Techniques

Usually used in the treatment of phobias, flooding and implosion techniques are based on classical conditioning and involve exposing an individual to a feared stimulus for an extended period of time. Because a person cannot stay anxious for long periods of time, the stimulus eventually becomes associated with a calm feeling. In flooding, the client either imagines being in the presence of the stimuli or actually places himself or herself "in vivo" with the stimuli (e.g., riding elevators in the Empire State Building, without desensitization, for those who have an elevator phobia!) (Zoellner, Abramowivtz, & Moore, 2003). Flooding seems to have had particular success with obsessive–compulsive disorders, post-traumatic stress disorders, generalized anxiety disorders, and social phobias.

Although sometimes used as a synonym to **flooding** (Levis & Krantwiess, 2003), the originators of **implosion therapy** (sometimes called **implosive therapy**) viewed this technique as intensifying the individual's anxiety by adding to the situation an unlikely, but plausible, scenario (Boudewyns & Shipley, 1983). For instance, in the following case example, a Vietnam veteran has post-traumatic stress disorder which is particularly focused on a fear of thunderstorms. A thunderstorm would often result in the client's going into his basement, driving away from the storm in his car, or drinking excessively—all in an effort to reduce his anxiety. In the following case, the therapist relates the client's fear to experiences in Vietnam when the client was startled by an explosion while he was standing near a tree. Then, the therapist exaggerates the fear by suggesting some particularly unpleasant anxiety-producing mental images (see Box 8.5).

Punishment to Effect Change in Children's Behavior

There are a number of techniques to effect change in children's behavior using punishment. However, because punishment may lead to unsuspected side effects (e.g., anger or other negative emotional responses), it is generally saved for particularly difficult or potentially harmful behaviors (e.g., head-banging, biting, aggression, tantrums, throwing) (Nye, 1992; Cooper et al., 2007). In addition, research over the years has shown that punishment is much more powerful when accompanied by the positive reinforcement of desired behaviors (Wacker, Harding, Berg, Cooper-Brown, & Barretto, 2003). Finally, when deciding whether to use

---

B o x 8.5   Implosive Therapy and PTSD

Therapist: Okay. I want you to feel this now. You can feel this in slow motion. You can hear that tremendous crash. It just keeps reverberating. Everything slows down now. You see a flash getting bigger and bigger. The noise sounds like thunder and it rumbles louder and louder. The pressure is pushing against you and you feel yourself losing control. Losing control and you are out of control and things start to go black. Your eyes are dim and you can't hear anything and you feel yourself floating. Floating and sailing into the air. You must be dying. You are dying. Feel that. Float into air. Feel that floating sensation. You can hear all your buddies yelling and screaming and see all of them. I want you to see the way it was. You can see them now all bloodied and you can feel your hot face and chest. You know that you had been hit too and you don't even know if your body is in one piece. It's as if it is flying apart. You are flying apart. Out of control. Concentrate on that. You're losing your grip. Floating and feeling the floating sensation. You are dying. "I am dying, I'm dying." You look down where you are and you are ripped apart. You feel your eyes, nose, and mouth bleed. You're just destroyed. You are destroyed and you are dying. You are gasping for air and you can't see. All you can feel is numbness now. You are blacking out and you can look down now as you float and see this massacre and see all of the bodies until you just THUD ... hit the ground. It is the last thing you feel before you just pass out. You're dead. You're dead. (Boudewyns & Shipley, 1983, pp. 129–130)

---

punishment with children, clinicians should consult with the children's parents to ensure that they feel comfortable using such techniques and to assess whether other, gentler techniques have been tried but failed (Blampied & Kahan, 1992). When the decision to use punishment has been made, a number of steps are suggested:

1. Carefully assess the desired behavior to be changed, using direct observation when possible.
2. Decide on the target behavior.
3. Develop a plan that is clearly understood by the recipient and the recipient's parents.
4. Make sure the recipient of the plan (and/or the recipient's parents) feels comfortable with the use of punishment.
5. Follow through on plan and assess its viability.
6. Make changes as necessary.

A quick overview of some punishment techniques often used today follows, and include response cost, social reprimands, time-out, overcorrection, physical punishment (e.g., spanking), and contingent electric stimulation. Some of these techniques can be taught to parents and practiced at home.

Response Cost.   With response cost, there is a "cost" for a certain behavior being exhibited. In these cases, the cost is the dispensing of a punishing consequence (negative or positive punishment; see Box 8.1) in order to cause a decrease in an undesired behavior and an increase in a desired behavior (Cooper et al., 2007; Little, 2003). Thus, in order to ensure that my daughter reads 30 minutes a day (the desired behavior), I do not allow her to instant message her friends ("pleasant" stimulus removed) unless she has read for 30 minutes The behavior she enjoys (the instant messaging) has thus been made contingent on her reading.

Social Reprimands.   We have all seen parents, teachers, and others use reprimands to try and change a child's behavior. However, the effectiveness of reprimands is mixed, depending on how they're used (Cooper et al., 2007). If a reprimand is used, it should be delivered firmly and infrequently; otherwise, individuals tend to habituate to it. When used, it should be clear to the recipient exactly what behavior is being focused upon, and positive reinforcement of other, appropriate behaviors should also be applied. In addition, when used in social spheres, code words or phrases can be used in place of the reprimand to lessen embarrassment. So, a child who consistently speaks out of turn in the classroom can be told by the teacher, "Jason, we've talked about you raising your hand prior to speaking; please do so in the future." Or, using a code word or phrase collaboratively chosen by Jason and the teacher, the teacher could say, "Jason, I'll call on you later," every time he speaks out of turn. Most important, when Jason appropriately does raise his hand, he must be positively reinforced for such behavior. The teacher could say, "Nice job raising your hand," or could smile at him, or give him a token that can be turned in at a later time for a reward.

Time-Out.   The most frequently used technique by parents in the United States (Friman & Finney, 2003), time-out (TO) involves the elimination of an undesired behavior (e.g., hitting) by removing a child from the situation in which he or she is exhibiting the behavior and placing the child in a new environment where there is little stimulation so that he or she may calm down. In administering TO, the following steps should be taken:

1. Be clear in advance with the child about what behavior warrants a TO.
2. Warn the child that a TO is imminent if the specific behavior does not cease.
3. Have a specific spot (e.g., a room or quiet space) where the child will be sent if the behavior does not cease.
4. Be clear on the amount of time that will be spent in the TO. One minute per age has been traditional, but Friman and Finney (2003) suggest ending a TO when the child has behaviorally shown that he or she is ready to leave TO (e.g., has calmed down).
5. Praise compliance when the child completes TO and positively reinforce appropriate behaviors.
6. Have an incentive for completing TO (although one must be careful not to reinforce TO!).

Overcorrection.   Overcorrection involves having a child engage in corrective behaviors that take effort and are contingent on and the result of exhibiting inappropriate behaviors (Cooper et al., 2007). For instance, a child who was asked to clean up his room once a week, and does not do so, is told to clean up his room every day for the next two weeks. Or, a child who hits a friend is told to apologize to the friend verbally, write a letter to the friend apologizing, and engage in an action that is helpful to the friend (e.g., giving the friend one of his toys, or helping the friend with homework) (see Box 8.6).

B o x 8.6 Overcorrection (A good thing?)

When I was about 10 years old, my mother caught me playing with matches. She took me into the bathroom and had me light a book of about 1,000 matches held in a special case she had. After I lit about 100, she said, "Okay, you've done enough." Well, I never arbitrarily lit matches again, but on the other hand, that "punishment" always stood out as something "mean" my mother did—something unlike her usual character.

Physical Punishment.   Perhaps the most controversial of the punishment techniques, physical punishment (e.g., spanking) is generally perceived by most as not being a particularly effective method of punishment (Blampied & Kahan, 1992). Oftentimes, spanking is done out of anger, not at the appropriate time, and can lead to repressed anger in a child. If spanking is to be considered, it should only be done for a targeted behavior that may be causing self-injury, or behavior that might cause harm to others. Thus, if a two-year-old is continually running in the street, spanking the child might reduce the frequency of this potentially dangerous behavior. On the other hand, effective parenting would have parents positively reinforcing the non-running-in-the-street behavior from the moment the child is able to walk. Such reinforcement should occur on a continual basis and takes effort—effort that many parents aren't willing to put out.

Contingent Electric Stimulation.   Although rarely used, brief electric shock to suppress a behavior that has been causing self-harm has shown dramatic results. For instance, Cooper et al. (2007) describe a number of studies in which such shock was used for individuals with behaviors that were longstanding and self-injurious, such as head- and face-banging. Such behaviors occur in some children on a continual basis to the point where they need to be restrained by helpers or parents, sometimes for hours. Obviously, the use of this type of punishment needs to be seriously considered only when it can remarkably improve an individual's well-being and in consultation with parents and experts in this kind of technique.

Aversion Therapy

Based on a classical conditioning paradigm, the basis of aversion therapy is to associate, on multiple occasions, a stimulus that is perceived to be highly noxious by the client with a behavior to be changed (Nathan, Gorman, & Salkind, 1999; Gifford & Shoenberger, 2003). Generally, aversive therapy is used with behaviors that put one at high risk of harming oneself or another. For instance, such therapy has had some success in treating smoking, alcoholism, sexual deviance, and, as discussed in the section on punishment, self-injurious behaviors such as head banging.

Using aversive therapy, Nathan et al. (1999) describes possible treatments for paraphilias (e.g., exhibitionists, pedophiles, sexual masochists and sadists). In such treatment, the client is first taught how to relax; is then aroused, usually through a mental image; is then presented an aversive stimulus; and finally escapes the aversive stimulus and the arousal. Thus, a pedophile might be first asked to relax comfortably, then told to imagine a situation which causes arousal, such as driving a car near a school and stopping to watch the children. Next, while in a state of arousal, the client is asked to imagine police-car lights whirling and sirens shrieking as police come running toward his car with guns in hand. No longer in a state of arousal, the client is next asked to imagine that the police run up to his car but, at the last minute, tell him it is a case of mistaken identity; they thought he was someone else they had been looking for. As sexually deviant behaviors are difficult to suppress and change, in addition to the aversive mental image, additional aversive stimuli, such as a noxious odor or electric shock, often need to be associated with the arousing mental image.

In a similar fashion, the drug Antabuse is an aversive stimulus taken by alcoholics to reduce their likelihood of drinking. When alcohol is ingested while the individual is on Antabuse, the individual has a wide range of negative bodily reactions, such as nausea, vomiting, indigestion, tachycardia, and heart palpitations.

Clearly, aversive stimuli should only be used with long-term behaviors that are particularly difficult to eliminate and that can cause the client and/or society serious harm.

Stimulus Control

Stimulus control occurs when a stimulus is altered and the new, healthier behavior that results from the altered stimulus is reinforced (Poling & Gaynor, 2003). Thus, whether we're talking about altering the sight of a drug, alcohol, or food to reduce an addiction; or rearranging furniture in a house to make it easier for an older person to live in his or her home; or labeling toys in a playroom with the first letter they start with so that a child is more likely to learn how to spell (a "doll" has a "D" placed on it), stimulus control can be quite powerful. When practicing stimulus control, it is critical to ensure that the individual is reinforced as a result of the changed stimulus. For instance, the sole act of removing alcohol from the home may not result in the new, desired behavior (reduction in drinking). At the very least, positive reinforcement for new, non-drinking behaviors should be occurring also. On the other hand, rearranging furniture in an older person's home might have some inherent reinforcing benefits, such as the person's not falling over furniture, finding it easier to get to the TV, or having an easier time getting to the food in the refrigerator. How might one reinforce new behaviors of the toddler so that the learning of the letters on the newly labeled toys is reinforced? (Hint: A parent's smile can be quite reinforcing.) Described in Box 8.7, my use of a lock to secure the kitchen is a type of stimulus control.

Self-Management Techniques

In this age of brief therapy, it is not surprising that self-management therapy (SMT), or providing a structured process in which the client can manage his or her own treatment plan, has become quite popular. Often undertaken within a

---

B o x 8.7   Stimulus Control of Night Eating

As a child I was overweight and would often find myself, in the middle of the night, at the refrigerator eating a snack. This behavior was clearly not healthy and as an adult, I decided to limit it. However, the addictive quality of waking up in the middle of the night and going to the refrigerator was quite strong. After I was married, and had two children, I devised a method of controlling this bad habit that has continued to work for me. I placed a lock on the kitchen door, bought a small safe, and had my wife and children learn the combination of the safe. Then, at an appropriate time every night, I would lock the kitchen door and place the keys in the safe. My wife and children would still have access to the kitchen at night, if they so chose, but I did not. This has substantially controlled my nighttime eating, and in the morning, when I wake up and feel good about myself and my body, I am reinforced for this new behavior.

B o x 8.8   Dr. Thompson's Work with Rayneer

Read or watch Dr. Thompson's work with Rayneer to see how Rayneer uses a heart sticker to ready herself (the self-managed controlling response) to practice her relaxation exercise that she learned in the therapist's office (the controlled target behavior response).

You can read this session by going to www.cengage.com/counseling/neukrug/CTP1e and click "student downloads." Or your instructor may show this session in class with the DVD that accompanies his or her copy of the text.

---

group setting (Rehm & Adams, 2003), SMT involves clients' learning how to accurately (1) select achievable goals, (2) monitor their progress toward their goals, (3) reward themselves as they make progress, (4) reassess the process if success is not achieved, and (5) plan for the future.

Over 50 years ago, Skinner (1953) described self-management as involving two responses: the **controlling response** and the **controlled response** (Cooper et al., 2007). The controlling response involves a self-managed behavior that prepares oneself to do the controlled response. The controlled response is the target behavior that one is wanting to exhibit. Thus, if I want to increase my ability to make empathic responses with my significant other, I might place red dots around my house to remind myself of the behavior that I want to change (making nonempathic responses). These dots ready me for the new behavior I want to adopt (making empathic response). The dots are the self-managed controlling response, while the actual empathic response is the controlled response or target behavior (see Box 8.8).

Operant Conditioning Techniques

A number of operant conditioning principles have been used to eliminate unwanted behaviors and to reinforce new, desired behaviors. After making an initial assessment of client concerns, behaviors to be eliminated are identified and newly desired behaviors are chosen to be adopted later. Then, the

T A B L E 8.2   Chart to Establish Baseline of Identified Undesirable Behaviors

Undesirable behavior	Amount	Time of day	Where	Intensity (1 = low, 10 = high)	Comments about
Overeating	List all foods eaten:				
Binge eating	Number of:				
Nighttime eating	Number of:				
Unhealthy foods	Types of:				
Negative body image	Thoughts about:				
Exercise	Types of:				

counselor will generally develop a baseline of the behaviors which are to be eliminated. Usually, such a baseline involves a count of the frequency and intensity of behaviors and is often completed through a charting and/or journaling process in which the client makes a notation every time the identified behavior is exhibited. Such a baseline helps to determine the extent of the behaviors and can also be used to measure progress made. Table 8.2 is an example of a chart that could be used by an overweight client who is assessing the baseline of a number of identified behaviors related to his or her eating habits.

Following the establishment of a baseline, the counselor works with the client to devise ways of extinguishing the identified unwanted behaviors and reinforcing new, desired behaviors. Abruptly stopping a behavior is usually very difficult; therefore a process of slow extinction along with the positive reinforcement of new behaviors is often established (of course, some behaviors are best eliminated by going "cold turkey," such as cigarette smoking). As an example, the overweight client just discussed might work with his or her therapist on extinguishing a number of the identified undesirable behaviors and reinforcing new, desirable behaviors (see Table 8.3). As you examine the strategies, note the many different types of behavioral techniques, discussed in this chapter, that are used to help the client reach his or her goals.

As clients adopt new behaviors, they can continue to chart their progress by using the baseline chart and/or by developing a new chart that assesses progress being made on their desired new behaviors. The use of operant conditioning can be very powerful, and the ways that it can be used are many and are probably limited only by our imaginations. However, change can be a formidable task and takes continual effort (see Box 8.9).

THE THERAPEUTIC PROCESS

Modern-day behavior therapy stresses the importance of a positive and caring relationship between the therapist and the client. This relationship is highlighted by the showing of acceptance, as described earlier under the "Therapeutic

TABLE 8.3   **Strategies to Extinguish Undesirable Behaviors and Reinforce New Behaviors**

New desirable behaviors	Strategies
Reduction of calorie intake	■ Write in journal when successful at calorie reduction (self-reinforcing) ■ Track calorie intake (helps to extinguish old eating behaviors)
Reduction in binge eating	■ At onset of binge, sit in designated room, away from food, for 15 minutes (time out strategy) ■ Situate pictures representing healthy body at strategic places to remind one not to binge (self-management technique) ■ Snap rubber band around wrist at onset of binge (aversive stimulus)
Reduction in nighttime eating	■ At onset of nighttime sit in designated room, away from food, for 15 minutes (time out strategy) ■ Clean whole house after nighttime eating (response cost technique) ■ Lock kitchen door at night and secure key to lock (stimulus control) ■ Situate pictures representing healthy body at strategic places to remind one not to binge (self-management technique)
Eating healthier foods	■ Purchase mostly healthy foods to control what is around home (stimulus control)
Body image/exercise	■ Exercise three times a week (self-reinforcing) ■ Weigh once a week for periodic reinforcement ■ Look in mirror at changes once a week (reinforcing)
For all behaviors	■ Positive self-talk ■ Positive reinforcement by significant others (e.g., spouse, parents, partner) ■ Join self-help/weight loss group to gain peer support and encouragement

Techniques" section of this chapter. This acceptance allows trust and rapport to be built and affords the therapist a greater opportunity to accurately assess problem areas. In addition, it is important for the therapist to collaborate with the client and direct the client toward techniques that would best ameliorate any identified problems. The therapist also acts as an objective scientist who assists the client in assessing the frequency, duration, and intensity of the behavior(s) and cognitions to be changed, and who helps the client assess progress from an objective viewpoint. The client therefore experiences the therapist as a caring and humane person who can effectively listen, assess problems, teach the client about techniques, and direct the client toward treatment goals. Such an approach tends to be active, directive, educative, and shorter than many of the more traditional approaches as the therapist attempts to have the client develop a

---

B o x 8.9   Sticker Charts and Other Helpful Reinforcers

Example 1

One of the most useful and powerful types of positive reinforcers for young children (aged two through eight) is the use of sticker charts and similar positive reinforcers. My wife was particularly skillful in her use of sticker charts and other positive reinforcers with our children. For instance, when our younger child, Emma, was exhibiting some inappropriate and nasty behavior toward others, my wife developed a method to reinforce helpful behaviors. After sharing her idea with me and our two children, we all agreed to the plan. It was decided that any time a family member did something positive for anyone else, a marble would be placed in a quart-sized jar. Any particularly altruistic or helpful behavior would yield an extra-large marble for the jar. It was also decided that any family member other than the person doing the altruistic behavior could make the judgment about what is "altruistic." After the jar was full, we would all go out to our favorite restaurant. So the marbles were quite reinforcing, as we all

enjoyed this event. And, not surprisingly, our younger child's behavior was slowly shaped, and she became a much more loving and polite child as she learned these new behaviors.

Example 2

Once, when working with a single mother of three children, I suggested she start using sticker charts to positively reinforce targeted behaviors of her children who were out of control in her home—constantly yelling and screaming. The mother would frequently respond by yelling back and periodically spanking the children. We assessed the situation and targeted some specific behaviors. After the first couple of weeks using the sticker charts, the mother was ecstatic—the home was peaceful. However, a week later, chaos again reigned. I quickly realized what went wrong: The mother had become tired of using the sticker charts. Sticker charts work, but they take work. And positive reinforcement takes consistency and effort.

---

series of new behaviors and cognitions and eventually manage these on his or her own. Such an approach can be visualized through a series of six stages:

Stage 1: Building the relationship. During this stage, the major goal is to build a strong relationship with the client and to begin to clearly define the goals of therapy. Building the relationship is done by showing an accepting attitude to the client, and today, it is usual to find behavior therapists demonstrating good listening skills and being empathic, showing concern and positive regard, and informing the client that any issue can be discussed in counseling. As a supportive, trusting relationship is developed, the therapist increasingly inquires about the hows, wheres, and whats of the presenting problem.

Stage 2: Clinical assessment. Critical to choosing the most effective technique for client change is to make a thorough assessment of client needs. Sometimes called a **functional behavior analysis (FBA)**, such an assessment should minimally include an in-depth structured interview that examines a broad range of predetermined areas in the client's life and particularly focuses on events that occur prior to and directly after the problematic behavior (Alberto & Troutman, 2006; Wolpe & Lazarus, 1966). In addition, it is often wise to incorporate the use of personality instruments, observation by the clinician, interviews with significant others, and self-monitoring by the client, who will later report back observations to the clinician (Neukrug & Fawcett, 2010). In other

---

B o x 8.10 Missing the Problem

John comes in for counseling complaining of stress, difficulty eating appropriately, marital problems, and children who are acting out. The clinician does not do a thorough assessment and, with the client's blessing, focuses on helping the client learn stress-management techniques, how to develop healthy eating habits, and how to communicate effectively. It is agreed with the client that if after a few months of counseling, marital and family issues are not better, they will reassess the situation. After three months of working on the identified issues, the client comes to the office clearly smelling of alcohol. During the next session, the therapist asks the client about his drinking habits, and the client relays that he drinks almost daily, and often is inebriated by the end of the day. The focus of counseling quickly changes. If the clinician had done a thorough assessment when the client first came in for counseling, this somewhat wasted time would probably not have occurred.

---

words, if it will broaden your understanding of the client to view his or her situation at home, go to the home. And if a parent's observation of a child will increase your ability to clearly see the problem, bring in the parent. Do what you need to do to ensure full understanding of the behaviors at hand, as errors in client assessment will lead to inaccurate treatment (Nay, 1979) (see Box 8.10).

During Stage 2, an overabundance of empathy, caring, and acceptance is limiting to the behavior therapist, as it does not allow for elaboration of the problem (Wolpe & Turkat, 1985). Examine the two responses below, one by a person-centered therapist and the second by a behavior therapist, and see how the second response could potentially elicit a fuller understanding of the problem situation—an understanding necessary for a definitive analysis of the problem at hand:

Example 1

CLIENT: I get very upset whenever my daughter takes out the car. I am convinced she is going to get into an accident and get hurt or die. I often end up with a panic attack.

PC THERAPIST: So, your anxiety really balloons whenever your daughter takes the car.

Example 2

CLIENT: I get very upset whenever my daughter takes out the car. I am convinced she is going to get into an accident and get hurt or die. I often end up with a panic attack.

BEHAVIOR THERAPIST: Interesting! So, are there other times when you have such panic attacks? (Client nods in the affirmative.) Explain them to me and describe what happens before each panic attack that you have.

Stage 3: Focusing on problem areas and setting goals. During the second stage, the therapist has completed a thorough assessment and defined potential problem area(s). Now, identified areas are further examined by obtaining a baseline of the frequency, duration, and intensity of the behaviors. Often, this is accomplished by having the client complete a journal and/or ledger of the behaviors in question. A careful analysis of problem behaviors can help to reveal their magnitude, sets parameters for how and when to change the behaviors, and is useful when assessing progress made. Completion of the baseline is also helpful in setting goals for treatment (see Tables 8.2 and 8.3). From an examination of the baseline, clients can better understand the magnitude of various problem behaviors, decide upon which they want to focus, and collaboratively set goals with the therapist.

Stage 4: Choosing techniques and working on goals. By drawing from social learning theory, operant conditioning, and classical conditioning, therapists have a large array of techniques to assist the client through the change process. At this stage in the therapeutic process, the therapist must carefully explain various techniques to the client and collaboratively choose those techniques which would be most efficacious for the problem at hand. Now the work begins as the client and therapist together devise a plan to use the techniques to reach decided-upon goals.

Stage 5: Assessment of goal completion. Now that goals have been decided upon, techniques chosen, and work is in progress, it becomes important to assess whether clients are reaching their stated goals. Because a baseline of the intensity, frequency, and duration of the problem behavior has usually been recorded, it is a relatively easy task to assess whether there is a lessening of the problem behavior. If no such progress is seen, it is important to reassess the problem and the techniques chosen (or recycle from Stage 3). If the problem was originally diagnosed accurately, and if appropriate techniques were chosen, the client should begin to see an amelioration of the problem.

Stage 6: Closure and follow-up. Reinforcement theory suggests that extinction of most behaviors will usually be followed by a resurgence of the targeted behavior called **spontaneous recovery** (Nye, 1992). Therefore, it is important to remain with the client long enough to ensure success and to prepare the client for a possible resurgence of the problem after therapy has ended. Therefore, many behaviorists build in follow-up sessions to the course of therapy. Of course, as in any therapy, when success is reached, it is important that the client experiences a sense of closure as he or she nears the end of therapy.

SOCIAL, CULTURAL, AND SPIRITUAL ISSUES

If a client comes from a culture that values action and the formulation of goals, that client is likely to feel an affinity toward behavioral and cognitive–behavioral approaches to counseling. In contrast, if a client's cultural background values the intrapsychic process and the importance of deep self-reflection and expression of feeling, that client might feel as if something is lacking when participating in this approach (Rosen & Weltman, 2005).

Even when a client comes from a culture that is comfortable with a goal-oriented approach, considering the client's unique needs as a function of his or her diverse background is critical to picking strategies that will be successful with clients (Ivey, D'Andrea, Ivey, & Sivek-Morgan, 2007). For example, when working with gay, lesbian, and bisexual clients, Balsam, Martell, and Safren (2006) suggest that the counselor raise the issue of the kinds of societal pressures these clients might be facing. Or, when working with Orthodox Jews, one should know that many of them have a stigma associated with having a mental disorder and also have a disdain for psychotropic medication (Paradis, Cukor, & Friedman, 2006). And when working with Latinos and African Americans, knowing about the legacy of their discrimination and how it might affect them today is crucial (Hays & Iwamasa, 2006; Iwamasa, 1996; Organista, 2006).

> In an early session describing her feelings of alienation on campus, she complained to her therapist that one of her professors described research investigating genetic causes of Black violence, as if African Americans were inferior and genetically prone to violence.... [T]he therapist tried to explain the teacher's perspective by saying, "It may help you to know that in the pursuit of knowledge, scientists should be able to study any topic." The student was offended and angrily quipped, "Well, I never heard about studies of a gene for violence in Whites back when they were lynching and conquering everybody." (Kelly, 2006, pp. 104–105)

Early behaviorism took pride in not examining "mentalistic" concepts. As a result, spiritual issues were notably absent from their work (Jones, 1988). Although some early behaviorists did not deny the concept of God, at the very least, spiritual issues were not seen as part of the behavioral paradigm, and the focus of therapy was solely on identification of problem behaviors and setting goals to change them. However, as behaviorists, over time, became more willing to allow other ideas to enter into the behavioral realm (e.g., cognitive therapy), they have slowly allowed the spiritual dimension to be up for discussion:

> As behavioral scientists, both of us were trained to turn a skeptical eye on mentalism and experiential constructs difficult to observe or operationalize.... Now here we are, editing a volume that discuses, self, ego, acceptance, forgiveness, surrender, and yes, even God. (Miller & Martin, 1988, p. 8)

The behaviorist of today is very different than the early radical behaviorist. Today, mentalistic concepts are fair game and even an unconscious can be discussed. But perhaps most interestingly, for the modern-day behaviorist, spirituality can become a central focus of therapy.

B o x 8.11   Luke's Experience in Behavior Therapy

Please review the Miller family's background, which can be found in Appendix B, and then read about Luke's encounter with a behavior therapist, which can also be found in Appendix B.

EFFICACY OF BEHAVIOR THERAPY

With a concentrated focus on the assessment of client needs, identifying specific problem areas, and treating clients with specific techniques, behavior therapy is one of the easiest approaches to research. Consequently, it is not surprising to find that compared to other forms of therapy, behavior therapy has allowed for some of the most productive research when examining outcomes in therapy (Wampold, 2001; Wilson, 1990; Wolpe, 1997). For instance, early research on behavior therapy showed it was successful in treating anxiety disorders, psychosomatic disorders, sexual dysfunction, and behavior problems with the developmentally delayed and delinquents, and when working with token economies with the mentally ill (Wampold, 2001; Wilson, 1997; Hirai & Clum, 2006). More recently, a mixture of cognitive and behavioral techniques have shown some success in treating borderline personality disorders, eating disorders, and depression, and in some forms of couples counseling. In addition, a quick review of the literature on cognitive–behavioral clinical outcomes shows that this approach may have some success in the treatment of a wide range of disorders.

Despite its clear success over the years, there are times when behavior therapy has been shown not to be particularly effective, such as in some forms of marital counseling, in controlling delusions and hallucinations with schizophrenics, and despite some initial success, in a 25 percent failure rate over time with obsessive–compulsive disorder (Fox & Kozak, 1997). Moreover, although the addition of a cognitive therapy component added depth and breadth to the behavioral approach, it appears as if initial thoughts that behavioral counseling would be successful in almost all realms of counseling has lessened. This may be partly due to the fact that there are biological limits to the treatment of certain disorders; that is, our biology defines us to such a degree that therapy cannot overcome it. Finally, for those who are examining such issues as unconscious motivations, self-awareness, identity development, sense of purpose, blocks in creativity, acceptance of sexual orientation, and "broad" issues, behavior and cognitive–behavior therapies are likely not as effective as, insight-oriented and in-depth approaches (see Box 8.11).

SUMMARY

Behavior therapy was developed during the first half of the twentieth century and is based on three types of behavioral paradigms: classical conditioning, first defined by Pavlov and later refined by such individuals as Watson and Wolpe;

operant conditioning, popularized by Skinner; and modeling, as originally presented by Bandura. Although initially viewed as a scientific, objective, deterministic,
and reductionistic approach to counseling, today's behavioral therapist is anti-
deterministic and has integrated what some consider to be humanistic concepts
into its approach in an effort to build a trusting and collaborative relationship.
Thus, it is not unusual to find behaviorists showing empathy and acceptance and
incorporating these attributes into the approach. In addition, we noted that because
the cognitive and behavioral approaches are based on learning theory, most therapists today incorporate the two approaches into what is called the cognitive–behavioral approach. Although this chapter focused mostly on the behavioral approach,
you were encouraged when reading the chapters on cognitive therapy to consider
how the two approaches could easily be combined.

Today's behavioral therapists have dozens of techniques from which to choose,
and in this chapter, we focused on some of the more popular behavioral techniques,
including acceptance; relaxation exercises and systematic desensitization; modeling;
token economy; flooding and implosion techniques; punishment to effect change in
children's behavior, such as response cost, social reprimands, time-out, overcorrection, physical punishment, and contingent electric stimulation; aversive therapy;
stimulus control; self-management techniques; and operant conditioning techniques.

The work of today's behavior therapists can be viewed through a series of
six stages in which they build the relationship, conduct a clinical assessment,
focus on problem areas and set goals, choose techniques and work on goals, assess
goal completion, and focus on closure and follow-up.

In relationship to social, cultural, and spiritual issues, we noted that those
clients who feel more comfortable with an intrapsychic approach would likely not
be at ease with the directive, objectivistic approach of the behaviorist. We also
noted that it is important to know the cultural background of one's client so that
techniques chosen have a natural fit to the values inherent in the client's culture.
We also pointed out the importance of considering the environmental impact on
clients, such as when forms of racism impinge negatively on the client's life. From a
spiritual perspective, we highlighted the fact that in recent years, there has been an
effort to integrate spiritual concerns into the behaviorist's repertoire of techniques.

Finally, we pointed out that behavioral therapy has had more research studies
supporting its work with clients than other types of therapy. We noted that particular
success has been found with the treatment of anxiety disorders, psychosomatic disorders, sexual dysfunction, and behavior problems with the developmentally delayed
and delinquents, and when working with token economies with the mentally ill.
Some success in the treatment of borderline personality disorders, eating disorders,
and depression, and in some forms of couples counseling, has also been noted. However, there has been limited success when conducting some types of marital counseling and when trying to control delusions and hallucinations with schizophrenics, and
a 25 percent rate of failure has been found over time with obsessive–compulsive disorder. We noted that for those who are looking for a more insight-oriented or in-
depth approach to counseling, behavior therapy is likely not a therapy of choice.

Behavioral therapy of today is a horse of a different color from its early
beginnings with Pavlov's experiments with dogs. Clearly, over the years, the

behavioral paradigm has changed, partly as a reflection of changes in society (e.g., the need for brief treatment approaches and our need to be results-oriented). Today, behavior therapy, along with its close cousin cognitive–behavioral therapy, can be applied in a variety of ways to help individuals deal with a wide range of disorders.

KEY WORDS

anti-deterministic
associative learning
aversion therapy
B. F. Skinner Foundation
"Baby in a Box"
baby-tender
behavioral rehearsal
black box
blank slate
Citation for Outstanding Lifetime Contribution to Psychology
classical conditioning
conditioned response
conditioned stimulus
controlled response
controlling response
deterministic
discrimination
extinction
fixed ratio or interval schedules
flooding

free choice
functional behavior analysis (FBA)
generalization
Gold Medal of the American Psychological Foundation
Humanist of the Year award
implosive therapy
learning theory
mentalistic concepts
modeling
National Medal of Science
negative punishment
negative reinforcement
neutral stimulus
operant conditioning
positive punishment
positive reinforcement
Project Pigeon
punishment
radical behaviorist

reciprocal inhibition
reinforcement contingencies
relaxation exercises
schedules of reinforcement
shaping
Skinner box
social learning
Society of the Experimental Analysis of Behavior
spontaneous recovery
subjective unit of discomfort
successive approximation
systematic desensitization
tabula rasa
unconditioned stimulus
variable ratio or interval schedules

KEY NAMES

Bandura, Albert
Blue, Yvonne
Buzan, Deborah Skinner

Jacobson, Edmund
Pavlov, Ivan
Skinner, B. F.

Vargas, Julie Skinner
Watson, John B.
Wolpe, Joseph

REFERENCES

Alberto, P., & Troutman, A. C. (2006). *Applied behavior analysis for teachers* (7th ed.). Upper Saddle River, NJ: Merrill Prentice Hall.

Ayllon, T., & Azrin, N. H. (1965). The measurement and reinforcement of behavior of psychotics. *Journal of Experimental Analysis of Behavior, 8*, 357–383.

Ayllon, T., & Azrin, N. H. (1968). *The token economy: A motivational system for therapy and rehabilitation.* New York: Appleton-Century-Crofts.

Balsam, K. F., Martell, C. R., & Safren, S. A. (2006). Affirmative cognitive-behavioral therapy with lesbian, gay, and bisexual people. In P. A. Hays & G. W. Iwamasa (Eds.), *Culturally responsive cognitive-behavioral therapy: Assessment, practice, and supervision* (pp. 223–244). Washington, D.C.: American Psychological Association.

Bandura, A. T. (1977). *Social learning theory.* Englewood Cliffs, NJ: Prentice Hall.

Bandura, A. T., Ross, D., & Ross, S. A. (1963). Imitation of film-mediated aggressive models. *Journal of Abnormal and Social Psychology, 67*, 3–11.

Bjork, D. W. (1997). *B. F. Skinner: A life.* Washington, D.C.: American Psychological Association.

Blampied, N. M., & Kahan, E. (1992). Acceptability of alternative punishments: A community survey. *Behavior Modification, 16*, 400–4135.

Boudewyns, P. A., & Shipley, R. H. (1983). *Flooding and implosive therapy: Direct therapeutic exposure in clinical practice.* New York: Plenum Press.

Brammer, L. M., & MacDonald, G. (2003). *The helping relationship: Process and skills* (8th ed.). Boston: Allyn & Bacon.

Cooper, J. O., Heron, T. E., & Heward, W. L. (2007). *Applied behavior analysis* (2nd ed.). Columbus, Ohio: Merrill.

Ferguson, K. E. (2003). Relaxation. In W. O'Donohue, U. J. Fisher, & S. C. Hayes (Eds.), *Cognitive behavior therapy: Applying empirically supported techniques in your practice* (pp. 330–340). Hoboken, NJ: John Wiley & Sons.

Fox, E. B., & Kozak, M. J. (1997). Beyond the efficacy ceiling? Cognitive behavior therapy in search of theory. *Behavior Therapy, 28*, 601–611.

Friman, P. C., & Finney, J. W. (2003). Time in (and time out). In W. O'Donohue, U. J. Fisher, & S. C. Hayes (Eds.), *Cognitive behavior therapy: Applying empirically supported techniques in your practice* (pp. 429–435). Hoboken, NJ: John Wiley & Sons.

Ghezzi, P. M., Wilson, G. R., Tarbox, R. S. F., & MacAleese (2003). Token economy. In W. O'Donohue, U. J. Fisher, & S. C. Hayes (Eds.), *Cognitive behavior therapy: Applying empirically supported techniques in your practice* (pp. 346–341). Hoboken, NJ: John Wiley & Sons.

Gifford, E. V., & Shoenberger, D. (2003). Rapid smoking. In W. O'Donohue, U. J. Fisher, & S. C. Hayes (Eds.), *Cognitive behavior therapy: Applying empirically supported techniques in your practice* (pp. 314–320). Hoboken, NJ: John Wiley & Sons.

Hayes, S. C., & Pankey, J. (2003). Acceptance. In W. O'Donohue, U. J. Fisher, & S. C. Hayes (Eds.), *Cognitive behavior therapy: Applying empirically supported techniques in your practice* (pp. 4–9). Hoboken, NJ: John Wiley & Sons.

Hays, P. A., & Iwamasa, G. W. (Eds.). (2006). *Culturally responsive cognitive-behavioral therapy: Assessment, practice, and supervision.* Washington, D.C.: American Psychological Association.

Head, L. S., & Gross, A. M. (2003). Systematic desensitization. In W. O'Donohue, U. J. Fisher, & S. C. Hayes (Eds.), *Cognitive behavior therapy: Applying empirically supported techniques in your practice* (pp. 417–422). Hoboken, NJ: John Wiley & Sons.

Hirai, M., & Clum, G. A. (2006). A meta-analytic study of self-help interventions for anxiety disorders. *Behavior Therapy, 37*(2), 99–111.

Holland, J. G., & Skinner, B. F. (1961). *The analysis of behavior: A program for self-instruction.* New York: McGraw Hill.

Ivey, A. E., D'Andrea, M., Ivey, M. B., & Simek-Morgan, L. (2007). *Theories of counseling and psychotherapy: A multicultural perspective* (6th ed.). Boston: Allyn & Bacon.

Iwamasa, G. W. (1996). Introduction to the special series: Ethnic and cultural diversity in cognitive and behavioral practice. *Cognitive and Behavioral Practice, 3*, 209–213.

Jacobson, E. (1938). *Progressive relaxation.* Chicago: University of Chicago Press.

Jones, S. L. (1988). A religious critique of behavior therapy. In W. R. Miller., & J. E. Martin, (Eds.). *Behavior therapy and religion: Integrating spiritual and behavioral approaches to change* (pp. 139–170). Newbury Park, CA: Sage Publications.

Kelly, S. (2006). Cognitive-behavioral therapy with African Americans. In P. A. Hays & G. W. Iwamasa (Eds.), *Culturally responsive cognitive-behavioral therapy: Assessment, practice, and supervision* (pp. 97–116). Washington, D.C.: American Psychological Association.

Levis, D. J., & Krantweiss, A. R. (2003). Working with implosive (flooding) therapy: A dynamic cognitive-behavioral exposure psychotherapy treatment approach. In W. O'Donohue, U. J. Fisher, & S. C. Hayes (Eds.), *Cognitive behavior therapy: Applying empirically supported techniques in your practice* (pp. 463–470). Hoboken, NJ: John Wiley & Sons.

Little, S. G. (2003). Classroom management. In W. O'Donohue, U. J. Fisher, & S. C. Hayes (Eds.), *Cognitive behavior therapy: Applying empirically supported techniques in your practice* (pp. 64–70). Hoboken, NJ: John Wiley & Sons.

Miller, W. R., & Martin, J. E. (1988). (Eds.). *Behavior therapy and religion: Integrating spiritual and behavioral approaches to change.* Newbury Park, CA: Sage Publications.

Nathan, P. E., Gorman, J. M., & Salkind, N. J. (1999). *Treatment of mental disorders: A guide to what works.* New York: Oxford University Press.

Naugle, A. E., & Maher, S. (2003). Modeling and behavioral rehearsal. In W. O'Donohue, U. J. Fisher, & S. C. Hayes (Eds.), *Cognitive behavior therapy: Applying empirically supported techniques in your practice* (pp. 238–246). Hoboken, NJ: John Wiley & Sons.

Nay, W. R. (1979). Multimethod clinical assessment. New York: Gardner Press.

Neukrug, E. S., & Fawcett, R. C. (2010). *Essentials of testing and assessment: A practical guide for counselors, social workers, and psychologists* (2nd ed.). Belmont, CA: Brooks/Cole.

Nye, R. D. (1992). *The legacy of B. F. Skinner: Concepts and perspectives, controversies and misunderstandings.* Pacific Grove, CA: Brooks/Cole.

Nye, R. D. (2000). *Three psychologies: Perspectives from Freud, Skinner, and Rogers* (6th ed.). Belmont, CA: Brooks/Cole.

O'Donohue, W., Fisher, U. J., & Hayes, S. C. (Eds.). (2003). *Cognitive behavior therapy: Applying empirically supported techniques in your practice.* Hoboken, NJ: John Wiley & Sons.

Organista, K. C. (2006). Cognitive-behavioral therapy with Latinos and Latinas. In P. A. Hays & G. W. Iwamasa (Eds.), *Culturally responsive cognitive-behavioral therapy: Assessment, practice, and supervision* (pp. 73–96). Washington, D.C.: American Psychological Association.

Paradis, C. M., Cukor, D., & Friedman, S. (2006). Cognitive-behavioral therapy with Orthodox Jews. In P. A. Hays & G. W. Iwamasa (Eds.), *Culturally responsive cognitive-behavioral therapy: Assessment, practice, and supervision* (pp. 161–176). Washington, D.C.: American Psychological Association.

Pavlov, I. P. (1927). *Conditioned reflexes: An investigation of the physiological activity of the cerebral cortex.* (G. V. Anrep, Trans.). London: Oxford University Press.

Poling, A., & Gaynor, S. T. (2003). Stimulus control. In W. O'Donohue, U. J. Fisher, & S. C. Hayes (Eds.), *Cognitive behavior therapy: Applying empirically supported techniques in your practice* (pp. 396–401). Hoboken, NJ: John Wiley & Sons.

Rehm, L. P., & Adams, J. H. (2003). Self-management. In W. O'Donohue, U. J. Fisher, & S. C. Hayes (Eds.), *Cognitive behavior therapy: Applying empirically supported techniques in your practice* (pp. 354–360). Hoboken, NJ: John Wiley & Sons.

Rosen, E. J., & Weltman, S. F. (2005). Jewish families: An overview. In M. McGoldrick, J. Giordano, & N. Garcia-Preto, *Ethnicity and family therapy* (3rd ed., pp. 667–680). New York: Guilford Press.

Sautter, R. A., & LeBlanc, L. A. (2006). Empirical applications of Skinner's analysis of verbal behaviors with humans. *The Analysis of Verbal Behavior, 22,* 35–48.

Skinner, B. F. (1938). *The behavior of organisms: An experimental analysis.* New York: Appleton-Century.

Skinner, B. F. (1948). *Walden Two.* New York: MacMillan.

Skinner, B. F. (1953). *Science and human behavior.* New York: MacMillan.

Skinner, B. F. (1957). *Verbal behavior.* New York, Appleton-Century-Crofts.

Skinner, B. F. (1960). Pigeons in a pelican. *American Psychologist, 15,* 28–37.

Skinner, B. F. (1968). *The technology of teaching.* New York: Appleton-Century-Crofts.

Skinner, B. F. (1969). *Contingencies of reinforcement: A theoretical analysis.* New York: Appleton-Century-Crofts.

Skinner, B. F. (1971). *Beyond freedom and dignity.* New York: Knopf.

Skinner, B. F. (1974). *About behaviorism.* New York: Knopf.

Skinner, B. F. (1976). *Particulars of my life: Part one of an autobiography.* New York: Knopf.

Skinner, B. F. (1978). *Reflections on behaviorism and society.* Englewood Cliffs, NJ: Prentice Hall.

Skinner, B. F. (1979). *The shaping of a behaviorist: Part two of an autobiography.* New York: Knopf.

Skinner, B. F. (1983). *A matter of consequences: Part three of an autobiography.* New York: Knopf.

Wacker, D. P., Harding, J., Berg, W., Cooper-Brown, L. J., & Barretto, A. (2003). Punishment. In W. O'Donohue, U. J. Fisher, & S. C. Hayes (Eds.), *Cognitive behavior therapy: Applying empirically supported techniques in your practice* (pp. 308–320). Hoboken, NJ: John Wiley & Sons.

Wampold, B. E. (2001). *The great psychotherapy debate: Models, methods, and findings.* Mahwah, NJ: Erlbaum.

Watson, J. B. (1925). *Behaviorism.* Chicago: University of Chicago Press.

Wilson, K. G. (1997). Science and treatment development: Lessons from the history of behavior therapy. *Behavior Therapy, 28,* 547–558.

Wolpe, J. (1958). *Psychotherapy by reciprocal inhibition.* Stanford, CA: Stanford University Press.

Wolpe, J. (1990). *The practice of behavior therapy* (4th ed.). New York: Pergamon Press.

Wolpe, J. (1997). Thirty years of behavior therapy. *Behavior Therapy, 28,* 633–635.

Wolpe, J., & Lazarus, A. A. (1966). *Behavior therapy techniques: A guide to the treatment of neuroses.* New York: Pergamon Press.

Wolpe, J., & Turkat, I. D. (1985). Behavioral formulation of clinical cases. In J. I. D. Turkat (Ed.), *Behavioral case formulation* (pp. 5–35). New York: Plenum Press.

Zoellner, L. A., Abramowitz, J. S., & Moore, S. A. (2003). Flooding. In W. O'Donohue, U. J. Fisher, & S. C. Hayes (Eds.), *Cognitive behavior therapy: Applying empirically supported techniques in your practice* (pp. 160–166). Hoboken, NJ: John Wiley & Sons.

Chapter 9

Rational Emotive Behavior Therapy

Learning Goals

- To gain a biographical understanding of Albert Ellis, one of the most
  influential therapists of all time and the creator of rational emotive behavior
  therapy (REBT).
- To understand the historical context in which Ellis created his active, directive,
  and psychoeducational approach to therapy.
- To review how child-rearing practices, family dynamics, societal influences,
  and innate biology can result in rational or irrational thinking, and to
  discuss the idea that individuals have the potential to overcome irrational
  thinking.
- To understand the anti-deterministic, existential, learning-based, and, some
  say, constructivist view of human nature of REBT.
- To review Ellis's twelve irrational and corresponding rational beliefs as well as
  three core "musturbatory" or grandiose irrational beliefs and the cognitive
  distortions that feed into them, such as absolutistic musts and shoulds,
  "awfulizing," "I-can't-stand-it-itis," demands, and people-rating (damning
  oneself and others).
- To review the following key concepts of REBT: philosophical conditioning;
  unconditional acceptance; irrational beliefs; cognitive distortions of events;
  the ABCs of feelings and behaviors; the rational, scientific approach of REBT
  using the Socratic dialogue method; and the importance of applying
  experimental methods.
- To highlight a number of techniques of REBT, including: showing
  unconditional acceptance; teaching the REBT philosophy; being active and
  directive; challenging clients; demonstrating the ABCs of feeling and
  behaving; encouraging the disputing of dysfunctional cognitions,
  behaviors, and emotions; using humor; using metaphors and stories; and
  homework.
- To review the five steps of the therapeutic process, including assessing the
  client's situation and hypothesizing how the ABCDEs apply, teaching the

REBT philosophy, demonstrating how the client's situation fits the REBT model, directing the change process, and reinforcing change and terminating the relationship.

- To highlight how this approach can be used cross-culturally, especially in light of the use of the terms "rational" and "irrational" and the stress that is placed on tolerance by REBT therapists.
- To discuss why this short-term, "rational" approach is likely to be most effective with certain types of clients.
- To see how REBT is applied through vignettes, DVDs, and case study.

I Wish I Were Not Crazy!
(Tune: "Dixie" by Dan Emmet)

Oh, I wish I were really put together—
Smooth and fine as patent leather!
Oh, how great to be rated innately sedate!
But I'm afraid that I was fated
To be rather aberrated—
Oh, how sad to be mad as my Mom and my Dad!
Oh, I wish I were not crazy! Hooray! Hooray!
I wish my mind were less inclined
To be the kind that's hazy!
I could, of course, agree to be less crazy—
But I, alas, am just too goddamned lazy!

Song's lyrics by Albert Ellis (1977). In A. Ellis, A garland of rational humorous songs *(cassette recording and songbook). New York: Institute for Rational-Emotive Therapy. Reprinted by permission of the Albert Ellis Institute.*

I was not introduced to REBT through a song, but I must admit, hearing the satire in some of the songs by Albert Ellis has helped me to remember the approach. As you might expect, REBT stands in stark contrast to the more psychodynamic approaches of Freud, Jung, Adler, or the existential–humanistic approaches of Frankl, Rogers, and Perls. And although some have called Dr. Ellis a "foul–mouthed sexual revolutionary," others have anointed him as "one of the most influential psychologists of the twentieth century" (Spiegel, 2004, para. 2; "The top 10," 2007). Whatever you call him, there's little doubt that you will have a strong opinion of both Dr. Ellis and the theory he developed. Let's take a look.

ALBERT ELLIS

Having recently passed away at the age of 93, Dr. Albert Ellis worked nonstop until the end of his life. And his last few years were as tumultuous as most of his life. For instance, when in his nineties, Ellis sued the board of the **Albert Ellis Institute**, which he founded over 50 years ago, for illegally removing him.

The Supreme Court of New York State agreed and insisted that he be reinstated (Carey, 2006). His removal coincided with attempts by the board to restrict Ellis's access to Institute money and to prevent him from doing his weekly REBT "live" therapy sessions in front of upward of 200 people (Hafetz, 2005). After years of developing the Institute and taking a modest salary, Dr. Ellis believed the board was trying to usurp his authority—and apparently the courts agreed. But what is the history behind this great icon of **cognitive therapy**?

Albert Ellis

Born in Pittsburg, Pennsylvania, on September 17, 1913, Albert Ellis was to become one of the most important theorists of all time (Hurley, 2004; "The top 10," 2007). The oldest of three children, Ellis moved with his family to New York City as a young child. Although Ellis states that his parents "seemed to love [him]" (Ellis, 2004a, p. 49), he quickly adds that they were distant and aloof, his father often away on business trips and his mother narcissistic and opinionated. A sickly and frail boy, Ellis had numerous hospitalizations during his childhood. In fact, at one point when he was about seven years old, he was hospitalized with chronic nephritis for 10 months, and remembers his father only visiting him once and his mother only once a week! However, even at this very young age, Ellis seemed to have had a propensity toward handling difficult times in a logical and rational manner. In fact, perhaps it was his parents' lack of attention that led him to become one of the greatest therapists of all time:

> I was anxious and somewhat depressed when my parents didn't show up regularly at the hospital, so I didn't want to be miserable. So I said to myself, what will I do not to be miserable and I figured out some of the rational techniques which I used later. My solutions were pretty good but not as good as the later REBT solutions. (Ellis as cited in Halasz, 2004, p. 326)

When Ellis was 12, he found out that his parents were divorced by overhearing a conversation between his aunt and mother (Ellis, 2004a; Halasz, 2004). Probably due to his lack of emotional involvement with his parents, he reports not being particularly affected by this. Ellis also notes that at around the same age, when studying for his Bar Mitzvah, he had a realization that God probably did not exist and that religion was not particularly important. He eventually became what he calls a "**probabilistic atheist**," and it is within this foundation that you can see the importance he places on scientific evidence:

> So, a probabilistic atheist is not a dogmatic atheist who says that there is no God and that there can't be. He says that in all probability there is none and therefore, since the probability of there being a God is 0.00001, I will assume there isn't any deity. If there is, and if he ever comes and talks to me, I'll ask him to prove that he really is God. (Ellis as cited in Halasz, 2004, p. 327)

You begin to get a sense of the foreshadowing of Ellis's methods when, at the relatively young age of 19, he decides to overcome his shyness of women by making himself talk to every woman who sat on a particular bench at the Bronx Botanical Gardens:

> Thirty walked away immediately.... I talked with the other 100 for the first time in my life, no matter how anxious I was. Nobody vomited and ran away. Nobody called the cops. (Ellis as cited in Hurley, 2004, para. 21)

After earning a degree in business during the 1920s from the City University of New York, Ellis spent a few years in the business field and saw himself as a political and economic revolutionary (Halasz, 2004). However, after becoming disillusioned with this profession, he became a writer, often writing about human sexuality, which was a relatively new field. Ellis soon gained notoriety from this expertise and saw himself as a sexual revolutionary. Not surprisingly, before long, people began to come to him for advice about their sexual problems. Feeling like he had finally found an occupational fit, in 1942, he decided to pursue a master's and Ph.D. in clinical psychology from Columbia University.

Due to Ellis's various phobias and neuroses, he became an avid reader of many different philosophies and "cured himself" using a variety of self-taught methods (Ellis, 2004b). However, like many graduate students of his era, Ellis decided to embrace the theory of his time and became trained in psychoanalysis. During this time, he also started a private practice. In 1943, he completed his Ph.D. and was soon writing voraciously, authoring dozens of articles on a variety of subjects, from testing to sexuality to the importance of using scientific methods in research.

Although Ellis went on to obtain additional training in psychoanalysis, and also underwent his own analysis, he soon began to question the effectiveness of this approach. Soon, he was writing articles that questioned the scientific basis of psychoanalysis and began to shape a new approach that had at its core how neuroses could be explained as conditioned thoughts and behaviors and treated through the use of directive techniques (cf. Ellis 1950, 1951a, 1956).

> My analyst used free association and really listening to his analysands. So I tried his method and ran up against all kinds of problems. I decided to give homework because I saw that people really didn't change unless they pushed their arse to do things differently. So I thought I would sneak in homework. But then I concluded in 1953 "this psychoanalysis is crap!" So I gave it up almost completely and went back to active-directive psychotherapy and started to develop REBT. (Ellis as cited in Halasz, 2004, p. 329)

In addition to his skepticism of psychoanalysis, early in his career, Ellis began to question the importance of some of the "new" nondirective techniques, such as client-centered counseling, that were gaining in popularity (Ellis, 1948). The volume of this critique would increase throughout Ellis's life as he became increasingly comfortable with his own approach.

In 1950, Ellis took a position as the chief psychologist for the state of New Jersey, but by 1952, he decided to devote all of his time to his private practice (Abrams & Abrams, 2005). Writing a number of books on human sexuality, Ellis became increasingly well-known, and his private practice began to flourish (see *The Folklore of Sex*, 1951b; *The American Sexual Tragedy*, 1954; *Sex Without Guilt*,

1958). In 1956, he founded and became the first president of the **Society for the Scientific Study of Sex**. A short time later, he became the American editor of the *International Journal of Sexology*. Perhaps ahead of his time, Ellis was found defending the publication of sexually explicit materials (probably modest by today's standards), and the lifestyles of gays and lesbians. His advocacy for the publication of sexually explicit materials helped the American Nudist Association win a 1958 Supreme Court decision that condoned the sending of magazines with sexually explicit information. However, the notoriety he gained resulted in his being denied speaking engagements and being banned from teaching positions at both his undergraduate and graduate schools.

In his young adulthood, Ellis was married twice and involved with many others (Ellis, 2004a). He saw these experiences as critical to his understanding of human sexuality and how to avoid being driven by the neediness that sometimes results when strong feelings toward another are not reciprocated. This discovery was critical to the development of his theory, as highlighted in his discussion around the ending of one of his marriages:

> For the rest of my life I have had very strong desires—many of them!— which I have striven to fulfill. But I have rarely thereafter thought that I *absolutely needed* what I wanted, nor *strongly needed* to avoid what I abhorred. And later I put antineediness, antiawfulizing, and antimusturbation solidly into REBT. (Ellis, 2004a, p. 94)

As Ellis continued to see clients in his private practice, he refined his therapeutic concepts and came to believe that even when clients understood their **irrational belief systems**, they would vehemently maintain them and continue feeling poorly about themselves. As his thoughts on this modified, he became convinced that it was how an individual came to view or understand his or her situation that caused disturbing, depressive, and upsetting emotions, not the situation itself. These beliefs, as Ellis himself said, were not new:

> … [I]f you have right opinions, you will fare well; if they are false, you will fare ill. For to every man the cause of his acting is opinion.…
> (Epictetus, ca. 100 A.D.)

During the 1950s, Ellis began to increasingly see himself as a "**rational therapist**" and no longer associated himself with psychoanalysis. His new **directive** and **cognitive** approach became known, in 1955, as **rational therapy**, and Ellis was soon seen as the first to practice cognitive therapy. His approach, which looked at how **self-defeating** and **irrational thinking** leads to negative feelings and emotional pain, was initially ignored, criticized, or mocked by many prominent theorists:

> I was hated by practically all psychologists and psychiatrists.… They thought it was superficial and stupid. They resented that I said therapy doesn't have to take years. (Ellis as cited in Hurley, 2004, para. 30)

Despite the animosity toward him and his approach, Ellis stubbornly continued on, and in 1957, he published his first book that highlighted his methods: *How to Live with a Neurotic* (Ellis, 1957a). Two years later, he founded the **Institute for Rational Living** in New York City. Calling himself an **experimentalist**, Ellis continually modified his approach to fit the knowledge he gained by applying his techniques to himself and with hundreds of the clients he saw. He also periodically collaborated with Aaron Beck, who was developing his own form of cognitive therapy independently from Ellis (Padesky & Beck, 2003). Although called a cognitive therapist, Ellis always said that thinking, feelings, and behaviors go hand in hand, and over the years, his approach began to incorporate more behavioral and feeling techniques. Over the years, Ellis changed the name of his approach from **rational therapy** to **rational emotive therapy** and, finally, to **rational emotive behavior therapy** to reflect this broader emphasis. The Institute would have parallel name changes until in recent years, when it became known as the Albert Ellis Institute.

From 1965 to 2002, Ellis lived with Janet Wolfe in an open relationship (Ellis, 2004a). She was 24 and he 51 when they met. The first office manager at the relatively new Institute, Janet would eventually obtain her Ph.D. in Clinical Psychology and become the executive director of the Institute. In 2002, she decided to leave the relationship, which Ellis described as somewhat shocking and sad, while also noting that he could cope effectively with her decision through his REBT philosophy (Ellis, 2004a). In 2004, Ellis married Debbie Joffe, an REBT-trained clinician who had been his assistant.

An innovative and prolific writer, over his lifetime, Ellis published over 800 articles, 75 books and monographs, and over 200 audio and video cassettes (Halasz, 2004). Listed as one of the most influential therapists of all time, Ellis was the recipient of the **American Psychological Association's Distinguished Professional Contribution award** and honored as a "**living legend**" by the American Counseling Association (Kaufman, 2007; "Remembering Albert Ellis," 2007). There is little question that his theory greatly shaped the field of cognitive therapy as well as the broader field of psychotherapy. And, although his scholarly writings will continue to affect the fields of counseling and psychotherapy, he will probably always be known for the quirky and interesting things he said over his lifetime, such as the time he learned that he had to have major intestinal surgery late in his life:

> They told me I'd have to have my major intestines out and I said, "Too fucking bad! So I'll have them out. It won't kill me, and if [it] does, I won't suffer after my death." There is nothing deeper than a person's philosophy. I refuse to make myself crazy. (Ellis as cited in Aviv, 2005, para. 13)

VIEW OF HUMAN NATURE

Believing we are **fallible human beings** who have the potential for rational or irrational thinking is the basis for the REBT's view of human nature. **Rational thinking**, say REBT therapists, leads to healthy ways of living, and results in people who show **unconditional acceptance** of self, of others, and of the way things are. Self-acceptance, says Ellis, is different from self-esteem, which Ellis sees as an unstable process related to how others see us (Ellis, 2006):

> Self-esteem is one of the worst evils known to man … because self-esteem means "When I do well and you love me, then I am a good person; but when I do poorly and you don't like me, back to shithood go I." (Ellis as cited in Davies, 2005, para. 7)

In contrast to rational thinking, **irrational thinking**, leads to emotional distress, dysfunctional behaviors, and neurotic ways of living, as well as people who tend to be critical of others and of themselves. Although early child-rearing practices, family dynamics, societal influences, and innate biology tend to be the basis for the development of rational or irrational thinking, REBT therapists believe that it is the individual who sustains his or her unique way of thinking (Ellis & MacLaren, 2005).

REBT therapists believe that there is a complex interaction between one's thinking, feeling, and behavioral states, and they view the interpretation of **cognitive processes** as being mostly responsible for **self-defeating emotions** and **dysfunctional behaviors**. Such interpretations, says Ellis, can be both conscious and unconscious. In other words, the reactions to events are filtered through one's belief system, and the individual responds consciously or unconsciously to the belief system, not to the event. If the belief system is irrational, the individual responds with self-defeating emotions and self-perpetuating dysfunctional behaviors. If the belief system is rational, the individual responds with emotions that perpetuate healthy ways of functioning in the world. Thus, strong emotions, such as grief after the loss of a dear friend or sadness if one's house is flooded from a hurricane, would be considered a reasonable response, whereas a deep depression after the ending of a relationship or road rage at a fellow driver would be seen as unreasonable responses and a reaction to an irrational belief system. Put simply, "… over-sensitivity is sensitivity plus disturbance" (Dryden & Neenan, 2003, p. 10). As you might expect, the depth at which and length of time for which one experiences a self-defeating emotion is related to one's beliefs about an event, with extremely negative, self-defeating emotions being related to strongly embedded irrational beliefs.

Although REBT therapists view an individual's belief system as generally being created early in life, they also believe it can be challenged and systematically changed by analyzing its philosophical basis and helping the individual gain awareness into the irrational beliefs that fuel maladaptive ways of living. Long-winded examination of the past is not necessary, and indeed, says Ellis, could be harmful and inhibit progress toward change.

> Freud was full of horseshit. He invented people's problems and what to do about them. Tell me one thing about the past. I'll prove it's not what upset you. It's how you philosophized about it that made you disturbed. (Ellis as cited in Aviv, 2005, para. 2)

As you can see from the above quote, the **insight-oriented** approach of REBT has a strong **anti-deterministic** philosophy that forwards the notion that we can choose new ways of thinking and ultimately feel better and act in healthier ways. This optimistic view of change has an *existential* flavor to it, although REBT is rarely placed within the existential schools. Perhaps REBT can best be seen as a philosophy that is a mixture of **learning theory** and **existential–humanistic philosophy**: learning theory in the sense that we learned a way of thinking, feeling, and acting that is self-perpetuating, and existential–humanistic because we can choose to learn new and healthier ways of thinking, feeling, and behaving.

More recently, Ellis has argued that REBT is a **constructivist approach** due to the fact that one can reconstruct one's meaning-making system by applying the theory (Ellis, 1996a, 1998). However, because the constructivist school minimizes the notion of an external reality, and because REBT suggests there are specific rational beliefs that should be taught to the client by the therapist, some in the constructivist school have challenged Ellis's assertion (Guterman, 1994; Watson, 1999). In response, Ellis stated that the teaching of a philosophy allows the client to have the tools to internalize the change process and create a new reality for himself or herself. At the very least, one can say that Ellis's approach has some constructivist leanings.

KEY CONCEPTS

Philosophical Conditioning

REBT therapists believe that the individual develops a way of understanding the world through his or her adherence to a unique philosophy (e.g., values, beliefs, understandings) generally developed early in life. Each person's philosophy has a tendency to become habitual, supports either rational or irrational beliefs, and is reinforced and sustained by the individual. Philosophies that support irrational beliefs lead to emotional distress and dysfunctional behaviors, whereas philosophies that support rational beliefs lead to healthy ways of living in the world. Philosophies are nondeterministic in that they can be scrutinized, analyzed, and changed at any point in a person's life.

Unconditional Acceptance

Since REBT therapists believe that individuals can change their philosophical conditioning, and ultimately their belief systems, no person is doomed to live a lifestyle that sustains emotional distress and dysfunctional behaviors. With this in mind, REBT therapists believe that it is critical that an individual be shown **unconditional acceptance** and not be berated for thinking, feeling, and acting in a certain manner. And perhaps more important, clients are encouraged and taught how to accept themselves and not rely on others for their self-esteem. Such an attitude helps to create an atmosphere where the client can develop a new, more effective belief system. As you can probably guess, this unconditional acceptance is very different from the unconditional positive regard seen from the person-centered (Rogerian) perspective:

> … Rogers thought he could get people to accept themselves just by listening to them and being nice to them, and I don't think that's enough. I think nine out of ten people who go through Rogerian therapy conclude wrongly that "I'm okay because my therapist approves of me." But that's conditional love. I get people to truly accept themselves unconditionally, whether or not their therapist or anyone loves them…. In REBT, we give clients unconditional acceptance but we also teach them how to give it to themselves. (Ellis, 2004a, p. 188)

Irrational Beliefs

Ellis originally identified ten irrational beliefs and later expanded these to **twelve irrational beliefs**, one or more of which most people have adopted (Ellis, 1962, 1989; Smith, 1989; see Table 9.1).

The following gives examples of two irrational beliefs from Table 9.1 that could have been incorporated into the cognitive belief system of a student who feels very badly about his or her exam results. In the first example, a feeling and possible behaviors that might result from irrational belief 8 are identified. What feelings can you identify and what behaviors might result if the same student had incorporated the second irrational belief listed (belief number 4)?

Irrational belief 8: "The idea that we should be thoroughly competent, intelligent, and achieving in all possible respects."

Possible feelings: depression

Possible behaviors: crying, sleeping too much, lack of interest in activities

Irrational belief 4: "The idea that human misery is invariable externally caused and is forced on us by outside people and events."

Possible feelings: _____

Possible behaviors: _____

In more recent years, Ellis reduced his twelve irrational beliefs down to what he has called **three core** (sometimes called mustabatory or grandiose) **irrational beliefs** (Ellis, 1989; Smith, 1989).

1. "I *absolutely must* under all conditions do important tasks well and be approved by significant others or else I am an inadequate and unlovable person!"

2. "Other people *absolutely must* under all conditions treat me fairly and justly or else they are rotten, damnable persons!"

3. "Conditions under which I live *absolutely must* always be the way I want them to be, give me almost immediate gratification, and not require me to work too hard to change or improve them; or else it is *awful*, I *can't stand*

T A B L E 9.1   Twelve Irrational Beliefs and Corresponding Rational Beliefs

Irrational Beliefs	Rational Beliefs
1. The idea that it is a dire necessity for adults to be loved by significant others for almost everything they do …	… instead of their concentrating on their own self-respect, on winning approval for practical purposes, and on loving rather than on being loved.
2. The idea that certain acts are awful or wicked, and that people who perform such acts should be severely damned …	… instead of the idea that certain acts are self-defeating or antisocial, and that people who perform such acts are behaving stupidly, ignorantly, or neurotically, and would be better helped to change. People's poor behaviors do not make them rotten individuals.
3. The idea that it is horrible when things are not the way we like them to be …	… instead of the idea that it is too bad, that we would better try to change or control bad conditions so that they become more satisfactory, and, if that is not possible, we had better temporarily accept and gracefully lump their existence.
4. The idea that human misery is invariably externally caused and is forced on us by outside people and events …	… instead of the idea that neurosis is largely caused by the view that we take of unfortunate conditions.
5. The idea that if something is or may be dangerous or fearsome we should be terribly upset and endlessly obsess about it …	… instead of the idea that one would better frankly face it and render it nondangerous and, when that is not possible, accept the inevitable.
6. The idea that it is easier to avoid than to face life difficulties and self-responsibilities …	… instead of the idea that the so-called easy way is usually much harder in the long run.
7. The idea that we absolutely need something other or stronger or greater than yourself on which to rely …	… instead of the idea that it is better to take the risks of thinking and acting less dependently.
8. The idea that we should be thoroughly competent, intelligent, and achieving in all possible respects …	… instead of the idea that we would better do rather than always need to do well and accept ourself as quite imperfect creature, who has general human limitations and specific fallibilities.
9. The idea that because something once strongly affected our life, it should indefinitely affect it …	… instead of the idea that we can learn from our past experiences but not be overly attached to or prejudiced by them.
10. The idea that we must have certain and perfect control over things …	… instead of the idea that the world is full of probability and chance and that we can still enjoy life despite this.
11. The idea that human happiness can be achieved by inertia and inaction …	… instead of the idea that we tend to be happiest when we are vitally absorbed in creative pursuits, or when we are devoting ourselves to people or projects outside ourselves.
12. The idea that we have virtually no control over our emotions and that we cannot help feeling disturbed about things …	… instead of the idea that we have real control over our destructive emotions if we choose to work at changing the musturbatory hypotheses which we often employ to create them. (Ellis, 1994)

them, and it is impossible for me to be happy *at all!*" (Ellis & MacLaren, 2005, pp. 32–33)

It should be noted that in the latter years of Ellis's life, he rarely made reference to his twelve original irrational beliefs, although often he would

---

B o x 9.1   Taking Awfulizing to the Extreme

Although REBT has certainly become one of the more popular theories of counseling and psychotherapy over the years, many have not agreed with some of the extreme stands that Albert Ellis took. Instead, many have adopted his views and have created a "softer" form of REBT. For instance, look at what he said about some things that many would consider "awful." Do you think he had a point?

We say that nothing is awful, nothing. Rape, incest, terrorism, Hitler—it isn't awful.... When something bad happens, you can easily upset yourself, but you always have a choice to feel sorry, regretful, frustrated, annoyed, and not depressed, anxious, and despairing. (Ellis as cited in Spiegel, 2004, para. 14, 16)

---

highlight his three core irrational beliefs. However, many therapists today continue to find the original twelve irrational beliefs helpful and use them in their practice.

Cognitive Distortion of Events

Ellis has identified a number of mechanisms that cause us to cognitively distort events and which we use to **indoctrinate** ourselves into thinking irrationally. Some of these include **absolutistic musts and shoulds, awfulizing, I-can't-stand-it-itis, demands,** and **people-rating (damning oneself and others)** (Ellis, n.d.; Ellis & MacLaren, 2005). As you read through these, consider the feelings and behaviors that might be associated with each.

Absolutistic musts and shoulds: This occurs when an individual believes that he or she must or should act a certain way in life (e.g., "I must be the best parent," or "I should always be polite"). Ellis suggests that people are not perfect, and absolutist thinking becomes a mechanism for setting ourselves up for failure.

Awfulizing: Awfulizing occurs when an individual exaggerates events by making them horrible, terrible, awful, or catastrophic (e.g., "If I don't get into that graduate program, my life will be shattered," or "It's so horrible, I can't even tell you what happened—okay, my husband abused me—I can't go on!"). REBT therapists assert that people are rarely faced with horrible, terrible, awful, or catastrophic events, and even when they are, they can choose to awfulize the situation or respond to it in a moderated manner (see Box 9.1).

I-can't-stand-it-itis: In a similar fashion to awfulizing, I-can't-stand-it-itis occurs when an individual continually sees events as being unbearable and generally exaggerates the event through his or her irrational belief system (e.g., "I just can't stand my daughter's behavior any more, she's going to drive me crazy!" or, "Those immigrants are taking jobs away from us; they're going to eventually take my job!"). Such exaggeration leads to depression and excessive worry.

Demands: The use of demands on oneself adds unnecessary stress to an individual because it assumes that a person should, must, or ought to act in a certain manner. Similarly, saying one "needs" as opposing to wanting or preferring something that is not critical for one's survival ("I *need* to have love") is another mechanism the individual uses to place excessive demands on oneself (see Box 9.2).

People-rating (damning oneself and others): A type of all-or-nothing thinking, people-rating occurs when an individual rates or views oneself, or another person, as having all or none of a quality (good, bad, worthless) (e.g., "My boss is a no-good idiot; I hate him," or "I loved that woman, she was perfect. Why did she do this to me?").

I don't damn any person, including Stalin, Hitler and President Bush....
I do damn and actively work against many of their thoughts, feelings, and behaviors. (Ellis, as cited in Green, 2003, para. 2)

The occurrence of an event, how we might distort that event, and the kinds of irrational thinking that takes place are intimately related, as shown in Figure 9.1:

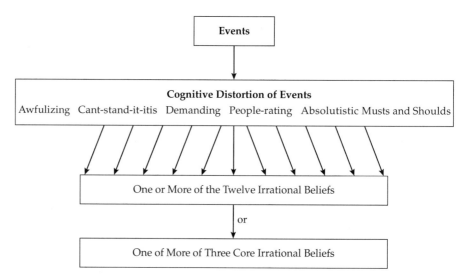

FIGURE 9.1 Relationships among Events, Cognitive Distortions of Events, and Irrational Beliefs

Now that we've examined some of the ways in which we cognitively distort events, let's go back to our earlier example about the student who did poorly on an exam, and consider how the following three cognitive distortions might be related to irrational beliefs 3, 4, and 8. You may also want to consider if any of the following examples might be related to other irrational beliefs listed in Table 9.1.

Example 1:

Possible cognitive self-statement: "I must do well on all my tests."
Cognitive distortion mechanisms at play in above statement: absolutistic musts, and placing unnecessary demands on self
Resulting irrational belief 8: the idea that we should be thoroughly competent, intelligent, and achieving in all possible respects

Example 2:

Possible cognitive self-statement: "I will never get anywhere in life due to this test—things are just a mess."
Cognitive distortion mechanism at play in above statement: awfulizing
Resulting irrational belief 3: the idea that it is horrible when things are not the way we like them to be

Example 3:

Possible cognitive self-statement: "My professor is a flaming idiot and doesn't know what he's doing."
Cognitive distortion mechanism at play in above statement: people-rating
Resulting irrational belief 4: the idea that human misery is invariably externally caused and is forced on us by outside people and events

The ABCDEs of Feelings and Behaviors

The REBT therapist addresses the client's irrational beliefs through the use of what Ellis called the **ABCDEs of feelings and behaviors** (Ellis & Harper, 1975). Using the ABCDEs, the REBT therapist first labels the **activating event**, (the situation that *seemed* to cause the consequential feelings and behaviors) "A," the **irrational** **belief** about the activating event as "iB" (irrational), and the **consequential** feeling or behavior as "C." Cognitive self-statements or beliefs that result in negative feelings are always rooted in one or more of the twelve irrational beliefs from Table 3.1, or the three core irrational beliefs from p. 291, and are also driven by the cognitive distortions.

For instance, for the following two examples, examine how the client's self-statements that result from the activating event are related to the three core irrational beliefs listed earlier on p. 291. To which of the twelve irrational beliefs listed in Table 3.1 might they also be related? To which cognitive distortions listed on p. 293 do you think they're related?

Example 1

Activating event (A): My lover has left me.
Cognitive self-statement or belief: I must have a lover, otherwise I am worthless.
Irrational belief (iB): Conditions under which I live *absolutely must* always be the way I want them to be, give me almost immediate gratification, and not require me to work too hard to change or improve them; or else it is *awful*, I *can't stand* them, and it is impossible for me to be happy *at all!*
Possible consequence (C):

> *Feelings consequence:* depression, panic
> *Behavioral consequence:* need to immediately seek out another person, even if the relationship may not be healthy or positive; or, isolation if depression is particularly bad

Example 2

Activating event (A): My boss didn't like the way I put that report together; I can tell in his tone of voice.
Cognitive self-statement or belief: I must be perfectly competent in everything I do.
Irrational belief (iB): I *absolutely must* under all conditions do important tasks well and be approved by significant others or else I am an inadequate and unlovable person!"
Possible consequence (C):

> *Feelings consequence*: depression or anger; low self-acceptance
> *Behavioral consequence*: inability to talk effectively with boss; compulsive work behaviors leading to stress

After the client understands the relationship between his or her irrational beliefs and affective and behavioral consequences, the therapist uses a wide range of techniques to **d**ispute (D) the irrational belief and to develop new **e**ffective responses (E) (see "Therapeutic Techniques" section for ways in which this is done). The result are new, **r**ational **b**eliefs (rB) or cognitions, and new consequences, that are less stressful and healthier, as noted below:

Example 1: After Cognitive Disputation

Activating event (A): My lover has left me.
Rational belief (rB): This is unfortunate, and things don't always work out in life the way that I want them to. However, I'll move on in my life and perhaps even meet someone I like more.
Possible consequence (C): feeling some sadness about the end of the relationship but looking forward toward meeting new people

Example 2: After Cognitive Disputation

Activating event (A): My boss didn't like the way I put that report together; I can tell in his tone of voice.
Rational belief (rB): Whatever my boss thinks of me, I know I have been working hard and I feel good about what I've done. I also know that I am not perfect, and feedback could help me do even better.
Possible consequence (C): high self-acceptance; seeking feedback from boss

Rational, Scientific Approach

Using the **Socratic dialogue method** to help clients rationally examine their philosophical precepts, REBT therapists attempt to identify cognitive distortions as well as their accompanying irrational beliefs (Ellis & MacLaren, 2005). In this method, the therapist leads the discussion, asks questions, and gently challenges the client to see how his or her thinking process is illogical and leads to emotional distress and dysfunctional behaviors. Through this philosophical discourse, clients are challenged to show evidence that their irrational beliefs are true. Since this is an impossibility (irrational beliefs are by their very nature false and thus disputable), the client has no recourse but to accept the irrationality of his or her self-statements. However, some clients take more convincing than others.

Application of Experimental Methods

Once a client has accepted the irrationality of his or her beliefs, he or she can begin to experiment with new ways of thinking, feeling, and acting that would result in living a healthier lifestyle. Irrational thoughts can be replaced with rational ones, and new ways of feeling and behaving can be adopted. The REBT therapist will actively teach the client about new, rational ways of thinking and encourage the client to experiment with new feelings and behaviors that match the new rational way of thinking. Thus, the client whose lover breaks up with him responds with a rational statement, such as: "It's sad that I won't have my lover around anymore, but I am perfectly lovable and can meet other people." Behaviors that match the new, rational self-statement would be designed and attempted (e.g., the client dresses nicely to go out and meet new people, and identifies places he or she can go).

THERAPEUTIC TECHNIQUES

REBT is a **psychoeducational** approach to counseling, which means that it teaches the individual more effective ways of living in the world and helps the individual learn about his or her psychological self. This approach relies on a number of techniques that enhance the client's learning about self, particularly ways in which the client distorts his or her cognitions and the accompanying irrational ways of thinking, and challenge the person to take on a new, rational approach to living. Some of the major techniques in this process include showing **unconditional acceptance; teaching the REBT philosophy; being active and directive; challenging clients; demonstrating the ABCs of feeling and behaving; encouraging the disputing of dysfunctional cognitions, behaviors, and emotions; using humor; using metaphors and stories;** and **homework**.

Showing Unconditional Acceptance

... [P]eople who achieve USA (unconditional self-acceptance) ... will not only fully accept themselves with their failings and "sins" but also will accept sinful and failing *others*. (Ellis, 2006, p. 22)

B o x 9.3   Teaching the REBT Philosophy

1. We are born fallible human beings and have the potential for rational or irrational thinking.
2. Although the past may have affected us, we are not bound by it.
3. Because we are fallible human beings, it is important to learn how to accept ourselves and others unconditionally and not berate ourselves or others for behaving in ways that cause emotional distress or dysfunctional behaviors.
4. "The ABCs:" The cognitive distortion of events, and not the event itself, is what causes irrational thinking, dysfunctional behaviors, and negative feelings.
5. Irrational thinking is the result of our cognitive distortions, which include: *absolutistic musts and shoulds, awfulizing, I-can't-stand-it-itis, demands, and people-rating (damning oneself and others)*. These distortions will cause irrational thinking.
6. Most of us have adopted one or more of twelve irrational beliefs or three core irrational beliefs that are a result of our cognitive distortions.
7. We are capable of adopting a new, more rational belief system that results in having appropriate feelings and functional behaviors.
8. Adopting a rational belief system will take practice, but we can overcome our past conditioning.

It is critical that from the moment a client steps into the REBT therapist's office, he or she is seen as a fallible human being who has done things that have upset himself or herself and others. This understanding allows the therapist to show **unconditional acceptance** toward the client, while at the same time recognize the inevitability of the fact that as fallible human beings, people will sometimes exhibit behaviors that are toxic for themselves and others. The acceptance of the individual by the therapist allows clients to freely discuss their thoughts, feelings, or behaviors.

Teaching the REBT Philosophy

As it is a psychoeducational approach, teaching about the philosophy of REBT is a critical piece of therapy. Thus, therapists will actively teach the philosophy of REBT, encourage clients to read books and printed materials, listen to audio and visual aids, and visit Web sites that explain the REBT philosophy. Some of the typical philosophical points that REBT therapists will teach clients about can be found in Box 9.3.

Being Active and Directive

Although listening and the use of empathy are not critical tools for the REBT therapist (see Box 9.4), some listening to understand the situation is, of course, always necessary. In addition, by using questions and encouraging the client to talk, the REBT therapist will conduct a client **assessment** that may include giving tests, gathering biographical information, and discussion of the client's life circumstances. The information obtained will be used to assess how the client distorts events and uses irrational thinking. In addition, the client might be directed to obtain materials that will increase his or her understanding of the REBT philosophy and is encouraged to practice specific interventions aimed at changing the way he or she thinks, acts, and feels. Often, this occurs by actively disputing the client's current way of thinking and teaching the client how to dispute on his or her own.

B o x 9.4 "Don't Give Me That Empathy Shit"

I was a few years out of my doctoral program and was considering doing advanced training in REBT. I decided to apply for a post-doctoral fellowship at the Albert Ellis Institute. Having been trained as a humanistic therapist, this was going to be a stretch for me. However, I believed that REBT had much to offer and that I could learn much from this experience. I was asked to come for an interview. After interviewing with some of the staff, I was told that I would next have the "obligatory interview" with Al. As you can imagine, I was nervous. I was taken to his office—there he is, an icon, sitting in his big easy chair. I said hello,

and we pretty quickly were into the role-play. I did what I thought I should do—listened and used empathy as I attempted to assess the situation prior to moving into the REBT approach. After a couple of minutes of empathy, Al looked at me and said, "Don't give me that empathy shit." I quickly changed— afterward, he said that I did a pretty good job. Well, I guess empathy really is not that important in REBT.

You can listen to this story, as well as other stories about Albert Ellis, by clicking on the link to Albert Ellis at the "Stories of the Great Therapists" Web site: http://www.odu.edu/sgt

---

Challenging Clients

From an REBT perspective, **challenging clients** should not be confused with heavy-duty confrontation. Challenging occurs when therapists suggest to their clients that they examine their current way of understanding their thinking, feeling, and behavioral processes. Subsequently, if they believe that change would be helpful, clients can choose to adopt more rational beliefs as well as healthier behaviors and feelings.

> You are not going to tell them what to feel, what to do or what to think. Rather, you are going to help them to understand what their options are about what to believe and what the likely emotional, be-havioral and thinking consequences are of each of these belief options. Once they have understood this, your job is to help them to choose the belief option that best helps them to achieve their healthy emotional, behavioral, and thinking goals. (Dryden & Neenan, 2003, p. 4)

Demonstrating the ABCs of Feeling and Behaving

Early on in therapy, the REBT therapist will use the "ABCs" to demonstrate to clients how irrational beliefs are causing emotional distress, not the situation or activating event. For instance, look at the following situation to see how the REBT therapist applies the ABCs to the problem being presented:

Client: I am having an ongoing problem with my mother. She turned seventy, my father (her husband) recently died, and I would like her to live with me. She's insistent that she wants to live on her own. She's healthy, but she can't live on her own forever. However, she never lis-tens to anything I say and refuses to move in with me. I know she is perfectly capable of making her own decisions, but if she lived with me, she would be much better off. I just think she is taking a risk with her life! If I don't do something soon, I know something bad will happen. What if she falls and can't get to a phone? I am waking up in the middle of the night having panic attacks about this. I haven't had a good night's sleep in months. Can you get her to listen to me?

In the above case, the client is concerned about his mother. The rational response would be to have some reasonable amount of worry about his mother's situation, and if his mother so chooses, offer some options to his mother. However, in this case, the mother does not want to do what her child wants, and she seems perfectly content with her situation. The REBT therapist formulates the possible ABCs of this client's dilemma and explains it to the client.

Activating event (A): Father recently died and Mom now lives alone.
Irrational belief (iB): This client is awfulizing the situation with his mother and placing demands on himself. The client believes that things must be the way he wants them to be (irrational belief 3), that unhappiness is caused by conditions outside of his control (irrational belief 4), and that he had better worry about these things; otherwise, they might happen (irrational belief 5). (See Table 9.1.)
Consequences (C): The client is having panic attacks and sleeping poorly— all the result of the irrational beliefs, not the activating event.

Encouraging the Disputing of Dysfunctional Cognitions, Behaviors, and Emotions

As clients learn the REBT philosophy, they realize that many of their cognitions, behaviors, and emotions have not been healthy. Thus, they are encouraged by the therapist to dispute the unhealthy ones and replace them with healthy ones. ***Disputations*** can occur cognitively, behaviorally, or emotionally.

Cognitive Disputation.   As clients begin to realize that it is not the event causing the feeling or behaviors, but the belief about the event, they are called upon to **dispute the irrational beliefs (DIBS)** that have been driving their emotional distress and dysfunctional behaviors. In helping clients challenge their existing irrational beliefs, Yankura and Dryden (1990) encourage clients to ask the following disputing questions:

- Where is the evidence for this belief?
- Is that really true?
- Why must it be so?
- Is there another way to think about this?
- What's the worst thing that could happen? Would that really be awful?
- What's this way of thinking about things going to get me? (p. 13)

Using the questions above, consider how our fictitious client might respond. The result of using these disputing questions is that the client's irrational beliefs are challenged. Eventually, the counselor can suggest that the irrational beliefs are replaced with rational ones. In our example, look at how new, rational beliefs replace the former irrational ones.

> *Activating event (A):* Father recently died and Mom now lives alone.
> *Rational belief (rB):* There is no evidence that Mom is doing poorly, and I can wait and see how she does. I cannot control her decisions and cannot excessively worry about something I cannot control.
> *Consequences:* Concern, but not excessive worry about mother's situation; offer help if she wants, but don't try to force my opinions on her.

Behavioral Disputations.   In addition to **cognitive disputations**, it is often beneficial to practice behavioral changes that coincide with the cognitive ones. Thus, clients are generally encouraged to practice behaviors that challenge the irrational beliefs that are responsible for the behaviors. **Risk-taking behaviors** are one kind of **homework assignment** often given to clients that encourage new ways of acting. Using our earlier example, instead of trying to convince his mother to move in with him, the client might ask her what kind of help, if any, she would like, given her new situation. Or, taking this technique to another level, why not have the son ask his mother if he can help her plan a cruise or assist her in meeting new people? Such **behavioral disputations** would be directly competing with the irrational fears he has been evoking.

Performing a **shame-attacking exercise**, which involves the purposeful acting out of a situation that might normally cause embarrassment, is a behavioral technique that reinforces the fact that approval from others is not necessary for self-acceptance. For instance, clients might be asked to walk down a street wearing outlandish clothes or go up to strangers and tell them how nice they look. With our fictitious case, the client might not contact his mother for a few weeks. This activity would allow the client to practice a different type of behavior than he is used to and reinforce his mother's independence.

Emotive Disputations.   The most commonly used emotive disputation in REBT is called **rational–emotive imagery** (Maultsby & Ellis, 1974). In this process, clients are asked to close their eyes and focus intensely on the situation that is causing them extreme emotional upset. When the client experiences the emotional upset, he or she signals the therapist, often by lifting a prearranged finger. The therapist then asks the client to change the self-defeating emotion to an appropriate emotion, usually assigned by the therapist. After the client accomplishes this, the therapist asks the client what he or she was able to do to change the feeling (Ellis, 1996b). Usually, the client responds by stating that he or she changed the way in which the situation was viewed. Thus, in our previous example with the older mother, the client would first experience the extreme worry and panic of imagining his mother's refusing to listen to his suggestions about moving and perhaps even seeing her falling and being taken to the hospital. Then, the therapist asks him to experience a different emotion— perhaps a feeling of calm or maybe even happiness. As the client experiences one of these feelings, the therapist asks him what he is imagining. In this case, the client might respond by saying that he sees his mother sitting in her apartment, contentedly reading the newspaper (which results in a calm feeling), or, alternatively, he might visualize her enjoying a cruise (which results in his feeling happy). Ultimately, rational–emotive imagery teaches a client that one can have control over one's thoughts, and ultimately, over one's emotions and behaviors.

Using Humor

> REBT assumes that people had better take things seriously, but not too seriously. (Ellis, 2004a, p. 95)

As one can see from the song at the very beginning of this chapter, Ellis loved to use **humor** in making his point. It is not unusual to be walking down the halls of an esteemed institution of higher education and hear a counseling theories class belting out one of Ellis's songs. Ellis also liked to quote the sixteenth-century philosopher, Michel Montaigne, who said: "My life has been filled with terrible misfortunes—most of which never happened."

REBT therapists see the humor that sometimes exists when individuals take on an irrational belief system. Unfortunately, many clients seem to want to wallow in their misfortune. Thus, REBT therapists will sometimes use humor to help clients see the ridiculousness of their "plight." Take the fearful son who is afraid of his mother's future. It's ironic, and almost funny, that she is perfectly satisfied in life, and he is the one with the pathology! Pointing out the humor of a situation can help clients see the pointlessness and irony of the situation.

Using Metaphors and Stories

Although a somewhat less direct method, **metaphors** and **stories** will sometimes be used in an effort to illustrate and reinforce points that the REBT therapist is trying to make (Yankura & Dryden, 1990). Thus, the son who is so concerned about his aging mother might be told something like: "You know, your mother reminds me of the Empire State Building. Despite the fact that the building is aging, and from another era, it still stands erect and strong in the middle of the city."

Homework

REBT therapists will often actively encourage their clients to practice many techniques at home. For instance, it would be common for REBT therapists to ask clients to practice, on their own, any of the disputation techniques mentioned or any of a number of other techniques, such as behavioral conditioning, bibliotherapy aimed at reading materials to reinforce new ways of being, expression of feelings, assertiveness training, or role-playing new behaviors. All of these techniques are tried with the intent of maintaining the new, more rational belief system.

THE THERAPEUTIC PROCESS

The REBT therapeutic process involves a series of steps that includes assessing the client's situation and hypothesizing how the ABCs apply, teaching the REBT philosophy, demonstrating how the client's situation fits the REBT model, directing the change process, and reinforcing change and terminating the relationship (cf. Dryden & DiGiuseppe, 1990).

Step 1: Assess Client's Situation and Hypothesize How the ABCs Apply

A client comes to therapy feeling upset, and it is the job of the REBT therapist to actively assess the client's situation, understand the client's upsetness, and come up with a hypothesis as to how the client is cognitively distorting events and causing himself or herself distress. **Assessment** occurs in a number of ways, including the use of standardized tests, biographical data inventories, client self-report, and interviewing (Ellis & MacLaren, 2005). The assessment process, which is ongoing throughout therapy, allows the therapist to consider how the ABCs apply to the client's situation. In this beginning phase of therapy, and ongoing throughout all the phases, the therapist shows acceptance toward the client, although constantly encouraging the client to examine his or her life and eventually take on a new philosophy of living.

Step 2: Teaching the REBT Philosophy

After the therapist formulates a hypothesis, he or she is ready to share it with the client. But first, the client must understand the broader philosophy of REBT. Therapists need to actively encourage clients to take on this philosophy if they are to make any substantive changes. Thus, REBT therapists teach the philosophy of REBT to clients (see Box 9.3). To reinforce the understanding of the REBT philosophy, pamphlets, books, Internet resources, and other aids that clients can review in the office or study at home might be suggested.

Step 3: Demonstrating How the Client's Situation Fits the REBT Model

Once understanding and acceptance of this philosophy occurs, clients are ready to hear how the therapist's hypothesis applies to the client's situation. This is generally done by having the therapist present his or her hypothesis in the ABC formulation, as noted earlier. To facilitate this process, a handout that addresses the twelve irrational beliefs (see Table 9.1) and/or three core irrational beliefs (p. 291) is sometimes distributed to clients.

Step 4: Directing the Change Process

Now that the client has taken on the REBT philosophy and sees how it specifically applies to his or her situation, it is time to actively work on making change. Change can occur on three levels—cognitive, feeling, and behavioral—and often occurs through the use of disputations, as noted earlier (the "D" of the ABCDEs, for "disputing"). Change occurs when clients are able to dispute their irrational thoughts, their dysfunctional

---

B o x 9.5   Dr. Allen and Rebekkah

To see the REBT process, read or watch Dr. Korrie Allen's work with "Rebekah."

    You can read this session by going to www.cengage.com/counseling/neukrug/CTP1e and click

"student downloads." Or your instructor may show this session in class with the DVD that accompanies his or her copy of the text.

---

behaviors, and their emotional distress, which leads to more effective responses (the "E" of the ABCDEs, for "effective"). In this process, using many of the techniques we discussed, the therapist actively suggests ways in which the client can rid himself or herself of irrational and dysfunctional thoughts, behaviors, and feelings, and adopt new, more rational and functional ones.

Step 5: Reinforcing Change and Terminating the Relationship

As clients increasingly become comfortable with REBT philosophy, they are able to apply it to other aspects of their lives. Although practice on their initial presenting problem should continue, they also are now able to understand how the basic principles of REBT can be applied to other problems in their lives. As they continue to make progress at working on their own issues, they develop an increasingly stronger acceptance of self and also are better able to accept others in their differences and fallibilities. Armed with the tools of change originating from the REBT philosophy, clients can terminate therapy and work on their own. Ultimately, the client will adopt a new style of relating to the world in which he or she replaces irrational beliefs with rational beliefs and the concurrent behaviors and feelings that go along with such beliefs (see Box 9.5).

SOCIAL, CULTURAL, AND SPIRITUAL ISSUES

REBT, like some other therapies, is largely a form of tolerance training. It encourages you to think, feel, and act the ways you want—but warns against rigidity and fanaticism. (Ellis, 2004c)

Mistakenly, many students believe that REBT is promoting a certain set of values. This is because Ellis uses highly charged words such as "irrational" and "rational" in his theory. However, if one takes a closer look at his theory, it is clear that Ellis is not telling any client what specific values to take on. He is, on the other hand, suggesting that some ways of living in the world are more likely to create frustration, emotional distress, self-hate, and hate of others. In essence, he is saying that certain ways of being are intolerant—intolerant and intolerable to ourselves, and intolerant and intolerable to others.

For instance, Ellis is not saying that you must believe in Jesus, or Allah, or God, or anyone. He is saying, however, that whatever you believe, do not do it in an absolutist manner. Truth is relative, and your beliefs are only *your* truth in a moment in time, says Ellis. And, if you feel like you must rigidly adhere to certain values (e.g., Jesus would never get angry), you're going to disappoint yourself—because as a fallible human being, you *will* get angry sometimes. Similarly, if you are walking around trying to get others to rigidly adhere to certain truths, you will piss people off. So, his REBT philosophy advocates for tolerance—tolerance toward self and tolerance toward others. How does he do this? By suggesting that certain "rational beliefs" are more likely to lend themselves to a philosophy of tolerance. Look at Table 9.1, and you'll see the "rational beliefs" are also tolerant beliefs.

Ellis is also suggesting that REBT is particularly suited for religious people (Nielsen, Johnson, & Ellis, 2001). He highlights the point that those who are religious are accustomed to dealing with a belief system, and he believes that his approach is uniquely suited for religious people in that he does not advocate changing their values. He does, however, suggest that the REBT therapist can respect a client's religious beliefs while at the same time challenging other beliefs that are causing emotional distress. In fact, Ellis goes on at length in describing how scripture is in line with many of the rational beliefs to which REBT adheres (e.g., accept others). Although others would argue that many religions are based, at least to some degree, on absolutist thinking, and thus would be at odds with REBT, for many religious people, the approach would be usable.

Overall, any person who holds firmly to absolutist thinking and rigid values will have a difficult time with REBT. For instance, if you come from a culture that promotes machismo at the expense of others, or believes that you have *your* bible that has *the* real "truth," or if you know the "correct" way of living, you will have a difficult time with REBT. So, if you're absolutist about your cultural values, your religious values, your terrorist or anti-terrorist values, or any other values, you will not do well in this approach (Ellis, 2004c). In fact, Ellis says, you are likely to fuel hatred toward the world. The bottom line: Understand differences and don't be absolutist or dogmatic, and don't rigidly practice "shoulds" or "musts" toward yourself or others.

EFFICACY OF RATIONAL EMOTIVE
BEHAVIOR THERAPY

In 1957, Ellis published the results of one of the first outcome studies of psychotherapy (1957b). Comparing his approach to psychoanalysis, orthodox psychoanalysis, and "psychoanalytically oriented" therapy, he found RT (**rational therapy**, as it was called then) to be considerably more effective than the other approaches, with 90 percent of these clients showing distinct or considerable improvement. Although methodological problems existed (Wampold, 2001), Ellis should be given credit for broaching the subject of outcome research.

B o x 9.6   Jake's Experience in Rational Emotive Therapy

Please review the Miller family's background, which can be found in Appendix B, and then read about Jake's encounter with an REBT therapist, which can also be found in Appendix B.

Since the 1950s, considerable research has been conducted on REBT. In numerous studies, REBT seems to compare favorably to other kinds of treatment (Silverman, McCarthy, & McGovern, 1997; Watson, 1999). Other studies have shown that clients treated with cognitive–behavioral therapies experience less disturbance and have improvement of their neurotic symptoms (Haaga & Davidson, 1989; Watson, 1999). Also, an examination of the *Journal of Rational-Emotive and Cognitive Behavior Therapy* shows that REBT has efficacy across a wide range of disorders and with a variety of cultural groups.

Although REBT is not a treatment of choice for highly educated individuals who have a strong desire to work on entrenched problems while exploring their pasts, it seems to be particularly efficacious for educated individuals who are relatively emotionally sound and would like to do focused therapeutic work quickly (Watson, 1999). For obvious reasons, it is also probably not particularly helpful with long-term entrenched problems and problems associated with severe thought disorders. And it is a difficult approach for resistant clients. Although I can imagine Ellis challenging a resistant client until he or she either walks out of the room or gives in, most therapists are not like Ellis, and the resistant client will clearly resist the taking on of a new philosophical way of being that includes rational thinking. Finally, because it is a brief approach that gives clients tools so they can continue to work on their own, it fits well in today's managed-health-care system (see Box 9.6).

SUMMARY

Albert Ellis, the originator of what was initially called rational therapy, developed his approach to therapy during the 1940s after developing a disdain for the long-term intrapsychic approach of psychoanalysis. Ellis found that he could help clients, in a relatively short amount of time, by suggesting that they change the manners in which they think about their situations. Experimenting with different techniques, Ellis soon developed an approach that was active, directive, and psychoeducational. Eventually, he expanded his approach and renamed it rational emotive behavior therapy to reflect the various dimensions he believed were important in the change process.

Although Ellis believed that early child-rearing practices, family dynamics, societal influences, and innate biology tend to be the basis for the development of rational or irrational thinking, his approach was unique in that he did not believe that spending time talking about the past was particularly important to the change process. Ellis saw people as fallible human beings who have the potential for rational or irrational thinking, and believed that rational thinking leads to healthy ways of living and results in people who show unconditional acceptance of self, of others, and of the way things are.

Ellis highlighted a number of mechanisms that fostered distorted thinking of events, including absolutistic musts and shoulds, awfulizing, I-can't-stand-it-itis, demands, and people-rating (damning oneself and others). In working with clients, Ellis suggested that therapists focus on the ABCs of feelings and behaviors, with the "A" representing an *activating* event, the "C" representing the emotional and behavioral *consequence* of that event, and the "B" representing the *belief* about the event. Irrational beliefs, suggested Ellis, were a result of distorted thinking and were responsible for maladaptive feelings and behaviors. Irrational thinking, as identified by the twelve irrational beliefs and later pared down to three core (sometimes called musturbatory or grandiose) irrational beliefs, could be replaced by rational thinking, stated Ellis.

In this chapter, a number of key concepts central to REBT philosophy were identified, including philosophical conditioning; unconditional acceptance; irrational beliefs; cognitive distortions of events; the ABCs of feelings and behaviors; the rational, scientific approach of REBT using the Socratic dialogue method; and the importance of applying experimental methods.

To help people change quickly, a number of techniques were identified, including showing unconditional acceptance; teaching the REBT philosophy; being active and directive; challenging clients; demonstrating the ABCs of feeling and behaving; encouraging the disputing of dysfunctional cognitions, behaviors, and emotions; using humor; using metaphors and stories; and homework.

It was noted that the REBT therapeutic process involves a series of steps that includes assessing the client's situation and hypothesizing how the ABCs apply, teaching the REBT philosophy, demonstrating how the client's situation fits the REBT model, directing the change process, and reinforcing change and terminating the relationship.

Ellis suggested that his approach has use with a wide variety of clients but would not be helpful for individuals who have strong, absolutist tendencies or ways of thinking. It was also suggested that highly educated individuals who are looking for long-term intrapsychic work would not be amenable to this approach. Ellis's approach has been shown to work with clients exhibiting a wide range of symptoms, although it is probably not as useful with those who have long-term entrenched problems or severe thought disorders, or resistant clients. It was suggested that this kind of brief approach fits well in today's managed-health-care system.

KEY WORDS

ABCDEs of feelings and behaviors

absolutistic musts and shoulds

activating event

Albert Ellis Institute

American Psychological Association's Professional Contribution award

anti-deterministic

application of experimental methods

assessment

awfulizing

behavioral disputations

being active and directive

challenging clients

cognitive disputations

cognitive distortion of events

cognitive processes

cognitive therapy

constructivist approach

damning oneself and others

demands

demonstrating the ABCs of feeling and behaving

directive disputations

dispute the irrational beliefs (DIBS)

dysfunctional behaviors

emotive disputations

encouraging the disputing of dysfunctional cognitions, behaviors, and emotions

existential–humanistic philosophy

experimentalist

fallible human beings

grandiose irrational beliefs

homework

homework assignment

humor, using

I-can't-stand-it-itis

indoctrinate

insight-oriented

Institute for Rational Living

International Journal of Sexology

irrational belief systems

irrational thinking

learning theory

living legend (ACA award)

metaphors and stories, using

musturbatory irrational beliefs

people-rating

philosophical conditioning

probabilistic atheist

psychoeducational

rational therapist

rational therapy

rational emotive therapy

rational emotive behavior therapy

rational thinking

rational scientific approach

rational–emotive imagery

risk-taking behaviors

self-defeating and irrational thinking

self-defeating emotions

shame-attacking exercise

Society for the Scientific Study of Sex

Socratic dialogue method

teaching the REBT philosophy

three core irrational beliefs

twelve irrational beliefs

unconditional acceptance, showing

KEY NAMES

Beck, Aaron   Epictetus   Joffe, Debbie   Wolfe, Janet

REFERENCES

Abrams, M., & Abrams, L. (2005). *A brief biography of Dr. Albert Ellis.* Retrieved from http://www.rebt.ws/albertellisbiography.html

Aviv, R. (2005, August 19). The interpretation of reams: Talking with Albert Ellis, world-renowned anti-Freud therapist. *The Village Voice.* Retrieved from http://www.villagevoice.com/people/0534,interview,67068,24.html

Carey, B. (2006, January, 31). Judge orders psychologist reinstated to institute. *New York Times.* Retrieved from http://www.nytimes.com/2006/01/31/nyregion/31ellis.html?ex=1180756800&en=4f0c1198ea0d7b91&ei=5070

Davies, A. (2005, July 21–27). Shrink raps. *TimeOut New York, 512* [Electronic version]. Retrieved from http://www.timeoutny.com/newyork/Details.do?page=1&xyurl=xyl://TONYWebArticles2/512/chill_out/shrink_wraps.xml

Dryden, W., & DiGiuseppe, R. (1990). *A primer on rational-emotive therapy.* Champaign, IL: Research Press.

Dryden, W., & Neenan, M. (2003). *The REBT therapist's pocket companion.* New York: Albert Ellis Institute.

Ellis, A. (n.d.). REBT by Albert Ellis, Ph.D.: 12 irrational ideas that cause and sustain neurosis. Retrieved from http://www.rebt.ws/REBT%20explained.htm

Ellis, A. (1948). A critique of the theoretical contributions of non-directive therapy. *Journal of Clinical Psychology, 4,* 248–255.

Ellis, A. (1950). An introduction to the principles of scientific psychoanalysis. *Genetic Psychology Monographs, 41,* 147–212.

Ellis, A. (1951a). Neurosis and human growth. *Psychological Bulletin, 48*(6), 542–544.

Ellis, A. (1951b). *The folklore of sex.* New York: Charles Boni.

Ellis, A. (1954). *The American sexual tragedy.* New York: Twayne Publishers.

Ellis, A. (1956). An operational reformulation of some basic principles of psychoanalysis. *Psychoanalytic Review, 43,* 163–180.

Ellis, A. (1957a). *How to live with a neurotic.* New York: Crown Publishers.

Ellis, A. (1957b). Outcome of employing three techniques of psychotherapy. *Journal of Clinical Psychology, 13,* 344–350.

Ellis, A. (1958). *Sex without guilt.* New York: Lyle Stuart.

Ellis, A. (1962). *Reason and emotion in psychotherapy.* Secaucus, NJ: Lyle Stuart.

Ellis, A. (1989). Comments on my critics. In M. E. Bernard & R. DiGiuseppe (Eds.), *Inside rational-emotive therapy: A critical appraisal of the theory and therapy of Albert Ellis* (pp. 199–235). New York: Academic Press.

Ellis, A. (1994). *The essence of rational emotive behavior therapy.* [Brochure]. New York: The Albert Ellis Institute.

Ellis, A. (1996a). A social constructionist position for mental health counseling: A reply to Jeffrey T. Guterman. *Journal of Mental Health Counseling, 18,* 16–28.

Ellis, A. (1996b). *Better, deeper, and more enduring brief therapy: The Rational Emotive Behavior Therapy approach.* New York: Bruner/Mazel.

Ellis, A. (1998). How rational emotive behavior therapy belongs in the constructivist camp. In M. F. Hoyt (Ed.), *The handbook of constructive therapies: Innovative approaches from leading practitioners* (pp. 83–99). San Francisco: Jossey-Bass.

Ellis, A. (2004a). *Rationale emotive behavior therapy*. Amherst, NY: Prometheus Books.

Ellis, A. (2004b). Why I (really) became a therapist. *Journal of Rational-Emotive Cognitive Behavior Therapy*, 22(2), 73–77.

Ellis, A (2004c). *The road to tolerance: The philosophy of Rational Emotive Behavior Therapy*. Amherst, NY: Prometheus Books.

Ellis, A. (2006). *The myth of self-esteem*. Amherst, NY: Prometheus Books.

Ellis, A., & Harper, R. A. (1975). A new guide to rational living. North Hollywood, CA: Wilshire.

Ellis, A., & MacLaren, C. (2005). *Rational emotive behavior therapy: A therapist's guide* (2nd ed.). Atascadero, CA: Impact Publishers.

Green, A. (2003, October 13). The human condition ageless, guiltless. *The New Yorker* [Electronic version]. Retrieved from http://www.rebt.ws/recentarticles.html

Guterman, J. T. (1994). A social constructionist position for mental health counseling. *Journal of Mental Health Counseling*, 16, 226–244.

Haaga, D. A., & Davison, G. C. (1989). Outcome studies of rational-emotive therapy. In M. E. Bernard and R. DiGiuseppe (Eds.), *Inside rational-emotive therapy* (pp. 155–195). San Diego, CA: Academic Press.

Hafetz, D. (2005, October 9). Star shrink, 92, is psyched out. *New York Post*, 5.

Halasz, G. (2004). Interview: In conversation with Dr. Albert Ellis. *Australasian Psychiatry*, 12(4), 325–333.

Hurley, D. (2004, May 4). Scientist at work: Albert Ellis. From therapy's Lenny Bruce: Get over it! Stop whining! *New York Times: Health Section*. [Electronic version]. Retrieved from http://www.nytimes.com/2004/05/04/health/psychology/04PROF.html?pagewanted=2&ei=5070&en=7f9ae346ae424997&ex=1180670400

Kaufman, M. T. (2007, July 25). Albert Ellis, 93, influential psychotherapist, dies. *New York Times*. Retrieved from http://www.nytimes.com/2007/07/25/nyregion/25ellis.html?ei=5088&en=fafd65d9cfba7311&ex=1343016000&partner=rssnyt&pagewanted=all

Maultsby, M. C., & Ellis, A. (1974). *Techniques for using rational-emotive imagery*. New York: Institute for Rational-Emotive Therapy.

Nielsen, S. L., Johnson, W. B., & Ellis, A. (2001). Counseling and psychotherapy with religious persons: A rational emotive behavior therapy approach. Mahwah, NJ: Lawrence Erlbaum Associates.

Padesky, C. A., & Beck, A. T. (2003). Science and philosophy: Comparison of cognitive therapy and rational emotive behavior therapy. *Journal of Cognitive Psychotherapy: An International Quarterly*, 17(3), 211–225.

Remembering Albert Ellis. (2007, August 31). *Counseling Today Online*. Retrieved from http://www.counseling.org/Publications/CounselingTodayArticles.aspx?AGuid=a66c5117-232e-41df-86ec-b1ceb1ace297

Silverman, M. S., McCarthy, M., & McGovern, T. (1992). A review of outcome studies of rational-emotive therapy from 1982–1989. *Journal of Rational-Emotive and Cognitive-Behavior Therapy*, 10(3), 86–111.

Smith, T. W. (1989). Assessment in rational-emotive therapy: Empirical access to the ABCD model. In M. E. Bernard & R. DiGiuseppe (Eds.), *Inside rational-emotive therapy: A critical appraisal of the theory and therapy of Albert Ellis* (pp. 135–152). New York: Academic Press.

Spiegel, R. (2004, June 2). Cognitive behavior therapy's controversial founder. *All Things Considered*. [Transcript]. Washington, D.C.: National Public Radio (NPR).

The top 10: The most influential therapists of the past quarter-century (2007, March/April). *Psychotherapy Networker*. Retrieved from http://www.psychotherapynetworker.org/index.php/magazine/populartopics/219-the-top-10

Wampold, B. E. (2001). *The great psychotherapy debate: Models, methods, and findings*. Mahwah, NJ: Erlbaum.

Watson, J. C. (1999). Rational emotive behavior therapy: Origins, constructs, and applications. (Report No. CG029710). (ERIC Document Reproduction Service No. ED436712) [Electronic version]. Retrieved from http://www.eric.ed.gov/ERIC Docs/data/ericdocs2/content_storage_01/0000000b/80/10/a0/16.pdf

Yankura, J., & Dryden, W. (1990). Doing RET: Albert Ellis in action. New York: Springer Publishing Company.

Chapter 10

Cognitive Therapy

Learning Goals

- To gain a biographical understanding of Aaron "Tim" Beck, the creator of cognitive therapy.
- To understand the historical context in which Beck developed cognitive therapy.
- To learn about the rational, pragmatic, educational, empirical, anti-deterministic, and—some say—constructivist view of human nature of cognitive therapy, and to understand the diathesis–stress model that suggests genetic predispositions, biological factors, and experiences combine to produce specific core beliefs.
- To learn a number of key concepts of cognitive therapy, including schemas; core beliefs; intermediate beliefs, including attitudes, rules and expectations, and assumptions; automatic thoughts, which result in behaviors, feelings, and physiological responses; cognitive distortions; coping (sometimes called compensatory) strategies; and cognitive conceptualization.
- To understand the cognitive conceptualization process, including the association between cognitive processes and mental disorders, the development of manuals to assist clinicians, the development of scales to measure treatment effects, and the conducting of clinical studies to measure effectiveness.
- To learn essential techniques of cognitive therapy, including building a strong therapeutic alliance (being collaborative; demonstrating empathy, caring, and optimism; adapting one's therapeutic style), Socratic questioning, educating the client about the cognitive model, identifying and challenging automatic thoughts and images, identifying and challenging cognitive distortions, identifying intermediate beliefs, identifying and challenging core beliefs, and doing homework assignments.
- To learn commonly used techniques of cognitive therapy, including thought-stopping, imagery-changing, rational–emotional role-play, and behavioral and emotive techniques.
- To learn about the four stages of the therapeutic process: (1) intake and evaluation, (2) the first session, (3) the second and subsequent sessions, and (4) termination.

- To understand cognitive therapy relative to cross-cultural counseling, especially in light of problems with diagnosing minorities and the "internal perspective" focus.
- To identify which disorders are likely to be particularly amenable to cognitive therapy.
- To see how cognitive therapy is applied through vignettes, DVDs, and case study.

> The thinking of the terrorist evidently shows the same kind of cognitive distortions observed in others who engage in violent acts, either solely as individuals or as members of a group. These include *overgeneralization*—that is, the supposed sins of the Enemy may spread to encompass the entire population. Also, they show *dichotomous thinking*—a people are either totally good or totally bad. Finally, they demonstrate *tunnel vision*—once they are engaged in their holy mission (e.g., jihad), their thinking, and consequently their actions, focuses exclusively on the destruction of the target. They behave like robots programmed for demolition with no attention to the value of the human lives that are destroyed. In fact, like the Japanese Kamikaze pilots of World War II, they are gratified by the heroic role that destiny has accorded them. Bin Laden, himself, stated in an interview that he would be happy to die as a martyr....
>
> We all have internal representations of ourselves and of other people. When we perceive ourselves or our group as threatened (often by a stigmatized minority), our internal representation of ourselves is usually of goodness and that of other people with whom we are in conflict with badness. Like the terrorists, we are disposed at these times to see ourselves as the victims victimized by the others, who are vulnerable and innocent. Over time our view of the other person or group progresses from *opponent* to *antagonist* to *Enemy*. We see the Enemy as dangerous, needing to be isolated, punished, or eliminated. We may seek revenge for the damage that we believe we have sustained or we may make a pre-emptive strike to forestall damage. The target of the violence is generally portrayed as the aggressor, as the victimizer. (Beck, A.T., 2002, pp. 211, 212)

This powerful piece by Aaron Beck speaks to how all of us have the ability to distort events and perceive the world in a dichotomous, "good and bad" fashion. As Beck asserts in his book *Prisoners of Hate* (Beck, A.T., 1999), such perceptions can lead to fights between people and wars between nations. Written prior

to 9/11, Beck knew that we *all* can develop distorted ways of viewing the world
and that only through our ability "to generate rational thought and benevolent
behavior" will we be able to develop "a more benevolent climate for the human
race" (p. 248). Although such rational thought can be nurtured at micro and
macro levels, this chapter will examine how cognitive therapy can be used to
help the individual understand and modify his or her cognitions in an effort to
live a more meaningful, satisfying, and peaceful existence.

AARON TEMKIN BECK

Courtesy of Aaron T. Beck

Aaron Beck

The third son of Jewish immigrants, Aaron Temkin Beck was
born in Providence, Rhode Island, on July 18, 1921 (Weishaar,
1993). His father, Harry, was in the printing business and known
as a socialist, and his mother, Lizzie, was a women's suffragist
who was described as having a strong and dominating
personality. Harry and Lizzie had four sons and one daughter,
with Aaron being their youngest (Krapp, 2005). However, their
first child, Bernard, died in infancy, and their second child,
Beatrice, died as a young child in the 1919 influenza epidemic. It
was said that Beck's mother never fully recovered from her
daughter's death and wished that Aaron had been a girl. At the
age of seven, Aaron broke his arm and eventually developed an
acutely serious bone infection that required surgery. Beck
remembers that although he was not fully unconscious from
the anesthesia, the surgeon started operating.

Beck's memories of his father and mother show parents with two very
different personality styles, with his father seeming "tranquil" and his mother
seeming emotional, erratic, and overprotective (Weishaar, 1993). He notes that
his emotion-filled relationship with his mother created a style of relating that
made him particularly sensitive to others with strong emotions. With his life-
threatening illness, and his mother's overprotectiveness and emotionality, it is
not surprising that Beck developed a number of self-defeating beliefs, phobias,
and anxieties early in life (Krapp, 2005). For instance, Beck remarks that his
absences from school due to his illness, along with memories of a very harsh
teacher yelling at him, were partially responsible for his creating an underlying
belief system that he was inept and incapable of achieving. Falling a year behind
in school, Beck tried to convince himself that he could do better in school, and
indeed was able to talk himself into overcoming his early negative beliefs about
his ineptness. In fact, he eventually ended up being one year ahead of his peers.
Beck's early beliefs and his ability to overcome them are seen as the origin for
his eventual theory that one's underlying **cognitive schema**, or floor plan,
leads to beliefs about oneself, and that one can challenge beliefs that lead to
self-destructive behaviors.

Fear of suffocation was another phobia Beck developed early in life. No doubt related to the fact that his brother Maurice would at times "playfully" try to suffocate him with a pillow until he could no longer breathe, this fear led to a tunnel phobia, where Beck felt as if his chest was being constricted. Similar to how he overcame his feelings of being academically inept, Beck again decided he would face his fear head-on by actively seeking out tunnels to drive through and "talking himself through" the anxiety-producing situation.

Beck's mother and father both valued education and pushed their children to achieve (Weishaar, 1993). Graduating first in his high school class, Beck ended up going to Brown University and graduated with honors in English and political science. Despite lacking the academic background to enter the medical field, he applied and was accepted to Yale medical school in 1942. However, while in medical school, another one of Beck's fears would rise up—a fear of blood. Being fearful of blood and going to medical school is clearly problematic, so again, Beck decided to face his fear. In fact, on reflection, Beck concludes that overcoming his fear was one of the reasons he entered medical school. And indeed, with sweat from anxiety dripping off his forehead while assisting during operations, Beck forced himself into situations in an effort to desensitize himself to them. Other fears that Beck overcame throughout his life include fears of public speaking, heights, and abandonment, which he also attacked head-on by doing such things as forcing himself to speak in front of large groups of people and climbing up the Leaning Tower of Pisa.

Although Beck initially decided to go into neurology, when doing his residence at Massachusetts General Hospital during World War II, there was such a need for psychiatric residents that he suddenly found himself immersed in the field of psychiatry. At the time, psychiatry was dominated by psychoanalysts, and when Beck suggested to his supervisors that he thought psychoanalysis was limited, he was told that it was his defenses talking. Thinking there might be some truth to this, he decided to embrace this approach he had formerly thought to be odd. Becoming increasingly involved in psychoanalysis, and even being supervised by the famous developmental psychologist and analyst Erik Erickson, Beck began to slowly embrace the psychoanalytic approach. Meanwhile, Beck had met Phyllis Whitman, and as the 1950s were ushered in, the two were married.

After finishing his residency at the hospital, Beck worked at the Valley Forge Army hospital just outside of Philadelphia. Here, he counseled soldiers who were dealing with post-traumatic stress disorder from the Korean War. Although he dabbled in the use of other techniques, Beck continued to be mostly analytically oriented. In 1959, he joined the faculty at the University of Pennsylvania and soon started to research the effectiveness of the psychoanalytic approach (Krapp, 2005; Weishaar, 1993). However, discouraged with some of his findings, and as he increasingly saw clients, Beck began to slowly question the efficacy and usefulness of psychoanalysis. This skepticism increased after he found that many of his clients had streams of private thoughts that commented on their experience. Others, not aware of their private thoughts, quickly became conscious of them once Beck began to probe with them the possibility that such thoughts were present. Calling them **"automatic thoughts,"** Beck realized that they "provided running commentary on the person's experience" (Weishaar, 1993, p. 20). Beck concluded that these thoughts were a function of an internal conversation with the self, and not associated with interpersonal dialogue. Thus, he came to believe that such thoughts, which seemed to affect how a person would think and ultimately act and feel, would likely not be expressed in response to most analytic techniques, such as free association or dream analysis (Beck, A.T., 1991).

Beck's transition to cognitive therapy happened somewhat slowly. First, as he began to give up some of the more traditional tenets of classical psychoanalysis, he attached himself to some of the more radical analysts of the time, like Alfred Adler and Karen Horney (Padesky & Beck, 2003; Weishaar, 1993). However, as the years passed, his interest in cognitive work grew, and in the 1960s, he began to write about his new cognitive approach to psychotherapy. Finding analysts dismissing his ideas, he had little professional support but great encouragement from his family, especially his brothers and wife. In 1961, Beck published the Beck Depression Inventory and started increasingly to write about the connection between depression and thinking. In 1963, Albert Ellis read some of Beck's publications, and realizing that the two of them were independently developing similar theories, began to correspond with Beck (Padesky & Beck, 2003). Although Beck and Ellis rarely wrote or researched together, they did share ideas and met professionally at times. In fact, at one point, Beck consulted Ellis for continued anxiety he had around public speaking.

Perhaps because Beck struggled with some mild depression of his own, he continued to study depression and how cognitive therapy could help with it. Obtaining grants to research his new approach, he soon was involved with a relatively large study that compared cognitive therapy with the use of anti-depressants in treating moderately depressed clients. Out of this research came the book *Cognitive Therapy of Depression* (Beck, Rush, Shaw, & Emery, 1979), which was one of the first books to draw attention to cognitive therapy and advocated for a relatively short-term approach to counseling. Beck's writings and research were soon to usher in what some called the "cognitive revolution in psychology" of the 1970s (Weishaar, 1993, p. 27).

As Beck's theory evolved, he realized that different disorders presented with specific **cognitive distortions**, or beliefs about the world that fueled the disorder. Thus, he hypothesized that individuals who had certain kinds of cognitive biases, vulnerabilities, or distortions were more likely to develop certain disorders (Hersen & Sledge, 2002). To show this was the case, Beck first conceptualized the cognitive processes involved in a number of disorders to identify the kinds of cognitive distortions these individuals likely had. Then, he developed manuals to assist in the training of clinicians to treat individuals with each of these disorders. To assess clinical effectiveness, Beck next developed a number of scales, including those that measure depression, hopelessness, anxiety, self-concept, sociotropy–autonomy, and suicide. Finally, to show the efficacy of clinicians' work, he conducted clinical trials to establish whether clients were improving. Some of the many disorders which Beck has researched using this approach include depression, suicide, anxiety and panic disorders, substance abuse, personality disorders, and schizophrenia (A. Beck, personal communication, October 17, 2009). Currently, he continues to research and be involved with numerous activities related to the advancement of cognitive therapy.

Called "Tim" by his family and friends, Beck is still active in research and writing. The honorary president of the **Academy of Cognitive Therapy**, Beck has published more than 500 articles and written 17 books (Beck Institute, 2008a). An unassuming man, over the years, Beck's research and writing have brought him praise and dozens of awards. A few of his more recent tributes have included the attainment of the prestigious **Lasker Award for Clinical Medical Research** in 2006 and the 2008 **American Psychiatric Association Distinguished Service Award**. Listed as the second most influential psychotherapist in recent times (just behind Carl Rogers), Aaron Beck has established his place in the annals of therapeutic history (The top 10, 2007).

Married for 58 years, Beck has four children and eight grandchildren. Beck's wife Phyllis, appointed the first female judge to the Superior Court of Pennsylvania, is often referred to by Beck as a person off whom he could bounce ideas while developing his theory (Krapp, 2005). His daughter, Judith Beck, received her doctorate in psychology from the University of Pennsylvania and has followed in his footsteps. Now directing education, clinical care, and research activities at the **Beck Institute**, she has written numerous books on cognitive therapy including the well-received *Cognitive Therapy: The Basics and Beyond* (Beck, J., 1995; Beck Institute, 2008b). She also has particular expertise in the use of cognitive therapy for weight loss and weight management (Beck, J., 2007; The Beck Diet Solution, 2007).

Finally, a number of variations of cognitive therapy that are often subsumed under the umbrella title "cognitive–behavioral therapy" have been developed over the years by other giants in the field, such as Arnold Lazarus, Michael Mahoney, and Donald Meichenbaum. At times in this chapter, we will refer to cognitive therapy's close cousin, cognitive–behavioral therapy, as their theoretical tenets are fairly similar.

VIEW OF HUMAN NATURE

Beck's writings suggest there is a **genetic and evolutionary predisposition** toward certain types of emotional responses. Although adaptive in the distant past, in today's world, their expression can sometimes be maladaptive (e.g., anxiety and anger) (Beck, A., 1967, 1976, 1999, 2005). Called the **continuity hypothesis**, the older, emotional responses are seen as "continuing" into the modern world (Weishaar, 1993), and when individuals in today's world exhibit large amounts of these emotional responses, they are often viewed as having a mental disorder. Beck also suggests that individuals who have a tendency toward exhibiting maladaptive emotional responses will not express them if they are taught effective skills by parents and others. And, taking a **rational**, **pragmatic**, and some say "**constructivist**" perspective, Beck assumes that even those who do exhibit maladaptive responses can change through therapeutic discourse with others, particularly if an individual learns how to modify his or her cognitive processes (Beck, J., 2005; Leahy, 2003). Thus, cognitive therapy is seen as an **anti-deterministic**, **active**, **educative**, and **empirical** approach to counseling that suggests that in a relatively short amount of time, people can manage and effect changes in their way of living in the world if given the tools to understand their cognitive processes and how they affect feelings and behaviors.

Beck posits a **diathesis–stress model** of mental disorders, which means that there is a genetic predisposition (diathesis) toward certain disorders that reveals itself under stressful conditions. Thus, Beck and other cognitive therapists believe that a combination of genetics, biological factors, and experiences combine to produce specific **cognitive schemas** and **core beliefs**, some of which may lie dormant and then suddenly appear as the result of stress and other conditions impinging on the person. Schemas and core beliefs are embedded, underlying beliefs that provide direction toward the manner in which one lives in the world (Beck, A., 1967, 1991), with negative core beliefs leading to negative feelings and dysfunctional behaviors, and positive core beliefs leading to healthy ways of living.

Beck suggests that most individuals are not aware of their core beliefs. Instead, such beliefs become the underlying mechanism for the creation of **intermediate beliefs**, which set the **attitudes, rules and expectations, and assumptions** we live by. These attitudes, rules and expectations, and assumptions can be understood by looking at how situations lead to what are called **automatic thoughts**, which result in a set of behaviors, feelings, and physiological responses that end up reinforcing core beliefs. And thus the cycle is continued. Over the years, Beck and others have spent time showing how certain mental disorders are related to specific core beliefs, intermediate beliefs, and automatic thoughts. Thus, if a counselor can accurately diagnose a client, that counselor can begin to make an educated guess as to some of the cognitive distortions, automatic thoughts, and core beliefs the client might have.

Although core beliefs are critical to the development of one's thinking processes, and ultimately to how one lives in the world, cognitive therapists believe that it is usually important to initially focus on automatic thoughts, not core beliefs. This is because core beliefs are seen as more embedded and less assessable than clients' automatic thoughts, consequently making automatic thoughts more easily "caught" and a more natural starting point (e.g., a core belief of "I am inadequate" is much more difficult for a client to initially grasp than an automatic thought of "I never will get this report done right"). By assessing and diagnosing the client, and by examining the client's automatic thoughts, the therapist can begin to hypothesize about the intermediate beliefs that produce the automatic thoughts and ultimately begin to understand the core beliefs that fuel the intermediate beliefs (see Figure 10.1).

Focusing minimally on the past, cognitive therapy initially shows clients how their current thinking affects their attitudes, feelings, and behaviors, and then has them learn how to change their cognitions so that they can live a more fully functioning and meaningful life. Although cognitive therapists do not

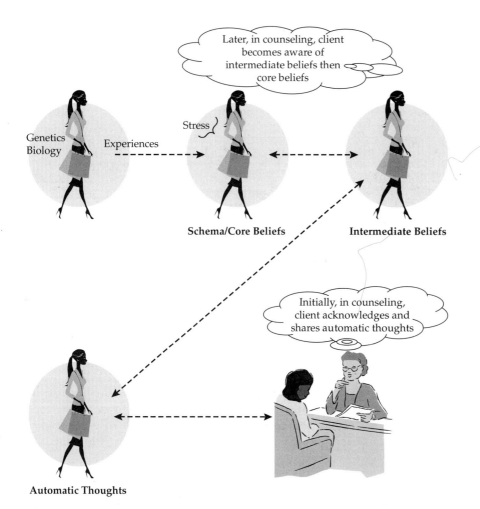

F I G U R E 10.1 The Development of Core Beliefs, Intermediate Beliefs, and Automatic Thoughts

From top-left to bottom-right: The diathesis–stress model suggests that biology and genetics, in conjunction with experiences, lead to certain core beliefs which can be activated under stress. Core beliefs lead to intermediate beliefs and eventually to automatic thoughts.

From bottom-right to top-left: The therapist first helps the client examine automatic thoughts, because those are most accessible. Later, intermediate thoughts and core beliefs are uncovered. Guesses can eventually be made about how certain stresses may have activated specific genetic predispositions.

spend a great amount of time examining the past, J. Beck (1995) suggests that there are three times when examining the past might be helpful: (1) when the client has a very strong desire to do so, (2) when the current focus produces little change, and (3) when examining the past can help in understanding current dysfunctional thinking.

Despite the fact that cognitive therapists view the development of cognitive processes as a critical piece to the shaping of certain behaviors and the emergence of specific emotions, cognitive therapists believe that it is important to address all aspects of the individual if change is to occur relatively quickly. Thus, many who practice Beck's approach, or other similar cognitive approaches, will use the more inclusive term cognitive–behavioral therapy (CBT).

KEY CONCEPTS

The Cognitive Model

As the name implies, cognitive therapy proposes that it is our cognitions, which includes our thoughts, beliefs, and the manner in which we perceive a situation, that are the basis for what we believe, how we act, and how we feel. Although cognitive therapists recognize the roles that genetics, biological factors, and experiences (e.g., the interactions with our parents) play in the formation of our cognitions, when working with clients, they focus on the *structure* of cognitions rather than the ways in which they were formed. In addition, cognitive therapists believe that stress can cause certain beliefs previously lying dormant to emerge at different times in a person's life (see Figure 10.1). The cognitive model describes three levels of cognitions: core beliefs, or the fundamental beliefs that underlie how we think, feel, and behave; intermediate beliefs, which consist of attitudes, rules and expectations, and assumptions that are outgrowths of our core beliefs; and automatic thoughts, which result in our behaviors, feelings, and physiological responses, and are the outgrowth of the attitudes, rules and expectations, and assumptions. Let's take a look at each of these.

Cognitive Schemas and Core Beliefs.   Aaron Beck originally defined a cognitive schema as a "structure for screening, coding, and evaluating the stimuli that impinge on the organism" (1967, p. 283). As such, schemas appear to affect how the individual responds to events in the world. Whereas some individuals will have schemas through which they interpret events in a positive manner, others will have schemas that will cause them to interpret the same events in a negative way. Unfortunately, negative schemas can result in lives that are debilitating, depressing, anger-evoking, anxiety-producing, and dysfunctional. Schemas can be seen as a master plan of the mind, a plan that turns certain core beliefs on or off. Core beliefs develop as we grow and lend direction to how we ultimately think, act, and feel. All of us have some positive core beliefs that lead toward positive ways of living (e.g., "I am an okay person," "I can control my life to a certain degree," "I can achieve"), and many of us have some negative core beliefs that lead to dysfunctional ways of living (e.g., "I am not okay," "I am not capable," "I am not likeable"). Those who are particularly distressed are largely governed by their negative core beliefs, and many of us, when stressed, can be dominated by these beliefs for short periods of time. Aaron and Judith Beck (Beck, J., 2005) propose that core beliefs are of three broad categories: helplessness, unlovability, and worthlessness (see Table 10.1).

T A B L E 10.1   Negative Core Beliefs

Helpless Core Beliefs

"I am inadequate, ineffective, incompetent; I can't cope."
"I am powerless, out of control; I can't change; I'm stuck, trapped, a victim."
"I am vulnerable, weak, needy, likely to be hurt."
"I am inferior, a failure, a loser, not good enough; I don't measure up to others."

Unlovable Core Beliefs

"I am unlikable, undesirable, ugly, boring; I have nothing to offer."
"I am unloved, unwanted, neglected."
"I will always be rejected, abandoned; I will always be alone."
"I am different, defective, not good enough to be loved."

Worthless Core Beliefs

"I am worthless, unacceptable, bad, crazy, broken, nothing, a waste."
"I am hurtful, dangerous, toxic, evil."
"I don't deserve to live."

SOURCE: Beck, J. (2005). *Cognitive therapy for challenging problems.* New York: Guilford Press. p. 22.

Let me offer one final note about schemas and core beliefs. If you're having trouble distinguishing the two, you're not alone. In fact, in the afterword of Riso, du Toit, Stein, and Young's (2007) book *Cognitive Schemas and Core Beliefs in Psychological Problems*, it is noted that "Theoretical development is inadequate at this time to make a sharp distinction between the schema construct and the notion of core beliefs" (pp. 221–223). And even Judith Beck (1995) hedges on the difference between the two when she says:

Core beliefs … are one's most central ideas about self. Some authors refer to these beliefs as schemas …" Aaron Beck (1964) differentiates the two by suggesting that schemas are cognitive structures within the mind, the specific content of which are core beliefs.

Given this ambiguity, for the purpose of this text, we are going to use the term "core beliefs" in lieu of the term "schemas." However, don't be surprised if you find *schemas* being used in addition to, or in place of, the term *core beliefs* in other readings that you might come across.

Intermediate Beliefs.   Our core beliefs affect the kinds of attitudes, rules and expectations, and assumptions we have in life, which Beck calls our intermediate beliefs. Thus, if one of my major positive core beliefs is that I am capable of working out my problems, when I face challenges, my attitude will be something like, "I'm okay, because I will make sure things will work out in the end." My rule and expectation might be, "Working hard resolves problems," and the assumption I live by is, "I assume things will work out if I work hard." On the other hand, consider the person who has the following negative core belief: "I am powerless to change my life." This person's attitude is something like, "Life sucks and there's little I can do about it." His or her rule and expectation is something like, "I expect that even if I try hard to change things, it will not work out, so why bother?" and the assumption is, "There is little I can do to make my lot in life better."

T A B L E 10.2 **Cognitive Distortions**

1. ***All-or-nothing thinking:*** Sometimes called *dualistic, black-and-white,* or *dichotomous* thinking, this occurs when individuals see the world in two categories, rather than in a more complex fashion.

   Example: "I am never good at my job." Or, "You are always happy."

2. ***Catastrophisizing:*** Making assumptions that something will go wrong rather than looking at situations more realistically or scientifically.

   Example: "I shouldn't have said that to my boss, I know I'll get fired." Or, "If I fly, the plane will crash."

3. ***Disqualifying or discounting the positive***: Even when a positive event occurs, assuming it means little in the total scheme of things.

   Example: "That award I won at work is meaningless, everybody wins awards."

4. ***Emotional reasoning***: Assuming that your feelings are always correct, even when there is evidence to the contrary.

   Example: "My wife and kids may tell me they love me, but I know I'm unlovable because I feel like no one can love me."

5. ***Labeling***: Defining oneself in terms of a "label" or "type" instead of seeing oneself in more complex and nuanced ways.

   Example: "I'm just a negative person." Or, "I'm always introverted."

6. ***Magnification/minimization***: Magnifying the negative or minimizing the positive about oneself, another, or a situation.

   Example: "I might have done well on that one test, but I know I'm not good in that subject." Or, "That incident at work proves that I am no good at what I do."

7. ***Mental filter:*** Focusing on one negative aspect of oneself, another, or a situation.

   Example: "I know why people stay away from me: They always see my disability."

8. ***Mind-reading:*** Making assumptions about what other people are thinking without considering other possibilities.

   Example: "She thinks I'm ugly."

9. ***Overgeneralization:*** Making large generalizations from a small event.

   Example: "That dinner for my kids was horrible; I'll never be a good parent."

10. ***Personalization***: Believing you are the cause for other person's negative behavior without taking into account other possible explanations.

    Example: "My colleague, James, was in a bad mood today because I didn't get that project to him in time."

11. ***"Should" and "must" statements***: Believing that oneself and others should act in a specific manner, and when they don't you believe it is horrible.

    Example: "My grandmother was outrageous today; she never should have acted so boldly in front of the company."

12. ***Tunnel vision:*** Only seeing the downside or negative aspect of a situation.

    Example: "Her expressing her opinion is uncalled-for. We'll never get friends that way."

Adapted from: Beck, J. (1995). *Cognitive therapy: Basics and beyond.* New York: Guilford Press.

Automatic Thoughts and Images. Automatic thoughts are the ongoing thoughts we have that cross our minds as we go through the day. When situations arise, individuals respond with automatic thoughts that are a consequence of their core beliefs and the attitudes, rules and expectations, and assumptions (intermediate beliefs) that are developed from their core beliefs. For instance, in the example just given, if the individual has a core belief that he or she is powerless to change his or her life, and that individual is suddenly faced with the breakup of a relationship, the situation (the breakup) will result in automatic thoughts based on the individual's intermediate beliefs. Thus, this person might "automatically" say to himself or herself: "Bad things always happen to me," "Life sucks," "Nothing ever works out," and "Even if I were to try, I'll find no one else." Automatic thoughts are generally related to one or more cognitive distortions (see Table 10.2) and are similar to the irrational beliefs and cognitive distortions identified by Ellis (see Chapter 8).

Similar to automatic thoughts are the ongoing images we have that cross our minds throughout our day. For instance, a person who has difficulty finishing a project for work might be saying to himself or herself, "I simply can't do this," or could have an image of his or her boss coming in with a disappointed look. Automatic thoughts and images result in behaviors, feelings, and physiological responses that reinforce core beliefs. Thus, a vicious cycle is developed. J. Beck (1995) has diagrammed the relationship between core beliefs, intermediate beliefs, automatic thoughts, and how they affect and are affected by situations in a person's life (see Figure 10.2). The arrows back to the core beliefs were added by me to show how such beliefs are often reinforced.

As an example, imagine the individual who has the core belief "I am powerless." This person has developed a series of attitudes, rules and expectations, and assumptions based on this core belief. And, when a situation occurs, automatic

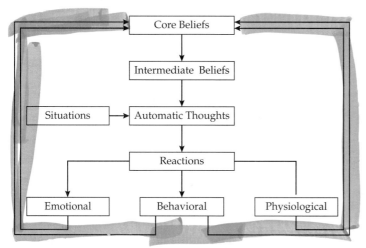

FIGURE 10.2 Relationships among Core Beliefs, Intermediate Beliefs, and Automatic Thoughts

Adapted from: Beck, J. (1995). *Cognitive therapy: Basics and beyond.* New York: Guilford Press. p. 18.

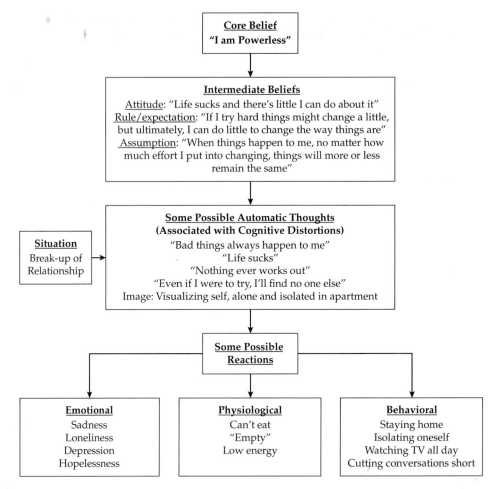

FIGURE 10.3 Example of the Relationships among Core Beliefs, Intermediate Beliefs, and Automatic Thoughts

thoughts or images related to one more cognitive distortions and based on the intermediate and core beliefs kick in (see Figure 10.3). After looking at Figure 10.3 and referring back to Table 10.2, what cognitive distortions do you think are at play?

Coping or Compensatory Strategies. Individuals who have negative core beliefs want to protect themselves from the pain such beliefs will inherently cause them (Beck, J., 2005). Thus, they develop **coping strategies** (also known as **compensatory strategies**) to steer them away from their negative core beliefs. For instance, if a person has a core belief that he or she is inadequate, that individual might develop the strategy of overachieving in an effort to not feel the emotions that result from having that core belief. Or, an individual who feels powerless might compensate by trying to become all-controlling. Such strategies are remarkably

similar to Alfred Adler's compensatory behaviors that are adapted by individuals in an effort to avoid feelings of inferiority. Perhaps it's not by chance that Aaron Beck developed these ideas after having been enamored, earlier in his life, by the Adlerian approach to counseling (Weishaar, 1993).

Generally, coping strategies develop early in life, and allow individuals to avoid dealing with the strong negative feelings that would result from their negative core beliefs. However, these behaviors do not rid the person of their negative core beliefs, and often, over time, these behaviors become increasingly maladaptive for individuals. For instance, consider two individuals. The first one is constantly striving to achieve in order not to feel inadequate, and the second is always trying to control others because he or she feels powerless. Over time, the first person might become more stressed as he or she compulsively tries to achieve, while the second person would likely have difficulty in relationships because he or she is constantly trying to control others (controlling behaviors do not work well in relationships).

Figure 10.4 shows the relationships among core beliefs, intermediate beliefs, coping strategies, automatic thoughts, and resulting feelings for a client described by Judith Beck (2005). In addition to the feelings the client would experience, you can imagine the kinds of behaviors that will result from this person's core beliefs and coping strategies (see Box 10.1).

Cognitive Conceptualization

> The cognitive specificity hypothesis proposes a distinct cognitive profile for each psychiatric disorder. (Beck, J., 2005, p. 954)

Over the years, Beck and others have suggested there are distinct cognitive processes for varying psychological disorders. Therefore, if the counselor can accurately assess a client's disorder, then specific automatic thoughts, intermediate thoughts, and core beliefs can be inferred. In addition, treatment plans can be matched to the specific disorder and to the cognitive processes that parallel the disorder, increasing the likelihood of success in counseling. Thus, from the moment the therapist meets the client, a process begins in which the therapist elicits information from the client so that he or she can hypothesize about the kinds of automatic thoughts, intermediate thoughts, and core beliefs that have been developed and continue to fuel the client's presenting problems. A number of activities can help in this process, including:

- Gathering important childhood data (understanding a person's history can help identify beliefs that have been developed).

- Accurately identifying client problems (certain problems lend themselves toward certain kinds of beliefs).

- Determining the client's diagnosis (diagnoses tend to correlate with specific beliefs).

- Having the client identify automatic thoughts (specific automatic thoughts are associated with underlying beliefs).

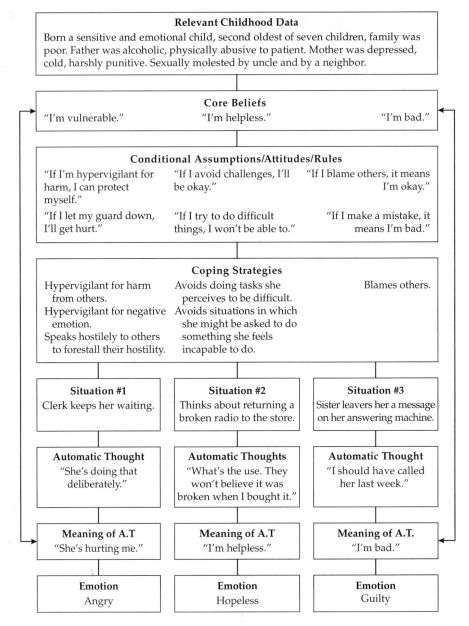

F I G U R E   10.4   Relationships among Beliefs, Coping Strategies, Automatic Thoughts, Behaviors, and Feelings

SOURCE: Beck, J. (2005). *Cognitive therapy for challenging problems.* New York: Guilford Press. p. 20. Reprinted by permission.

- Identifying resulting emotions, physiological responses, and behaviors related to the automatic thoughts (responses tend to cluster as a function of specific beliefs).

- Identifying past and current stressors that might have led to the development of specific beliefs (see Box 10.2).

B o x 10.1   Deciphering Your Core Beliefs

Use Figure 10.4 as a template. Then, consider your major childhood events and reflect on your emotions and automatic thoughts to determine what core beliefs might be driving your feelings and behaviors.

B o x 10.2   Dr. McAuliffe's Work with Karen

Read or watch Dr. McAuliffe's work with "Karen." Try to identify some of the automatic thoughts and core beliefs with which Karen is struggling. How do you think her automatic thoughts and her core beliefs affect her relationships?

You can read this session by going to www.cengage.com/counseling/neukrug/CTP1e and click "student downloads." Or your instructor may show this session in class with the DVD that accompanies his or her copy of the text.

THERAPEUTIC TECHNIQUES

This section is divided into "essential techniques," or those techniques that are almost always used by cognitive therapists, and "commonly used techniques," which are techniques used by cognitive therapists a good portion of the time. However, dozens of other techniques have been identified. Leahy (2003), for instance, describes 88 techniques in his book, *Cognitive Therapy Techniques*. In point of fact, any technique from different theoretical perspectives that may seem successful in assisting the client in changing his or her beliefs and in living a more comfortable life is fair game for the cognitive therapist. Clearly, to list them all would be impossible.

Essential Techniques

These techniques, used by most cognitive therapists almost all the time, include **building a strong therapeutic alliance, Socratic questioning, educating the client about the cognitive model, identifying and challenging automatic thoughts and images, identifying and challenging cognitive distortions, identifying intermediate beliefs, identifying and challenging core beliefs,** and **doing homework assignments.**

Building a Strong Therapeutic Alliance.   Cognitive therapists see a strong therapeutic relationship as critical to an effective outcome in counseling (Beck, J., 2005). A number of ways are suggested to accomplish this, including being collaborative; demonstrating empathy, caring and optimism; and adapting one's therapeutic style.

   Being Collaborative: Collaboration, or viewing the counselor–client alliance as a team and assuming "the role of guide with a certain expertise" (Beck, J., 2005, p. 65), is one of the key skills of the cognitive therapist. In addition, the cognitive therapist is open to eliciting feedback from the client. In fact, it is usual for cognitive therapists to ask their clients at the end of each session such things as, "How has this session been for you?" or, "Does what we did today make sense to you?" or, "Are the goals we set in sync with where you think we should be going?"

Demonstrating empathy, caring, and optimism: These basic counseling skills are important for most forms of therapy. For the cognitive therapist, who can easily slip into a role of objective scientist, it is particularly important to remember not to view therapy as "clinical process" but as a joint therapeutic venture in which two people are sitting together in an effort to help one of them feel better. Clients who work with detached, objective scientists would be more likely to give up than clients who work with therapists who show deep understanding and caring, and who are hopeful about the future.

Adapting one's therapeutic style: Cognizant of the fact that clients respond differently to varying personality styles, J. Beck suggests that therapists adjust their style based on how the client presents to the therapist. For instance, it is probably better to approach a client who is mistrusting with calm, good listening skills, and a little bit of humility, while an overly dependent client "usually appreciates a therapist who takes charge in the session and is fairly directive ..." (Beck, J., 2005, p. 67). Although this might initially feed into the client's dependency style, it will help build the relationship and, in the long run, as the client improves, help the client become more independent.

Socratic Questioning.   Socratic questioning involves the use of questions to challenge clients to think rationally about their situation in order to illuminate alternative ways of understanding predicaments. Conducted with a helpful spirit, such questioning is mostly used after the relationship has been established in an effort to challenge the client's use of dysfunctional automatic thoughts, rigid rules and assumptions, and negative core beliefs. For example, if a client has an automatic thought such as, "I am not as smart as my co-workers," which leads to feelings and behaviors that are self-destructive (feeling unmotivated, not working hard), which then results in poor supervisor evaluations, the therapist might ask such questions as:

- "Are you really not as smart as your co-workers?"
- "What evidence do you have that you're not as smart as your co-workers?"
- "My experience has been that people have different strengths. What are your strengths at work?"
- "How might this belief stop you from being smarter?"
- "What do you think your life would look like if you didn't have these thoughts?"

Educating the Client about the Cognitive Model.   Early in counseling therapists should educate their clients about the cognitive model. Starting with the basics, therapists explain automatic thoughts and help clients identify some of the thoughts they might be having. As clients begin to understand their automatic thoughts, therapists can then show clients how those thoughts are related to their intermediate beliefs. Finally, therapists can demonstrate connections between intermediate beliefs and core beliefs. Often, graphics such as those in Figures 10.1 through 10.4 can be used to help facilitate this process. As clients learn to apply this cognitive model to themselves, they gain a deep understanding of the relationship among thoughts, feelings, behaviors, intermediate beliefs, and the more entrenched core beliefs.

Identifying and Challenging Automatic Thoughts and Images. Since cognitive therapists "work backwards" toward helping clients see how their core beliefs affect the very basis of who they are, the first step after building the relationship and educating the client is to help clients identify their automatic thoughts and images. These thoughts and images are the most readily understood aspect of the cognitive model because clients can easily "catch" them, and because clients can quickly see the direct connection between their thoughts and their negative feelings and dysfunctional behaviors. For example, the client who has just broken up with his or her lover comes in feeling depressed. After gathering basic information about the client, the counselor might ask the client such questions as:

- "Are you aware of anything that you are saying to yourself that may be causing you to feel this badly?"
- "Can you imagine what kinds of self-statements, thoughts, or images you are having that could cause you to feel this way?"
- "Have you noticed any thoughts or images you have that kind of drift through your mind while you have been feeling this way?"

Even clients who have not been aware of their automatic thoughts and images can generally become conscious of them. Ultimately, counselors teach clients a variety of techniques to challenge their automatic thoughts and images, such as thought-stopping and imaging work (discussed later).

Identifying and Challenging Cognitive Distortions. Since automatic thoughts are often based on one or more cognitive distortions identified in Table 10.2, after identifying automatic thoughts, therapists will often suggest which cognitive distortions are likely to be associated with the client's thoughts. Sometimes, they may do this by simply handing the client the list of distortions and reviewing it with them. After one or more distortions have been identified, the therapist and client will often engage in a discussion about the irrationality of such distortions and how changing one's automatic thoughts can help to moderate or even eliminate the cognitive distortions and their debilitating results.

Identifying Intermediate Beliefs.   Once clients are able to identify and challenge their automatic thoughts and associated cognitive distortions, they can move to the next level of beliefs by examining the attitudes, rules and expectations, and assumptions that drive their thoughts and associated distortions. Often, a worksheet, such as that used in Figure 10.3, can be helpful for the client, as the therapist tests out hypotheses with the client about the kinds of attitudes, rules and expectations, and assumptions that tend to run his or her life. Identifying such beliefs moves the client toward the next phase of therapy, which is identifying and challenging core beliefs.

Identifying and Challenging Core Beliefs.   Usually, seamless movement occurs from the client's awareness of his or her attitudes, rules and expectations, and assumptions (intermediate beliefs), to an understanding of the core beliefs that set them up. Thus, as soon as intermediate beliefs are acknowledged, the therapist shows the logical connection between those beliefs and the client's core beliefs. The next challenge is to confront the core beliefs. One method of doing this is by completing a **core belief worksheet** in which the client identifies a negative core belief that has consumed his or her life, highlights a new positive core belief that the client can strive toward, and shows evidence that contradicts or reframes the client's old core belief and moves the client toward a new positive core belief. For instance, look in Table 10.3 to see how Juan contradicts his old core belief, "I am ineffective."

Homework.   An active, ongoing process, homework is critical to the cognitive therapy process, as it helps the client practice what he or she has learned in the office and facilitates client movement toward managing his or her own problems. Homework can take many forms and should focus on the issue being addressed in therapy at the time. For instance, the major focus of homework assignments might progress from catching automatic thoughts and images, to challenging automatic thoughts and images, to challenging intermediate beliefs, and, finally, to challenging core beliefs. There are hundreds of different kinds of homework assignments that can be given, and all of the "commonly used techniques" highlighted in the next section are often given as homework assignments.

Commonly Used Techniques

The following represent some of the techniques commonly used by many cognitive therapists much of the time. They include **thought-stopping,** **imagery-changing, rational–emotional role-play,** and **behavioral and emotive techniques.**

Thought-Stopping.   A major strategy of cognitive therapy is for the client to realize that automatic thoughts are related to negative feelings and dysfunctional

T A B L E 10.3   Core Belief Worksheet

Old core belief: "I am ineffective."

"How much do you believe the old core belief right now?"	(0–100): *25%*
"What's the most you've believed it this week?"	(0–100): *55%*
"What's the most you did *not* believe it this week?"	(0–100): *90%*

New belief: "I am pretty good at most things I do and I usually try hard."

"How much do you believe the new belief right now?"	(0–100): *75%*

Evidence Contradicting Old Belief/ Supporting New Belief	Reframing Old Belief
Went to daughter's child–parent conference Helped kids with homework Spent time making children their lunches Researched an important paper for work Boss praised me three times Kids gave me lots of hugs this week Wife told me I'm a great father Worked hard to fix things around the house Took kids and wife bowling	Had trouble understanding new project at work. But, asked for help from co-workers and believe I am capable of understanding it and doing a good job. Only put the kids to bed once this week. But had a hard week at work, and wife and kids didn't seem to mind. I can do more next week, and I have other signs that I am a good dad. Couldn't fix the broken back door. But, I realize I'm not perfect at everything, and I did a lot of other things around the house this week.

Adapted from: Beck, J. (1995). *Cognitive therapy: Basics and beyond.* New York: Guilford Publications. p. 177.

behaviors. Thus, it is often suggested that clients find ways to prevent their negative thoughts. One method of doing this is through thought-stopping, which can be accomplished in a variety of ways, such as:

- replacing a negative thought with a newly identified positive one
- yelling to oneself, or out loud, "Stop it!" when a negative thought is identified
- placing a rubber band on one's wrist and snapping it whenever one has a negative thought
- actively diverting one's thoughts to more pleasant thoughts
- participating in a relaxation exercise in order to "move" one's thoughts to a different place

Imagery-Changing.   As noted earlier, like thoughts, mental images are a product of one's core beliefs and can produce distressing feelings and dysfunctional behaviors. To address disturbing mental images, a number of techniques have been developed. Using the following scenario, eight imagery-changing techniques are described (Beck, J., 1995).

Vanessa has a bridge phobia and becomes extremely anxious when driving over a bridge. Even when her husband is driving, she begins to get panicky as they get close to a bridge. As they drive over, she begins to have images of her husband losing control of the car, and imagines the car veering off the side of the bridge and plunging into the water. She sees them struggling to get out of the car as it fills with water. Her heart beats frantically as they drive over the bridge, the images deeply embedded in her mind.

Following Images to Completion.   In this technique, the client tells the story about the image to its completion. Generally, one of two things happen: either the client resolves the story (e.g., Vanessa sees them crashing off the bridge, looks at the therapist, and says, "This is really silly—this will never happen," and begins to challenge the image), or the image is taken to its catastrophic end, which provides important new material the client can work on (e.g., Vanessa sees herself and her husband dying in the crash and worries about what will happen to the children— the underlying concern in the image is worry about ensuring her children's safety).

Jumping Ahead in Time.   In this case, the client jumps ahead in time in an effort to "jump over" the distressing image. For instance, while driving over the bridge, Vanessa learns how to image herself safely at the end of the bridge.

Coping in the Image.   Here we have Vanessa change her image so that she is coping in the image. For instance, as she and her husband near the bridge, she can imagine herself saying to him, "Can I drive? I love going over this bridge." Then, she can imagine herself driving over.

Changing the Image.   In this case, the image is changed to one which does not result in distress. This can be done realistically or as a "magical" image. As an example of a magical image, Vanessa might see herself in a fancy convertible going over a golden bridge that has safety nets on the side to catch cars that could fall over. Her hair flows in the wind as she enjoys the ride over the bridge.

Reality-Testing the Image.   Here the therapist uses Socratic questioning to bring the client "back to reality." For instance, the therapist might ask Vanessa, "What is the likelihood of this happening?" "Do you think your anxiety is in line with the probability that this will occur?"

Repeating the Image.   By describing a distressing image multiple times, the image will often change on its own, sometimes becoming more subdued. For instance, when Vanessa is asked to continually describe the image of the car driving over the bridge, she slowly changes it in her mind's eye to one in which she is still anxious, but is able to successfully make it over the bridge.

Image-Stopping.   Similar to thought-stopping, this technique has the client use mechanisms to stop the image in its tracks. For instance, Vanessa might yell out "Stop it!" as she begins to imagine the car veering off the road, or she might snap a rubber band she has placed around her wrist—the snapping being a signal to herself to stop imagining the car veering off the bridge.

Image-Distracting.   Here the client does something that is incompatible with the anxiety-producing image. So, Vanessa might play Sudoku as she rides in the car. One cannot play Sudoku and be anxious at the same time. Or, she might have a planned phone call to her supervisor to discuss a work situation at the time she knows she will be going over the bridge.

Rational–Emotional Role-Play.   Even though clients sometimes come to the realization that their beliefs are dysfunctional, they are not always able to counteract them, because they continue to feel emotionally attached to them. Rational–emotional role-play allows clients to have a debate between the rational and emotional parts of themselves. Often, the therapist will first debate the client by role-playing the rational part while the client responds with the emotional, dysfunctional part. Then, in order to allow the client to counteract his or her own dysfunctional part, the therapist will switch roles with the client. The following role-play shows the first part of this process, with the therapist playing the rational part and the client playing the emotional, dysfunctional part. As you read it, consider what a client might take from such a role-play.

COUNSELOR: How about we role-play the emotionally dysfunctional and the rational parts of your dilemma around feeling incompetent at parenting because sometimes you lose your cool and yell at your children? I'll be the rational part, and you start by being the emotional, dysfunctional part. As that person, tell me how you feel about your parenting.

CLIENT: I'm a horrible mother. I'm always screaming at my kids.

COUNSELOR: I am not! Most of the time I'm not screaming at my kids. In fact, most of the time I'm a pretty good parent.

CLIENT: Well, I may not be screaming at them all the time, but when I do, I know they just hate me and I know it's not good for their self-esteem.

COUNSELOR: I know that yelling is not the best thing, but I also know that it's only a small part of who I am as a parent, and I can put that part in perspective.

CLIENT: My friends don't yell at their kids. They must be much better parents.

COUNSELOR: I don't see my friends yelling at their kids as much as I do, but I also know that they have other issues with their kids. And besides, I'm in therapy working on my issues trying to better myself.

CLIENT: Well, I still just don't feel good about yelling at my kids as much as I do.

COUNSELOR: I don't like that I yell at my kids as much as I do, but I'm working on that; learning how to deal with my emotions and learning other ways of responding to myself. In fact, I'm pretty proud of myself for doing this.

CLIENT: Well, yelling even some of the time is just a horrible thing to do.

COUNSELOR: Certainly yelling less is better than yelling more. And, let's not forget all the other times that I don't yell. Actually, usually I'm a damned good parent.

CLIENT: Actually, that is true; I am good at those other times. I'm really empathic, nurturing, and caring with them.

COUNSELOR: So we have a little bit of a broader picture here, don't we?

CLIENT: Well, yes, I guess we do.

In the above role-play, notice the various cognitive distortions that make up the client's thinking process (see Table 10.2 to identify specific distortions). How can identification of such distortions and associated automatic thoughts help the client? With what core beliefs might this client be struggling? Also, consider what it would be like if the client and therapist switch roles, with the client now being able to be the more rational, functional part of self.

Behavioral and Emotive Techniques.   Throughout this chapter, I have discussed the connections among beliefs, automatic thoughts, and how one feels and acts. With negative automatic thoughts come negative feelings and dysfunctional behaviors. And it makes sense that if a client is to change his or her automatic thoughts, he or she should also address the emotions and behaviors that have resulted from them. Such a multifaceted approach can help the change process occur more rapidly.

For instance, the mother who insists that she is a bad mother because she yells too much can begin to consider other ways of dealing with her feelings and changing her children's behaviors so that she doesn't feel compelled to yell. For example, a behavioral approach for this mother could be to develop additional parenting skills, such as the use of a sticker chart. An emotive technique could be to yell into a pillow every time she becomes overwhelmed with her children. Yelling at your children does not make you a failure, but finding other ways to discipline your children and deal with your out-of-control emotions will make you a better parent.

As another example of a behavioral technique, consider the man who has a core belief that he is unlovable. From this core belief he has developed a set of behaviors that prevents him from getting close to people. As this person works on addressing his negative core belief, he can also approach his problem behaviorally. For instance, he might set a goal for himself of finding a support group where he can meet others. And, as an emotive technique, once he finds this group, he can have a secondary goal of sharing deeper feelings with some of the people in the group in an effort to develop intimacy.

There are literally hundreds of behavioral and emotive techniques that cognitive therapists can use in conjunction with their cognitive techniques. They are only limited by the imagination of the therapist in consultation with the client. In fact, a large number of the techniques described elsewhere in this text can be applied in this manner. To find an appropriate technique, the therapist must have a good sense of the client's underlying cognitive processes (often deduced from a diagnosis and good client history) and then match an appropriate technique.

THE THERAPEUTIC PROCESS

The therapeutic process in cognitive therapy can be seen as a series of stages that includes intake and evaluation, the first session, the second and subsequent sessions, and termination.

Intake and Evaluation

This first part of the therapeutic process occurs prior to actual therapy taking place and is focused on doing a thorough assessment of the client. This process, which may or may not take place with the client's eventual therapist, helps the therapist orient himself or herself to the client's problem prior to the actual beginning of counseling. This is important because certain problems and diagnoses are indicative of specific kinds of underlying beliefs. So, if the therapist can make an accurate diagnosis and clearly identify issues, he or she can begin the process of deciphering the core beliefs with which a client might be struggling. Some areas the therapist will focus on during this session include (1) the presenting problem, (2) a description of symptoms and level of current functioning, (3) a history related to the presenting problem, (4) DSM diagnosis, and (5) having the client take appropriate assessment instruments (e.g., a depressed client might take the **Beck Depression Inventory** II) (Beck, Steer, & Brown, 2003). During the intake, initial information is being gathered in an effort to complete as many aspects of Figure 10.4 as possible in an effort to gain a broad understanding of the client's history and belief system and how they affect his or her current day functioning.

The First Session

The structure of the first session varies from subsequent sessions because it focuses on building the relationship, instilling hope in the client, and educating and orienting the client to the cognitive model. J. Beck (1995) suggests the following structure for the first session in order to accomplish this:

1. *Setting the agenda:* This part of the session involves the therapist's informing the client about what will occur during the first session.

2. *Conducting a mood check:* Here the therapist reevaluates the client with the same assessment instrument given during the intake or with a subjective index (e.g., "On a scale of 0 to 100, with 100 being extremely depressed, how depressed do you feel today?").

3. *Review of presenting problem(s) and goal setting:* This next part of the first interview is involved with reviewing the initial problems identified during the intake interview and assuring that no other issues need to be addressed.

After a thorough assessment of the presenting problem(s) is finished, the problems are turned into goals. For example, a depressed client who is missing work and feeling lonely might have the broad goals of feeling less depressed, making new friends, and missing less time at work.

4. ***Educating the client about the cognitive model:*** Here the therapist teaches the client the relationships among thoughts, feelings, and behaviors. Thoughts are broadly defined as what one is thinking about as well as images or pictures that pass through one's mind, and the therapist uses examples from the client's life to show that situations affect thoughts and that thoughts will often lead to strong feelings and actions. And, the therapist might use a drawing to highlight this point:

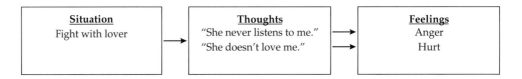

| **Situation**
Fight with lover | **Thoughts**
"She never listens to me."
"She doesn't love me." | **Feelings**
Anger
Hurt |

At this point, the focus is on teaching the client how to catch his or her automatic thoughts. Later sessions will focus upon cognitive distortions (and their relationship to automatic thoughts), intermediate thoughts, coping or compensatory strategies, and core beliefs. Because the therapist has conducted a thorough assessment, he or she is equipped with one or more hypotheses about the client's belief system. As therapy progresses and as the client increasingly sees the connections among automatic thoughts, intermediate beliefs, and core beliefs, the therapist will share some of these hypotheses with the client.

5. ***Expectations for therapy:*** Because clients often come into therapy with the idea that the therapist will "cure" them in some magical fashion, during this first session, the therapist seeks to de-mystify the therapeutic process by describing therapy as a rational and empirical process in which the client examines how he or she can feel better by changing his or her cognitions. Based on the kind of presenting problem, the therapist also offers a realistic estimate of how long this process should take.

6. ***Educating the client about his or her disorder:*** Most clients "want to know their general diagnosis, that they are not crazy, and that their therapist has helped others like them before …" (Beck, J., 1995, p. 38). Normalizing their experience is critical because it allows clients to realize that others have experienced and successfully tackled similar problems in therapy. In addition, letting clients know that therapy is rational and logical, that therapy has specific goals, and that the therapist has helped clients with similar problems gives the client a sense of hope and purposefulness.

7. ***Summarizing and developing homework:*** Near the end of this session, the therapist summarizes what was talked about and collaboratively develops tasks which the client can work on at home prior to the next session.

Tasks should be achievable, and if the therapist senses that the client will not work on one or more specific tasks, he or she should modify the task(s) or come up with others.

8. *Feedback:* Asking for feedback helps to reinforce the collaborative nature of the relationship and assures that the therapist is on target with the direction of therapy. Feedback can be asked for orally or in writing. Judith Beck (1995) suggests that the following kinds of questions be asked when feedback is requested in writing:

   - What did you cover today that's important to you to remember?
   - How much did you feel you could trust your therapist today?
   - Was there anything that bothered you about therapy today? If so, what was it?
   - How likely are you to do your homework?
   - How much homework had you done for therapy today?
   - What do you want to make sure to cover at the next session?

   Adapted from: Beck, J. (1995). *Cognitive therapy: Basics and beyond.* New York: Guilford Press. p. 42.

Information from the initial intake and the first session allows the therapist to put the pieces of the puzzle together as he or she completes all aspects noted in Figure 10.4. This allows the therapist, and eventually the client, to increasingly understand how the client's history, belief system, coping strategies, and automatic thoughts affect the client's daily life.

Second and Subsequent Sessions

These sessions focus on strengthening the therapeutic alliance and on symptom relief. In that light, the therapist hopes to continue to familiarize the client with the cognitive therapy model, work collaboratively, help the client solve identified problems, and, as symptom relief is obtained, work toward termination. As sessions continue, this work becomes increasingly focused as the pieces of the puzzle, as highlighted in Figure 10.4, are completed. Judith Beck (1995) suggests the following structure for the second and subsequent sessions:

1. *Update and mood check:* Here the therapist checks in with the client to see how he or she is progressing since the last session. In addition to gathering verbal feedback, the therapist asks the client to retake the same instrument that was taken during their last session (e.g., Beck Depression Inventory). In this manner, the therapist can assess progress toward goals.

2. *Bridge from previous session:* To ensure that the therapist and client are "on the same page," the therapist asks the client to recall important points from the previous session. If differences are evident, they are discussed and new goals are created. To facilitate this process, Judith Beck (1995) suggests that clients write out responses to the following:
   - What did we talk about last session that was important? What did you learn?
   - Was there anything that bothered you about our last session? Anything you are reluctant to say?

- What was your week like? What has your mood been like, compared to other weeks?
- Did anything happen this week that is important to discuss?
- What problems do you want to put on the agenda?
- What homework did you do/not do? What did you learn?

Adapted from: Beck, J. (1995). *Cognitive therapy: Basics and beyond.* New York: Guilford Press. p. 49.

3. ***Setting the agenda:*** In the earlier sessions, the therapist sets more of the agenda as he or she teaches the client about the cognitive model. As the client learns more about the model, as well as techniques that can be used to address cognitive distortions, coping strategies, and negative core beliefs, it is the client who increasingly sets the agenda.

4. ***Review of homework:*** Compliance in doing homework is facilitated by the therapist's reviewing all homework assignments. When a homework assignment has not been completed, it is important for the therapist to understand the reason why it was ignored. Ignoring a homework assignment due to a family emergency is quite different from ignoring one because the goals were inappropriate. As sessions continue, the client takes more responsibility for developing his or her own homework assignments.

5. ***Feedback:*** As in the first session, feedback is critical in every session if the client is to feel as if he or she is a collaborator and if therapy is to be on track (see "The First Session").

Termination

Because it is predicated on the alleviation of identified symptoms, cognitive therapy tends to be short-term, and from the very first session, there is an eye to the last session. Although the therapist takes a more directive and educative role early on in this process, as the client increasingly learns how to work independently on his or her issues, the therapist takes a lesser role. Figure 10.5 graphically depicts this process.

As therapy continues, the therapist should expect client setbacks as the client struggles to work on his or her problems and as the hypotheses that originally were formed become slightly changed. As the client nears the last session, the therapist should explore his or her thoughts about termination and help the client develop a process in which he or she is conducting **self-management** sessions.

SOCIAL, CULTURAL, AND SPIRITUAL ISSUES

With cognitive–behavioral therapy, cognitive therapy's close cousin, being the most frequently used approach to counseling (Hays, 2006), it is particularly important that this approach is shown to be effective with a wide range of cultural groups. However, research on cognitive–behavioral therapy and

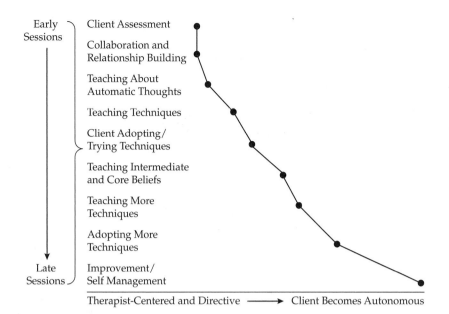

Early Sessions
- Client Assessment
- Collaboration and Relationship Building
- Teaching About Automatic Thoughts
- Teaching Techniques
- Client Adopting/ Trying Techniques
- Teaching Intermediate and Core Beliefs
- Teaching More Techniques
- Adopting More Techniques

Late Sessions
- Improvement/ Self Management

Therapist-Centered and Directive ⟶ Client Becomes Autonomous

F I G U R E 10.5 Movement of Client toward Termination over Sessions

cognitive therapy has almost exclusively been conducted on whites, with only a few studies looking at its effectiveness with minorities. In a positive light, cognitive therapy stresses the importance of tailoring the approach to each client based on the assessment conducted early in counseling. However, two red flags are raised with this emphasis. First, cognitive therapy stresses the importance of making a diagnosis and subsequently using this diagnosis as one aspect of conceptualizing the client's issues, and later using this conceptualization to match the client to specific techniques. Since there is some evidence that minorities and women may be misdiagnosed at higher rates than whites (Leah & Sullivan, 2001; Li, Jenkins, & Sundsmo, 2007; Paniagua, 2005), the inherent flaws in this process are obvious. Second, clinicians need to know which techniques are most suited to specific cultural groups. With multicultural training still being relatively new in the mental health professions, there are still many therapists who have not been exposed to cross-cultural training that targets specific skills needed for varying cultural groups.

Another cross-cultural issue related to cognitive therapy is that it focuses mostly on how one's internal cognitive structures (e.g., core beliefs, automatic thoughts) affect one's behaviors and feeling states. This traditional view minimizes the possibility that for many individuals, especially minorities and the poor, problems exist due to psychosocial and environmental issues. These include such issues as racism, discrimination, natural disasters, poverty, exposure to crime, and "inadequate health care or social services; legal problems, and exposure to disasters or war" (Hays, 2006, p. 9). It is critical that today's cognitive therapists take these external events into consideration when working with clients.

Because cognitive therapy tends to focus almost exclusively on the individual, those clients who view themselves from the lens of their family or from a broader community context may be less amenable to this approach, unless the cognitive therapist can adapt to this broader perspective. In addition, minority clients often bring with them values and experiences specific to their cultural group. Those therapists who are not familiar with different cultural groups may conceptualize their clients incorrectly, misinterpret the meanings clients ascribe to their thoughts and beliefs, and have difficulty building relationships with minority clients. Clearly, as with all approaches, cognitive therapists need to have the knowledge, skills, and attitudes necessary to work with a wide range of clients (Roysircar, Arredondo, Fuertes, Ponterotto, & Toporek, 2003).

Relative to one's spirituality, there are a broad range of beliefs regarding how one's spirituality may affect one's belief system. Some, such as many Unitarians and Reform Jews, believe that one's belief system is mostly a function of internal structures in interaction with experiences. On the other hand, others, such as some Asian Americans, evangelical Christians, and Orthodox Muslims believe that the spiritual world directly affects their lives (Iwamasa, Hsia, & Hinton, 2006; G. McAuliffe, personal communication, June 22, 2009). Clearly, such disparate beliefs will affect how a therapist works with the client. For instance, where many Unitarians and Reform Jews will find a logical connection between their beliefs and cognitive therapy theory, therapists would have to make adjustments with some Asian Americans, evangelical Christians, and Orthodox Muslims by understanding that "other forces" can also be shaping the client's life. As with cross-cultural issues, the cognitive therapist needs to understand how the client comes to understand his or her spirituality and make necessary changes to the approach based on this understanding.

EFFICACY OF COGNITIVE THERAPY

Cognitive therapy uses a case conceptualization process in which the therapist assesses the client and then applies a specific treatment plan based on this assessment that is fairly well spelled out. In addition, instruments to assess and measure progress in treatment have been developed. Thus, assessing the effectiveness of cognitive therapy can seem rather straightforward: Assess, apply your model, and use your instrument to measure change. It is not surprising, therefore, that hundreds of studies to measure the effectiveness of cognitive therapy have been conducted over the years.

In an attempt to make sense out of all this research, one study examined 16 meta-analyses that looked at the success of cognitive therapy with 10,000 subjects (Butler, Chapman, Forman & Beck, 2006). The authors note that the results demonstrate strong evidence of the success of cognitive therapy with "unipolar depression, generalized anxiety disorder, panic disorder with or without agoraphobia, social phobia, post-traumatic stress disorder, and childhood depressive and anxiety disorders" (p. 17). They also suggest moderate success when used to

---

B o x 10.3   Jake Sees an REBT Therapist

Please review the Millder family's background which can be found in Appendix B, and then read about

Jake's encounter with an REBT therapist, which can also be found in Appendix B.

---

treat marital problems, somatic disorders in children, and chronic pain. They note that cognitive therapy was more effective than antidepressants for adult depression (although, medication and therapy combined, is generally more effective than either alone), as effective as behavior therapy in the treatment of obsessive-compulsive disorders and in the treatment of depression in adults, and somewhat effective in treating bulimia and schizophrenia. In addition, the authors point to evidence that cognitive therapy seems to have staying power, in the sense that after treatment is discontinued, it shows long-term positive effects for a number of disorders.

Despite the large number of studies with positive results, few have been controlled studies that compare the effects of cognitive therapy with other forms of treatment. In addition, despite the bold statements by Butler et al. (2006), as well as by Beck himself (2005), others are not so willing to assume it is the specific approach of cognitive therapy that is causing change in clients (Wampold, 2001). They suggest a number of confounding factors may exist that are actually at the heart of the positive changes, including such things as the ability to build a relationship with clients, the use of empathy, and the therapist's allegiance to his or her approach—or the belief of the therapist that his or her approach will work.

Finally, as an approach that tends to target symptoms, it is clear that cognitive therapy has some advantages over other forms of therapy when addressing certain kinds of problems. Its protocol of defining the problem, focusing on it, and working on it can quickly ameliorate a number of symptoms. In addition, the development of manuals by Beck to assist in the treatment of specific disorders is clearly helpful. However, cognitive therapy may not be the treatment of choice for some problems faced in therapy. For instance, when working with a client who is resistant, dealing with a sexual identity disorder, dealing with a recent loss, or wanting to focus on an increase in personal growth, the "cookbook" approach may not be helpful, as these approaches do not lend themselves to specific negative core beliefs. The bottom line is that cognitive therapy probably works well for certain problems, but should be used on a limited basis for other kinds of issues (see Box 10.3).

SUMMARY

Born in Providence, Rhode Island, in 1921, Aaron Temkin "Tim" Beck is considered the founder of cognitive therapy. Going to medical school and struggling with some of his own fears and phobias early in life, Beck initially became a psychoanalyst. However, becoming disillusioned over the years with psychoanalysis, and finding that his clients were often aware, or could easily become aware, of "automatic thoughts," he began to develop his own theory that focused on how one's cognitive processes mediate how one acts and feels. Over the years, he has recognized his wife's role in helping him refine his theory, and in recent years, his daughter Judith Beck has become one of the leaders of cognitive therapy.

In coming up with his model, Beck was careful to develop a process that could be thoroughly researched. Through his research he found that different disorders presented with cognitive distortions that were specific to that disorder. Thus, in examining the efficacy of his approach, Beck came up with a logical process that included hypothesizing about the cognitive processes associated with different disorders, developing manuals to assist clinicians in the treatment of various disorders, developing scales to measure the disorder (e.g., depression), and conducting clinical studies to assess the effectiveness of therapeutic interventions with the manuals that were developed.

Positing a diathesis–stress model of mental disorders, cognitive therapy suggests that a combination of genetic predispositions, biological factors, and experiences combine to produce specific cognitive schemas and core beliefs, some of which may lie dormant and then suddenly appear as the result of stress and other conditions impinging on the person. Cognitive therapy is seen as a rational, pragmatic, educative, empirical, and anti-deterministic approach that proposes that people can manage and effect changes in the way they live in the world in a relatively brief amount of time. Believing that genes, biology, and experiences affect the development of the person, this approach has elements of a constructivist perspective when it states that through discourse with others, individuals can change their cognitions and overcome their predispositions.

Cognitive therapists believe that one's core beliefs become the underlying mechanism for the creation of intermediate beliefs that set the attitudes, rules and expectations, and assumptions we live by. These attitudes, rules and expectations, and assumptions can be understood by looking at how situations in life lead to what are called automatic thoughts that result in a set of behaviors, feelings, and physiological responses that end up reinforcing core beliefs. Beck also suggests there are a number of cognitive distortions that tend to be associated with the automatic thoughts that we have. Finally, coping or compensatory strategies, usually created early in life, are often developed by individuals to steer themselves away from experiencing their negative core beliefs. However, these strategies do not rid the person of his or her core beliefs, and over time, the strategies become maladaptive for the individual. Beck and other cognitive therapists believe that, through a process called cognitive conceptualization, the therapist can assess the client thoroughly and begin to make some hypotheses about the kinds of automatic thoughts and intermediate and core beliefs that define the person. Then, strategies can be developed to help the individual change his or her thoughts and beliefs.

In practicing cognitive therapy, the therapist generally uses a number of essential and commonly used techniques. Some of the essential techniques include building a strong therapeutic alliance (being collaborative; demonstrating empathy, caring, and optimism; and adapting one's therapeutic style); Socratic questioning, educating the client about the cognitive model, identifying and challenging automatic thoughts and images, identifying and challenging cognitive distortions, identifying intermediate beliefs, identifying and challenging core beliefs, and doing homework assignments. Some of the commonly used techniques include thought-stopping, imagery-changing, rational–emotional role-play, and behavioral and emotive techniques. In addition, it was noted that hundreds of other specific techniques can be used to help with the change process.

The therapeutic process can be viewed through a series of four stages: (1) intake and evaluation; (2) the first session, which includes setting the agenda, conducting a mood check, review of presenting problem(s) and goal setting, educating the client about the cognitive model, defining expectations for therapy, educating the client about his/her disorder, summarizing and developing homework, and feedback; (3) the second and subsequent sessions, which includes update and mood check, bridge from previous session, setting the agenda, review of homework, and feedback; and (4) termination.

Relative to social, cultural, and spiritual issues, it was noted that, although hundreds of studies have been conducted, few have included substantial numbers of minorities. Also, it was stressed that, because cognitive therapy relies on making a diagnosis, minorities might be particularly at risk when participating in this approach, as some evidence shows that they are misdiagnosed at higher rates than whites. Also, many therapists may not be adequately trained to apply cognitive therapy to minority clients. In addition, cognitive therapy has traditionally viewed clients solely from an "internal perspective," which tends to devalue the importance of external factors differentially affecting minorities and women. Finally, relative to spirituality, those who stress more of a logical view of religion and who see the importance of going "within" may find a fit with cognitive therapy, however, those who see "other forces" as shaping their lives may have a more difficult time with this approach.

Finally, we noted in this chapter that cognitive therapy is particularly amenable to being researched because of the direct relationship between diagnosis, cognitive conceptualization, and the development of treatment strategies. Thus, hundreds of studies have been conducted over the years. Recent meta-analyses have shown it to be effective across a wide range of disorders and to seem to show persistence even after treatment has ended. However, some have suggested that it may be more the qualities of the therapist that are responsible for its efficacy, including the ability of the therapist to build a relationship, show empathy, and be committed to an approach. Others question whether such a symptom-focused approach is adaptable to problems that are not so easily identified or are longerterm in their nature.

KEY WORDS

Academy of Cognitive
    Therapy
active
adapting one's
    therapeutic style

all-or-nothing
    thinking
American Psychiatric
    Association
    Distinguished Service
    Award

anti-deterministic
attitudes, rules and
    expectations, and
    assumptions
automatic
    thoughts

automatic images

Beck Depression
Inventory

Beck Institute

behavioral and emotive
techniques

being collaborative

bridge from previous
session

building a strong
therapeutic alliance

catastrophisizing

cognitive
conceptualization

cognitive distortions

conducting a mood
check

constructivist

continuity hypothesis

compensatory strategies

coping strategies

core beliefs

core belief worksheet

demonstrating empathy,
caring, and optimism

diathesis–stress model

disqualifying or
discounting the
positive

educating the client
about cognitive
model

educative

emotional reasoning

empirical

expectations for therapy

feedback

educating client about
his/her disorder

genetic and
evolutionary
predisposition

homework

identifying and
challenging
automatic thoughts
and images

identifying and
challenging cognitive
distortions

identifying and
challenging core
beliefs

identifying intermediate
beliefs

imagery-changing

intake and evaluation

intermediate beliefs

labeling

Lasker Award for
Clinical Medical
Research

magnification/
minimization

mental filter

mind-reading

overgeneralization

personalization

pragmatic

rational

rational–emotional

role-play

review of homework

review of presenting
problem(s) and goal
setting

schemas

"should" and "must"
statements

self-management

setting the agenda

Socratic questioning

summarizing and
developing
homework

termination

the cognitive model

the first session

the second and
subsequent sessions

thought-stopping

tunnel vision

update and mood check

KEY NAMES

Adler, Alfred

Beck, Harry

Beck, Judith

Beck, Lizzie

Beck, Maurice

Erickson, Erik

Horney, Karen

Whitman, Phyllis

REFERENCES

Beck, A. T. (1964). Thinking and depression: II. Theory a
 Psychiatry, 10, 561–571.

Beck, A. T. (1967). *Depression: Clinical, experimental, and t*
 Harper and Row. Republished as *Depression: Causes*
 University of Pennsylvania Press, 1972.

Beck, A. T. (1976). *Cognitive therapy and the emotional dis*
 Universities Press.

Beck, A. T. (1991). Cognitive therapy: A 30-year retro
 46(4), 368–375.

Beck, A. T. (1999). *Prisoners of hate: The cognitive basis*
 New York: HarperCollins.

Beck, A. T. (2002). Prisoners of hate. *Behaviour Resea*

Beck, A. T. (2005). The current state of cognitive th
 Archives of General Psychiatry, 62, 953–959.

Beck, J. (1995). *Cognitive therapy: Basics and beyond*. New York: Guilford Press.

Beck, J. (2005). *Cognitive therapy for challenging problems*. New York: Guilford Press.

Beck, J. (2007). *The Beck diet solution: Train your brain to think like a thin person*. Birmingham,
 AL: Oxmoor House Publications.

Beck, A. T., Rush, A. J., Shaw, B. F., & Emery, G. (1979). *Cognitive therapy of depression*.
 New York: Guilford Press.

Beck, A. T., Steer, R. A., & Brown, G. K. (2003). *BDI-II manual*. San Antonio, TX:
 Psychological Corporation.

Beck, A. T., Arthur, F., & Denise, D. D. (2004). *Cognitive therapy of personality disorders*
 (2nd ed.). New York: The Guilford Press.

Butler, A. C., Chapman, J. E., Forman, E. M., & Beck, A. T. (2006). The empirical
 status of cognitive–behavioral therapy: A review of meta-analyses. *Clinical Psychology
 Review, 26*(1), 17–31.

Hays, P. A. (2006). Introduction: Developing culturally responsive cognitive-behavioral
 therapies. In P. A. Hays & G. Y. Iwamasa (Eds.), *Culturally responsive cognitive-
 behavioral therapy: Assessment, practice, and supervision* (pp. 3–21). Washington, DC:
 American Psychological Association.

Hersen, M., & Sledge, W. H. (Eds.). (2002). Beck, A. T. In M. Hersen & W. H. Sledge,
 Encyclopedia of psychotherapy (vol. 1, p. 177). Boston: Academic Press.

Iwamasa, G. Y., Hsia, C., & Hinton, D. (2006). Cognitive-behavioral therapy with
 Asian Americans. In P. A. Hays & G. Y. Iwamasa (Eds.), *Culturally responsive
 cognitive-behavioral therapy: Assessment, practice, and supervision* (pp. 117–140).
 Washington, DC: American Psychological Association.

Krapp, K. (Ed.). (2005). Beck, Aaron Temkin. *Psychologists and their theories for students*
 (vol. 1, pp. 67–91). Detroit, MI: Gale Cengage Publishers.

Leah, M. M., & Sullivan, A. (2001). The intersection of race, class, and gender on diagnosis. In D. B. Pope-Davis & H. K. Coleman (Eds.), *The intersection of race, class, and
 gender in multicultural counseling* (pp. 353–384). Thousand Oaks, CA: Sage.

(2003). *Cognitive therapy techniques: A practitioner's guide*. New York: Guilford cations.

., Jenkins, S., & Sundsmo, A. (2007). Impact of race and ethnicity on the expression, assessment, and diagnosis of psychopathology. In M. Hersen, S. M. Turner, & D. C. Beidel (Eds.), *Adult psychopathology and diagnosis* (pp. 101–121). Hoboken, NJ: John Wiley & Sons.

McAuliffe, G., Grothaus, T., Pare, D., & Wininger, A. (2008). The practice of culturally alert counseling. In G. McAuliffe (Ed.), *Culturally alert counseling: A comprehensive introduction* (pp. 570–631).

Padesky, C. A., & Beck, A. T. (2003). Science and philosophy: Comparison of cognitive therapy and rational emotive behavior therapy. *Journal of Cognitive Psychotherapy: An International Quarterly, 17*(3), 211–225.

Paniagua, F. A. (2005). *Assessing and treating culturally diverse clients: A practical guide* (3rd ed.). Thousand Oaks, CA: Sage.

Riso, L. P., du Toit, P. L., Stein, D. J., & Young, J. E. (2007). *Cognitive schemas and core beliefs in psychological problems: A scientist-practitioner guide*. Washington, DC: American Psychological Association.

Roysircar, G., Arredondo, P., Fuertes, J. N., Ponterotto, J. G., & Toporek, R. L. (Eds.). (2003). *Multicultural counseling competencies 2003: Association for Multicultural Counseling and Development*. Alexandria, VA: Association for Multicultural Counseling and Development.

The Beck Diet Solution (2007). Home page. Retrieved from http://www.beckdietsolution.com/Library/InfoManage/Guide.asp?FolderID=1&SessionID={DAF1BA1B-C32D-4D0C-8677-D7FC386C7C10}

The Beck Institute (2008a). Dr. Aaron T. Beck's biography. Retrieved from http://www.beckinstitute.org/InfoID/302/RedirectPath/Add1/FolderID/196/SessionID/%7B129FFEEF-B6FF-447C-9B57-DD2EE25F144F%7D/InfoGroup/Main/InfoType/Article/PageVars/Library/InfoManage/Zoom.htm

The Beck Institute (2008b). *Dr. Judith S. Beck's biography*. Retrieved from http://www.beckinstitute.org/InfoID/252/RedirectPath/Add1/FolderID/196/SessionID/%7B05E33117-AB8E-4E1A-A944-FC6AA69608B9%7D/InfoGroup/Main/InfoType/Article/PageVars/Library/InfoManage/Zoom.htm

The top 10: The most influential therapists of the past quarter-century (2007, March/April). *Psychotherapy Networker*. Retrieved from http://www.psychotherapynetworker.org/index.php/magazine/populartopics/219-the-top-10

Wampold, B. E. (2001). *The great psychotherapy debate: Models, methods, and findings*. Mahwah, NJ: Lawrence Erlbaum Associates.

Weishaar, M. E. (1993). *Aaron T. Beck*. Thousand Oaks, CA: Sage Publications.

Chapter 11

Reality Therapy/Choice Theory

Learning Goals

- To gain a biographical understanding of William Glasser, the creator of reality therapy and choice theory.
- To understand the historical context in which Glasser developed reality therapy and then choice theory.
- To understand the relationship between one's need-strength profile and the anti-deterministic, present-focused, internal-control, and choice-based view of human nature of choice theory.
- To learn about key concepts of choice theory, including the basic needs of survival (self-preservation), love and belonging, power (inner control), freedom (independence), and fun (enjoyment); internal and external control and their relationships to the seven caring habits and seven deadly habits; choice; quality world; and total behavior, which includes behaviors, thoughts, and their resulting feelings and physiological responses.
- To learn how current-day reality therapy applies Wubbolding's WDEP system, which includes the **w**ants of the client (W), what the client is **d**oing in his or her life's **d**irection (Ds), **e**valuating if what the client is doing is working (E), and developing a **p**lan of action that can be implemented (P).
- Relative to the WDEP system, to understand the importance of exhibiting certain attitudes and techniques of the environmental elements while avoiding others ("tonics and toxins of the counseling relationship").
- To examine the strengths and weaknesses of reality therapy relative to cross-cultural counseling and religion, especially in light of the emphasis on internal control in reality therapy.
- To examine the efficacy of reality therapy relative to the kinds of research studies completed and the need for more controlled studies.
- To see how reality therapy is applied through vignettes, DVDs, and case study.

… [N]one of the people described in the DSM-IV, the official diagnostic and statistical manual of mental illness published by the American
Psychiatric Association, are mentally ill. I don't deny the reality of their
symptoms; I deny that these symptoms, whatever they may be, are an
untreatable component of an incurable brain malfunction. I do not see
their symptoms as mental illness but as an indication that they are not
nearly as mentally healthy as they could learn to be.

… [T]he basic human problem has nothing to do with the structure
of physiology of our brain. We are by our nature social creatures and to
be mentally healthy or happy, we need to get along with the people in
our lives. Unhappy people like John Nash [the "schizophrenic" physicist
portrayed in the movie *A Beautiful Mind*], and all those whose disorders
appear in the DSM-IV, are not mentally healthy. They are lonely or
disconnected from the people they need.

[These people] express their unhappiness in the symptoms described
in the DSM-IV plus many others like pain and anger. For them to become more mentally healthy and happier, we have to offer compassion,
social support, education, and counseling. They do not need brain drugs
and electric shocks, all of which harm their brains. (Glasser, 2003, p. xxii)

The above bold statements made by William Glasser show the strength of his
beliefs concerning his theory. Symptoms people exhibit, which we tend to call
"mental disorders," are reflective of the pain, anger, and unhappiness in their lives,
not a sign that something is inherently wrong with them, asserts Glasser. There is no
chemical imbalance or difference in brain structure that causes some of us to act in
ways that we sometimes label as "pathological." And, perhaps most important, we
don't need drugs or other brain-altering approaches to bring us back to what some
would call "normalcy." We need a compassionate, caring person who can teach us
healthier ways of getting our needs met. But where did this man come from who
unflinchingly challenges the mainstream beliefs of the majority of today's mental
health professionals? Let's take a look.

WILLIAM GLASSER

The youngest of three children, William Glasser was born in Cleveland,
Ohio, on May 11, 1925. Glasser's mother and father emigrated separately from
politically unstable Eastern Europe in the early 1900s when they were young
teenagers (Wubbolding, 2000). Wealthy in Russia, his father's family struggled
in the U.S. Although not poor, when his parents eventually married, they had to
work hard to make a living. Despite, or perhaps because they were not highly

educated, they stressed the importance of learning, and all three children were eventually to seek post-secondary educations.

Prior to the age of six, Glasser remembers his parents having violent fights, and even recalls times when, in a rage, his father broke things, and one time when he hit his mother. Although frightened by the violence, he states, "Whatever difficulty they had with each other, they were always loving toward me" (Glasser, 1998, p. 89). Although the fights subsided, the animosity between his parents seemed palpable in the household. Despite his father's periodic outbursts, Glasser remembers his father as a gentle soul and his mother as controlling. In fact, in references to his father's accepting attitude toward others, Glasser states, "[Never] in the more than sixty years that I knew him did I ever see him try to control another person except when he was being goaded by my mother" (Glasser, 1998, p. 90). It is not a great leap to believe that Glasser's theory, which underscores the importance of not controlling others, was influenced by these early perceptions.

William Glasser

Courtesy of The William Glasser Institute

A shy child, in early adolescence and young adulthood, Glasser points to a few people who had a particularly positive effect on his life. For instance, he describes having a warm and loving relationship with his sixth-grade teacher, Ms. Sheehan, who encouraged him and boosted his confidence (Glasser, 2003). Eventually, Glasser went on to receive his bachelor's degree in engineering from Case Western Reserve University in Ohio. After working for a year, he decided that psychology was more of a match for him, and he went back and obtained his M.S. in Clinical Psychology from Case Western. He notes that while working on his master's degree, the dean of his college encouraged him to go into psychiatry, despite Glasser's lack of confidence about getting into medical school. Listening to his dean's advice, he applied and was accepted to medical school at Case Western and obtained his degree in 1953. As with his sixth-grade teacher, Glasser points to this relationship as having a significant positive effect on his life.

In 1953, most psychiatrists were trained in the traditional psychoanalytical approach to therapy, and this was also the case with Glasser (Wubbolding, 2000). However, while working with clients during his residency, Glasser began to believe that they were struggling with basic human problems in response to which they developed symptoms, not the intrapsychic conflicts or organic deficits that many psychiatrists alleged. Taking a risk, he began to share his unconventional beliefs about psychiatry with his supervisor, Dr. G. L. Harrington. To his surprise, he found encouragement and mentorship that would last for years. Glasser cites all of these formative relationships as critical to his ability to feel good about himself and ultimately forge a new approach to psychotherapy (Glasser, 2003).

In 1957, Glasser completed his residency and went into private practice. In 1960, he wrote his first book, *Mental Health or Mental Illness*, and it is here that we see Glasser question, in print, the traditional role of psychiatry, which he had begun to question verbally during his residency (Lennon, 2000). As he expanded his practice, he also worked on developing his ideas, and in 1965, published his first book on his theory, *Reality Therapy*. A sensation early on, this book changed the ways in which multitudes of counselors and therapists would approach their clients. When first coming up with his theory, Glasser believed that mental illness was an inability to meet two basic needs: "the need to love and be loved and the need to feel that we are worthwhile to ourselves and to others" (Glasser, 1965, p. 9). Agreeing with Thomas Szasz in his classic book *The Myth of Mental Illness* (1961), Glasser criticized the psychiatric profession for propagating the belief that mental illness was the result of some inherently flawed biological brain functioning. Instead, he suggested that individuals labeled as mentally ill, as well as those having daily living problems, were exhibiting irresponsible behaviors because they had not formed relationships that had helped them learn how to effectively meet their needs:

> The guiding principles of reality therapy are directed toward achieving the proper involvement, a completely honest, human relationship in which the patient, for perhaps the first time in his life, realizes that someone cares enough about him not only to accept him but to help him fulfill his needs in the real world. (Glasser, 1965, p. 21)

While in private practice, Glasser became gradually more involved with applying his theory in educational settings. Starting as early as 1956, Glasser had been consulting with the **Ventura School of Girls**, a correctional facility for girls between the ages of 15 and 19 (Glasser, 2006; Wubbolding, 2000). There he was able to convince the staff to apply his theory, which increasingly focused on building trust and respect, the use of discipline (e.g., having consequences for not following through on the change process), the elimination of punishment (not imposing pain following a behavior a person in power doesn't like), highlighting successes, and helping the girls make good choices that would better meet their needs. As his reputation spread, he was offered a substantial amount of grant money by the **W. Clement Stone Foundation** of Chicago to develop and implement his ideas. This money was critical to the establishment, in 1967, of the **Institute for Reality Therapy and Educator Training Center**. Then, in 1969, while still consulting with the Ventura School, Glasser published his revolutionary book, *Schools without Failure*, which highlighted how his ideas could be used in educational settings (Lennon, 2000; Wubbolding, 2000). Quickly, Glasser's reputation extended to the education field as schools around the country adapted his methods of working with children. Although changed over the years, Glasser's positive approach to working with children continues to be used in schools worldwide (Glasser, 2006).

During the 1970s, Glasser continued to write books that expanded some of his core ideas, such as the book *The Identity Society* (1972), which elaborated on some of the practical techniques of reality therapy, and *Positive Addiction* (1976), which highlighted the importance of choosing important positive behaviors in one's life. During this decade, Glasser also became intrigued by William T. Powers's **perceptual control theory**, which looked at how perceptions influence the manner in which we control our environment in an effort to get our needs met (Powers, 1973). Adapting many of Powers's ideas, Glasser developed his own version of control theory that became the underlying principles to the practice of reality therapy. Some of Glasser's books that reflected these changes included

Stations of the Mind (1981), *Control Theory* (1984), *Control Theory in the Classroom* (1986), and *Control Theory in the Practice of Reality* (1989).

During the 1990s, intrigued by Edward Deming's **total quality management (TQM)** approach, which applied humanistic and systems principles to business and industry (Deming, 1986), Glasser again adapted his theory by highlighting the importance of clients' making choices that would enable them to live in a world that matched their internal image of what the world should look like. Calling this the **quality world**, Glasser suggested that clients could best make positive choices that matched their quality worlds if they were afforded a supportive environment free of coercion and criticism. At this point, Glasser changed the name of his institute to the **Institute for Reality Therapy, Control Theory, and Total Management** (Wubbolding, 2000).

Although Glasser incorporated many of Powers's ideas into his theory, he also had differences with him (Wubbolding, 2000). With this in mind, and finding that the word "control" was a hot button for many people, in 1996, Glasser decided to use the name **choice theory** instead of **control theory** (Glasser, n.d.; Wubbolding, 2000). His books *Choice Theory* (1998) and *Counseling with Choice Theory* (2001) reflect these changes. Today, Glasser states that the practice of reality therapy is "firmly based on **choice theory** and its successful application is based on a strong understanding of choice theory" (The William Glasser Institute, 2009a, para. 1). At around the same time that Glasser started using the name choice theory, he again changed the name of his institute, this time to the **William Glasser Institute**, highlighting the fact that reality therapy and choice theory are based on the ideas of William Glasser.

As Glasser learned from others, he adapted his theory. For instance, his original theory had humans possessing two basic needs, but now has them possessing five. His ideas that individuals should not behave irresponsibly and that they should face their unique "reality" has morphed to a theory that suggests that individuals examine their needs and their quality worlds and develop what he calls **internal-control language** to direct their lives more efficiently (Glasser, W., & Glasser, C., 2000; Van Nuys, 2007). Also, Glasser now asserts that we all make the best choices we know how to make as we attempt to meet the pictures in our quality worlds, and almost all of us could make better choices if placed in an environment that could teach us how to do so (Glasser, 1998, 2001; Glasser, W., & Glasser, C., 1999; Lennon, 2000; Van Nuys, 2007).

Over the years, Glasser's reputation has grown. In 2003, Glasser received the **Professional Development Award** from the American Counseling Association (ACA) for significant contributions to the field of counseling. In 2004, he was given the **ACA's A Legend in Counseling Award** in 2005, the esteemed designation "**Master Therapist**" was given to him by the American Psychotherapy Association, and also in 2005, he obtained the **Life Achievement Award** by the International Center for the Study of Psychiatry and Psychology. Clearly, William Glasser has been one of the leaders in the fields of counseling and psychotherapy.

Today, William Glasser's ideas have spread worldwide as his books have been translated into several languages and his workshops presented throughout the world. Having trained over 75,000 people in his approach, his ideas have been integrated into education, counseling, and even business (The William Glasser Institute, 2009b). Although in semi-retirement, Glasser periodically lectures and continues applying his theory through his writing, such as his recently published book *Eight Lessons for a Happier Marriage* (Glasser, W., & Glasser, C., 2007).

Although William Glasser has been the driving force behind choice theory and reality therapy, many have assisted him and even expanded on his ideas. For instance, over the years, he had two important women in his life who helped him sort through his ideas and assisted him in writing and editing some of his books. His first wife, Naomi Glasser, was by his side until her death in 1992. In more recent years, his second wife, Carleen Glasser, has assisted him as he has continued to refine his ideas. Also, over the years, there have been numerous associates who have helped in training others in reality therapy, in applying the theory to educational and organization consultation, and in clarification and expansion of the theory. Bob Wubbolding, one of the first to be trained in reality therapy at the Institute, has been particularly noteworthy, especially in his adaptation and expansion of the theory (Wubbolding, 2000) (see Box 11.1).

VIEW OF HUMAN NATURE

Reality therapy posits that we have five genetically based needs, the original of which is the **survival** or **self-preservation** need that helped us endure thousands of years ago in a difficult world. From the survival need spun off the needs for **love and belonging**, **power** (or **inner control**), **freedom** (or **independence**), and **fun** (or **enjoyment**), each of which has helped the human species thrive in distinct ways. Today, the strength of all five needs is said by Glasser to be "fixed at birth and does not change" (1988, p. 91). The manner in which each of us learns to meet our unique **need-strength profile** is said to be a reflection of our personality.

Glasser (1998, 2001) suggests that from the moment we are born, we begin to create our quality worlds, which contain pictures in our minds of the people, things, and beliefs most important to us in meeting our unique need-strength profiles. Since these pictures are unique, they represent each person's take on reality (Brickell, 2007; Wubbolding, 2010; Wubbolding & Brickell, 1999). As some examples, these pictures might include the life partner we want, the car we want to buy, and a religious belief to which we want to adhere. If the individual is able to choose behaviors that match the pictures in his or her quality world, that person will satisfy one or more of the five needs and feel content, at least for a short period of time. The quality world does not have a moral base to it; it simply provides us pictures of what we want. These pictures can and do

---

B o x 11.2   Interview with a Hit Man

Here is a portion of an interview between a mob hit man, Richard Kuklinski, and psychiatrist Dr. Dietz in which we see Dr. Dietz responding to Mr. Kuklinski's question regarding why he viciously murdered over two hundred people. Similar to how a helper who practices reality therapy might respond, the psychiatrist suggests that Mr. Kuklinski's personality was not destined, but developed as a result of the parenting style he received.

> But the fact that you're born with a genetic predisposition toward fearlessness doesn't mean that it's inevitable for you to become a criminal, because some people who have the genetic predisposition toward fearlessness become pro-social

risk takers. They do things like drive racecars, test-fly planes, [become] fighter pilots, bomb disposal technicians. Those are all jobs where it helps to have a lot of fearlessness and in fact, some people in law enforcement are brave and have that same capacity to be fearless.... If you raise a kid with love and kindness and affection most of the time you have got a good shot at their growing up to be a decent, caring, loving human being, and treating their own kids well. But if you raise a kid the way Stanley [Kuklinski's father] raised you, with no love, no affection, constant abuse, beatings for no reason, all you teach is hatred.

SOURCE: HBO. The Iceman Interviews. Dr. Park Dietz with Richard Kuklinski, 2003.

---

change throughout one's lifetime, and pictures that previously satisfied us can remain in our minds for long periods of time and can sometimes become a source of pain if we cannot satisfy them. For instance, it can take a long time to rid oneself of the image of a lover who has left when this person symbolizes the satisfaction of certain needs in a person's quality world.

Central to reality therapy is the idea that our **total behavior** is chosen and generated from within in an effort to match the pictures in our quality worlds. By total behavior, Glasser means our actions, our thinking process, our feelings, and our physiological responses. Glasser goes on to state that we can only choose our actions and thoughts, which are jointly called **doing**, and that our feelings and our physiology result from those choices. Keep in mind, however, that feelings and physiology can be motivating in the sense that they can affect the kinds of actions and thoughts made; thus, the four elements are considered inseparable.

Glasser suggests that the language a person uses is reflective of how that person makes choices in an attempt to meet his or her needs (Glasser, W., & Glasser, C., 1999). **Internal-control language** is accepting, respectful, and supportive of others, and reflects a person who is clear about the choices that will best meet his or her needs. Contrast this with **external-control language**, which is blaming, critical, and threatening of others, and reflects a person who has not learned how to make choices that best meet his or her needs. These individuals tend to spend energy trying to control others and see their lives as controlled by others and by events. However, because external control is all that they know, they have "chosen" the best they can. Those who come to counseling are often struggling with language and behaviors that reflect external control, which was generally adopted from the environment to which they were exposed as they grew up (Wubbolding, 2000) (see Box 11.2). Therefore, one role of the counselor is to provide an atmosphere conducive to teaching about internal control and **choice** and to help clients broaden the behaviors they generate in an effort to satisfy the pictures in their quality worlds.

Since language reflects how a person makes choices, Glasser has long suggested that clients and others use language that more clearly reflects the fact that we choose our behaviors. For instance, instead of saying something like "My depression is making me sleep all the time," or "I have a mental illness that has stopped me from working," or "My anger makes my blood pressure go up," Glasser suggests that individuals say such things as, "I am depressing myself and choosing to sleep much of the time," "I make myself mentally ill and choose not to work," and "I anger myself and make my blood pressure rise." The use of language that clearly shows that a person is responsible for his or her state in life is in conflict with the contemporary view held by many in mainstream psychiatry that suggests that mental disorders are the result of some intrinsic, organically based problem (e.g., genetic differences in brain function) or that individuals are determined by such things as early childhood experiences.

As you can probably tell, Glasser's approach is **anti-deterministic**, because at any point in life, a person can evaluate his or her total behaviors and learn how to make new choices that better matches his or her quality world and need-strength profile. And, since Glasser believes that needs can only be satisfied in the **here and now**, the approach is focused mostly on the present. Even if an individual had been traumatized and learned maladaptive ways of behaving in an attempt to meet his or her needs, that person can learn new ways of choosing that can lead to more effective satisfaction of needs. Generally, people can learn these new ways of choosing through the development of relationships that are accepting, loving, and caring, such as one might find in therapy. Such relationships teach internal-control language, how to make better choices, and how to best match one's quality world.

As you read this view of human nature, you may be wondering why this approach is considered cognitive–behavioral, and not existential–humanistic—and you would be correct in questioning why it is in this section. Clearly, this approach has a cognitive bent, as it focuses on people's perceptions of their quality worlds. It also has a strong behavioral focus, as it spends much time on finding new behaviors that are better at meeting needs in one's quality world. However, it clearly has an existential orientation, with its focus on the present and its emphasis on choice. So, you can see how it is somewhat arbitrarily placed in this section, and if you think this approach fits better elsewhere, you could have a strong argument for moving it. For now, we'll keep it here.

KEY CONCEPTS

Glasser continually adapted his approach to the practice of reality therapy as he massaged the philosophical underpinnings of his theory. Today, Glasser views choice theory as the basis to the practice of reality therapy (Glasser, 2001; The William Glasser Institute, 2009b). This section of the chapter reviews key concepts of choice theory, and the next two sections, on therapeutic techniques and the therapeutic process, will examine how reality therapy applies these concepts.

Choice Theory

Choice theory is the theoretical foundation for the practice of reality therapy. Therefore, when conducting reality therapy, therapists will often explain choice theory to their clients, the ten main principles of which are listed below. For the most part, these principles are an outgrowth of five concepts, which are central to the understanding of reality therapy and will be discussed in the rest of this section: basic needs, internal control, choice, quality world, and total behavior.

The Ten Axioms of Choice Theory

1. The only person whose behavior we can control is our own.

2. All we can give another person is information.

3. All long-lasting psychological problems are relationship problems.

4. The problem relationship is always part of our present life.

5. What happened in the past has everything to do with what we are today, but we can only satisfy our basic needs right now and plan to continue satisfying them in the future.

6. We can only satisfy our needs by satisfying the pictures in our Quality World.

7. All we do is behave.

8. All behavior is Total Behavior and is made up of four components: acting, thinking, feeling, and physiology.

9. All Total Behavior is chosen, but we only have direct control over the acting and thinking components. We can only control our feeling and physiology indirectly through how we choose to act and think.

10. All Total Behavior is designated by verbs and named by the part that is the most recognizable. (The William Glasser Institute, 2009c)

Basic Needs.   Five needs have been identified by Glasser as critical to human functioning, including **survival** (sometimes called **self-preservation**), **love and belonging**, **power** (sometimes called **inner control**), **freedom** (frequently referred to as **independence**), and **fun** (or **enjoyment**). Glasser hypothesizes that survival was the original need, with the other four needs spinning off from it. Today, all are basic to our ability to thrive in productive ways. Glasser also suggests that each of us has a specific need-strength profile that is based on our genetics, and that the kinds of choices we make to meet our needs defines our personality.

Needs can conflict with one another. For instance, my need to feel a sense of belonging with my family is sometimes in conflict with my need for power that I fulfill through my writing, and I sometimes feel conflicted about whether I should work (write) or spend time with my family. Which needs we satisfy are basic to the kinds of choices we make from moment to moment, help define who we are, and are important to whether we feel content. As you read about the needs, consider *your* specific need-strength profile, how you go about meeting your needs, and which needs of yours compete with one another.

Box 11.3   The Seven Caring Habits and the Seven Deadly Habits

Caring Habits	Deadly Habits
supporting	criticizing
encouraging	blaming
listening	complaining
accepting	nagging
trusting	threatening
respecting	punishing
negotiating differences	bribing

Survival (self-preservation).   Survival is basic to our existence and includes survival of the species through sex and self-preservation by ensuring we have food, shelter, safety, and health. To live in a civilized world, the mechanisms we use to survive have had to be managed in ways to ensure mutual survival. Thus, we recognize that harming others is usually not the best mechanism to ensure our own survival, as it will generally bring the wrath of others upon us. Glasser (1998) suggests that the other four needs separated from the survival need because they increased the likelihood of survival. Thus, those who can successfully, love, be powerful, enjoy freedom, and have fun are more likely to survive.

Love and Belonging.   As humans evolved, building relationships with one another to ensure that we could mutually survive, and even thrive, became ever more important. Today, in developed countries, the survival needs of most individuals are mostly met. However, the need for love and belonging is often the one need with which people struggle the most. And if this need is not fulfilled, it is difficult to fulfill the other three needs of power, freedom, and fun, because these needs generally involve relationships. Thus, one major focus of reality therapy is to help clients examine how they are fulfilling their relationships needs.

Glasser (2007) and Van Nuys (2007) suggest that one goal of reality therapy is to help clients build relationships modeled on the **seven caring habits** while avoiding the **seven deadly habits** (see Box 11.3). Such relationships can be an anchor for clients and gives them the strength to examine which of theirs needs are not being satisfied.

Although most of us may not be masters at displaying the seven caring habits, our ability to practice at least some of these behaviors allows us to accomplish tasks with colleagues, enjoy our friendships, and love our partners. In intimate relationships, our ability to love becomes intertwined with sexual love, which is related to the need for survival. And, sometimes the inability to exhibit the caring habits leads to distress in our love relationships although our sexual desires may continue. This can lead to difficulties in our relationships (e.g., affairs, "faking" love to have sex, etc.). Thus, the ability to embrace and exhibit caring habits and build strong bonds with our partners is critical if we are to maintain honest, caring, loving, sexual relationships with our partners.

Power (inner control).   Animals, including humans, use power to ensure attainment of basic needs, such as food, shelter, and sometimes sex. However, this brute force use of power is more closely related to the survival need, in contrast to the uniquely human quality of "power for the sake of power" (Glasser, 1998, p. 37). Wubbolding and Brickell (1999) suggest that power is similar to the French word *pouvoir*, which means "to be able or capable." Power comes from within, and we alone can control it. In this sense, it is related to the ability of one to have "a sense of empowerment, worthiness, self-efficacy, and achievement" (Wubbolding & Brickell, 1999, p. 8). Power is motivating, and can be used for the good of the individual and for the good of all. Power of this kind is felt by the person who attempts to beat his or her personal record, by the individual who competes with others, and by the person who strives to discover something new or accomplish a difficult personal goal. Power such as this has been the motivating force for exploring the solar system and for the invention of a multitude of products that have led to the betterment of all societies. On the other hand, as you well know, power is easily abused, such as the autocratic leader who commits genocide, the corrupt Wall Street broker who uses illegal means to attain money, and the teacher who takes pride in failing his or her students to "show them" the results of not "properly" achieving. Power can be life-sustaining and creative, and can help us feel good about ourselves, or it can be destructive and life-threatening.

Freedom (independence).   Freedom is the ability to do what we want when we want as long as it does not interfere with someone else's ability to do what he or she wants when he or she wants. Glasser (1998) suggests that the enemy of freedom is when one tries to control another, and that true freedom follows the **Golden Rule**, whose universality can be found in many cultures and religions (see Table 11.1).

Many see freedom and independence as a basic human right as reflected in a democracy. Such freedom allows us to express ourselves in any way that we wish, as long as we respect our interdependence (e.g., not yelling "fire" in a crowded movie theatre, stopping at red lights, vaccinating our children to ensure that we are all safe). Freedom promotes creativity, for if we are free to experiment with different ways of being in the world, we allow ourselves to be imaginative and inventive. People who allow themselves personal freedom are rarely selfish and generally share their creativity easily and readily with others. Personal freedom is particularly important in choice theory, as it reminds us that we freely choose all of our behaviors and are ultimately the makers of our own destiny.

Fun (enjoyment).   Stating that "fun is best defined by laughter" (Glasser, 1998, p. 41), Glasser also believes that fun is a learning process. Our innate ability to laugh and have fun is seen in the infant, as he or she laughs at a smiley face or at a new task not before undertaken. Adults have fun, especially when they love, as

TABLE 11.1   The Golden Rule

Religion	Source	Statement
Christianity	Luke 6:31	Do to others as you would have them do to you.
	Matthew 7:12	So in everything, do to others what you would have them do to you, for this sums up the Law and the Prophets.
Islam	The Hadith	No one of you is a believer until he desires for his Brother that which he desires for himself.
Judaism	The Talmud, Shabbat 31a	What is hateful to you, do not do to your fellow men. This is the entire Law; all the rest is commentary.
Hinduism	The Mahabharata	This is the sum of duty: do naught to others which if done to thee would cause thee pain.
Baha'i Faith	Epistle to the Son of the Wolf	And if thine eyes be turned towards justice, choose thou for thy neighbor that which thou choosest for thyself.
Confucianism	Analects 15:23	Tsekung asked, "Is there one word that can serve as a principle of conduct for life?" Confucius replied, "It is the word *shu*—reciprocity: Do not do to others what you do not want them to do to you."
	Mencius VII.A.4	Try your best to treat others as you would wish to be treated yourself, and you will find that this is the shortest way to benevolence.
Zoroastrianism	Shayas-na-Shayas 12:29	Whatever is disagreeable to yourself do not do unto others.

SOURCE: Johnson, D.W. (2003). *Reaching out: Interpersonal effectiveness and self-actualization* (8th ed.). New York: Allyn & Bacon. p. 379.

they allow one another to try new ways of being with one another and experiment together with new activities in the world. Lack of fun, suggests Glasser, is a symbol of a relationship's souring.

Fun and enjoyment can be obtained in countless ways. It is experienced when we read something interesting and novel, or when we feel a sense of satisfaction as we slowly master a new sport and later experience the joy of playing it. It is felt in the laughter we experience over a new amusement park ride or when we make sense of a joke. And fun is apparent when we feel a sense of curious joy as we discover how a new electronic device works and take pleasure in its use. We continually experience the fun and joy involved in the process of uncovering new ideas, learning new tasks, or discovering new things about other people, and our lives would be stagnant if this were not the case.

Internal Control.   From the moment we are born, choice theory asserts, how we feel is a reflection of the behaviors we choose in our attempts to satisfy our needs (Glasser, 2001). Unfortunately, many of us erroneously believe that external

---

B o x 11.4   External Control and the Abusive Spouse

Abusive spouses/partners have erroneously learned, generally from their abusive parents, that external factors are the cause of a person's happiness in life. As their parents unsuccessfully attempted to live more satisfying lives by controlling each other and their children, they unknowingly and mistakenly taught their children to believe that controlling others would lead to a more satisfying life. So, when their children grow and eventually partner, a cycle of abuse begins where one spouse/partner emotionally or physically abuses the other spouse/partner in an attempt to get his or her needs met. Sometimes, these behaviors result in the abused spouse/partner acting in accord to the other's wishes. However, this leaves the abused spouse/partner feeling resentful toward the other spouse/partner and extremely unlikely to want to build a relationship with him or her. Such resentment, of course, prevents a sense of love and belonging, and this important need is not fully met through the relationship. In contrast, consider the couple who allow each other to make choices about what each of them wants. Although each person's immediate needs will not always be satisfied by the other, in the long run, partners will feel more loving toward each other as they recognize the freedom they have been given.

---

factors control our behaviors and are responsible for how we feel. These individuals believe that when the doorbell rings, the ringing causes them to answer the door, instead of believing that the ringing provides them information to which they can respond. These individuals blame their negative feelings on such things as a "mental disorder" or identify them as the result of someone else's behaviors. "If only I was not depressed," or, "If only she would act differently," or, "If only my parents were nicer," are the mantras these individuals live by.

In contrast, those who live by an **internal-control** philosophy thoughtfully and actively choose their behaviors, considering all along how their choices will affect fulfillment of their needs, how they will feel, and how their actions will affect others. The language they use is also reflective of this internal orientation. For instance, instead of saying, "I can't," these individuals might say "I won't." Or, instead of saying "I'm too depressed to go out," these people might say, "I am depressing myself and choosing not to go out." Or, instead of saying, "He makes me crazy," these persons might say, "I make myself crazy whenever I'm around him." Learning to identify the language of external control and changing one's language to reflect internal control and choice is one of the goals of counseling using choice theory (Glasser, 2001; Glasser, W., & Glasser, C., 1999; Wubbolding, 2000) (see Box 11.4).

> … [I]f our behaviors are chosen, it is inaccurate to describe them by using nouns and adjectives. To be accurate, verbs are the only part of speech that should be used to describe behavior. For example, the commonly used terms *depression* (a noun) or *depressed* (an adjective) are inaccurate. Following choice theory, we would use the verb forms *depressing* (a gerund) or choosing *to depress* (an infinitive). (Glasser, 2001, p. 25)

In relationships, people who live by an **external-control** philosophy will often blame, criticize, bribe, complain, punish, be passive–aggressive, torture, or in other ways try to manipulate others in an attempt to change the external factors they believe are the cause of their unhappiness (see "seven deadly habits," Box 11.3).

However, such attempts at controlling friends, colleagues, lovers, and others results in relationships marked by control issues and power disparities, and relationships that lack the caring that can come from allowing a person to be himself or herself (Glasser, W., & Glasser, C., 2007; Van Nuys, 2007). On the other hand, those who live by a philosophy of internal control embody the seven caring habits (see Box 11.3), habits that are incompatible with the use of coercion. These habits build thoughtful and caring relationships that are more likely to result in mutual understanding and a sense of love and belonging with others. Such relationships are also the basis for the satisfaction of our other needs.

Choice

All we do from birth to death is behave, and every behavior is chosen. (Glasser, W., & Glasser, C., p. 24)

Of course, basic to choice theory is the idea that we are constantly making choices that lead to a range of behaviors resulting in anything from satisfaction to dysfunctional ways of living in the world. However, reality therapy's definition of **choice** is carefully nuanced. For instance, Wubbolding (2000) stresses the fact that choice means that "behavior is generated from within the person for the purpose of need satisfaction" (p. 67), that all behaviors are treated as choices, and that there is a difference between the kinds of "choices" an infant makes and the kinds of choices an adult makes.

[Infants] send out their best signal to the persons in the external world, that is, their immediate environment, in an attempt to get what they want relative to their needs. As children grow and develop language, they discover through their creative behavioral system that other behaviors are available.... They choose to attempt these behaviors at appropriate developmental and maturational points as more effective ways to fulfill their needs.... As a person grows and develops, choices become more conscious and explicit and adults become more clearly aware of choices. (Wubbolding, 2000, pp. 66–67)

Because many of us have learned the language of external control, lack of awareness of the choices that lead to self-destructive behaviors is common. Although making the best choices they know how to make, these individuals choose poorly, usually because they had significant people in their lives who modeled external control, and they have subsequently grown to believe that one's fate is not in one's hands. Put simply, in their attempts to control others, they have not made good choices for themselves. Highlighting this point, Wubbolding (2000) notes that people only choose "the good or the apparent good" (p. 67). In other words, what is a seemingly a good choice for many is actually a choice that is entrenched in a world of external control and results in the attempted manipulation of others. Such individuals end up depressing themselves, angering themselves, making themselves neurotic or psychotic, and so forth, all the while believing that it is not their doing.

Due to the fact that reality therapy is anti-deterministic and forward-looking, helpers who practice this approach believe that individuals can relatively quickly learn

---

B o x 11.5   Can the Abusive Partner/Spouse Change?

Go back and re-read Box 11.4. Do you think an abusive spouse/partner can give up his or her external control language and adopt new, caring habits? If you think this person can, you are a prime candidate to be a reality therapist.

---

that they have been choosing behaviors built on the fallacious belief that external control works. And, they also know that once the language of internal control is learned, clients can begin to make more effective choices. At any point in one's life, reality therapy maintains that one can choose to build new relationships anchored in internal control and based on respect and caring (see the seven caring habits in Box 11.3). Such relationships have the ingredients for individuals to make positive choices in their lives—choices that bring need satisfaction (see Box 11.5).

> William Glasser tells us with absolute clarity that happiness and fulfill-ment depend on the quality of our relationships, that choice determines the kinds of relationships we have and will have, and that controlling others is not the way to get what we want. (Glasser, 2001, p. xii)

Quality World.   From birth, each of us has a model or pictures in our mind of what the world would look like if our needs were satisfied. Called our **quality world** (Glasser, 1998), the pictures in it reflect what is important to us and what we most desire or want, including "(1) the *people* we most want to be with, (2) the *things* we most want to own or experience, and (3) the *ideas or systems* of belief that govern much of our behavior" (p. 45).

> All day long our minds drift back and forth to the images in our quality worlds; we can't get them off our minds. Examples of these pictures are the new homes we are saving for; the new jobs we want so much; the good grades that are so important to our future; the men and women we plan to marry; and our sick children, who are recovering their health. For alcoholics, the image is the alcohol they crave so much; for gamblers, the run at the crap table that is always on their minds; for revolutionaries, a new political system to replace the one they hate so much, and for religious people, the picture of heaven or paradise in which they hope to spend eternity. (Glasser, 1998, p. 45)

The people, things, and ideas that have emerged in our quality worlds are based on our unique need-strength profiles and the ways in which we have been taught to meet our needs. There is no moral base to the quality world; it simply wants what it wants. If we have learned how to make choices using an internal-control philosophy, our language will reflect the seven caring habits and we will make smart choices that directly meet our needs. However, if we have learned to make choices based on external-control philosophy, our choices will be mired in control issues, because we see our lives as being directed by outside forces. These individuals will try to manipulate these outside forces (e.g., a lover, a colleague) in an effort to get their needs met. These choices do not bode well for relationships or long-term satisfaction of needs.

Changing pictures in one's quality world is not easy, because they are based on our limited knowledge of the world and generally represent the only way individuals have learned to meet their needs. However, in contrast to our genetically based need-strength profile, pictures are not an inherent aspect of who we are and, with effort and new knowledge, old pictures can be discarded and new ones established to meet the same needs the old pictures had served. For instance, a person who has not learned how to develop loving relationships may become a drug addict, using a drug to feel a false sense of "love" in his or her life. This person needs to discard the picture of the drug currently in his or her quality world, learn how to develop relationships that will bring him or her a sense of love and belonging, and develop new pictures that will reflect this new way of being in the world. In addition, sometimes, pictures that were placed in one's quality world become obsolete and no longer serve a need-satisfying function. In fact, pictures in one's quality world can become painful. For instance, the picture of my mom making me dinner, which used to motivate me to find ways of being with her so that I could satisfy my need for love and belonging, remains in my quality world despite the fact that she is no longer alive. Unless I modify or remove this picture, I will feel depressed because I can no longer choose behaviors to make this happen. Can you think of things I can do to modify or remove this picture?

Understanding the quality world of the client is critical to helping the client find ways of most effectively meeting his or her needs and to help the client discover those pictures that may no longer be serving a need-satisfying purpose.

Total Behavior. When helpers who use reality therapy use the word "behavior," they are almost always referring to what they call **total behavior**, which is composed of four elements: acting, thinking, feeling, and our physiology. Reality therapy maintains that we can only choose how we act and think (which they call **doing**), and that we generally have more control over our actions than our thinking (Wubbolding, personal communication, May 10, 2009). Reality therapy also asserts that our feelings and our physiology are the result of how we act and think. However, even though one cannot actively choose feelings and physiology, they are factors related to the kinds of actions one takes and thoughts one has. Therefore, there are intimate relationships among our actions, thoughts, feelings, and physiology; that is, our actions, thoughts, feelings, and physiological responses all impact one another (see Box 11.6). Certainly, this makes some intuitive sense. If I'm depressed and lethargic and I suddenly decide to start going to an aerobics class, I am *doing* something different. My actions are changed, what I think about will be different, my feelings will likely be affected in a positive way, and as my blood pumps rapidly through my system, my physiology will be affected on multiple levels. Thus, in counseling, if we want to change how we feel and if we want to affect our physiology, we must do something different—which entails making new and better choices about how we act and think.

B o x 11.6   The Inseparability of Our Actions, Thoughts, Feelings, and Physiology

Consider the possible interconnections among actions, thoughts, feelings, and physiology for a depressed person. For instance, what might some typical behaviors be of a person who is depressed? What kinds of "self-talk" might that person have? What kind of feelings will that person tend to have? Discuss the possible implications that acting, thinking, and feeling in those ways will have on a depressed person's physiology. Be as specific as possible. When you have finished, discuss the other people listed.

- a person with obsessive-compulsive disorder
- a person with a thought disorder (e.g., "diagnosed" as schizophrenic)
- a person who is "bipolar"
- a person who is a compulsive liar
- a content person
- a person who is competitive at work and has little concern for how he or she outdoes others

---

The Relationships among Key Concepts of Choice Theory.   As you can tell by Glasser's ten axioms as well as your reading, the key concepts of choice theory are interrelated. Figure 11.1 offers a visual representation of many of these concepts and graphically shows how they fit together.

THERAPEUTIC TECHNIQUES

Today, a common method of training reality therapists is the **WDEP system** developed by Bob Wubbolding (Wubbolding, 2000; Wubbolding & Brickell, 1999). This system stands for **w**ants of the client, what the client is **d**oing in his or her life's direction, **e**valuating if what the client is doing is working, and developing a **p**lan of action that can be implemented. Wubbolding suggests that for a client to effectively involve himself or herself in the WDEP cycle, the helper must be firm, friendly, and fair and build a strong therapeutic relationship based on trust and hope (see Figure 11.2). This is accomplished by the counselor's demonstrating the techniques and embodying the attitudes of what Wubbolding calls the **environmental elements**, which includes exhibiting the 25 "**tonics of the counseling relationship**" and avoiding the 8 "**toxins of the counseling relationship**" (see Figure 11.2). The following describes these environmental elements while the next section of the book, on therapeutic processes, describes the actual WDEP cycle.

Environmental Elements

Tonics of the Counseling (See Figure 11.2)
Attending Behaviors. This basic counseling skill includes paraphrasing what the client has said, tracking client nonverbals, and showing through body language that the counselor has heard the client. Other typical attending skills include having an open body stance, maintaining good eye contact, and showing a sense of interest through one's facial features.

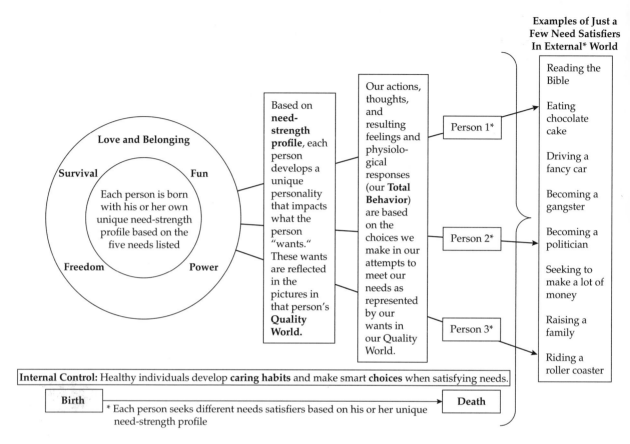

F I G U R E 11.1   Relationships among Internal Control, Needs, Quality World, Wants, Choices, Total Behaviors, and External World

AB-CDE.   Wubbolding and Brickell (1999) suggest that helpers should **a**lways **b**e **c**onsistent, **c**ourteous, and **c**alm; be **d**etermined that there will be a positive outcome, and **e**nthusiastic about the client's future.

Suspend Judgment.   When therapists convey an accepting and nonjudgmental attitude, clients feel free to discuss deeper thoughts and feelings and are more likely to understand the kinds of debilitating choices they have made. Wubbolding and Brickell (1999) also note that within this nonjudgmental framework, counselors should be able to share thoughts with their clients about how some of their behaviors may not be healthy (e.g., a substance abuser, a person with anger management issues).

Do the Unexpected.   Doing the unexpected can motivate clients. So, for the depressed client, a counselor suddenly might say, "Tell me the time you last laughed out loud." After the client's response, the client is asked to see if he can make that happen again. Another counselor might suddenly ask a client with agoraphobia to go for a walk with the counselor on a busy street. Sometimes associated with the technique of paradoxical intention (prescribing the symptom to induce change), doing the unexpected can have unexpected positive responses.

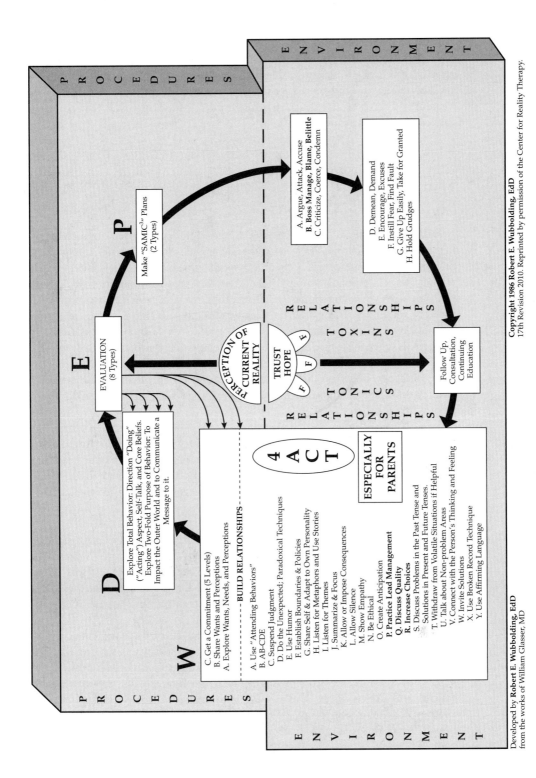

Procedures: Build Relationships

C. Get a Commitment (5 Levels)
B. Share Wants and Perceptions
A. Explore Wants, Needs, and Perceptions

- - - - - - BUILD RELATIONSHIPS - - - - -

A. Use "Attending Behaviors"
B. AB-CDE
C. Suspend Judgment
D. Do the Unexpected; Paradoxical Techniques
E. Use Humor
F. Establish Boundaries & Policies
G. Share Self & Adapt to Own Personality
H. Listen for Metaphors and Use Stories
I. Listen for Themes
J. Summarize & Focus
K. Allow or Impose Consequences
L. Allow Silence
M. Show Empathy
N. Be Ethical
O. Create Anticipation
P. Practice Lead Management
Q. Discuss Quality
R. Increase Choices
S. Discuss Problems in the Past Tense and Solutions in Present and Future Tenses.
T. Withdraw from Volatile Situations if Helpful
U. Talk about Non-problem Areas
V. Connect with the Person's Thinking and Feeling
W. Invite Solutions
X. Use Broken Record Technique
Y. Use Affirming Language

4 A C T

ESPECIALLY FOR PARENTS

EVALUATION (8 Types)

Explore Total Behavior: Direction "Doing" ("Acting") Aspect, Self-Talk, and Core Beliefs. Explore Two-Fold Purpose of Behavior: To Impact the Outer World and to Communicate a Message to it.

Make "SAMIC³" Plans (2 Types)

PERCEPTION OF CURRENT REALITY

TRUST HOPE

RELATIONSHIPS FATOXIONS

RELATIONSHIPS FATOXIONS

A. Argue, Attack, Accuse
B. Boss Manage, Blame, **Belittle**
C. Criticize, Coerce, Condemn

D. Demean, Demand
E. Encourage, Excuses
F. Instill Fear, Find Fault
G. Give Up Easily, Take for Granted
H. Hold Grudges

Follow Up, Consultation, Continuing Education

PROCEDURES

ENVIRONMENT

Developed by Robert E. Wubbolding, EdD
from the works of William Glasser, MD

Copyright 1986 Robert E. Wubbolding, EdD
17th Revision 2010. Reprinted by permission of the Center for Reality Therapy.

FIGURE 11.2 Cycle of Psychotherapy, Counseling, Coaching, Managing, and Supervising

Use Humor.   Humor that is "good-natured and never sarcastic, critical or patro-nizing" (Wubbolding & Brickell, 1999, p. 20) can go far in building a relationship and motivating a client to work on change. Although clearly a technique that should be used carefully (e.g., one does not use humor when a client is discussing the death of a loved one), humor is a skill that counselors can use to their advantage.

Establish Boundaries.   Letting clients know about the rules of the counseling relationship, such as through an informed consent statement, can help clarify what can and cannot be done in counseling and helps define the limits of the relationship as clients work toward change.

Share Self and Adapt to Own Personality.   Although certain aspects of a counselor's life are clearly off-limits, there are times when self-disclosure can strengthen the relationship. For instance, if a client is a sports enthusiast, and so is the counselor, talking about a particular sport might strengthen the relationship. Self-disclosure can also involve giving honest feedback to the client. For instance, the reality therapist might say to the addict: "Clearly, shooting heroine is not good for you. This behavior is not getting you what you want." Or, paraphrasing Glasser, "It is congruent with the principles of reality therapy for someone to tell the blind person that he or she cannot become an airline pilot" (Wubbolding, 2000, p. 148). Lastly, sharing oneself occurs in unique ways and is dependent on the personality style of the helper. Counselors need to know their own style of relating and use what works for them.

Listen for Metaphors and Stories.   A client's quality world is often represented by the metaphors and stories told to the counselor. For instance, a counselor might discuss a client's unmet love and belonging needs after the client states, "I keep trying to work on my marriage, but I feel like I'm a turtle in its shell, afraid to come out."

Listen for Themes.   Like listening for metaphors, a good ear can give insight into the client's world. For instance, when a client tells the counselor, "My kids only want me to help them with their homework," and, "My wife just sees me as a person to fix things around the house," and, "Even fishing is boring these days," the client might be saying, "I am not having fun in my life."

Summarize and Focus.   Summarizing and focusing all of what the client has told the counselor can help clients see the kinds of needs and wants that are not being fulfilled and can also help to reinforce new choices clients have made or will make. For instance, a counselor might say, "As I listen to you today, I hear the control and power issues you're having in many of your relationships." Or, another counselor might say, "You know, you have really worked hard and I hear what progress you have made toward building solid relationships in your life."

Allow or Impose Consequences.   Allowing a client to experience consequences of behaviors can raise consciousness about how destructive certain behaviors have been. For instance, a client's lover may be enabling the client's drinking by hiding alcohol and making excuses for the client who is consistently late to work. Having the client experience the consequences of his or her behavior (e.g., hitting bottom) can "push" the client toward working on the problem behaviors. Allowing or imposing consequences is often used in institutional settings (e.g., schools) to help students understand how their behaviors can be destructive.

Allow Silence.   Silence is golden, as it allows clients to hear themselves, reflect on what they are saying, and consider the consequences of their behaviors. Finally, it allows clients to think about new ways of acting.

Show Empathy.   Empathy is hearing the client fully, understanding deep, sometimes unexpressed feelings, and seeing the complexity of themes related to what the client is saying. From a reality therapy perspective, empathy is also understanding "where the client can be in the future" (Wubbolding, personal communication, May 10, 2009). Using empathy can help clients understand their needs and wants before they develop new ways of living in the world.

Be Ethical.   All counselors should practice ethical behaviors in their counseling relationships. Wubbolding and Brickell (1999) suggest that some of the more important ethical issues for helpers who practice reality therapy are making sure they include professional disclosure statements, obtaining informed consent, and ensuring that they avoid dual relationships.

Create Anticipation and Hope.   Therapists who use reality therapy enter the relationship with optimism and a sense that clients can and will change. This sense of anticipation and hope can be seen in both the verbal and nonverbal communication of the helper and is contagious as it instills optimism and a desire for change in the client.

Practice Lead Management, Discuss Quality, and Increase Choices.   These three elements are particularly important when using reality therapy in organizations (e.g., schools, workplaces, etc.). These qualities speak to the importance of having a leader in the setting who is nonauthoritarian and noncoercive, and who encourages an atmosphere that is respectful, democratic, participatory, transparent, and appreciative of differentness, and one in which there is a sense that individuals have choices concerning their behaviors.

Discuss Problems in the Past Tense and Solutions in Present and Future Tenses.   Focusing on the past tends to mire one in past symptoms and complaints. Thus, reality therapists tend to focus on the present and the future. Although it may sometimes be prudent to focus on the past in an effort to strengthen the relationship, generally, the focus on therapy should be on changing behaviors that are currently preventing the client from getting what he or she wants and needs.

Withdraw from Volatile Situations If Helpful.   Some problems have no easy solutions and clients may try to draw the counselor into an issue that cannot be resolved. It is best to avoid such situations, and instead, help clients focus on problems that have solutions and needs that can be met.

Talk About Non-Problem Areas.   Like withdrawing from volatile situations, sometimes it's prudent not to talk about problems, as "problem talk" sometimes leads to an ongoing focus on the problem as opposed to a focus on fixing the problem.

Connect with the Person's Thinking and Feeling.   Reality therapists are encouraged to focus on thinking and feeling, while, at the same time, emphasizing how it is the behaviors that are preventing the client from thinking and feeling in ways that they want.

Invite Solutions.   Reality therapy is about finding solutions, not about focusing on the past or spending an inordinate amount of time focusing on problems. Thus, clients are invited to focus on how they can change their behaviors and find solutions to their problems.

Use the Broken-Record Technique.   Counselors should be committed to their clients and continually help them focus on directing their lives toward new ways of behaving that better meets their needs.

Use Affirming Language.   Be positive and affirm the work your client is doing in therapy.

Toxins of the Counseling Relationship

Elements to avoid. A number of behaviors can go far in destroying a therapeutic relationship and relationships in general. Based on external control, many of these behaviors are similar to those that Glasser highlights in his list of "seven deadly habits" (see Box 11.3). These behaviors should be avoided by counselors and clients alike. Wubbolding use the acronym "**ABCDEFGH**" when discussing each of the following attitudes and behaviors, almost all of which need little explanation (see Figure 11.2):

Avoid <u>a</u>rguing, <u>a</u>ttacking, or <u>a</u>ccusing	Don't encourage <u>e</u>xcuses
Don't <u>b</u>oss manage, <u>b</u>lame, or <u>b</u>elittle*	Don't instill <u>f</u>ear or Find <u>f</u>ault
Don't <u>c</u>riticize, <u>c</u>oerce, or <u>c</u>ondemn	Don't <u>g</u>ive up easily or take for <u>g</u>ranted
Don't <u>d</u>emean or <u>d</u>emand	Don't <u>h</u>old grudges

*Often used to explain behaviors in business and in schools by those in power. However, a therapist or a client should also not be bossy, blaming, or belittling.

THERAPEUTIC PROCESS

By demonstrating the techniques and embodying the attitudes highlighted in the environmental elements, clients should be able to successfully involve themselves in the WDEP cycle. Remember, the acronym stands for the <u>w</u>ants of the client, what the client is **d**oing in his or her life's **d**irection, **e**valuating if what the client is doing is working, and developing a **p**lan of action that can be implemented (see Figure 11.2). The following describes each aspect of this cycle. Let's examine it in a little more detail.

Implementing the WDEP System

(W) Discovering Wants.   In this part of the cycle, counselors are interested in clients fully understanding the kinds of wants in their quality worlds. Typically, counselors will first teach clients about the quality world and how wants become associated with it, discuss issues related to these concepts, and suggest reading materials to elaborate on them. As clients slowly begin to understand the concepts of the quality world and wants, they are better able to identify their unique wants, which are based, if you remember, on the client's individual need-strength profile. Some questions that can be used to clarify client wants include:

- We talked about your "quality world" and the kinds of wants that the pictures represent. Can you tell me some of the wants in your world?
- What do you think are some of your most important wants in life?
- What kind of wants do you believe motivate you to do things?
- What is it that you want for your _____?

For the last question, Wubbolding (2000, p. 99) suggests that clients specifically be asked about wants in ten areas of their lives, including what they want for:

- themselves
- the world around them
- the therapy process itself
- parents, children, teachers, school
- spouse, partner
- job manger, supervisor, or co-workers
- friends, relatives
- associates or acquaintances
- religion/spirituality/higher power
- any institution that impinges upon their lives

These questions represent a few of the many different kinds of responses a counselor can make to help clients begin to understand their quality worlds and explore their wants. Other ways of exploring wants is through visualization, journaling, creative tasks (e.g., working with clay) and so forth.

As clients gain clarity about their quality worlds and their associated wants, they are in a better position to assess their levels of commitment to the therapeutic process. Wubbolding (2000) suggests that there are five levels of commitment that range from "I don't want to be here" to "I'll do whatever it takes." Clarity on commitment by both the client and the therapist will clearly affect how work in therapy proceeds.

(D) Analyzing the Direction in Which the Client is Moving and What the Client Is Doing to Get There.   After identifying wants in their clients' quality worlds, counselors can begin to ask their clients to describe what they are doing to fulfill their wants.

> So, when partners feel distant from one another, they are asked where they are headed: towards a better relationship or towards separation. The chemically dependent person can be asked, "If your use of drugs continues to increase at the current rate, where will you be in five years?" The student who refuses to study or who makes little attempt to get along in the school can be asked, "If you continue down this same pathway, where will you be at the end of the school year?" (Wubbolding & Brickell, 1999, p. 41)

It is at this point that clients begin to identify what they are doing to have their wants in their quality worlds fulfilled. For example, assuming that the first client states that he wants to have a better relationship, the second wants to stop using, and the third wants to do well in school, here are some examples of questions that can be asked to help clients identify how they are going about trying to have their wants fulfilled.

- *Client 1*: Can you describe your day to me and tell me what you did, or did not do, to make your relationship more of what you want it to be?

- *Client 2*: You're saying you're wanting to stop using; take me through your typical day and what you have done, or not done, to make yourself move in that direction.

- *Client 3*: So, school has not been working for you; tell me what a typical day looks like and what you do to make friends and to study.

(E) Self-Evaluation Techniques.
> The essential aspect of self-evaluation is a personal, inner judgment about behavior or "quality world" wants. (Wubbolding & Brickell, 1999, p. 45)

After identifying what clients are doing to have their wants fulfilled, they can begin the process of evaluating if what they are doing is working for them; that is, if what they are doing is successfully meeting their needs as identified by their wants in their quality world. For instance, the client who wants a better relationship with his lover might write in a journal all his interactions during one day with his lover, only to discover that he talks to her critically and does not find alone-time with her. The chemically dependent person might make a list of times she uses and who she is around, and realize that she spends more time around enablers than other people. And the student might write down all of the free times she has and the ways she interacts with other students, and find out

---

B o x 11.7   Select Techniques to Evaluate Whether Client Is Having Wants Fulfilled

1. **Asking the client specific questions**
   Counselors can ask clients to engage in evaluation of their behaviors by asking them specific questions, such as:
   a. "Is what you're doing working for you?"
   b. "Has that behavior been helpful in having your wants fulfilled?"
   c. "Have the choices you made moved you in the direction you've wanted to go in life?"
2. **Suggesting client do self-reflection**
   Clients can be asked to find time during the week to reflect on their lives and consider if what they are doing is working for them.
3. **Using a behavioral checklist**
   Clients can be given a behavioral checklist and check those behaviors which are positive and those which are negative in reference to getting their wants fulfilled.

4. **Using a "feeling word" checklist**
   Clients can be given a "feeling word" checklist and identify which feelings they have most often and examine what behaviors are associated with those feelings. Behaviors associated with negative feelings can be evaluated and new behaviors that lead to better feelings chosen.
5. **Monitoring thoughts**
   Clients can monitor and identify which thoughts are associated with particular actions and whether those specific thoughts are effective at getting their wants fulfilled.
6. **Physiological monitoring**
   Clients can be asked to take periodic blood pressure readings and note what actions or thoughts are associated with a rise or fall in blood pressure. High blood pressure readings may be associated with inefficient ways of having a specific want fulfilled.

---

that she spends little time studying and makes virtually no attempts to be friendly with fellow students.

There are an endless number of techniques that clients can use to help them examine if what they are doing is working for them. Although behaviors are often the easiest and most direct method of examining the effectiveness of meeting one's wants, thoughts, feelings, and physiological responses can also be used. Box 11.7 offers just a few examples of how clients can evaluate if what they are doing is working for them.

(P) Make Specific, Workable Plans.   As clients begin to focus on the changes they want to make, in collaboration with the counselor, they can develop a plan to change what they are doing. Wubbolding (2000) identifies three levels of planning: those initiated solely by the client, those developed with the counselor, and those developed by the counselor. Although all are acceptable, Wubbolding suggests that generally, those initiated solely by the client are most effective (see Figure 11.3).

Wubbolding (Wubbolding, 2000; Wubbolding & Brickell, 1999) suggests two types of plans: those that are linear and those that are paradoxical. **Linear plans** are to the point; they address the problem directly, and are often client-initiated. For instance, if a client wants to have a better relationship and finds that he is spending little time with his partner, a linear plan would be to focus directly on finding ways to make more time. **Paradoxical plans**, on the other hand, work with the problem indirectly and are generally counselor-initiated.

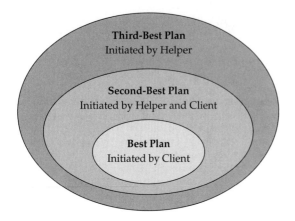

FIGURE 11.3 Effectiveness of Plans

SOURCE: Wubbolding, R. (2000). *Reality therapy for the 21st century*. Philadelphia, PA: Brunner-Routledge. p. 151.

Two types of paradoxical plans are **paradoxical intention** and **reframing** (Robbins, n.d.). As an example of paradoxical intention, an individual who is constantly worrying about others and therefore not able to build friendships, is told to spend more time worrying about others and to write down all of her worries. This has the effect of the client's realizing the ridiculousness of her problem. And for reframing, a mother who thinks her child is withdrawn is offered a reframe by her therapist when the therapist says, "Seems like your daughter is very self-reflective—maybe she'll make a good therapist some day." Although helpers practicing reality therapy tend to use linear plans more frequently than paradoxical plans, all can be helpful in assisting clients to change.

Plans come in many shapes and sizes, and whatever type of plan is decided upon needs to be workable. Wubbolding and Brickell (1999) use the acronym **SAMIC³** to examine whether a plan is workable (see Figure 11.2). Using this acronym, the plan should be:

S: *Simple* (unambiguous and clear)

A: *Attainable* (realistic and doable)

M: *Measurable* (exact and clear about when it will take place)

I: *Immediate* (completed as quickly as possible)

C: *Controlled* (the client is in the driver's seat)

C: *Consistent* (can be repeated if necessary)

C: *Committed* (client is dedicated to doing the plan)

Finally, it should be remembered that plans are not set in stone, but are a road map for how the client might change. If the plan is not effective, counselors should discuss with the client why it was not workable and, when necessary, help the client devise a new plan.

A Final Word about the WDEP System.   When using the WDEP system, it is important to remember that one can revisit any aspect of the cycle at any point in the change process. Thus, clients may want to suddenly take a new look at the

---

B o x 11.8   Dr. Gilchrist's Work with Todd

Read or watch Dr. Gilchrist's work with "Todd." Try to identify what aspects of the WDEP system Dr. Gilchrist used.

You can read this session by going to www.cengage.com/counseling/neukrug/CTP1e and click

"student downloads." Or your instructor may show this session in class with the DVD that accompanies his or her copy of the text.

---

wants, reexamine their direction and what they are doing, reevaluate their progress, or make new plans. Whatever clients decide to do, the therapist should be committed to the client and never give up helping the client make new choices that will lead to a life with greater satisfaction (see Box 11.8).

SOCIAL, CULTURAL, AND SPIRITUAL ISSUES

In a chapter entitled "Multicultural Dimensions in Reality Therapy," Wubbolding (2000) suggests that all helpers who practice reality therapy need to adapt to a diversity-sensitive approach when working with clients. In doing this, Wubbolding et al. (1998) offer a number of guidelines, including viewing the approach as flexible and adaptable based on the client's needs and culture; being sensitive to the client's worldview; knowing how the helper's attitudes, skills, and knowledge will affect the counseling relationship; and having a solid base in choice theory and reality therapy so that the therapist is facile in adapting the approach with different clients.

Wubbolding (2000) gives some examples of how reality therapy is adapted for diverse clients. For instance, recognizing that in Japanese culture the helper is revered and respected, the helper who works with a Japanese client can use this deference to facilitate delving into the quality world of the client. As another example, when talking with an Irish-Catholic American female who hesitatingly states that she no longer has sexual relations with her husband, a priest (who is also a counselor), uses a less direct response when he says, "You wouldn't want to talk about it, would you?" This indirect response has the result of allowing the woman to either talk about the problem or move on to something else. And, when working with Native Americans who are familiar and comfortable with medicine cards (pictures of animals with medicinal powers), the helper can use these cards to identify needs and clarify wants. Wubbolding and others (2004) also offer compelling evidence for the acceptance of this approach with different ethnic groups and in different settings, such as with African Americans and Koreans, and with juvenile delinquents in Hong Kong and residents in a correctional institution in Slovenia. Finally, Wubbolding (2000) also states that reality therapy is sensitive to the larger system from which the client comes. For instance, he states, "Reality therapy has evolved over the years to the point where it incorporates a systemic world view" (p. 179).

Despite the assertion that reality therapy views the client systematically, there is still a strong emphasis on how the client is choosing his or her current predicament. This is because reality therapy sees the construction of one's reality as an internal. In fact, Wubbolding (2000) states that regardless of the external pressures or even oppression, reality therapy always assumes that the individual has choices. This focus, some might argue, diminishes the negative impact that society has on minorities and women because it maintains that each person is responsible for the larger system, rather than saying that there are some aspects of larger systems over which we have little power and control. On the other hand, because reality therapy often will establish new systemic rules for organizations, such as schools, one could argue that the approach strongly advocates for its clients by making deep-rooted changes in how the system treats all of its clients.

Despite some criticism, it is to Glasser's credit, and to that of the William Glasser Institute, that the popularity of reality therapy has spread worldwide. In fact, reality therapy has been successfully taught and practiced in many countries around the world, and reality therapy institutes from Singapore to Jerusalem to New Zealand, and elsewhere, have been developed to promote the theory (Wubbolding et al., 2004; The William Glasser Institute, 2009d). This fact illustrates the multicultural application and acceptability of choice theory and reality therapy.

Relative to religion and spirituality, it was noted earlier in this chapter that Glasser recognized the importance of the Golden Rule in ensuring that all people are free and recognizing that when meeting individual needs, it is important that we don't harm others. However, religion and spirituality are rarely discussed in most of Glasser's writings. For religious clients who believe there is external truth, reality therapy may be problematic, with its adherence to the belief that reality is the result of the choices we make and not based on an external reality. On the other hand, reality therapy can be viewed as reinforcing of an existing religious belief system. Imagine, for instance, the religious person who holds a certain belief system in his or her quality world and has not made choices to support it. Through therapy, this person may find new behaviors that would strengthen the beliefs that already exist in his or her quality world. Perhaps it is not surprising that after reading the book *Choice Theory*, the well-known pastor Dr. Robert Schuller stated, "A few weeks after I received this book, I showed it to my television audience and said, 'This is a fabulous book." (Glasser, 1998, back cover). Wubbolding suggests that reality therapy should strive to be more inclusive of those with strong religious beliefs and spiritual values, and goes on to state that perhaps there should be another fundamental need added to reality therapy—the need for purpose, meaning, and faith (Wubbolding, personal communication May 10, 2009).

EFFICACY OF REALITY THERAPY

Litwack (2007) cites a number of studies, particularly doctoral dissertations, that speak to the significant amount of research that has examined the efficacy of reality therapy from 1970 to 2007. Unfortunately, most of the published research to date

---

B o x 11.9   Markus Meets a Reality Therapist

Please review the Miller family's background, which can be found in Appendix B, and then read about | Markus's encounter with a reality therapist, which can also be found in Appendix B.

---

has not been controlled studies, and that is the major reason it was not included in Wampold's book, *The Great Psychotherapy Debate* (2001), which examined the efficacy of the major psychotherapeutic approaches (Wampold, personal communication, January 18, 2009). The few controlled studies that have been completed are almost exclusively looking at institutional settings, mostly schools. These studies show reality therapy demonstrating a "medium effect" and is of "practical significance" (Radtke, Sapp, & Farrell, 1997, p. 4).

In speaking to the research that highlights the importance of the therapeutic relationship to client outcomes (cf. Wampold, 2001), Wubbolding (2000) notes the importance that reality therapy places on building a therapeutic relationship. He also cites a number of mostly uncontrolled studies, conducted on a wide variety of populations, which show that reality therapy has had wide-reaching effects. A few of these studies demonstrated the following:

- reduction in substance abuse
- decrease in recidivism for juvenile offenders
- reduction in domestic violence
- increase in socialization and rehabilitation for inmates
- decrease in depression
- increase in ability to manage pain for clients with arthritis
- increase in ability to maintain an exercise program
- increase in appropriate behaviors for students
- increase in self-concept for students
- helpful in improving quality education

Although a significant amount of research has been done, most of it has been completed by those who have a vested interest in reality therapy and, as noted, the use of control groups has been minimal. It is clear that the time is here for controlled studies that examine the relative effect of reality therapy as compared to other approaches (see Box 11.9).

SUMMARY

William Glasser, the creator of reality therapy, grew up in Cleveland, Ohio, with parents whom he describes as having a tumultuous relationship. Despite his parents' arguing, he remembers his parents as being loving toward him. He also remembers a number of important people who mentored him along his way. Although Glasser was trained in psychoanalysis, he questioned many basic notions of analytical therapy and created a novel and revolutionary approach to counseling that was anti-deterministic and present-focused, and had a belief in the ability of the person to make changes. With influences from Powers's perceptual control theory and Deming's total quality management theory, Glasser would eventually develop reality therapy based on choice theory, which was used in schools, business, and counseling settings. Some people who helped Glasser to shape his theory over the years were his first wife, Naomi Glasser, his second wife, Carleen Glasser, and Bob Wubbolding, who expanded on Glasser's ideas.

Choice theory, the basis of reality therapy, suggests that there are five basic needs, including survival (self-preservation), love and belonging, power (inner control), freedom (independence), and fun (enjoyment), all of which help humans survive and thrive. Each individual has a genetically based need-strength profile, which is fixed at birth. The choices we make in an effort to fulfill these needs are represented by pictures in our quality worlds. Glasser suggests that an individual's "total behavior" is chosen and generated from within in an effort to match the pictures in his or her quality world. Total behavior includes our actions, our thinking process, our feelings, and our physiological responses. However, we can only actively change our actions and thoughts, which Glaser jointly calls what we are "doing." Our feelings and physiology result from those choices. Glasser suggests that the individual operates from an internal-control position, although many people mistakenly believe they are externally controlled. One goal of therapy is to move clients from an external- to an internal-control philosophy, and for clients to adopt the seven caring habits as opposed to living by seven deadly habits. The basic ideas of choice theory are summarized through Glasser's "ten axioms," which are an outgrowth of five concepts central to the understanding of reality therapy: basic needs, internal control, choice, quality world, and total behavior.

The standard method of implementing reality therapy using choice theory is the WDEP system. To build a firm, friendly and fair therapeutic relationship that includes trust and hope, the counselor demonstrates the environmental elements related to the "tonics of the counseling relationship" which includes 25 attitudes and techniques. In addition, the helper tries to avoid the eight ("ABCDEFGH") "toxins of the counseling relationship." The 25 tonics should be exhibited throughout the implementation of the procedures of the WDEP system, which includes the **w**ants of the client (W), what the client is **d**oing in his or her life's **d**irection (Ds), **e**valuating if what the client is doing is working (E), and developing a **p**lan of action that can be implemented (P).

Wubbolding suggests that counselors need to be adaptable when working with diverse clients and offers a variety of examples of how the approach can be applied to clients from different backgrounds. In addition, reality therapy has shown an international presence with Glasser's book being translated into many languages and reality therapy institutes popping up around the world. Some criticism of reality therapy is its strong emphasis on internal control and de-emphasis of the notion that external events can have a negative impact on the individual.

Relative to religious and spiritual issues, reality therapy is fairly silent; however, it would make sense that some helpers who practice reality therapy would have problems with the belief in an external truth, especially if it the "truth" is contrary to the individual's pictures in his or her quality world. On the other hand, reality therapy is a fit for those religious people who want to make choices that match beliefs already existing in their quality world. Also, Wubbolding suggests that it is time for reality therapy to be more inclusive of those with strong religious beliefs and spiritual values, and that adding another fundamental need to reality therapy—the need for purpose, meaning, and faith, should be considered.

Finally, most of the research on reality therapy does not use controlled studies, although what is available does show efficacy in a number of areas. However, it is clear that controlled studies, especially some that compare reality therapy to other psychotherapeutic approaches, are called for.

KEY WORDS

ABCDEFGH

A Legend in Counseling Award (ACA)

anti-deterministic

basic needs

choice

choice theory

control theory

direction and doing (D)

doing

enjoyment (also called "fun")

environmental elements

evaluation (E)

external control

external-control language

freedom (also called "independence")

fun (also called "enjoyment")

Golden Rule

here and now

independence

inner control (also called "power")

Institute for Reality Therapy and Educator Training Center

Institute for Reality Therapy, Control Theory, and Total Management

internal control

internal-control language

Life Achievement Award: International Center for the Study of Psychiatry and Psychology

linear plans

love and belonging

Master Therapist designation

need-strength profile

paradoxical intention

paradoxical plans

perceptual control theory

plan (P)

power (also called "inner control")

Professional Development Award (ACA)

quality world

reframing

SAMIC^3

self-disclosure

self-evaluation techniques (E)

self-preservation need (also called "survival")

seven caring habits

seven deadly habits

survival (also called "self-preservation")

ten axioms of choice theory

tonics of the counseling relationship (see Figure 11.2)

toxins of the counseling relationship (see Figure 11.2)

total behavior

total quality management (TQM)

use humor

Ventura School of Girls

W. Clement Stone Foundation

wants (W)

WDEP system

William Glasser Institute

KEY NAMES

Deming, Edward

Glasser, Carleen

Glasser, Naomi

Harrington, G. L.

Powers, William T.

Sheehan, Ms.

Szasz, Thomas

Wubbolding, Robert

REFERENCES

Brickell, J. (2007, February). Reality therapy: Helping people take more effective control of their lives. *Counseling at Work*, 6–9.

Deming, W. E. (1986). *Out of the crisis*. Cambridge, MA: MIT Center for Advanced Engineering Study.

Glasser, W. (1960). *Mental health or mental illness: Psychiatry for practical action*. New York: Harper & Row.

Glasser, W. (1965). *Reality therapy: A new approach to psychiatry*. New York: Harper & Row.

Glasser, W. (1969). *Schools without failure*. New York: Harper & Row.

Glasser, W. (1972). *The identity society*. New York: Harper & Row.

Glasser, W. (1976). *Positive addiction*. New York: Harper & Row.

Glasser, W. (1981). *Stations of the mind: New directions for Reality therapy*. New York: Harper & Row.

Glasser, W. (1984) *Control theory*. New York: Harper & Row.

Glasser, W. (1986). *Control theory in the classroom*. New York: Harper & Row.

Glasser, W. (1989). *Control theory in the practice of reality therapy: Case studies*. New York: Harper & Row.

Glasser, W. (1998). *Choice theory: A new psychology of personal freedom*. New York: HarperCollins.

Glasser, W. (2001). *Counseling with choice theory: The new reality therapy*. New York: HarperCollins.

Glasser, W. (2003). *Warning: Psychiatry can be hazardous to your mental health*. New York: HarperCollins.

Glasser, W. (2006). *Every student can succeed*. Chatsworth, CA: William Glasser, Inc.

Glasser, W. (n.d.). *Development of the ideas*. Retrieved from http://www.wglasser.com/images/glasser_forms/develop_ideas.pdf

Glasser, W., & Glasser, C. (1999). *The language of choice theory*. New York: HarperCollins.

Glasser, W., & Glasser, C. (2000). *Getting together and staying together*. New York: HarperCollins.

Glasser, W., & Glasser, C. (1999) *The language of choice theory*. New York: HarperPerrenial.

Glasser, W., & Glasser, C. (2007). *Eights lessons for a happier marriage*. New York: HarperCollins.

Lennon, B. (2000). From "reality therapy" to "reality therapy in action." *The International Journal of Reality Therapy, 20*(1), 41–46.

Litwack, L. (2007). Research review: Dissertations on reality therapy and choice theory – 1970–2007. *International Journal of Reality Therapy, XXVII*(1), 14–16.

Powers, W. T. (1973). *Behavior: The control of perception*. Chicago: Aldine Publishing Company.

Radtke, L., Sapp, M., & Farrell, W. C. (1997). Reality therapy: A meta-analysis. *Journal of Reality Therapy, XVII*(1), 4–9.

Robbins, L. B. (n.d.). *The art of promoting choice: A counseling workbook*. Oakland, TN: Author.

Szasz, T. (1961). *The myth of mental illness*. New York: Paul B. Hoeber, Inc.

The William Glasser Institute. (2009a). *Reality therapy*. Retrieved from http://www.wglasser.com/index.php?option=com_content&task=view&id=13&Itemid=28

The William Glasser Institute. (2009b). *The William Glasser Institute: Home of choice theory*. Retrieved from http://www.wglasser.com/

The William Glasser Institute. (2009c). *Choice theory: The ten axioms of choice theory*. Retrieved from http://www.wglasser.officewebsiteonline.com/index.php?option=com_content&task=view&id=12&Itemid=27

The William Glasser Institute. (2009d). *International locations*. Retrieved from http://www.wglasser.com/index.php?option=com_content&task=view&id=32&Itemid=62

Van Nuys, D. (2007). *An interview with William Glasser, MD and Carleen Glasser on happier marriages*. Retrieved from http://www.mentalhelp.net/poc/view_doc.php?type=weblog&id=283&wlid=9&cn=289

Wampold, B. (2001). *The great psychotherapy debate: Models, methods, and findings*. Mahwah, NJ: Lawrence Erlbaum Associates.

Wubbolding, R. (1998). Professional issues: The use of questions in reality therapy. *Journal of Reality Therapy, 16*(1), 122–127.

Wubbolding, R. (2000). *Reality therapy for the 21st century*. Philadelphia, PA: Brunner-Routledge.

Wubbolding, R. (2008). Cycle of managing, supervising, counseling and coaching (16th rev.). [Chart]. Cincinnati, OH: Center for Reality Therapy.

Wubbolding, R. (in press). *Reality therapy: Monograph psychotherapy series*. Washington, DC.: American Psychological Association.

Wubbolding, R. E., Basheer, A., Brickell, J., Kakitani, M., Kim, R. I., Lennon, B., … Tham, E. (1998). Multicultural awareness: Implications for reality therapy and choice theory. *International Journal of Reality Therapy, XVII*(2), 4–6.

Wubbolding, R., & Brickell, J. (1998). Qualities of the reality therapist. *International Journal of Reality Therapy, XVII*(2), 47–49.

Wubbolding, R., & Brickell, J. (1999). *Counselling with reality therapy*. Oxon, UK: Winslow Press.

Wubbolding, R., Brickell, J., Imhof, L., Kim, R., Lojk, L., & Al-Rashidi, B. (2004). Reality therapy: A global perspective. *International Journal for the Advancement of Counselling, 26*(3), 219–228.

Post-Modern Approaches

Narrative therapy and solution-focused brief therapy, the two approaches we will examine in this section, are recent additions to the therapeutic milieu and are based on the philosophies of social constructionism and post-modernism. Social constructionism suggests that individuals construct meaning in their lives from the discourses they have with others and the language that is used in their culture and in society. Post-modernism suggests that all reality should be questioned. Those with this philosophy doubt many of the basic assumptions of past popular therapies, which suggest that certain structures cause mental health problems (id, ego, superego, core beliefs, lack of internal locus of control, etc.). Rather than harp on past problems that tend to be embedded in oppressive belief systems, post-modern approaches suggest that clients can find exceptions to their problems and develop creative solutions. Post-modern approaches tend to be short-term therapies, with solution-focused brief therapy being considered a particularly brief approach, sometimes lasting fewer than five sessions.

Chapter 12

Narrative Therapy

Learning Goals

- To review the biographical sketch of Michael White, one of the originators of narrative therapy.
- To understand the historical context in which Michael White developed his approach.
- To understand the constructionist, post-modern, and post-structuralist influences on the anti-deterministic, anti-objectivist view of human nature of narrative therapy, and to see how they reflect the ideas that realities are socially constructed, realities are constituted through language, realities are organized and maintained through narrative, and there are no essential truths.
- To review the following key concepts related to narrative therapy: post-modernism, post-structuralism, social constructionism, narratives, dominant and problem-saturated stories, deconstruction, thin or thick descriptions, relativism, power, unique outcomes, re-authoring, and lack of neutrality.
- To review a number of important techniques used in narrative therapy, including showing mystery, respectful curiosity, and awe; use of questions; collaboration and reflexivity; reflection, empathy, and verbatim responses; encouraging clients to tell their stories; externalizing the problem and mapping its effects; having clients identify unique outcomes or exceptions; absent but implicit responses and double listening; considering social and political issues; scaffolding; use of therapeutic documents and other paraphernalia; re-membering; definitional ceremonies; reflective teams; and telling and retelling.
- To understand the four broad phases of narrative therapy, which include joining, examining patterns, re-authoring, and moving on.
- To examine social and cultural issues, especially in light of how language is used in the creation of reality and how transmission of values from those in power tends to oppress people from nondominant groups, such as individuals of color; women; gays, lesbians, and bisexuals; and other historically oppressed groups.
- To understand the relationship between the philosophical underpinnings of narrative therapy and the social justice stance that most narrative therapists take.

- To examine how, for those who experience their religions as oppressive, their spiritual lives can be "re-storied."
- To examine biases in research and to discuss the application of quantitative and qualitative research to narrative therapy.
- To see how narrative therapy is applied through vignettes, DVDs, and case study.

> The Icarus Project envisions a new culture and language that resonates with our actual experiences of "mental illness" rather than trying to fit our lives into a conventional framework. We are a network of people living with experiences that are commonly labeled as bipolar or other psychiatric conditions. We believe we have mad gifts to be cultivated and taken care of, rather than diseases or disorders to be suppressed or eliminated. By joining together as individuals and as a community, the intertwined threads of madness and creativity can inspire hope and transformation in an oppressive and damaged world. Our participation in The Icarus Project helps us overcome alienation and tap into the true potential that lies between brilliance and madness. (The Icarus Project, 2008)
>
> *Beyond the medical model:* While we respect whatever treatment decisions people make, we do not define ourselves as essentially diseased, disordered, broken, faulty, and existing within the bounds of DSM-IV diagnosis. We are exploring unknown territory and don't steer by the default maps outlined by docs and pharma companies. We're making new maps. (The Icarus Project, 2006, para. 1)

Like the grassroots Icarus Project that seeks to redefine mental illness as a "gift" based in brilliance and madness, there is a wave of treatment approaches that empower clients by having them reexamine their own life stories. In fact, even calling these ways of working with clients "treatment approaches" may be a disservice to the optimistic and forward-looking ways that these approaches offer. But where did these approaches come from, and why now? Understanding the life of Michael White, a founder of one of these approaches, narrative therapy, may help us see why.

MICHAEL KINGSLEY WHITE

Born in 1948 in Adelaide, Australia, this Baby Boomer was not a child you would have imagined would eventually develop a theory that would change the way many modern-day therapists work. Michael came from a working-class home. His father, Neil, had served in World War II and was considered more traditional and sometimes strict, and his mother, Joan, a housewife, was viewed as more liberal (Chamberlain, 2003; Park, 2008). She, in particular, would greatly influence her son's life, and was seen as loving, compassionate, accepting, hard-working, and hopeful that her children would have opportunities she never did. Michael, the second-born, had an older sister, Sue, who describes herself as the "bookworm" in the family, and two younger siblings: a sister Julienne, and a brother Paul, with whom he was very close. Although suffering from asthma as a child, Michael was quite active, and he and Paul would often spend hours playing

Michael White

and sometimes getting involved in mischievous activities. Often playing soccer together, the family seemed to be close-knit and had an upbeat attitude toward life, and throughout his adult life, Michael would maintain a relatively close relationship with his family of origin and their offspring. Interestingly, Michael's bouts with asthma seemed to motivate him to become a fitness enthusiast for most of his life. Perhaps his attitude of "turning lemons into lemonade" was one of the reasons he ended up developing a positive approach to therapy.

After high school, White worked as a landscape gardener, laborer, and mechanical draftsman. It was also during this time that White began to stand up for what he saw as perceived injustices as he, along with his older sister and sometimes mother, protested the Vietnam War (Park, 2008). In fact, White met his future wife and life-work partner, Cheryl, at an anti-war demonstration in 1971. They married in 1972, and Cheryl's ongoing involvement in feminism and social justice was to be a major influence on White's life and work. In fact, many of White's ideas can be directly traced to the ongoing conversations between the two of them. White's involvement with Cheryl, his compassionate and liberal mother, the family environment, and his coming of age during the turmoil and changes of the 1960s all likely influenced White's thoughts about narrative therapy as well as his eventual focus on social justice issues.

During the early 1970s, White worked briefly as a probation and welfare officer, and then went on to become a psychiatric social worker (Pearse, 2008; White, 2008). It was also at this time that White began to deal with his own depression. After being poorly treated and humiliated by the mental health system, White was certain that there was a more effective way to work with clients. It was then that he became keenly interested in how clients were often diagnosed and treated in an objective and seemingly inhumane manner, and in the inherent power inequities in hospital practices, particularly those between staff and clients (Chamberlain, 2003).

In 1974, White obtained his diploma of technology in social work from the University of South Australia and soon after became a senior psychiatric social worker at the Adelaide Children's Hospital in Australia. Here he was encouraged to practice his skills, and he soon was developing innovative ways of working with children, particularly those with anorexia, encopresis (fecal soiling), and night terrors. While at the hospital, he obtained his bachelor's degree in social work. It was then that White began to challenge some of the traditional ways in which clients were treated and power was used and abused. In 1978, Michael and Cheryl had a daughter, Penni. A devoted father, White devised fun games with a child who was physically fragile while Cheryl put her career on hold to be with Penni in her early years, only returning to full-time work later (Chamberlain, personal communication, March 14, 2008).

In 1979, White became the first editor of the *Australian and New Zealand Journal of Family Therapy* (ANZJFT). During the 1970s and early 1980s, he was particularly enamored with how people communicate in systems and was influenced by such individuals as Gregory Bateson, who wrote extensively on this subject ("Family therapy" n.d.; Hart, 1995). Then, in 1981, White decided to leave the hospital setting to open a private practice with a group of colleagues at **Oxford House**, with members of that group becoming the first private-practice social workers in Australia. Here they began to develop training programs on his emerging theory, which increasingly looked at a systemic approach to working with individuals. During this time, White came up with the notion of **externalizing the problem**, a process whereby a client would give a name to a problem so that it did not seem to reside within the person. For instance, a person could call his or her depression "the black box," where sad things are kept. Externalizing a problem allows people to see it as something that is not inherently embedded in them and allows them to both separate from their problem and focus keenly on finding solutions.

In 1983, Michael and Cheryl founded the **Dulwich Centre for Narrative Therapy** (Bhat, 2008; Chamberlain, 2003). After Michael stepped down as editor of ANZJFT, Cheryl created **Dulwich Centre Publications**. This eventually became the vehicle through which most of White's works were published (Chamberlain, personal communication, March 14, 2008). In fact, without Cheryl's "behind-the-scenes" involvement with the publication of White's work, narrative therapy would likely be less widely known today.

During the early 1980s, White developed a deep friendship with David Epston, a Canadian-born émigré to New Zealand. Epston was trained as an anthropologist but, like White, eventually worked as a social worker. Also like White, Epston focused on working with children and adolescents. Both White and Epston were married to strong, feminist women and saw as part of their roles in life being politically active in an effort to change what they saw as the oppressive political systems that subjugated and brought chaos to many individuals, particularly minorities. Epston describes his relationship with White as "blood brothers" (Epston, 2009), and although they never actually did therapy together (Chamberlain, personal communication, May 15, 2008), they would eventually write a number of books that were instrumental to the development of narrative therapy (cf. Epston & White, 1992; White & Epston, 1990). Today, David Epston is a visiting professor at the UNITEC Institute of Technology in Auckland, New Zealand, and is co-director of the **Family Therapy Centre of Auckland**. His work continues to be foundational in the field of narrative therapy.

B o x 12.1 "Good" and "Bad" English?

Power and truth are intimately related. For instance, most of us have been brought up with the belief that a certain type of spoken English reflects the "correct" way to speak and is an indication of level of intelligence and social status. Although controversial in his own way, Barack Obama's former minister, Reverend Jeremiah Wright, highlighted this by noting that when President Kennedy would use uncommon English he would not be criticized, but "only to a black child would they say you speak bad English" (Wright, 2008, para. 30). In fact, when minorities use uncommon English, they are often said to be lazy, stupid, or rebellious.

As White evolved, so did his theory (Hart, 1995). In the mid 1980s and on, White became particularly interested in the social construction of reality and how individuals develop their meaning-making systems, or the notion that our sense of self is at least partially formed by our broader social system. From the late 1980s, White became interested in **post-modernism**, which challenges many of the assumptions of **modernism**, the lens through which many scientists and theorists from a wide variety of disciplines had come to view reality. Post-modernists believe that there are multiple ways to understand the world, no foundational rules defining who we are, and no one method of communication that would guarantee a better understanding of another person. Questioning truth, wondering how truth reverberates in society, and exploring how clients create reality as a function of such truths are some of the issues focused upon by the post-modern, narrative therapist. It is not surprising that during this time, White became particularly interested in the work of the French philosopher Michel Foucault, who spoke of how language is subtly created and used by the privileged to support their understanding of what is truth, and that such truth maintains the roles of the privileged and often results in the oppression of others (Miller, 2008; White, 2002).

White's interest in post-modernism also brought him in close contact with **social constructionism**, or how the values transmitted through language by the social milieu (e.g., family, culture, and society) are intimately connected with the development of the person. Such an approach suggests that the person is constantly changing with the ebb and flow of the influences of significant others, culture, and society. Ultimately, principles inherent in post-modernism and social constructionism became foundational to narrative therapy. As an outgrowth of these philosophies, the approach took a keen interest in understanding how power affects all of us in subtle but pervasive ways by dictating the kinds of truths we come to hold and the narratives (stories) we create as a function of such truths (see Box 12.1). Therefore, one of the functions of the narrative therapist becomes trying to understand clients' **dominant narratives** and assisting clients in making choices about establishing counter-narratives in order to live a more satisfying life.

The post-modern and social constructionist influences on White became increasingly evident, such as when he applied his theory to his work with Aborigines in New South Wales, Australia (Chamberlain, 2003). Greatly

---

B o x 12.2   Retelling Stories to Make One Stronger

The following paragraph shows how stories, such as those of the Aborigines, can be retold in ways that make them stronger. Look in particular at how "Grief" has been externalized and seen as separate from as these indigenous people retell their story:

> As Indigenous people of this country, we have faced so many losses due to past and present injustice. Grief's presence has been with us for

a long time. Now we are seeking ways of speaking about Grief that are consistent with our cultural ways of doing things. We are remembering those who have died, we are honouring Indigenous spiritual ways, and we are finding ways of grieving that bring us together. We are telling our stories in ways that make us stronger. (Wingard, 2001, para. 1–2)

---

influenced by the anthropologist Barbara Myerhoff, who studied the stories of a group of mostly elderly and frail Jewish immigrants in California (Myerhoff, 2007), White found that by listening to the stories of the Aborigines' dispossession and relocation, he could help them create new stories which reframed their understanding of these horrendous events (Winslade, personal communication, May 6, 2008) (see Box 12.2).

Because post-modernism and social constructionism are particularly interested in how the social milieu's use of language creates a dominant reality, there is a natural tendency for those who adopt this approach to focus on **social justice issues** in their efforts to challenge many of the basic assumptions that have been held out as truth (e.g., certain ethnic groups cannot achieve). From this perspective, differences among people are seen as a reflection of the transmission of dominant values and beliefs through language, and not as some inherent pathological state that dwells within any single person or group. It's therefore not surprising that White and his fellow narrative therapists spent much time visiting other countries and cultures and helping those who were oppressed and disadvantaged, such as the poor, minorities, gays and lesbians, and women. Narrative practice has therefore grown more extensively in places outside of the therapeutic mainstream (Winslade, personal communication, May 7, 2008).

Ultimately, the narrative approach that White helped to establish has clients examine and understand their narratives, deconstruct their embedded stories, and create new narratives. One of the ways he did this was to encourage clients to "externalize" the problem in order to separate them from the problem and see it more clearly. Along these lines, White often stated, "**The person is not the problem; the problem is the problem,**" and would communicate with clients in a way that would assist them in **re-authoring** their narratives in order to achieve a new sense of who they are and develop increased satisfaction in life (Hart, 1995). His innovative ideas and work with children and families was one of the reasons he won the **Distinguished Contribution to Family Therapy and Theory and Practice** award from the American Family Therapy Academy in 1999 (White, 2008).

White had some help in the development and dissemination of narrative therapy. Of course, there was David Epston, his friend and colleague. In addition, Karl Tomm, Director of the **Family Therapy Program at the University of Calgary**, mentored and encouraged White as he saw in the young Australian an original therapist whose ideas were worthy of a hearing (Chamberlain, personal communication, May 14, 2008). Tomm helped to open doors of international teaching for White and remained a friend to both Cheryl and Michael. Others, like John Winslade and Gerald Monk, have continued the narrative tradition. And, of course, White had his wife who helped and encouraged him along the way.

In 2007, White published his most recent book, *Maps of Narrative Practice*. At around this time, Michael and Cheryl separated. Then, in January of 2008, White set up the **Adelaide Narrative Therapy Centre** because he wanted to focus more keenly on his work, particularly his focus on family therapy, while Cheryl decided to continue her social justice and community work at the Dulwich Centre (Chamberlain, personal communication, May 14, 2008; White, 2008). His own best advocate for his approach, White could often be found traveling the world presenting case histories and lectures on narrative therapy. It was on such a sojourn to San Diego that he died of a heart attack in April of 2008.

VIEW OF HUMAN NATURE

> In the traditional scientific framework, truth is discovered, and in the postmodernist framework, truth is constructed. (Shapiro, Friedberg, & Bardenstein, 2006, p. 136)

From a narrative perspective, there is no one view of human nature; there are views of human nature. This reflects the post-modern and social-constructionist perspective that there are multiple realities in the sense that all individuals create their realities through interactions or discourses within their social circles. This point of view also implies that values held by power-holders in society tend to become the norms by which individuals compare themselves, and such norms are reinforced through the language that we share. For instance, mental health professionals who hold positions of power create a diagnostic manual, the DSM-IV-TR, and most mental health professionals, and others, use it and "speak" its language. It becomes the discourse of a particular professional community. Over time, it becomes the norm that professionals, and even most laypersons, use when considering whether one has what is called a "mental disorder." Ultimately, the DSM is reflective of the values of the power-holders who created it and its worth, say the narrative therapists, should be looked at with that in mind.

From the narrative point of view, individuals are constantly in discourse with others within their social milieu, and it is through such interactions that they develop their sense of self. Although people are deeply affected by the language used in their social spheres, narrative therapy is **anti-deterministic** because it assumes that people can understand the realities that have been created, deconstruct their foundations (take them apart), and develop or re-author new stories that are empowering. Since the major focus of narrative therapy is "where people want to go" rather than "where they have been" (Hoyt, 1994, p. 1), narrative therapy is seen as more optimistic than many other approaches. In fact, narrative therapists are considered **anti-objectivists**, which means that they oppose those approaches that develop a theoretical model that explains reality and then uses that hypothetical model to define the experience of others (e.g., psychodynamic approaches, the DSM-IV-TR). This objectification of others, which almost always focuses on the client's past, often results in the disdain for or oppression of those being looked at:

> The objectivists and monumentalists, on the other hand, prefer to stand above the fray, where they can assume a position of omniscience, and work in the "clean" realm of detachment and ethical neutrality. To me, the attitudes embodied in their "standing above it all" range from mild condescension through active surveillance to brute domination....
> (Rosaldo, 1993, p. 221)

Freedman and Combs (1996) offer a further understanding of the narrative approach by proposing a view of human nature based on four premises: realities are socially constructed, realities are constituted through language, realities are organized and maintained through narrative, and there are no essential truths.

Realities Are Socially Constructed. The narrative therapist believes that the psychological makeup of the person—that is, beliefs, values, customs, habits, personality style, and so forth—is created from the ongoing interaction and discourse individuals have with their families and the larger cultural "soup" from which they come (e.g., ethnic group, community, society). People then tend to categorize these created understandings of the world and then separate themselves from the knowledge that they were the ones who actually created the categories, as if the resulting truth is separate or outside themselves. For instance, many people place various religions in different categories based on their understanding of each religion's closeness to holding the truth about God. They subsequently place these varying religions in a hierarchy from "good" to "bad." They even point to "evidence" of these categorizations as if the evidence exists outside of themselves, not realizing that the evidence is actually a result of the discourse they have had (the received knowledge and "truth") from within their family and cultural milieu.

Realities Are Constituted through Language. Narrative therapists believe that as individuals become increasingly networked within their social milieu, they develop a particular reality, or point of view, as a function of the language used within that milieu. Examples of how language creates reality are many. For instance, consider how the use of nonsexist language has changed our perceptions of what is real. Today, instead of saying the "nature of man," we often say the "view of human nature;" instead of "men working," we say "people working;" and instead of "stewardess" we say "flight attendant." Even high-ranking politicians use this "new" language. Now consider how the picture in one's mind of a work crew on a highway might change because signs now say "people working" instead of "men working."

Since language is closely related to what we come to perceive and to know, one's psychological style is seen as a pliable product of the language used in one's social milieu, not as something inherent within the person. And since context can change, people can change or even have multiple styles or identities depending on the context in which they find themselves. Consequently, the therapeutic environment can offer a new context in which new realities can potentially be created for the client and for the therapist as they dialogue with one another.

Realities Are Organized and Maintained through Narrative. The narrative therapist views reality as a creation of the individual's discourse with others and a function of the language used in those conversations. The resulting stories people create about themselves then maintain their reality. In addition, the cultural context from which one comes has **dominant stories** that are often integrated by the person and become a part of the life story of the individual. So, to understand a person, listen to his or her stories. For instance, many Jewish people have heard the words "never again" as part of the story related to the Holocaust and other oppressive experiences over the generations. Certain Jewish holidays acknowledge these experiences, encourage memories of them, and honor the ability of the Jewish people to free themselves from the oppressors while also stating that all peoples should be free. Consider how this dominant narrative may have affected a Jewish person's ways of knowing the world, with vigilance about oppression and mistrust of authority being woven into Jewish culture. Narrative therapy suggests that, like reading a good novel, one should "read" or listen to the client's stories and join the client in trying to understand his or her dominant stories.

There Are No Essential Truths. Rejecting the notion of an external truth that underlies the way we all come to know the world, narrative therapists believe that we define our realities from the discourses in our unique, contained world. Although we all tend to have dominant stories that dominate our lives and define the reality we live most of the time, we also have other stories that play a lesser role in our lives. In essence, we are multistoried. Our stories define who we are, and reality or truth can change as a function of the particular story with which one is identifying in the moment. For instance, consider the different dominant stories of African Americans and white Americans during the O. J. Simpson trial of the mid-1990s. Relative to the police, stories of many African Americans had to do with oppression, police bias, and racist acts being carried out against them, while white Americans had stories around police protection and truth and justice always being on their side. Is it any wonder than many African Americans and whites saw this trial through different lenses? And, more recently, consider the biracial lens through which Barack Obama likely views the world. He appears to have multiple stories that allow him to have an understanding of different groups of people.

Since we are all multistoried, by listening to clients' nondominant stories and by helping them create new stories, counseling can help new realities emerge. Consider the implications this has for those who have been called "mentally ill." If when listening to a person's stories, one finds some contexts and times in which the person is not "mentally ill," is this person really "mentally ill?" This way of viewing mental illness contrasts sharply with the traditional view, which assumes that there is something permanent and fixed within the person that makes him or her mentally ill (all the time). The narrative therapist believes that through dialogue and by adopting different language, a formerly "mentally ill" person can identify a new, *preferred story* and can begin to identify himself or herself as mentally healthy.

KEY CONCEPTS

Post-Modernism

In the Woody Allen movie *Sleeper*, the main character is placed in a cryogenic apparatus and wakes up in the future only to find that much of what used to be bad for him is now good:

Dr. Melik: You mean [in the past] there was no deep fat? No steak or cream pies or hot fudge?

Dr. Agon: Yes, but these things were considered unhealthy. Precisely the opposite of what we now know to be true. (Allen & Brickman, 1973, p. 20)

Like in the movie *Sleeper*, **post-modernism** suggests that what we come to know as truth can and likely will change as a function of the context in which we find ourselves. Post-modernism suggests that modernism, which had as its basis a belief that progress could be made through analysis, experimentation, and scientific knowledge, needs to be questioned. It does not necessarily mean that what was has been learned or discovered is "wrong," but that it is important to question how "truth" became known and what it means that we now have this new knowledge. In fact, by some, post-modernism is defined as the questioning of modernism, particularly such ideas as empiricism and that scientific method can find "the truth" (Weinberg, 2008). The truths of science, the truth of a psychotherapeutic theory, and the belief that we can understand our existence are all questioned by post-modernists.

The post-modern revolution (well, uprising, at least) over the past 30 years has us questioning the foundation for our beliefs. Although we might all agree that an apple will fall "down" from a tree, there is much we can question. For instance, concepts such as Freud's psychosexual stages, or Rogers's concept of the "congruent self," or the existentialist notion of choice all grew out of a certain context and time period and have meaning within that context. And, despite the fact that they might, at times, offer us helpful models for understanding self, they are all contingent on a certain way of understanding the world that is bound by the contexts from which they arose. Post-modernism, as understood through narrative therapy, suggests that our individual truths are reflected in our constantly changing narratives as our lives move on and our context changes. And they suggest that our individual truths are often reflective of the collective knowledge that has been transmitted to us through language. Thus, how we come to make meaning in the world is reflective of the larger system which holds a certain view of truth, or epistemology.

Post-Structuralism

Considered part of the post-modern movement, **post-structuralism** is a reaction to **structuralism**, which was a concept closely aligned with the scientific revolution and later adopted by the social sciences and other disciplines (Payne, 2006; Russell & Carey, 2004). In counseling and psychology, structuralism suggests the existence of inherent structures that affect personality development. The description of these structures is seen through a particular theory's view of human nature. Think of the "structures" that exist in psychoanalysis, or person-centered counseling, or cognitive theory. Each of these theories has a particular belief about the human species' meaning-making system, or ways of understanding the world. These structures are seen as real; that is, they exist within the context in which they are presented. So, beliefs about repression, self-actualization, or cognitive schemas are all structures that fit neatly into a larger system or theory that adherents to those theories believe molds how we come to know the world.

The post-structuralists challenged this prevailing view. They disputed the notion that the psychodynamicists, existentialists, cognitive–behaviorists, or most other theorists held a monopoly on the truth about the nature of people. And they went a step further: They suggested that beliefs in these truths encourage a myopic way of knowing. Thus, individuals struggling to become less repressed, or self-actualized, or to know their cognitive schemas become enveloped by these very processes, and it is these very processes that end up dictating how these individuals come to understand the world. They do not see other ways of knowing as possibilities. In fact, language in society tends to reinforce many "truths" from structural thinking, and those who do not accept these truths are often seen as psychotic, stupid, defensive, immoral, or rebellious. Think of the counseling-related words and phrases that now exist and that we take for granted from this structural revolution: *unconscious, id, ego, repression, defensiveness, superego, internality, self-esteem, self-actualization, need hierarchy, inner drives, cognitive schemas, mental disorder, neurotic, psychotic*, and on and on. If you don't believe in the meaning behind these words, you are seen as being outside of the norm—not in the mainstream—a nonbeliever.

> So, where does poststructuralist inquiry take us? … It takes us into considerations of how it is that lives are actually constituted through this triumvirate—to how persons' lives are shaped by these notions and the practices of living that are associated with them, to how these notions and practices style acts of living.… The joining of claims about nature, repression and psychological emancipation powerfully ties persons to the reproduction of our culture's "truths" of identity in their

pursuit of liberation—persons are ever more tightly bound to their subjectivities through their efforts to liberate themselves. (White, 1997, pp. 223–224)

A word of warning. Keep in mind that the post-structuralists are not saying these systems do not exist; they are saying, let's view them as particular knowledge systems, or as one way of understanding the world. And let's take a look at what believing in any therapeutic system means for the person, his or her family, his or her culture, and society. In the end, the post-structuralists have offered an alternative perspective that has a relativistic outlook—that is, a perspective that suggests there are many ways of knowing, none of which hold absolute truth, and all of which can impact the person in different ways. Not labeling the person as *wrong* or *unhealthy*, regardless of the person's views, they suggest that identities are constantly in formation as individuals interact with others over time (see "Social Constructionism"). Based on a comparison made by Russell and Carey (2004), Table 12.1 compares and contrasts the structuralist and post-structuralist positions.

Social Constructionism

The realities that each of us take for granted are the realities that our societies have surrounded us with since birth. The realities provide the beliefs, practices, words, and experiences from which we make up our lives, or as we say in post-modernist jargon, "constitute our selves." (Freedman & Combs, 1996, p. 16)

Social constructionism became popularized during the 1960s and suggested that language and discourse form mental concepts become the basis for what is believed to be truth. These "truths" are held in high esteem by institutions in society as they take on particular power and are used to influence decision-making (Berger & Luckmann, 1966; Gergen, 1999). For instance, many in the United States believe that "we are the creators of our own fate," "we are individually responsible for what happens to us," and "if we dig deep enough, we can understand why we do certain things." These beliefs have been promulgated by a number of Western-based counseling theories that assert that there is something inherent that makes us who we are. Humanists put forth this philosophy by emphasizing an inherent "self-actualizing tendency" and the importance of having an "internal locus of control." Psychodynamic theorists argue that there are certain intrapsychic functions that affect who we are (e.g., the id, ego, and superego). These beliefs have taken on particular power in our field and are often promulgated as truths. The social constructionists, however, question these truths. They view knowledge as always changing, a function of the historical and cultural milieu from which the individual comes, and passed down through cultures to individuals by language (Winslade & Geroski, 2008). Thus, these concepts are seen as having taken on power as a result of the historical and cultural context from which they came and not based on reliable facts or truth.

T A B L E 12.1   **Comparing the Structuralist and Post-Structuralist Schools**

	Structuralism	Post-Structuralism
Purpose of inquiry	To examine underlying issues of self and deep structures inherent within the person that give the person direction in life.	To examine how the language that we use and the language that others use help to shape our lives.
Objectivity	One can understand another through the development of a model that describes the nature of the person.	There is a constant dialogue that occurs among people, which results in a continuous redefinition of who we are. Who we are can be understood through the stories we tell.
Normative comparisons	Normative comparisons are important because they help us see how different we are from others and identify possible problem areas.	We should not compare ourselves to others or to social norms, but instead listen to what our own stories tell us.
Creation of ideas, problems, and qualities	Ideas, problems, and qualities are manufactured by deep structures inherent within us. Objective models describe how ideas, problems, and qualities are developed through the deep structures (e.g., I'm neurotic because my "real self" is not congruent with my "false self").	"Our ideas, problems, [and] qualities are all products of culture and history. They have been created over time and in particular contexts." (p. 96) Therapy can help us focus attention to stories that are not problem-saturated, help us focus on positive qualities, and empower us.
identity	Identity is deep within ourselves, predictable, fairly fixed, and changes little over time.	Identity is a function of the language that we use in relationship with others and the power dynamics in culture and society. It changes as a function of who we are with and over time.
Purpose of therapy	To use a preset model to understand and diagnose a client.	To "[c]onsider how stories describe the lives of our clients and how therapy can enable the development of 'preferred stories of identity'" (p. 97).

The social constructionist sees the individual as constantly changing throughout life as he or she has an ongoing discourse with others. Rather than an "'I' can pick myself up by the bootstrap" attitude, the social constructionist says that, as people interact with one another, they have an ongoing conversation through which meaning is made (Drewey & Winslade, 1997). Thus, the social constructionist sees identity as constantly in formation and changing as a function of the language that is used in interaction with others. In fact, from this perspective, one can have a number of "identities" or "selves" depending on the discourses one

Social Constructionism

Parental Values

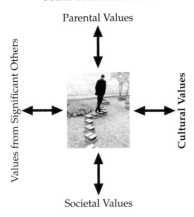

Values from Significant Others

Cultural Values

Societal Values

F I G U R E 12.1 Social Constructionism

Through ongoing discourse within a person's social and cultural milieu, a person constructs his or her sense of self, which changes over time. The person's narratives reveal this changing sense of self.

finds oneself in over time. I am not an ongoing "Ed." Instead, I have an "Ed" with my partner, a different "Ed" with my colleagues, another Ed ("Dad") with my children, and another Ed ("Eddie") with my siblings; and the Eds, the Dad, and the Eddie change over time. And my sense of self is not embedded within me; it is a changing and evolving self in relation to the various groups within which I find myself. And, to take it one step further, the word "Ed" is not sufficient enough to define all of who "Ed" is (see Figure 12.1).

Narratives

> … [W]e live by the stories that we have about our lives … [T]hese stories actually shape our lives, constitute our lives, and … "embrace our lives." (White, 1995, p. 14)

A **narrative** is a story. In the case of narrative therapy, our narratives are the stories that define who we are, and we are continually engaged in "storying" during our lives. There are many narratives or stories that "embrace" us along our paths in life, and our stories can and do change as we move along. In fact, narrative therapists like to say that our lives are *multistoried*; that is, there are many stories that define who we are, and sometimes, the stories contradict each other. Some narratives are **unhelpful stories** in the lives of clients, as they feed into oppressive narratives, while other narratives can be **helpful stories** in that they are empowering (Brown, 2007). Understanding the many different stories that exist within a person as well as being able to identify stories that contradict and deny other stories is critical to the narrative therapist's work. For instance, a therapist can try to uncover other, more helpful stories that contradict a **problem-saturated** story that is over-whelming and causing problems in a person's life. Thus, it is often said that people can **re-story** or **re-author** their lives through the narrative therapy process.

As you might assume, one of the goals of narrative therapy is to help the individual identify his or her problem-saturated and unhelpful stories, lessen their significance, and develop what are called **preferred stories**, which are healthier and can become the client's dominant narratives.

Dominant and Problem-Saturated Stories

Although we are multistoried, our lives are often saturated by **dominant stories** to which we ascribe our identity. These stories are generally passed along to us by significant people in our lives, our culture, our community, and our society. They are entrusted to us in subtle ways, perhaps subtler than some of us would like to believe. Yet in other ways, they are obvious in that we can quickly identify them when we begin to look for them. Since many of the stories are representative of values or normative ways of being within the larger community or in society, many of us have similar stories to which we ascribe to our identity. And when we don't meet the normative way of being as suggested in the story, we sometimes believe there is something wrong with us. So, we hear that "girls should be one way" and "boys should act a different way," and if we do not adhere to the ways that we have been "told" to act, there is something wrong with us. That is why so many people believe that a woman who acts assertively is "bitchy" but a man who acts assertively is "effective," and a man who is mild-mannered is "gay" and a similarly behaved woman is "sensitive."

Dominant stories can become **problem-saturated** when they are causing some amount of pain, distress, and dysfunction. For instance, consider a boy who, when sometimes acting in a sensitive manner, becomes verbally abused by his father and is told he'd better act more like a "man." This boy may now carry those negative views of himself, which are passed on to him by his father through language. This young man sees his sensitive self as "wrong," and society does little to contradict that view when it defines male sensitivity as "gay" and implies that there's something wrong with being gay. Whether this man is gay may or may not be important. What is important is how the language and its associated values used by his father and in society become integrated into the boy's sense of who he is. In counseling, one step toward helping this young man is through what's called the **deconstruction** of the dominant, problem-saturated story.

Deconstruction

… [D]econstruction has to do with procedures that subvert taken-for-granted realities and practices; those so-called "truths" that are split off from the conditions and the context of their production, those disembodied ways of speaking that hide their biases and prejudices, and those familiar practices of self and of relationship that are subjugating of persons' lives. (White, 1991, p. 27)

Deconstruction is the process of taking apart a dominant story in an effort to understand the beliefs, values, ideas, or social discourses that have been supporting it. Stories are generally kept alive by values and ideas within families, culture, and society, and then internalized by the client (Freedman & Combs, 1996). It is usually important to help the client understand how the story was developed so that he or she can see the relationship between the story that has been internalized and the broader social milieu that "handed" the story over to the client.

> From this perspective, it is proposed that persons' lives are shaped by the meaning that they ascribe to their experience, by their situation in social structures, and by the language practices and cultural practices of self and of relationship that these lives are recruited into. (White, 1991, p. 27)

As the narrative therapist listens to the dominant story with a different ear than the client's, the therapist hears the "gaps" in the stories and realizes that other stories intertwine, parallel, and even contradict the dominant story. Through a combination of listening and asking questions, the narrative therapist evokes other stories that have been in the background in the client's life, stories that deny, contradict, and oppose the dominant story. And as the narrative therapist begins to have some ideas about how the dominant story took on so much power to begin with, he or she might raise questions about them while being respectfully curious. As this process proceeds, the strength of the dominant story lessens because it is being "deconstructed," or taken apart slowly and seen in a new light.

Thin or Thick Descriptions

> It is almost as if we are born with an inconclusion, and until we fill the gap with story, we are not entirely sure, not only what our lives mean, not only what secrets require our attention, but that we are there at all. (Myerhoff, 2007)

Our understanding of ourselves is often based on what's called a **thin description** of our life stories. Such descriptions, which generally evolve out of our problem-saturated stories, leave little room for alternative explanations, lend themselves toward narrow explanations of events, and tend to "dominate" the way we come to understand who we are. **Thick descriptions**, on the other hand, are complex descriptions of our lives and the stories that describe our lives, and show an understanding that our lives are multistoried. In narrative therapy, the therapist hopes to examine alternative stories that deny or contradict the dominant, thin stories, which are often problem-saturated. For instance, the "sensitive" man discussed earlier initially focuses mostly on his abusive father's comments about him, which leads to his "thin" conclusion about who he is. By helping the client identify other memories that contradict the dominant, problem-saturated story, the client can begin to develop a more complex and richer story about self that includes multiple aspects of self.

Relativism

> We are moving towards a dictatorship of relativism which does not recognize anything as for certain and which has as its highest goal one's own ego and one's own desires. (Pope Benedict XVI, 2005)

Pope Benedict implies that **relativism** could present havoc for society, for, in its basic form, relativism suggests that all truths, attitudes, and beliefs are equally valid (Freedman & Combs, 1996). However, narrative therapists have a different spin on relativism. They suggest that there are multiple truths, and that truth is seen from the perspective of the discourse from which the individual emerges. They go on to say that an individual's sense of the world is often dominated by one or two stories, which have become the client's basis for truth. These dominant stories are generally linked to cultural imperatives (family, community, religion, society) and result in the oppression of certain groups of individuals. Narrative therapists help individuals look at how they have been negatively and positively impacted by the language of their cultural milieu and of the society in which they have been immersed (Drewey & Winslade, 1997).

The narrative therapist also suggests that, despite being dominated by one or two stories, we actually all have multiple stories that contain multiple truths, and they help clients examine how their dominant stories may have affected themselves and others. In addition, the narrative therapist has conversations with the client about other "background" stories in the client's lives. In this manner, the narrative therapist can help the client examine the impact of the dominant stories and can engage in discourses with the client about what "storylines" they may choose to live in their lives. In that sense, they can now begin to "re-author" their lives.

Power

The narrative therapist's ideas concerning relativism are closely associated with issues of **power** and inequities in society, as dominant societal "truths," which many of us end up believing in, are just one take on the truth. And, say the narrative therapists, it is these same truths that tend to maintain the power structure in society and are responsible for the oppression of nondominant groups. For the narrative therapist, dominant stories from society are internalized by individuals, cause people to live out and believe stories that tend to oppress the underclass, and blind clients to other possible stories and opportunities (Freedman & Combs, 1996; White, 1993, 1995; White & Epston, 1990). Thus, stories about how certain clients of color are "lazy," "stupid," "rebellious," and so on are often subtly, and sometimes blatantly, passed down. They become part of the dominant stories of those in power and are even sometimes internalized and "believed" by the very people whom the stories are about. Since those in power are often unaware of their privileged position, it is also helpful for them to examine the stories they have developed in their own lives. Enlightening those in power to their narratives can help them see how their story is one that has been used to oppress others. You can see why narrative therapists are particularly sensitive to how oppressed groups are treated and how that treatment becomes part of the individual's sense of identity.

Unique Outcomes (Sparkling Outcomes and Exceptions)

Helping clients identify times that deny, contradict, or modify the dominant, problem-saturated story is one of the major roles of the narrative therapist (Payne, 2006). The therapist does this by asking the client when in his or her life there were **unique outcomes** (sometimes called **sparkling outcomes** or **exceptions**) to the narrative that is "dominating" the client's life (White & Epston, 1990). Then, through respectful inquiry, the therapist explores and invites the client to magnify those unique outcomes. This process invites the client to develop new strands, or new stories, based on those unique outcomes or exceptions.

Re-Authoring

> Re-authoring conversations invite people to continue to develop and tell stories about their lives, but they also help people to include some of the more neglected but potentially significant events and experiences that are "out of phase" with their dominant storylines. (White, 2007, p. 61)

As clients tell their life stories and reveal their dominant, problem-saturated stories that are filled with thin descriptions of who they are, they also provide small glimpses of other stories that contradict the dominant, thinly descriptive story. As the therapist hears these unique outcomes or exceptions to the dominant story, questions are used to focus upon how these unique outcomes or exceptions might yield alternative stories that lead to new conclusions about the client. As these unique outcomes and exceptions get pieced together into other stories, the client sees that he or she is a much more complex person and is not simply defined by the dominant, thinly descriptive story. For instance, look at Figure 12.2, which shows the problem-saturated story as well as two new alternative stories being generated by the "sensitive" man. As with the client illustrated in Figure 12.2, awareness of new but already existing parts of self through the new stories that have been identified helps clients re-author their lives as they increasingly redefine themselves in broader, more complex ways.

Lack of Neutrality

> ... [T]here is no neutrality on the part of therapists. Every response you take comes from a particular point of view. In fact, the assumption of neutrality is likely reinforcing the gender and cultural biases inherent in society. (White, Epston, & Andrews, 1994)

Narrative therapists believe that we are never neutral (Winslade & Geroski, 2008). We bring our assumptions about the world into play every time we

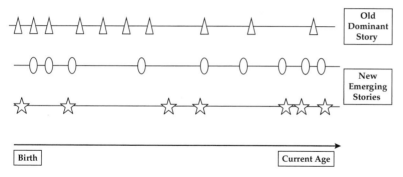

F I G U R E 12.2   Identification of New, Alternative Stories

The line with the triangles are symbolic of times John remembers being verbally abused by his father for being sensitive—his dominant story. The line with
the ovals represents times John remembers being a content, sensitive child or
man. And the line with stars reflects times John remembers being a content
"strong" child or man. John is now beginning to re-author or redefine who he
is, and the problem-saturated story is beginning to become less meaningful.

interact with a client. Any theory or cultural assumption that we have been
taught and have embedded into our ways of knowing becomes the lens from
which we see others and becomes part of the toolbox into which we reach in
our relationship with clients. So, whether it is a counseling theory, a theory of
development, or a theory about cultural identity, our understanding of others is
filtered through such theories, shapes our conversations with others, and affects
our work in ways of which we sometimes may not be aware. Thus, given that
we are not neutral, it is important to consider how our biases shape our
conversations with our clients. Perhaps more important, narrative therapists
suggest that neutrality allows "isms," which are pervasive in society, to affect the
client's life. Therefore, one role of the narrative therapist is to be non–neutral
and to carefully suggest, or wonder with the client, what roles certain "isms"
may be have played in the development of the client's stories.

THERAPEUTIC TECHNIQUES

Showing Mystery, Respectful Curiosity, and Awe

Traditionally, it has been common for clients to look up to, idealize, and perceive the
therapist as being powerful due to the therapist's status and knowledge (Brammer &
MacDonald, 2003). And therapists have commonly fed into this notion as they
objectified their clients by applying their particular theoretical orientation to them
(Winslade, Crocket, & Monk, 1997). Narrative therapists, on the other hand,
recognize this perception on the part of clients and enter the relationship with a sense
of **respectful curiosity**, **mystery**, and **awe** as they position themselves toward
hearing the client's story (Payne, 2006). They assume that clients have the tools and
ability to assist themselves in reducing their own problems and do not find fault with

the client for his or her situation (Morgan, 2000). This role helps to de-mystify the relationship and to define it as a discourse between individuals in which both can change. The use of specific questions that foster this kind of relationship are particularly important here (see "Use of Questions").

Use of Questions

> ... [I]n a therapy of oral tradition, the re-authoring of lives and rela-tionships is achieved primarily, although not exclusively, through a process of questioning. (White & Epston, 1990, p. 17)

The **use of questions** is one of the most critical tools for the narrative therapist, as questions help to set the tone for the direction the relationship will take. Questions near the beginning of the relationship will reflect respectful curiosity, mystery, and awe about the client's reason for coming to counseling, and serve to encourage the client to discuss his or her problem-saturated story. As the relationship continues, questions will focus on externalizing the problem and on mapping its effects. Then, the focus of questions becomes an exploration of unique outcomes or exceptions to the client's problem-saturated story. Later, questions will focus on how the client might be able to re-author his or her story. Table 12.2 offers some typical kinds of questions that might be asked at different points in the therapeutic relationship.

Collaboration and Reflexivity

In an effort to lessen the power differential between the client and the therapist, and to ensure that the direction of counseling is helpful for the client, therapists will often take steps to "check in" with the client. This is generally done through the use of specific questions. For instance, Morgan (2000) notes that the following questions may be asked at any point during the relationship:

- How is this conversation going for you?
- Should we keep talking about this, or would you be more interested in ...?
- Is this interesting to you? Is this what we should spend our time talking about?
- I was wondering if you would be more interested in my asking you some more about this, or whether we should focus on X, Y, or Z? [X, Y, Z being other options] (pp. 3–4)

Along these lines, an explanation will sometimes be offered by the therapist regarding what he or she is doing as a way of "checking in" with the client and making sure that the client understands and feels comfortable with what is happening in counseling (White, Epston, & Andrews, 1994). In addition, using a process called **reflexivity**, the client is also invited to comment on the helping process so that the helper can learn from the client the impact the helping process is having on the client. In this process, respect for the client's perspective

T A B L E   12.2   Sampling of Types of Questions Used at Different Points in the Relationship

Time of Relationship	Focus of Questions	Type of Question
Beginning	respectful curiosity, mystery, and awe	■ Can you tell me what brings you here today? ■ How did you come to have this problem? ■ How do you think this problem has affected you? ■ I'm interested in knowing as much detail about your problem as possible; can you explain it to me? ■ What about that problem is so powerful for you? ■ That is really interesting; can you tell me more about how this happened to you? ■ I'm wondering how this problem got so big for you? ■ How do you think the problem has affected you? ■ Do you like what the problem has been doing or do you object to it? Why?
Late beginning	externalizing the problem and mapping the effects of the problem	■ How did this problem enter your life? ■ If we were to give a name to this problem, what do you think that might be? (e.g., "the black box") ■ What is it about ["the black box"] that you object to? ■ How has ["the black box"] altered your life? ■ How does ["the black box"] affect your life? ■ What do you think the implications for ["the black box"] are for your life? ■ What would your world look like without ["the black box"]? ■ Any thoughts about how you might tackle ["the black box"]? ■ If you had any means at your disposal what would you do to rid yourself of ["the black box"]?
Middle	unique outcomes or exceptions	■ What would you prefer? ■ If you were to not have this problem, how would your life look? ■ Have there been any times in your life when you did not have this problem? ■ What was so unique about the times that you did not seem so affected by the problem? ■ It's amazing how much of your life was taken up by the problem, yet I think I hear that there were times when that was not the case. Can you tell me about those times? ■ What was happening in your life during the times when you did not have this problem?
Late	re-authoring	■ Now that we've identified a series of times when you were free of this problem, any ideas how you can make this happen in the future? ■ What name would you give to this counter-story? ■ How can we expand these other unique and positive times in your life and minimize these problem-saturated times? ■ How might be able to expand these other storylines you've shared with me? ■ What would your life look like if it were dominated by these other stories rather than [the name of the problem]?

on what is occurring in counseling is paramount (Besley & Edwards, 2005; Winslade, 2005). This is considerably different from many approaches in which the helper takes on an "expert role" and the reasons for what the helper is doing is often hidden from the client.

Reflection, Empathy, and Verbatim Responses

Watch Michael White work with clients and you will see a mixture of questions, reflections, and empathy as he attempts to connect or **join** with them as they explore their stories (cf. White, Epston, & Andrews, 1994). Empathy in this context should not be viewed as a tool to try and understand what is "underneath" the problem, but an important technique that shows you have heard the client accurately. The use of reflection and empathy is a powerful tool that helps therapists connect with their clients, encourages clients to talk about their stories, assists clients in deepening the level of trust, fosters the exploration of the clients' stories in new detail and in new ways, and helps to reinforce clients' development of new stories. Reflection and empathy are not neutral tools, as what counselors decide to reflect mirrors their own biases and beliefs (Freedman & Combs, 1996). In fact, many times, the therapist will repeat verbatim what the client has stated in an effort not to influence the client and to ensure that the client clearly hears his or her own problem-saturated story (Winslade, personal communication, August 29, 2009). Accurate **reflection**, **empathy**, and **verbatim responses**, it is hoped, will assist clients in their re-authoring of new stories that are not problem-saturated.

Encouraging Clients to Tell Their Stories

Encouraging clients to tell their stories comes naturally if one believes that such stories are the road to understanding how clients have developed their sense of self. Storytelling can be a starting point for the journey between the therapist and client. During this beginning phase of therapy, counselors should keep in mind that clients present a "thin description" of their stories; that is, they are generally not fully aware of the complexity of their problem-saturated story or that other stories may contradict or deny the problem-saturated story. In addition, early in therapy, much is omitted from clients' initial descriptions due to forgetfulness or feelings of mistrust and embarrassment about sharing intimate details. Thin descriptions of stories often lead clients to thin conclusions about their lives, as they tend to view the world in simple, often dualistic ways (Morgan, 2000). As clients continue to tell their stories, the narrative therapist can help them expand on the problem-saturated stories. This is generally accomplished through the therapist's ability to be respectfully curious, show wonderment, and ask questions about their stories. Such therapist qualities tend to invite clients to more fully describe their stories. Reflections, empathy, and verbatim responses can also be a useful tool in understanding clients' stories and in encouraging them to more fully describe their experience.

B o x 12.3   Beating Sneaky Poo

In a sometimes funny manner, Heins and Ritchie (1988) have taken ideas developed by Michael White and have written a short book with comic book–like illustrations that helps children deal with the serious issue of encopresis (fecal soiling). By externalizing the problem, "sneaky poo" becomes the focus of the concern that children, parents, and sometimes medical professionals work together to solve. By focusing on "sneaky poo" rather than the child, children stop experiencing the blame that often comes with encopresis as they separate themselves from the problem. After externalizing the problem, the authors give hands-on ways that children and their parents can help "sneaky poo" not be a problem any longer.

B o x 12.4   Dr. Milliken Helps Shane Externalize His Problem

Read or watch how Dr. Milliken helps to name Shane's problem as "darkness."

You can read this session by going to www. cengage.com/counseling/neukrug/CTP1e and click "student downloads." Or your instructor may show this session in class with the DVD that accompanies his or her copy of the text.

Externalizing the Problem and Mapping Its Effects

The language used today in the fields of counseling and psychology is based on Western values. Such language tends to view problems as being entrenched in some form of intrapsychic experience, related to some unconscious drive, a function of something out of the client's control, or seen as something inherent in the client. This view of reality, as understood by narrative therapists, is a myth that should be challenged. Thus, it is critical that therapists help clients view their problems as not being inherent in self. "The person is not the problem; the problem is the problem," asserted Michael White. Thus, it is important to extricate the problem, or "get it out of us!" (see Box 12.3). This is generally done by having the client give the problem a name, which is the first step toward externalizing it and redefining how the problem is understood (White & Epston, 1990). Then, through the use of specific questions (see "Use of Questions"), the therapist can help the client map the effects that the problem has had on him or her. As noted earlier, externalizing the problem helps clients separate from the problem and also helps them focus keenly on solving the problem (see Box 12.4).

Unique Outcomes or Exceptions

As clients feel increasingly comfortable revealing their stories, and through the use of questions and discussion (see "Use of Questions"), they begin to examine key aspects of their lives that are not problem-saturated. Identifying times that seem to be at odds with, rebuff, or demonstrate a smaller impact of the problem-saturated story helps to reframe a client's sense of identity. While some narrative therapists will specifically ask if there were times when the problem was not as prevalent or did not exist, others will wait for clients to generate times on their own when the problem was not dominating the client's life. Eventually, the therapist can help the client string together aspects of the client's life that are not problem-saturated so that he or she can embrace alternative stories.

Absent but Implicit Responses and Double Listening

Absent but implicit responses are related to the notion that every experience and expression we have in life has multiple layers or multiple stories, some of which are obvious (explicit) while others are less obvious but may be implied (White, 2000). Thus, the therapist has an opportunity not only to listen to the story that is being told, but to listen ("**double listen**") and inquire about the less obvious, implied story of the client. This opens up opportunities for clients to discover other meanings to their problem-saturated story which can lead to other, thicker descriptions of their lives.

For instance, Preston, who initially came to counseling because he felt his anger was causing him problems in his relationships, has externalized his problem as the "angry red monster." He describes a series of incidents in which he felt like he or others were treated poorly and he "lost his cool." Just a few of these included:

- Screaming on the phone at the person who works for the health insurance company because the company did not pay for a doctor's visit that he "knew" should be included in his coverage.

- Yelling at his wife for instances where he states she was spending an inordinate amount of time with their children and his in-laws.

- Walking out of a class he was taking in graduate school and yelling to the students and the professor "you're all a bunch of racists" during a discussion on multiculturalism.

- Becoming irate at a Dunkin Donuts teller for charging him "inappropriately."

As Preston continues to discuss the "angry red monster," the therapist asks Preston a series of questions that focuses on that which is **absent but implicit**, rather than the direct content being offered by the client. In this sense, the therapist is "double listening"—listening to the content of what Preston has said but also listening to that which is absent but implicit.

Choosing to focus on the absent but implicit, the therapist might ask Preston a series of questions that can help develop new conversations about Preston's angry red monster. For instance, the therapist might ask, "What do you think your anger wants from you?" or, "How do you imagine these situations would be best resolved?" or, "What is it about each of these situations that are egging you on?" or, "What would life be like if these situations didn't exist?" To these questions, Preston responds that he has always felt that life was filled with injustices. The therapist then invites Preston to discuss what injustice means to him and to relay any stories in his life that may have to do with injustice. Preston quickly describes a series of stories about the importance of fighting injustice. Being African American and growing up in the South, Preston talks about a number of discussions, when he was young, concerning injustices done to his "people." He remembers "endless" conversations with his grandfather about segregation and describes how his grandfather had to "kowtow" to the "white man." He goes on to talk about how his family and extended culture stressed the importance of fairness and justice. He notes that he married a woman who was an "activist" who fought injustice. He then notes, "Most of my adult life I have been fighting injustices—they just make me so angry." As Preston says this, he suddenly blurts out, "I take injustices very seriously, whether they are to others or to me. I guess I see how my life has been filled with themes that involve injustices. I see how I have been treated unjustly, and I also see how some of my reactions have been unjust to others."

Preston is examining his dominant, problem-saturated story and is beginning to see how his life is multistoried and much more complex than he originally viewed it when first describing his anger. He can now find other ways of elevating other, unique stories in his life and limiting his problem-saturated story, if he so chooses.

Considering Social and Political Issues

Narrative therapists believe that there are a wide range of social and cultural issues that affect an individual's experiences. However, because the Western world has a legacy of viewing problems from an intrapsychic perspective, such issues often get hidden as individuals blame themselves for predicaments that may be partly or fully outside of their control. Narrative therapy helps a person identify issues of sexism, racism, classism, heterosexism, and elitism, as well as other ways in which individuals have problems created for them due to abuses of power. Usually sometime after the client has begun to externalize the problem, narrative therapists will use questions to help clients consider how their dominant, problem-saturated stories are shaped by cultural issues and biases in society (White, Epston, & Andrews, 1994). A small sampling of such questions might include the following:

- Can you describe times when you have been discriminated against?
- How do you think gender roles have affected your relationship with your spouse (or lover) or with others?
- Do you think there are any societal values that work against your living a more peaceful and loving life?
- Do you think that issues of race may have been responsible for you not being promoted at work?
- Do you think societal attitudes towards gays, lesbians, and bisexuals has affected you?

Scaffolding

The gap between what is known and familiar and what might be possible for people to know about their lives can be considered a "zone of proximal development." … The zone can be traversed through conversational partnerships that provide the necessary scaffolding to achieve this…. (White, 2007, p. 264)

Moving from a dominant, problem-saturated story to a new way of seeing self is one of the major goals of narrative therapy. This process takes time and occurs by identifying unique outcomes and exceptions, and building on past, positive events. By weaving together events not linked to the problem-saturated story, the client slowly builds new stories. Although the problem-saturated story still exists, it begins to take on different meaning and a smaller role as the client builds new, more positive stories. Slowly, the client begins to view himself or herself through a new lens that is jointly developed through collaboration with the therapist.

In explaining this process, White (2007) talked about the importance of developing tasks for the client that slowly distance him or her from the problem-saturated story. Over time, White suggests that clients can move from **low-level distancing tasks** to **high-level distancing tasks**. Thus, the woman who has a story that she is worthless and not deserving of love might be asked to consider a time when this was not the case, and asked to share that memory. Finding exceptions to her problem-saturated story would be the beginning of a new story, and a low-level distancing task. Contrast this with the woman who now sees that she is deserving of love, and the therapist dialogues with her about various ways in which she can find loving relationships in her life and then suggests a high-level task such as a ceremony where loving friends are brought in to share their thoughts with her, thus building on her newfound "loving" identity.

Use of Therapeutic Documents and Other Paraphernalia

To acknowledge progress and describe change, written documents are often encouraged or provided (Payne, 2006). For instance, clients might journal about how they now view their lives as compared to how their lives were when the problem dominated their lives, or they might write biographies that show the shifting changes in their lives. Therapists can also use documents to show client progress, such as writing letters to clients that affirm their changes, providing medallions that acknowledge shifts in thinking, or giving certificates that acknowledge new ways in which clients now understand themselves (see Box 12.5).

B o x 12.5 Was the Wizard of Oz a Narrative Therapist?

... [A] heart is not judged by how much you love, but by how much you are loved by others. – The Wizard

I was always taken by the Wizard of Oz's use of documents and paraphernalia to acknowledge aspects of the Tin Man, Scarecrow, and Lion that they, themselves, did not focus upon. Each of these characters had his own problem-saturated story. The Tin Man saw himself living a heartless life, the Scarecrow thought he was brainless, and the Lion saw himself as a coward. Pointing out to each of these individuals times when they were not who they thought they were underscored the notion that they did not have to continue accenting their problem-saturated stories. And to accentuate the importance of their new identities, the Wizard gave each of them something important. To the Tin Man, he gave a large, red, heart-shaped clock that hung from a golden chain; the Scarecrow received a diploma so he would always be reminded that he was smart; and to the Lion, he gave a medal signifying how brave he was.

Re-membering

A term coined by Barbara Myerhoff (1982), **re-membering** has to do with helping individuals reconstruct their identities by accenting and expanding on specific positive memories and by limiting problem-saturated memories (Russell & Carey, 2004). Re-membering allows clients to call up powerful positive images from the past, connects clients to something going on in the present, and provides a road map for the future. For instance, a client might have a memory of a time he or she did something heroic. This image can be called on, focused upon, and used as a metaphor for who he or she is now and how he or she will act in the future. Clients may also re-member individuals who have had positive influences on their lives but have been lost due to death, changes in location, loss of contact over time, and so forth. Clients can re-member through many avenues, including journaling, writing stories, meditating or reflecting, viewing videos, and so forth. In addition to re-membering positive memories, clients can delimit memories that have had negative influences on their lives.

Definitional Ceremonies (Outsider Witness Groups)

The term **definitional ceremonies**, sometimes called **outsider witness groups**, was originated by Barbara Myerhoff's (1982, 1986) work with elderly Jews in California as she watched them "reinvent themselves" at a community center (Russell & Carey, 2004). In narrative therapy, such a ceremony generally occurs after a client has begun to develop new, thick stories that start to reshape the client's sense of self and involves the retelling and witnessing of the client's new stories. Generally, this retelling is to a group of carefully chosen friends, significant people in the client's life, or individuals who had previously sought consultation for a similar difficulty and have expressed a desire to assist others in the future. Such witnessing by the group reinforces and solidifies the client's sense that he or she is moving on.

During such a definitional ceremony, White (2007) warns against using traditional methods of responding and suggests that the witnesses not applaud, affirm, congratulate, or interpret the client's stories. Instead, the purpose of the witness is to have dialogue with the client around images that may have surfaced and emotions that were evoked within the listener. This will generally lead to a discourse between witnesses and the individual that helps to "thicken" and solidify stories of all involved.

Reflective Teams

> Our new way of working makes us feel that we are participants in a process in which family members become our equals. We do not feel we can or should control the therapy process, and we accept that we are merely a part of it. (Andersen, 1987, p. 427)

Reflective teams are when individuals observe clients with their therapists and later share their thoughts about what they have observed and experienced with the client and the therapist. Reflective teams can include significant others, therapists, or individuals who have experienced similar issues in their lives. Originally used as a family therapy technique by Tom Andersen (1987), and sometimes considered a type of definitional ceremony, reflective teams offer clients a mechanism to consider new ways of re-authoring their lives. White (1993, 1995) suggested that reflective team discussions be structured in four parts during one interview:

Part 1: The reflective team quietly observes the client with the therapist from behind a one-way mirror, via a closed-circuit TV, or as they sit in the same room as the client and therapist.

Part 2: The reflective team members introduce themselves to the client and then switch places with the client and therapist. While the client and therapist observe, the reflective team participates in a discussion that focuses upon exceptions to the dominant stories of the client, highlighted by their sense of wonderment and mystery about the client's narrative. Then, the reflective team members discuss possible alternative stories they think could be a potential outgrowth of the exceptions they have heard. Finally, the reflective team "deconstructs" one another's responses in an effort to question the inherent power that is sometimes experienced by clients from "experts." This process allows the client to see the reflections as possible alternative ways of viewing the client's narrative and not as advice or heavy-handed suggestions. It also allows team members to examine their own lives.

Part 3: The reflective team again switches places with the therapist and client. Then, the therapist and client have an opportunity to jointly discuss any aspects of the reflective team's responses that seem meaningful and helpful. This process allows for possible new realizations about the client's life that could bring new potential actions.

Part 4: All participants join together and ask each other why certain ideas were discussed, certain questions asked, and other questions not asked. As this interview concludes, the client can inform the "interviewer and team members of those ideas which were of most interest, to give an indication of those lines of questioning that they believe hold the most promise, and to provide feedback about any speculation on the possibilities that might be taken up at the next session" (White, 1995, p. 195).

Telling and Retelling

Telling and retelling new stories to self, to the therapist, and to others reinforces the client's newfound sense of identity. This can be done in an informal way, through discourse with others; by writing letters or e-mails to self and others; by writing an autobiography; through creative outlets, such as drawings or sculpting; by making video recordings or computer blogs; by using outside witnesses; by having definitional ceremonies; and so forth.

THERAPEUTIC PROCESS

The lack of belief in absolute truth negates the idea of an absolute process of therapy. Therefore, it is unlikely that you would find narrative therapists identifying specific stages of therapy. However, White (1993) and Payne (2006) do offer a sense

---

B o x 12.6 Dr. Milliken's Work with Shane

Read or watch Dr. Milliken's work with Shane and identify the phases of the relationship and which narrative techniques Dr. Milliken uses with Shane.

You can read this session by going to www.cengage.com/counseling/neukrug/CTP1e and click

"student downloads." Or your instructor may show this session in class with the DVD that accompanies his or her copy of the text.

---

of a general direction in which clients move in counseling. Based on their ideas, I have generated four broad phases that most clients experience in the narrative therapy process. Phase 1 is the **joining** phase, when the therapist meets the client, begins to build a relationship, and invites the client to share his or her problem-saturated story. In Phase 2, **examining patterns**, the client is invited to examine stories that contradict, deny, or oppose the problem-saturated story. Phase 3, **re-authoring**, is when the client begins to build new, more positive stories, and Phase 4, **moving on**, is when the client has developed a new, more positive outlook on life and is ready to leave therapy. Figure 12.3 maps the likelihood of specific techniques being used within the phases. However, keep in mind that narrative therapy is a free flowing process where phases can re-emerge as the therapeutic process continues (see Box 12.6).

SOCIAL, CULTURAL, AND SPIRITUAL ISSUES

The discourses of pathology make it possible for us to ignore the extent to which the problems for which people seek therapy are the outcome of certain practices of relationship and practices of the self, many of which are actually informed by modern notions of "individualism" … [and] are so often mired in the structures of inequality of our culture, including those pertaining to gender, race, ethnicity, class, economics, age, and so on. (White, 1995, p. 115)

Is there a person? or groups of persons, who do not like to tell their stories? Narrative therapists will listen to anyone's story, and listen with an ear that shows respect, curiosity, awe, and an invitation to "please tell me more." And they don't pass judgments on the stories, but they will ask clients to consider how their story has been influenced by others, particularly how it may have been influenced by power brokers in society and significant others in their lives. And, because the narrative therapist enters the therapeutic relationship with the knowledge that dominant narratives in society often deleteriously affect people of color, women, gays, lesbians, bisexuals, and other historically oppressed groups, they are particularly attuned to issues of discrimination and inequality when working with clients (Semmler & Williams, 2000).

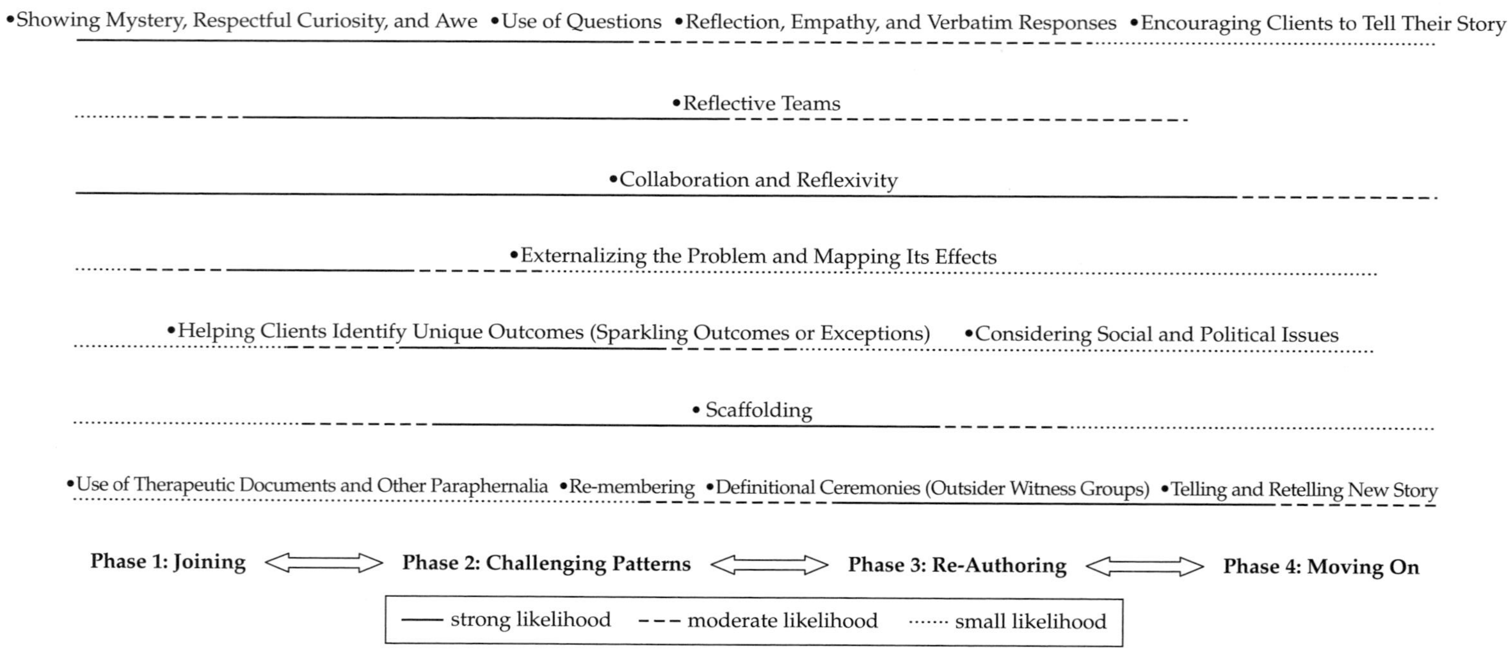

FIGURE 12.3 Likelihood of Techniques Occurring as a Function of Phase*

*The use of every technique or series of techniques listed is associated with the whole line it is above.

Although narrative therapists do not push their values onto their clients, they are not "neutral." In fact, narrative therapists believe that when therapists are "neutral," they are subtly supporting the "isms" of society. This stance lies in the belief that issues of power and subjugation occur in both obvious and subtle ways, are endemic throughout society, and are particularly harmful to clients from diverse backgrounds. Although they will not push their agendas onto clients, they will, in collaboration with the clients, ask questions that might raise issues about oppression. Some of the underlying issues that fuel such questions include the following (Russell & Carey, 2004; Raheim et al., n.d.):

- how depression or other symptoms are supported by the broader culture (e.g., women are often "encouraged" to be depressed rather than have a strong voice)
- the societal influences that impinge on the individual and feed into his or her dominant, problem-saturated story
- how medications are used to "quell" the voice of the client
- how traditional mental health treatment methods support male, hetero-sexist, and racist notions
- ensuring that acts of violence and abuse perpetrated on the client are not seen as something for which he or she is blamed
- ensuring that there is a sense of equality in the therapeutic relationship and that the client feels as if her or his voice is heard
- ensuring that clients have choices relative to the gender and ethnic background of the therapist
- recognizing that therapists are often privileged and clients often are not
- examining how lack of privilege has affected a client's life
- examining how "mainstream values" support certain ways of functioning and oppress many minorities

To be a narrative therapist is to be a social justice activist. If you believe that language creates reality and that language sometimes results in the overt and covert oppression of certain groups, there is no other choice but to advocate for those who are oppressed and to recognize the advantages of those who are privileged.

Relative to spirituality and religion, one role of the narrative therapist may be to help the client feel empowered through his or her spiritual and/or religious stories. Although religion can be disempowering and abusive in the lives of some clients, there are other aspects of religion or spirituality that can be examined and uplifting for a client and may have been ignored by the client. In fact, Carlson and Erickson (2000) suggest a series of questions to help clients find unique outcomes and alternate stories on their way to re-authoring their spiritual lives. Being able to disengage from old, oppressive stories and develop new, empowering stories that re-engage a person in his or her religion, or in a newfound religion or spirituality, can be a goal of narrative therapy

(Nelson-Becker, 2004). In the end, the narrative therapist does not see religion as holding exclusive truth, but it can be meaningful in defining how clients live their lives.

> We want to know the truth about reincarnation, we want proof of the survival of the soul, we listen to the assertion of clairvoyants and to the conclusions of psychical research, but we never ask, *never*, how to live.... (Krishnamurti, 1969, p. 76)

EFFICACY OF NARRATIVE THERAPY

As you might guess, traditional, quantitative ways of researching are not particularly amenable to the narrative therapy approach (Gergen & Gergen, 2008). In fact, narrative therapists would argue that there is inherent bias in this method of researching. For instance, although quantitative research has brought us many advances, its so-called "purity" must be called into question when we realize that every decision a quantitative researcher makes in designing, implementing, analyzing, and interpreting a study is a reflection of the discourses that dominate in his or her world. The subject matter that is chosen, the population to be examined, the kinds of designs that are chosen, even the statistical analysis used, can lead a researcher to certain conclusions. In fact, from a narrative therapy perspective, how would one even decide what "variable" to research, or even what the goal of therapy might be that could be measured when a client initially comes into the office?

Whereas **quantitative research** assumes that there is an objective reality within which research questions can be formulated and scientific methods used to measure specified variables, **qualitative research** holds that there are multiple ways of viewing knowledge and that one can make sense of the world by immersing oneself in a relationship in an attempt to provide possible explanations for the problem being examined (Heppner, Kivlighan, & Wampold, 1999). This approach is much more aligned with the narrative therapist's way of understanding the world. Table 12.3 combines information from tables presented by Heppner et al. (1999, p. 242) and McMillan and Schumacher (2006, p. 13), who distinguish qualitative and quantitative research. You can see how well the qualitative research model fits the narrative therapist's approach to doing therapy.

Although a qualitative research approach seems to be a good fit for narrative therapy, it should be noted that there is a dearth of good qualitative studies examining this approach. Read most articles on narrative therapy, and you find the authors anecdotally describing the process of their work with clients instead of applying qualitative research principles. Perhaps narrative therapists prefer it this way, as they would likely question the efficacy of whatever research approach was taken. However, others might argue that the time for good qualitative research that examines the efficacy of narrative research is here (see Box 12.7).

T A B L E 12.3   Distinctions between Quantitative and Qualitative Research

	Quantitative	Qualitative
Assumptions about the world	Truth exists and reality can be measured.	Reality is socially constructed, and there are multiple realities.
How knowledge is applied	Knowledge is used to develop hypotheses. Deductive process.	Past knowledge can bias results. Inductive process.
Research methods and process	Mathematical, statistical, and logical.	Philosophical, anthropological, and flexible. Method changes and emerges as data are collected.
Biases and validity	Bias is problematic. Increased control of study to increase validity to reduce bias.	Bias is acknowledged. Reduced through the use of multiple methods of attaining data and examining results.
Goals and generalizability	To discover truth and generalize to larger audience.	To uncover information and describe findings to enlighten public.
Researcher role	Detached, objective scientist.	Researcher is immersed in social situation and describes and interprets findings.
End product	Scientific report usually published in peer-reviewed journal.	Report accessible to many audiences, including lay public. May or may not be published in peer-reviewed journal.

SUMMARY

Narrative therapy is a relatively new approach to counseling that was originated by Michael White and David Epston. After personally experiencing the negative effects of the mental health system, White began to develop his own approach to therapy that was much more sensitive to the personal stories of his clients, more optimistic, and future-oriented. Some of the people that influenced him included Michel Foucault, Barbara Myerhoff, Gregory Bateson, and Karl Tomm. White's wife, Cheryl, was also a particularly important influence on White's work, and she and White eventually established the Dulwich Center for Narrative Therapy in South Australia. White's approach evolved from a systems to a

---

B o x 12.7   Celia Meets with a Narrative Therapist

Please review the Miller family's background, which can be found in Appendix B, and then read about Celia's encounter with a narrative therapist, which can also be found in Appendix B.

communication to a post-modern approach. In recent years, John Winslade and Gerald Monk have continued work on this important approach.

Narrative therapy is based on post-modernism, social constructionism, and post-structuralism. Post-modernists question modernism, such as the "truths" that are often attributed to empiricism and the scientific method. Post-modernism suggests that there is no one way to understand the world, no foundational set of rules to make sense of who we are, and no one approach to communication in understanding a person. Social constructionism has to do with how values are transmitted through language by the social milieu (e.g., family, culture, and society) and suggests that the person is constantly changing with the ebb and flow of the influences of significant others, culture, and society. Post-structuralism questions the inherent "truth" of such things as intrinsic psychological structures to which many psychological theorists point in explaining their view of human nature. Narrative therapy is anti-deterministic, anti-objectivist, and more positive than most past therapies. In addition, narrative therapists believe that realities are socially constructed, realities are constituted through language, realities are organized and maintained through narrative, and there are no essential truths.

In addition to post-modernism, social constructionism, and post-structuralism, some of the key concepts we examined in narrative therapy included narratives, and the fact that we are all multistoried and that some stories are helpful, while others are unhelpful; the dominant and problem-saturated stories with which clients often present; the importance of deconstruction of stories when working with clients; helping clients move from thin to thick stories; understanding relativism and the nature of multiple realities; how power dynamics in society as seen by the dominant stories are internalized; the importance of therapists' looking for unique outcomes or exceptions; helping clients re-author their stories; and the importance of not being neutral, because neutrality supports the existing oppressive power structure endemic in society.

There is a range of techniques which the narrative therapist can use at varying times, including showing mystery, respectful curiosity, and awe; use of questions; collaboration and reflexivity; reflection, empathy, and verbatim responses; encouraging clients to tell their stories; naming and externalizing the problem and mapping its effects; helping clients identify unique outcomes or exceptions; absent but implicit responses and double listening; considering social and political issues; saffoldng; use of therapeutic documents and other paraphernalia; re-membering; definitional ceremonies (outsider witness groups); reflective teams; and telling and retelling.

Narrative therapy can be viewed in four phases. Phase 1, the joining phase, occurs when the therapist meets the client, begins to build a relationship, and invites the client to share his or her problem-saturated story; Phase 2, examining patterns, is when the client is invited to examine stories that contradict, deny, or oppose the problem-saturated story; Phase 3, re-authoring, is when the client begins to build new, more positive stories; and Phase 4, moving on, is when the client has developed a new, more positive outlook on life and is ready to leave therapy. Although some techniques tend to be used more frequently at certain points in counseling, it was suggested that narrative therapy is a free-flowing process where phases can re-emerge as the therapeutic process continues.

Relative to cross-cultural issues, it was suggested that being neutral is actually siding with the oppressive powers of the larger social system. Instead, narrative therapists help clients look at how language in their social milieu and society may have negatively impacted them and might be intimately related to their problem-saturated story. Therefore, narrative therapists tend to be social justice advocates. In reference to spiritual issues, one role of the narrative therapist is to help clients look at how they may have been oppressed by certain religious values, but also to help clients feel empowered by developing new religious and/or spiritual stories.

Finally, it is suggested that quantitative research relies on a modernist paradigm by objectifying and having a myopic view of the research process. Qualitative research, on the other hand, seems a natural fit with the narrative tradition and can potentially offer much to our understanding of narrative therapy. However, to date, there have been few good qualitative research studies that have explored the efficacy of narrative therapy.

KEY WORDS

absent but implicit responses

Adelaide Narrative Therapy Centre

anti-deterministic

anti-objectivists

Australian and New Zealand Journal of Family Therapy

awe

collaboration

considering social and political issues

deconstruction

definitional ceremonies

Distinguished Contribution to Family Therapy and Theory and Practice

dominant narratives

dominant stories

double listening

Dulwich Centre for Narrative Therapy

Dulwich Centre Publications

empathy

encouraging clients to tell their stories

examining patterns phase (phase 2)

exceptions

externalize the problem

externalizing the problem and mapping its effects

Family Therapy Centre of Auckland

Family Therapy Program at the University of Calgary

helpful stories

high-level distancing tasks

join

joining phase (phase 1)

lack of neutrality

low-level distancing tasks

modernism

moving on phase (phase 4)

multistoried

mystery

narratives

outsider witness groups

Oxford House

post-modernism

post-structuralism

power

preferred stories

problem-saturated

qualitative research

quantitative research

questions

realities are constituted through language

realities are organized and maintained through narrative

realities are socially constructed

re-authoring

re-authoring phase
(phase 3)
reflection
reflective teams
reflexivity
relativism
re-membering
respectful curiosity
re-story

scaffolding
social constructionism
social justice issues
sparkling outcomes
structuralism
telling and retelling
the person is not the
problem; the
problem is the
problem

therapeutic documents
and other
paraphernalia
there are no essential
truths
thick descriptions
thin descriptions
unhelpful stories
unique outcomes
verbatim responses

KEY NAMES

Andersen, Tom

Bateson, Gregory

Epston, David

Foucault, Michel

Monk, Gerald

Myerhoff, Barbara

Tomm, Karl

White, Cheryl

White, Joan

White, Julienne

White, Neil

White, Paul

White, Penni

Winslade, John

REFERENCES

Allen, W., & Brickman, M. (1973). *Sleeper.* [Original film script]. Culver City, CA: Rollins & Joffe Productions.

Andersen, T. (1987). The reflecting team: Dialogue and meta-dialogue in clinical work. *Family Process, 26,* 415–428.

Berger, P. L., & Luckmann, T. (1966). *The social construction of reality: A treatise in the sociology of knowledge.* Garden City, NY: Anchor Books.

Besley, A. C. T., & Edwards, R. G. (2005). Editorial: Poststructuralism and the impact of the work of Michel Foucault in counselling and guidance. *British Journal of Guidance & Counselling, 33*(3), 277–281.

Bhat, N. (2008, March 27). Problems are treated from the outside in. *San Diego Union Tribune.* Retrieved from http://www.signonsandiego.com/uniontrib/20080327/news_1c27therapy.html

Brammer, L. M., & MacDonald, G. (2003). *The helping relationship: Process and skills* (8th ed.). Boston: Allyn & Bacon.

Brown, C. (2007). Situating knowledge and power in the therapeutic alliance. In C. Brown & T. Augusta-Scott (Eds.), *Narrative therapy: Making meaning, making lives* (pp. 3–22). Thousand Oaks, CA: Sage Publications.

Carlson, T. D., & Erickson, M. J. (2000). Re-authoring spiritual narratives: God in persons' relational identity stories. *Journal of Systemic Therapies, 19*(2), 65–83.

Chamberlain, S. (2003). *A tale of narrative therapy.* Retrieved from http://therapy.massey.ac.nz/175772/narrative/mod1web/3hour1.html

Drewey, W., & Winslade, J. (1997). The theoretical story of narrative therapy. In G. Monk, J. Winslade, K. Crocket, & D. Epston (Eds.), *Narrative therapy in practice: The archaeology of hope* (pp. 32–52). San Francisco: Jossey-Bass Publishers.

Epston, D. (2009). *David Epston remembers Michael White.* Retrieved from http://www.narrativeapproaches.com/White%20Memorial_files/epston%20remembers.pdf

Epston, D., & White, M. (1992). *Experience, contradiction, narrative, and imagination: Selected papers of David Epston and Michael White, 1989–1991.* Adelaide, South Australia: Dulwich Centre Publications.

Family therapy. (n.d.). *Therapist profiles: Michael White.* Retrieved from http://www.abacon.com/famtherapy/white.html

Freedman, J., & Combs, G. (1996). *Narrative therapy: The social construction of preferred realities.* New York: W. W. Norton and Company.

Gergen, K. (1999). *An invitation to social construction.* Thousand Oaks, CA: Sage Publications.

Gergen, K. J., & Gergen, M. M. (2008). Social construction and psychological inquiry. In J. A. Holstein & J. F. Gubrium (Eds.), *Handbook of constructionist research* (pp. 171–188). New York: The Guilford Press.

Hart, B. (1995). Re-authoring the stories we work by: Situating the narrative approach in the presence of the family of therapists. *Australian and New Zealand Journal of Family Therapy, 16*(4), 181–189.

Heins, T., & Ritchie, K. (1988). *Beating sneaky poo: Ideas for faecal soiling.* Retrieved from http://www.narrativetherapylibrary.com/img/ps/spoo1.pdf

Heppner, P. P., Kivlighan, D. M., & Wampold, B. E. (1999). *Research design in counseling* (2nd ed.). Belmont, CA: Wadsworth.

Hoyt, M. F. (1994). Introduction: Competency-based future-oriented therapy. In M. F. Hoyt (Ed.), *Constructive therapies.* New York: Guilford Press.

Krishnamurti, J. (1969). *Freedom from the known* (M. Lutyens, Ed.). New York: Harper & Row.

McMillan, J. H., & Schumacher, S. (2006). *Research in education: Evidence-based inquiry* (6th ed.). Boston: Allyn & Bacon.

Miller, L. (2008). Foucauldian constructionism. In J. A. Holstein & J. F. Gubrium (Eds.), *Handbook of constructionist research* (pp. 251–274). New York: The Guilford Press.

Morgan, A. (2000). *What is narrative therapy? An easy-to-read introduction.* Adelaide, South Australia: Dulwich Centre Publications.

Myerhoff, B. (1982). Life history among the elderly: Performance, visibility, and re-membering. In J. Rub (Ed.), *A crack in the mirror: Reflexive perspectives in anthropology* (pp. 99–120). Philadelphia: University of Pennsylvania Press.

Myerhoff, B. (1986). "Life not death in Venice": Its second life. In V. W. Turner & E. M. Bruner (Eds.), *The anthropology of experience* (pp. 261–286). Chicago: University of Illinois Press.

Myerhoff, B. (2007). *Stories as equipment for living: Last talks and tales of Barbara Myerhoff* (rev. ed.). Ann Arbor, MI: University of Michigan Press.

Nelson-Becker, H. B. (2004). Spiritual, religious, nonspiritual, and nonreligious narratives in marginalized older adults: A typology of coping styles. *Journal of Religion, Spirituality, and Aging, 17*(1/2), 21–38.

Park. S. (2008). *More words.* Retrieved May 5, 2008, from http://www.adelaidenarrative therapycentre.com.au/more_words.html

Payne, M. (2006). *Narrative therapy.* Thousand Oaks, CA: Sage Publications.

Pearse, J. (2008, April 28). Michael White dies: Used stories as therapy. *The New York Times.* Retrieved from http://www.nytimes.com/2008/04/28/us/28white.html

Perry, W. G. (1968). *Forms of intellectual and ethical development in the college years: A scheme.* New York: Holt, Rinehart, and Winston.

Raheim, S., Carey, M., Waldegrave, C., Tamase, K., Tuhaka, F., Fox, H., … Denborough, D., (n.d.). *An invitation to narrative practitioners to address privilege and dominance.* Retrieved from http://www.narrativetherapylibrary.com/img/ps/Privdom.pdf

Rosaldo, R. (1993). *Culture and truth: The remaking of social analysis.* Boston: Beacon Press.

Russell, S., & Carey, M. (2004). *Narrative therapy: Responding to your questions.* Adelaide, South Australia: Dulwich Centre Publications.

Semmler, P. L., & Williams, C. B. (2000). Narrative therapy: A storied context of multicultural counseling. *Journal of Multicultural Counseling and Development, 28,* 51–62.

Shapiro, J. P., Friedberg, R. D., & Bardenstein, K. K. (2006). *Child and adolescent therapy: Science and art.* Hoboken, NJ: John Wiley & Sons.

Sparks, A. C., & Smith, B. (2008). Narrative constructionist inquiry. In J. A. Holstein & J. F. Gubrium (Eds.), *Handbook of constructionist research* (pp. 295–314). New York: The Guilford Press.

The Icarus Project. (2008). *Icarus project: Welcome to Icarus.* Retrieved from http://theicarusproject.net/

The Icarus Project. (2006). *Icarus project: Mission statement.* Retrieved from http://theicarusproject.net/about-us/icarus-project-mission-statement

Weinberg, D. (2008). The philosophical foundations of constructionist research. In J. A. Holstein & J. F. Gubrium (Eds.), *Handbook of constructionist research* (pp. 13–40). New York: The Guilford Press.

White, M. (1991). Deconstruction and therapy. *Dulwich Centre Newsletter, 3,* 21–40. Adelaide, South Australia: Dulwich Centre Publications.

White, M. (1993). *Narrative therapy using a reflective team.* [Video]. Alexandria, VA: American Counseling Association.

White, M. (1995). *Re-authoring lives: Interviews and essays.* Adelaide, South Australia: Dulwich Centre Publications.

White, M. (1997). *Narratives of therapists' lives.* Adelaide, South Australia: Dulwich Centre Publications.

White, M. (2000). *Reflections on narrative practice: Essays and interviews.* Adelaide, South Australia: Dulwich Centre Publications.

White, M. (2002). Addressing personal failure. *International Journal of Narrative Therapy and Community Work, 3,* 33–76.

White, M. (2007). *Maps of narrative practice.* New York: Norton Books.

White, M. (2008, May 6). *Curriculum vitae.* Sent via e-mail by Jane Hales, assistant to Cheryl White, Dulwich Centre, Adelaide, South Australia.

White, M., & Epston, D. (1990). *Narrative means to therapeutic ends.* New York: Norton.

White, M., Epston, D., & Andrews, J. (1994). *The best of friends: A live interview with Michael White.* [Video]. Los Angeles: Master's Works Video Productions.

Wingard, B. (2001). *Telling our stories in ways that make us stronger.* Retrieved from http://www.narrativetherapylibrary.com/catalogue.asp?id=11

Winslade, J. M. (2005). Using discursive position in counselling. *British Journal of Guidance & Counselling, 33*(3), 351–364.

Winslade, J., Crocket, K., & Monk, G. (1997). The therapeutic relationship. In G. Monk, J. Winslade, K. Crocket, & D. Epston (Eds.), *Narrative therapy in practice: The archaeology of hope* (pp. 53–81). San Francisco: Jossey-Bass Publishers.

Winslade, J., & Geroski, A. (2008). A social constructionist view of development. In K. Kraus (Ed.), *Lenses: Applying lifespan development theories in counseling* (pp. 88–113) Boston/New York: Lahaska Press.

Wright, J. (2008). *Transcript of Jeremiah Wright's April 26th, 2008 speech to NAACP.* Retrieved from http://edition.cnn.com/2008/POLITICS/04/28/wright.transcript/index.html

Chapter 13

Solution-Focused Brief Therapy

Learning Goals

- To review the biographical sketches of Insoo Kim Berg and Steven de Shazer, two of the originators of solution-focused brief therapy (SFBT).
- To understand the historical context in which Berg and de Shazer developed their approach.
- To understand the constructionist and post-modern influences on the pragmatic, anti-deterministic, future-oriented, and optimistic view of human nature of SFBT.
- To understand how Wittgenstein's philosophy concerning language and its relationship to reality affected the development of SFBT and its tendency to normalize problems and believe in the strengths of the client.
- To review a number of key concepts related to SFBT, including the post-modern and social-constructionist basis of the approach; the fact that the approach is non-normative in that it does not attempt to compare a person's problems to a norm group; the tendency not to pathologize; its solution-focused and future orientation; looking at exceptions to clients' problems and identifying their strengths; looking at clients in terms of readiness, not resistance; and an examination of the 10 basic assumptions of SFBT.
- To learn about a number of techniques basic to SFBT, including pre-session changes; being an ambassador by showing curiosity, respect, and acceptance; using listening and empathy; being tentative; asking preferred goals questions, coping questions, exception-seeking questions, and solution-oriented questions; reframing; amplification; complimenting clients; and scaling.
- To understand the six stages of SFBT: pre-session change, forming a collaborative relationship, describing the problem, establishing preferred goals, problem-to-solution focus, reaching preferred goals, and ending therapy.
- To show how SFBT honors the subjective worldview of clients and is likely an approach that can be used with a wide range of diverse clients.
- To examine the efficacy of SFBT, especially in light of its relative newness to the field of counseling and psychotherapy and, to date, the relative lack of controlled studies.
- To see how SFBT is applied through vignettes, DVDs, and case study.

The master therapist Milton Erickson was known for practicing unusual interventions that were brief and often at the client's home or workplace. For instance, there is the story of how he once spent less than an hour at the home of a woman who was depressed, lonely, and shy. By visiting her home, he realized she was an expert at cultivating African violets and that she was a committed member of her church. He quickly came up with an intervention: every time there was a birth, wedding, or death at the church, she was to send one of her flowers. She did this religiously, which dramatically changed her life as other church members began to get to know and appreciate her. At her death, the newspaper noted that hundreds of people attended the funeral of the "African Violet Lady." (paraphrased from Gordon & Meyers-Anderson, 1981).

In the beginning, there was Freud. Soon followed disciples, many of whom had profound ideas about the "psyche." As years passed, psychoanalysis lost some of its glitter but still maintained a large base. Slowly, other approaches arose, also mostly concerned with the "inside" of the person, and generally those who practiced these therapies would spend months or years helping clients examine and understand "the problem." Then, one day, an unconventional psychiatrist, Milton Erickson, started to practice a new form of therapy. As reflected in the story above, he focused on client strengths, not deficits, and he worked quickly. His work was to greatly affect those at the **Mental Research Institute** (MRI) in Palo Alto, California. Established in 1959 by Don Jackson, MRI included a number of therapists and researchers who would become household names, such as Virginia Satir, Gregory Bateson, and Jay Haley (Cade, 2007; Goldenberg & Goldenberg, 2008). Unconventional in their focus, these individuals looked at how communication and rules in systems, particularly family systems, affected individuals within those systems.

In 1966, within MRI, the **Brief Family Therapy Center** (BFTC) was established. Led by Paul Watzlawick, John Weakland, and Dick Fisch, BFTC focused solely on helping families solve their problems as opposed to "underlying" issues or global communication and system patterns (Cade, 2007; Goldenberg & Goldenberg, 2008). Although they realized that families were trying their best to fix the "problem," they also saw that the solutions families tried usually resulted in entrenching the problem more. Approaching families with an attitude of experimentation, these therapists were highly active and felt free to use any methods that were ethical and legal to solve problems or lessen presenting symptoms.

Unknown to each other at the time, Insoo Kim Berg and Steve de Shazer would end up at BFTC for advanced training, eventually meet, fall in love, and marry. What they learned at BFTC would greatly affect the development of

SFBT, and although many individuals like Bill O'Connell, Bill O'Hanlon, Jeffrey Guterman, Peter De Jong, and others impacted the methods and practices of solution-focused counseling, Berg and de Shazer are often cited as the early pioneers of this approach. Let's take a look at this couple who would change the way in which many therapists work.

INSOO KIM BERG AND STEVE DE SHAZER

Suppose that one night, while you were asleep, there was a miracle and this problem was solved. How would you know? What would be different? (de Shazer, 1988, p. 5)

Insoo Kim Berg

Steve de Shazer

Born on July 25, 1934, in Korea, Insoo Kim Berg grew up in what most would have called a prosperous and even privileged family in Korea. A few years later, on June 25, 1940, thousands of miles away in Milwaukee, Wisconsin, Steve de Shazer was born to an electrical-engineer father and opera-singing mother (Dolan, 2006).

As a young teenager, Berg's world would be shattered when her family's home was bombed during the Korean War. It was at that point that she realized, "It is people, not things, that are important in life" (Dolan, 2007, p. 130). Berg would initially study pharmacy at Ewha Women's University in Seoul. Then, in 1957, she decided to leave Korea for the United States, where she would earn her bachelor's degree in 1967 and her master's of science in social work (MSSW) in 1969 from the University of Wisconsin–Milwaukee (Berg, n.d.a; "Tribute to Insoo Kim Berg," 2007). Meanwhile, de Shazer, growing up in Milwaukee, would earn his BFA in 1964 and, like Berg, his MSSW from the University of Wisconsin–Milwaukee in 1971 (de Shazer, n.d.), But the two had not met—yet.

With her MSSW in hand, Berg secured a job at Family Services of Milwaukee, where she worked until 1980. Paralleling her work at Family Services, in 1974, she took advanced training programs at the **Menninger Institute** and at the **Family Institute of Chicago**. Here she was required to meet with one family for an entire year and then have her supervisor and a class watch her work with this family. Relying heavily on an insight-oriented approach, Berg increasingly began to question the length of treatment and the intense focus on insight. "These primarily working class families were in a great deal of pain and they were not interested in gaining insight but wished for the pain to go away, and quickly, too, not to wait for weeks, months, even a year" (Berg, n.d.b, para. 6). Enthralled by the writings of Jay Haley and John Weakland, and others who offered a briefer lens through which to view therapy, Berg moved to the MRI in Palo Alto, where she began to study with those at BFTC.

Like Berg, de Shazer also decided to do additional training at MRI and, over the years, was mentored by John Weakland. And despite the fact that he and Berg both had roots in Milwaukee, it was actually Weakland who introduced them to each other. This union was to be the main impetus for their lasting marriage and for the beginning of SFBT.

De Shazer was a Ludwig Wittgenstein enthusiast. Considered by some to be one of the major philosophers of the twentieth century, Wittgenstein's ideas are often seen as a precursor to **post-modernism** (Wittgenstein, 1963). In fact, Wittgenstein was one of the first to challenge the modernist view of the world, such as the primacy of the scientific method. He also suggested that language shapes reality and that reality is always changing as a function of the interactions individuals have with others. De Shazer adapted Wittgenstein's ideas to the therapeutic setting. From this perspective, Wittgenstein's ideas suggest one should not try to have a "deep understanding" of the client's reality or think in terms of internal mechanisms that help to create reality. Instead, if a client says he or she is depressed, the therapist should accept that is how the client feels and help the client get undepressed through language and discourse. Most important, the therapist would help move the client toward his or her **preferred goals** so the client feels better (O'Connell, 2003).

Influenced by Wittgenstein and intrigued by the work being done at BFTC–MRI, de Shazer, Berg, and three others decided to start the Brief Family Therapy Center of Milwaukee, which initially mirrored what was happening at MRI. Mentored by Weakland and others, the center slowly began to grow. As the team began to treat large numbers of clients, they noticed that interventions that were solution-focused, not problem-focused, seemed to have better and quicker results. In fact, the group realized that the average number of sessions clients spent in therapy was six, yet most therapists, with their insight-oriented approaches, expected clients to be in therapy for months, if not years (Gingerich, 2006). They also realized that most therapists saw clients as diseased and were continually hypothesizing about their clients as if the therapist knew something about them that they did not know about themselves (Cade, 2005). Deciding that clients were their own best resources and that they could be helped in a short amount of time, they decided to use videotapes and live observation to examine what techniques seemed to have the quickest and best results. In fact, this is how de Shazer (1988) came up with his famous **miracle question** that is quoted at the beginning of this biographical sketch.

Knowing they could quickly and effectively work with clients, the team decided to contract with one health insurance company for a flat fee of $500 per client, regardless of how long the treatment took (United Kingdom Association..., 2006). As they continued to work, they increasingly began to think that clients could be seen from a more positive frame of reference and helped in a short amount of time. In fact, de Shazer came to be called the "man with **Occam's razor**," which is the belief that the simplest solution is often the best solution (Berg, n.d.b). Eventually, conducting informal follow-up studies of their clients, de Shazer was able to show that his new approach to counseling was effective in a short amount of time (Gingerich, 2006).

As their successes grew with this new solution-focused approach, the group decided to publish the **Underground Railroad**, a newsletter highlighting their novel ways of working with clients. Their success with the newsletter and with clients, and the popularity of Berg and de Shazer's publications, would make the couple nationally and internationally known. Berg wrote numerous articles, served on editorial boards, developed multimedia resources demonstrating solution-focused counseling, and wrote 10 books, some of which include *Family Based Services: A Solution-focused Approach* (Berg, 1994), *Solutions Step-by-Step* (Berg & Reuss, 1998), *Tales of Solutions* (Berg & Dolan, 2001), *Interviewing for Solutions* (De Jong & Berg, 2002), *Children's Solution Work* (Berg & Steiner, 2003), and *Brief Coaching for Lasting Solutions* (Berg & Szabo, 2005). Similarly, de Shazer lectured worldwide, served on editorial boards, and wrote a number of popular books, some of which include *Patterns of Brief Therapy* (1982), *Keys to Solutions in Brief Therapy* (1985), *Clues: Investigating Solutions in Brief Therapy* (1988), *Putting Difference to Work* (1991), *Words Were Originally Magic* (1994), and *More than Miracles: The State of the Art of Solution-focused Therapy* (de Shazer & Dolan, 2007)

Although consumed by his work, de Shazer was also a person whose heart was in the arts, a classically trained musician, and at one point in his life, earned a living from playing jazz on his saxophone. He also was a gourmet cook, artist, baseball fan, and philosophy enthusiast. Sadly, while on one of his lecture trips, he contracted pneumonia and died in Vienna on September 11, 2005. Although Berg was also constantly busy with her work, she managed to find time to involve herself in activities as varied as yoga, classical music, gardening, physical activities, and reading. Known as a caring, funny, warm, optimistic, and enthusiastic professional, Insoo Kim Berg passed away peacefully on January 10, 2007.

VIEW OF HUMAN NATURE

Solution-focused brief therapy is a **pragmatic, anti-deterministic,** and **future-oriented** approach that offers optimism and hope about the ability of the client to change. This positive approach rejects the notion that individuals have an inherent tendency toward mental health problems or illnesses and focuses almost exclusively on solutions and on client strengths, not on client deficits or problems (Fernando, 2007). Trusting that change can occur quickly, this approach believes that individuals can find **exceptions** to their problems and build on those exceptions to find new ways of living in the world (O'Hanlon & Weiner-Davis, 2003).

De Shazer and Dolan (2007) have suggested that SFBT is "not theory-based" (p. 1), and one can understand this argument when remembering that most of the techniques were pragmatically chosen after the Milwaukee group realized clients could be helped quickly. In fact, although most modern-day solution-focused therapists would likely identify themselves as **social constructionists** and **post-modernists**, in the case of SFBT, which came first—the techniques or the philosophy—is uncertain. Despite the assertion that SFBT is not theory-based, it is clear that de Shazer and others have been influenced by Wittgenstein, **social constructionism**, and **post-modernism**, and this is where the approach has its philosophical home (Bidwell, 2007; Guterman, 2006).

As noted in Chapter 11, the post-modern, social-constructionist approach assumes that reality is a function of social interaction, which is especially influenced by the language used within an individual's social sphere as well as the language that is endemic in cultures and society. In fact, they would argue that the nature of reality is limited by language, as ideas and concepts, which have their basis in language, are affected by the context in which they evolve (Gergen, 1985, 2009). Similar to the Heisenberg Uncertainty Principle in physics that suggests the act of observing a phenomenon may change the phenomenon in ways that make it difficult to be understood, our very attempts at understanding ourselves are likely affected by the context through which we have come to understand reality and the language that we use to describe this understanding. Thus, reality is particularly malleable and must always be questioned. This approach differs from most other theories, which assume there is something inherent that functions to create one's reality. Such inherent structures put forth by other theorists range from a tendency for the individual to actualize himself or herself, as the humanists suggest, to a genetically based cognitive map that lends direction to the manner in which one sees the world, as some cognitive therapists assert, to an id, ego, and superego that jointly form the individual's personality structure, which psychoanalysts put forth.

The post-modern, social-constructionist position asserts that pathology, for all practical purposes, does not exist, since one cannot prove that it is inherently found within the person. Thus, this perspective assumes that problems can be viewed as challenges that are inherent in a language-based system (Gergen, 1985, 2009; Guterman, 2006; Wittgenstein, 1963). Seen from this viewpoint, how the counselor brings himself or herself into the relationship is critical to helping the individual overcome his or her problems. If the counselor believes that pathology exists within the person, he or she will find this pathology; if the counselor believes that the problems are system-based (e.g., residing within the family), he or she will find this to be the case; but if the counselor assumes that problems are a function of the language used by the client within his or her social sphere (including the counselor's office!), opportunities for change through the use of a new language are plentiful. Thus, "SFBT eschews the 'medical model' perspective and takes a **nonpathological approach**" (Watts & Pietrzak, 2000, p. 443).

Given the pragmatic and future-oriented focus, as well as the philosophical assumptions inherent in social constructionism and post-modernism, most solution-focused therapists believe that clients can change quickly; the client is the expert; the client has strengths which can be expanded upon; it is important to focus on solutions, not problems; when developing solutions, it is important to focus on the future; and the client, in dialogue with the counselor, can create a new problem-free language as he or she moves toward creating a new reality (O'Hanlon & Weiner-Davis, 2003).

KEY CONCEPTS

Post-Modernism and Social Constructionism

Like narrative therapy, SFBT has a strong post-modern and social-constructionist perspective, and the reader is referred to Chapter 12 to read the sections on **post-modernism, post-structuralism** (a subcategory of **post-modernism**), and

---

B o x 13.1   Difference in Boys' and Girls' Math Scores: Science or Myth?

When I grew up, except for those careers that were traditionally gender-specific (e.g., nursing), there were few women who went into math and science careers. In fact, over the years, it was assumed that one of the many reasons women did not go into these careers was because of their heavy emphasis on math. The "conversation" in society was that girls and women simply did not have the innate ability to do math; this was believed to be reality. As recently as 2005, the then-president of Harvard questioned women's intrinsic ability in science, stating that this may be due to inherent differences in math ability (Dobbs, 2005). Now, a new meta-analysis shows that differences in math scores between grades 2 and 11 are indistinguishable as a function of sex (Hyde, Lindberg, Linn, Ellis, & Williams, 2008). So, what used to be seen as a genetic reality now appears to be a belief system that many of us (including many girls and women) bought into!

---

social constructionism under "Key Concepts." Here, I offer a quick overview of those philosophies and how they relate to SFBT.

Post-modernism has sometimes been defined as the questioning of modernism, which states that truth can ultimately be uncovered and that underlying structures are responsible for shaping how one comes to understand the world. Post-modernists suggest that much of what has been handed to us as "truth" by the modernists is only the modernists' particular "take" on reality. Therefore, therapists who act in an "objective" manner and assume that there are certain inherent mechanisms that lead a person down a path toward a particular personality style have become entrenched in believing that particular truth.

Social constructionism views knowledge and truth as something that is constructed through conversations (Gergen, 1985, 2009; Rudes & Guterman, 2007). Fitting comfortably alongside post-modernism, this philosophy suggests that language used and the discourses we have with others are key factors in the development of reality. In other words, nothing is fixed (see Box 13.1).

Since language creates reality through discourse, the major responsibility of a therapist would be to recognize that the language he or she uses will likely impact the client (as the client's language will likely impact the therapist). Therefore, the therapist must carefully choose his or her words, knowing the influence of language on the person. In fact, *not* saying certain things will reinforce existing ways of being for the client. Also, since reality is constantly changing and is a function of language, it is assumed that one can never fully know the inner world of another; "all one can know is the verbal expressions of another's experiences" (Rudes & Guterman, 2007, p. 388). For post-modernists and social constructionists, even the idea of an "inner world" is seen as a cultural by-product, not something that necessarily exists. From this perspective, it would make sense to question any therapist who states that he or she knows the client's inner world as a result of understanding the functioning of some hypothesized inner structures (e.g., id, ego, superego; incongruent vs. congruent self). Hypothetically, what I say is the color blue may be someone else's red, and what I say is depression may be experienced differently by another, and what I say is happiness also may be experienced differently by another (see Box 13.2).

B o x 13.2   Color Therapy

Imagine there was a therapy that stated color preference was an indication of mental health, and the closer a person's favorite color was to "red," the healthier he or she was. Those who liked red most were very healthy, those who liked orange were pretty healthy, those who liked yellow were somewhat healthy, and so forth down the spectrum to green, then blue, and then to those who liked violet, who were really unhealthy. Now imagine that this therapy became so popular that it was accepted throughout the land, and most people "knew" that color preference was related to mental health.

Now, imagine a client sees a therapist who is a "color therapist." Naturally, one of his first questions is to ask the client what her favorite color is. She says "blue." Well, immediately, the therapist assumes the client is not mentally healthy. After all, blue is way down the list toward violet. So, the therapist begins to treat her and tries to change her favorite color. He even has a systematic way of having her work up the hierarchy toward red. If she practices the system every day, she will eventually get closer to red, says the therapist. After a few months, she has worked her way up to green, and the therapist says he thinks that she might want to consider taking some medication, for medication will help her experience the red more often. The therapist tells her that after a few years

of experiencing more red, she can try to reduce her medication as she may begin to like red on her own.

Frustrated that she is not making progress rapidly enough, the client decides to see a new therapist. The new therapist is clearly unconventional and does not even believe in color therapy. She asks the client to tell her what her problem is. The client states "Well, everyone says that liking blue is bad, and so I must be mentally ill. What do you think?" This therapist replies by saying, "How about we don't focus on the color right now. Instead, let me ask you: What do you want your life to look like? Where do you want to take therapy? What do you want as your end goal? What would make you happier?"

With the first therapist, there is an external reality based on preconceived notions about colors. This reality has been bought into by many. In fact, a whole system of working with clients has been developed. Almost everyone "knows" and believes in this approach. The second therapist, however, does not have these preconceived ideas, and indeed even questions the moral authority, which asserts that this reality exists. This therapist does not believe there are any internal structures that mediate mental health based on color. She questions its basis and wants the client to focus on future goals. This is the basis of SFBT!

Finally, Freedman and Combs (1996) suggest four premises that summarize much of what has been said: realities are **socially constructed**, **realities are constituted through language**, **realities are organized and maintained through narrative**, and **there are no essential truths** (see Chapter 12 for a longer discussion of these premises).

Non-Normative

Since reality is in the eye of the beholder, there is no normative way of being that is the "correct" way to act. Therefore, SFBT therapists do not compare their clients' behaviors to the behaviors of others in an effort to try and have their clients act like "most people." However, Thomas and Nelson (2007) note that it is sometimes important to let clients know that others have experiences similar to theirs. Thus, a client who is experiencing panic attacks might want to know that the symptoms he or she has seem similar to the symptoms thousands of other people have. These types of comparisons can alleviate the anxiety some clients have when they believe they are the only ones who have them.

Non-Pathologizing

Thomas and Nelson (2007) note that one key assumption of SFBT is to embrace a nonjudgmental stance regarding the problems clients bring with them to therapy. Such a stance is based on the belief that no reality is better than another—they are just different. Thus, therapists should avoid viewing client problems as pathological, even when the client presents with behaviors that traditionally have been classified in such a manner. In fact, SFBT asserts that embracing a point of view that assumes client pathology and views clients as inherently deficient is the result of a kind of professional "group think":

> … [W]hen a counselor describes clients in terms of pathological categories, this indicates that he or she has conversed within the context of a professional community that, in turn, has chosen to organize its knowledge accordingly. (Guterman, 2006, p. 16)

Even though a counselor may take a **non-pathologizing** stance with clients, he or she will still have opinions about client actions. For instance, clients whose behaviors are in some manner harming themselves or others may be alarming to a therapist. And, as in the case of abusive behaviors or suicidal and homicidal behaviors, therapists may decide to discuss their concerns with their clients, and in the case of foreseeable harm, respond in a manner that assures no harm occurs to the client or to others.

Solution Focused and Future Oriented

Today, most clinicians are trained to focus on problems, likely because the earliest psychotherapists were physicians trained as analysts who examined the underlying causes of disease. Partly due to its success in medicine, this problem-focused model became embedded in the mental health professionals' work. Thus, many counselors today see clients as diseased or deficient due to problems from the client's past. They believe such clients must be diagnosed appropriately and treated for their past problems. These counselors tend to use disease-laden, problem-focused language. SFBT therapists, on the other hand, focus on client strengths and help clients identify their **preferred goals** (O'Connell, 2003). Table 13.1 contrasts the use of questions from a problem focus with those from a solution focus.

Although some have suggested that the use of a diagnostic manual like the DSM-IV-TR reinforces the disease model, others suggest that it is not the DSM-IV-TR that is problematic but rather the manner in which a counselor approaches the manual (McLaughlin, 2006). A counselor who has a disease focus sees the manual as identifying diseases and client deficits; on the other hand, an SFBT therapist who has a positive, strength-based focus can see benefit from such a manual as well as other assessment processes (Guterman, 2006):

> Accordingly, my solution-focused counseling approach involves conducting a formal intake, including a comprehensive psychosocial history, a thorough mental status examination, formulating a multiaxial diagnostic impression, and making psychiatric referrals for clients who meet

T A B L E 13.1   Contrasting a Problem Focus with a Solution Focus

Problem-focused	Solution-focused
▪ How can I help you?	▪ How will you know that coming here today has been helpful?
▪ Could you tell me about the problem?	▪ What would you like to change?
▪ Is the problem a symptom of an underlying issue	▪ Can we dig deep to discover solutions?
▪ How are we to understand the problem in light of the past?	▪ What will the future look like without the problem?
▪ What defense mechanisms are operating?	▪ How can we use the skills and strengths of the client?
▪ How many sessions will we need?	▪ Have we achieved enough to end?

From: O'Connell, B. (2005). *Solution-focused therapy* (2nd ed.). Thousand Oaks, CA: Sage. p. 20.

the criteria for certain diagnoses (e.g., major depression, bipolar disorder, and schizophrenia). When I complete the intake, however, I proceed to co-construct a problem with the client in keeping with a solution-focused approach to counseling. (p. 16)

In short, the SFBT therapist sees value in obtaining information and then, with the client, discussing how to use that information to focus on solutions.

Exceptions and Client Strengths

Similar to narrative therapy, one focus of SFBT is to help clients recognize that their lives have not been filled only with problems; there have been times when they have been strong, felt good about themselves, and have dealt effectively with issues that have arisen. Therefore, one role of the solution-focused therapist is to inquire about those times and to help clients see how they have effectively coped so that such mechanisms can potentially be amplified and used in the future. Thus, the solution-focused therapist is vigilant about looking for times when the problem has not saturated the client's life—looking for **exceptions** to what is sometimes described by narrative therapists as the "dominant, problem-saturated" way of living (Payne, 2006).

Readiness, Not Resistance

When working on my doctorate, I went to a workshop on how to counsel resistant adolescents. As the workshop leader started to present, the first thing he said was, "There are no resistant adolescents, only bad therapists." I was taken aback. After all, aren't adolescents known to be resistant? Well, given the state of many adolescents, I would still argue that adolescent clients are probably more difficult to work with than many other clients. However, there is no doubt that

---

B o x 13.3   Tim Grothaus Works with Latonya

Read or watch Dr. Tim Grothaus's work with Latonya, and consider whether Latonya is a customer, complainant, or visitor.

You can read this session by going to www. cengage.com/counseling/neukrug/CTP1e and click

"student downloads." Or your instructor may show this session in class with the DVD that accompanies his or her copy of the text.

---

the workshop leader had a point. He was saying that every adolescent, even the most "resistant," could be helped by some therapist. Solution-focused therapy makes a similar point. Rather than labeling a client "resistant," solution-focused therapy suggests that clients who have not been able to change have simply not yet found an available mechanism to change (Guterman, 2006). In fact, given a different counselor, a client who has difficulty changing could indeed be able to change.

Instead of viewing clients as resistant, De Jong and Berg (2002) and de Shazer (1988) describe three types of clients and relate their ability to change as more of an issue of readiness, not resistance. **Customers** are ready to work on defining their preferred goals and on problem-solving. **Complainants** are often able to identify their problems and come to a consensus with the counselor about what needs to be addressed but have trouble coming up with solutions. **Visitors** are shopping around—testing the waters to see if they want to try out therapy. These clients may not be able to identify or want to talk about problems and cannot come up with goals for treatment. However, complainants can become customers, and visitors can become complainants, under the right circumstances (see Box 13.3). And what is the right circumstance? It's probably finding the right therapist who can connect with the client and subsequently help that client move toward identifying issues and focusing on solutions. O'Connell (2005) offers a graphic presentation of the differences between a person who is ready for change and one who is not (see Figure 13.1).

Knows what to change	Does not know what to change
Knows how to recognize signs of change	Does not know how to recognize signs of change
Wants to change	Does not want to change
Knows how to change	Does not know how to change
Aware of obstacles to change	Unaware of obstacles to change
Confident of making changes	Lacks confidence about making changes
Ready to make changes	Not ready to make changes

From: O'Connel, B. (2005). *Solution-focused therapy* (2nd ed.). Thousand Oaks, CA: sage, p. 27.

F I G U R E 13.1 Client Positions about Change
SOURCE: O'Connell, B. (2005). Solution-focused therapy (2nd ed.). Thousand Oaks, CA: Sage.

Box 13.4 Assumptions

---

1. Change is constant and inevitable.
2. If it ain't broke, don't fix it.
3. If it works, do more of it.
4. If it's not working, do something different.
5. Clients come to us with resources and strengths.
6. Small steps can lead to big changes.

7. There is not necessarily a logical relationship between the solution and the problem.
8. The language for solution development is different from that needed to describe a problem.
9. No problems happen all the time; there are always exceptions that can be utilized.
10. The future is both created and negotiable.

Basic Assumptions

With its post-modern and social-constructionist philosophical basis, and its pragmatic, strength-based, future-oriented, and brief focus, a number of basic assumptions about how to work with clients have been identified by de Shazer, Berg, O'Hanlon, and others (cf. O'Hanlon & Weiner-Davis, 2003; de Shazer & Dolan, 2007; Thomas & Nelson, 2007). Box 13.4 highlights these assumptions, and descriptions of each follow.

1. *Change is constant and inevitable.* Our lives are filled with changes—from the developmental changes, we undergo as we move through life, to the unexpected changes that occur from some unforeseen event to the changes we choose to make because we believe they will better our lives. Recognizing the importance of change to feel better, SFBT therapists see change as opportunity. Thus, in therapy, clients can try out new behaviors and new ways of being as they direct their lives in directions they want to take them.

2. *If it ain't broke, don't fix it.* Some approaches to therapy look for problems, even when they don't exist, and assume that there are additional issues "underneath" even when the client isn't presenting symptoms. The solution-focused approach makes no assumptions about underlying issues and does not look to change behaviors that the client has not identified as problematic.

3. *If it works, do more of it.* As obvious as this might sound, clients sometimes have not focused on what does work in their lives, and conversations about what is working and the possibility of doing more of what works can be an important focus in therapy.

4. *If it's not working, do something different.* In other, more traditional approaches, when what the client is doing is *not* working, the client is often labeled as "resistant." SFBT, on the other hand, assumes that when current ways of living are not bringing the client what he or she wants, the client needs to try other behaviors until some are found that do work for the client.

5. *Clients come to us with resources and strengths.* Clients are experts about themselves—they know what has been working and what has not been working in their lives, although they have not always focused on identifying

those behaviors. And, in contrast to many therapeutic approaches that view therapists as experts in identifying client pathology, this approach sees therapists as experts in problem solving. Therefore, SFBT therapists help clients identify their strengths and resources so that they can make positive changes in their lives.

6. *Small steps can lead to big changes.* If you've seen the movie *What About Bob*, you'll understand how small steps can lead to big changes—well, at least in theory. In the movie, Richard Dreyfus plays a psychiatrist who wrote a book called *Baby Steps* and is treating the multiphobic Bo Wiley (Bill Murray). Like in the movie, SFBT embraces a commonsense assumption that if clients accomplish small steps over time, they can move "gradually and gracefully forward … to subsequently be able to describe things as 'better enough' for therapy to end." (de Shazer & Dolan, 2007, p. 2)

7. *There is not necessarily a logical relationship between the solution and the problem.* Thomas and Nelson (2007) note that traditional therapies will spend extraordinary amounts of time dealing with issues that seemingly "caused" the problem. Offering the analogy of a flat tire that needs to be fixed, they note that it does not matter how the tire got flat; what's important is that it get fixed. SFBT therefore focuses on fixing the problem by asking the client to focus on solutions, not by focusing on problems that often have little effect on helping the client feel better.

8. *The language for solution development is different from that needed to describe a problem.* Since solutions, not problems, are being focused upon, this approach uses a tone that is optimistic, future-oriented, positive, and hopeful. In contrast, problem-oriented approaches tend to focus on deficits and pathology and are filled with negative language and depressive symbols and words.

9. *No problems happen all the time; there are always exceptions that can be utilized.* Although clients often feel they are engulfed by their problems, in actuality, all people have times when there are exceptions to their problems. One role of the counselor is to help explore these exceptions, help determine what is different in the client's life during those exceptions, and elicit new solutions from this newly found information.

10. *The future is both created and negotiable.* As opposed to the more traditional view of therapy, which sees individuals as "locked into" a way of being based on their inherent ways of living in the world, this approach believes that people are the "architects" of their destiny, and in conversation with the therapist, can co-create a new future.

THERAPEUTIC TECHNIQUES

There are a vast number of techniques that a solution-focused therapist would use, as long as the focus of the session was congruent with the general philosophy of the solution-focused approach, which assumes that one should show respect and appreciate the client, believe that clients can change quickly, help to identify client strengths, and focus mostly on solutions rather than problems. The following highlights some of the more popular techniques.

Requesting That Clients Note Pre-Session Changes

Solution-focused therapists assume that when a client seeks counseling, he or she is ready for change. Therefore, prior to the first sessions therapists will often ask clients to note any change that may occur between the time they made the appointment and the time they actually showed up for the appointment (O'Connell, 2003). Then, when the client does arrive for the first appointment, the therapist generally prompts the client by asking what change, if any, has been noticed.

Being an Ambassador (Showing Curiosity, Respect, and Acceptance)

In contrast to therapeutic models, where therapists approach the client as the "expert," the solution-focused therapist enters the relationship as an ambassador to a foreign country might (Murphy, 2008). For instance, an ambassador would be respectful, curious, and accepting of people in another culture in his or her attempt to understand the ways of the people. In a similar fashion, the solution-focused therapist enters the relationship humbly and is curious about the client's predicament, respectful of the client's ways of being, and accepting of what the client tells him or her. Ultimately, such an approach helps to elicit information from the client and strengthens the therapeutic alliance.

Listening and Empathy

As in many other approaches, listening and empathy are important skills for the solution-focused therapist, particularly at the beginning of the relationship (O'Connell, 2005). This is because when clients initially enter counseling, their talk is often problem-saturated, and they generally want to discuss their problems in detail. Giving clients the opportunity to talk about their problems is respectful and an important aspect to building the relationship and understanding their problems (De Jong & Berg, 2002). However, such a problem focus should not be extensive and should change in a relatively short amount of time to **solution talk**.

Being Tentative

> SFBT therapists do not marry their ideas or techniques; instead, they hold loosely to assumptions, apply techniques lightly, and are cautious with their language…. (Thomas & Nelson, 2007, p. 8).

Similar to what De Jong and Berg (2002) call holding a **not-knowing posture,** being tentative means that the therapist approaches the client with an attitude that the client is the expert and that any hypotheses or interpretations about

---

B o x   13.5   Phil

Phil, a 35-year-old single male, is currently depressed and has suffered with depression most of his adult life. He is the youngest of three children and describes growing up in a family that was marked by "lots of complaining and family members feeling disgruntled." He notes that his parents did not have a loving relationship and often walked around with a "sour look on their faces." He has tried a number of ways to alleviate his depression but states none have worked. In fact, he spent three years in a "depth-oriented" therapy and also has tried taking "SSRI" antidepressants. In addition, he states that he has attempted to "fix the problem on his own" by continually reading self-help books. He reports constantly trying to do "thought-stopping" so he would no longer have any depressive thoughts.

---

why the client might be struggling should be cautiously held (cf. Anderson & Goolishian, 1992). The therapist demonstrates tentativeness by being humble, respectful, and curious; by not acting as the "expert;" and by the types of response he or she gives. For instance, solution-focused therapists can often be heard starting sentences with such phrases as:

- Could it be that … ?
- Am I correct in assuming that … ?
- Correct me if I'm wrong that …
- I would guess that …

Use of Questions

Questions are an important skill that all solution-focused therapists need to learn how to use, and how a therapist frames a question has far-reaching effects on the tone and direction of the relationship (De Jong & Berg, 2002). From a solution-focused perspective, questions generally be classified in one of five areas: (1) what the client is hoping his or her future will look like **(preferred goals questions)** (2) what the client is doing and whether it is working for him or her **(evaluative questions)**, (3) how the client has coped in the past with his or her problem **(coping questions)**, (4) when exceptions to the problems have occurred **(exception-seeking questions)**, and (5) how the client's life would be if the problem did not exist **(solution-oriented questions)**. Box 13.5 offers a scenario concerning Phil, who has sought out counseling due to ongoing depression. This scenario will be used to exemplify how different kinds of questions might be used.

Preferred Goals Questions.   Having its roots in the narrative therapy concept of preferred stories, which seeks to help clients identify and adopt healthier, non–problem-saturated stories (Freedman & Combs, 1996), the purpose of solution-focused counseling is to help clients reach their **preferred goals**, which are new ways of being that will result in their feeling better (Bertolino & O'Hanlon, 2002). Therefore, it is important that the therapist have a sense of how the client's life will look when these goals are reached and how long the client believes it will take for these outcomes to be reached. Otherwise, "therapy could reasonably go on forever" (de Shazer, 1988, p. 93). When devising these preferred goals questions, the problem is not focused on, but the client's hoped-for future is. Some questions that O'Connell (2003) suggests include:

- How will you know that coming here has been worthwhile for you?

- What are your best hopes for this session?

- What will be the first sign for you?

- How will you know when things are getting better?

- How long do you think it will take before things get better?

- How will you know when things are getting better? (p. 7)

Evaluative Questions.   These questions focus on whether client behaviors have had a positive effect on the client's life and in what manner they have helped the client achieve his or her goals. For instance, in Phil's case, the following questions might be asked:

- How successful have you been in trying to alleviate your depression?

- How helpful was the use of antidepressants?

- What aspects of "depth" therapy were helpful to you?

- How do you think "thought-stopping" has helped lessen your depression?

- What about reading self-help books has helped you with your depression?

- Out of all the ways that you have tried, what was the most effective in alleviating your depression?

Notice that when asking evaluative questions about Phil, they are not focused on the depressive family atmosphere or his parents' lack of a loving relationship, as such questions would be problem-focused, not solution-focused. Instead, the focus is on aspects of Phil's life that may have been at least somewhat helpful in his attempt to find solutions. In the same vein, when Phil responds, it is important to spend only a limited amount of time on what has not worked, as such discussions are wasteful and rehash past failures. For instance, if Phil says, "Depth therapy just made me feel worse," then a discussion of depth therapy would be limited, although it would be okay to ask a question like, "Although depth therapy was not helpful overall, what aspect *was* helpful for you?" Overall, the therapist should focus on those behaviors that have worked for Phil and have expanded discussions around those responses that can be used in solution-building.

Coping Questions.   Coping questions ask clients to think about and describe times in which they have been able to cope with the problem effectively. In asking these types of questions, solution-focused therapists will sometimes use **pre-suppositional questions**, which make the assumption that there have been times when the problem did not saturate the client's life. So, instead of asking, "Have there been times when you were able to cope with [the problem]?"

a client is asked, "What ways have you found to cope with [the problem]?" For instance, in Phil's case, he might be asked the following pre-suppositional, coping questions:

- What ways have you found to help manage or alleviate your depression?
- What other ways have you tried that were successful in alleviating your depression?
- I know you had trouble getting out of bed this morning because you were so depressed. Can you tell me what enabled you to be able to get yourself up?
- Your depression seems to have impacted your eating, and you've lost some weight. How is it that you are able to eat sometimes?

Exception-Seeking Questions. Exception-seeking questions, one of the most well-known solution-focused skills, explore what is going on in the client's life when he or she is not experiencing the problem. Using this type of question helps to quickly focus on the task at hand—finding solutions. As with coping questions, rather than asking *if* the client has exceptions, there is the pre-supposition that the client *has* had exceptions in his or her life. In Phil's case, the following questions could be used:

- I bet there have been times in your life when you have not felt depressed. Can you describe them for me?
- What was going on in your life when you did not feel depressed?
- When undergoing hardships, people often have moments when they feel good. Can you describe times like that for me? What is going on with you during those times?

Solution-Oriented Questions. These questions have clients zero in on how their lives would be different if the problem did not exist. One kind of solution-oriented question, the "miracle question," has gained much notoriety. Mentioned in the biographical sketch, in Phil's case, the "miracle question" would be:

- Phil, suppose a miracle happened while you were sleeping and the problem that brought you here was solved. What would your life look like? How would things be different?

In addition to the miracle question, other types of solution-oriented questions can be asked of clients. For instance, Phil can be asked the following:

- How would your life look different if you were not depressed?
- If you were given a magic pill that would somehow make everything better, how would your life look?
- If you could change anything in your life so you would feel better, how would things be different?

Amplification

In order to stay away from problem talk, therapists will amplify client successes by encouraging them to have expanded discussions about solutions that have worked for them. For instance, referring back to Phil in Box 13.5, if Phil had remarked that exercise had been effective in alleviating his depression, the therapist might respond by saying any of the following:

- Exercise really seemed to help you through your depression; tell me more about how that worked for you.
- I'm impressed with your ability to deal with your depression with exercise; can you give me more details on how you were able to do that?
- That's a really interesting way of changing your life; how exactly do you think that materialized for you?

Complimenting

Complimenting, or reinforcing client strengths and resources, is a basic skill that solution-focused therapists will use to encourage clients in their continued efforts at solution-building. For instance, relative to Phil's past "exercise" regime, his therapist might say, "Sounds like you did a great job at scheduling exercise into your life so that it would alleviate some of your depression." Or, if Phil has worked on increasing his communication skills with the person he was dating, and if this led to a decrease in depression, the therapist might say, "I am really impressed with your newfound ability to effectively communicate with Jaime. It really seems to have enriched your relationship and made you feel better." Compliments can be a natural part of therapy and, unfortunately, have too often been avoided.

Reframing

Many clients come into therapy with an attitude that there is something wrong with them—that they're deficient in some manner. In fact, it is not unusual for clients to view themselves as having a mental disorder. Since social constructionism believes that this kind of thinking is often the result of dominant language that has been perpetuated by power-holders in society and is ultimately suppressive of other ways of viewing the world, they will sometimes reframe clients' understanding of their problems by offering alternative ways of viewing a mental disorder. For instance, Ivey and Ivey (1998) offer a reframe of a number of personality disorders to show how they can be viewed as a "logical response to developmental history" (p. 334). In doing this, they point out the positive aspects of what they call **personality styles** (instead of **personality disorders**) (see Box 13.6).

B o x 13.6   Positive Reframe of Personality Disorders

Personality Style	Paranoid	Schizoid	Schizotypal	Antisocial	Borderline	Histrionic
Positive Frame	It is important to watch out for injustice.	It is useful to be a loner or independent of others at times.	Ability to see things differently than others see them.	It is sometimes necessary to be impulsive and take care of our own needs.	Intensity in relationships is desirable at all times.	All could benefit at times with open access to emotions.

Personality Style	Narcissistic	Avoidant	Dependent	Obsessive–Compulsive	Passive–Aggressive
Positive Frame	A strong belief in ourselves is necessary for good mental health.	It is useful to deny or avoid some things.	We all need to depend on others.	Maintaining order and a system is necessary for job success.	All of us are entitled to procrastinate at times.

From: Ivey, A., & Ivey, M. (1998). Reframing DSM-IV: Positive strategies from developmental counseling and therapy. *Journal of Counseling and Development*, 76, 338.

Scaling

Although a type of evaluative question, this technique has become so popular that we have listed it separately from that part of the chapter. In fact, use of scaling has become a widely used technique in many forms of counseling and has a wide range of applications. Scaling involves asking clients to subjectively rate themselves between a 0 and a 10 on an imaginary scale that assesses any of a number of experiences, feelings, or behaviors from the past, present, or future. Scaling helps to more easily see where the client has been and if the client is making progress (De Jong & Berg, 2002). For instance, referring back to Phil in Box 13.5, we could ask him the following scaling questions:

- With 0 being equal to the worst your depression ever was and 10 being equal to the best you could possibly feel, can you tell me, Phil, where on a scale of 0 to 10 you are today?

- Phil, on the scale of 0 to 10, how effective do you think the thought-stopping has been for you?

- Phil, being that today you rated yourself a 2, where do you think you could end up on your imaginary scale of 0 to 10?

- I know, Phil, that when you first started counseling, you rated yourself at a 2 on our imaginary scale. Where do you think you are today?

THERAPEUTIC PROCESS

Solution-focused counseling can be viewed through a series of stages, which include **pre-session change**, **forming a collaborative relationship**, **describing the problem**, **establishing preferred goals**, **problem-to-solution focus**, **reaching preferred goals**, and **ending therapy** (De Jong & Berg, 2002; O'Connell, 2005). Let's take a look at each of these stages and examine techniques typically used with each stage. Table 13.2 summarizes the techniques most likely found during the different stages.

Stage 0: Pre-Session Change

With the knowledge that clients are generally ready to change when they seek counseling, prior to the first session, the therapist and client decide on an appointment time, and the therapist asks the client to become cognizant of any changes that are made prior to their first meeting.

Stage 1: Forming a Collaborative Relationship

Solution-focused therapists downplay potential power differentials between counselors and clients and prefer to view clients as having the strengths and

TABLE 13.2   Stages and Most Likely Used Techniques

Stages	Techniques
Stage 0: Pre-session change	▪ Requesting that clients note pre-session changes
Stage 1: Forming a collaborative relationship	▪ Being an ambassador (showing curiosity, respect, and acceptance) ▪ Listening and empathy ▪ Being tentative
Stage 2: Describing the problem	▪ Being an ambassador (showing curiosity, respect, and acceptance) ▪ Listening to the identified problem for a short amount of time ▪ Being tentative
Stage 3: Establishing preferred goals	▪ Preferred goals questions
Stage 4: Problem-to-solution focus	▪ Evaluative questions ▪ Coping questions ▪ Exception-seeking questions ▪ Solution-focused questions ▪ Reframing ▪ Amplification ▪ Compliments
Stage 5: Reaching preferred goals	▪ Scaling ▪ Listening and empathy ▪ Compliments
Stage 6: Ending therapy	▪ Scaling ▪ Listening and empathy ▪ Compliments

resources to find their own preferred goals. Instead of being an expert at knowing a particular theory that posits why a client might respond in a certain manner, the solution-focused therapist is seen as an expert at helping the client identify his or her own strengths and resources. Techniques that help to initially build a collaborative and trusting relationship that will foster this point of view include being an ambassador (showing curiosity, respect, and acceptance), being a good listener, using empathy, and being tentative.

Stage 2: Describing the Problem

Obviously, most clients do not seek out counseling unless they are struggling with some problem. Although the focus of therapy is almost exclusively on solutions, it is important that when clients first enter counseling they feel heard, so many of the same skills that are used to form the collaborative relationship are initially used to listen to clients' problems. De Jong and Berg (2002) suggest that problems only need to be listened to for about 15 minutes before solutions are focused upon. Although others might argue that a longer time is needed for clients to feel like their problems are heard, what is most critical is that clients feel comfortable during the beginning phase of therapy, especially during the first session. Rather quickly, the therapist will begin to use other techniques that will move clients toward focusing on preferred goals.

Stage 3: Establishing Preferred Goals

One of the first steps toward helping clients focus on preferred goals is to have them begin to respond to questions about what they would like to see in the future. Letting go of the problem-saturated way of viewing the world is critical for clients if they are to make progress quickly. Thus, it is important that questions that focus on preferred goals, such as those noted earlier by O'Connell (2003), are asked of clients early in therapy.

Stage 4: Problem-to-Solution Focus

To help clients increasingly focus on solutions instead of problems, a number of different types of questions are employed, including evaluative questions, which help clients distinguish behaviors that have led to identified preferred goals from those that have not; coping questions, which help clients focus on past behaviors that have been successful in dealing with problems; exception-seeking questions, which help clients take a fresh look at what actions in their lives have led to preferred goals; and solution-focused questions, which are future-oriented and offer clients the opportunity to develop new, positive ways of reaching their preferred goals.

Therapists support clients in their new solution-building focus in a number of ways, including amplification, which encourages clients to give more detail concerning how they have used their strengths and resources so that they can increasingly employ these strategies as they work toward their preferred goals; reframing, which provides a different take on past behaviors in an effort to normalize and de-pathologize how clients view themselves; and complimenting, in an effort to reinforce clients' efforts toward reaching their preferred goals.

B o x 13.7   Tim Grothaus Works with Latonya

Read or watch Dr. Tim Grothaus's work with Latonya, and review which techniques he used and how many of the stages he completed with her.

You can read this session by going to www.cengage.com/counseling/neukrug/CTP1e and click

"student downloads." Or your instructor may show this session in class with the DVD that accompanies his or her copy of the text.

Stage 5: Reaching Preferred Goals

By the end of the first session, clients have developed a new outlook and have shifted from focusing on problems to focusing on solutions. Between their first and subsequent sessions, they work on implementing and reaching their preferred goals. Therapists can help clients evaluate the effectiveness of their new solution focus by using scaling and can tweak goals in future sessions, with the focus being on clients working quickly to implement their changes. Therapists reinforce clients by being good listeners and showing empathy and by complimenting them on their efforts.

Stage 6: Ending Therapy

> … [B]rief therapy means, among other things, "as few sessions as possible and not one more than necessary" (de Shazer as cited in Hoyt, 1996, p. 61)

Since therapy is brief, as soon as the preferred goals are reached, therapy is finished. Follow-up can be conducted to ensure that clients are continuing their solution-focused orientation (see Box 13.7). As in Stage 5, the chief techniques include listening and empathy, complimenting, and scaling.

SOCIAL, CULTURAL, AND SPIRITUAL ISSUES

> Clients are given the opportunity to educate the therapist about their perspectives, about life in general, about what they think the therapist should know of their problems and about details of the problem-free futures they would like. As far as possible the therapist "speaks the language" of the client, clarifying the meaning the client attaches to particular phases. (Lethem, 2003, p. 122)

Since SFBT stresses the importance of curiosity, respect, and acceptance, and honors the subjective worldview of the client, one can see how it lends itself toward working with a wide range of clients. In fact, De Jong and Berg (2002) stress the importance of the "not-knowing posture" when working with *all* clients. This means that one approaches the client tentatively and with the sense that the client is the expert about his or her life. It means a deep respect for cultural differences and an understanding that the client's reality is always different from the therapist's.

Although SFBT has not been extensively used outside of developed and Western countries, it seems to have an advantage theoretically over other approaches since it has a basic belief that there are multiple realities. Because of this, success is measured as a result of the client's own subjective experience of how well he or she is doing (e.g., scaling) as opposed to some "externally imposed 'yardstick' that may not be culturally relevant" (Fiske, 2007, p. 321).

When working with women, Lethem (2003) points to the advantages of the positive focus of SFBT, especially relative to how it concentrates on clients' strengths and resources and how it de-pathologizes and normalizes client experiences. These, she states, are particularly helpful with women as, historically, women have had a tendency to blame themselves for their problems. In addition, she notes that this approach challenges the traditional stereotype of women as victims who are incapable of coping with their problems. Instead, SFBT is uplifting to women and helps them direct their lives.

Relative to religious and spiritual issues, the SFBT therapist should be effective with a wide range of religious and spiritual people—even those who hold very rigid religious convictions. This is because SFBT does not have a stake in what any religious group believes; instead, it cares about what each client wants for his or her preferred goals, including preferred goals relative to a client's religious and spiritual life. So, people of all different religions who want to better their lives can be effectively treated in solution-focused counseling (Gallagher, 2007).

For whom would this not work? SFBT would probably not be particularly beneficial for clients who want to spend a considerable amount of time "getting to the root" of their problems. For instance, clients who believe that ongoing "in-depth" work with a therapist is critical to knowing oneself would not make good candidates for this brief approach. Also, clients who are not seeking to change (e.g., "the visitor") would not be particularly helped by this approach, although sometimes "visitors" can become "complainants" or even "customers."

EFFICACY OF SOLUTION-FOCUSED
BRIEF THERAPY

In its relatively short lifespan, a number of studies have examined the efficacy of solution-focused therapy and have generally found it to be fairly effective for a broad range of individuals. For instance, client self-report data from the Brief Family Therapy Center at Milwaukee that was gathered in the early 1990s showed that for 136 clients, success rates generally hovered between 75 and 80 percent for 22 different types of problems (De Jong & Berg, 2002). Type of problems ranged from such things as depression to job-related problems to sexual abuse to blended family issues. In addition, type of DSM-IV diagnosis did little to predict outcome. Results were similar for males and females across a wide range of ages and across different ethnic groups.

Finding similar results to De Jong and Berg, MacDonald (1994) found that clients who had undergone solution-focused type of counseling found "a good outcome in 65% of cases as reported by patients themselves" and that positive

> **B o x 13.8 Angela's Experience in Solution-Focused Brief Therapy**
>
> Please review the Miller family's background, which can be found in Appendix B, and then read about | Angela's encounter with an SFBT therapist, which can also be found in Appendix B.

outcomes seemed "associated with longer attendance, the mean being 5.47 sessions against 3.71 in the unimproved group" (p. 423). Perhaps not surprising, those with long-standing problems fared less well. In summarizing much of the early work of solution-focused therapy, George, Iveson, and Ratner (1999) found that "research shows good outcomes of between 65% and 83% across a range of referrals" (p. 136).

Despite the apparent positive results in the literature, caution needs to be used when assessing the efficacy of SFBT, as many of the studies examined had procedural problems, few were experimental in nature, the use of control or comparison groups were rare, and almost all were completed by individuals invested in finding positive outcomes for SFBT (Cade, 2007; Corcoran & Pillai, 2007). For example, Gingerich and Eisengart (2000) examined 15 controlled outcome studies of SFBT and found some to be methodologically weak, concluding that "the 15 studies provide preliminary support for the efficacy of SFBT but do not permit a definitive conclusion" (p. 477).

Corcoran and Pillai's (2007) review of solution-focused research found that despite the fact that hundreds of studies had been completed since 1985, only 10 were experimental in nature and used more than one treatment group. When looking at these 10 studies, they found that "50% of the studies can be viewed as showing improvement over alternative conditions or no-treatment control" (p. 7). In addition, in a meta-analysis of 22 experimental studies that used a control or comparison group, it was found that SFBT was effective for "internalizing behavior problems such as depression, anxiety, self-concept, and self-esteem but does not appear to be effective with externalizing behavior problems such as hyperactivity, conduct problems, or aggression or family and relationship problems" (Kim, 2008, p. 113). Also, what may be most telling is the fact that two major books on outcome research and evidenced-based practice do not list any research for solution-focused counseling (Freeman & Powers, 2007; Wampold, 2001).

In summary, less-controlled and more informal research on solution-focused counseling has been very positive, whereas the limited number of more-controlled studies shows mixed results. Clearly, outcome research for this kind of therapy is in its infancy (see Box 13.8).

SUMMARY

The precursor to the development of SFBT can be traced back to the master therapist Milton Erickson as well those who worked at the Mental Research Institute. However, it was Insoo Kim Berg and Steve de Shazer who are seen as the originators of this approach to therapy. Both having spent some time at

MRI, the couple eventually developed their own brief therapy center in Milwaukee. Noticing that clients could be helped in much shorter times than had been previously thought, the couple and their colleagues experimented with new forms of treatment. From their newsletter, the *Underground Railroad*, as well as the numerous books that the couple wrote, SFBT quickly gained national and international recognition.

The view of human nature of SFBT is pragmatic, anti-deterministic, future-oriented, and optimistic about the possibilities of client change. Most of the techniques are based on a social-constructionist and post-modern view of the world. Of particular influence was the philosopher Wittgenstein, who believed that language was critical to the development of a person's reality and that there was no objective reality, a view that tended to normalize each person's problems in the sense that problems were not viewed as inherent, or within the person, but instead as a function of the conversations people had with others and of endemic beliefs in culture and society.

A number of key concepts were stressed in this chapter, including the postmodernist and social-constructionist basis of the approach; the fact that the approach is non-normative in that it does not attempt to compare a person's problems to a norm group; the tendency not to pathologize; a solution focus and future orientation; the importance of looking at exceptions to clients' problems and their strengths; looking at clients in terms of readiness, not resistance; and an examination of 10 basic assumptions to SFBT.

In this chapter, a number of techniques were expounded upon, including requesting that clients note pre-session changes; being an ambassador (showing curiosity, respect, and acceptance); using listening and empathy; being tentative; asking preferred goals questions, coping questions, exception-seeking questions, and solution-oriented questions; reframing client responses; amplification of client solutions; complimenting clients; and using scaling to assess progress. It was shown how these techniques might fit into six stages that included pre-session change, forming a collaborative relationship, describing the problem, establishing preferred goals, problem-to-solution focus, reaching preferred goals, and ending therapy.

Relative to social, cultural, and spiritual issues, it seems that SFBT could be helpful to a broad range of clients, particularly because it stresses showing curiosity, respect, and acceptance, and honors the subjective worldview of the client. In addition, it was noted that because it concentrates on clients' strengths and de-pathologizes clients' experiences, it may be particularly helpful with women. It also challenges the traditional stereotype that women are victims who are incapable of coping with their problems. It probably would be less helpful with those who are seeking self-reflective, long-term psychotherapy that looks at "intrapsychic" issues.

Finally, a number of research studies have looked at the efficacy of SFBT and although research is relatively young in this area, and many of the studies were methodologically weak, they seem to show that SFBT has a moderate to high success rate with a broad range of clients for a wide range of diagnostic categories.

KEY WORDS

acceptance

ambassador

amplification

anti-deterministic

basic assumptions

being tentative

Brief Family Therapy
Center of Palo Alto

Brief Family Therapy
Center of Milwaukee

client strengths

complainant

complimenting

coping questions

customer

empathy

evaluative questions

exceptions

exception-seeking
questions

Family Institute of
Chicago

future-oriented

listening

Menninger Institute

Mental Research
Institute (MRI)

miracle question

non-normative

non pathological

non-pathologizing

not-knowing posture

Occam's razor

personality disorder

personality style

post-modernism

post-modernist

pragmatic

preferred goals

preferred goals questions

pre-session changes

pre-suppositional
questions

readiness, not resistance

realities are constituted
through language

realities are organized
and maintained
through narrative

realities are socially
constructed

reframing

respect

scaling

showing curiosity

social constructionism

social constructionists

solution-focused

solution-oriented
questions

solution talk

Stage 0: Pre-session
change

Stage 1: Forming a
collaborative
relationship

Stage 2: Describing the
problem

Stage 3: Establishing
preferred goals

Stage 4: Problem-to-
solution focus

Stage 5: Reaching
preferred goals

Stage 6: Ending therapy

there are no essential
truths

Underground Railroad

use of questions

visitor

KEY NAMES

Bateson, Gregory

De Jong, Peter

Erickson, Milton

Fisch, Dick

Guterman, Jeffrey

Haley, Jay

Jackson, Don

O'Connell, Bill

O'Hanlon, Bill

Satir, Virginia

Watzlawick, Paul

Weakland, John

Wittgenstein, Ludwig

REFERENCES

Anderson, H., & Goolishian, H. (1992). The client is expert. A not-knowing approach to therapy. In S. McNamee & K. J. Gergen (Eds.), *Therapy as social construction* (pp. 25–39). Newbury Park, CA: Sage.

Berg, I. K. (1994). *Family based services: A solution-focused approach*. New York: W. W. Norton.

Berg, I. K. (n.d.a). *Insoo Kim Berg Vita*. Retrieved from http://educationandcounseling. sdstate.edu/CHRDtribute.aspx

Berg, I. K. (n.d.b). *For students only*. Retrieved from http://educationandcounseling. sdstate.edu/CHRDtribute.aspx

Berg, I. K., & Dolan, Y. M. (2001). *Tales of solutions: A collection of hope-inspiring stories*. New York: Norton.

Berg, I. K. & Reuss, N. (1998). *Solutions step-by-step: Substance abuse treatment manual*. New York: W. W. Norton.

Berg, I. K., & Steiner, T. (2003). *Children's solution work*. New York: W. W. Norton.

Berg, I. K., & Szabo, P. (2005). *Brief coaching for lasting solutions*. New York: W. W. Norton.

Bertolino, B., & O'Hanlon, B. (2002). *Collaborative, competency-based counseling and therapy*. Needham Heights, MA: Allyn & Bacon.

Bidwell, D. R. (2007). Miraculous knowing: Epistemology and solution-focused therapy. In T. S. Nelson & F. N. Thomas (Eds.), *Handbook of solution-focused brief therapy: Clinical applications* (pp. 65–87). New York: The Haworth Press.

Cade, B. (2005). *Obituary: Steve de Shazer: 1940–2005*. Retrieved from http://www.ebta. nu/page28/page32/page32.html

Cade, B. (2007). Springs, streams, and tributaries: A history of the brief, solution-focused approach. In T. S. Nelson & F. N. Thomas (Eds.), *Handbook of solution-focused brief therapy: Clinical applications* (pp. 25–64). New York: The Haworth Press.

Corcoran, J., & Pillai, V. (2007). A review of the research on solution-focused therapy. *British Journal of Social Work* Advance Access [Electronic Version]. Retrieved from http://bjsw.oxfordjournals.org/cgi/reprint/bcm098v1?maxtoshow=&HITS= 10&hits=10RESULTFORMAT=&fulltext=corcoran&searchid=1& FIRSTINDEX=0&resourcetype=HWCIT

De Jong, P., & Berg, I. K. (2002). *Interviewing for solutions* (2nd ed.). Pacific Grove, CA: Brooks/Cole.

de Shazer, S. (1982). *Patterns of brief family therapy: An ecosystemic approach*. New York: The Guilford Press.

de Shazer, S. (1985). *Keys to solutions in brief therapy*. New York: W. W. Norton & Company.

de Shazer, S. (1988). *Clues: Investigating solutions in brief therapy*. New York: W. W. Norton & Company.

de Shazer, S. (1991). *Putting difference to work*. New York: W. W. Norton & Co Inc.

de Shazer, S. (1994). *Words were originally magic*. New York: W. W. Norton & Company.

de Shazer, S. (n.d.). Steve de Shazer vita. Retrieved from http://educationandcounseling. sdstate.edu/CHRDtribute.aspx de Shazer, S., & Dolan, Y. V. (2007). *More than miracles: The state of the art of solution-focused therapy*. Binghamton, NY: Haworth Press.

Dobbs, M. (2005, January 19). Harvard chief's comments on women assailed: Academics critical of remarks about lack of gender equality. *Washington Post*, A02.

Dolan, Y. (2006). Steve de Shazer: In memoriam. *Journal of Marital and Family Therapy*, *32*(1), 1–2.

Dolan, Y. (2007). Tribute to Insoo Kim Berg. *Journal of Marital and Family Therapy*, *33*(2), 129–131.

Fernando, D. M. (2007). Existential theory and solution-focused strategies: Integration and application. *Journal of Mental Health Counseling*, *29*(3), 226–241.

Fiske, H. (2007). Solution-focused training: The medium and the message. In T. S. Nelson & F. N. Thomas (Eds.), *Handbook of solution-focused brief therapy: Clinical applications* (pp. 317–342). New York: The Haworth Press.

Freedman, J., & Combs, G. (1996). *Narrative therapy: The social construction of preferred realities*. New York: W. W. Norton and Company.

Freeman, E., & Powers, M. (Eds.). (2007). *Handbook of evidence-based psychotherapies: A guide of research and practice*. West Sussex, England: John Wiley & Sons.

Gallagher, D. (2007). Solution-focused brief therapy in faith-based communities. In T. S. Nelson & F. N. Thomas (Eds.), *Handbook of solution-focused brief therapy: Clinical applications* (pp. 225–248). New York: The Haworth Press.

George, E., Iveson, C., & Ratner, H. (1999). *Problem to solution: Brief therapy with individuals and families*. London: Brief Therapy Press.

Gergen, K. J. (1985). The social constructionist movement in modern psychology. *American Psychologist*, *40*, 266–275.

Gergen, K. M. (2009). *An invitation to social construction* (2nd ed.). Thousand Oaks, CA: Sage.

Gingerich, W. (2006). Obituary: Steve de Shazer. *Research on Social Work Practice*, *16*, 549–550.

Gingerich, W. J., & Eisengart, S. (2000). Solution-focused brief therapy: A review of the outcome research. *Family Process*, *39*, 477–498.

Goldenberg, H., & Goldenberg, I. (2008). *Family therapy: An overview*. Belmont, CA: Brooks/Cole.

Gordon, D., & Meyers-Anderson, M. (1981). *Phoenix: Therapeutic patterns of Milton H. Erickson*. Cupertino, CA: Meta Publications.

Guterman, J. T. (1996). Reconstructing social constructionism: A response to Albert Ellis. *Journal of Mental Health Counseling*, *18*, 29–40.

Guterman, J. T. (2006). *Solution-focused counseling*. Alexandria, VA: American Counseling Association.

Hoyt, M. F. (1996). Solution building and language games: A conversation with Steve de Shazer. In M. F. Hoyt (Ed.), *Constructive therapies* (vol. 2, pp. 60–86). New York: Guilford Press.

Hyde, J. S., Lindberg, S. M., Linn, M. C., Ellis, A. B., & Williams, C. C. (2008). Gender similarities characterize math performance. *Science*, *321*, 494–495.

Ivey, A., & Ivey, M. (1998). Reframing DSM-IV: Positive strategies from developmental counseling and therapy. *Journal of Counseling and Development*, *76*, 334–350.

Kim, J. S. (2008). Examining the effectiveness of solution-focused brief therapy: A meta-analysis. *Research on Social Work Practice, 18,* 107–116.

Lethem, J. (2003). Using solution-focused therapy with women. In B. O'Connell & S. Palmer (Eds.), *Handbook of solution-focused therapy* (pp. 118–128). Thousand Oaks, CA: Sage.

MacDonald, A. J. (1994). Brief therapy in adult psychiatry. *Journal of Family Therapy, 16,* 415–426.

McLaughlin, L. E. (2006). The pros and cons of viewing formal diagnosis from a social constructionist perspective. *Journal of Humanistic Counseling, Education and Development, 45*(2), 165–173.

Murphy, J. J. (2008). *Solution-focused counseling in schools* (2nd ed.). Alexandria, VA: American Counseling Association.

O'Connell, B. (2003). Introduction to the solution-focused approach. In B. O'Connell & S. Palmer (Eds.), *Handbook of solution-focused therapy* (pp. 1–11). Thousand Oaks, CA: Sage.

O'Connell, B. (2005). *Solution-focused therapy* (2nd ed.). Thousand Oaks, CA: Sage.

O'Hanlon, B., & Weiner-Davis, M. (2003). *In search of solutions: A new direction in psychotherapy* (rev. ed.). New York: Norton.

Payne, M. (2006). *Narrative therapy.* Thousand Oaks, CA: Sage Publications.

Rudes, J., & Guterman, J. T. (2007). The value of social constructionism for the counseling profession: A reply to Hansen. *Journal of Counseling and Development, 85,* 387–392.

Thomas, F. N., & Nelson, T. S. (2007). Assumptions and practices within the solution-focused brief therapy tradition. In T. S. Nelson & F. N. Thomas (Eds.), *Handbook of solution-focused brief therapy: Clinical applications* (pp. 3–24). New York: The Haworth Press.

Tribute to Insoo Kim Berg. (2007). Retrieved from http://www.sfbta.org/insookimberg

United Kingdom Association for Solution Focused Practice. (2006). Riding the underground railroad: Insoo Kim Berg talks about the origins and future of the solution focused approach. *Solution News, 2*(3), 3–6. Retrieved from http://www.solution-news.co.uk/issues/solutionnews2(3).pdf

Wampold, B. E. (2001). *The great psychotherapy debate: Models, methods, and findings.* Mahwah, NJ: Erlbaum.

Watts, R. E., & Pietrzak, D. (2000). Adlerian "encouragement" and the therapeutic process of solution-focused brief therapy. *Journal of Counseling and Development, 78,* 442–447.

White, M., & Epston, D. (1990). *Narrative means to therapeutic ends.* New York: Norton.

Wittgenstein, L. (1963). *Philosophical investigations* (G. E. M. Anxcombe, Trans.) New York: Macmillan.

Extensions, Adaptations, and Spin-offs

This section offers a brief overview of a number of approaches, which, for various reasons, have maintained popularity in recent years. Chapter 14 examines individual approaches to counseling and psychotherapy. First, we examine four psychodynamic approaches: Erikson's psychosocial theory of development, object-relations theory, self-psychology, and the relational and intersubjectivity perspective. Next, we examine four extensions and adaptations to cognitive–behavioral therapy: multimodal therapy, dialectical behavior therapy, acceptance and commitment therapy, and constructivist therapy. The chapter concludes with a review of a few approaches that pull from cognitive–behavioral, existential–humanistic, and post-modern therapy, including eye movement desensitization response (EMDR) therapy, motivational interviewing, gender aware therapy (feminist therapy and counseling men), positive psychology, and complementary, alternative, and integrative therapies. Chapter 15 examines a number of popular family therapy approaches, including structural family therapy, strategic family therapy, human validation process model, multigenerational approaches, experiential family therapy, psychodynamic family therapy, behavioral and cognitive–behavioral family therapy, narrative family therapy, and solution-focused family therapy.

Chapter 14

Individual Approaches To Counseling and Psychotherapy

Learning Goals

To offer a brief overview of four areas that extended and adapted psychodynamic theory, including:

- Erikson's psychosocial theory of development
- object-relations theory
- self-psychology
- the relational and intersubjectivity perspective

To offer a brief overview of four extensions and adaptations to cognitive–behavioral therapy, including:

- multimodal therapy
- dialectical behavior therapy
- acceptance and commitment therapy
- constructivist therapy

To offer a brief overview of five new directions in therapy that tend to be loosely associated with cognitive–behavioral therapy, existential–humanistic therapy, and/or post-modern therapy, including:

- eye movement desensitization response (EMDR) therapy
- motivational interviewing
- gender-aware therapy: feminist therapy and counseling men
- positive psychology
- complementary, alternative, and integrative therapies

For those of us who are really ticked, there's
   autogenic, bioenergetic, holotropic, and character-analytic.
And for those of us who are really, really riffed, there's
   psychoanalysis, Daseinsanalysis, Sophia analysis, and Radix.
And if you are scolding, there's therapy that takes place by
   holding, focusing, and neurolinguistic programming.
But if you're a little more rational, you can partake in
   transpersonal, ecological, developmental, or transactional.
And, if you're a little more psychological, there's
   ecological, dialectical, developmental, and conversational.
If your body needs some work, there's
   integrative, integral, internal, and sometimes interpersonal.
And if that's not enough, body work that's rough can get into your psyche
   while doing some Reiki, pulsing, Rolfing, or orgonomy.
And if you want to talk about your mama, there's
   psychedelic, psychosynthesis, psychosystems, and, of course, psychodrama.
But if it's your dad of whom you need to be wary, why don't you get
   involved in some hypnotherapy, vegetotherapy, expressive, or feminist
   theory.
Alas, in the end, if we want to relax, we can be a little less radical, and
   participate in character-analytical, contemplative, concentrative, or
   conversational.

So many therapies to choose from and so little time. With hundreds of approaches to counseling and psychotherapy out there (Gabbard, 1995; O'Leary, 2006; "List of psychotherapies," 2009), even if we spent the rest of our lives in therapy, we could only participate in a small number of them. But why is it that some theories make it into a book such as this one, while hundreds are left out? Probably, a combination of factors are at play. First, the theories that are in a textbook usually have some history to them—they've been used and people believe they are helpful. Second, these approaches usually have some research, or significant clinical experience, to back them up. Third, the theorists who created these theories have usually written a great deal, thus publicizing their theories. Fourth, many of the theorists were entrepreneurs in the sense that they wrote, developed institutes, initiated journals, and were out on the road giving workshops about their theories. And finally, the public seems to have a thirst for certain theories at a specific time in history. For some theories, it's just the right time. For instance, while teaching, I recently asked my students, "How many of you have ever heard of transactional analysis?" Out of a class of 25, one older student raised her hand. Transactional analysis, or "TA," had been in all the books. It was the rage during the 1960s and 1970s, and it had much to offer. Now, hardly anyone has heard of it. That's the way of many theories. On the other hand, those that have had staying power probably have something to offer.

In this chapter, we will look at a number of adaptations and spin-offs of the theories discussed in the book. In addition, we will look at some theories that are taking us in new directions. Some of these theories have had staying power and appear to have much to offer. Others are very new and are riding a wave of popularity. Only time will tell if these newer theories will have staying power. But why, out of hundreds of possibilities, were some of these theories chosen for this chapter? A number of reasons: some have been shown to be effective, some are riding that wave of popularity, and some are just interesting and are the newest "breakthrough" theories. The chapter will be loosely arranged by conceptual approaches. So, the first four theories come out of the psychodynamic tradition, and the next four theories have cognitive–behavioral leanings. Within the last six "newer" approaches, you can find pieces of cognitive–behaviorism, existential–humanism, and post-modern theory.

PSYCHODYNAMIC APPROACHES

Many of the post-psychoanalytic models of therapy moved away from the Freudian concept that the id is the primary motivator of behavior and focused on how the ego is affected by psychosocial and interpersonal factors (Wallerstein, 2001). The ones we will take look at include **Erikson's psychosocial theory of development**, **object-relations therapy**, **Kohut's self-psychology**, and **relational psychoanalysis and intersubjectivity.**

Erikson's Psychosocial Theory of Development

Although Erik Erikson started out studying Freud's psychoanalytic approach, he later developed a model that dramatically revised Freud's understanding of the developing ego. Contrary to psychoanalysis, he felt that the influence of instincts and the unconscious were not as great as many had posited and that **psychosocial forces**, in combination with biological and internal psychological factors, were major contributors to the development of a healthy personality. Suggesting that individuals pass through eight life stages, Erikson viewed the individual as changing throughout his or her life and placed considerably more emphasis on the influence of social factors than did any of his predecessors (see Table 14.1). In addition, Erikson's approach was more positive than traditional psychoanalysis, as he believed that when previous stages were not successfully traversed, they could be revisited at a later date (Erikson, 1963, 1968, 1980, 1982).

Erikson suggested that as individuals pass through the eight stages, they are faced with a **task**, sometimes called a **crisis**. Portrayed as a pair of opposing forces, Erikson described the first opposing task in each stage as **syntonic**, or of positive emotional quality, and the second task as **dystonic**, or of negative emotional quality. He suggested that individuals needed to experience both the syntonic and dystonic qualities. However, in the end, one has to find a balance between the two, with individuals leaning toward the syntonic quality. For instance, trust

T A B L E 14.1   **Erikson's Psychosocial Stages of Development**

Stage	Name of Stage (Ages)	Virtue of Stage	Description of Stage
1	Trust vs. Mistrust (birth – 1)	Hope	In this stage, the infant is building a sense of trust or mistrust, which can be facilitated by significant others' ability to provide a sense of psychological safety to the infant.
2	Autonomy vs. Shame and Doubt (1–2)	Will	Here, the toddler explores the environment and is beginning to gain control over his or her body. Significant others can either promote or inhibit the child's newfound abilities and facilitate the development of autonomy or shame and doubt.
3	Initiative vs. Guilt (3–5)	Purpose	As physical and intellectual growth continues and exploration of the environment increases, a sense of initiative or guilt can be developed by significant others who are either encouraging or discouraging of the child's physical and intellectual curiosity.
4	Industry vs. Inferiority (6–11)	competence	An increased sense of what the child is good at, especially relative to his or her peers, can either be reinforced or negated by significant others (e.g., parents, teachers, peers), leading to feeling worthwhile or, discouraged highlighted by feelings of inferiority.
5	Identity vs. Role Confusion (adolescence)	Fidelity	Positive role models and experiences can lead to increased understanding of temperament, values, interests, and abilities that define one's sense of self. Negative role models and limited experiences will lead to role confusion.
6	Intimacy vs. Isolation (early adulthood)	Love	A good sense of self and self-understanding leads to the ability to form intimate relationships that are highlighted by mutually supporting relationships, which encourage individuality with interdependency. Otherwise, the young adult feels isolated.
7	Generativity vs. Stagnation (middle adulthood)	Caring	Healthy development in this stage is highlighted by concern for others and for future generations. This individual is able to maintain a productive and responsible lifestyle and can find meaning through work, volunteerism, parenting, and/or community activities. Otherwise, the adult feels stagnant.
8	Ego Integrity vs. Despair (later life)	Wisdom	The older adult who examines his or her life either feels a sense of fulfillment or despair. Successfully mastering the developmental tasks from the preceding stages will lead to a sense of integrity for the individual.

is a critical factor in all people's lives, as we must generally trust others if we are to get along with one another. However, a certain amount of mistrust is also important. For instance, if you are walking down a dark street and see an ominous figure, you should react with a fair amount of mistrust. More generally, Erikson believed that too much trust would lead to what he called *sensory distortion*, while too much mistrust would lead to *withdrawal* (see Table 14.1). Similarly, too much autonomy would lead to *impulsivity*, while too much shame and doubt would lead to *compulsion*, and so forth. Clearly, the role of significant others in the early stages had much influence over the individual's ability to find the correct balance between the syntonic and dystonic qualities.

Erikson believed that the development of a healthy ego is contingent on the individual's ability to master these critical periods of development and is highlighted by a particular **virtue** or **strength** that is associated with successful passage through each stage (see Table 14.1). If a positive identity is created and the virtue embraced, the individual can successfully move on to the next critical period. On the other hand, the individual who is not able to cope with age-specific developmental tasks will develop a low self-image and a bruised ego, and will carry these dysfunctions into the next levels of development, therefore making it difficult to successfully complete later developmental tasks. Erikson's eight life-span stages are often referenced as a means of assisting the helper in understanding typical developmental tasks of the client. Such understanding can assist the helper in developing strategies for clients as they attempt to successfully pass through the stages.

Object-Relations Therapy

An adaption and extension to psychoanalysis, object-relations theory suggests that instead of being primarily driven by their sexual and aggressive drives, as posited in classical psychoanalysis, the primary motivator for humans is the need to be in relationships (Glickauf-Hughes & Wells, 2007). Other instincts may impinge on people, but they are seen as being secondary to, or driven by, the **need to be in relationships**. Thus, our sex drive is primarily driven by our need to be with others. From an object-relations perspective, we are each born into the world with a genetic predisposition or script that can be altered by our early relationships. As we take in these relationships, we begin to build a **self**. Some of the major object-relations theorists have included Melanie Klein, W. R. D. Fairbairn, Harry Guntrip, Donald Winnicott, Margaret Mahler, Otto Kernberg, and Harry Stack Sullivan, among others (Glickauf-Hughes & Wells, 2007).

Object-relations therapists use the word **objects** to describe external objects and internal representations of objects to which individuals become attached early in life (Glickauf-Hughes & Wells, 2007). As early objects (e.g., mother, father, significant others), or aspects of those objects, become internalized, the individual begins to develop a unique character or self (Sullivan, 1953). One external object that tends to have a major impact on most people is one's mother. Object-relations theorists talk about **"good-enough" mothering** (or parenting), which means that the mother provides a positive **holding environment** for the child, especially in times of need (Winnicott, 1958, 1965). Such mothers are able to soothe, show empathy, be loving, and adequately care for their young children and do not take a child's behavior personally. Thus, the angry or anxious child is seen by the good-enough mother as a child in need, not a child who is doing something to harm or upset the mother. Through good-enough parenting skills, this child learns how to contain and manage his or her feelings. A child who has good-enough parenting is eventually able to develop a sense of self that is based on healthy ego functioning (Guntrip, 1969).

Object-relation theorists often talk about stages of development that tend to move from a **symbiotic, undifferentiated relationship** with mother (or early caretaker) toward **individuation, separation of self** and what is called **object constancy** (Fairbairn, 1952/2001; Mahler, 1968; Mahler, Pine, & Bergman, 1975/2000). Object constancy means that as the child moves into adulthood, he or she increasingly gains the ability to see self as separate from others, has a clear sense of who he or she is, and does need to be immediately gratified by others. These individuals have learned how to manage and contain their emotions. As one moves toward object constancy, you will often see them go through transitional stages. For instance, children will often become attached to **transitional objects**, like blankets, stuffed animals, and pacifiers, as they move from their dependency to their mothers toward increasing autonomy (see Box 14.1). A transitional object is one that children simultaneously feel as part of themselves and as something different or "other" than themselves; thus, the transition is one of increasing awareness and understanding of the external world, including the world of other people. Early in life, for example, a "sad" stuffed animal might reflect a child's sadness, whereas when older, the child will see the stuffed animal as just that: a toy.

Many object-relations theorists believe that the infant separates self–object experiences into categories of good or bad (Klein, 1975; Kernberg, 1980; Weininger, 1992). In essence, the mom (or primary caregiver) is two persons: at one time good (e.g., when she's feeding the child) and at another time bad (e.g., when the child doesn't have his or her immediate needs met). Known as **splitting**, this defense mechanism allows the very young child, who does not yet have the capacity to see individuals as complex, to split the person (the internalized object!) into either "all-good" or "all-bad."

We all, to some degree, carry splitting into adulthood. For instance, I sometimes "split" (see) my wife as a "bad person," such as when I get into an argument with her. However, my ego has the capacity to say, "you're splitting her—she is not a bad person—you are just upset right now and resorting to a former, old internalized image, and it is this image that is trying to paint a picture of her as all-bad." Others will have more difficulty with splitting (e.g., those with narcissistic personality disorder). These persons will struggle in relationships as they flip-flop—at one moment loving the "good person" and at the next moment hating the same "bad person." In actuality, there is no good or bad person—it is the projection of early unresolved experiences with primary caretakers who did not provide good-enough parenting. One major challenge for the client is to gain the capacity to integrate bad and good images of others and be able to develop a sense of self that does not need constant "feeding" by others.

B o x 14.1   Emma's Transition

My daughter Emma was (and is) greatly loved by me and my wife. And, until first grade, she was in a very humanistically oriented daycare that provided much empathy, love, and a good number of hugs. In first grade, she went to public school, where they provided desks, structure, academics, a "friendly" teacher but no hugs and not much time for empathy. She regressed. In fact, she lost it totally. Every day, we would take her to school, and she would cry hysterically as we left—and cry for the rest of the day at school. Realizing she needed to make the transition and develop independent ego functioning, we devised a number of methods that included some transition objects. We did many things to help her in this process:

1. I would drop her off at school, rather than her mother, to ease the separation from her primary love object—her mother.
2. Emma would be taken out of the classroom to be with the counselor twice a day. This would help her receive the empathy and caring she needed.
3. The counselor started a small group of students from her class to help Emma, and others in her class, adjust to the new school and to one another. This would help her transition from "mother object" to "student object."
4. I would give Emma a "gold" dollar after she successfully peeled herself off me in the morning. At the end of the week, she could purchase a toy. Although a reinforcement technique, the coins also acted as a transition object.
5. The teacher would arrange Emma's desk so that she sat near the one student Emma knew, and the teacher would place Emma near students with whom she would most easily relate. This would allow her to build relationships with other students.
6. We would place notes in her lunchbox encouraging her and telling her we loved her.
7. We would give Emma a locket with our pictures for her to hold onto and look at during the day. This would act as a transition object.

As with most change, the plan did not work overnight. However, Emma slowly became adjusted to her new school as she gained an increased sense of separateness from her mother and me.

As the person grows, his or her unique self seeks out other people who will affirm who the person is. Thus, individuals tend to find others in life who will support their early blueprint or sense of self. Individuals who have been traumatized early in life and had poor parenting tend to become locked in their way of relating and have a more difficult time changing than those who have had more positive and flexible parenting, such as those who have had good-enough parenting. One important purpose of object-relations therapy is to resolve early traumatic experiences so the individual can build a new self-structure. In a sense, you might say that clients need to be re-parented by taking in new "objects" (the therapist), which can then serve as a new blueprint for the self in relationship with others. However, attachment to old objects can be strong, and it is often not easy to move on.

Because object-relations therapies maintain many of the tenets of traditional analysis, their approach to therapy can be seen as a long-term, in-depth, analytical process that attempts to have the person understand early experiences in terms of separation and individuation. This is accomplished by having the therapist develop an empathic therapeutic relationship while the client slowly relives early childhood conflicts with parents. Through the building of this relationship and the use of interpretation, the client can integrate a new parental model and become individuated. In essence, the therapist becomes the healthy parent the client never had (Kohut, 1977; Masterson, 1981).

Self-Psychology*

Classical or Freudian psychoanalysis, as well as early object-relations therapy, were the springboards for Heinz Kohut's *Self-Psychology* (Kohut, 1977, 1984). Kohut focused on the development of the self, as opposed to the importance of drives. He also believed that one's self is not the internal representation of an image or object, as the object-relations theorists posited, but an inner experience that has a sense of continuity over time. **Selfobjects**, said Kohut, were the ongoing inner experience of another person as represented in the self. Kohut believed that to grow into healthy adults, three basic needs had to be met: to feel special (**recognition**), to believe that parents are strong, capable, and self-assured (**idealizing parents**), and to be like others and to belong (**twinship**).

Kohut, like his predecessors, believed that there was no such thing as a perfect parent (or therapist!), but he did believe that **good-enough parenting** would give children what they needed to develop a strong sense of self so they would be able to soothe themselves through difficult times and not need constant reassurance and praise throughout their lives. However, he believed that if children's needs were not met, problems would arise. For instance, if a child had not been prized and given attention ("recognition"), he or she would experience low self-esteem, a sense of worthlessness, and occasional feelings of unwarranted grandiosity instead of feeling strong and capable. Along the same lines, Kohut felt that the inability to internalize idealized images of parents would result in children who did not feel capable and worthwhile, whereas those who did successfully internalize such images would feel vibrant, strong, creative, and compassionate about life. Finally, Kohut believed that children who didn't have adequate twinship experiences would feel odd and out of place rather than experiencing healthy feelings of belonging (Kahn, 1991).

Kohut believed that clients needed a **corrective emotional experience** to develop a healthy self that had not been developed due to poor parenting. A term coined earlier by Franz Alexander (1950, 1956), Kohut saw therapist empathy as central to this corrective experience. Calling this ability **"experience-near,"** Kohut believed therapist empathy has the ability to come close (near) to understanding deeply the experience of the client. This ability, said Kohut, was critical to repairing past failures and other disruptions to the development of the self. Of course, even the expert analyst would periodically make empathic failures, because no one can be perfect. And, said Kohut, it was these very failures that could be used in repairing the client's self. As the client develops a transference relationship with the therapist, reactions to these failures can be interpreted to him or her, and the client can begin to build a new, healthier self that is based on this new relationship.

The Relational and Intersubjectivity Perspective†

As with object-relations theory and self-psychology, the relational and intersubjectivity perspective suggests that individuals have **internalized images** of significant,

---

*Contributed by Cheree Hammond.
†Contributed by Cheree Hammond and Ed Neukrug.

early relationships in their lives (e.g., parents) and that the remnants of those images impact how individuals relate to others and themselves and the decisions they make in their lives. However, they also suggest that these early patterns can change as individuals relate and interact with others. In fact, Stolorow and Atwood (1992) suggested that the older psychodynamic models bought into the **myth of the independent mind**. They argued that personality and the patterns of understanding and relating to others in the world do not develop in isolation but within the mutually influencing subjectivities of the people in relationship (Kahn, 1991; Stolorow & Atwood, 1992).

> Freud views mind as fundamentally monadic; something inherent, wired in, prestructured, is pushing from within. Mind for Freud emerges in the form of endogenous pressures. Relational-model theories view mind as fundamentally dyadic and *interactive*; above all else, mind seeks contact, engagement with other minds. Psychic organization and structures are built from the patterns which shape those interactions. (Mitchell, 1988, pp. 3–4)

Some of the more prominent theorists in these areas include Lew Aron, Jessica Benjamin, Phillip Bromberg, Irwin S. Hoffman, Thomas Ogden, Stephen Mitchell, and Paul Wachtel. A whole journal, *Psychoanalytic Dialogues*, is now devoted to this perspective.

Influenced somewhat by feminist theory, those who embrace this perspective believe that people are primarily driven by a need to be in relationship with others (Safran, 2009; Wachtel, 2008). The adherents of this approach believe that **"the self" is formed in relationship**, is only known through relationships, and continually grows and changes through relationships. Unfortunately, since our early relationships are often flawed and are our templates for how we believe all relationships should be, we generally sabotage any attempt at healing by recapitulating our past, flawed relationships. In addition, we generally choose others who do not have the tools to promote healing. Relational and intersubjectivity therapists are able to provide a new relationship with the client that can help the client heal.

Relational and intersubjectivity therapists believe in the importance of having a **deep, personal encounter** with the client as the two engage in dialogue (Mitchell, 1993, 2002). This perspective gives attention to the notion that the therapist is subject to the same subjective experience as the client sitting across from him or her. Therapists who embrace this perspective give attention and voice to both transference within the therapeutic relationship and to carefully timed **self-disclosures** of their countertransference. **Transference** and **countertransference** are understood to both elicit experiencing and be responses to the feelings elicited by the other. Consequently, the dynamic relational process between the therapist and client becomes grist for the mill (Kahn, 1991; Natterson & Friedman, 1995; Stolorow & Atwood, 1992. Indeed, it is this deep and often unconscious sharing (or conflict) that serves as the staging area for recognizing and integrating disowned parts of self, denied emotional experiencing, and counterproductive **relational patterns**. This perspective uses empathy to help the therapist hear the client and to help the client hear himself or herself. Carefully expressed self-disclosure, concerning how the client impacts the therapist, helps the client see his or her role in relationships more clearly.

The timing of self-disclosure is critical and must be offered when the client is able to hear such feedback. Through such disclosures, clients can begin to understand how certain relational patterns are remnants of early relationships and continue to cause dysfunctional ways of relating. In addition to self-disclosing to the client, the therapist encourages the client to self-disclose and share his or her feelings about the therapist. The ongoing relationship of empathy and self-disclosure allows the client, as well as the therapist, to understand how each relates to one another, and it is through this interaction that both can change. This process is painful, hopeful, and empowering as the client experiences wounds from the past that continue to affect his or her life and subsequently learns how to transcend them.

COGNITIVE–BEHAVIORAL APPROACHES

Dozens of adaptations and extensions of cognitive–behavioral therapy have been developed over the years, with four of the more popular approaches being **multimodal therapy**, **dialectical behavior therapy**, **acceptance and commitment therapy**, and **constructivist therapy**.

Multimodal Therapy

Feeling that behavior therapy had a limited range of techniques and strategies, Arnold Lazarus developed what he called **multimodal therapy** (Lazarus, 1976, 2002; Wolpe & Lazarus, 1966). Today, multimodal therapy employs a vast array of techniques and has been identified by many as a systematic, relatively brief, eclectic approach to therapy (Lazarus, 1976. 1997a, 1997b; Lazarus & Beutler, 1993; Mahalik, 1990). Because of Lazarus's attempts to clearly define the problem, set goals, identify techniques, and measure success, he seems in many ways to fit the modern-day definition of behaviorism. In addition, his theoretical leanings toward **social learning theory** and his lack of focus on "dynamic processes" point his theory more toward a behavioral orientation (Lazarus, 1986, 2008). However, as you will see, Lazarus's formulations have gone far beyond the more traditional work of the behavior therapist.

Lazarus's approach is based on a careful analysis of the client within seven modalities known by the acronym **BASIC ID**. In assessing a client's needs in therapy, Lazarus asks a client to develop his or her own modality profile by responding to questions in the following domains:

Behavior: Make a list of those overt behaviors such as acts, habits, gestures, responses, and reactions that you want to increase and those that you would like to decrease. What would you like to start and stop doing?

Affect: Write down your unwanted emotions, moods, and strong feelings (e.g., anxiety, guilt, anger, depression).

Sensation: Make a list of any negative sensations related to your senses of touching, tasting, smelling, seeing, and hearing (e.g., tension, dizziness, pain, blushing, butterflies in stomach).

Imagery: Write down any bothersome recurring dreams or vivid memories and any negative features about your self-image. Make a list of any mental images or auditory images that may be troubling you.

Cognition: Make a list of any attitudes, values, opinions, and ideas that get in the way of your happiness. Include negative things you often say to yourself (e.g., "I am a failure.").

Interpersonal relationships: Write down any bothersome interactions with other people (relatives, friends, lovers, employers, acquaintances). Any concerns you have about the way other people treat you should appear here.

Drugs/biology: Make a list of all drugs you are taking, whether prescribed by a doctor or not. Include any health problems, medical concerns, and illnesses that you now have or have had in the past. (paraphrased and shortened from Lazarus, 1986)

Following a thorough analysis of the client's BASIC ID, straightforward treatment strategies and treatment goals are developed for each of the modalities. Although each modality will be addressed, some modalities will likely be stressed over others. Clearly, Lazarus's approach is pragmatic and can be adopted by any therapist who has an in-depth knowledge of treatment interventions and is able to effectively match them with clients' profiles.

Dialectical Behavior Therapy

… [T]he DBT therapist must be able to inhibit judgmental attitudes and practice radical acceptance of the client in each moment while keeping an eye on the ultimate goal of the treatment: to move the client from a life in hell to a life worth living as quickly and efficiently as possible. (Dimeff & Linehan, 2001, p. 11)

Dialectical behavior therapy (DBT) was originally developed by Marsha Linehan for use with clients who have particularly difficult problems or disorders, such as borderline personality disorders (Fruzzetti & Fruzzetti, 2003; Linehan, 1993; Dimeff & Linehan, 2001). More recently, it has been applied to a wide range of disorders. At first glance, the term *dialectical behavior therapy* seems like an oxymoron. *Dialectical* means to examine the meaning of truth and create new knowledge through this examination. This seems like a far cry from how we typically understand behavior therapy. However, the actual practice of DBT seems to successfully link these two. Let's take a look at how.

Based on a **biosocial theory** of personality development, DBT assumes that some people are born with heightened emotional sensitivity. When such individuals are placed in an environment that invalidates their sensitive emotional core, they bounce between **emotional inhibition** (in an attempt to be accepted) and **emotional overexpressiveness** (in an attempt to have their feelings understood). As you might expect, such individuals end up having a difficult time maintaining relationships, because they are constantly looking to be validated but are continually disappointed that there is no person who has the ability to give them the constant validation they crave. Despite their disappointment, they earnestly try to maintain some semblance of a relationship by controlling their disappointment and discouragement. However, they can control these feelings for just so long before their ability to inhibit their emotional responsiveness gives out. Soon, their disappointment leads to blame and anger, as they see the other's lack of validation as the cause of their emotional distress. They lash out blaming the other, but soon realize they are overly needy. They feel guilt-ridden and ashamed of themselves for their reactions. Oscillating between attempting to inhibit their emotions and being overly emotionally expressive is distressing and tiring and often leads to self-abusive behaviors (e.g., suicide, cutting, addictions) as such individuals attempt to soothe their pain. Clearly, clients such as these can be difficult to work with, as they can be emotional roller-coasters who have difficulty maintaining a therapeutic relationship, will often blame themselves or the therapist for lack of progress, and are more likely than most clients to act out, often in some manner that would cause them harm.

Because the client is often emotionally labile and has experienced others as being invalidating, a primary role of the DBT therapist is to consistently show a sense of **acceptance** of the client while encouraging the client to change. Generally, the therapist does this by demonstrating empathy, genuineness, caring, warmth, and understanding. In addition, the therapist practices and teaches **mindfulness**, an Eastern practice characterized by a sense of tranquility and a calm awareness of one's emotions, self, consciousness, perceptions, and body. Ultimately, the therapist attempts to be mindful with the client, and the client learns how to be mindful with himself or herself and with others. The therapist must also help the client develop strategies for change. Some of the strategies used to help the client change include **behavioral analysis**, the **teaching of problem-solving skills**, **cognitive restructuring**, and the use of a wide range of **operant conditioning techniques**. To add to the change process, clients are often asked to participate in **behavioral skills groups** in addition to individual therapy.

A major aspect of this type of therapy is the **commitment** of the therapist to the health of the client. This is shown through the therapist's caring and realness in the relationship, the therapist's willingness to share limited aspects of his or her life through **self-disclosure** in the **ongoing dialogue**, and the therapist's willingness to receive periodic telephone contacts between sessions to discourage self-destructive patterns and encourage new, healthier behaviors. However, through an open and ongoing dialogue, the therapist also clearly lets the client know that there are limits to what the therapist can do. The therapist models the fact that, like the loved ones with whom the client so wants to connect, the therapist is not perfect and cannot meet all of the client's needs. Consultation teams are often used to help counselors stay motivated with and committed to their clients.

DBT is a relatively new form of therapy that helps clients feel accepted and gently challenges them to change their ways of being in the world and to act on specific cognitive and behavioral change strategies. It takes a well-seasoned professional who can consistently listen to and love a "difficult" client, openly share his or her own frailties, help clients see how problems can hold solutions, assist clients in developing specific change strategies, and be committed to having an ongoing, deep dialogue with another human being who happens to be a client.

Acceptance and Commitment Therapy: ACT

God [or higher power] grant me the Serenity to accept the things
I cannot change, the courage to change what I can, and the wisdom
to know the difference. (The Serenity Prayer)

Considered the third wave of the cognitive–behavioral therapies (behavior therapy being the first and cognitive therapy the second) (Hayes, 2004), acceptance and commitment therapy (ACT), pronounced "act," is based on **relational frame theory**, which explains behaviors and cognitions as a complex web of relational associations. Developed by Steven Hayes and others in the late 1980s (Hayes & Smith, 2005; Hayes & Strosahl, 2004; Hayes, Strosahl, & Wilson, 1999), ACT uses a mixture of cognitive techniques, behavioral techniques, and Eastern philosophy and applies it in novel ways. Despite its strong theoretical base and rigorous research, its popularity and pop-psychology appeal has led some to liken it to a cult (Cloud, 2006).

Believing that cognitive–behavioral therapy had much to offer, the originators of ACT also realized that although traditional cognitive–behavioral techniques appeared to have some short-term positive effects, clients would often not find the long-term contentment they were seeking. It was theorized that the difficulty with traditional cognitive–behavioral techniques was that they took a rather myopic view of symptoms, assuming that symptoms could be treated in isolation from the complex web of interactions we have in life (Eifert & Forsyth, 2005). This snapshot view saw symptoms as something that occurred at a moment in time, an "event," not as part of a long-term process that is a least partly the nature of being human.

Because traditional cognitive–behavioral therapists viewed symptoms as events, they would attempt to associate symptoms with specific cognitive distortions that they assumed "caused" or were responsible for the symptoms (Ciarrochi & Bailey, 2008; Hayes & Strosahl, 2004). In contrast, the ACT therapist sees cognitive distortions and "symptoms" being reinforced in dozens, hundreds, or maybe even thousands of ways, which would make them nearly impossible to change or extinguish. Therefore, the ACT therapist has the client become aware of his or her symptoms and encourages the client to accept them. ACT suggests that focusing on trying to change symptoms, as the traditional cognitive–behavioral therapists do, often increases the strength of the symptom. They suggest that the more you struggle with the symptom, the more it binds you, much like the Chinese finger trap.

Paradoxically, they assert, accepting the symptom can have somewhat of a calming effect, although not necessarily eliminating the symptom.

Just let them [your negative feelings] be there without struggling against them, and instead of investing your energy in trying to control how you feel, invest it in acting on your values—in doing the things that make life rich and meaningful. And there's a great bonus that comes from taking this approach: even though you're not trying to get rid of your negative feelings, you'll find they commonly reduce in frequency and intensity. (Harris as cited in Flora, 2009, p. 69)

The goal of ACT is to help "create a rich and meaningful life, while accepting the pain that inevitably goes with it" (Harris, 2006, p. 2). This goal is reached by applying six core principles toward the development of **psychological flexibility**: defusion, acceptance, contact with the present moment, self as context, values, and committed action (see Figure 14.1). Briefly, **defusion** has to do with being able to observe our language, thoughts, and emotions from a detached perspective so that they don't have quite the impact on us that they usually do; **acceptance** means that we accept ourselves with our feelings and sensations, even when they are unpleasant; **contact with the present moment** is related to allowing oneself to fully experience oneself in the here and now; the **self as context**, sometimes called the **transcendent self**, is related to seeing ourselves as more than just our feelings, thoughts, or behaviors, and being in touch with a higher consciousness that sometimes occurs through the practice of **mindfulness**, meditation, and related techniques; **values** is the process of determining what is most important and meaningful in a person's life; and **committed action** is the process of setting goals based on one's values and taking action to reach those goals responsibly. The process of reaching increased psychological flexibility has been broken down into three steps by Eifert and Forsyth (2005) and includes:

1. *Accept thoughts and feelings* in an effort to end the struggle that occurs when we try to change or eliminate our thoughts and feelings.
2. *Choose directions* based on what is really important in the client's life—what a person values most.
3. *Take action* by being committed to making the needed changes based on what was identified as being most important in the client's life.

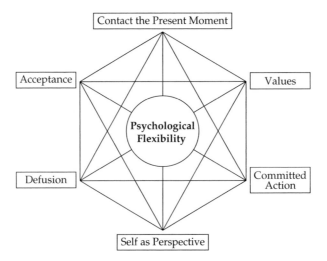

FIGURE 14.1 Six Core Processes: The ACT Hexaflex Model

SOURCE: Bach, P. A., & Moran, D. J. (2008). *ACT in practice: Case conceptualization in acceptance and commitment therapy.* Oakland, CA: New Harbinger Publications, p. 7.

ACT therapists have developed numerous workbooks, self-help resources, and practical techniques to help clients live lives that reflect their core values. With an approach that is deliberate, thoughtful, and uses mindfulness, ACT clients are not expected to eliminate problems and symptoms but rather to moderate them as they work toward living a more meaningful life.

Constructivist Therapy

From a constructivist perspective, rationality is intrinsically relativistic, and, as such, it can only refer to contextually and historically situated efforts to attain meaning and coherence. (Guidano, 1995, p. 93)

Developed by Michael Mahoney (1995a), constructivist therapy is usually placed within the cognitive therapy conceptual framework despite the fact that it is often at odds with the more traditional, rational cognitive approaches of Ellis and, to a lesser degree, Beck. Mahoney, who himself started out as a more traditional cognitive therapist, highlights some of the following concepts related to constructivist notions of psychotherapy (Mahoney, 1995b; Mahoney, Miller, & Arciero, 1995; Neimeyer, 1995):

- **There is no single reality:** Constructivist theory challenges the assertion of a single, authenticated, external reality.

- **We constantly recreate reality:** Through the process of living and interacting with the environment, and as a function of our cognitive processes, people are continually creating and recreating their understanding of reality.

- **Schematas can change:** Deep underlying schemata, such as unconscious processes and a person's sense of self and identity, are more difficult to change than surface structures.

- **Thoughts, feelings and actions are inseparable:** There is a complex and inseparable interaction among one's thoughts, feelings, and actions.

- **We are our thoughts:** We do not simply have thoughts and interpretations of the world; we are our thoughts and interpretations, and they are constantly undergoing reconstruction as we interact with others in the world.

Comparing the more traditional rational approach with the constructivist approach, we find some major differences (Goncalves & Machado, 1995; Mahoney, 1995b; Mahoney et al., 1995) (see Table 14.2).

The goal of therapy for Mahoney and other constructivists would be to assist the client in understanding his or her unique ways of knowing and making sense out of the world and to help the client create new constructions that may work better for him or her. This is attained through a **dialectical process** in which the client shares his or her **meaning–making system** as the therapist attempts to understand and discusses with the client new ways for the client to make meaning or create a new reality. Partly, the therapist does this by attempting to understand how the client views significant past and present relationships. The **narratives** the client reveals about these relationships hold the meaning to the client's ways of

T A B L E 14.2   Comparison of Rationalist and Constructivist Views

Rationalist Views	Constructivist Views
Humans are mostly rational beings who are beset by irrational thoughts. Thoughts can overpower feelings and behaviors.	Humans are complex, with thoughts, feelings and behaviors being interdependent.
The thinking process obeys logical reasoning, which therefore means that illogical/irrational beliefs can be replaced by logical/rational ones.	Thoughts are metaphors about our existence and how we make meaning. Understand a person's meaning-making system, and you stand a chance of assisting him or her in new and profound ways.
Psychotherapy involves understanding one's inner thoughts and replacing illogical thinking with logical/rational thinking that will lead to a mentally healthy individual.	Individual meaning-making can be understood through the stories the person makes. Through a variety of psychotherapeutic techniques, new constructions of reality can be developed.

knowing the world and to his or her unique cognitive structures. As meanings and deep structures become understood, the client may choose to change his or her ways of being in the world. The therapist can facilitate this process through a variety of techniques, including use of empathy, metaphor and analogy, hypnotherapy, traditional cognitive therapy, and any other techniques that may assist in revealing deeper structures and supporting the client through the change process.

APPROACHES LOOSELY BASED ON COGNITIVE–BEHAVIORAL THERAPY, EXISTENTIAL–HUMANISTIC THERAPY, AND/OR POST-MODERN THERAPY

In the past 30 years, a number of new approaches have been developed that have borrowed some of their ideas from cognitive–behavioral therapy, existential–humanistic therapy, and/or post-modern therapy. In this section, we will examine six approaches that have gained some recognition, including **eye movement desensitization response therapy; motivational interviewing; gender-aware therapy (feminist therapy and counseling men); positive psychology;** and **complementary, alternative, and integrative therapies**.

Eye Movement Desensitization and Reprocessing Therapy

The seed of EMDR sprouted one sunny afternoon in 1987, when
I took a break to ramble around a small lake…. I noticed that when
a disturbing thought entered my mind, my eyes spontaneously started
moving back and forth. They were making rapid repetitive movements

on a diagonal from lower left to upper right. At the same time, I noticed that my disturbing thought had shifted from consciousness, and when I brought it back to mind, it no longer bothered me as much....

... [A]s I worked with the first seventy people, I discovered that I had to develop a procedure around the effect of the eye movements to resolve the anxiety consistently. Over time, the method came to include important elements of all the major schools of psychotherapy: psycho-dynamic (based on Freud's work), behavioral, cognitive, systems, and body-oriented. (Shapiro & Forrest, 1997, pp. 9–10)

Developed by Francine Shapiro in 1987, EMDR is a relatively new therapy that was originally used to help clients who were struggling with traumatic events (Shapiro & Forrest, 1997). However, in recent years, it has been expanded to treat a wide variety of problems, including such issues as depression, eating disorders, sports performance, addictions, and some problems a partner or spouse might discover through couples counseling (Shapiro, 2002a, 2005, 2009).

One of the more rapidly spreading therapies of the twenty-first century, EMDR has the client focus on **rapid eye movements** or some other **rhythmic stimulation** (e.g., tapping) while simultaneously imagining a traumatic or troubling event. This process begins to lessen the symptoms associated with the event. In addition, new, positive **core beliefs** are substituted for older, negative beliefs, and other new behaviors are encouraged to maintain change. EMDR uses a combination of theories to explain its success. First, it suggests that past traumas can become embedded in our psyche, a view that has similarities to psycho-dynamic theory. Second, it suggests that core beliefs maintain negative experiences, which is similar to cognitive therapy. Also, it proposes that new cognitions and behaviors can help a person adopt new ways of being in the world, which is cognitive–behavioral. Finally, it states that **neural pathways** in the amygdala and hippocampus store traumatic memories, which become **depoten-tiated**, or blocked, during treatment. Using all of these theories in an integrative fashion, EMDR treatment involves eight phases that sometimes can be completed within a few sessions, but often take longer (Lipke, 2000; Shapiro, 2002b).

Phase 1: Client History and Treatment Planning

In this phase, an in-depth history of the client is taken, and a treatment plan is formed. In particular, the therapist focuses on what the problem is, as well as the symptoms of the problem, situations from the past that caused the problem, current issues that continue distress, and those behaviors and skills needed in the future to alleviate the problem. In-depth discussion of the problem is not necessary; however, the client does need to identify what the problem is. Usually, this phase takes one to two sessions.

Phase 2: Preparation

Generally lasting one to two sessions, but sometimes longer (depending on the issue), this phase involves building a trusting relationship with the client as well as beginning to teach the client a range of relaxation and coping techniques. Although EMDR is known mostly for the use of eye movements to alleviate trauma, the relationship should not be underestimated, as it is critical that the client "buy into" the process if it is to be successful. Thus, building a strong therapeutic alliance through the use of such skills as empathy and positive regard is critical at this phase (Dworkin, 2005). In addition, teaching a variety of cognitive–behavioral relaxation techniques and coping skills helps clients begin the process of self-managing their anxiety.

Phase 3: Assessment

Using the problem situation identified in Phase 1, in this phase, the client isolates negative beliefs associated with the event. Similar to the negative beliefs discussed by Beck and Ellis, the client is asked to identify negative self-statements that the client has relative to the event. Such self-statements or core beliefs could be things like, "I am not lovable," "I am worthless," or "I am not capable." After picking one or more negative beliefs, the client then identifies positive beliefs that contradict the negative ones. Using the **subjective units of discomfort (SUD) scale**, the client rates his or her level of discomfort from 0 to 10, with 0 being the most relaxed within the context of the problem and a 10 being the most upset. The client can relay his or her rating when thinking about the negative event, negative self-statements, or the newly identified positive self-statement.

Phase 4: Desensitization

During Phase 4, the therapist has the client focus on upsetting images, negative beliefs, emotions, and physical sensations related to a traumatic or upsetting event. At the same time, the therapist directs the client in a series of eye movements or related stimulations (e.g., tapping, listening to rhythmic tones). Then, the therapist tells the client to **"blank it out"** (or "let it go") and take a deep breath and then asks, "What do you get now?" (Shapiro, 2002b, p. 38). At this point, the therapist will continue with treatment based on the type of response the client gives. If the client is still bothered by the initial upsetting image and related symptoms, desensitization will be repeated. However, clients will often leave the initial image and move on to another image related to the traumatic event. A decision to move on is made if a there is a SUD level of 0, 1, or 2.

Phase 5: Installation

As clients' level of upset decreases, there is a natural increase in the positive cognitive beliefs they identified in Phase 3. Thus, the purpose of this phase is to strengthen those cognitive beliefs. Using what is called the **validity of cognition (VoC) scale**, which runs from a 1 (completely false) to a 7 (completely true), the goal is to have clients reach the high end of the scale in reference to their newly chosen positive cognitive beliefs. In this phase, the therapist encourages the pairing of the positive cognition with the traumatic event. So, a person who was verbally abused as a child and always told he was "stupid" will pair the image of being told he or she was stupid with a statement like "I am capable and smart." Other activities might also be used at this time to reinforce the positive self-statement, such as the client's deciding to confront his or her parent directly about the statements made in early life. This confrontation, if done correctly, could help to anchor the positive belief.

Phase 6: Body Scan

Because the body will sometimes continue to hold the tension from traumatic or upsetting events beyond what our minds are consciously saying, clients are asked to scan their bodies while remembering the target event. If tension is still present, additional processing is done (Phases 4 and 5).

Phase 7: Closure

The closure phase ensures that the client finishes each session feeling better than when the session was started and helps clients focus on ongoing feelings of **psychological stability**. Thus, at the end of each session, clients are encouraged to practice the self-management techniques learned in Phase 2. In addition, clients are encouraged to keep an ongoing journal to record their progress, to practice the self-management techniques at home, and to use relaxation recordings at home to maintain their stability. These techniques, in conjunction with the earlier work done in Phases 5 through 7, ensure ongoing progress.

Phase 8: Reevaluation

At the beginning of each EMDR session, the therapist reviews the client's journal with the client and talks with the client about any additional targets (problems) that need to be addressed through processing. As processing continues, new issues will arise, and the focus of treatment will change. As new issues emerge, clients will re-cycle through Phase 3 to Phase 8. As new targets are dealt with, over time, client anxiety will lessen, and psychological stability will be maintained without further treatment being necessary.

Although a relatively young therapy, much research has been completed on EMDR, especially in the area of post-traumatic stress disorders (PTSDs) and related traumas. This research suggests that EMDR is as or more effective than medication alone or other kinds of treatment. In fact, the Department of Defense and the American Psychiatric Association's practice guidelines suggest that EMDR is one treatment of choice for trauma (EMDR Institute, 2005). In addition, EMDR has become increasingly used with other disorders not directly related to trauma. Finally, recent brain research indicates that eye movement, or other rhythmic stimulation, is able to block the memories produced by specific neural pathways, and it is hypothesized that stimulation of specific parts of the brain may be able to do the same (Rasolkhani-Kalhorn & Harper, 2006). Thus, in the near future, studies that examine the use of noninvasive brain stimulation and use a similar protocol to that noted in the eight phases of EMDR therapy are likely.

Motivational Interviewing

Rooted in person-centered counseling, but also incorporating aspects of psychodynamic and cognitive–behavioral therapy, motivational interviewing (MI) is a relatively new approach to counseling that was developed by W. R. Miller and S. Rollnick. Originally developed for the treatment of substance abuse (Miller, 1983, 1999; Miller & Rollnick, 1991), in recent years, the application of MI has expanded and, today, it is most often seen in the treatment of "gambling, eating disorders, anxiety disorders, chronic disease management, and health-related disorders" (Arkowitz & Miller, 2008, p. 1). A number of assumptions about motivation that drive MI theory have been identified. Miller (1999) suggests that they include the following:

■ *Motivation is a key to change:* Motivation is a complex construct that includes a number of factors, all of which can be important to the change process. Some include the individual's sense of self, biological factors, social factors, developmental issues, etc.

■ *Motivation is multidimensional:* Motivation is effected by internal urges, external pressures and goals, perceptions of risks and benefits, and cognitive assessment of the situation.

■ *Motivation is dynamic and fluctuating:* Motivation can vary over time and can vacillate in intensity.

■ *Motivation is influenced by social interactions:* Internal factors are critical for change, but external factors help create conditions for change.

■ *Motivation can be modified:* A wide variety of elements can modify a person's motivation, and a skilled clinician can assist in setting up those conditions.

■ *Motivation is influenced by the clinician's style:* The ability of the counselor to build a therapeutic relationship is probably as or more important than the specific skills the clinician uses.

■ *The clinician's task is to elicit and enhance motivation:* Clinicians should have a wide range of techniques to assist the client in the change process.

To a large degree, the nonmotivated client is seen as a myth in MI. Instead, the client is viewed as an individual who waxes and wanes in his or her motivation and one who can become motivated under the right circumstances. MI theorists argue that creating the right circumstances is done partly by the clinician's having an attitude or "spirit" that is solicitous of the client. This attitude includes being **collaborative**, where there is a partnership between the client and counselor; **evocative**, where the counselor uses a client-centered approach to elicit the personal goals and dreams of the client; and **honoring** the client's autonomy, in the sense that the counselor is accepting of the client, caring toward the client, and respectful of the client's decisions and goals (Rollnick & Miller, 1995; Rollnick, Miller, & Butler, 2008).

In describing the change process in substance abusers, Miller presents a **five-stage model** and suggests that clients will often re-cycle through the stages prior to being successful (see Figure 14.2). Using this model, clients are seen on a continuum that includes **precontemplation**, or the point where they do not realize there is a problem; **contemplation**, when they begin to become aware that a problem exists but are ambivalent about the need for change; **preparation**, when clients realize change is needed and begins to consider strategies for change; **action**, when strategies are implemented; and **maintenance**, when efforts are made to maintain the gains that have been achieved. Finally, **recurrence** (not shown in the figure) is the awareness that change is

Permanent Exit

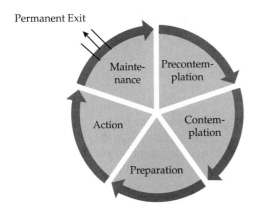

F I G U R E 14.2 Five Stages of Change

Adapted from: Miller, W. R. (1999). *Enhancing motivation for change in substance abuse treatment.* Rockville, MD: U. S. Department of Health and Human Services, p. 17.

difficult and that clients will often slip or relapse into their change process. In this case, re-cycling through the stages is needed.

Four basic principles of MI have been described by Miller and Rollnick (2002); they include **expressing empathy** in an effort to build a relationship and hear the client; **developing discrepancies**, which is helping clients hear how their behaviors and values may not always be in sync (a gambling-addicted father who values saving money for his child to go to college); **rolling with resistance**, where the counselor tries to understand the importance of the client's resistance and what purpose it serves for him (the gambler gets a "rush" because he or she has no meaning in life); and **supporting self-efficacy** or believing and supporting that the client has the necessary skills to make change and is the final decider in the change process.

At the beginning stages of the change process (e.g., precontemplative and contemplative), the counselor tends to use many basic counseling skills such as open-ended questions, listening, empathy, affirming, and summarizing (Arkowitz & Miller, 2008). Slowly, as the client moves toward the preparation stage, the therapist will encourage the client to talk about change. Change talk will often focus on the ambivalence that the client has toward change, and in some cases, clinicians will examine underlying reasons why a client may not want to change. This intrapsychic focus can be a critical part of the change process. As clients become increasingly ready to make change, counselors will use any of a variety of skills to help in the change process as the client moves toward taking action. Often, cognitive–behavioral techniques will be implemented at this point.

As you can see, MI integrates a number of approaches in its effort to help clients change. Although MI is a relatively young therapy, initial research seems to supports its efficacy (Arkowitz & Miller, 2008). You might want to consider using MI if you will be working with clients identified as benefitting from this kind of approach.

GENDER AWARE THERAPY

Whether working with a man or a woman, knowledge of gender biases can allow a counselor to be effective at what some have called gender-aware therapy (Good, Gilbert, & Scher, 1990; Seem & Johnson, 1998). Such therapy **considers gender central to counseling; views problems within a societal context; encourages counselors to actively address gender injustices; encourages the development of collaborative and equal relationships;** and **respects the client's right to choose the gender roles appropriate for himself or herself** regardless of their political correctness (Kees, 2005; Mejia, 2005). Let's look at two variations of gender aware therapy: feminist therapy and counseling men.

Feminist Therapy*

Feminist therapy had its basis in the feminist political movement of the 1960s and 1970s, which sought to offer women a new vantage point that was not based on traditional gender-role expectations (Funderburk & Fukuyama, 2002). Broadly, feminist theory recognized the **impact of gender**, the **oppression of women**, and the **influence of politics**. It sought to liberate women from the kitchen and the side of a crib and to bring them front and center to a more prominent and fulfilling place in society. Feminist therapy understood that as a function of a male-dominated society, women were often devalued, and therefore, awareness of gender issues and the battle to decrease oppression against women and other minorities through **social justice actions** became significant principles of feminist theory (Robinson-Wood, 2009).

Today, the overarching goal of feminist therapy is **empowerment** of female clients (Brown & Bryan, 2007). Feminist helpers believe that empowering a client involves awakening the client to her own intrinsic power. Indeed, Brown (2006) states:

> Feminist therapy, speaking out loud about power, disrupts the trance of despair that has become so common in today's culture. Feminist therapy requires its practitioners to think in a complex and nuanced manner about how power and powerlessness are the roots of distress. (p. 17)

Several components comprise feminist theory and the empowerment of women. The first is viewing the **person as a political entity** (Funderburk & Fukuyama, 2002). Specifically, this refers to the fact that no client is an isolated individual but rather is impacted by the political and social environments. Historically and currently, women and minorities have been at a disadvantage politically, and one focus of feminist therapy is to encourage these marginalized clients to find their voice and create societal change.

A second guiding principle of feminist therapy is **recognition of the power and authority the counselor holds** in the relationship (Brown & Bryan, 2007). The feminist counselor actively seeks to establish a therapeutic alliance that is collaborative and effectively balances the relationship's power dynamics (Brown,

---

*Contributed by Julia Forman.

Weber, & Ali, 2008). Educating the client about what counseling entails, examining the influence of society's expected gender roles, and genuinely and appropriately self-disclosing serve to create an egalitarian relationship. Also, feminist counselors will often use **feminist contracting** in an effort to build an **egalitarian, cooperative, and trusting** relationship that empowers the client by allowing the client to determine the nature and timing of what will be discussed (Brown, 1993). Feminist contracting enables helpers and clients to cooperatively create agreed-upon actions and objectives to effectively treat a challenge in the client's life.

The third critical component of feminist therapy is to **focus on a wellness** model (Brown & Bryan, 2007). Feminist helpers do not see problems arising from psychopathology, otherwise termed the "disease model." On the contrary, feminist therapists tend to view problems as a function of external factors; that is, symptomatic behaviors are seen as coping responses to societal and political stress and oppression. Viewing female clients from a wellness perspective may lead to questions concerning the feminist therapist's relationship with the *Diagnostic and Statistical Manual* (DSM-IV-TR) (Brown, 2006). Carolyn Enns (1993), a leading feminist therapist, gives several reasons why feminist therapists should eschew formal diagnosis, despite current pressures to diagnose. For instance, she notes that focusing on psychopathology moves the attention away from the client's societal context and dilutes the need for systemic change, that expectations for traditional gender role behaviors may be reaffirmed by diagnoses, and that the use of diagnosis may lend itself to an unequal balance of power. Furthermore, Enns asserted that the DSM-IV-TR is a symbol of oppression, as it was created by Caucasian males in the mental health field, and that diagnoses may taint a helper's view of the client.

In addition to the three critical components of feminist therapy just discussed, in 2007, the American Psychological Association (APA) adopted **Guidelines for Psychological Practice with Girls and Women** that should be integrated into the practice of feminist therapy. The guidelines, which are listed in Table 14.3, contain three sections: (1) diversity, social context, and power, (2) professional responsibility, and (3) practice applications.

Finally, in the actual practice of feminist therapy, Neukrug (2007) offers **12 steps** to consider that take into account the critical components of feminist therapy and the APA guidelines in counseling:

1. *Have the right attitudes and beliefs, gain knowledge, and learn skills.* Be prepared to work with women by embracing the appropriate knowledge, skills, and beliefs prior to meeting with them (e.g., know and incorporate the APA guidelines in Table 14.3).

2. *Ensure that the counseling approach you use has been adapted for women.* Conduct an inventory of your theoretical approach for any inherent sexist leanings it may have. Discard it or adapt as necessary.

3. *Establish a collaborative relationship, give up your power, and de-mystify the counseling process.* Recognize the importance that power plays in all relationships, and attempt to equalize the counselor–client relationship. This can be done by downplaying the "expert" role, by encouraging women to trust themselves, and through self-disclosure. Within this relationship, the

T A B L E 14.3   APA Guidelines for Psychological Practice with Girls and Women

Section 1:
Diversity, Social Context, and Power

Guideline 1: Psychologists strive to be aware of the effects of socialization, stereotyping, and unique life events on the development of girls and women across diverse cultural groups (p. 35).

Guideline 2: Psychologists are encouraged to recognize and utilize information about oppression, privilege, and identity development as they may affect girls and women (p. 37).

Guideline 3: Psychologists strive to understand the impact of bias and discrimination upon the physical and mental health of those with whom they work (p. 39).

Section 2:
Professional Responsibility

Guideline 4: Psychologists strive to use gender and culturally sensitive, affirming practices in providing services to girls and women (p. 46).

Guideline 5: Psychologists are encouraged to recognize how their socialization, attitudes, and knowledge about gender may affect their practice with girls and women (p. 50).

Section 3:
Practice Applications

Guideline 6: Psychologists are encouraged to employ interventions and approaches that have been found to be effective in the treatment of issues of concern to girls and women (p. 52).

Guideline 7: Psychologists strive to foster therapeutic relationships and practices that promote initiative, empowerment, and expanded alternatives and choices for girls and women (p. 55).

Guideline 8: Psychologists strive to provide appropriate, unbiased assessments and diagnoses in their work with women and girls (p. 58).

Guideline 9: Psychologists strive to consider the problems of girls and women in their sociopolitical context (p. 60).

Guideline 10: Psychologists strive to acquaint themselves with and utilize relevant mental health, education, and community resources for girls and women (p. 62).

Guideline 11: Psychologists are encouraged to understand and work to change institutional and systemic bias that may impact girls and women (p. 64).

SOURCE: American Psychological Association. (2007). *Guidelines for psychological practice with girls and women.* Washington, D.C.: Author.

counselor and client should work toward a relationship that focuses on cooperatively created actions and objectives.

4. *Identify social/political issues related to client problem(s), and use them to set goals.* Women tend to internalize problems that are sometimes of an external nature. Help women understand the nature of the problem within its socio-cultural context and help them see how the unique dynamics of women tend to cause them to internalize these issues. For instance, it is common for abused

women to blame themselves for the abuse. Help them see that they are not responsible for the abuse, and help them set goals to break free of the abuse.

5. *Use a wellness model and avoid the use of diagnosis and labels.* Diagnosis and labels can be disempowering to women and tend to focus treatment toward psychopathology. A wellness orientation that uplifts women can help them get in touch with their strengths.

6. *Validate and legitimize a woman's angry feelings toward her predicament.* As women begin to recognize how they have internalized social and political issues, they begin to understand how they have been victimized. Helpers should assist women in combating feelings of powerlessness, helplessness, and low self-esteem and help them identify their strengths.

7. *Actively promote healing through learning about women's issues.* Helpers should encourage women to learn more about women's issues. This can be done by providing written materials to women, suggesting seminars for them to attend, and providing a list of women's groups or women's organizations that support women's issues.

8. *Provide a safe environment to express feelings as clients begin to form connections with other women.* As female clients gain clarity regarding their situations, they see how society's objectification of women has led to fear and competition among women. This newfound knowledge will lead to a desire to have deeper, more meaningful connections with other women. Helpers can validate feelings of fear and competition with other women that result from society's objectification of women. As these feelings dissipate, clients will move toward strong and special connections with women. At this point in counseling, helpers should consider the possibility of providing a women's support group.

9. *Provide a safe environment to help women understand their anger toward men.* As women increasingly see that a male-dominated society has led to the objectification of women, they will begin to express increasing anger toward men. However, helpers can assist clients in understanding the difference between anger at a man and anger at a male-dominated system. Slowly, women will see that some men can also be trusted.

10. *Help clients deal with conflicting feelings between traditional and newfound values.* As women increasingly get in touch with newfound feminist beliefs, they will become torn between those beliefs and values that do not seem congruent with those beliefs (e.g., wanting to stay home to raise the children). Helpers should validate these contradictory feelings, acknowledge the confusion, and assist clients to fully explore their belief systems.

11. *Facilitate integration of the client's new identity.* Helpers can assist clients in integrating their newfound feminist beliefs with their personal beliefs, even those personal beliefs that may not seem to be traditionally feminist. Clients are able to feel strength in their own identity development and no longer need to rely on an external belief system.

12. *Say goodbye.* It is important to help women move on with their newfound identities, and helpers should encourage women to try being in the world without counseling. Counseling is always an option for the future.

Counseling Men

> In order for us to be able to "hold" others as men, we have to imagine ourselves being held by our fathers, perhaps the first male we wanted to hold and be held by. (Osherson, 1986/2001, 195)

Although concerns of men are generally quite different from those of women, they are no less important, especially in light of the fact that compared to women, **men seek counseling less** and **have a more negative attitude toward the helping process** (Addis & Mahalik, 2003; Berger, Levant, McMillan, Kelleher, & Sellers, 2005). As with women, men need to feel supported in therapy and not feel judged for having their own issues—**issues that are common to the male experience** and that cut across all racial, ethnic, and cultural groups. For instance:

- Men tend to be more comfortable with angry feelings, aggression, and competitiveness, and less comfortable with sad feelings, collaboration, self-disclosure, and intimacy.

- Men are sometimes ostracized for expressing feelings, especially those considered to be traditionally feminine feelings, and yet criticized for not being more sensitive.

- Men are criticized for being too controlling and self-reliant and are made to feel inadequate if they do not take control.

- Men are socialized to be more aggressive and individualistic and are thus more prone to accidents, suicide, early death through wars, and acts of violence.

- Men are encouraged to be competitive and controlling (take charge), and yet these very behaviors lead to increased stress and likely play a factor in men's shorter life expectancy

- Men are socialized not to be engaged in child-rearing and yet are criticized for being distant fathers.

- Men have biological problems unique to them (e.g., prostate cancer, prostatitis, higher rates of stress-related diseases, and testicular cancer).

As with women, counselors need to be aware of men's issues and have empathy for a man's situation. A number of ideas that can be incorporated into a set of guidelines when working with male clients are listed below (Brooks, 1998; Berger et al., 2005; Greer, 2005; McCarthy & Holliday, 2004; Mejia, 2005; Osherson, 1986/2001; Pollack & Levant, 1998):

1. *Have the right attitudes and beliefs, gain knowledge, and learn skills.* Embrace the appropriate knowledge, skills, and beliefs prior to meeting with a male client.

2. *Accept men where they are, as this will help build trust.* Men, who are often initially very defensive, will work hard on their issues once they trust the counselor.

3. *Don't push men to express what may be considered "softer feelings."* Don't push a man to express feelings, as you may push him out of the helping relationship. Men tend to be uncomfortable with certain feelings (e.g., deep sadness, feelings of incompetence, feelings of inadequacy, feelings of closeness) but more at ease with "thinking things through," problem-solving, and expressing some feelings such as anger and pride.

4. *Early on in therapy, validate the man's feelings.* Validate whatever feelings a man expresses, and remember that in order to protect their egos, men may initially blame others and society for their problems.

5. *Validate the man's view of how he has been constrained by male sex-role stereotypes.* Help to build trust by validating a man's sense of being constrained by sex-role stereotypes (e.g., he must work particularly hard for his family).

6. *Have a plan for therapy.* Collaborate with men, and together build a plan for therapy. Men like structure and a sense of goal-directedness even if the plan is changed later on.

7. *Begin to discuss developmental issues.* Introduce male developmental issues so a man can quickly express concerns that may be impinging upon him (e.g., midlife crises) (Levinson, 1985).

8. *Slowly encourage the expression of new feelings.* As you reinforce the expression of newfound feelings, men will begin to feel comfortable sharing what are considered to be more feminine feelings (e.g., tears, caring, feelings of intimacy).

9. *Explore underlying issues and reinforce new ways of understanding the world.* Explore underlying issues as they emerge (e.g., childhood issues, feelings of inadequacy, father–son issues).

10. *Explore behavioral change.* As insights emerge, encourage men to try out new behaviors.

11. *Encourage the integration of new feelings, new ways of thinking, and new behaviors.*

12. *Encourage new male relationships.* Encourage new male friendships in which the client can express his feelings while maintaining his maleness (e.g., men's group).

13. *Say goodbye.* Be able to say goodbye, and end the relationship. Although some men may want to continue therapy, many will see it as time-limited, a means to a goal.

Positive Psychology and Well-Being Therapy

One evening, an old Cherokee Indian told his grandson about a battle that goes on inside people. He said, "My son, the battle is between two 'wolves' inside us all. One is Evil. It is anger, envy, jealousy, sorrow, regret, greed, arrogance, self-pity, guilt, resentment, inferiority, lies, false pride, superiority, and ego. The other is Good. It is joy, peace, love, hope, serenity, humility, kindness, benevolence, empathy, generosity, truth, compassion and faith." The grandson thought about it and then asked his grandfather, "Which wolf wins?" The old Cherokee simply replied, "The one you feed." (traditional Cherokee story)

After 100 years of the field of psychology focusing almost exclusively on problems, in 1998, Martin Seligman, the then-president of the American Psychological Association, decided it was time for a change. It was then that Seligman decided to launch the positive psychology movement by encouraging research and articles in the field and developing a section on positive psychology in the counseling psychology division of APA (Seligman & Csikszentmihalyi, 2000). Seligman had been known for his experiments on **learned helplessness** (Seligman, 1975; Seligman & Maier, 1967), where it was shown that dogs that had received electric shocks in a situation they could not avoid would subsequently avoid escaping a situation in which evading the shock was possible. Subsequent research on humans showed that certain types of cognitive styles tend to lead to learned helplessness in people. After years of research on learned helplessness, Seligman shifted perspectives and realized that individuals can modify their thinking and actions and learn how to be optimistic and positive. He called this **learned optimism** (Seligman, 1990).

Positive psychology didn't pop out of nowhere, and its beginning can be found in the writings of many of the humanistic psychologists who came before the positive psychology movement (Seligman, 2009). One of the important distinctions between positive psychology and the early humanists was the assumption made by the humanists that people were inherently good. The philosophy behind positive psychology suggests that we are all capable of many things, including both good and bad feelings and actions, and our actual behaviors are likely a function of a multitude of factors, including situational factors, the system in which we live, our culture, our genes, how we grew up, and perhaps a little bit of mystery. So, if we're **capable of being bad or good**, the positive psychology movement questions, Why not make efforts to focus on the strengths and positive feelings of the person? The current wave of those involved in positive psychology has emphasized focusing on how to help people experience more positive emotions, the study of positive traits, and mechanisms for establishing institutions that focus on the positive (Peterson, 2006). The **Positive Psychology Center** (2007, para. 3) at the University of Pennsylvania suggests that the goals of positive psychology include building a science that supports:

- families and schools that allow children to flourish
- workplaces that foster satisfaction and high productivity
- communities that encourage civic engagement
- therapists who identify and nurture their patients' strengths
- the teaching of positive psychology
- dissemination of positive psychology interventions in organizations and communities

From a positive psychology perspective, **symptoms are not a sign of pathology**. For instance, depression in adults, aggressive behavior in children, or post-traumatic stress disorder are not seen as symptoms that are interminably embedded in the person but as qualities any of us might exhibit under certain circumstances, as well as qualities that individuals can transcend if taught how to do

B o x 14.2   Positivity Ratio
Want to determine your positivity ratio? Go to http://www.positivityratio.com/single.php and take the quiz!

so. Therefore, positive psychology researchers have focused on how people can make a shift from negative thoughts and behaviors to positive emotions and actions.

Along these lines, Barbara Fredrickson has conducted a considerable amount of research on the importance of positive emotions, with some interesting results (Fredrickson, 2001; Fredrickson & Losada, 2005). For instance, positive emotions increase happiness and psychological growth, result in longer life, increase intuition and creativity, increase resilience to adversity, and decrease health problems. Fredrickson warns, however, that negative feelings are also important, because one cannot experience the positive unless there is a contradictory feeling to compare it to (Fredrickson, 2009). Her research suggests that, optimally, there should be a **three-to-one ratio of positive to negative feelings** (see Box 14.2). However, she also cautions that one should not attempt to "act" positively, as others will pick up on this artificiality and will likely feel bitter toward these attempts to be something one is not. She goes on to state that developing a positive outlook takes time and intention. She encourages **loving-kindness meditation** and other purposeful acts, which will increase one's ability to genuinely feel positive emotions.

Using positive psychology within a therapeutic context is relatively new, and little research on this approach has been conducted. However, Giovanni Fava (Fava, 2009; Fava & Ruini, 2003; Ruini & Fava, 2009) has developed and conducted preliminary research on a type of therapy that targets client strengths. Called **well-being therapy**, this approach focusses on **Ryff's (1989) six dimensions of psychological well-being: autonomy**, **personal growth**, **environmental mastery**, **purpose in life**, **positive relations**, and **self-acceptance** (see Table 14.4).

A short-term approach to therapy, well-being therapy usually lasts for eight sessions and "emphasizes self-observation, with the use of a structured diary, and is directive and problem-oriented, based on an educational model" (Ruini & Fava, 2009, p. 512). The therapy can be viewed through three phases:

Initial sessions: During these sessions, clients are asked to identify times when they have experienced a sense of well-being. Using a structured diary that can be completed at home, they are asked to record those episodes and rate them on a scale of 0 to 100 (100 = the most intense well-being that the individual could experience).

Intermediate sessions: Lasting for two or three sessions, in this phase, clients are asked to examine how their moments of well-being had been interrupted prematurely and are taught how to observe their thoughts, especially those irrational or automatic thoughts that prevented them from continuing to experience a sense of well-being. This phase helps the therapist distinguish which aspects of Ryff's dimensions are being hindered by irrational and automatic thoughts. At this point, the counselor might challenge the client's irrational or automatic thoughts; however, the main focus for the client is on learning how to observe his or her sense

T A B L E 14.4   Modification of the Six Dimensions of Psychological Well-Being According to Ryff's Model

Dimensions	Impaired Level	Optimal Level
Environmental mastery	The subject has or feels difficulties in managing everyday affairs; feels unable to change or improve surrounding context; is unaware of surrounding opportunities; lacks sense of control over external world.	The subject has a sense of mastery and competence in managing the environment; controls external activities; makes effective use of surrounding opportunities; is able to create or choose contexts suitable to personal needs and values.
Personal growth	The subject has a sense of personal stagnation; lacks sense of improvement or expansion over time; feels bored and uninterested with life; feels unable to develop new attitudes or behaviors.	The subject has a feeling of continued development; sees self as growing and expanding; is open to new experiences; has sense of realizing own potential; sees improvement in self and behavior over time.
Purpose in life	The subject lacks a sense of meaning in life; has few goals or aims, lacks sense of direction, does not see purpose in past life; has no outlooks or beliefs that give life meaning.	The subject has goals in life and a sense of directedness; feels there is meaning to present and past life; holds beliefs that give life purpose; has aims and objectives for living.
Autonomy	The subject is overconcerned with the expectations and evaluation of others; relies on judgment of others to make important decisions; conforms to social pressures to think or act in certain ways.	The subject is self-determining and independent; able to resist social pressures; regulates behavior from within; evaluates self by personal standards.
Self-acceptance	The subject feels dissatisfied with self; is disappointed with what has occurred in past life; is troubled about certain personal qualities; wishes to be different than what he or she is.	The subject has a positive attitude toward the self; accepts his/her good and bad qualities; feels positive about past life.
Positive relations with others	The subject has few close, trusting relationships with others; finds it difficult to be open and is isolated and frustrated in interpersonal relationships; is not willing to make compromises to sustain important ties with others.	The subject has warm and trusting relationships with others; is concerned about the welfare of others; is capable of strong empathy affection, and intimacy; understands give-and-take of human relationships.

SOURCE: Fava, G. A., & Ruini, C. (2003). Development and characteristics of a well-being enhancing psychotherapeutic strategy: Well-being therapy. *Journal of Behavior Therapy and Experimental Psychiatry, 34*, 51.

of well-being. It is here that the client begins to learn how to "feed" his or her good feelings and positive sense of well-being. Finally, in this phase, the therapist might begin to suggest pleasurable activities to encourage a continued sense of well-being.

Final sessions: Ryff's six psychological dimensions are increasingly explained to the client, and the therapist tries to zero in on those dimensions that are compromising a sense of well-being (e.g., a person who is being dominated by another individual in his or her life may be experiencing a low sense of well-being on the autonomy dimension) (see Table 14.4). Cognitive–behavioral techniques are used to confront negative thoughts and to work on developing new behaviors. Then, and most important, the client is asked to continue to observe and "feed" his or her sense of well-being by keeping a journal, reflecting on moments of well-being, expanding his or her problem-solving skills, and partaking in activities that lead to an increased sense of well-being.

Although a new approach to therapy, well-being therapy shows promise in helping clients expand their sense of well-being and good feelings by focusing mostly on positive aspects of self.

Complementary, Alternative, and Integrative Approaches*

Today, we may be in the midst of a paradigm shift as emerging complementary, alternative, and integrative therapeutic approaches become ever more popular. Complementary medicine or therapy includes products, systems, or practices that are used in conjunction with conventional methods to treat biological and mental health problems, whereas alternative approaches are used instead of conventional methods. An integrative approach suggests that **traditional healing** methods are integrated with complementary or alternative approaches in an effort to promote **physical**, **emotional**, and **psychological well-being** (Weil, 1995).

Complementary and alternative approaches take a **holistic approach** to healing, which means that they focus on the whole person as opposed to one aspect of the person. The overall emphasis of these new (and sometimes very old) approaches is to focus on a client's overall wellness (Myers & Sweeney, 2004, 2005) while being cognizant of and attending to the client's cultural background and beliefs. Ultimately, these "new" theories and approaches offer a different framework for conceptualizing client issues and the sources of these problems. For instance, rather than dealing with "depression," one might focus on the **total range of an individual's wellness**, such as one's **creative self** (e.g., thinking, emotions, control or personal mastery, work, positive humor); **coping self** (e.g., leisure, stress management, self-worth, realistic beliefs); **social self** (e.g., friendship, love); **essential self** (e.g., spirituality, gender identity, cultural identity, self-care); and **physical self** (e.g., nutrition, exercise) (Myers & Sweeney, 2004, 2005). These approaches will tend to integrate contemporary medical and behavioral therapies, alternative approaches from other cultures, and new approaches based on age-old ideas and modes of treatment in addressing the whole person. In addition, these approaches underscore the notion that no one method or model is all-encompassing. Physicians, therapists, energy healers, or shamans do not have all the answers.

In 1998, the federal government created the **National Center for Complementary and Alternative Medicine** (NCCAM, 2009) for scientific

---

*Contributed by Suzan Thompson.

research on complementary and alternative medicine. According to NCCAM, an increasing number of Americans are using complementary and alternative medicine or therapies to treat a variety of chronic conditions such as depression, anxiety, dysthymia, panic disorder, generalized anxiety disorder, insomnia, chronic pain, substance abuse, and dementia/cognitive impairment (Kessler et al., 2001; Mamtani & Cimino, 2002; Oken, Storzbach, & Kaye, 1998; Unutzer et al., 2000). In fact, statistics show that nearly 30 percent of Americans are using alternative therapies, and Americans are spending upward of 48 billion dollars a year on such therapies (Frontline, 2003). It seems apparent that alternative and complementary care is here to stay. With this in mind, it behooves mental health practitioners to be aware of this trend, educate themselves about these approaches, and consider using such techniques, where appropriate, in their own practices to better respond to client needs.

Some complementary and alternative techniques might surprise you and may include a number of popular as well as lesser-known therapies. NCCAM categorizes these approaches into five main domains, although some approaches might fit into more than one category (NCCAM, 2007):

- *Biologically based systems* (vitamins and minerals, herbs and supplements, animal products, special diets, chelation therapy)

- *Manipulative and body-based* (chiropractic, osteopathy, reflexology, massage)

- *Mind-body medicine* (yoga, guided imagery, meditation, hypnotherapy, spirituality, art, dance, and music therapies, tai chi)

- *Alternative medical systems* (Ayurvedic medicine, naturopathy, homeopathy, traditional Chinese medicine)

- *Energy therapies* (qigong, Reiki, therapeutic touch, thought-field therapy, emotional freedom techniques, EMF Balancing Technique, electromagnetic fields)

When working with clients who might be interested in complementary, alternative or integrative approaches, it's helpful to consider the following prior to choosing an approach:

- What is its modality?

- What is it used for?

- What is it effective with?

- What are the cautions or contraindications?

- What training and/or credential is required?

- How will you integrate it into the therapeutic process?

- What is the ethical use of the modality?

- What is the research on the approach?

One way of informing yourself on these approaches is to consult information from NCCAM, which continues to fund and publish studies on the approaches (see http://nccam.nih.gov). Notable books on these approaches include: *Spontaneous Healing* (Weil, 1995), *Reinventing Medicine* (Dossey, 1999), *Energy Medicine* (Eden & Feinstein, 2008), *Healing with Complementary and Alternative Therapies* (Keegan, 2001), and the *Handbook of Complementary and Alternative Therapies in Mental Health*

(Shannon, 2002). Associations that offer conferences and publications related to alternative, complementary, and integrative health include **Alternative Therapies in Health and Medicine** (http://www.alternative-therapies.com), the **Association for Humanistic Psychology** (http://www.ahpweb.org), the **Association for Comprehensive Energy Psychology** (http://www.energypsych.org), the **American Holistic Health Association** (http://www.ahha.org), and the **Center for Noetic Sciences** (http://www.noetic.org). Interesting, this latter was created by astronaut Edgar Mitchell in 1971 after he returned from his Apollo 14 mission to the moon with a deep knowledge that something greater than himself existed. Through his leadership, research was initiated that looks into the possibility that "reality is more complex, subtle, and inexorably mysterious than conventional science had led him to believe" (Noetic Sciences, 2009, para. 3).

As we seek our own mind–body–spirit health, we need to be aware of all the tools that are available to us, and complementary, alternative, and integrative health care offers us a multitude of choices for healing, growth and development.

SUMMARY

This chapter reviewed a number of adaptations, extensions, and spin-offs of the major theories already discussed in the text. We started with a look at a number of extensions and adaptations to classical psychoanalysis that generally de-emphasize the role of the id in personality development. We noted that Erikson's psychosocial theory suggested that individuals pass through eight stages and that social forces play a bigger role in development than Freud or earlier psychoanalysts had suggested. Erickson believed that the influence of instincts and the unconscious were not as great as many had suggested. In passage through the stages, people were faced with a task, or crisis, that could be seen as representing opposing forces (e.g., trust vs. mistrust). Erikson described the tasks as "syntonic" or "dystonic." He also believed that the development of a healthy ego is contingent on the individual's ability to master these critical periods and is highlighted by a particular virtue or strength that is associated with successful passage through each stage.

We then moved on to object-relations theory, which stresses the importance of relationships (as opposed to sexual aggressive drives) in motivating people. Object-relations theorists talk about good-enough mothering and providing positive holding environments for children in the development of the self through a series of stages that tend to move from symbiosis to separation of self. We also noted how "splitting" plays an important role in the development of the self. The purpose of object-relations therapy is to resolve early traumatic experiences so the individual can build a new self-structure. Clients are re-parented by taking in new "objects" (the therapist), which can then serve as a new blueprint for the self.

Looking at Kohut's self-psychology next, we stated that Kohut gave attention to the development of the self and did not focus on drives or instincts. Kohut believed that three basic needs had to be met by the child: to feel special (recognition), to believe that parents are strong, capable, and self-assured (to idealize the parent), and to be liked by others and to belong (twinship). He also believed that clients needed a corrective emotional experience to develop a healthy self and said that empathy and interpretation of the transference relationship was critical to the repairing of the client's self. Like the object-relations therapists, Kohut thought that clients could be re-parented and the needs that hadn't been adequately provided by parents could be provided by the therapist through a corrective emotional experience.

The relational and subjectivity perspective speaks on the importance of an ongoing dialogue between the client and the therapist. These therapists suggest that we have internalized images of significant, early relationships (e.g., parents) and that those images impact how individuals relate. However, they also argue that personality and the patterns of understanding and relating to others in the world do not develop in isolation from others but rather within the mutually influencing subjectivities of people in relationships. They highlight the myth of the independent mind and suggest that it is through interactions that the "self" is formed. Those who practice this perspective develop a deep, intimate, self-disclosing relationship with their clients and give attention to transference and to carefully timed self-disclosures of the therapist's countertransference as well. Mutually sharing is geared to elicit experiencing, which can then be understood in terms of past patterns in relationships and how it affects current relationships.

From the cognitive–behavioral perspective, four approaches were examined. Multimodal therapy, developed by Arnold Lazarus, approaches the client by assessing seven modalities, known as the BASIC ID. Following a thorough analysis of the client's BASIC ID, straightforward treatment strategies and treatment goals are developed for each of the modalities.

Dialectical behavior therapy was designed to treat borderline personality disorders but is now used for other disorders. Based on a biosocial theory of personality development, DBT assumes that some people are born with heightened emotional sensitivity. DBT therapists are accepting while encouraging the client to change. Therapists do this by demonstrating empathy, genuineness, caring, warmth, and understanding, and by teaching mindfulness. Therapists are committed to clients, as shown by their caring, realness, willingness to self-disclose, and willingness to receive telephone contacts between sessions to discourage self-destructive patterns and encourage new, healthier behaviors.

Acceptance and commitment therapy is based on relational frame theory, which explains behaviors and cognitions as a complex web of relational associations. Developed by Steven Hayes and others in the late 1980s, ACT uses a mixture of cognitive techniques, behavioral techniques, and Eastern philosophy, and applies it in novel ways. The goal of ACT is to help create a rich and meaningful life, while accepting the pain that inevitably goes with it, and is reached by applying six core principles of psychological flexibility: defusion, acceptance, contact with the present moment, self as context, values, and committed action. ACT can be viewed through three stages: accepting thoughts and feelings, choosing direction, and taking action.

Constructive psychotherapy, developed by Michael Mahoney, suggests that people are continually creating and recreating their understanding of reality. Constructive therapists believe that deep underlying schemata are more difficult to change than surface structures. In addition, they suggest that there is a complex and inseparable interaction between one's thoughts, feelings, and actions, and that we do not simply have thoughts and interpretations of the world; we are our thoughts and interpretations. Such thoughts and interpretations are constantly undergoing reconstruction as we interact with others. Using a dialectical process to examine the client's meaning-making system, the goal of therapy is to assist the client in understanding how he or she makes sense out of the world and to help the client create new constructions that may work better for him or her.

From the cognitive–behavioral, existential–humanistic, and post-modern perspective, five approaches were identified. Eye movement desensitization therapy, developed by Francine Shapiro, has clients focus on rapid eye movements, or some other rhythmic stimulation (e.g., tapping), while imagining a traumatic or troubling event. In addition, new, positive core beliefs are substituted for older, negative ones, and new behaviors are encouraged. EMDR suggests that past traumas become embedded in our psyche, core beliefs maintain negative experiences, new cognitions and behaviors can help a person adopt new ways of being in the world, and there are neural pathways that store traumatic memories, which become depotentiated or blocked during treatment. Integrating these theories, EMDR treatment involves eight phases that sometimes can be completed within a few sessions.

Motivational interviewing is generally used with substance abuse, gambling, anxiety disorders, eating disorders, chronic disease management, and health-related disorders. Some assumptions include that motivation is a key to change, is multidimensional, is dynamic and fluctuating, is influenced by social interactions, can be modified, and is influenced by the clinician's style, and that the clinician's task is to elicit and enhance motivation. Clinicians are seen as collaborative, evocative, and honoring of the client. Five stages include precontemplation, contemplation, preparation, action, and maintenance, and four basic principles include expressing empathy, developing discrepancies, rolling with resistance, and supporting self-efficacy.

Gender-aware therapy encompasses feminist therapy and counseling men and includes the following common elements: gender is central to counseling, problems are viewed within a societal context, counselors actively address gender injustices, collaborative and equal relationships are developed, and clients choose their gender roles regardless of their political correctness. Feminist therapy has its basis in the feminist movement and recognizes the impact of gender, the oppression of women, and the influence of politics. The goal of feminist therapy is empowerment of female clients through the use of a wellness model. To help understand how to work with women, the American Psychological Association's *Guidelines for Psychological Practice with Girls and Women* were reviewed, and steps for working with women were given. Relative to counseling men, it was noted that men have unique issues that impinge on them and affect their way of viewing the world. These were highlighted and, as with feminist therapy, a number of steps for working with men were given.

Positive psychology is a recent addition to the field of therapies, officially launched in 1998 by the then-president of the APA, Martin Seligman. Although its roots can be traced to the humanistic therapies, positive psychology suggests that we're capable of good and bad and that clients can learn how to focus on the positive aspects of the self. Recent research by Fredrickson supports this approach, as she has shown that positive emotions increase happiness and psychological growth, result in longer life, increase intuition and creativity, increase resilience to adversity, and decrease health problems. One therapeutic model recently developed by Giovanni Fava, well-being therapy, suggests that clients be viewed through three phases along Ryff's six dimensions of well-being: autonomy, personal growth, environmental mastery, purpose in life, positive relations, and self-acceptance. This approach attempts to replace negative thoughts and behaviors with positive ones by identifying the problematic areas of the six dimensions and then helping the client develop positive aspects in his or her life in those areas.

The last approaches we examined were complementary, alternative, and integrative approaches. Complementary medicine or therapy includes products, systems, or practices used in conjunction with conventional methods to treat biological and mental health problems. Alternative therapy is that when alternative approaches are used instead of conventional methods. An integrative approach suggests that traditional healing methods are integrated with complementary or alternative approaches. The overall emphasis of these approaches is to focus on a client's overall wellness, such as one's creative self, coping self, social self, essential self, and physical self. It was noted that the National Center for Complementary and Alternative Medicine categorizes these approaches into five main domains: biologically based systems, manipulative and body-based approaches, mind–body medicine, alternative medical systems, and energy therapies.

KEY NAMES AND WORDS

Erikson's Psychosocial Stages of Development

Key Words

Autonomy vs. Shame and Doubt

crisis

dystonic

Ego Integrity vs. Despair

Generativity vs. Stagnation

Identity vs. Role Confusion

Industry vs. Inferiority

Initiative vs. Guilt

Intimacy vs. Isolation

psychosocial forces

strength

syntonic

task

Trust vs. Mistrust

virtue

Key Name

Erik Erikson

Object-Relations Therapy

Key Words

good-enough mothering

holding environment

individuation

need to be in relationships

object constancy

objects

self

separation of self

splitting

symbiotic, undifferentiated relationship

transitional objects

Key Names

Donald Winnicott

Harry Guntrip

Harry Stack Sullivan

Margaret Mahler

Melanie Klein

Otto Kernberg

W. R. D. Fairbairn

Self-Psychology

Key Words

corrective emotional
    experience

development of self

experience near

good-enough parenting

idealizing parents

recognition

selfobject

twinship

Key Names

Franz Alexander

Heinz Kohut

Relational and Intersubjectivity Perspectives

Key Words

countertransference

deep personal encounter

internalized images

myth of independent
    mind

relational patterns

self-disclosure

"self" formed in
    relationships

transference

Key Names

Irwin S. Hoffman

Jessica Benjamin

Lew Aron

Paul Wachtel

Phillip Bromberg

Stephen Mitchell

Thomas Ogden

Multimodal Therapy

Key Words

affect

BASIC ID

behavior

cognition

drugs/biology

imagery

interpersonal
    relationships

sensations

social learning theory

Key Name

Arnold Lazarus

Dialectical Behavior Therapy

Key Words

acceptance

behavioral analysis

behavioral skills groups

biosocial
    theory

cognitive restructuring

consultation teams

commitment

emotional inhibition

emotional
overexpressiveness

mindfulness

ongoing dialogue

operating conditioning

self-disclosure

teaching of problem-
solving skills

Key Name

Marsha Linehan

Acceptance and Commitment Therapy ("ACT")

Key Words

acceptance

accept thoughts and
feelings

choose directions

committed action

contact with the present
moment

defusion

Hexaflex Model

mindfulness

psychological flexibility

relational frame theory

self as context

take action

transcendent self

values

Key Name

Steven Hayes

Constructivist Therapy

Key Words

constructivist vs.
rationalist views

dialectical process

meaning-making system

narratives

schematas can change

there is no single reality

thoughts, feelings, and
actions are
inseparable

we are our thoughts

we constantly recreate
reality

Key Name

Michael Mahoney

Eye Movement Desensitization Therapy (EMDR)

Key Words

blank it out

core beliefs

depotentiated

neural pathways

Phase 1: Client History
and Treatment
Planning

Phase 2: Preparation

Phase 3: Assessment

Phase 4: Desensitization

Phase 5: Installation

Phase 6: Body Scan

Phase 7: Closure

Phase 8: Reevaluation

psychological stability

rapid eye movements

rhythmic stimulation

subjective units of discomfort (SUD) scale

validity of cognition (VoC) scale

Key Name

Francine Shapiro

Motivational Interviewing

Key Words

action stage

collaborative

contemplation stage

developing discrepancies

elicit and enhance motivation

evocative

expressing empathy

five-stage model

four basic principles

honoring

maintenance stage

motivation can be modified

motivation is a key to change

motivation is dynamic and fluctuating

motivation is influenced by social interactions

motivation is influenced by the clinician's style

motivation is multidimensional

precontemplation stage

preparation stage

recurrence

rolling with resistance

supporting self-efficacy

Key Names

S. Rollnick

W. R. Miller

Gender-Aware Therapy

Key Words

considers gender central to counseling

encourages counselors to actively address gender injustices

encourages development of collaborative and equal relationships

respects the client's right to choose the gender role appropriate for him or her

views problems within a societal context

Feminist Therapy

APA Guidelines for Psychological Practice with Girls and Women

egalitarian, cooperative, and trusting

empowerment

feminist contracting

focus on wellness

impact of gender

influence of politics

liberation of women

oppression of women

person as a political
entity

recognition of power/
authority of
counselor

social justice actions

12 steps to working
with women

Key Name

Carolyn Enns

Counseling Men

issues that are common
to the male
experience

men have a more
negative attitude
toward the helping
process

men seek counseling less

13 steps to working
with men

Positive Psychology

Key Words

3:1 ratio of positive to
negative feelings

autonomy

capable of being good or
bad

environmental mastery

learned helplessness

learned optimism

loving kindness
meditation

personal growth

positive relations

Positive Psychology
Center

purpose in life

Ryff's six dimensions of
psychological well-
being

self-acceptance

symptoms not a sign of
pathology

well-being therapy

Key Names

Barbara Fredrickson

Giovanna Fava

Martin Seligman

Complementary, Alternative, and Integrative Approaches

Key Words

alternative medical
systems

alternative therapies
in health and
medicine

American Holistic
Health Association

Association for
Comprehensive
Energy Psychology

Association for
Humanistic
Psychology

biologically based
systems

Center for Noetic
Sciences

coping self

creative self

energy therapies

essential self

holistic approach

manipulative and body-
based

mind–body medicine

National Center for
Complementary and
Alternative Medicine
(NCCAM)

physical self

| physical, emotional, and psychological well-being | social self

total range of individual's wellness | traditional healing |

Key Name

Edgar Mitchell

REFERENCES

Addis, M. E., & Mahalik, J. (2003). Men, masculinity, and the contexts of help seeking. *American Psychologist, 58*(1), 5–14.

American Psychological Association. (2007). *Guidelines for psychological practice with girls and women*. Washington, D.C.: Author.

Alexander, F. (1950). Analysis of the therapeutic factors in psychoanalytic treatment. *Psychoanalytic Quarterly, 19*, 482–500.

Alexander, F. (1956). Psychoanalysis and psychotherapy. Developments in theory, technique, and training. New York: Norton.

Arkowitz, H., & Miller, W. R. (2008). Learning, applying, and extending motivational interviewing. In H. Arkowitz, H. A. Westra, W. R. Miller, & S. Rollnick (Eds.), *Motivational interviewing in the treatment of psychological problems* (pp. 1–25). New York: Guilford Press.

Bach, P. A., & Moran, D. J. (2008). *ACT in practice: Case conceptualization in acceptance and commitment therapy*. Oakland, CA: New Harbinger Publications.

Berger, J. M., Levant, R., McMillan, K. K., Kelleher, W., & Sellers, A. (2005). Impact of gender role conflict, traditional masculinity ideology, alexithymia, and age on men's attitudes toward psychological help seeking. *Psychology of Men & Masculinity, 6*(1), 73–78.

Brooks, G. R. (1998). *A new psychotherapy for traditional men*. San Francisco: Jossey-Bass.

Brown, C. (1993). Feminist contracting: Power and empowerment in therapy. In C. Brown & K. Jasper (Eds.), *Consuming passions: Feminist approaches to weight preoccupation and eating disorders* (pp. 176–194). Toronto, ON: Second Story Press.

Brown, C. G., Weber, S., & Ali, S. (2008). Women's body talk: A feminist narrative approach. *Journal of Systemic Therapies, 27*(2), 92–104.

Brown, L. S. (2006). Still subversive after all these years: The relevance of feminist therapy in the age of evidence-based practice. *Psychology of Women Quarterly, 30*, 15–24.

Brown, L. S., & Bryan, T. C. (2007). Feminist therapy with people who self-inflict violence. *Journal of Clinical Psychology: In Session, 63*(11), 1121–1133.

Ciarrochi, J. V., & Bailey, A. (2008). *A CBT practitioner's guide to ACT: How to bridge the gap between cognitive behavioral therapy and acceptance and commitment therapy*. Oakland, CA: New Harbinger Publications.

Cloud, J. (2006, February 5). The third wave of therapy. *Time Magazine*. Retrieved June 2, 2009, from http://www.time.com/time/magazine/article/0,9171,1156613,00.html

Dimeff, L., & Linehan, M. M. (2001). Dialectical behavior therapy in a nutshell. *The California Psychologist, 34*, 10–13.

Dossey, L. (1999). *Reinventing medicine: Beyond mind-body to a new era of healing.* San Francisco: HarperSanFrancisco.

Dworkin, M. (2005). *EMDR and the relational imperative: The therapeutic relationship in EMDR treatment.* New York: Routledge.

Eden, D., & Feinstein, D. (2008). *Energy medicine: Balancing your body's energies for optimal health, joy, and vitality* (updated and expanded ed.). New York: Penguin Group.

Eifert, G. H., & Forsyth, J. P. 2005). *Acceptance and commitment therapy for anxiety disorders.* Oakland, CA: New Harbinger.

EMDR Institute. (2005). *The efficacy of EMDR.* Retrieved from http://www.emdr.com/efficacy.htm

Enns, C. Z. (1993). Twenty years of feminist counseling and therapy: From naming biases to implementing multifaceted practice. *The Counseling Psychologist, 21*(1), 3–87.

Erikson, E. H. (1963). *Childhood and society* (2nd ed.). New York: Norton.

Erikson, E. H. (1968). *Identity: Youth and crisis.* New York: Norton.

Erikson, E. H. (1980). *Identity and the life cycle.* New York: Norton.

Erikson, E. H. (1982). *The life cycle completed.* New York: Norton.

Fairbairn, W. R. D. (2001). Psychoanalytic studies of the personality. New York: Taylor & Francis. (Original work published 1952)

Fava, G. A. (2009, June 19). *Well-being therapy.* Workshop presented at the First World Congress on Positive Psychology. Philadelphia, PA.

Fava, G. A., & Ruini, C. (2003). Development and characteristics of a well-being enhancing psychotherapeutic strategy: Well-being therapy. *Journal of Behavior Therapy and Experimental Psychiatry, 34,* 45–63.

Flora, C. (2009, January/February). The pursuit of happiness. *Psychology Today, 42*(1), 60–69.

Fredrickson, B. (2001). The role of positive emotions in positive psychology: The broaden-and-build theory of positive emotions. *American Psychologist, 56,* 218–226.

Fredrickson, B. (2009, June 19). *Positivity: The path to flourishing.* Workshop presented at the First World Congress on Positive Psychology. Philadelphia, PA.

Fredrickson, B., & Losada, M. F. (2005). Positive affect and the complex dynamics of human flourishing. *American Psychologist, 60,* 678–286.

Frontline (2003, November 6). *The alternative fix.* Retrieved from http://www.pbs.org/wgbh/pages/frontline/shows/altmed/etc/synopsis.html

Fruzzetti, A. R., & Fruzzetti, A. E. (2003). Dialectics in cognitive and behavior therapy. In W. O'Donohue, U. J. Fisher, & S. C. Hayes (Eds.), *Cognitive behavior therapy: Applying empirically supported techniques in your practice* (pp. 121–128). Hoboken, NJ: John Wiley & Sons.

Funderburk, J. R., & Fukuyama, M. A. (2002). Feminism, multiculturalism, and spirituality. *Women & Therapy, 24*(3), 1–18.

Gabbard, G. O. (1995). Are all psychotherapies equally effective? *The Menninger Letter, 3*(1), 1–2.

Glickauf-Hughes, C., & Wells, M. (2007). *Object relations psychotherapy: An individualized and interactive approach to diagnosis and treatment.* Lanham, MD: Rowman & Littlefield.

Goncalves, O. F., & Machado, P. P. (1995). Cognitive narrative psychotherapy: Research foundations. *Journal of Clinical Psychology, 55*(10), 1179–1191.

Good, G. E., Gilbert, L. A., & Scher, M. (1990). Gender aware therapy: A synthesis of feminist therapy and knowledge about gender. *Journal of Counseling and Development, 68*, 376–380.

Greer, M. (2005, June). Keeping them hooked in. *APA Monitor, 36*(6), 60.

Guidano, V. F. (1995). Constructivist psychotherapy: A theoretical framework. In M. J. Mahoney (Ed.), *Cognitive and constructive psychotherapies: Theory, research, and practice* (pp. 89–102). New York: Springer.

Guntrip, H. (1969). *Schizoid phenomena, object relations, and the self.* New York: International Universities Press.

Harris, R. (2006). Embracing your demons: An overview of acceptance and commitment therapy. *Psychotherapy in Australia, 12*(4), 2–8.

Harris, R. (2008). *The happiness trap: How to stop struggling and start living.* Boston: Trumpeter Books.

Hayes, S. C. (2004). Acceptance and commitment therapy, relational frame theory, and the third wave of behavioral and cognitive therapies. *Behavior Therapy, 35*, 639–665.

Hayes, S. C., & Smith, S. X. (2005). *Get out of your mind and into your life: The new acceptance and commitment therapy.* Oakland, CA: New Harbinger.

Hayes, S. C., & Strosahl, K. D. (Eds.). (2004). A practical guide to acceptance and commitment therapy. New York: Springer.

Hayes, S. C., Strosahl, K. D., & Wilson, K. G. (1999). *Acceptance and commitment therapy: An experiential approach to behavior change.* New York: Guilford Press.

Kahn, M. (1991). *Between therapist and client: The new relationship, revised edition.* New York: Holt Paperbacks.

Keegan, 2001. *Healing with complementary and alternative therapies.* Albany, NY: Delmar Thomson Learning.

Kees, N. L. (Ed.). (2005). Special issue on women and counseling. *Journal of Counseling and Development, 83*(3).

Kernberg, O. (1980). *Internal world and external reality.* New York: Jason Aronson.

Kessler, R. C., Soukup, J., Davis, R. B., Foster, D. F., Wilkey, S. A., Van Rompay, M. I., & Eisenberg, E. M. (2001). The use of complementary and alternative therapies to treat anxiety and depression in the United States. *American Journal of Psychiatry, 158*(2), 289–294.

Klein, M. (1975). *Psychoanalytic theory: An exploration of essentials.* New York: International Universities Press.

Kohut, H. (1977). *The restoration of self.* New York: International Universities Press.

Kohut, H. (1984). *How does analysis cure?* Chicago: University of Chicago Press.

Lazarus, A. A. (1976). *The practice of multimodal therapy.* Baltimore: Johns Hopkins University Press.

Lazarus, A. A. (1986). Multimodal therapy. In U. C. Norcross (Ed.), *Handbook of eclectic psychotherapy* (pp. 65–93). New York: Brunner/Mazel.

Lazarus, A. A. (1997a). *Brief but comprehensive psychotherapy: The multimodal way.* New York: Springer Publishing.

Lazarus, A. A. (1997b). Brief, focused, solution-oriented, and yet comprehensive? In J. K. Zeig (Ed.), *The evolution of psychotherapy: The third conference* (pp. 83–89). New York: Brunner/Mazel.

Lazarus, A. A. (2002). The multimodal assessment therapy approach. In F. Kaslow (Ed.), *Comprehensive handbook of psychotherapy* (vol. 4, pp. 241–254). New York: Wiley.

Lazarus, A. A. (2008). Multimodal therapy. In R. J. Corsini & D. Wedding, *Current psychotherapies* (8th ed., pp. 368–401). Belmont, CA: Brooks/Cole.

Lazarus, A. A., & Beutler, L. E. (1993). On technical eclecticism. *Journal of Counseling and Development, 71*(4), 381–385.

Levinson, 1985.

Linehan, M. M. (1993). *Cognitive behavioral treatment of borderline personality disorder.* New York: Guilford Press.

Lipke, H. (2000). *EMDR and psychotherapy integration: Theoretical and clinical suggestions with focus on traumatic stress.* New York: CRC Press.

List of psychotherapies. (2009). The Wikipedia free encyclopedia. Retrieved May 5, 2009, from http//enwikipediaorg/wiki/List_of_psychotherapies

Mahalik, J. R. (1990). Systematic eclectic models. *The Counseling Psychologist, 18*(4), 655–679.

Mahler, M. S. (1952). On child psychosis and schizophrenia: Autistic and symbiotic infantile psychosis. In R. S. Eissler, A. Freud, H. Hartmann, & E. Kris (Eds.), *The psychoanalytic study of the child* (vol. 7, pp. 286–305). New York: International Universities Press.

Mahler, M. S. (1968). *On human symbiosis and the vicissitudes of individuation* (Vol. I: Infantile psychosis). New York: International Universities Press.

Mahler, M. S., Pine, F., & Bergman, A. (2000). *The psychological birth of the human infant: Symbiosis and individuation.* New York: Basic Books. (Original work published 1975)

Mahoney, M. J. (1974). *Cognition and behavior modification.* Cambridge, MA: Ballinger.

Mahoney, M. J. (1991). *Human change processes: The scientific foundation of psychotherapy.* New York: Basic Books.

Mahoney, M. J. (Ed.). (1995a). *Cognitive and constructive psychotherapies: Theory, research, and practice.* New York: Springer.

Mahoney, M. J. (1995b). Theoretical developments in the cognitive and constructive psychotherapies. In M. J. Mahoney (Ed.), *Cognitive and constructive psychotherapies: Theory, research, and practice* (pp. 3–19). New York: Springer.

Mahoney, M. J. (1997). Psychotherapists' personal problems and self-care patterns. *Professional Psychology Research and Practice, 28*(1), 14–16.

Mahoney, M. J., Miller, H. M., & Arciero, G. (1995). Constructive metatheory and the nature of mental representation. In M. J. Mahoney (Ed.), *Cognitive and constructive psychotherapies: Theory, research, and practice* (pp. 195–208). New York: Springer.

Mamtani, R., & Cimino, A. (2002). A primer of complementary and alternative medicine and its relevance in the treatment of mental health problems. *Psychiatric Quarterly, 73*(4), 367–381.

Masterson, J. F. (1981). *The narcissistic and borderline disorders: An integrated developmental approach.* New York: Brunner/Mazel.

McCarthy, J., & Holliday, E. L. (2004). Help-seeking and counseling within a traditional male gender role: An examination from a multicultural perspective. *Journal of Counseling and Development, 82*, 25–30.

Mejia, X. (2005). Gender matters: Working with adult male survivors of trauma. *Journal of Counseling and Development, 83,* 29–40.

Miller, W. R. (1983). Motivational interviewing with problem drinkers. *Behavioural Psychotherapy, 11,* 147–172.

Miller, W. R. (1999). *Enhancing motivation for change in substance abuse treatment.* Rockville, MD: U. S. Department of Health and Human Services.

Miller, W. R., & Rollnick, S. (1991). *Motivational interviewing: Preparing people to change addictive behavior.* New York: Guilford Press.

Miller, W. R., & Rollnick, S. (2002). *Motivational interviewing: Preparing people for change* (2nd ed.). New York: Guilford Press.

Mitchell, S. A. (1988). *Relational concepts in psychoanalysis: An integration.* Cambridge, MA: Harvard University Press.

Mitchell, S. A. (1993). *Hope and dread in psychoanalysis.* New York: Basic Books.

Mitchell, S. A. (2002). *Can love last? The fate of romance over time.* New York: W. W. Norton.

Myers, J. E., & Sweeney, T. J. (2004). *Counselors for wellness: Theory, research, and practice.* Alexandria, VA: American Counseling Association.

Myers, J. E., & Sweeney, T. J. (2005). The indivisible self: An evidence-based model of wellness. *Journal of Individual Psychology, 61*(3), 269–278.

National Center for Complementary and Alternative Medicine (2007). *What is CAM?* Retrieved July 13, 2009, from http://nccam.nih.gov/health/whatiscam/overview.htm#types

National Center for Complementary and Alternative Medicine (2009). *About NCCAM.* Retrieved July 13, 2009, from http://nccam.nih.gov/about/

Natterson, J. M., & Friedman, R. J. (1995). *A primer of clinical inter-subjectivity.* Northvale, NJ: Aronson Press.

Neimeyer, R. A. (1995). An appraisal of constructivist psychotherapies. In M. J. Mahoney (Ed.), *Cognitive and constructive psychotherapies: Theory, research, and practice* (pp. 163–194). New York: Springer.

Neimeyer, R. A., & Mahoney, M. (Eds.). (1999). *Constructivism in psychotherapy.* Washington, D.C.: American Psychological Association.

Neukrug, E. (2007). *The world of the counselor.* Belmont, CA: Brooks/Cole.

Noetic Sciences. (2009). *About IONS: History.* Retrieved from http://www.noetic.org/about/history.cfm

Oken, B. S., Storzbach, D. M., & Kaye, J. A. (1998). The efficacy of ginkgo biloba on cognitive function in Alzheimer disease. *Archives of Neurology, 55,* 1409–1415.

O'Leary, E. (2006). The need for integration. In E. O'Leary & M. Murphy, *New approaches to integration in psychotherapy* (pp. 3–12). New York: Routledge.

Osherson, S. (2001). *Finding our fathers: How a man's life is shaped by his relationship with his father.* New York: McGraw-Hill. (Original work published 1986)

Peterson, C. (2006). *A primer in positive psychology.* New York: Oxford University Press.

Pollack, W. S., & Levant, R. F. (1998). *New psychotherapy for men.* New York: Wiley.

Positive Psychology Center. (2007). *Home page.* Retrieved June 21, 2009, from http://www.ppc.sas.upenn.edu/

Rasolkhani-Kalhorn, T., & Harper, M. L. (2006). EMDR and low frequency stimulation of the brain. *Traumatology*, *12*(1), 9–24.

Robinson-Wood, T. L. (2009). Advocacy and social justice. In T. L. Robinson-Wood (Ed.), *The convergence of race, ethnicity, and gender: Multiple identities in counseling* (3rd ed., pp. 284–294). Upper Saddle River, NJ: Merrill.

Rollnick, S., & Miller, W. R. (1995). What is motivational interviewing? *Behavioural and Cognitive Psychotherapy*, *23*, 325–334.

Rollnick, S., Miller, W. R., & Butler, C. C. (2008). *Motivational interviewing in health care: Helping patients change behavior.* New York: Guilford Press.

Ruini, C., & Fava, G. A. (2009). Well-being therapy for generalized anxiety disorder. *Journal of Clinical Psychology*, *65*, 510–519.

Ryff, C. D. (1989). Happiness is everything, or is it? Explorations on the meaning of psychological well-being. *Journal of Personality and Social Psychology*, *6*, 1069–1081.

Safran, J. (2009, March). IARRP eNEWS: President's column, 8(1). Retrieved June 2, 2009, from http://www.iarpp.org/library/download/enews15.pdf

Seem, S. R. & Johnson, E. (1998). Gender bias among counseling trainees: A study of case conceptualization. *Counselor Education and Supervision*, *37*, 257–268.

Seligman, M. E. P. (1975). *Helplessness: On depression, development, and death.* San Francisco: W. H. Freeman.

Seligman, M. E. P. (1990). *Learned optimism.* New York: Knopf.

Seligman, M. E. P. (2009, June 18). Positive education. Open event at the First World Congress on Positive Psychology. Philadelphia, PA.

Seligman, M. E. P., & Csikszentmihalyi, M. (Eds.). (2000). Positive psychology [Special issue]. *American Psychologist*, *55*(1).

Seligman, M. E. P., & Maier, S. F. (1967). Failure to escape traumatic shock. *Journal of Experimental Psychology*, *74*, 1–9.

Shannon, S. (2002). *Handbook of complementary and alternative therapies in mental health.* San Diego, CA: Academic/Harcourt.

Shapiro, F. (2002a). (Ed.). *EMDR as an integrative psychotherapy approach: Experts of diverse orientations explore the paradigm prism.* Washington, D.C.: American Psychological Association.

Shapiro, F. (2002b). EMDR treatment: Overview and integration. In F. Shapiro (Ed.). *EMDR as an integrative psychotherapy approach: Experts of diverse orientations explore the paradigm prism* (pp. 27–56). Washington, D.C.: American Psychological Association.

Shapiro, F., & Forrest, M. S. (1997). *EMDR: The breakthrough "eye movement" therapy for overcoming anxiety, stress, and trauma.* New York: Perseus Books.

Shapiro, R. (2005). (Ed.). *EMDR solutions: Pathways to healing.* New York: W. W. Norton and Company.

Shapiro, R. (2009). (Ed.). *EMDR solutions II: For depression, eating disorders, performance, and more.* New York: W. W. Norton and Company.

Stolorow, R., & Atwood, G., (1992). *Cases on being: The intersubjective foundations of psychological life.* Psychoanalytic Inquiry Book Series (vol. 12). New York: Analytic Press.

Sullivan, H. S. (1953). *The interpersonal theory of psychiatry.* New York: Norton.

Teyber, E. (2001). *Interpersonal process in psychotherapy: A relational approach.* Belmont, CA: Brooks/Cole.

Todd, J., & Bohart, A. C. (2003). *Foundations of clinical and counseling psychology* (3rd ed.). Long Grove, IL: Waveland Press.

Unutzer, M. P. H., Klap, R., Sturm, R., Young, A. S., Marmon, T., Shatkin, J., & Well, K. B. (2000). *American Journal of Psychiatry, 157*, 1851–1857.

Wachtel, P. L. (2008). *Relational theory and the practice of psychotherapy*. New York: The Guilford Press.

Wallerstein, R. S. (2001). The growth and transformation of American ego psychology. *Journal of the American Psychoanalytic Association. 50*, 135–169.

Weil, A. (1995). *Spontaneous healing: How to discover and enhance your body's natural ability to maintain and heal itself.* New York: Knopf.

Weininger, O. (1992). *Melanie Klein, from theory to reality*. New York: Karnac Books.

Winnicott, D. W. (1958). *Through paediatrics to psychoanalysis*. London: Hogarth.

Winnicott, D. W. (1965). *The maturational process and the facilitating environment*. New York: International Universities Press.

Wolpe, J., & Lazarus, A. (1966). *Behavior therapy techniques*. New York: Pergamon.

Chapter 15

Couples and Family Counseling

Learning Goals

- To provide a brief history of the field of couples and family therapy that addresses how a number of events and people affected the development of the field.
- To understand the variety of views of human nature espoused by family therapists and to review 12 basic assumptions to which most family therapists adhere when practicing couples and family therapy.
- To examine a number of key concepts that fuel the way most family therapists work, including general systems theory, cybernetics, boundaries and information flow, rules and hierarchy, communication theory, scapegoating and identified patients, stress, developmental issues, and social constructionism.
- To offer an overview of a number of popular couples and family therapy approaches and to highlight the individuals most associated with them, including:
  - human validation process model of Satir
  - structural family therapy as presented by Minuchin
  - strategic family therapy as developed by Haley, Madanes, and the Milan Group
  - multigenerational approaches of Boszormenyi-Nagy and of Bowen
  - experiential family therapy of Whitaker
  - psychodynamic family therapy of Ackerman and of Skynner
  - behavioral and cognitive–behavioral family therapy
  - narrative family therapy of White and of Epston
  - solution-focused therapy of Berg, de Shazer, O'Hanlon, and others
- To examine a number of social, cultural, and spiritual issues related to the use of family therapy.
- To examine the efficacy of couples and family therapy.
- To see how couples and family therapy is applied, through vignettes and case study.

Once upon a time, therapy involved lying on a couch before a bearded fellow who sighed and said, "I wonder why you said that." Therapy today is a viable option for constructing real solutions to real problems. It also might include a group behind a one-way mirror and a family in front of it with a video camera for a supervisor to study later.

Unlike other approaches to mental health and psychology, family therapy focuses on the *interpersonal* relationship of the members of a system called a *family*. Changing the system involves bringing the whole family together at times and attempting to make changes to reduce misery and distress.

Participation in family therapy does not suggest that something serious is wrong with a family. The family therapist serves as an agent to deal with simple adjustments or a system in misery. The therapy that is *interpersonal* is different from the therapy that is *individual*. Hundreds if not thousands of researchers and therapists are clarifying the cause of family distress and what to do about it. (Haley, 2009, para. 1–3)

In contrast to the other approaches discussed in this text, which focused on how to help *individuals* with their problems, couples and family therapy tends to see "the problem" as residing in the system and thus focuses on the interpersonal nature of "the problem." This chapter offers a brief history of how couples and family therapy evolved and how it challenged many of the traditional ways of doing therapy. In addition, an overview of some of the more important concepts and common approaches to couples and family therapy will be presented.

FAMILY THERAPY: A BRIEF HISTORY

Although the emergence of couples and family therapy as a profession began around the middle part of the twentieth century, there were a number of events that led up to its birth. For instance, during the 1800s, two approaches to working with families and communities evolved (Burger & Youkeles, 2008). **Charity Organization Societies** had volunteers visiting the poor to assist in alleviating conditions of poverty. These **friendly visitors** would often spend years assisting one family by aiding in educating children, giving advice and moral support, and providing small amounts of necessities. At about the same time, the **settlement movement**, which had staff who lived in the poorer communities, began to arise (Leiby, 1978). These idealistic staff believed in community action and tried to persuade politicians to provide better services for the poor. One of the best-known settlement houses was **Hull House**, established by social activist Jane Addams (1860–1935) in 1889 in Chicago (Addams, 1910). Out of this involvement with the underprivileged, articles and books arose concerned with finding methods of meeting the needs of the poor and how to work with destitute families within the larger social system. It is here that we see the beginning of social casework and the first time that the "system" is acknowledged as an important component to take into account when helping individuals and families overcome their difficulties.

Paralleling the work of these early social workers was the psychotherapeutic approach of Alfred Adler, who believed that external forces greatly affected personality development and that through education, one could help to alleviate problems. In fact, Adler's approach to working with children is often cited as an early precursor to family therapy models (Goldenberg & Goldenberg, 2008; Sherman, 1999). At Adler's child guidance clinics, parents would often meet with therapists to discuss problems with their children, although generally the parents and children were not all in the same room together (Bottome, 1957). For the first time, counselors were suggesting that problems in one family member had a significant effect on the whole family.

Despite these early efforts at working with families, the embeddedness of psychoanalysis and other individual-oriented approaches to counseling and psychotherapy made it difficult for novel therapeutic approaches to take a hold (Guerin, 1976). Thus, until the late 1940s and early 1950s, therapists who saw the value of working with the whole family often felt pressure to see the "patient" separately from the rest of the family. Soon, however, this new approach to psychotherapy began to take shape.

> [At first, s]ome hospitals had a therapist to deal with the carefully pro-tected intrapsychic process, another psychiatrist to handle the reality matters and administrative procedures, and a social worker to talk to relatives. In those years this principle was a cornerstone of good psy-chotherapy. Finally, it became acceptable to see families together in the context of research. (Bowen as cited in Guerin, 1976, p. 3)

As increasing numbers of therapists believed it was useful to see the "whole" family together, a variety of approaches to family counseling developed during the 1950s that began to use this new model of working with clients (Guerin, 1976). Although some of these evolved independently, there was a core group of early therapists and family therapists who influenced one another and whose training often overlapped. The inside cover of Bitter's (2009) book, *Theory and Practice of Family Therapy and Counseling*, offers a fascinating series of genograms that shows an intricate maze of close to 100 of these early, and somewhat later, family therapists.

Not surprisingly, although treating the whole family slowly became accepted, with the continued popularity of psychoanalysis, many of the early pioneers of couples and family therapy combined a systemic approach with basic psycho-analytic principles. Probably the most well-known of these was Nathan Ackerman (1958, 1966), a child psychiatrist. Another psychoanalytic trained therapist, Ivan Boszormenyi-Nagy (1973, 1987), stressed the importance of having ethical relationships in families and highlighted the notion that our senses of fairness and our loyalties are unconsciously passed down through generations and create a specific view of the world which may, or may not, match our spouses' views. Establishing the **Eastern Pennsylvania Psychiatric Institute** (EPPI), Boszormenyi-Nagy's **contextual family therapy** would sometimes include grandparents and other significant individuals when examining these cross-generational issues, with the goal of helping families develop healthier and more loving ways of communicating. At around the same time, Murray Bowen (1976, 1978) developed what some would later call **multigenerational family counseling**. Working initially at the **Menninger Clinic** in Kansas and later at the **National Institute of Mental Health** (NIMH) in Washington, D.C., Bowen was interested in communication in families who had a family member who was schizophrenic. Working with all members of a family, but one member at a time, his experiences with these families, and later with families struggling with "normal" problems, resulted in new ideas about how family dysfunction is passed on through generations.

Probably the group that was to have the most profound influence on the evolution of couples and family therapy was led by an anthropologist, Gregory Bateson, in Palo Alto, California (Guerin, 1976; Mental Research Institute, 2008). Fascinated by human communication, in the early 1950s, Bateson hired Jay Haley, John Weakland, Don Jackson, and William Fry, and this team began to look at how individuals communicate in systems, particularly families that had schizophrenic members. Their **double-bind theory** attempted to explain how schizophrenics are often caught in a web of mixed messages from family members who hold power. The first to apply principles of **general systems theory** and **cybernetics** to an understanding of family communication, their ideas would fuel the manner in which a generation of couples and family therapists would work and continues to influence how family therapists work today. Out of this project came the **Mental Research Institute** (MRI) at Palo Alto. Led by Don Jackson, and joined by a number of research associates, most notably Jay Haley, Virginia Satir, and later Cloé Madanes, this group focused on communication and family process. Satir's work at MRI, as well as an earlier collaboration she had with Murray Bowen and influences from humanistic psychology, would eventually lead to the development of her **human validation process model**, which emphasized communication and self-esteem in couples and families (Satir, 1967, 1972a, 1972b). Meanwhile, Haley (1973, 1976) and Madanes (1981) would take a different route. Concentrating mostly on making strategic behavioral changes, their **strategic therapy** became one of the most popular and intriguing approaches to couples and family counseling.

At around the same time, the Palo Alto group was formulating their ideas, a somewhat different approach to working with families began to take shape under the auspices of Carl Whitaker. Influenced by individuals as varied as Gregory Bateson, Carl Jung, the psychoanalyst Melanie Klein, and Buddhist philosopher Alan Watts, Whitaker was known to be unconventional in his approach and willing to freely experiment with his responses during sessions. With the concurrent spread of humanistic psychology during the 1950s and 1960s, it is not surprising that this **experiential family therapy** approach, which drew from a belief in intrapsychic forces, humanistic philosophy, and systems thinking, was to evolve at this time (Napier & Whitaker, 1972, 1978; Whitaker, 1976).

Having worked with families in Israel and low-income and minority families in New York City, and influenced by Bateson and others at Palo Alto, during the 1960s, Salvador Minuchin (1974, 1981) developed one of the most widely respected approaches to couples and family therapy at the **Philadelphia Child Guidance Clinic**. An Argentinean-born psychiatrist, Minuchin would become known for his work with minorities and the poor in Philadelphia as he applied his **structural family therapy** approach that sought to understand how problems in family could be explained by problems in the family's structure. Eventually, Jay Haley joined Minuchin, and the two shared their ideas on working with families. It is also here that Jay Haley and Cloé Madanes met, and eventually married.

In 1966, within MRI, the **Brief Family Therapy Center** (BFTC) was established. Led by Paul Watzlawick, John Weakland, and Dick Fisch, BFTC focused solely on helping families solve their problems, as opposed to spending an inordinate amount of time on "underlying" issues, communication sequences, or systemic patterns (Cade, 2007; Goldenberg & Goldenberg, 2008). These individuals realized that the solutions families tried generally resulted in entrenching the problem more. Approaching families with an attitude of experimentation, these therapists were highly active and felt free to use any methods that were ethical and legal to solve problems or lessen presenting symptoms. Steve de Shazer (1982) and Insoo Kim Berg (1994), both of whom did postgraduate studies at BFTC, became two leading figures in the development of **solution-focused family therapy**.

Intrigued by Gregory Bateson and inspired by the work of Jay Haley, the early 1970s saw an Italian group, known as the **Milan Group**, become popular (Palazzoli, Boscolo, Cecchin, & Prata, 1978). With Watzlawick from BFTC acting as their consultant, this group would borrow many ideas from Bateson's original work but were also influenced by the work of cognitive and constructivist therapists, who believed that language usage is critical to meaning-making and how one comes to make sense of one's family.

As you might expect, with the expansion of behavioral and cognitive approaches to individual therapy in the latter part of the twentieth century, we concomitantly saw these philosophies applied within the family context. Finally, with what has come to be known as the "post-modern" movement, we see the recent rise of what is called **narrative family therapy**. Influenced by Michael White and David Epston (White, 1995; White & Epston, 1990), this approach attempts to understand a family's narrative, or story, and helps them to **deconstruct problem-saturated stories** and then reconstruct how the family comes to understand itself.

In recent years, the field of couples and family therapy has taken off, with 48 states having licensure for marriage and family counseling, according to the **American Association of Marriage and Family Therapy** (AAMFT, 2009). Today, AAMFT and the **International Association for Marriage and Family Counselors** (IAMFC), a division of the American Counseling Association, are the two main couples and family therapy associations in the country. These associations, along with their respective accreditation bodies (COAMFTE and CACREP), lead the field in setting curriculum standards for accreditation, making recommendations to state licensing boards, defining best practices and ethical standards, and helping to set credentialing requirements in the field of couples and family therapy. Today, training in couples and family therapy is commonplace in almost all programs that train helpers.

VIEW OF HUMAN NATURE

Because family therapists can have as their basis any number of theoretical orientations, their views of human nature can vary dramatically. For instance, a family therapist can be psychodynamically oriented and believe that the unconscious plays an important role in one's life; behaviorally focused and view the individual as conditioned by his or her environment; existential–humanistically oriented and see the individual and the family as having a growth force that can be actualized; or have leanings toward social constructionism and believe that there is no one reality and that individuals construct their sense of meaning from language. Despite these differences, most (but not necessarily all!) family therapists believe in a number of assumptions about families and about systems that are integrated into their theoretical orientations. These are summarized below (Barker, 2007; Turner & West, 2006).

- The interactional forces in families are complex, and cannot be explained in a simple, causal fashion.

- Families have **overt** and **covert rules** that govern their functioning.

- Understanding the **hierarchy** in a family (e.g., who's "in charge;" who makes the rules) can help one understand the makeup and communication sequences of a family.

- Understanding the **boundaries** of the family system and the subsystems (e.g., spousal, sibling) can help one understand the makeup and communication sequences of a family.

- Understanding whether boundaries are **rigid** or **semi-permeable** (e.g., how information can get in and out of families) can help one understand how communication and change occurs in families.

- Understanding how family members communicate can give insight into how a family maintains its way of functioning.

- Each family has its own unique **homeostasis** that describes how the family typically interacts. This homeostasis is not "bad" or "good." It simply is.

- Communication in families is complex, and the language families use is a message about who they are.

- Change occurs by changing the homeostasis, or the usual patterns in the family.

- Issues passed down by language in families, in culture, and in society affects how families come to define themselves.

- **Stress** from the expected developmental milestones through which most families pass can wreak havoc on the family, and family therapists should be aware of the particular issues involved in such developmental milestones.

- In addition to being equipped to deal with stress from **developmental milestones**, family therapists should have the tools to help families deal with the unexpected stresses of life.

KEY CONCEPTS

The assumptions listed in the "View of Human Nature" section are an outgrowth of a number of ideas that have been generated over the years and will be expanded upon in this section. They include the following concepts: **general systems theory, cybernetics, boundaries and information flow, rules and hierarchy, communication theory, scapegoating and identified patients, stress, developmental issues,** and **social constructionism.**

General Systems Theory

> Living systems are processes that maintain a persistent structure over relatively long periods despite rapid exchange of their component parts with the surrounding world. (Skynner, 1976, pp. 3–4)

The amoeba. The family. The universe. What do these seemingly dissimilar entities have to do with couples and family therapy? Although knowledge of the amoeba and of the universe may seem like a far cry from helping us to understand the family, in actuality, they all have something in common: They obey the rules of a system. The amoeba has a **semi-permeable boundary** that allows it to take in nutrition from the environment. This delicate animal could not survive if its boundaries were so rigid that they prevented it from ingesting food or so permeable that they would not allow it to maintain and digest the food. As long as the amoeba is in balance, it will maintain its existence.

The universe is an exceedingly predictable place, and it has a certain cadence to it. It maintains a persistent structure over a long period of time. However, remove a star, planet, moon, or asteroid, and the system is shaken, momentarily disequilibrated as it moves to reconfigure itself. As long as the universe is in balance, it will maintain its existence.

Like the amoeba and the universe, what occurs in the family is predictable, because the family too has boundaries and structure that maintains itself over long periods of time. As long as the family system is in balance, it will maintain its existence.

> The concept of system thus treats people and events in terms of their interactions rather than their intrinsic characteristics. The most basic principle underlying the systems viewpoint has been understood for some time. An ancient astronomer once said, "Heaven is more than the stars alone. It is the stars and their movements." (Baruth & Huber, 1984, p. 19)

General systems theory (von Bertalanffy, 1934, 1968) was developed to explain the complex interactions of all types of systems, including living systems, family systems, community systems, and solar systems. Each system has a boundary that allows it to maintain its structure while the system interacts with other systems around it. So the action of the amoeba, one of the smallest of all living systems, affects and is affected by surrounding **suprasystems**, while the universe, the largest of all systems, is made up of **subsystems** that have predictable relationships to one another. Similarly, the action of subsystems in families will affect other subsystems (e.g., the parental subsystem will affect the child subsystem); family units will affect other families; families make up communities that affect society; and so on.

Cybernetics

The study of **cybernetics**, or control mechanisms in systems, has been used to explain the regulatory process of a system (Becvar & Becvar, 2009). The distinctive manner that each system has to maintain its stability is called its **homeostasis**. One type of cybernetic system of which we are all aware is the thermostat. As it becomes colder, the temperature drops, and the thermostat turns on the heating system; as the temperature goes up, the thermostat shuts down the heat. This type of cybernetic system is called a **negative feedback loop** because it keeps the irregularities within the system at a minimum. **Positive feedback loops** occur when change in one component in a system leads to a change in another component within the same system, which leads to a change in the first component, and so on. On the relationship level, cybernetics explains how couples and families regulate themselves using their unique ways of communicating as they maintain their homeostasis. Although most couples and families are engaged in negative feedback loops most of the time, sometimes you will see a positive feedback loop such as when spouses egg each other on in a continual escalation of a fight. Look at Box 15.1 for an example of a couple engaged in a positive feedback loop.

Based on the example in Box 15.1, you might conclude that negative feedback loops are good and positive feedback loops are bad. Actually, this is not the case (Becvar & Becvar, 2009). Negative feedback loops are good if they result in healthy behaviors in families (good communication, good feelings, etc.). However, negative feedback loops will sometimes maintain dysfunctional behaviors (lack of communication, negative feelings), and although positive feedback loops can lead to abuse, they also can be the impetus for shaking up the system and having it move toward healthier ways of communicating. In fact, couples and family therapists will often encourage the disequilibration of the "safe" yet unhealthy ways of relating that can be found in some negative feedback loops so that the couple or family can take on new ways of relating. Each family has its unique way of interacting, which includes negative and sometimes positive feedback loop systems. If you examine communication sequences in any family, you can begin to understand the unique boundaries, feedback loops, and homeostatic mechanisms involved.

B o x 15.1 Joyce and Antonio: A Positive Feedback Loop

In the dialogue below, Joyce and Antonio are discussing going out to a play. As they realize that their expectations about the evening differ, they begin to get angry at each other. Eventually, there is an altercation, at which point Antonio defuses the situation by leaving.

JOYCE: Are you going to the play with me tonight?

ANTONIO: Well, I was actually thinking I might go out with my friends. You know, I haven't really seen them for a while. Besides, I didn't really think that I committed myself to the play.

JOYCE: Well, you did say you thought you would go with me.

ANTONIO: I don't remember saying that. I was thinking all along that I would go out with my buddies.

JOYCE: I remember distinctly you telling me you would go. It's clear as day to me. You're either lying or have early dementia.

ANTONIO: Look, I don't want to get into a fight. You're always forcing me to get into a fight with you. I don't know why you egg me on like this. You must have a need to fight with me. I bet it has to do with the fact that you never felt loved by your father—you know, we've talked about that before.

JOYCE: Not being loved by my father! Who are you kidding? The only one I don't feel loved by is you. At least my father was around. You just take off whenever you damn please! Half of the time you leave me with the kids, as if you have no responsibility around here. You just go out, get blasted and God knows what else.

ANTONIO: Look, I'm no slacker around here. You don't do a damn thing around this house. Look at it. It's a mess. I do plenty, and you can't even keep this house together. I work hard to fix this place up, and you can't even run a vacuum once in a while. You … it's disgusting!

JOYCE: Don't call me disgusting!

ANTONIO: I didn't! I said *it's* disgusting—the house.

JOYCE: No, I heard you, you were going to say I'm disgusting. I hate you! You and your drinking, you and your friends. You and those sluts you hang out with at work. I know what you're doing behind my back!

ANTONIO: Screw you!

JOYCE: Go to hell! (Swings at him.)

ANTONIO: (Grabs her arm as she swings and throws her on the floor.)

JOYCE: You abusive bastard!

ANTONIO: Screw you…. I'm getting out of here. (Leaves the house.)

JOYCE: (Sobs as Antonio leaves.)

Boundaries and Information Flow

A healthy system has **semi-permeable boundaries** that allow new information to come into the system, be processed, and then incorporated into the system. When a system has **rigid boundaries**, information is not able to easily flow into or out of the system, and change becomes a difficult process. Alternatively, a system that has **diffuse boundaries** allows information to flow too easily into and out of the system, causing the individual components of the system to have difficulty maintaining a sense of identity and stability (Nichols & Schwartz, 2009; Turner & West, 2006). Rigid boundaries will often lead to disengagement on the part of family members and a heightened sense of autonomy. In extreme cases, such families will have family secrets (e.g., child abuse), with their rigid boundaries maintaining the secret within the family. Diffuse boundaries, on the other hand, often lead to enmeshment and a lack of independence on the part of family members.

B o x 15.2   Jim Jones and the Death of a Rigid System

During the 1950s and early 1960s, Jim Jones was a respected minister in Indiana. However, over the years, he became increasingly paranoid and grandiose, believing he was Jesus. He moved his family to Brazil and later relocated to California, where approximately 100 of his church followers from Indiana joined him. In California, he headed the "People's Church" and began to set rigid rules for church membership. Slowly, he became more dictatorial and continued to show evidence of paranoid delusions. Insisting that church members prove their love for him, he demanded sex with female church members, had members sign over their possessions, sometimes had members give their children over to him, and had members inform on those who went against his rules. In 1975, a reporter uncovered some of the tactics Jones was using and was about to write a revealing article about the church. Jones learned about this and, just prior to publication of the article, moved to Guyana, taking a few hundred of his followers with him. As concerns about some of the church practices reached the United States, California Congressman Leo Ryan and some of his aides went to Guyana to investigate the situation. Jones and his supporters killed Ryan and the aides, and Jones then ordered his followers to commit suicide. Hundreds killed themselves. Those who did not were murdered.

Jim Jones had developed a church with an extremely rigid set of rules. The writing of a revealing article as well as the congressman's flying into Guyana were perceived as threats to the system. As with many rigid systems, attempts at change from the outside were seen as potentially lethal blows to the system. Jones dealt with the reporter's threat to the system by moving his congregation to Guyana. Then, rather than allow new information into the system, Jim Jones killed off the system, first killing the congressperson and then ordering the church members to commit suicide. The members had become so mired in the rules of the system that nearly 900 of them ended up committing suicide or being murdered. (Axthelm, 1978)

American culture allows for much variation in the permeability of various systems, but systems that have boundaries that are too diffuse or too rigid tend toward dysfunction. In the United States, it is common for us to find families and community groups (e.g., some religious organizations) with a fairly rigid set of rules that maintain their functioning in relatively healthy ways. Alternatively, we may also find families and community groups that allow for a wide range of behaviors within a fairly diffuse system (e.g., communes). Unfortunately, all too often, we have seen the dysfunction that results from a system whose boundaries are too rigid or too diffuse (see Box 15.2).

Rules and Hierarchy

Families have **universal** and **idiosyncratic rules**, which can be overt or covert, that are partly responsible for determining the nature of the family. Universal rules are those rules that all families tend to follow and are often related to hierarchical structure. For instance, almost all cultures have a hierarchy in which parents, guardians, or an older "wise" person is on a higher level of authority than children. Not following this rule has a consequence, although the kinds of consequences will vary as a function of the culture. Idiosyncratic rules are unique to the family. For instance, a family might have a rule that whenever there is tension in the couple's relationship, the youngest child is yelled at for doing something wrong. In a situation such as this, it is likely that the child is being **scapegoated** in an effort to diffuse tension between the couple. There are an infinite number of idiosyncratic rules, and they usually happen in an automatic manner.

Communication Theory

The work of Paul Watzlawick and others at Palo Alto greatly changed the manner in which therapists understood the communication process (cf. Watzlawick, Beavin, & Jackson, 1967; Watzlawick, Weakland, & Fisch, 1974). Understanding the complexities of human communication helps therapists recognize the unique characteristics of couples and families and is often the first step toward developing a plan for change. Some of the principles of communication highlighted by Watzlawick and others include the following (Barker, 2007):

- "Normal" or "abnormal" is a contextual phenomenon, not an objective state of being.
- Behaviors tell a story about communication between people and are often more a sign of what's going on than the actual words that are communicated.
- One cannot *not* communicate. Not saying anything is a communication about communication.
- A message sent is not necessarily the message received. A person might send one message, but a different message might be heard.
- Communication has two ways of expression: digitally, or the exact meaning of the words, and analogically, or the meaning about the meaning, often expressed nonverbally. For example, a person may be angry and say "I love you" in an angry tone. The digital message "I love you" is at odds with the analogical message.
- Communication makes a statement about the content of the conversation and about the relationship one is in. In other words, each statement a person makes is an expression about the relationship.
- A series of communications gives important meaning about the relationship (a husband might always discuss issues with a flat affect to his wife; this continual flat message may be more important than the actual words he says).
- Any intervention made within the system, be it with one or more of the family members, will reverberate throughout the system.
- The unconscious is not an important factor in working with individuals; instead, what is important are the current behaviors people are exhibiting.
- The *whys* are not as important as *what* is going on between people.

Scapegoating and Identified Patients

All couples bring unfinished business to their relationship. The more serious the issues, the more likely they will affect their relationship and others in the family.

For instance, a wife who was sexually molested as a child and as a result feels mistrust toward men may choose a man who is emotionally distant (and safe). Perhaps he is a workaholic. Alternatively, a man who has fears of intimacy might choose a wife who allows him to be distant (and safe). Perhaps she was sexually molested and distrusts men. As the relationship unravels, the issues that each spouse brings to the marriage will get played out on one another or on the children. The emotionally distant workaholic husband may become stressed at work, irritable, and nasty toward his wife and/or children. The distrustful wife may become discontented with her marriage due to its lack of intimacy and subsequently become depressed and nonresponsive toward her husband and children. Is it surprising that there are so many affairs and divorces?

When family members are discontented with one another and when they directly or indirectly take out this unhappiness on a specific family member, that member is said to have been **scapegoated** (Nichols & Schwartz, 2009). Sometimes, when a family member is scapegoated, that person takes on the role of **identified patient** (IP), or the family member who is believed to have the problem. System theorists, however, view the whole family as having the problem. For instance, when a child acts out in the family, in school, or in the community, couples and family therapists will typically view that child as the family member who is carrying the pain for the family. Why is someone in a family scapegoated? Usually because it has become too painful for the couple or family to look at some other painful issue (Hull & Mather, 2006). Rather than sharing their concerns within the family or seeking marital counseling, the couple or family scapegoats a member in the family, often a child (see Box 15.3).

> Psychotherapy, particularly marital psychotherapy, threatens to "uncover" the anxious turmoil in the marriage. "If we seek help as a couple," the partners say silently to themselves, "it will all come out." The anger, the bitterness, the hurt, the sense of self-blame that each carries—this will be the harvest of the opening up to each other. "Maybe it will destroy what we have" is their fear. They dread not only losing the stability of the marriage, but damaging their fragile self-images. Rather than risk their painful and tenuous security, they suppress the possibility of working on their marriage together. (Napier & Whitaker, 1978, p. 148)

Stress

Living is stressful, and at some point in the life of the family, it will be faced with mild to oppressive **stress**. Families with semi-permeable boundaries, clearly defined subsystems and suprasystems, little scapegoating, good communication skills, and a healthy hierarchical structure will have an easier time managing stress (see Box 15.3). On the other hand, families with ill-defined boundaries and poor communication skills will tend to blame others for their problems, not take responsibility for their feelings and actions, and have a difficult time dealing

---

Box 15.3   A Situational Family Crisis

When I was between the ages of 8 and 13, I had a heart disorder called pericarditis. This was a somewhat debilitating illness that enlarged my heart, caused me much chest pain, and left me periodically bedridden with a resulting mild depression. Although not considered extremely serious, this illness certainly affected my life in a major way. However, it also affected my parents' lives and the lives of my siblings.

Although my illness potentially could have been a threat to the homeostasis in the family, it became clear that the family was healthy enough to deal effectively with this situation. As my parents' marriage was solid, the added stress did not dramatically affect their relationship. In addition, they were able to maintain the functioning of the family in a relatively normal way. This normalization of family patterns during a period of stress speaks highly of the health in the family.

---

with stress. Minuchin (1974) identified four types of stress with which families typically struggle at some point in their development:

- *Stressful contact of one member with extrafamilial forces* (e.g., difficulty at work)
- *Stressful contact of the whole family with extrafamilial forces* (e.g., a natural disaster such as a hurricane)
- *Stress at transitional or developmental points in the family* (e.g., puberty, midlife-crises, retirement, aging)
- *Idiosyncratic (situational) stress* (e.g., unexpected illness)

Developmental Issues

All families face **developmental milestones** that will result in some amount of stress. Becvar and Becvar (2009) suggest that families traverse nine stages of a family cycle, each of which has its own critical emotional issues and tasks that need to be addressed (see Table 15.1).

Whereas some families have developed ways of communicating that allow them to effectively deal with stressful situations, others have not (Turner & West, 2006). One function of the family therapist is to be aware of potential developmental crises that may affect a family and understand how families tend to respond to stress that results from these normal developmental tasks. Having the skills to help families change their response from one that is harmful to one that allows the family to function at an optimal level is an important role of the family therapist.

Social Constructionism

The addition of social construction to systems theory, then, helps address the criticism that systems theory focuses too much on stability, ignores cultural context, and operates as though the research can find objective truth. (Turner & West, 2006, p. 70)

T A B L E 15.1   Stages of the Family Life Cycle

Stage	Emotional Issues	Stage-Critical Tasks
1. Unattached adult	Accepting parent-offspring separation	a. Differentiation from family of origin b. Development of peer relationships c. Initiation of career
2. Newly married adults	Commitment to the marriage	a. Formation of marital system b. Making room for spouse with family and friends c. Adjusting career demands
3. Childbearing adults	Accepting new members into the system	a. Adjusting marriage to make room for child(ren) b. Taking on parenting roles c. Making room for grandparents
4. Preschool-age child(ren)	Accepting the new personality	a. Adjusting family to the needs of specific child(ren) b. Coping with energy drain and lack of privacy c. Taking time out to be a couple
5. School-age child(ren)	Allowing child(ren) to establish relationships outside the family	a. Extending family-society interactions b. Encouraging the child(ren)'s educational progress c. Dealing with increased activities and time demands
6. Teenage child(ren)	Increasing flexibility of family boundaries to allow independence	a. Shifting the balance in the parent-child relationship b. Refocusing on mid-life career and marital issues c. Dealing with increasing concern for older generations
7. Launching center	Accepting exits from and entries into family	a. Releasing adult children into work, college, marriage b. Maintaining supportive home base c. Accepting occasional returns of adult children
8. Middle-aged adults	Letting go of children and facing each other again	a. Rebuilding the marriage b. Welcoming children's spouses, grandchildren into family c. Dealing with aging of one's own parents
9. Retired adults	Accepting retirement and old age	a. Maintaining individual and couple functioning b. Supporting middle generation c. Coping with death of parents, spouse d. Closing or adapting family

SOURCE: Becvar, D. S., & Becvar, R. J. (2009). *Family therapy: A systemic integration* (7th ed.). Boston: Allyn & Bacon. p. 111. Reprinted by permission of Pearson Education, Inc.

In recent years, there has been a shift for some family therapists in their understanding of how families are formed and make sense of themselves (Tomm, 1998; Turner & West, 2006). Having a **social constructionist** philosophy, these family therapists believe that systems theory, and its close cousin, cybernetics, placed too much emphasis on causal factors and did not stress cultural context enough. The social constructionists suggested that these earlier family therapists tended to see themselves as experts and objective observers who make interventions on the family. In contrast, the social constructionists focus on the ongoing, changing manner in which family members come to understand themselves. They believe that families continually co-construct (construct together through ongoing dialogue and nonverbal interactions) their understanding of who they are, and that this construction is a function of the language used in the family and beliefs from their culture and society. Change occurs, therefore, by the therapist's entering the family with a respectful curiosity and exploring, with the family, how they co-construct a sense of meaning for themselves. Then, through the use of thoughtful and respectful questioning, social constructionists believe that they and the family can co-construct a new language for the family that is positive and focuses on solutions. Although many family therapists today integrate this perspective into their existing systems framework (Becvar & Becvar, 2009), some, such as the narrative and solution-focused purists, question these earlier theories (e.g., systems theory, communication theory) and discard them for a belief in the importance of how language defines the person and the family.

MODELS OF FAMILY THERAPY

The key concepts just discussed are the driving force behind the various approaches to family counseling. As some approaches adhere more to certain concepts than others, as you read the theories, reflect on which key concepts are most driving a particular theory. With many theories of couples and family therapy to choose from, included in this chapter are the most popular ones as well as those that are most associated with some of the major players in the history of couples and family therapy. The theories we will look at include the **human validation process model, structural family therapy, strategic family therapy, multigenerational family therapy, experiential family therapy, psychodynamic family therapy, behavioral and cognitive–behavioral family therapy, narrative family therapy,** and **solution-focused family therapy.**

Human Validation Process Model of Family Therapy

All of the ingredients in a family that count are changeable and correctable—individual self-worth, communication, system, and rules—at any point in time. (Satir, 1972a, p. xi)

In addition to Salvador Minuchin and Jay Haley, Virginia Satir is considered to be one of the pioneers of couples and family therapy. Her **human validation process model**, which has also been called a *communication theory* and a *change process model*, integrates many ideas from family systems theory and communication theory, while adding a sense of caring and a focus on self-esteem that is emphasized in the existential–humanistic approaches (Satir, 1972b).

Virginia Satir

Courtesy of The Virginia Satir Global Network

Satir believed that a **primary survival triad** exists that includes parents and the child, with each child's sense of well-being and self-esteem the result of this triad. Low self-esteem eventually leads individuals to take on one of four unhealthy universal communication patterns: (1) **the placater**, who appeases people so others won't get angry at him or her; (2) **the blamer**, who accuses others in an effort to diffuse hurt; (3) **the computer**, who acts cool, calm, and collected in an attempt to deal with the world as if nothing could hurt him or her; and (4) **the distracter**, who goes off on tangents in an effort to treat threats as if they do not exist (Satir, 1972a). On the other hand, Satir also believed that children who had healthy parenting would grow into adults who were congruent—in sync with their feelings, thoughts, and behaviors—and could thus communicate clearly with others.

Believing that communication and behavioral patterns are a result of complex interactions among family members and the legacy from past generations, Satir felt it was important to obtain graphic information about important past events in one's family. Thus, she would often have families complete a **family life fact chronology**, which is a history of important events within the extended family. Similar to a **genogram**, the family life fact chronology could be analyzed and reflected upon by all involved in therapy. Additionally, Satir was one of the first therapists to use **family sculpting** in an effort to bring forth blocked and unexpressed emotions (Piercy, Sprenkle, & Wetchler, 1996). This experiential work involves each family member taking a physical position that nonverbally represents how that member interacts with the rest of the family. For instance, a child who is withdrawing might stand near a door as if she were about to leave the room; a mother trying to control her son might stand over him with her finger pointed at him; and a father who is detached through drinking might sit at a table with a make-believe glass of beer in his hand.

Satir believed that a family therapist should be caring and respectful, believe in the ability of the family to heal, actively encourage the family to change, be spontaneous, and act "as a facilitator, a resource person, an observer, a detective, and a model for effective communication" (Becvar & Becvar, 2009, p. 199). By creating a trusting atmosphere that encouraged the letting-down of defenses, Satir hoped to open up communication patterns, look at past hurts, and help clients learn how to be more effective and open communicators. Ultimately, through this process, Satir hoped that individuals in couples and families could have mature relationships in which each person could (Satir, 1972a):

- be responsible for oneself and have a strong sense of self.
- make decisions based on an accurate perception of self, others, and the social context.

- be able to make wise choices for which one takes full responsibility.
- be in touch with one's feelings.
- be clear in one's communication.
- be able to accept others for who they are.
- see differences in others as an opportunity to learn, not as a threat. (adapted from Satir, 1967, p. 91)

Structural Family Therapy

Courtesy Minuchin Center for the Family

Salvador Minuchin

Although many well-known family therapists see themselves in the structural school, certainly the most renowned is Salvador Minuchin (1974, 1981). Minuchin (1974) states that all families have **interactional** and **transactional rules** that are maintained by the kinds of boundaries in the family, as noted through the structure and hierarchy that exists. He also asserts that all families experience stress, which is handled differently by each family as a function of the existing rules, boundaries, and structure and hierarchy in the family (see p. 511). In order to make change in families, structural family therapists must join with the family, map the family, and provide interventions for restructuring.

Joining. Minuchin believes that change in the family can occur only if the therapist is able to "join" with the family. **Joining** is when the counselor is accepted by the family and wins its confidence. Joining can be done in many ways, such as through empathy, being friendly, or sharing common stories with the family. Joining the family allows the counselor to understand the family's rules, boundaries, structure and hierarchy, and stress. It is only then that the counselor can begin the process of mapping and later restructuring the family.

Mapping.   **Mapping** a family can be done formally or informally, and involves an examination of how the family communicates, who is in charge, rules used in the family to maintain its homeostasis, and an understanding of the structure and hierarchy of the family. Mapping is the first step toward restructuring, as one cannot make change unless one understands the current way in which the family relates.

Restructuring. **Restructuring** the family occurs after the counselor has joined the family and mapped its structure. It involves creating healthier boundaries, and changing structure and hierarchy, in order to help the family deal with stress and function in a healthier manner. Restructuring can occur in numerous ways. Box 15.4 describes the restructuring of one family.

Structural family therapy is a deliberate and purposeful approach to working with families and relies on many of the basic principles discussed under "Key

---

B o x 15.4   An Example of Family Restructuring

Mom and Dad have three children, aged 15, 12, and 1. Since the birth of their new child, the two oldest children have been fighting constantly and having problems at school. The husband and wife seem depressed. Assessing the situation, you find that the whole family is dealing with transitional and idiosyncratic stress. The baby was not planned, and the family is stretched financially. The therapist notes that the family hierarchy has changed, that the spousal subsystem is showing depression, and that the parental subsystem is not able to maintain control over the two older children. The therapist wants to strengthen the spousal and parental subsystems. The current map of the family is shown to the left of the legend.

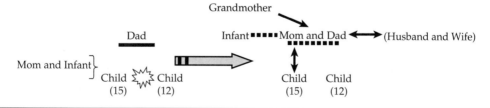

The family therapist prescribes the following actions:

- Have the oldest child take a certification course in babysitting to assist with child care.
- Ask the grandmother to assist with child care to relieve some pressure on Mom.
- Have Dad take on some of the responsibilities related to the problems with the oldest children. He must meet with the teachers and school counselors.
- Suggest that Mom, who now has assistance with child care, take on a part-time job to relieve some of the economic stress (she has always worked in the past).

- Establish one evening a week when the grand-mother or oldest child will watch the other two children so the parents can go out.

The goal is to reestablish the spousal subsystem while strengthening the parental subsystem. The grand-mother and oldest child will periodically take on a position of power in the family, with their power being time-limited. The extra money and reduction of stress for Mom will result in reduced stress in the family. The family map eventually looks like the diagram below:

Concepts." Many family therapists who are first starting out are trained in this approach, as it helps the therapist view the family from a systemic perspective.

Strategic Family Therapy

The steps involved in strategic therapy are based on an understanding of communication and systems theory; and, because unconscious motivations play

Courtesy of Dr. Sonja Benson

Jay Haley

Courtesy of Cloé Madanes

Cloé Madanes

little if any role in this type of therapy, the approach is relatively pragmatic. Relative to the therapeutic process, the strategic approach is not particularly concerned with feelings (although the therapist wants the client to end up having good feelings!). This approach is based on how individuals communicate with one another, how communication sequences can be changed to help people feel better, and how power is dispersed in the family. Power for the strategic therapist is defined in some very nontraditional ways:

> Power tactics are those maneuvers a person uses to give himself influence and control over his social world and to make that world more predictable. Defined thus broadly, a man has power if he can order someone to behave in a certain way, but he also has power if he can provoke someone to behave that way. One man can order others to lift and carry him while another might achieve the same end by collapsing. (Haley, 1986, p. 53)

The therapist most associated with the strategic approach has been Jay Haley (1973, 1976), although others, like Cloé Madanes and the Milan Group, have also become well-known. Haley was greatly affected by Milton Erickson, a legend as a therapist because of his uncanny ability to induce change in clients. In Haley's 1976 book, *Problem-Solving Therapy*, he describes four stages of the first interview that lay the groundwork for the change process. Although unique to the way Haley implements strategic therapy, these stages provide a picture of how all strategic family therapists work.

Haley's Stages of The First Interview

1. *The social stage.* During this stage, the therapist invites the whole family to counseling and asks each member to introduce himself or herself. At this point, the therapist can observe where family members sit, interactions among family members, and the overall mood of the family. During this stage, the therapist should not share his or her observations with the family, and all formulations about the family should be tentative.

2. *The problem stage.* During the problem stage, each family member is asked to describe his or her perceptions of the problem. The therapist should carefully listen, as the problem is often defined differently by family members. Interactions among family members should be carefully observed, and therapist interpretations about the problem should not be shared.

3. *The interaction stage.* The interaction stage is highlighted by the therapist's attempt to get the family to interact during the session in the same manner in which they might at home. This process assists the therapist in viewing how the family is organized around the problem.

4. *Goal-setting stage.* During this stage, the family is asked to be clear about what they would like to change, and, in collaboration with the therapist, a problem is agreed upon. This problem is important and needs to be addressed;

however, it also tells us something about how the family communicates and the hierarchies in the family (Foster & Gurman, 1985; Haley, 1973, 1976). Therefore, how the therapist addresses the problem may vary based on an assessment of the structure and communication sequences in the family. Remember, the focus is on having people change the way they communicate so they will feel better, and sometimes what the family thinks they *should* do will actually make the problem worse. Thus, the role of the therapist is to help the family change based on the therapist's understanding of the communication problems and how power is used (and abused) in the family. The family need not know why the therapist is prescribing certain tasks, but the family does need to "buy into" the change process. Haley addresses this change process through the use of **directives**.

Directives

It is important to emphasize that directives can be given directly or they can be given in a conversation implicitly by vocal intonation, body movement, and well-timed silence. Everything done in therapy can be seen as a directive. (Haley, 1976, p. 50)

Directives are the kinds of instructions given to a family to foster change. If enough progress has been made, directives can be made at the end of the first session, although sometimes it may take two or three sessions. Haley (1976) identifies two types of directives: "(1) telling people what to do when the therapist wants them to do it, and (2) telling them what to do when the therapist does not want them to do it because the therapist wants them to change by rebelling" (p. 52).

In the first case, a therapist can either give good advice or give a directive that changes the structure of the family. Haley admits that advice, even good advice, is rarely followed by families. Therefore, he suggests giving directives in which the family wants to participate, directives that will address both the presenting problem and also broader problems inherent in the family organization and communication sequencing. The therapist generally does not reveal to the family his or her agenda of restructuring family dynamics, as this is not generally found to expedite change. For instance, parents might identify a problem as their daughter's use of drugs. However, in therapy, it soon becomes clear that the family isolates and cuts off the daughter from the rest of the family. The therapist could give good advice, such as suggesting to the daughter that she take a drug education class. However, this would most likely be a wasteful suggestion, as it is unlikely to be followed by the rebellious daughter. Therefore, it would be more useful to offer a directive that deals with the drug use *and* the family organization—a directive in which all would participate. For example, the therapist might ask the family to include the daughter in as many family activities as possible in an effort to ensure that she is not doing drugs. The parents will appreciate this directive, as it is dealing with the problem, and the daughter will appreciate it, as she is finally being included in the family.

The second type of directive, called a **paradoxical directive**, involves asking clients to do something opposite of what might seem logical, with the expectation that the directive is likely to fail and that this failure will lead to success in therapy. Put simply, "some clients are more invested in the 'cons' of change, not the 'pros' of change" (Jack Grimes, personal communication, July 14, 2009). If clients actually do follow the directive, success is also ensured. For instance, a family has a child who is constantly angry and screaming. The therapist might reframe the situation by stating that this child is actually quite healthy in that he is expressing his feelings. The therapist suggests that listening to the child's feelings is not likely to be helpful because the child needs to release his healthy anger. Probably, the therapist remarks, it would be helpful instead to encourage the child to scream more. Parents who rebel against this suggestion end up listening to the child. On the other hand, parents who go with the suggestion are now compliant clients who have reframed the problem into a healthy behavior and are praised at the next session for being such good clients.

Another technique to induce change of this kind is through the **use of metaphor**. Look at how Haley (1976) uses metaphor to deal with a couple's uncomfortable feelings about talking directly to their son about his being adopted:

> [The therapist] talked to the boy about "adopting" a dog who had a problem of being frightened.... When the boy said the family might have to get rid of the dog if he became ill and cost doctor bills [the boy had been ill], the therapist insisted that once adopted the family was committed to the dog and would have to keep him and pay his doctor bills no matter what. Various concerns the boy might have had about himself as well as the parents' concerns about him were discussed in metaphoric terms in relation to the proposed adoption of the puppy. (p. 65)

Course of Treatment.   Strategic therapy tends to be a short-term approach to counseling because it focuses almost exclusively on presenting problems, does not spend time dealing with intrapsychic processes, and uses directives to facilitate the change process (Carlson, 2002). Usually, directives can be made within the first few sessions, with follow-up and revision to the original directives sometimes calling for only a few more sessions.

Clearly, to be a strategic therapist takes a great deal of training and confidence in one's ability at suggesting effective directives. It is interesting to watch some of the more well-known strategic therapists work. Criticized as manipulative by some, today's strategic therapists stress collaboration, not manipulation (Carlson, 2002). In fact, their directives, even ones with hidden agendas, appear to come from a real and caring place for these master therapists.

Multigenerational Family Therapy

Family counselors who take on a multigenerational approach to family therapy focus on how behavioral patterns and personality traits from prior generations have been passed down in families. Therefore, many multigenerational family counselors may encourage bringing in parents, grandparents, and perhaps even cousins, uncles, and aunts.

Although multigenerational family counselors focus on intergenerational conflicts, the way they go about this may differ. For instance, Ivan Boszormenyi-Nagy (1973, 1987) believes that families are relational systems in which **loyalties**, a sense of **indebtedness**, and ways of relating are passed down from generation to generation. Couples enter relationships with a **ledger of indebtedness and entitlements** based on their families of origin and what was passed down to those families. A couple who enters a relationship with an imbalanced ledger will invariably attempt to balance the ledger with each other. This is almost always unsuccessful, as the imbalance is a result of unfinished business from the family of origin, not from the spouse. For instance, one who felt unloved by his mother might attempt to settle up his account with her by trying to have his wife shower him with love. However, because this is unfinished business with the mother, the husband will continue to feel a sense of emptiness, even if the wife fulfills this request. Boszormenyi-Nagy believes that it is crucial for all family members to gain the capacity to hear one another, communicate with one another, and have the ability to understand their interpersonal connectedness to the current family as well as their families of origin.

> When each generation is helped to face the nature of the current relationships, exploring the real nature of the commitments and responsibility that flow from such involvements, an increased reciprocal understanding and mutual compassion between the generations results. The grandchildren, in particular, benefit from this reconciliation between the generations; they are helped to be freed of scapegoated or parentified roles and they have a hope for age appropriate gratifications plus a model for reconciling their conflicts with their parents. (Friedman, 1989, p. 405)

Another multigenerational family therapist, Murray Bowen, believed that previous generations could dramatically affect one's ability to develop a healthy ego. He considered the ultimate goal of couples and family therapy to be the **differentiation of self**, which included differentiation of self from others and the differentiation of one's emotional processes from one's intellectual processes (Bowen, 1976, 1978; Guerin & Guerin, 2002). He believed that there was a **nuclear family emotional system** made up of all family members (living, dead, absent, and present), which continued to have an emotional impact upon the system. Such an emotional system, said Bowen, is reflective of the level of differentiation in the family, and is called the **undifferentiated ego mass**. Thus, previous generations could continue to have an influence on current family dynamics (Klever, 2004). Bowen used the **genogram** to examine details of a family's functioning over a number of generations. Although the basic genogram includes such items as dates of birth and death, names, and major relationships, along with breakups or divorces, the therapist will usually also ask the family to include such things as where various members are from, who might be scapegoated and/or an

Murray Bowen

© Cengage Learning

B o x 15.5   Who's More Dysfunctional?

Bowen's belief that individuals generally find others of similar psychological health has always intrigued me. Many times, I have seen clients come for therapy, complaining and even diagnosing their lover or spouse whom they have left. At these times, I've often thought that if the partner were there, that person would likely have a comparable complaint or diagnosis. And it certainly makes some intuitive sense. After all, why would someone who is psychologically healthier

than my clients want to be with them? (Or, for that matter, why would someone psychologically healthier than you, or me, want to be with us?) And why would my clients choose to be with someone less healthy than them? (Or, why would we choose to be with those less healthy than us?) Have you ever found yourself diagnosing a person you are with or used to be with? Any thoughts about what they may have been saying about you?

---

identified patient, mental illness, physical diseases, affairs, abortions, and stillbirths. Such genograms are excellent tools for examining how families evolve over time and for identifying current issues in families (McGoldrick, 2005) (see Figure 15.1).

Bowen believed that individuals find others of similar psychological health with whom to form significant relationships. Therefore, an undifferentiated person will find a person with a similar level of undifferentiation, each hoping he or she will find completeness in the other. What initially seems like a perfect fit usually ends up as a major disappointment and often ends in divorce. When undifferentiated parents do not deal with their issues, which by their very nature are frequent, a **family projection process** occurs in which parents unconsciously **triangulate** their children or project their own issues onto the children. The purpose of this projection is to reduce stress within the parental relationship while maintaining each spouse's level of undifferentiation. This allows the couple to continue to avoid their issues. An unhealthy relationship obviously leads to problems with child-rearing, and ultimately the child grows into an undifferentiated self, thus continuing the cycle. This process could continue *ad infinitum* (see Box 15.5).

From a Bowenian perspective, therapists should be detached and take on the role of teachers and consultants, helping their clients to understand family dynamics and systems theory from an intellectual framework. Bowen mostly worked with couples, generally did not include children in the process, and kept emotionality at a minimum during the sessions by having the clients talk to and through the therapist. Bowen's goal was to help family members see themselves as they truly are and to help them move toward differentiation of self.

Experiential Family Therapy

As the name implies, **experiential family therapy** stresses the experience of self, of one another, and of the therapist within the family therapy milieu (Napier, 2002). Based mostly on humanistic and existential psychology, this type of therapy has a positive view of human nature, believes that the individual (and the family) has a natural growth tendency, and relies on the relationship between the therapist and the family to induce change. The most well-known experiential family

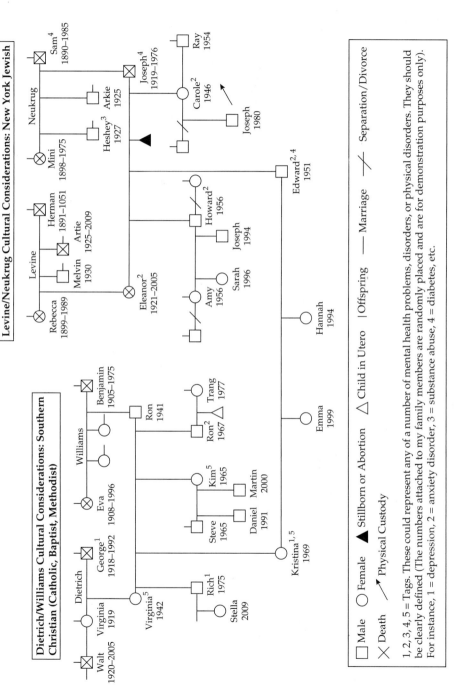

FIGURE 15.1 Hannah Virginia Williams Neukrug's Abbreviated Genogram

Carl Whitaker

therapist is Carl Whitaker, who prided himself on his lack of a theoretical approach: "I have a theory that theories are destructive and I know that intuition is destructive" (Whitaker, 1976, p. 154). Despite this bold statement, it is clear that when working with families, Whitaker conceptualizes families from a systems perspective:

> The major problem we see in the individual approaches is they fail to take into account the powerful interdependence between family members.... The "symptom" is merely a front for the family's larger stress. (Napier & Whitaker, 1978, pp. 270–271)

In fact, if you read any of Whitaker's writings, it quickly becomes evident that his approach is strongly influenced by humanistic psychology with a touch of psychodynamic theory. For instance, Whitaker believes that counselors should:

- Respect each family member's self-actualizing process.
- Respect the family's ability to unravel itself if placed in a trusting environment.
- Create an atmosphere of oneness and nondefensiveness in order to make it difficult for the family to flee into defensive patterns.
- Assist families in resolving the pain and anger that brings them to therapy.
- Assist families in looking at their ghosts from the past.
- Be powerful enough to "invade the family" in order to be part of the family and assist in breaking roles that have become solidified over time (Whitaker, 1976, p. 163).
- Have an "I–Thou" relationship with co-therapists and the family. This real relationship models openness, the ability to dialogue and to express feeling. "Why should the family expose their tender underbelly if the therapist plays coy and self-protective?" (Whitaker, 1976, p. 164).
- Not offer any particular framework or preconceived way in which the family should operate in an effort to have the family develop their own structure.
- Model playfulness, craziness, and genuineness, in an effort to get family members to loosen up and be themselves, and ultimately push them toward individuation.
- Assist families in establishing a generation gap, or boundaries between parents and children.

Sometimes sounding strikingly like Carl Rogers, Whitaker suggests that at first, the family is defensive and closed to the therapist. As the therapist invades and then joins the family, the family begins to see him or her as a genuine person and begins to open up. This is when past inner hurts and conflicts begin to emerge, and it is at this point that the therapist can facilitate the family members' exploration of these hurts and help the family understand how this pain has affected each member of the family. Each family member can now begin to work on his or her own problems and move toward individuation. In fact,

Napier and Whitaker (1978) note that the later stages of family counseling seem more like a number of individual sessions occurring at the same time:

> At the end of therapy the family should have resolved their major relationship conflicts, and the individuals should really be individuals in a psychological sense. (Napier & Whitaker, 1978, p. 274)

Whitaker believes it is usually wise to have a co-therapist, as this will allow counselors to model the I–Thou relationship. In addition, such a "real" relationship enables therapists to discuss their understanding of the family with each other—usually in front of the family (Napier & Whitaker, 1978). Also, because of the sheer numbers of people involved in family therapy, co-therapy enables counselors to periodically attend to each member of the family. Showing his psychodynamic leanings, Whitaker also suggests that co-therapists will often be perceived as the "parents" of the family, allowing families to make analogies to their families of origin, which can then be discussed. However, co-therapists can also be perceived in other roles, allowing family members to project their issues onto them (Napier & Whitaker, 1972):

> Carl can be a very big-breasted, tender mother at times and a stern, tough grandfather at others, and I myself don't make a bad rebellious adolescent at times. It's a lot more complicated than the simplistic way in which we often identify personality with biology. (Napier & Whitaker, 1978, p. 92)

Watch Whitaker work, and you see a master therapist who is witty, bright, reflective, real, strong, and willing to take risks. Despite the fact that he says he has no theory, you see consistency in his work, a consistency in the way he presents himself to the family that allows the family to grow, learn, deal with painful issues, dialogue, and ultimately change.

Psychodynamic Family Therapy

Family therapy, from a psychodynamic perspective, attempts to merge many of the concepts from systemic thinking with psychodynamic theory. For instance, when viewing psychoanalysis contextually, family dynamics is seen as a reflection of each family member's personality development through the psychosexual stages. The major difference between psychodynamic family therapists and traditional, individual-oriented psychodynamic therapists is that the family therapist places great emphasis on how the client projects his or her internal world onto the family and the subsequent interactional processes that take place, whereas the individual-oriented therapist almost exclusively emphasizes the internal world of the client and projections onto the therapist (Becvar & Becvar, 2009).

Nathan Ackerman (1958, 1966) and Robin Skynner (1981) are two well-known psychodynamic family therapists. Like Ackerman and Skynner, most psychodynamically oriented therapists have generally been trained in traditional psychoanalysis methods but also saw value in

Nathan Ackerman

Courtesy of the Ackerman Institute for the Family

taking a systemic view when working with clients. Most converts to the systems approach have found that this combination offers a broader perspective that allows for direct involvement with the cast of characters. A combination such as this seems to speed up the usual slow process of most psychodynamically oriented individual approaches.

For the psychodynamic family therapist, there is generally an emphasis on how effective parents were in assisting their children through the developmental stages (Foster & Gurman, 1985). Because of this underlying assumption, unresolved issues through the developmental stages are thought to be reflected in the family in unconscious ways. Therefore, psychodynamic family therapy has as its major goal "to free family members of unconscious constraints so that they'll be able to interact with one another as healthy individuals" (Nichols & Schwartz, 2008, p. 248).

Although strategies and techniques for the psychodynamically oriented therapist will vary, the major thrust is to have the couple or family explore their interactions and begin to understand how their behaviors result from unresolved conflicts from childhood. These conflicts may be multigenerational, in the sense that the parents pass on their conflicts to their children. It is therefore common for psychodynamically oriented therapists to encourage their clients to bring in grandparents or other extended family members for a session and to encourage clients to continue to discuss unresolved issues while at home with their immediate and extended family members.

Behavioral and Cognitive–Behavioral Family Therapy

Much like individual approaches to behavior therapy, **behavioral family therapy** is oriented toward symptom relief and does not focus on intrapsychic processes, underlying issues, or the unconscious. This approach tends to be highly structured and focuses on specific behaviors and techniques. As in individual behavior therapy, the family behavior therapist has at his or her disposal a wide array of techniques taken directly from operant conditioning, classical conditioning, and social-learning theory or modeling. Also, as in individual behavioral therapy, in recent years, there has been a trend toward the inclusion of cognitive therapy as an aspect of behavioral family therapy (Becvar & Becvar, 2009). Cognitive–behavioral family therapists believe that mediating cognitions can also affect family members and therefore should be addressed in treatment. For instance, when a parent is continually dismissive of a child, this child begins to make negative self-statements concerning his or her self-worth. Therefore, in addition to behavioral change for the parents, cognitive–behavioral family therapists believe that the child's negative automatic thoughts also need to be addressed.

Whereas many traditional behavioral therapists have viewed problem behaviors in a linear, cause-and-effect fashion, most behavioral and cognitive–behavioral family therapists integrate systems theory with cognitive and behavioral theory and view problem behaviors as the result of a number of feedback loops in which the dysfunctional behavior becomes reinforced from a number of different sources, including the family (Barker, 2007; Goldenberg & Goldenberg, 2008). Because the behavioral and cognitive–behavioral family therapist is dealing with the family and not just one individual, it is particularly important to identify symptoms and target behaviors that the whole family will agree are important to change, and to understand how various behaviors are reinforced in the system:

> The cognitive–behavioral approach is compatible with systems theory and includes the premise that members of a family simultaneously influence and are influenced by each other. Consequently, the behavior of one family member triggers behavior, cognitions, and emotions in other members, which in turn elicit reactive cognitions, behavior, and emotions in the original member. As this process plays out, the volatility of family dynamics escalates, rendering the family vulnerable to negative spirals of conflict. (Nichols & Schwartz, 2008, p. 284)

Although many different models of **behavioral** and **cognitive–behavioral family therapy** have been developed, some common elements that are typically identified in this approach include the following (Foster & Gurman, 1985; Gladding, 2007; Goldenberg & Goldenberg, 2008; Nichols & Schwartz, 2008):

- The importance of building a working relationship.
- Viewing therapy as an active approach that elicits the collaboration of the family.
- Believing that basic learning theory principles can be applied in a systems framework.
- Viewing therapy as brief and time-limited.
- Focusing on specific behaviors or cognitions that will be targeted in the treatment.
- Stressing the increase of positive behaviors over the elimination of negative behaviors.
- Teaching and coaching clients about the relationships among events in their lives, behaviors, cognitions, and consequences (e.g., negative or positive feelings).
- Setting goals that are clear, realistic, concrete, and measurable.
- Actively teaching and supervising the change process within the family.
- Helping families to learn how to self-manage and monitor changes in behaviors and cognitions.
- Evaluating the effects of specific techniques in an effort to measure progress.

Whereas some family therapists believe it is always important to include the whole family in the treatment, regardless of the problem (Napier & Whitaker, 1978; Satir, 1967), behavioral and cognitive–behavioral family therapists take into account what the presenting problem is and tend to include only those members who seem to be directly related to the change process (Nichols & Schwartz, 2008).

For instance, if a child is having behavior problems at home and correction of the problem involves only parenting skills training, there may be no need to include the child. Similarly, if a couple is having marital problems, although their problems will be spilling over to the children, the correction of the problem may not be directly involved with the children, and therefore they may not have to be included. In this process, it is most important for the behavioral and cognitive–behavioral family therapist to make a good assessment of the problem in an effort to determine correct treatment strategies and decide who in the family should be included in therapy (Becvar & Becvar, 2009; Nichols & Schwartz, 2009).

Narrative Family Therapy

The person or the family is not the problem; the problem is the problem. (Michael White, paraphrased)

This quote speaks to one of the newest trends in family therapy—**narrative family therapy**. Based on some of the most recent developments in the counseling field, such as **social constructionism**, **post-modernism,** and what is called **narrative reasoning** (Gladding, 2007), narrative family therapy has at its core the belief that there are no absolute truths and that it is critical to understand the stories that people and families tell in order to help them **deconstruct** how they come to understand their family. Ultimately, the goal of narrative family therapy is to recreate how the family comes to understand itself.

Photo by Jill Freedman

Michael White

Two of the early founders of narrative therapy were Michael White and David Epston (White, 1995; White & Epston, 1990), both of whom decided to discard some of the rule-based procedures found in the more traditional family therapy techniques that tended to follow general systems and cybernetic theory (Nichols & Schwartz, 2009). This approach has some similarities to solution-focused therapy in that it takes an optimistic, proactive, future-oriented approach to working with people. Therapists who practice this kind of therapy tend to do the following (Fenell & Weinhold, 2003; Nichols & Schwartz, 2009):

- Show interest and develop a strong collaborative relationship with the family.

- Understand a family's history through the stories it tells and examine how the problem has been dysfunctional for the family.

- Ask questions in a nonjudgmental manner in order to understand the issues in the family and begin to help the family redefine the problem.

Courtesy of David Epston

David Epston

- Have the family **externalize the problem**. For instance, instead of defining the problem as "people in the family don't value each other," the problem becomes "time"—there's not enough *time* for everyone to show each other how much they care.

- Begin to look for **exceptions to the problem**.

- Find evidence in the family's history to show how the family has been competent and resourceful and able to combat problems such as this.

- Help the family reframe the place the problem has played in the family and help them to redefine or re-author their understanding of themselves by focusing on their existing strengths and their possibilities for the future.

- Help the family reinforce existing strengths and newfound narratives through ceremonies and other ways of acknowledging the changes the family has made.

The end goal of narrative family therapy is to help families understand how their history had defined who they were and how they interacted, and to help them find their own unique, new way of being in the world. Ultimately, the family decides what is considered a healthy way of functioning as they deconstruct their past ways of being and find new and better ways of relating.

Insoo Kim Berg

Photo courtesy of the Brief Family Therapy Center

Solution-Focused Family Therapy

Solution-focused family therapy is very similar to solution-focused therapy discussed in Chapter 13 and was originated by Insoo Kim Berg, Steve de Shazer, Bill O'Hanlon, and others (Berg, 1994; de Shazer, 1982). As you may remember from Chapter 13, solution-focused therapy is a pragmatic and future-oriented approach that assumes that clients can change quickly. Because the approach focuses on solutions, not problems, discussion of the past is very limited, as such discussion is believed to keep the client mired in the problem. Viewing the client as the expert, this approach believes that the client has strengths that can be expanded upon. Somewhat based on **social constructionism** and **post-modernism**, in dialogue with the counselor, the solution-focused family therapist believes that he or she can help the client create a new, **problem-free language** associated with new behaviors as he or she finds **exceptions to the problem**, develops solutions, and moves toward creating a new reality.

Steve de Shazer

Photo courtesy of the Brief Family Therapy Center

Like narrative therapy, but unlike most other forms of family therapy we examined in this chapter, solution-focused family therapy does not rely on the assumptions of general systems theory, cybernetics, boundary or information flow, or many of the other theoretical underpinnings listed at the beginning of this section of the chapter (Nichols & Schwartz, 2009). In fact, solution-focused family therapists question the "truth" of those who rely on such theory and do not view problems as being inherently caused by flaws in the family's structure. Instead, they believe that language and perception of problems is related to the development of problems. Therefore, solution-focused family therapists have clients examine alternative ways of viewing themselves and focus solely on helping clients find solutions to their problems based on their existing strengths. Since each member can do this on his or her own, solution-focused therapists do not need to see

Bill O'Hanlon

Courtesy of Bill O'Hanlon

the whole family in therapy, but rather only those who want to work on their own solutions. Underlying assumptions of this type of therapy were listed in Chapter 13 and are repeated, in brief, here:

- Change is constant and inevitable.
- The client is the expert on his or her experience.
- Clients come to us with resources and strengths.
- If it ain't broke, don't fix it.
- If it works, do more of it; if it's not working, do something different.
- Small steps can lead to big changes.
- There is not necessarily a logical relationship between the solution and the problem.
- The language for solution development is different from that needed to describe a problem.
- No problems happen all the time; there are always exceptions that can be used.
- The future is both created and negotiable.

As you may remember from Chapter 13, solution-focused therapy can be viewed through a series of six stages that included pre-session change, forming a collaborative relationship, describing the problem, establishing preferred outcomes, problem-to-solution focus, reaching preferred outcomes, and ending therapy. With therapy occurring rapidly, the therapist enters the initial session asking if any pre-session changes were noted, and takes an **ambassador** position with the client in which he or she is curious, respectful, and accepting. Using listening and empathy skills and being tentative in his or her approach, the solution-focused therapist forms a collaborative relationship and slowly moves the client from a description of the problem toward the establishment of **preferred outcomes**. Solutions are eventually determined through the use of a number of **questioning techniques** that include asking preferred outcome questions, evaluative questions, coping questions, exception-seeking questions, and solution-oriented questions. In addition, therapists will also reframe client responses to view them in a positive light, amplify exceptions, compliment clients around solutions that work, and help clients assess progress through the use of **scaling**, where clients subjectively rate their progress on a scale from 0 to 10. With solution-focused family therapy being very similar to solution-focused therapy, you can refer to Chapter 13 for a more in-depth look at this approach.

SOCIAL, CULTURAL, AND SPIRITUAL ISSUES

Any comprehensive attempt to understand personal or family functioning must take into account the fundamental influences of gender, culture, and ethnicity in shaping the lives and experiences of men and women. These issues have assumed center stage for family therapists in recent years, extending their thinking beyond observing internal family interaction processes to include the impact of the outside social, political, and historical forces in the belief systems and everyday functioning of family members. (Goldenberg & Goldenberg, 2008, p. 54)

Regardless of the couples and family therapy approach being applied, when working with families from diverse cultures and religious orientations, a number of issues should be considered (Goldenberg & Goldenberg, 2008; Hines, Petro, McGoldrick, Almeida, & Weltman, 2005; Ho, Rasheed, & Rasheed, 2004; McGoldrick, Giordano, & Garcia-Petro, 2005). The following highlights but a few of the major concerns:

- Racism, poverty, and lower-class status are widespread for many diverse clients and can dramatically affect how families feel about themselves and their relationship to the counselor.

- Language used by the dominant culture is often covertly or overtly oppressive of culturally and ethnically diverse families and affects how others see the family, how the family sees itself, and how the family sees and lives in society.

- Many culturally and ethnically diverse families are bicultural, and all families face issues surrounding, conflicting value systems between their culture of origin and the larger culture.

- Language differences may cause problems of miscommunication and even misdiagnosis for clients in families.

- Clients from culturally and ethnically diverse families may be less likely to attend counseling and more likely to end therapy early. Therefore, therapists need to be particularly vigilant about reaching out to such clients and ensuring that they are treating them effectively.

- Gender role issues play an increasingly large role in families from all cultures.

- Sexual orientation plays an increasingly large role in families from all cultures.

- Religion, religious values, and spirituality play significant roles in many cultures, and it behooves the effective family therapist to understand the impact religion and spirituality has on the family.

- Families may differ dramatically around a number of key elements, including how the family dresses and value appearances, embraces specific beliefs and attitude, relates to family and significant others, plays and make use of leisure time, learns and uses knowledge, communicates and uses language, embraces certain values and mores, uses time and space, eats and uses food in its customs, and works and applies themselves.

The astute cross-cultural family counselor needs to have the knowledge necessary to work with different kinds of families, the awareness of his or her cultural biases, and the unique skills needed to work with couples and families from diverse backgrounds.

Finally, a quick word about the title of this chapter. You'll notice that the title was "Couples and Family Therapy," not "Marriage and Family Therapy." This is because the term *marriage therapy* excludes all of those thousands of gay and lesbian couples who still cannot become married in this country. Thus, I have used a more inclusive term that is in sync with the American Counseling Association's, American Psychological Association's, and National Association of Social Worker's stands on the normalization of homosexuality. One has to wonder why the AAMFT and IAMFC have continued to use titles that are exclusive of a substantial portion of our population.

EFFICACY OF COUPLES AND FAMILY THERAPY

Research on the effectiveness of couples and family therapy has not been overabundant; however, meta-analyses of the research that has been conducted found some interesting results (Carr, 2004, 2005; Fenell & Weinhold, 2003; Shadish & Baldwin, 2003). Summarizing some of the major findings, this research suggests the following:

- Couples and family therapy seems as effective as individual therapy.
- Couples and family counseling is clearly more effective than no treatment.
- Couples and family therapy is as good, and in some cases better than, other forms of treatment (e.g., individual counseling).
- Although no one approach to couples and family therapy is particularly better than another, there are some approaches that work more effectively with specific problems.
- The ability of the therapist to build a relationship with the family is one of the key factors in successful outcomes.
- Rates of deterioration in couples and family therapy are about the same as those in individual therapy.
- Couples therapy is better than each partner's seeing a clinician separately.
- Brief therapy is as effective as open-ended therapy.
- When fathers are in therapy with the family, treatment outcomes improve.
- Co-therapy does not seem to be more effective than one therapist seeing the family.
- When an individual in a couple or family has been diagnosed as having a severe psychological problem, successful outcomes are less likely.
- Interaction styles of a family and family demographics are not related to outcomes in treatment.

SUMMARY

This chapter began with a brief history of the development of couples and family therapy. We started with a discussion of how Charity Organization Societies and "friendly visitors" were some of the first to view the systemic nature of problems in families and communities. We pointed out that these early approaches to helping the poor led to the development of social casework from a systemic perspective.

We noted that Alfred Adler was one of the first to include the family when treating individuals, although family members were usually in separate rooms from the client. We also noted that the hold psychodynamic approaches had on the individual perspective of doing therapy was strong, and that early family therapy approaches tried to adapt this individual approach to working with the family. We noted that the shift toward family therapy being acceptable was probably related to the impact of those who worked at Palo Alto. It was here that communication in systems was researched, and a number of individuals who worked and consulted at Palo Alto became some of the most well-known family therapists.

The original work at Palo Alto, as well as the subsequent research at MRI, influenced the development of a number of family therapy approaches, including strategic family therapy, structural family therapy, and the human validation process model. At around the same time, other approaches to family therapy evolved, including multigenerational family therapy and experiential family therapy. A few years after MRI was founded, the Brief Family Therapy Center at Palo Alto was formed and became the impetus for the development of solution-focused family therapy. Other approaches to family therapy that later took hold included behavioral and cognitive–behavioral family therapy, and narrative family therapy.

As the chapter continued, a number of important concepts that underlie most approaches to couples and family therapy were examined. These included general systems theory, which examines the unique properties of many systems, including family systems; cybernetics, or control mechanisms in systems, which has been used to explain the regulatory process in systems and includes positive and negative feedback loops; boundaries and information flow in systems; the importance of rules and hierarchy in systems; the development of communication theory in the understanding of interpersonal relations; how individuals are scapegoated and become identified patients; how families deal with stress; developmental milestones through which families typically pass; and an understanding of social constructionism and how some recent family therapists have adopted this new and somewhat different way of understanding the family.

We examined some of the more popular approaches to couples and family therapy in this chapter, including the human validation process model, which was made popular by Virginia Satir; strategic family therapy used by Jay Haley, Cloé Madanes, and the Milan Group; structural family therapy, which was popularized by Salvador Minuchin; multigenerational family therapy, as practiced by Murray Bowen and Ivan Boszormenyi-Nagy; experiential family therapy, as popularized by Augustus Napier and Carl Whitaker; psychodynamic family therapy, such as that offered by Nathan Ackerman and Robin Skynner; behavioral and cognitive–behavioral family therapy; narrative family therapy of White and Epston; and solution-focused family therapy as popularized by Berg, de Shazer, and O'Hanlon.

This chapter examined issues related to multicultural counseling within a family context. It was stressed that family counselors need to understand their own values and biases and the unique worldviews of the families with whom they work. Also, helpers must be able to apply appropriate intervention strategies as a function of the family's cultural background. In addition, it was stressed that family counselors should be aware of a number of unique issues related to families and how they might affect family treatment.

The chapter concluded with a discussion of the efficacy of couples and family therapy, and noted that overall, couples and family therapy seem as efficacious or more efficacious than many other approaches. Other specific issues related to its efficacy were discussed.

KEY WORDS

ambassador

American Association of Marriage and Family Therapy (AAMFT)

behavioral family therapy

boundaries

Brief Family Therapy Center (BFTC)

Charity Organization Societies

cognitive–behavioral family therapy

contextual family therapy

covert rules

communication theory

cybernetics

deconstruct

developmental issues/ milestones

differentiation of self

diffuse boundaries

directives

double-bind theory

Eastern Pennsylvania Psychiatric Institute (EPPI)

exceptions to problems

experiential family therapy

externalize the problem

family life fact chronology

family projection process

family sculpting

friendly visitors

general systems theory

genogram

Haley's Stages of the First Interview

hierarchies

homeostasis

Hull House

human validation process model

idiosyncratic rules

idiosyncratic stress

indebtedness

identified patient

information flow

International Association For Marriage And Family Counselors (IAMFC)

interactional rules

joining

ledger of indebtedness and entitlements

loyalties

mapping

Menninger Clinic

Mental Research Institute (MRI)

Milan Group

multigenerational family therapy

narrative family therapy

narrative reasoning

National Institute of Mental Health (NIMH)

negative feedback loop

nuclear family emotional system

overt rules

paradoxical directive

Philadelphia Child Guidance Clinic

positive feedback loop

post-modernism

preferred outcomes

primary survival triad

problem-free language

problem-saturated
stories

psychodynamic family
therapy

questioning techniques
(solution-focused
therapy)

restructuring

rigid boundaries

rules

scaling

scapegoating

semi-permeable
boundaries

settlement movement

social constructionism

solution-focused family
therapy

strategic therapy

stress

structural family therapy

subsystem

suprasystem

the blamer

the computer

the distracter

the placater

transactional rules

triangulate

undifferentiated ego
mass

universal rules

use of metaphor

KEY NAMES

Ackerman, Nathan

Addams, Jane

Alfred, Adler

Bateson, Gregory

Berg, Insoo Kim

Boszormenyi-Nagy,
Ivan

Bowen, Murray

de Shazer, Steve

Epston, David

Erickson, Milton

Fisch, Dick

Fry, William

Haley, Jay

Jackson, Don

Madanes, Cloé

Minuchin, Salvador

Napier, Augustus

O'Hanlon, Bill

Satir, Virginia

Skynner, Robin

Watzlawick, Paul

Weakland, John

Whitaker, Carl

White, Michael

REFERENCES

Ackerman, N. W. (1958). *The psychodynamics of family life*. New York: Basic Books.

Ackerman, N. W. (1966). *Treating the troubled family*. New York: Basic Books.

Addams, J. (1910). *Twenty years at Hull House*. New York: Macmillan.

American Association of Marriage and Family Therapy. (2009). Directory of MFT licensure and certification boards. Retrieved from http://www.aamft.org/resources/Online_Directories/boardcontacts.asp

Axthelm, P. (1978, December 4). The emperor Jones. *Newsweek*, pp. 54–60.

Barker, P. (2007). *Basic family therapy* (5th ed.). Ames, IO: Blackwell Science Ltd.

Baruth, L. G., & Huber, C. H. (1984). *An introduction to marital theory and therapy*. Pacific Grove, CA: Brooks/Cole.

Becvar, D. S., & Becvar, R. J. (2009). *Family therapy: A systemic integration* (7th ed.). Boston: Allyn & Bacon.

Berg, I. K. (1994). *Family based services: A solution-focused approach.* New York: W. W. Norton.

Bitter, J. R. (2009). *Theory and practice of family therapy and counseling.* Belmont, CA: Brooks/Cole.

Boszormenyi-Nagy, I. (1973). *Invisible loyalties: Reciprocity in intergenerational family therapy.* New York: Harper & Row.

Boszormenyi-Nagy, I. (1987). *Foundations of contextual therapy.* New York: Brunner/Mazel.

Bottome, P. (1957). *Alfred Adler: A portrait from life.* New York: The Vanguard Press.

Bowen, M. (1976). Theory in the practice of psychotherapy. In P. J. Guerin (Ed.), *Family therapy: Theory and practice* (pp. 42–90). New York: Gardner Press.

Bowen, M. (1978). *Family therapy in clinical practice.* New York: Jason Aronson.

Burger, W., & Youkeles, M. (2008). *Human services in contemporary America* (7th ed.). Belmont, CA: Brooks/Cole.

Cade, B. (2007). Springs, streams, and tributaries: A history of the brief, solution-focused approach. In T. S. Nelson & F. N. Thomas (Eds.), *Handbook of solution-focused brief therapy: Clinical applications* (pp. 25–64). New York: The Haworth Press.

Carlson, J. C. (2002). Strategic family therapy. In J. Carlson & D. Kjos (Eds.), *Theories and strategies of family therapy* (pp. 80–97). Boston: Allyn & Bacon.

Carr, A. (2004). Thematic review of family therapy journals in 2003. *Journal of Family Therapy, 26*(4), 430–445.

Carr, A. (2005). Thematic review of family therapy journals in 2004. *Journal of Family Therapy, 27*(4), 399–421.

de Shazer, S. (1982). *Patterns of brief family therapy: An ecosystemic approach.* New York: The Guilford Press.

Fenell, D. L., & Weinhold, B. K. (2003). *Counseling families: An introduction to marriage and family therapy* (3rd ed.). Denver, CO: Love.

Foster, S., & Gurman, A. S. (1985). Family therapies. In S. J. Lynn & J. P. Garske (Eds.), *Contemporary psychotherapies: Models and methods* (pp. 377–418). Columbus, OH: Merrill.

Friedman, M. (1989). Martin Buber and Ivan Boszormenyi-Nagy: The role of dialogue in contextual therapy. *Psychotherapy, 26,* 402–409.

Gladding, S. T. (2007). *Family therapy: History, theory, and practice* (4th ed.). Upper Saddle River, NJ: Merrill.

Goldenberg, H., & Goldenberg, I. (2008). *Family therapy: An overview* (7th ed.). Belmont, CA: Brooks/Cole.

Guerin, P. (1976). Family therapy: The first twenty-five years. In P. J. Guerin (Ed.), *Family therapy: Theory and practice* (pp. 2–23). New York: Gardner Press.

Guerin, P., & Guerin, K. (2002). Bowenian family therapy. In J. Carlson & D. Kjos, *Theories and strategies of family therapy* (pp. 126–157). Boston: Allyn & Bacon.

Haley, J. (1973). *Uncommon therapy.* New York: Norton.

Haley, J. (1976). *Problem-solving therapy.* San Francisco: Jossey-Bass.

Haley, J. (1986). *The power tactics of Jesus Christ and other essays* (2nd ed.). Rockville, MD: Triangle.

Haley, J. (2009). *Jay Haley: The family therapist.* Retrieved from http://www.jay-haley-on-therapy.com/html/family_therapy.html

Hines, P. M., Petro, N. G., McGoldrick, M., Almeida, R., & Weltman, S. (2005). Culture and the family life cycle. In B. Carter & M. McGoldrick (Eds.), *The expanded family life cycle: Individual, family, and social perspectives* (3rd ed., pp. 69–87). Boston: Allyn & Bacon.

Ho, M. K., Rasheed, J. M., & Rasheed, M. N. (2004). *Family therapy and ethnic minorities* (2nd ed.). Thousand Oaks, CA: Sage.

Hull, G. H., & Mather, J. (2006). *Understanding generalist practice with families*. Belmont, CA: Brooks/Cole.

Klever, P. (2004). The multigenerational transmission of nuclear family processes and symptoms. *The American Journal of Family Therapy, 32,* 337–351.

Leiby, J. (1978). *A history of social welfare and social work in the United States*. New York: Columbia University Press.

Madanes, C. (1981). *Strategic family therapy*. San Francisco: Jossey-Bass.

McGoldrick, M. (2005). History, genograms, and the family life cycle: Freud in context. In B. Carter & M. McGoldrick (Eds.), *The expanded family life cycle: Individual, family, and social perspectives* (3rd ed., pp. 47–68). Boston: Allyn & Bacon.

McGoldrick, M., Giordano, J., & Garcia-Preto, N. (2005). *Ethnicity and family therapy* (3rd ed.). New York: Guilford Press.

Mental Research Institute. (2008). *About us*. Retrieved from http://www.mri.org/about_us.html

Minuchin, S. (1974). *Families and family therapy*. Cambridge, MA: Harvard University Press.

Minuchin, S. (1981). *Family therapy techniques*. Cambridge, MA: Harvard University Press.

Napier, G. (2002). Experiential family therapy. In J. Carlson & D. Kjos, *Theories and strategies of family therapy* (pp. 296–316). Boston: Allyn & Bacon.

Napier, A., & Whitaker, C. (1972). A conversation about co-therapy. In A. Ferber, M. Mendelsohn, & A. Napier (Eds.), *The book of family therapy* (pp. 480–506). New York: Jason Aronson.

Napier, A., & Whitaker, C. (1978). *The family crucible*. New York: Harper & Row.

Nichols, M. P., & Schwartz, R. C. (2008). Family therapy: Concepts and methods (8th ed.). Boston: Allyn & Bacon.

Nichols, M. P., & Schwartz, R. C. (2009). *The essentials of family therapy* (4th ed.). Boston: Allyn & Bacon.

Palazzoli, S. M., Boscolo, L., Cecchin, G., & Prata, G. (1978). *Paradox and counterparadox*. New York: Jason Aronson.

Piercy, F. P., Sprenkle, D. H., & Wetchler, J. L. (1996). *Family therapy sourcebook* (2nd ed.). New York: Guilford.

Satir, V. (1967). *Conjoint family therapy*. Palo Alto, CA: Science and Behavior Books.

Satir, V. (1972a). *Peoplemaking*. Palo Alto, CA: Science and Behavior Books.

Satir, V. (1972b). Family systems and approaches to family therapy. In G. D. Erickson & T. P. Hogan (Eds.), *Family therapy: An introduction to theory and technique* (2nd ed., pp. 211–225). Pacific Grove, CA: Brooks/Cole. (Original work published 1967)

Shadish, W. R., & Baldwin, S. A. (2003). Meta-analysis of MFT interventions. *Journal of Marital and Family Therapy, 29*(4), 547–570.

Sherman, R. (1999). Family therapy: The art of integration. In R. E. Watts (Ed.), *Intervention and strategies in counseling and psychotherapy* (pp. 101–134). Philadelphia: Taylor and Francis.

Skynner, A. C. R. (1976). *Systems of marital and family psychotherapy*. New York: Brunner/Mazel.

Skynner, A. C. R. (1981). An open-systems, group-analytic approach to family therapy. In A. S. Gurman & D. P. Kniskern (Eds.), *Handbook of family therapy* (pp. 39–84). New York: Brunner/Mazel.

Tomm, K. (1998). A question of perspectives. *Journal of Marital and Family Therapy, 24*(4), 409–413.

Turner, L. H., & West, R. (2006). *Perspectives on family communication* (3rd ed.). Boston: McGraw-Hill.

von Bertalanffy, L. (1934). *Modern theories of development: An introduction to theoretical biology*. London: Oxford University Press.

von Bertalanffy, L. (1968). *General systems theory*. New York: Braziller.

Wallerstein, J. S., & Blakeslee, S. (1989). *Second chances: Men, women, and children a decade after divorce*. New York: Ticknor & Fields.

Wallerstein, J. S., & Blakeslee, S. (2004). *Second chances: Men, women, and children a decade after divorce* (rev. ed.). New York: Houghton Mifflin.

Watzlawick, Beavin, & Jackson, 1967.

Watzlawick, Weakland, & Fisch, 1974.

Watzlawick, P., Beavin, J. H., & Jackson, D. D. (1967). *Pragmatics of human communication: A study of interactional patterns, pathologies, and paradoxes*. New York: Norton.

Watzlawick, P., Weakland, J. H., & Fisch, R. (1974). *Change; Principles of problem formation and problem resolution*. New York: Norton.

Whitaker, C. (1976). The hindrance of theory in clinical work. In P. J. Guerin (Ed.), *Family therapy* (pp. 154–164). New York: Gardner Press.

White, M. (1995). *Re-authoring lives: Interviews and essays*. Adelaide, South Australia: Dulwich Centre Publications.

White, M., & Epston, D. (1990). *Narrative means to therapeutic ends*. New York: Norton.

Appendix A

Assessment of Your Theoretical and Conceptual Orientations

The following offers you a way to determine which of the 12 theories of counseling (as reflected in Chapters 2–13) and broad conceptual orientations (psychodynamic, existential-humanistic, cognitive-behavioral, post-modern) you are most affiliated. If you prefer, a similar scale that is somewhat more user-friendly can be found at http://www.odu.edu/~eneukrug/therapists/survey.html.

To discover your theoretical and conceptual orientations, read each of the following items and, using the scale below, write in the spaces provided how strongly you feel about each item (write in a 1, 2, 3, 4, or 5).

I Don't Believe This   1   2   3   4   5   I Feel Extremely Certain
Statement at All   That This Statement Is True

_____ 1. Instincts (e.g., hunger, thirst, survival, sex, and aggression) are very strong motivators of behavior.

_____ 2. Psychological symptoms represent a desire to regain repressed parts of ourselves as well as parts of self that have never been revealed to consciousness.

_____ 3. Environmental influences on the child can lead to the development of a neurotic character, but through education and therapy, the person can change.

_____ 4. Children learn behaviors through conditioning (e.g., positive reinforcement, punishment).

_____ 5. We are born with the potential for rational or irrational thinking.

_____ 6. We are born with a predisposition toward certain disorders that could reveal itself under stressful conditions.

_____ 7. We are born with five needs: survival, love and belonging, power, freedom, and fun.

_____ 8. We are born into a world that has no inherent meaning or purpose, and we subsequently create our own meaning and purpose.

_____ 9. An inborn actualizing tendency lends direction toward reaching our full potential.

_____ 10. We are born with the capacity to embrace an infinite number of personality dimensions.

_____ 11. Reality is created through interactions or discussions within one's social circle.

_____ 12. Change can occur in fewer than six sessions. Extended therapy is often detrimental.

_____ 13. Deciding how to satisfy instincts (e.g., hunger, thirst, survival, sex, and aggression) occurs mostly unconsciously.

_____ 14. Revealing unconscious material to consciousness allows for an integrated "whole" person.

_____ 15. We all are striving for perfection in our effort to be whole and complete.

_____ 16. Past and present conditioning makes us who we are.

_____ 17. Irrational thinking leads to emotional distress, dysfunctional behaviors, and criticism of self and others.

_____ 18. By understanding one's cognitive processes (thinking), one can manage and change the way one lives.

_____ 19. We all have a quality world containing mental pictures of the people, things, and beliefs, which are most important in meeting our unique needs.

_____ 20. We all struggle with the basic question of what it is to be human.

_____ 21. Children continually assess whether interactions are positive or negative to their actualizing process or way of living in the world.

_____ 22. The mind, body, and soul operate in unison; they cannot be separated.

_____ 23. Values held by those in power are disseminated through language and become the norms against which we compare ourselves.

_____ 24. Individuals can find exceptions to their problems and build on those exceptions to find new ways of living in the world.

_____ 25. Our personality is framed at a very young age and is quite difficult to change.

_____ 26. Primordial images that we all have interact with repressed material to create psychological complexes (e.g., mother complex; Peter Pan complex).

_____ 27. Children's experiences by age 5 years, and memories of those experiences, are critical factors in personality development.

_____ 28. Behaviors are generally conditioned and learned in very complex and subtle ways.

_____ 29. Although learning and biological factors influence the development of rational or irrational thinking, it is the individual who sustains his or her type of thinking.

_____ 30. Core beliefs (underlying beliefs that map our world) are the basis for a person's feelings, behaviors, and physiological responses.

_____ 31. We can only choose our actions and thoughts; our feelings and our physiology result from those choices.

_____ 32. We are born alone, will die alone and, except for periodic moments when we encounter another person deeply, we live alone.

_____ 33. The "self" has a need to be regarded positively by significant others.

_____ 34. From birth, the individual is in a constant state of self-regulation through a process of need identification and need fulfillment.

_____ 35. Psychopathology (mental disorders) is a social construction. There is no separate reality that supports its existence.

_____ 36. Although many therapies describe structures that affect functioning (e.g., id, ego, self-actualizing tendency), there is no objective reality proving their existence.

_____ 37. The development of defense mechanisms (repression, denial, projection) are ways of managing instincts.

_____ 38. Archetypes, or inherited unconscious primordial images, provide the psyche with its tendency to perceive the world in certain ways that we identify as human.

_____ 39. As children, how we learn to cope with inevitable feelings of inferiority affects our personality development.

_____ 40. Conditioning (e.g., positive reinforcement, punishment) can lead to a multitude of personality characteristics.

_____ 41. When our cognitive processes result in irrational thinking, we tend to have self-defeating emotions and exhibit dysfunctional behaviors.

_____ 42. Genetics, biological factors, and experiences combine to produce specific core beliefs that affect how we behave and feel.

_____ 43. At any point in one's life, one can evaluate one's behaviors, thoughts, feelings, and physiology and make new choices that better meet one's needs.

_____ 44. Meaningfulness, as well as a limited sense of freedom, comes through consciousness and the choices we make.

_____ 45. Because they want to be loved, children will often act in a way in which significant others want them to act instead of acting in a manner that is real or congruent with themselves.

_____ 46. Parental dictates, social mores, and peer norms can prevent a person from attaining satisfaction of a need. This unsatisfied need can affect us in ways of which we are unaware.

_____ 47. Constant discourse and interactions with others within one's social milieu leads to the development of a sense of self.

_____ 48. Language endemic in culture, society, and the individual's social sphere determines the nature of reality.

_____ 49. Because we spend the majority of our time unconsciously struggling to satisfy our unmet needs, happiness is an elusive feeling experienced infrequently.

_____ 50. We are born with the mental functions of sensation–intuition and thinking–feeling, which affect our perceptions. Their relative strengths are affected by how we were raised.

_____ 51. At an early age, we develop a private logic that moves us toward dysfunctional behaviors or towards wholeness.

_____ 52. By carefully analyzing how behaviors are conditioned, one can understand why an individual exhibits his or her current behavioral repertoire.

_____ 53. It is not events that cause negative emotions, but the belief about the events.

_____ 54. We all have automatic thoughts (fleeting thoughts about what we are perceiving and experiencing) that result in a set of behaviors, feelings, and physiological responses.

_____ 55. When language shows caring and the taking of responsibility, good choices are made. When language is blaming, critical, and judgmental, poor choices are made.

_____ 56. We sometimes avoid living authentically and experiencing life fully because we are afraid to look squarely at how we are making meaning in our lives.

_____ 57. Anxiety, and related symptoms, can be conceptualized as a signal to the individual that he or she is acting in a nongenuine way and not living fully.

_____ 58. Breaking free from defenses (e.g., repression) allows one to fully experience the present and live a saner life.

_____ 59. Reality is a social construction, and each person's reality is organized and maintained through his or her narrative and discourse with others.

_____ 60. Pathology, in all practical purposes, does not exist and is not inherently found within the person.

_____ 61. Early child-rearing practices are largely responsible for our personality development.

_____ 62. People are born with a tendency to be either extroverted (e.g., being outgoing) or introverted (e.g., being an observer, looking inward).

_____ 63. Child experiences, and the memories of them, impact each of our unique abilities and characteristics integral to the development of our character or personality.

_____ 64. By identifying what behaviors have been conditioned, one can eliminate undesirable behaviors and set goals to acquire more functional ways of acting.

_____ 65. The depth at which and length of time for which one experiences a self-defeating emotion is related to one's beliefs about an event, not to the event directly.

_____ 66. Automatic thoughts (fleeting thoughts about what we are perceiving) reinforce core beliefs we have about the world.

_____ 67. Needs can only be satisfied in the present, so focusing on how past needs were not met is useless.

_____ 68. People can gain a personally meaningful and authentic existence by making new choices that involve facing life's struggles honestly and directly.

_____ 69. Being around people who are real, empathic, and show positive regard results in the individual's becoming more real.

_____ 70. The ultimate way of living involves allowing oneself access to all of what is available to one's experience. Essentially, Now = Awareness = Reality.

_____ 71. Problems individuals have are a function of their problem-saturated stories or narratives. However, new preferred stories can be generated.

_____ 72. Problems are the result of language passed down by families, culture, and society, and dialogues between people.

SCORING

Scoring I (Psychodynamic Theories): Place the numbers you chose across from the respective item. In each column, add up your score for each theory and divide the total by 30. That will give you the percentage score for that approach. Place your percentage in the parentheses. For the "psychodynamic score," add the total scores from each of the bottom rows, and place it in the far right column. Divide that score by 90, and that will give you the percentage score for psychodynamic therapy. Place that percentage in the parentheses next to *psychodynamic.*

Psychoanalysis ( )	Analytical ( )	Individual Psychology ( )	Score for Psychodynamic ( )
1 _____	2 _____	3 _____	
13 _____	14 _____	15 _____	
25 _____	26 _____	27 _____	
37 _____	38 _____	39 _____	
49 _____	50 _____	51 _____	
61 _____	62 _____	63 _____	
TOTAL: _____	_____	_____	_____

Scoring II (Existential–Humanistic Theories): Place the numbers you chose across from the respective item. In each column, add up your score for each theory and divide the total by 30. That will give you the percentage score for that approach. Place your percentage in the parentheses. For the "existential–humanistic score," add the total scores from each of the bottom rows, and place it in the far right column. Divide that score by 90, and that will give you the percentage score for existential–humanistic therapy. Place that percentage in the parentheses next to *existential–humanistic.*

Existential ( )	Person-Centered ( )	Gestalt ( )	Score for Existential–Humanistic ( )
8 _____	9 _____	10 _____	
20 _____	21 _____	22 _____	
32 _____	33 _____	34 _____	
44 _____	45 _____	46 _____	
56 _____	57 _____	58 _____	
68 _____	69 _____	70 _____	
TOTAL: _____	_____	_____	_____

Scoring III (Cognitive–Behavioral Theories): Place the numbers you chose across from the respective item. In each column, add up your score for each theory and divide the total by 30. That will give you the percentage score for that approach. Place your percentage in the parentheses. For the "cognitive–behavioral score," add the total scores from each of the bottom rows, and place it in the far right column. Divide that score by 120, and that will give you the percentage score for cognitive–behavioral therapy. Place that percentage in the parentheses next to *cognitive–behavioral*.

Behavioral ( )	REBT ( )	Cognitive ( )	Reality Therapy ( )	Score for Cognitive– Behavioral ( )
4 _____	5 _____	6 _____	7 _____	
16 _____	17 _____	18 _____	19 _____	
28 _____	29 _____	30 _____	31 _____	
40 _____	41 _____	42 _____	43 _____	
52 _____	53 _____	54 _____	55 _____	
64 _____	65 _____	66 _____	67 _____	
TOTAL _____	_____	_____	_____	_____

Scoring IV (Post-Modern Theories): Place the numbers you chose across from the respective item. In each column, add up your score for each theory and divide the total by 30. That will give you the percentage score for that approach. Place your percentage in the parentheses. For the "post-modern score," add the total scores from each of the bottom rows, and place it in the far right column. Divide that score by 60, and that will give you the percentage score for post-modern therapy. Place that percentage in the parentheses next to *post-modern*.

Narrative ( )	Solution-Focused ( )	Score for Post-Modern ( )
11 _____	12 _____	
23 _____	24 _____	
35 _____	36 _____	
47 _____	48 _____	
59 _____	60 _____	
71 _____	72 _____	
TOTAL: _____	_____	_____

RESULTS

Your scores represent the percent of items you endorsed in each theoretical area as well as the percent of items you endorsed for the combined theories in a specific conceptual orientation (psychodynamic, existential–humanistic, cognitive–behavioral, and post-modern)

DESCRIPTIONS OF THEORETICAL ORIENTATIONS

Psychoanalysis

Developed by Sigmund Freud, psychoanalysis suggests that instincts, such as hunger, thirst, survival, aggression, and sex, are very strong motivators of behavior. The satisfaction of instincts is mostly an unconscious process, and defense mechanisms are developed to help manage our instincts. Because we are in a constant and mostly unconscious struggle to satisfy our instincts, psychoanalysts believe that happiness is elusive. Early child-rearing practices are responsible for how we manage our defenses and for normal or abnormal personality development. The fact that early childhood experiences forms personality and that our behaviors are mostly dictated by the unconscious lends a sense of determinism to this approach.

Analytical Psychology

Analytical psychology was developed by Carl Jung, who believed that psychological symptoms represent a desire to regain lost parts of self, as well as parts that have never been revealed to consciousness, so that the person can become whole. Analytical therapists believe that we have primitive or primordial images that interact with repressed material to cause "complexes." We inherit these images, or archetypes, and they provide the psyche with its tendency to perceive the world in certain ways that we identify as human. In addition, we are born with the mental functions of sensation–intuition and thinking–feeling, which affect our perceptions and whose relative strengths are affected by child-rearing patterns. We are also born with a tendency to be extroverted (outgoing) or introverted (observer; inward).

Individual Psychology

Developed by Alfred Adler, individual psychology suggests that early childhood experiences, and the memories of those experiences, result in our character or personality. If early experiences, and the memories of them, enhance our innate abilities and characteristics, we will have a tendency to move toward wholeness, completion, and perfection. However, a person's response to early feelings of inferiority can result in the creation of private logic and compensatory behaviors that lead toward maladaptive or neurotic behaviors. Although early experiences influence the development of personality, education and therapy can be effective in helping a person change.

Behavior Therapy

Developed by B. F. Skinner, John Wolpe, Albert Bandura, Ivan Pavlov, and others, behavior therapy is based on classical conditioning, operant conditioning, and social learning (or modeling), which suggest that how individuals are conditioned affects their personality development. Behaviorists believe that conditioning is very complex and can happen in subtle ways. By carefully analyzing how behaviors are conditioned, one can understand why an individual exhibits certain behaviors and develop goals to eliminate undesirable behaviors while reinforcing new desirable behaviors.

Rational Emotive Behavior Therapy (REBT)

Developed by Albert Ellis, REBT suggests that we are born with the potential for rational or irrational thinking, and it is the belief about an event that is responsible for one's reaction to the event, not the event itself. Beliefs about an event can be rational or irrational, with irrational thinking leading to emotional distress, dysfunctional behaviors, and criticism of self and others. Although individuals have a tendency to sustain the type of thinking they previously learned, irrational thinking can be challenged, and individuals can adopt rational thinking if given the opportunity through counseling.

Cognitive Therapy

Developed by Aaron "Tim" Beck, cognitive therapy suggests that we are born with a predisposition toward certain emotional disorders that reveals itself under stressful conditions. Cognitive therapists also believe that genetics, biological factors, and experiences combine to produce specific core beliefs that are responsible for automatic thoughts (fleeting thoughts about what we perceive and experience), which result in a set of behaviors, feelings, and physiological responses. By understanding one's cognitive processes (e.g., core beliefs, automatic thoughts), one can address and change automatic thoughts and core beliefs that lead to dysfunctional behaviors and distressful feelings.

Reality Therapy

Developed by William Glasser, reality therapy suggests that we are born with five needs—survival, love and belonging, power, freedom, and fun—which can only be satisfied in the present. Reality therapists believe that we have a "quality world" that contains pictures in our mind of the people, things, and beliefs, which are most important in meeting our needs. We make choices based on these pictures, although we can only choose actions and thoughts; feelings and our physiology result from those choices. At any point in one's life, one can evaluate one's behaviors, thoughts, feelings, and physiology, and make new choices. Language we use reflects the kinds of choices we have made.

Existential Therapy

Developed by Viktor Frankl, Rollo May, Irvin Yalom, and others, existential therapy states that we are born into a world that has no inherent meaning or purpose, that we all struggle with the basic question of what it is to be human, and that we alone can create our own meaning and purpose. Existential therapists believe that we all have the ability to live authentically and experience fully, but we sometimes avoid such an existence out of our fears of looking squarely at how we are making meaning in our lives. They state that meaningfulness, as well as a limited sense of freedom, comes through consciousness and the choices we make.

Person-Centered Counseling

Carl Rogers founded this approach, which states that we have an inborn actualizing tendency that lends direction to our lives as we attempt to reach our full potential. However, this tendency is sometimes thwarted as individuals act in ways in which significant others want them to act due to the individual's desire to be loved and regarded by those significant others. This results in the creation of an incongruent self. Anxiety and related symptoms are signals that the person is acting in a non-genuine way and not living fully. Being around people who are real, empathic, and who show positive regard can help individuals become real or genuine.

Gestalt Therapy

Founded by Fritz Perls, Gestalt therapy suggests that we are born with the capacity to embrace an infinite number of personality dimensions. With the mind, body, and soul operating in unison, from birth, the individual is in a constant state of need identification and need fulfillment. However, parental dictates, social mores, and peer norms can prevent a person from attaining a need and results in defenses that block the experiencing of needs. Gestalt therapy highlights the importance of accessing one's experience because the "now" of experience = awareness = reality. Experiencing allows one to break free from defenses and live a saner life.

Narrative Therapy

Narrative therapy, developed by Michael White, suggests that reality is a social construction and that each person's reality is organized and maintained through his or her narrative or language discourse. Within this context, values held by those in power are often disseminated through language and become the norms against which individuals compare themselves. Therefore, problems individuals have, including mental disorders, are a function of problem-saturated stories or narratives people have in their lives, and these are created through the individual's social discourse. However, individuals can deconstruct their problem-saturated stories and discover new narratives and re-author their lives.

Solution-Focused Brief Therapy

Steve de Shazer and Insoo Kim Berg, two founders of solution-focused brief therapy, suggested that problems are the result of language passed down by families, culture, and society, and dialogues between people. Therefore, pathology, in all practical purposes, is not inherently found within the person, as is professed by many therapies that describe structures that affect functioning (e.g., id, ego, self-actualizing tendency). Believing there is no objective reality, they suggest that individuals can find exceptions to their problems and build on those exceptions to find new ways of living in the world. They suggest that change can occur in fewer than six sessions and that extended therapy is often detrimental.

DESCRIPTION OF BROAD CONCEPTUAL ORIENTATIONS

Psychodynamic Approaches (psychoanalysis, analytical therapy, and individual psychology)

Developed near the beginning of the twentieth century, but maintaining widespread popularity today, psychodynamic approaches vary considerably but contain some common elements. For instance, they all suggest that an unconscious and a conscious affect the functioning of the person in some deeply personal and "dynamic" ways. They all look at early child-rearing practices as being important in the development of personality. They all believe that examining the past, and the dynamic interaction of the past with conscious and unconscious factors, are important in the therapeutic process. Although these approaches have tended to be long-term, in recent years, some have been adapted and used in relatively brief treatment modality formats.

Cognitive–Behavioral Approaches (behavior therapy, rational emotive behavior therapy (REBT), cognitive therapy, and reality therapy)

Cognitive–behavioral approaches look at how cognitions and/or behaviors affect personality development, behaviors, and emotional states. All of these approaches believe that cognitions and/or behaviors have been learned and can be relearned. They tend to spend a limited amount of time examining the past, as they focus more on how present cognitions and behaviors affect the individual's feelings, thoughts, actions, and physiological responses. They all believe that after identifying problematic behaviors and/or cognitions, one can choose, replace, or reinforce new cognitions and behaviors that result in more effective functioning. These approaches tend to be shorter than the psychodynamic or existential–humanistic approaches.

Existential–Humanistic Approaches (existential therapy, Gestalt therapy, and person-centered counseling)

Loosely based on the philosophies of existentialism and phenomenology, these approaches were particularly prevalent during the latter part of the twentieth century but continue to be widely used today. Existentialism examines the kinds of choices one makes to develop meaning and purpose in life and, from a psychotherapeutic perspective, suggests that people can choose new ways of living at any point in their lives. Phenomenology is the belief that each person's reality is unique and that to understand the person, you must hear how that person has come to make sense of his or her world. These approaches tend to focus on the "here and now" and gently challenge clients to make new choices in their lives. Although generally short-term than the psychodynamic approaches, these therapies tend to be long-term than the cognitive–behavioral approaches.

Post-Modern Approaches (narrative therapy and solution-focused brief therapy)

Narrative therapy and solution-focused brief therapy are recent additions to the therapeutic milieu and are based on the philosophies of social constructionism and post-modernism. Social constructionism suggests that individuals construct meaning in their lives from the discourses they have with others and the language that is used in their culture and society. Post-modernism suggests that all realities should be questioned. Those with this philosophy even doubt many of the basic assumptions of past popular therapies, which suggest that certain structures cause mental health problems (id, ego, superego, core beliefs, lack of internal locus of control, etc.). Rather than harbor on past problems that tend to be embedded in oppressive belief systems, post-modern approaches suggest that clients can find exceptions to their problems and develop creative solutions. Post-modern approaches tend to be short-term therapies, with solution-focused brief therapy being considered a particularly brief approach, sometimes lasting fewer than five sessions.

Appendix B

The Millers

A Therapeutic Journey

BY CHEREE HAMMOND, PH.D.

TABLE OF CONTENTS

INTRODUCTION

In the chapters you are reading, you are learning about key concepts and basic procedures used when providing counseling from a number of different theoretical perspectives. Now you will have an opportunity to see, firsthand, how each of these approaches is applied, by reading the story of how one or more members of the Miller family experiences each of the therapeutic approaches described.

Following the family members through the different therapeutic approaches will give you the advantage of thinking about a client from a number of different perspectives. You will also have an opportunity to think about theory application across generations and how gender and ethnicity may play a role in the lives of your clients. But before you read the case studies, here's some background on the family we call the "Millers."

THE MILLERS

Jake and Angela Miller recently celebrated their fifteenth anniversary with their friends, parents, and children. Jake's father and mother, Ted and Ann, were there, and they brought Jake's sister, Justine. Ted and Ann met in Atlanta and have been married for 42 years. Ted earned a law degree and has worked in corporate law ever since, while Ann worked as a piano teacher until her twins, Jake and Justine, were born. They are now 41.

Angela's parents, Dexter and Evangeline, celebrated with the family. Dexter and Evangeline met at college in California 41 years ago. Dexter, whose parents were from Nigeria, is an English professor at a mid-sized private university. Evangeline worked as a social worker facilitating adoptions. Due in part to her work, Evangeline and Dexter eventually adopted two African American children when Angela was 5: Lillian, who was just an infant, and Markus, who was 2. Angela is their only biological child and is now 40 years old. Lillian is a social worker, married, and has two children. Markus is gay, lives with his partner, Rob, and just left his job as a high school science teacher to pursue his Ph.D. in physics.

Jake and Angela met in graduate school, and today Jake works as a structural engineer and Angela is an art teacher at an elementary school. They have two children, Luke (10) and Celia (7). Recently, Jake has had some bouts with anxiety, which have begun to affect his relationship with his wife and children. The situation has become so difficult that it has placed a strain on Jake and Angela's relationship. In addition, their growing tensions might be contributing to problems their children have experienced at school.

The following offers more specific information about Jake, Angela, Luke, and Celia, which is followed by a genogram of the extended family. The genogram is then followed by highlights of some of the issues the Millers are facing.

Jake Until the age of 10, Jake remembers a happy childhood. From what he could tell, his parents, Ted and Ann, got along well. Ann seemed to have many friends whom she saw often and was active in the community; Ted seemed content in his work. Jake describes his childhood like this: "I don't really remember anything *bad* happening until I was 10. My parents seemed like they had a lot of fun together, they got along well, teased each other—they were affectionate and all that. What stands out for me is how much fun my twin sister,

Justine, and I had when we were kids. We were into everything, climbing on the roof of the house or digging holes under the shed until the floor caved in— that kind of thing. There was nothing that Justine wouldn't try; she was funny, real quick, you know, and so brave. Nothing scared her. That was before the accident. One day, Justine got it in her head that we would take Dad's car out of the garage and park it on the other side of the wooded area across the interstate. It was a joke for April Fool's day. We were only 10, and of course I was scared, but Justine was sure it would be a good trick so before I knew it, we were in the car and I was driving! Justine was laughing; I remember that she had her bare feet curled up under her and, as always, no seatbelt. I guess I didn't look or something 'cause right after I pulled the car out onto the interstate, a semi hit the car and Justine went through the windshield. She was never the same. She was out for a long time and when she finally came out of her coma she had a serious brain injury. She had to learn to talk again and all that. When she did talk … well, she wasn't Justine anymore."

Today, Justine is cared for by her parents and is able to maintain a job at a local fast-food restaurant. However, she continues to have serious cognitive impairment. Although Jake tends to get along with her, he periodically quips at her, telling her he thinks she can do better than she's been doing.

After the accident, Jake began to have problems with anxiety. He had a hard time sleeping through the night and had nightmares. "Things changed a lot at our house. It seemed like no one ever laughed anymore and we didn't *do anything*. Before the accident, my parents would come up with something spontaneous and fun and we would get up and go! But after Justine changed, well, things at the house got real quiet, and I always felt that something bad was going to happen. I was afraid to leave the house sometimes." Jake's parents took him to a psychiatrist briefly to address the nightmares and anxiety, but they did not talk about his feelings together as a family and rarely referred to the accident.

As the years passed, Jake's anxiety lessened and he was only occasionally disturbed by anxiety or nightmares. He seemed to move on with his life and he successfully finished high school, college, and graduate school. He met and married his wife while in graduate school. Soon after he married and had children, he became involved with a national association that advocates for child-safe automobiles, "Just so nothing like what happened to Justine could happen to anyone else again."

Although Jake sounds proud when describing his wife and children, in recent months, he has been struggling with a number of issues. Jake notes, "We've been having problems with Luke. He's fearless, like Justine was—and always into something! He's not bad, just mischievous, but lately he's been getting in trouble at school. A couple of months ago, Luke and Celia were playing in the car and Luke knocked the car out of park. I was mowing the lawn and came around the corner just in time to see the car roll into the street. I felt my chest tighten, I couldn't breathe. I thought I was having a heart attack! Since the incident with the car, I am anxious all the time. I can't sleep, and when I do, I have nightmares. I have been afraid for Angela to take the car and … I guess I've been difficult to deal with."

Since this incident Jake is constantly checking all of the locks, making sure the car is in "park," and always "checking" on the children. He has asked Angela a number of times to home-school the children in order to make sure that they are safe. He is also aware that his relationship with Angela is different: "Angela and I just seem kind of disconnected lately." Jake has noticed that his anxiety has caused him to miss work lately, and he is very concerned he will get a poor performance evaluation.

Angela Angela is feeling at a loss. One afternoon, she confided to the school counselor, "I really don't know what is happening to our family. Jake has just gotten so anxious that it is a full-time job keeping up with all his fears. He gets so angry with me for insisting Celia go to school, and Luke just won't listen to him at all. I feel like I'm a character in one of those really bad movie-of-the-week things. Sometimes I go into the bathroom, turn on the water in the tub and cry. I don't want to live my life this way."

When Angela was growing up, she spent the fall and spring on a university campus and spent summers in Nigeria with her father's family. "I enjoyed spending time with my grandparents," she says, "but somehow I always felt out of place. When I was in Nigeria, my cousins treated me differently because as far as they were concerned I was 'white' and an American, but when I was back in America I was 'black.' But, I really didn't feel 'black' either. In fact, most of the time I felt more like a Nigerian kid than an American. You'd never catch me talking to my parents or teachers the way the kids at school talked to adults!

"No matter where we were, there was always one constant, my role as caretaker. Lillian, my adopted sister, was born with a congenital hip deformity that made walking difficult. It was my job to see to Lillian and make sure she had what she needed. I was never free to just go out and play with the other kids. I always had to stay near Lillian. I felt so trapped when I watched the other children on their bikes or playing chase. That's how I feel now, with Jake's demands; I feel trapped watching everyone else live their lives and still, after all these years, not really knowing who I am."

Luke Luke is 10; he's starting fifth grade this year. Luke has been a vibrant, active little boy since day one. He is curious and bright. His mother, Angela, has delighted in his willingness to try anything. He seems to live life fully and to feel things deeply. His laughter is contagious, but when Luke is angry, he can be difficult to reason with.

Luke's father spends a lot of time trying to rein Luke in. "He's like a wild horse sometimes," he says. "He can be so out of control." Luke doesn't always listen to warnings about safety, like staying out of the car, for instance. If something breaks or someone is hurt, it is often Luke who is at the bottom of it. These incidents make Jake furious. Angela isn't comfortable with the way Jake yells at Luke, and lately, they have been fighting over it.

Celia Celia is 7 and is going to be in the second grade. Her mother explains, "Right away, we could see a difference between the two children. Celia is much more cautious; an observer. She tends to absorb whatever feeling is around her. She gets caught up in Luke's excitement and she likes to join Luke in his adventures and pranks. Celia worries though, and her hesitation sometimes makes Luke angry. A lot of the time, Luke and Celia start out playing together but end up in an argument."

Recently, Celia has had problems with anxiety. What began as a mild resistance to going to school has become a real problem. More and more often, her mother gets a phone call from the school nurse saying that Celia has a stomachache and wants to come home. Angela became really worried when Celia got so anxious one morning about getting on the bus to go on a field trip that she wet her pants.

Genogram and Highlights of Nuclear Family

The following is a genogram of the Miller family as well as a brief listing of some of the major issues facing each family member.

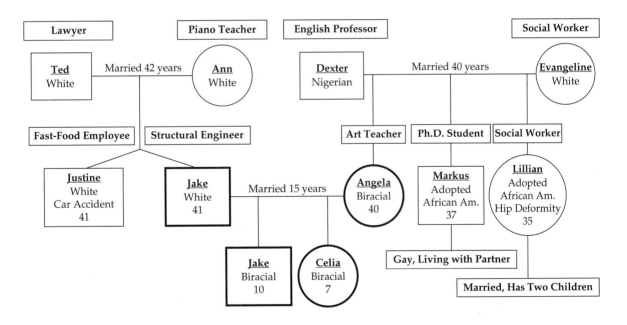

JAKE: At twin sister's (Justine's) prodding, when 10, drove car with her in it into interstate. "Semi" hit car. Caused brain damage for Justine. Remembers "happy" family until the age of 10. Family became solemn after accident. Recent panic attack when car rolled with children in it. Anxiety and sleeplessness since incident. Angry at son frequently. Disconnected from wife.

ANGELA: Feeling at a loss, and doesn't know what to do about problems in the family. Particularly concerned about Celia and Jake. Caretaker. Feels trapped and not happy with life. Not clear who she is. Identity issues around being biracial. Always played the "good" person.

LUKE: Starting fifth grade. Vibrant, curious, bright, a risk-taker, and adventurous. Reminds Jake of twin sister Justine before the accident. Angela likes Luke's personality. Can be funny but also has tendency to lose his temper. Jake tries to rein him in. Differences between Angela's and Jake's parenting is bone of contention.

CELIA: Starting second grade. Cautious, an observer, and absorbs whatever feeling is around her. Often "joins in" with Luke's pranks and adventure. When she doesn't, Luke gets upset. Recently, has been struggling with anxiety manifested by problems at school, such as stomachaches and enuresis. Increasingly becoming school-phobic.

The Miller family isn't really all that unusual. As they say, a little rain must fall into every life. But things have gotten difficult enough for Jake, Angela, Luke, and Celia that counseling might offer them one way of knowing themselves better and be a method for the family to find a sense of renewal while providing a healthier way of living with one another. In the following chapters, you will have an opportunity to see how different theories might be applied to the various members of this family. And, near the end of the book, you will see how a family therapist might work with the Millers. These case studies will allow you to contrast some of the advantages and disadvantages of the different approaches to counseling and psychotherapy, and also give you an opportunity to compare an individualistic approach and a systemic approach to counseling. Enjoy!

JAKE'S EXPERIENCE WITH
A PSYCHOANALYTIC THERAPIST

Dr. Eckman, a short, white-haired man in his early seventies, motions Jake toward a squat, squarish, earth-colored couch perched behind a deeply stained oak coffee table. The corner desk is piled with folders and old books and an array of mismatched coffee mugs. As he takes in the figurines and artwork in the office, Jake notices the surreal quality of the moment, unsure exactly how things had gotten bad enough that he needed therapy. Dr. Eckman has a surprisingly warm and welcoming look as he gestures Jake to sit in on the couch. "I thought I was supposed to lie down on the couch," Jake says in a half-joking voice. Dr. Eckman looks at Jake and, with a soft, trusting voice, says, "You can if you like, but I usually don't work that way. Mostly, I just want you to feel comfortable so we can take a look at what's going on with you. Based on our brief phone conversation, it sounds like you're a bit discouraged, Jake. Can you tell me a little about what has brought you to therapy?"

"I was just wondering that myself." Jake smiles slightly before continuing. "I guess I've always been a bit of a worrier, but things are much worse now.

As I mentioned on the phone, I recently had a panic attack. I'm almost more worried about having another one than I am about something happening to the kids—well, almost. I'm completely powerless when it happens," Jake begins. Jake explains the circumstances around his last panic attack, when Luke and Celia knocked the family car out of gear and were sitting inside as it rolled into the street in front of their house. "When my sister and I were their age, we were messing around in my dad's car and my sister was nearly killed," Jake shakes his head as if to erase the thought from his mind. "I think seeing those kids in the street like that just flipped me out." Dr. Eckman continues to listen as Jake shares, "I know I have been unreasonable at home, but I can't seem to control my fear that something horrible might happen to Angela or the kids. A part of me wishes that Angela and the kids would just stay home, never leave…. I asked Angela to home-school Celia and we had a big fight about it. Part of me knows how unrealistic and unfair that sounds, but the other part really wants it. It just seems like all this anxiety is getting in the way of our relationship."

Despite developing some hypotheses about Jake's situation, initially, Dr. Eckman is concerned about building a relationship with Jake and helping Jake feel comfortable enough to share some of his deepest thoughts and feelings. At the same time, Dr. Eckman is already hypothesizing to himself about Jake's predicament. For instance, he wonders about the unconscious forces that he believes are feeding Jake's anxiety. He considers how Jake's early childhood development shapes the configuration of the structure of personality (the id, ego, and superego), which ends up creating a template for how he deals with relationships throughout his life. Dr. Eckman is particularly interested in how the ego fends off real and perceived anxiety motivated by urges from the id and the demands from the superego.

At the opening of the second session, Dr. Eckman comments, "Jake, you seem to be favoring your right leg. What happened?"

"Oh, that," Jake says, reddening a bit. "That happened in the accident I was in with my sister." Jake swallows and continues, "When the semi hit Dad's car, Justine went through the windshield. The front end of the car was smashed in, and there was some damage to my hip. I broke a couple of ribs, and I had a bad concussion."

"You hadn't mentioned that before. It sounds like it was pretty bad," Dr. Eckman prompts.

"Yeah, I guess, so. I don't ever really talk about what happened to me. It was Justine that really had it bad, you know. She has a brain injury and—well, it was just bad, that's all."

"You had quite a long recovery, and it sounds like you are lucky to be alive," Dr. Eckman probes. "How did you two end up in the car in the first place?"

"Wow, I haven't thought that far back in a long time." Jake's expression grows serious. "Well, you know, Justine was about the bravest girl I ever knew. There was never a challenge that she wasn't ready to tackle. She was incredible. And she was really, really smart, too." Jake's glance drifts to a cluttered corner of the room as he begins to share his memories, almost as if he is talking to himself. "Justine really wanted to play a trick on Dad and take the car and hide it in the woods. As usual, I was scared and tried to talk her out of it, but she was sure it would be really funny. So finally, I caved. I remember she had her bare feet curled up under her in the front seat—the seatbelt hanging loose at her side. I told her to buckle up, but she just laughed at me." Looking up at Dr. Eckman, Jake pauses and says, somewhat taken aback, "Dr. Eckman, you look so sad."

"Jake, I'm just reflecting the sadness I feel from you." Jake swallows and feels the tears rising in his throat, breaking finally in sobs.

As their work continues, Dr. Eckman is able to identify a number of defense mechanisms that have served an important role in Jake's life by staving off anxious feelings emerging from his unconscious. His use of free association, dream analysis, exploration of memories and fantasies, and interpretation and has exposed four primary defense mechanisms: repression, idealization, reaction formation, and denial. Sitting down with Jake's chart, Dr. Eckman begins to make sense of Jake's defensive responding. After the session, he summarizes his understanding of Jake's defenses this way:

Repression: In his sessions, Jake is able to remember his sister's insistence that the two of them take their father's car, including a vivid memory of her sitting next to him moments before the accident. However, as he has been able to recall more of the incident, he has begun to remember that Justine had to bully him into doing the prank in the first place. Jake has gained access to the (id-based) anger and resentment he felt toward Justine directly after the accident for "making him" do the prank and has realized that he repressed this anger because it is in conflict with how he thought he "should" feel (superego: he should feel bad for his sister). Over the years, Jake's repression has not been entirely successful in containing the unacknowledged anger and resentment. It has seeped out in his anxiety and panic attacks, in his dreams, in periodic quips he aims at his sister, and in his sometimes obsessive-compulsive behavior toward making sure that his wife and children are "safe."

Idealization: Jake appears to have had a realistic relationship with his sister prior to the accident. However, since the accident, he has idealized her. He now always speaks highly of her and often refers to the bold and fearless behaviors that she had as a child. He can no longer see her as she was or as she is today. His idealization of her allows him to sidestep his full range of feelings, which include anger, guilt, sadness, and love.

Reaction formation: Jake unconsciously has anger toward his sister for "making" him drive the car. He also feels guilt for being the driver. The guilt is tremendous, given the severity of Justine's injuries and his parents' values for "always doing the right thing" that he has introjected. One way he appears to avoid these unacceptable feelings is by almost *always* being nice to his sister, although once in a while he quips at her (parapraxes!). His idealization of her makes it easier for him to maintain this mask of niceness.

Denial: Although Jake was nearly killed when the semi slammed into his father's car, he has been unable to talk about this aspect of the accident, or even discuss his own extensive injuries. Until now, they have been denied altogether.

Coming so close to death himself, Jake is terrified of death. However, these thoughts, and their associated fears, are now slowly seeping into preconsciousness. His "edginess" toward his wife and his anger toward his "wild" and "impossible-to-control" son are indications that his denial is no longer working for him.

Dr. Eckman believes that all people with healthy egos use defense mechanisms at one time or another; however, he believes that psychopathology develops when defense mechanisms fail to contain anxiety or are used to avoid or distort reality, or when defensive attempts to contain anxiety become self-destructive. By Jake's own admission, his fears have become so exaggerated as to be out of sync with reality. As his defense mechanisms begin to falter, he has exhibited feelings and behaviors, like anger, edginess, and a need to control others, that have deleteriously affected his relationships with his family, particularly his wife and son.

As Dr. Eckman considers the sessions to follow, he will work to illuminate Jake's defense mechanisms and bring Jake's unconscious thoughts and feelings into his conscious awareness. He believes that he must help Jake learn new ways of understanding and containing his anxiety, as the old ways are not working. He and Jake will continue to spend a great deal of time exploring his past and making connections between these early experiences and the ways in which he responds to his family now. Although issues concerning the accident have been highlighted early in therapy, ultimately, Dr. Eckman hopes to uncover earlier relational issues with Jake's parents and others that have served to form the structure of Jake's personality. Dr. Eckman hopes this process will put an end to Jake's demands that Angela stay near the house, his constant reprimanding of Luke, and his recent decision to ask Angela to home-school Celia.

For You to Consider

1. What techniques do you see Dr. Eckman using at the beginning of the relationship?

2. What techniques do you see Dr. Eckman using as the relationship continues and as Jake feels more comfortable sharing deeper thoughts and feelings?

3. Do you see Jake using any other defense mechanisms other than the four that were highlighted?

4. What types of transferences might you expect?

5. From a psychoanalytic perspective, how would you explain Jake's experience of Dr. Eckman's feeling sad and Jake's subsequent sobbing after Dr. Eckman says he's just reflecting Jake's sadness?

6. Are you in touch with any feelings that you might have that could cause countertransference toward Jake? (e.g., irritation, wanting to nurture Jake, feelings of blame toward Jake, a desire to rescue Jake)

7. What do you think the course of treatment will be like?

8. Relative to the course of treatment, how much time do you think Jake will need to discuss his presenting problem versus the time he will take to examine his general personality style as it relates to early child-rearing issues? Explain.

9. How long do you think treatment will last?

10. Do you think that medication might be an effective means of controlling Jake's anxiety while he works on the underlying causes?

11. What cross-cultural factors could affect the analyst's relationship with Jake?

12. From a psychoanalytic perspective, if Jake came to you saying he suddenly decided that he needs to become more religious to rid himself of the sin that he has perpetrated on his sister Justine, what would you think? How might you react?

13. What do you think the prognosis is for Jake?

14. Although psychoanalysis is considered a long-term therapy as compared to many other forms of treatment, do you think there could be short-term gains that Jake might experience in this form of therapy?

15. Do you think it is ethical and professional to work with Jake alone when other members of his family are hurting? What types of treatment might be best for the rest of the family?

ANGELA'S EXPERIENCE IN JUNGIAN THERAPY

Angela immerses her hands in the deep, sudsy water; something about doing dishes by hand seems to help her clear her mind. Lifting a cereal bowl from the bottom of the sink, her thoughts move to family. "I think I feel like I'm falling apart," she says to her brother Markus, who is sitting at the breakfast table sipping on his coffee. "I don't know if you noticed, but it seems like Jake is constantly on a verge of a panic attack or so irritable that he's impossible to talk with."

"I guess I did notice he was a little different," Markus offers, "and what in the world is going on with the kids? How long has Luke been throwing things in the house?"

"I wish I knew. It's been going on for a couple of months. It's so embarrassing. I have the school calling about both kids—Luke's mouth and Celia's stomach!" Angela says, moving the bowl to the drying rack. "Did you hear Jake talking about me home-schooling Celia at breakfast again this morning? I feel so guilty. You know, if I had Celia home, she'd be doing better, but honestly, I think I'd go out of my skull at home all day."

"It's you I'm worried about," Markus offers frankly. "I haven't seen you this blue in a long time. Have you thought of maybe talking to someone? You could go see Dr. Bertram. She helped a lot when I was trying to figure out how to come out to the rest of the family. She's a feminist, but not the kind who criticizes men all the time. I think you'd like her. She's a good sounding board."

As she sits down to meet with Dr. Bertram for the first time, Angela takes in the blends of sage, tan, and beige colors in her office. The soft, steady sound of an air filter draws Angela's eye to a tank holding exotic fish. Floor-to-ceiling windows overlook a small park filled with flowerbeds and flowering trees. Dr. Bertram, a slender woman with sparkling hazel eyes, sits down across from Angela, looks at her warmly, and says, "Tell me what has brought you."

Angela swallows and begins, "Well, doctor, I'm just at my wits' end. You see, my family—we're just not doing well."

"You know, you can call me 'Naomi,' if you like, or 'Dr. Bertram,'" she offers. "Just wanted to give you the option—but tell me about your family."

Before she knows it, the session is nearly at its end, and Angela has opened herself up to Dr. Naomi—the name she has come to call her. With Dr. Naomi's help, Angela has described their struggles in a way that makes more sense even to her. "Dr. Naomi, thank you for listening to me this morning; you really helped me get a new perspective on myself and on Jake, too. I feel some of the sadness I had coming in, lifting a little. I had been feeling so inadequate as a wife and as a mom."

"It seems to me that you and your husband just have different ways of looking at the world. Your empathy and your desire to understand how everyone is feeling—and to take care of them—is an important part of your character." Dr. Naomi continues, "Jake's character is just a bit different. From the way you describe him, he seems more concerned with making sure everything is in order and in taking charge. It sounds like he's less concerned with relationships and more concerned with making sure that Luke is behaving and Celia is less anxious."

Dr. Naomi notices that as their therapy progresses, Angela seems to feel more and more trusting. Soon she is revealing things she has never talked to anyone about. In their last session, she had shared the shame and embarrassment she felt as a child for not being a good enough caretaker for her little sister, Lillian. Today, she seems to be covering some new ground and talking about things she had not given herself permission to think about.

"When I was in college, I always seemed to be taking care of men. My boyfriends always seemed to be guys who needed a lot from me and took a lot, too. Sometimes, they were abusive, and I just took it because I thought they needed me. To be honest, I felt like it was my job to make sure they felt good. I'm sure that's why I started having sex as early as I did. I wasn't ready." Angela sits quietly for a long time and then continues. "I was willing to do anything to make sure they would be okay. I didn't want to hurt their feelings. Sometimes, I think that's why I married Jake. He seemed so willing to take things slowly; so respectful of me and my family. After all, a lot of men wouldn't even look twice at a biracial women—both white and black men. You'd be surprised. But he didn't care at all about that. And, he didn't want to jump in bed with me. He was so, so nice to me and my family. My family has loved him for that. But now, he just seems to want to be in control. His anxiety has certainly gotten the best of him—and of me. I feel like I have to be the 'caretaker' again. On the other hand, I have another part of me—a part that doesn't want to let others tell me what to do."

"You know, Angela, you aren't alone in all this. Lots of people get kind of caught up in one aspect or another of their character. It gets twisted around a bit by bad experiences," Dr. Naomi explains. "What happens is that a strong part of our character can begin to take over where it doesn't need to. We call it a 'complex.' Everyone's models for how to be in the world, say as a man or a woman, a father or a mother, are based on archetypes that have been around forever. Sometimes, when we have bad experiences that relate to that archetype, we develop a complex that ends up getting in the way."

"Maybe I have a 'caretaking complex!'" Angela says.

"That would be a good way to describe it, I think," Dr. Naomi offers, smiling.

"I did have bad experiences around caretaking. My grandmother, and even my parents, were often nasty to me—telling me I wasn't a good child because I didn't take good enough care of my sister. I tried my best—really!"

"Angela, it is clear to me that you took very good care of your sister and you take good care of your family. That's not really in question. This 'caretaking complex' is still such a large part of your 'self.' It leaves you with a lot of guilt for not home-schooling the kids or taking away Jake's anxiety for him."

One afternoon, a couple of months into therapy, Angela comes into Dr. Naomi's office carrying a large canvas of heavy paper and lays it on the coffee table that sits in the middle of the floor. Dr. Naomi leans forward and examines the canvas. "The paper seems to be hand-made. Did you make this?" she asks, noticing the delicate scattering of embedded leaves and petals within the paper's fibers. Angela nods. Depicted on the canvas in pastel is the long, slender figure of a cocoa-skinned woman dressed in a silken gown. The woman is surrounded by countless children in hues ranging from creamy beige to mustards to red clay to a spectrum of browns. Also depicted is the figure of a man placed among the children. The woman towers over the children and the male figure. "I had a dream, Dr. Naomi, and when I woke up, I had to draw it. When I was in college I used to draw and paint, and even made paper. I haven't had time to do that in years. This canvas is one I made before Jake and I were married. I used plants from my grandparents' home in Nigeria to dye the paper and used them to add texture."

"Tell me about the dream," Dr. Naomi invites, still examining the canvas.

"In my dream, I was married to Jake and we had adopted, like, a dozen children. They were all of different ethnicities—white, black, Asian, and more. They seemed to be everywhere and they were making a lot of noise. They clearly wanted to be taken care of. Of course, they reminded me a little of my upbringing, with me being lighter-skinned, my brother and sister being black, my father being Nigerian, and my mom being white. Anyway, they were making all this noise, but I was very tall, and the noise was just in the distance. I was dressed in that silken gown I drew—kind of sensual—you could see the trees and the grass and the sky reflected in it. Jake was much smaller than me, but taller than the kids. I looked at him, and said, with this deep, strong voice: 'Well, Jake, aren't you going to take care of the kids?' And, in the dream—I couldn't believe it—he said: 'Yes, dear, of course I am.' I was so powerful!"

"So, in this dream, it's kind of like a different you?" prompts Dr. Naomi.

"I think this is another side of me; a side in which I was not the caretaker. A side that is strong and powerful. It reminded me of some men I have known, but in the dream I was still definitely a woman. I felt beautiful and sexy in the dream, but I was also strong. I woke up from that dream and felt like I could do anything."

"You seem to be getting in touch with your 'shadow' and your 'animus.' You are beginning to see that there are many parts of you. In your dream, you seem to be ready to embrace these parts," Dr. Naomi suggests.

As the weeks pass, Dr. Naomi believes Angela has made great strides in her Jungian analysis, and she looks forward to continuing her therapy with her. Angela has grown stronger emotionally, and has started to have an intense curiosity about finding new parts of herself during their sessions. Angela has become more comfortable exploring her fantasies and dreams in therapy and has been able to connect these to parts of herself that she had repressed. As she continues in her therapy, Angela's artwork has become more important to her. "I cleared out a guest room at the rear of the house," she says. "Jake helped me move the furniture and the kids helped me paint the walls. We transformed it into a small art studio. I never thought I would have a studio of my own, and now I do."

One afternoon, Angela is talking to Markus about Dr. Naomi. "She says that therapy can sometimes last for years. I trust her opinion, but slowly I'm trusting my opinion more and more. We'll see how long this takes—and where it takes me!"

For You to Consider

1. Can you identify Angela's "psychological type?" What behaviors give you insight into the type that you think she is?

2. Can you identify Jake's "psychological type?" What behaviors give you insight into the type that you think he is?

3. How often do you think differences in psychological type cause problems in relationships? Do you think that if two people have similar psychological types they would be more likely to get along?

4. Can you identify how Angela's caretaking complex was formed?

5. Do you think there may be other hidden meanings to Angela's dream? Based on your understanding of Angela, what else might you get out of the dream?

6. Do you think it's inevitable that one has a persona, shadow, animus or anima, and a self? What evidence is there that these exist? What about a personal unconscious and collective unconscious?

7. Jung often talked about the first half and second half of a person's life, and said that in the second half, particular emphasis can be placed on understanding the personal unconscious and the collective unconscious. Psychologically, do you think Angela is in her first or second half of life?

8. Ultimately, where do you think therapy will take Angela? Do you think if she "grows" in therapy that she might ultimately grow away from Jake? What implications does this have for her and her family?

9. Jung had a strong belief in finding the opposite side of self. Although he had what today would be considered an outdated view on homosexuality, do you think that we all may have another side to our sexuality? For instance, do you think if we're "gay" we have a "straight" side" and if we're "straight" we have a "gay" side?

10. What is your guess about how long Angela would need to be in therapy?

JAKE IN ADLERIAN THERAPY

As Jake sits behind the wheel of his SUV and watches his children disappear into the front entrance of East Elementary, he is aware of a nagging sense of dread. "I just know something is going to happen to those kids. Why won't Angela just teach them at home? It doesn't make any sense!" His heart begins to pound. Jake takes some deep breaths, checks the rearview mirror, and pulls out of the parking lot, feeling helpless and guilty somehow. Jake's life has become consumed by his anxiety. Lately, he has felt on the verge of panic, constantly distracted by fantasies of potential catastrophe and ways to prevent disaster. Though his relationship with Angela and his children, Luke and Celia, had once been a source of connectedness, satisfaction and pride, he finds himself completely distracted by what he feels sure are irrational fears.

Ken Roberts, an Adlerian counselor, a stout man in his mid-forties, offers Jake a seat. The room is warm and reminds Jake of his parents' house, with its wood paneling and orange shag carpet that has seen better days. "I haven't been able to get the landlord to change that carpet, but I'm working on it," Ken says, noticing Jake's gaze. "Why don't you tell me a little about why you are here, Jake."

"Sure—well—um," Jake stumbles, "I was dropping the kids off at school a couple of days ago, and as they were walking into the building, I just started to worry about all the things that could happen to them, especially Celia. I think about that a lot; it has been really distracting me lately. Well, as I watched them go into the building, I felt my breathing get faster and faster and my heart was pounding like crazy." Jake catches his breath and continues, "The cars behind me started to honk, and I felt really confused. I stepped on the gas and a kid ran out in front of me! I stopped in time and the kid wasn't hurt but … I just think this is getting out of hand. I felt a little like that this morning before I came here, you know, a little panicked when the kids went to school. Anyway, that was the morning I decided I had to talk to someone, so I called you."

"Sounds like nearly hitting that kid in the parking lot was the last straw. This anxiety about your kids seems to have you by the throat," Ken replies.

"That's exactly what it's like, as if someone has his hands around my throat all the time! Is this something that you can fix, Dr. Roberts? I've had anxiety problems before, this time I want them gone for good."

"Jake, I think this is something we can work on together; it is certainly something you can get a handle on and move on to another chapter in your life," Ken reassures. "I think a good place to start might be to find out a bit more about you. I wonder if you would be willing to take this home." Ken hands Jake a packet. "It is a 'lifestyle assessment.' If you don't mind, fill it out and bring it with you next time so we can talk about it."

Ken is just beginning his work with Jake and is in the first phase of the relationship: building the therapeutic relationship. To build the relationship, he has used most of the skills important at this phase, including showing empathy and being nonjudgmental, respectful, optimistic, and egalitarian. He is also preparing Jake for the next phase: assessing and understanding the lifestyle.

When Jake returns the next week, he has the packet with him. He places it on the coffee table. "You should have warned me about that thing. It really got me thinking about my family and my childhood," Jake says, easing into a frayed brown chair. "And, it took a long time," Jake says in a somewhat irritated voice.

"I guess you were caught off-guard by this homework. I'm curious about what this activity brought up for you," Ken begins.

"Thinking back to when I was a kid kind of threw me. I think a lot about my sister's accident and even talked to a counselor once about it. She had a brain injury when we were young. But I hadn't thought a lot about much of anything in my childhood and what was surprising was all the memories it brought back. I was really surprised when I realized … this is going to sound funny … how distant our folks were from us before the accident. Justine and I just had our own world with no one else in it. And after the accident, I felt really alone. In a way, I lost a lot from that accident, just as Justine did, really. It's really confusing. I felt so angry, so scared, and so guilty all at once, you know."

"I hear all the strong feelings you had both before and after the accident," Ken says. "Sounds like you had a special relationship with Justine, and the accident really impacted you in many ways. I also see that you had listed some traits for yourself and some for your sister Justine on the assessment. I noticed that you have put both 'helpless' and 'brave' for Justine, and 'fearful' and 'responsible' for yourself. Can you tell me a little more about that?" Ken asks, handing Jake the packet he had filled out the week before.

"That sounds contradictory, I know, but Justine was really brave when we were kids, to the point of being reckless, actually. But, like I said, she isn't really independent anymore since that accident, so she is also 'helpless.' On the other hand, I guess I started out being kind of scared all the time when we were kids—I mean, before the accident. I guess I have my fears now, too. But I'm responsible."

"When you say *responsible*, what does that word mean to you?" Ken asks.

"You know! Guilty, the cause of Justine's injuries," Jake says, sounding vaguely irritated.

"I guess I asked, Jake, because that's a word that can mean accountable, like you said, or it can mean someone who is conscientious or trustworthy, or even the person who is expected to deal with problems," Ken offers.

"You know, that's about the size of it. I felt guilty and responsible and now I feel like I have to take responsibility to see that nothing bad ever happens again," Jake says. "Sometimes, that need to keep control over everything pushes me so much it gets in the way of everything else."

In his work with Jake, Ken is hypothesizing that Jake has tried to compensate for his early fears and feelings of inferiority through a need to control others. He can see how he has developed his own private logic that tells him that if he could only be in control, nothing bad will happen. This private logic has led to a subjective final goal of wanting to be the perfect protector. It is at this point that Ken points out to Jake that his efforts to protect his family by controlling them are not working for him. His anxiety and panic attacks have Jake and his family in a virtual prison of fear.

When Jake enters Ken's office for his next appointment, he pauses a moment before taking a deep breath and sitting down. "You seem really wiped out, Jake, what's up?" asks Ken.

"I didn't sleep well last night," Jake begins. "Well, yesterday at dinner everything seemed fine, when all the sudden I found myself in the middle of another argument with Angela. I had been bossing her around and telling her how she ought to be doing something—I can't really remember what it was. Luke started acting out, so I yelled at him and sent him to his room. Angela and I have been fighting a lot lately, but there was something about this fight—I don't know, I just couldn't sleep."

"You found yourself in the same old pattern of fighting with Angela, but there was something that struck you about it that you just can't put your finger on. Jake, do you remember what you were feeling before the fight began?" Ken asks curiously.

"Well, now that you mention it, I remember before dinner Angela had said that it might not be a good idea for me to go to this conference I was thinking of going to. She said that I seemed really stressed lately, and she thought I should take some vacation time to rest and just let someone else at the office go to the conference. I was irritated but I also thought she was right. After all, I can't go to Los Angeles and have a panic attack, can I? I felt so worthless."

"What did it remind you of?" Ken probes.

"In the moment, I don't know if it reminded me of anything, but now that you mention it, it was just like when Justine would talk to me in a way when she knew that I wasn't up to the challenge—or worse yet, that I was scared and she wasn't. I don't know if this makes sense, but it seems like every time I start to feel inferior, I take it out on Angela. It's kind of interesting—I act that way toward my mother and other women, too."

Jake has moved successfully into the third phase, insight and interpretation. Ken feels that by exploring dreams, early memories, and Jake's family constellation, Jake will become more aware of the childhood feelings of inferiority he had toward his more outgoing and daring sister. Ken hopes that as Jake begins to realize that he is compensating for his feelings of inferiority with his attempts at controlling others, particularly women such as his wife, he will want to change his behaviors.

It is nearing the end of their weekly session, and Ken and Jake sit together for some time before Jake breaks the silence. "If only I had just said 'no!' I could have stopped the whole accident from happening. I can't let something like that happen to my wife or kids. I have to put my foot down, especially with Luke."

"It sounds to me that you think that it is somehow possible for you to prevent all possible disasters if you can just perfect your job as the protector. I'm not sure that it is really possible for anyone to have that much power over the universe," Ken offers.

"I guess I didn't realize how much of a problem trying to protect her and the kids had gotten to be in my marriage and with my family," Jake says, sounding surprised. "I came in here thinking my problem was my anxiety, but it's my marriage and how I treat my kids, too. I'm afraid I'm going to lose my wife and that my kids will hate me."

"Jake, what if you tried doing something different when you started to feel inferior or worthless, something other than acting superior to Angela or trying to control the kids?"

"I don't know if I can do anything different. I've been doing this so long." Jake sighs, sounding defeated.

"I'll tell you what, Jake, sometimes we don't have to know how to do things differently—sometimes just acting as if we do paves the way to making changes," Ken offers.

"You mean like *fake it till you make it*?" Jake asks.

Ken laughs. "Yep, that's a good way to describe it. Jake, there is something else we can try, too. We could do some role-playing; that would give you a chance to try out doing things differently without worrying about making mistakes. If you like, we could start next week," Ken offers.

As Jake's awareness and understanding has grown, Ken has encouraged him to begin to make changes in his life. As they enter the fourth phase, reeducation and reorientation, Ken challenges him to try to respond differently at home with his wife and children. Ken "spits in Jake's soup" by pointing out how his attempt to control his wife's behavior ends up distancing her—something Jake clearly does not want. As they work together, Ken believes Jake will be able to transform his deeply entrenched style of living. Ultimately, Jake is encouraged to try new, more effective ways of communicating with his wife and children and to let go of his attempts to control their behavior. Ken feels that by encouraging Jake to "act as if" he is a person who can communicate effectively and can allow his wife and children to have their own identities, Jake can begin to let go of his old style of life and adopt a new, healthier one.

"You look like you are bursting with something," Ken comments as Jake takes a seat. Jake hands him an opened envelope and motions for him to open it. Ken skims the letter. "Well, congratulations, Jake. I'm not sure what all this means, but it looks exciting."

"A couple of weeks ago, I got an e-mail. It was my boss asking me if I would be interested in sitting on a new committee for the National Association for Child Safety. They were looking for an engineer to consult on some of their upcoming initiatives. At first, I thought it must be some kind of mass e-mail. It looked really interesting, but I just didn't think it was something I could do. But then I remembered what you said about acting as if I could. I talked to my boss and he said he thought of me for the committee right away. I was really not sure I was up to it, but I filled out the application anyway. Well, they called me and I'll tell you—at first, I felt really intimidated, but I remembered how we had practiced in those role-plays about being confident and persuasive, but not bossy—it must have worked. I got this letter this morning. I'm going to be part of something that might really make a difference to my kids' safety and to the safety of others. I can't wait!" Jake is grinning from ear to ear.

"I've noticed some changes with Angela, too. I've been trying to listen to her, and I do my best to control my temper when I start to get that inferiority feeling coming over me. I'm not sure Angela has noticed, but we haven't been fighting as much. It's been nice," Jake says with a look of relief. "I am also trying to let go of controlling everything my kids do. I actually let them play out in the yard the other day—and I wasn't even watching them—well, hardly watching, at least.

Ken is excited for Jake; he believes that Jake has made a lot of progress in a short amount of time. He is beginning to try to act differently with Angela by improving his communication skills and not using a controlling tone with her. He has begun to let go of his need to watch over his kids every minute of the day. And he has become active in a program that will benefit both his kids and the larger community. His letting go of his narcissistic need to control has allowed him to begin to see outside of himself. His anxiety is no longer controlling him, and he is a calmer person—both calmer for himself and calmer with others. Ken believes that Jake is on his way to feeling whole and to gaining a sense of purpose in life as he focuses on and develops this new style of life, which is more in line with who he really is rather than a reaction to his early feelings of inferiority.

For You to Consider

1. How did Dr. Roberts change the focus of Jake's problems?

2. What was the purpose of the lifestyle assessment?

3. What early experiences and early memories have combined to develop Jake's current style of life?

4. How has Jake compensated for his early feelings of inferiority?

5. What kind of subjective final goal has Jake developed, and how has his private logic supported this goal?

6. Why is Jake's current style of life dysfunctional?

7. Do you believe Jake's career choice and his decision to become involved with the National Association for Child Safety is a function of his subjective final goal? Why or why not?

8. What stumbling blocks might you foresee occurring with Jake as he goes through the therapeutic process using this approach?

9. Using Jake as an example, make an argument for why this type of therapy could be considered psychodynamic, existential–humanistic, or constructivist.

10. Adlerian therapy has often been applied with children. Using Celia or Luke as examples, from an Adlerian framework, respond to the following questions if you were to see them in therapy.

    a. How might you gain their trust?

    b. What techniques would you use to gather information from them?

    c. Given the information you already have from the introduction to the family, what clues do you have to their developing lifestyles?

    d. How might you help these children gain insight into their behavior?

    e. In what ways are Celia's anxiety and Luke's reluctance to listen a function of the family dynamics? How do these behaviors work for them? How are the dysfunctional?

    f. How might you help each child develop healthier ways of being?

11. Do you see any advantages to all members of the family getting together and discussing their issues? Why or why not?

12. How might the process of working with Angela differ from that of working with Jake?

13. Come up with some possible thoughts on how issues of ethnicity and culture might affect this family's relationships with one another.

14. Can you identify your style of life and some of the memories and experiences you have that have gone into creating it?

JAKE MEETS AN EXISTENTIAL THERAPIST

Jake feels his world falling apart around him. As he grabs the front doorknob, he flinches at the absolute quiet of the house. Once filled with the noise of Luke's antics and decorated with Celia's dolls and stuffed bears, the house is barren, silent, and empty. At work, Jake has been dragging himself around his office half-dazed since Angela took the kids to Philadelphia for the summer to stay with her sister Lillian while she recovered from hip surgery due to her congenital hip problem. Jason, a colleague, thought it would be a good idea for Jake to go and talk to someone, Mr. Landes, but Jake hasn't realized how much Angela's leaving has affected him until this morning. It seems like the world he has worked so hard to hold together is shattered in pieces around him.

"He looks awfully young," Jake thinks to himself as he shakes Mr. Landes's extended hand.

"Hey, call me 'Chris.' Just take a seat anywhere," Chris offers, motioning Jake inside. Jake looks around the office, a hodgepodge of mismatched furniture and odd-looking art. "You look kind of distraught, Jake. What's going on? Your message said something about your wife leaving?" Jake realizes he is wearing yesterday's rumpled shirt, and he'd neglected to run a comb through his hair before leaving the house.

Jake, feeling somewhat unsure about Chris, but also out of options, takes a deep breath and begins, "I've been married 15 years; her name is Angela. We have two great kids, Luke and Celia. I love Angela a lot, and I think she loves me too, but for the last year we've been having problems. Angela just doesn't seem to understand that it is important that we keep our kids out of harm's way. There is too much at stake! I know, I've seen what can happen when kids make one foolish choice—it can affect their whole lives." Jake goes on to explain about the panic attack he had when Luke and Celia rolled the family car into the street. "Angela should have been watching the kids! That never should have happened." Jake's voice rises and then falls again as he explains how that experience had reminded him of what had happened to his sister, Justine, when they were children. "You know, it still makes me a little sick to think about Justine in her coma. I was pretty banged up myself, and my parents had to roll me in a wheelchair to see Justine; she was laying there with all those tubes and casts … and black and blue. I realized, *that could have been me*. It didn't make any sense that she was laying there practically dead and I was going to be okay," Jake says, looking off into the distance as if he can see the whole scene playing out in front of his eyes. "You know, she never was the same; her whole life has just been a waste, no point, nothing."

"Jake, how have you made sense of what happened to Justine?" Chris asks.

"It doesn't make sense, at least none that I can see. She's like the walking dead. She doesn't have any real purpose, no one in her life, and nothing to do but put burgers on a bun, wrap them up and hand them to customers. All she cares about is making the perfect burger." Jake's voice betrays a building anger; he clenches and unclenches his fist and looks out the window at the tall unkempt grass blowing gently in the breeze.

"I guess I see it a little differently," Chris begins cautiously. "It seems to me that Justine has made something out of her life. It seems like she gets pleasure from doing her work and doing it well. And it seems like you are also trying to make something out of your life and that your meaning comes from doing what you can to keep your family safe, but somehow that hasn't been satisfying to you; it seems that the harder you try, the more anxious you feel."

Chris, taking an existentialist perspective, thinks of therapy as more or less unfolding in eight phases. In his first meeting with Jake, he has been able to make *contact* with Jake, he's made good progress in *understanding* how Jake experiences the world, and he's made some first steps into *education and integration*, Phases I, II, and III, respectively. He believes that by offering Jake his empathy and understanding, they can build a strong therapeutic relationship, something he believes is the essence of what makes existential therapy effective. Chris understands that for Jake, the world is unpredictable and dangerous, and requires his vigilant attention. On one level, Chris agrees with Jake: The world is full of unknowns, and it seems tragedy does seem to find its way into every life. Chris, however, believes that life's difficulties offer opportunities to make choices about how to respond. He believes that each of us has the choice to respond with courage and authenticity or to respond in fear and avoidance.

As therapy continues, Chris continues to educate Jake about the basics of the existential philosophy that underlies existential therapy. He makes some suggestions about what Jake might read (Jake promises to dust off his copy of *Man's Search for Meaning*—"I remember reading that when I was in college; it's still on my bookshelf."). In the coming weeks, Chris continues to build their therapeutic relationship, hoping to create an I–Thou connection with Jake in which each of them can connect to one another authentically. As therapy moves into Phase IV, *awareness*, Chris begins to challenge Jake to see how his choices to avoid facing the existential angst inherent in living and in knowing that we are eventually going to die are actually creating his panic. In other words, he hopes that Jake will understand that by avoiding the acknowledgment of these fears he has developed neurotic behaviors that have driven a wedge between him and the rest of his family.

Borrowing a technique from solution-focused therapy that Chris thinks fits nicely into the existential framework, Chris asks: "Jake, if you were to wake up in the morning and realize that something has happened as you slept, some change has come over you—as you opened your eyes, you realize you have adopted a whole new way of being in the world … What would that look like?"

"A whole new way of being—hmm, good question." Jake looks thoughtful for a moment. "Well, the first thing I think I'd do is make love to my wife. Instead of starting the day with my list of worries and nagging her about what to do and not do with the kids, I would just want to be there with her." Jake thinks a moment and then says, "If I really had a whole new way of being, like you said, I think I would really be so different. I wouldn't be waiting for something terrible to happen or trying to devise ways to avoid disaster. I think the thing that would be most different would be that I would *do something*, just make a decision about something and do it. Maybe I'd take Luke up to the state park and go hiking; he's always asking me if we can do that."

As Chris works with Jake, he hopes he will be able to help Jake understand and become accepting of how his avoidance of dealing with his "existential angst" has prevented him from living authentically, making choices in his relationships, and taking responsibility for his actions. Chris realizes the importance of remaining empathic to Jake's experiencing while still challenging him to gain greater *self-acceptance*, Phase V in Jake's progress toward meaning and change.

"So I guess one of the first things that would be different in life, if you had a whole new way of being in the world, would be that you would be closer to Angela and to your kids, especially Luke?" Chris asks.

"Yeah, that's right," Jake says, "I guess I can really see how my crazy need to keep everyone safe and close to me has driven my wife away. It is really hard to hear myself say that, but I think it's true. Angela didn't really have a choice; she had to get away. I think I was driving her up the wall!" Jake sighs deeply.

"I guess there is an upside to all of this. At least now I know, now I understand, that I have some choice in how I deal with my fears and how I relate to Angela and the kids. If she comes back, I think I can turn this around."

"And if she doesn't?" Chris asks.

"Well, Chris, I don't know; maybe she won't. I would hate that, but you know, at least now I can go into whatever happens with my eyes open, knowing that I have choices about how I deal with our problems."

Chris realizes Jake is moving into Phase VI, *responsibility*, when Jake begins the session by saying, "I've had a rough couple of days, Chris. You know, when we talked last week, I thought it was all coming together for me. I was thinking, 'Okay, yeah, I have choices here. I can decide how I want to be in the world. All I have to do is choose.' That felt pretty good, but then I started to think about what that meant."

Chris prompts Jake to go on.

"You know," Jake continues, "I realized that if I have choices, well, then, it is up to me to do the choosing. That feels like a real burden. I mean, even if Angela does come back, I still have to depend on myself to decide what my life means and to shape it into something I can be proud of."

Jake has begun to think more deeply about the relationship between his choice to live in a world mastered by his anxiety or to master his anxiety by being more fully in a world that is not always easy to live in. Together with Chris, Jake is able to explore what this freedom means to him and what kind of life he would like to build for himself. Chris and Jake are now in Phase VII, *choice and freedom*, of their therapeutic journey. One afternoon, Jake comes to the office excited: "Last Monday, I was lying in bed looking up at the blackness of the ceiling, and it felt like a weight pressing down on me. I started to feel myself getting more and more anxious about it when something you said several weeks ago popped into my head: 'Everyone dies sometime, there isn't really anything I or anyone else can do about it.'" Jake explains to Chris, "The strange thing was that somehow, that was comforting. I realized that all the efforts I had put into trying to control something that can't be controlled had been such a waste."

"Something seemed to change for you by really understanding that death is inevitable. So, what sense have you made of that?" Chris asks, curious.

"Well, I decided to just get out of bed to read some of that other book you suggested," Jake offers.

"You mean the Sartre?" Chris clarifies.

"Yeah, the Sartre. I had ordered it a couple of weeks ago but hadn't opened it yet. Anyway, I came across this passage where he said something like *it is death that gives life meaning*. That shifted everything in my head somehow. I was thinking that maybe that was true; maybe because we do die we have to make the most of every day."

"So you were caught up in those old familiar feelings of anxiety and thoughts about death when you decided at some level to take a turn, just try it a different way. Instead of getting more and more upset, you decided to get out of bed and read Sartre; have I got that right?"

Jake nods.

"I'm really impressed that you were able to make that shift, Jake."

Jake looks at Chris shyly. "So, do you want to know what I did?"

Chris smiles.

"Well, I took the rest of the week off of work, and I flew to Philadelphia. I know it sounds a little crazy, but when I got there, I rented a car and took Luke, Celia, and Lillian's two kids to a theme park a couple of hours away."

"That was spontaneous; you just had the feeling you needed to be with your family and went! What happened between you and Angela?" Chris asks.

"She was surprised, I can tell you that! When Luke told her I took the kids on the roller-coasters, her jaw dropped open. After the kids were in bed, she and I went for a long walk. In some ways, it was like the old days. It was so nice to have her close to me again," Jake says, gazing out the window. "I told her I've been working on trying to be different in my life. I told her I was tired of being afraid to live." Jake pauses. "You know, I felt completely different about myself, too. I had an excited feeling about being so spontaneous; that was new, but the feeling that really surprised me was the feeling I had about myself. I felt real and solid. I felt like I knew who I was and why I was in the world. I think before I always had this feeling that anxiety was holding me together, like I might break into really tiny pieces and get blown away in the slightest breeze. I don't feel that now. And one other thing—you know, I had this other funny thought also. I was thinking about going back to church. Not the same church I went to before, one in which I could just go and find some inner solace and peace. Someplace where I can reflect on my life and its meaning and God. I'm not sure where I'm going with this, but I know it's something I want to pursue."

In the following weeks, Jake and Chris move into Phase VIII of the therapeutic process, *separation*. Jake has begun to understand his values, is starting to see where he draws meaning for his life, and feels he has some clarity on the ways in which he can get sucked into avoiding meaning and the importance of being real and taking responsibility for how he will relate to others. When Jake is ready to end therapy with Chris, he admits, "I'm still not sure how things will work out between Angela and me, but I know that I can choose to continue to do things that drive her away from me and move me further and further from living the life I want to live, or I can be real with her and with myself. I can choose every morning when I step out of bed how I want to be in the world.... I guess I do make that choice every morning!"

For You to Consider

1. Early in therapy, Chris explains to Jake the paradox of the world he lives in by saying, "It seems that the harder you try, the more anxious you feel." How does focusing on symptoms result in maintaining neurotic ways of being in the world?

2. In his work with Jake, how effective do you think it would have been if Chris had used "paradoxical intention" by asking him to try and be even more vigilant about assuring his and his family's safety?

3. In Phase I of Jake's therapy, Chris broaches the topic of Justine's work and how that helps put a sense of meaning in her life. If you were Jake's existential therapist, how might you explore this further with Jake? Do you think Jake might be able to learn something from Justine?

4. In Phase III, Chris begins to educate Jake about existential philosophy. How comfortable are you with teaching a philosophy to your client? What methods might you use to explain the basic tenets to your client?

5. How comfortable would you have felt if Chris decided to share some of his own struggles in life as an example of how life is often riddled with conflicts and struggles, and as a mechanism to show how one has to constantly make choices in dealing with these difficulties? How comfortable would you be sharing some of your struggles in life with a client?

6. The chapter lists a number of ways in which people avoid taking responsibility in their lives, including compulsivity, displacement, playing the victim, losing control, avoiding autonomy, willing-denial, and physical disease. Which of these methods has Jake used? Explain.

7. Do you think Jake would have been as motivated to change if Angela had not left for Philadelphia? What do you think the relationship is between external factors and the internal change process?

8. What do you think of Jake's possible newfound embracing of religion? Do you think he can be avoiding something through his religion? How do you believe his new faith experience will be different from how he once viewed faith?

9. Do you think Angela could benefit from existential therapy? In what ways has Angela been living inauthentically? What symptoms does Angela use to avoid her existential angst? How might you help Angela gain insight into the ways she has avoided making choices about how to be in the world?

10. How do you feel about making use of books, movies, poetry, and music to help clients gain access to their own meaning-making? How might talking about a book, a movie, or music in a session look? In what ways would this be different from talking about the same subjects with a friend? What types of questions might help your clients make connections between what is happening in a movie, a book, or music with what is happening in their own lives?

11. Of the following methods of avoiding responsibility in life, which do you use: compulsivity, displacement, playing the victim, losing control, avoiding autonomy, willing-denial, and physical disease? Are there other ways in which you may be avoiding living authentically in your own life? Explain.

12. What could you do differently that would bring authenticity into your life?

ANGELA'S EXPERIENCE IN GESTALT THERAPY

Driving down the long country lane, Angela hears the gravel popping beneath her tires as she takes one curve and then another. She realizes that she hasn't been alone with her thoughts like this in years. Normally, her two children,

Luke and Celia, would be in the backseat of the car, creating a steady din requiring her frequent intervention. Generally, Jake would sit behind the wheel confessing to her one fear after another and his take on how to avoid disaster. But today, Angela is in the driver's seat. She feels her foot press gently on the gas and is exhilarated as the car races forward. By the time she reaches Dr. Davis's office, her heart is pounding.

Dr. Davis is a rosy-cheeked woman of about 50; her eyes dance as she invites Angela to sit in one of the overstuffed chairs in the middle of the room. "You seem flushed," Dr. Davis notes, handing Angela a glass and motioning to the pitcher of water sitting on the coffee table next to her. Angela sits, looks shyly into her lap, and begins, "I had such a strange experience driving here today. It was as if there was a part of me aching to be free; I felt myself pushing the car forward faster and faster, pulling around those tight corners. I don't think I've ever done anything so reckless. I don't know what got into me." After drinking deeply from her glass, Angela begins to explain why she has come. She describes Jake's anxiety and the pressure and tensions that have resulted between them and with their two children. She tells Dr. Davis about some of her experiences in childhood of caring for her sister on long, hot afternoons in Nigeria, wishing she could go outside and play with the other children.

Dr. Davis is a Gestalt therapist. She believes that each of us strives to fulfill our most basic needs but that our needs can be thwarted by familial and social expectations. She believes that based on these expectations, our identities are formed and are comprised of polarities of contrasting traits, some of which we find acceptable and work to express, and others which we submerge or deny. As Dr. Davis listens to Angela, she is aware of the ways in which Angela has closed off parts of herself that she finds unacceptable, the parts of her that would like to acknowledge her own needs, and the part of her that feels angry.

"You seem far away right now. What are you feeling now?" Dr. Davis prompts.

"I feel guilty—ashamed, too, I guess. I don't think I should be feeling the way I do, you know—wanting to be free and all. After all, I should be a good support for my family—that's my job," she says, playing with her hands nervously.

"You are doing something with your fingers there," Dr. Davis comments, noticing Angela twisting her wedding ring in circles up toward her knuckle and back down again. "Do that more." Angela blinks curiously at Dr. Davis and begins twisting the ring more. Dr. Davis leans forward. "Now, Angela, with more gusto!" Angela focuses on her ring, twisting it more quickly and with more energy; tears gather in her eyes. "What are your fingers telling you, Angela? Have them talk to you, Angela. What are they saying?"

Angela looks at Dr. Davis puzzled, then, almost as if her fingers are looking at her and talking, they shout, "Break free!" Dr. Davis prompts Angela to have her fingers repeat this a number of times: "Break free. Break free. Break free." The sound vibrates the room. As she repeats herself a third and fourth time, Angela's tears begin to stream down her cheeks.

"It seems you've liberated your tears," says Dr. Davis. "Tell me, what do you want to be free of?"

Angela goes on to talk about how she was always placed in the caretaking role, and now that she is an adult, she has continued this role. She shares that she wants to be free of all of the responsibilities she feels in life, including those to her children and husband.

Dr. Davis would like to help Angela to more fully experience her life and the full richness of her emotional self in the here and now, including her repressed feelings of a need to be autonomous. As a Gestalt therapist, Dr. Davis views Angela's difficulties as unfinished business. She believes that because Angela's early needs for freedom and fun were thwarted by cultural and parental expectations, Angela's unmet needs were blocked from her awareness and became unfinished business. She believes that Angela's inability to acknowledge and experience these needs has led her to live a phony and inauthentic life as she plays the role of the perfect wife, mother, daughter, and granddaughter. In order for Angela to become more authentic, she will have to be able to work on the unfinished business that maintains her inauthentic way of being, her mask of niceness and unflagging nurturance.

In the weeks that follow, Dr. Davis works to help Angela see that she has introjected her parents' expectations, swallowing whole their demand that she always be ready to care for others. She works with Angela to acknowledge her needs by making use of specialized techniques and experiments, like the exaggeration technique described earlier. Dr. Davis encourages Angela to remain in the here and now as she expresses her feelings and experiencing.

One afternoon, Angela comes to the session trembling. She seems to be having difficulty looking at Dr. Davis as she sits in her usual spot on the couch and looks at her hands resting in her lap.

"Angela, help me understand what is happening with you right now," Dr. Davis asks softly.

"I feel like I am back at square one. I've been wasting my time here!"

Dr. Davis waits as Angela sits crying into a tissue and is able to continue talking again. "Yesterday, my grandmother called. She told me that Lillian, my younger sister, needs help. She just had hip surgery and I went to Philadelphia to help her out with her kids. Now my grandmother is telling me to go back there and help her out some more; she just isn't doing well enough on her own. This is really bad timing. I don't know if it is a good idea to leave Jake and the kids to fend for themselves just when Jake is starting to get help for his anxiety. I feel like there are two parts of me—the independent me, and the connected and sometimes dependent mother and wife. And, I guess if I were to be honest, I feel a little resentful because of your need to have me be independent. I don't think that you really understand that my obligations to Jake and the kids, and to Lillian and my extended family, are more than just obligations. They *are* my connections to them, and it is the way that I am bound to my family and them to me. It is a part of my culture and I don't think that I can just reject that part of me and still be *real*. My obligations to Jake and the kids are a part of me, too."

Dr. Davis listens to Angela's feelings, then says, "You've felt that to be real with me you had to be *independent Angela*, and the Angela who ignores her family obligations and ignores her culture? Angela, can you tell me how angry you are at me for pushing you to be independent?"

"It makes me furious! I come here so you can help me and you haven't really tried to understand at all!" Angela responds.

"Angela, now tell me what the real Angela looks like," Dr. Davis says, nodding her encouragement.

"Well, the real Angela can decide how I am going to take care of my kids, Lillian, and *myself* all at the same time." Angela pauses, then says, "I guess this hasn't been about trading in the part of me that cares for others and supports my family for the part that needed attention and needed to be heard. No, this has been about letting both parts of myself have a voice."

"Say that again, Angela," Dr. Davis prompts. "Say it loudly."

Together, Angela and Dr. Davis have been working to help Angela discover how to integrate polarities into a cohesive whole, a genuineness that allows Angela full contact with the world and with her own experiencing. Angela's cultural frame is a big part of who she is, and giving this aspect of herself adequate attention in therapy has been vital for Angela in being able to understand how her polarities of self- and other-care can be integrated so that she can make decisions about her life that are consistent with her needs, those she has been aware of as well as those she had once submerged.

"I've made my decision," Angela begins. "The school year will end in six weeks. I will go to Philadelphia and help Lillian on the weekends. I'll take care of the big chores and she can rest. And then, if she still needs help when school lets out, I will take the kids up there for another couple of weeks."

Dr. Davis smiles. "But this time, you are making your decision aware of all parts of yourself—the strong, autonomous part, and the strong, committed-to-family part."

For You to Consider

1. When Angela came in to see Dr. Davis, she said she wanted to "break free." What do you believe Angela needed to be free of?

2. Angela's need for freedom and autonomy was not fully experienced due to one or more of the following resistances or blockages to her own experience: introjection, projection, retroflection, desensitization, deflection, egotism, and confluence. Explain these different mechanisms and identify which one(s) Angela likely used to prevent herself from experiencing this need fully.

3. What special attention did Dr. Davis need to give to Angela's cultural frame in order to help her fully integrate all parts of herself? If you were working with Angela, how do you think you would help Angela make sense of her American and Nigerian identities?

4. Do you think that Dr. Davis wanted Angela only to be independent, as Angela asserted?

5. How comfortable would you feel asking a client to "talk to their fingers" or other body part?

6. What other techniques do you think would be effective for Angela's work in dealing with her unfinished business and integrating repressed parts of herself?

7. Using Perls's notion of the structure of neuroses, explain the therapeutic process as Angela experienced it.

8. When you consider Jake's personality, what parts of himself does Jake seem to reject? Which parts does he embrace?

9. Do you think that Jake and Angela's expectations of Luke may lead Luke to begin to cut off parts of himself? How might rejecting parts of himself look for Luke as he grows to adulthood? How about Celia?

10. Do you think this approach would be effective with the whole family present at the same time? Why or why not?

11. What polarities do you experience in your own personality? What parts of you do you think of as *bad*? What would integrating or embracing those parts look like in your life right now?

12. Are there times when you feel you are wearing a mask, or being phony? What makes it difficult to let go of these masks and be real in your relationships with others?

13. Using Perls's notion of the structure of neuroses, explain where on the circle you see yourself most of the time.

14. Being a Gestalt therapist requires a bit of the theatrical and some risk-taking. Do you think this is something you could do? If not, is it because you have cut off a part of yourself?

ANGELA'S EXPERIENCE WITH A PERSON-CENTERED COUNSELOR

Sitting in the somewhat cramped waiting room surrounded by glossy magazines, a cover featuring a mother and daughter, cheek to cheek, wearing broad toothy smiles, catches Angela's attention. A feeling sweeps over her as if she might burst into tears before she even gets a chance to introduce herself to her counselor. When she confided how lost she felt, her brother, Markus, had suggested that she see Henry Denshaw. "I heard that he is just a really great listener, and that seems like something you could use right now." Angela is relieved when Henry retrieves her from the waiting room and leads her to his office.

Angela sits on the bright-red loveseat situated against the tall built-in bookcases lined with volumes of books and family photos. Angela sits silently, taking in the room, while across from her, Henry settles comfortably in a chair that is showing its wear. Henry's concerned expression seems to mirror Angela's hurt. An understanding nod seems to invite the tears that are welling up behind Angela's eyes. After a moment, Angela is able to speak, "I just feel at such a loss for what to do."

"The feeling of being lost and hurt is written all over your face. It is pretty clear this is a difficult time for you right now," Henry offers.

Henry, a person-centered therapist, is most concerned with providing Angela the space and the time to describe what she is feeling. Refraining from offering direction or questioning her, Henry believes that given the chance, Angela, like all clients, will be able to voice her innermost concerns and feelings. Henry strongly believes that given the right conditions, people will naturally realize their authentic selves. He believes that in order to give Angela what she needs, he first must try to fully understand her and convey that understanding to Angela. Henry tries to be attuned to what Angela is saying as well as the feelings that Angela is able to name and those that are just beyond her awareness. While Angela doesn't say much initially, her body language speaks volumes. Henry hopes that as Angela begins to open up, he will be able to convey his understanding and his unconditional positive regard while remaining authentic and present with her.

Henry believes that Angela's confusion and sadness is a symptom of the conflict between her natural tendency toward actualizing who she is (her "self") and her need for positive regard (satisfying a role for others in order to win their love and approval).

"Things have been a little rough for my daughter, Celia. She's 7 years old now and has so much anxiety at school that she has been getting stomachaches a lot. At least once a week, the nurse calls for me to pick her up. The situation is really stressing my husband. He really got upset when she had an accident at school—she wet herself when she was boarding the bus to go on a field trip. The final straw came when Jake asked me to home-school Celia. I'm pretty sure that wouldn't be good for her. She needs friends. Somehow, though, I feel I *should* want to be home helping Celia."

"This is a familiar struggle for you," Henry offers.

"Well, yes. As I think about it, I feel exactly the same way I felt the summer when I was 8 years old or so. We were visiting my grandparents in Nigeria. My parents had gone to the market and my father had left me in charge of my sister Lillian—she was 3—and Markus was out playing in the yard with the other children. I had been watching her all summer long; at least, it felt that way. My parents were so concerned about her because of her bad hip. She had a hard time getting around on her own until she was able to get the first of her surgeries. At first, I felt like a grownup taking care of Lillian, but after a while, I really wanted to go out with my cousins. One afternoon, I asked my grandmother if I could leave Lillian in the house with her and go with my cousins and the other kids to the river to fish. My grandmother gave me a very stern look and reminded me about my responsibility to my sister. It was just a look, you know, but I felt so … ashamed.

"I guess in a lot of ways, I agree with my grandmother now that I am older. Maybe I should have felt more responsible and wanted to take care of Lillian. After all, family is our first responsibility. Certainly mine is—well, at least, should be. The family's needs should come before mine. I know I need to protect Celia and make sure she is safe and learning. It can't be good for her to go to school every day feeling so anxious, can it? Maybe I'm just a bad mother, but I just really don't know what to do—what do you think?"

Leaning forward in his chair, Henry begins, "Angela, I know that you would very much like to know what I think you should do. But I believe that only you can know what is right for you and your family. Maybe I can help you discover that."

As Henry reflects on his session with Angela, he returns to the belief that if he provides an environment of empathy, acceptance, and unconditional positive regard, Angela will feel safe to explore her predicament and to discover what it is she believes is the best course for her and her family.

As the session continues, Angela begins to see how being a caretaker has been a condition of worth that she felt strongly while growing up, both while in Nigeria and in the United States. Angela seemed to feel her family's love and approval most when she was caretaking. Any time she didn't want to be the caretaker, she felt rejected and ashamed. Now she feels some of the same conditions placed on her by Jake. As long as she agrees to go along with what Jake wants, Jake will love her. When she is assertive with Jake, he criticizes her and questions her commitment to the family.

As their second session opens, Angela is able to be more open about her frustrations with Jake. "Right now, I am so angry with Jake I can barely think straight. I guess I'm on the fence about what is best for Celia—for her to stay home or go to public school—but it makes me furious that he is putting me in this position," Angela explains. "It is hard to admit this, but sometimes I get so frustrated with Jake and his anxiety. At first, I had a lot of sympathy for him, I really did. But now his problem is really our problem. I think he expects me and the kids to change so that he doesn't have to feel anxious."

"So you are left feeling like an emotional yo-yo, going from sympathy, to anger, and then guilt, and at times just real confusion about how you *should* feel," Henry says.

"Yes, yes! That's right. It seems like I feel all these different feelings. But one thing I know—when Jake starts talking to me about home-schooling Celia, I get angry. Angry, because I feel like he doesn't at all value my job—my work! It isn't that I'm overjoyed about my job, but it is mine. But then when I really think about it, my work isn't all that important, not as important as Celia, anyway."

"You are really backed up against a wall. In order to get Jake's love and support you have to give up what is meaningful to you and be responsive to his needs and feelings. Somewhere along the way, your own needs and feelings stopped being part of the equation," Henry offers. "I guess at this point, it is pretty difficult to figure out not only what you want to do for Celia, but what you want for yourself."

"You know, Henry, I don't think I can remember a time when I've had a chance to really consider who I am outside of all these demands," Angela confesses.

Henry hopes to help Angela feel supported and accepted as she explores her own needs and desires for the first time. He believes that, together, they can begin to make sense of her feelings of confusion, sadness, and guilt. As therapy continues, Henry is aware of how important it has been to provide her with the unconditional positive regard that would allow her to be free to explore her own struggles and to understand herself.

As Henry considers how their sessions might unfold, he expects that he will be challenged to help her unearth a clearer vision of who she actually is, to assist her in the development of a self image that incorporates both American and Nigerian cultures, to help her build greater confidence in her ability to make important decisions for herself and for her family, and to help her decide what roles in her family and in her career make sense for her.

For You to Consider

1. Sometimes, when we work with a client like Angela who is torn and unsure about how to proceed, the answer may seem very clear to us, but our answer may not be right for the client. Did you have a feeling about how Angela should respond to Jake's request that she home-school Celia? If you were Angela's person-centered counselor, how would you help her to find her way to an answer to this dilemma?

2. If you had struggled with issues similar to those with which Angela is struggling, from a person-centered perspective, do you think it would ever be justified to share your similar struggles?

3. Take a look at each of Henry's responses. Do you think that they were empathic? Why or why not? How might you have responded if you were Angela's person-centered counselor?

4. How difficult might it be for you not to ask questions of Angela, and instead to use empathy and other nondirective techniques to help her find her own solutions?

5. Do you think empathy is enough in Angela's case? Why or why not?

6. Considering Jake's recent struggles, how effective do you think a person-centered approach would be for him, especially the use of the core conditions of genuineness, unconditional positive regard, and empathy?

7. If you were to use a person-centered approach with Jake, are there any ways in which you might adapt it for his unique situation?

8. How might you adapt a person-centered approach if you were working with Celia and Luke?

9. How long do you think Angela would need to spend in counseling to resolve some of her concerns? Is it feasible for her to be in counseling for an extended period of time?

10. How important do you think it is for you to learn about the Nigerian culture? From a person-centered perspective, do you think that knowledge of that culture will help you relate more effectively with Angela?

11. If you found yourself having strong feelings, either negative or positive, toward Angela, as a person-centered therapist, what might you do with those feelings?

12. If you felt strong feelings about how Angela should act, would you share them? Under what circumstances might you share your feelings with her?

LUKE'S EXPERIENCE IN BEHAVIOR THERAPY

Recently, Luke's natural tendency to question, explore, and enjoy his freedom has begun to get in his way at home and at school. Luke argues regularly with his father and sometimes refuses to do what his mother asks him to do. Luke's behavior has begun to carry over into the school setting, and his teachers have started to complain. One day, Luke's teacher, Ms. Parson, approaches the school counselor, Lia Harper, telling her, "That kid is just a bad seed; there's nothing I can do with him. I've just about had it." Lia, a behaviorist, privately disagrees, believing instead that children are neither inherently good nor bad. She believes that behavior is simply learned and continues only because children find the behavior rewarding. However, hearing Ms. Parson's frustration with Luke, she simply listens. Lia is aware that African American children are much more likely to be identified as emotionally disturbed than white children. She would like to help Luke turn his behavior around before his already irritated teacher begins to frame Luke's behavior in this way. She decides to invite the teacher to a meeting with Luke's parents, Jake and Angela.

As the meeting opens, the school counselor notices Angela's look of embarrassment and Jake's thinly veiled anger at Luke, who waits for them in the lobby. After Ms. Parson finishes her list of complaints about Luke's increasingly difficult behavior, Lia explains that she would like to help Luke get back on track before he enters middle school, where she is afraid that Luke's behavior may lead to more serious consequences. As the meeting progresses, Angela confides, "Luke has become so disrespectful at home that I don't see how we can take him to my grandparents' house for the summer like we had planned. My grandparents are Nigerian; our culture holds authority in very high regard. They won't tolerate Luke's sassing and disobedience."

Jake snaps, "Well, *I* hold respect in pretty high regard, too! I've just about had it with Luke's behavior."

Angela remarks, while looking into her lap, "Well, I don't think it helps that you are yelling at him all the time."

Luke's school counselor offers to do a functional behavioral analysis (FBA) to help them all better understand why Luke behaves the way he does. She explains that children behave in ways that are rewarding, or have some kind of payoff, and that an FBA may help them discover what reward Luke is getting from his outbursts. She explains that once the behavioral analysis is complete, a behavioral intervention plan (BIP) can be developed that will help Luke get what he needs in more productive ways.

In the following two weeks, Lia meets with Luke's teachers and observes Luke in class a few times. She asks the teachers to keep a baseline of how many times Luke acts out during the week. She takes careful note of Luke's classroom environment and particularly how he responds to different children, adults, and activities throughout the day. She also meets with Jake and Angela to talk about Luke's behavior at home and hopes to get more specifics about when and with whom Luke is likely to begin to act out, and what happens afterward. She believes that by gathering accurate data, she can form a hypothesis about the function of Luke's behavior. Luke's parents agree to keep a log of Luke's behavior so that they can all gain a clearer picture of what is happening when Luke misbehaves at home. Lia is interested in finding out how Luke's environment is shaping his behavior as he responds to both positive and negative attention. She is convinced that Luke's behavior is learned and that, with an appropriate behavior plan, they can help Luke behave differently.

Once Lia has collected her observations, the baseline data from the teachers, and the log that Luke's parents are keeping, she considers all the information carefully and begins to notice a number of patterns. For instance, she notices that Luke seems to react with outbursts and refusal (e.g., yelling loudly, "I won't do that!") whenever there is a great deal of structure, like in a highly structured classroom activity, some sports activities in his physical education class, and certain chores at home. When Luke acts out at school, or defies his parents, he is often sent into the hallway or, at home, straight to his room. Lia believes that Luke's behavior is rewarded by his exclusion from highly structured activities and, apparently, Luke does not find being alone too high a price to pay for his avoidance of these tasks. She notices, however, that when Luke has more than one option in how to approach a job, activity, or assignment, he is often receptive and sometimes even eager to give it a shot. She also found that Luke doesn't tolerate tension well. Based on the logs kept by his parents, Lia notices that when his parents argue, Luke will often look sullen and then act out by throwing things in the house. At that point, his parents tell him to go to his room. In these situations, Luke has found that drawing attention to himself effectively draws attention away from the conflict at home. It seems he doesn't mind being sent to his room, where the world seems a lot less hostile. This response seems to have generalized to school; when the classroom teacher reprimands a student, Luke will often look sullen, and subsequently become irritated and blurt out something negative toward the teacher. The teacher responds by giving Luke a "time-out" and having him stand in the hallway. The time-out is actually reinforcing for Luke, as he enjoys being in the calm atmosphere of the hallway, feeling special, and looking at the artwork. Finally, Lia keeps a mental note that the baseline kept by the teachers shows that the average number of acting-out behaviors for each week was 19 (17 the first week, and 21 the next).

In addition to observing, gathering data, talking with the teachers, and talking with the parents, Lia hopes that Luke can be motivated to change his behavior if she can identify something that Luke finds rewarding, so she arranges for them to meet. After talking with Luke, she learns that he really likes feeding the hedgehog that Mr. Rodriguez, the art teacher, keeps in the back of his classroom. Luke even shows up sometimes when it is time to change the bedding in the cage.

Based on the behavior analysis, Lia has come up with a number of recommendations to help change Luke's behaviors. She places this in a chart and sets up a meeting time to review it with Luke's teacher, the physical education and art teachers, and Luke's parents (see Table B.1). The counselor knows that she will run into some resistance on the part of the teachers and the parents. For instance, she suspects that Luke's teachers will not want to extinguish Luke's behavior by ignoring it, because they will feel like they have to respond in the moment to his outbursts. And she expects that the parents will balk at giving him a hug when he acts out.

Initially, the teachers and parents might not want to participate in some of the other interventions, either. However, she knows that if she can get everyone to "buy into" the tasks, Luke is going to feel better. In actuality, everyone will probably feel better as Luke's negative behaviors diminish, and she hopes that some of the activities will result in the teachers and the parents responding differently around Luke (e.g., the teachers giving "choices," the parents going into counseling). However, knowing that there might be some resistance, Lia will approach the task of giving out the assignments with two goals in mind: educating and persuading Luke's parents and

T A B L E B.1   Behavior Intervention Plan

Stimulus	Luke's Response	New Stimulus/New Reinforcement
Teachers asking Luke to do a specific task	Yelling "I won't do that!"	▪ Teacher gives "choices" to Luke ▪ Extinction: Ignoring Luke's acting-out response ▪ Token economy: Token for every hour there is no outburst (total number of tokens possible = 35). 25 tokens in a week allows Luke to care for hedgehog for the week.
Teacher reprimanding other student	Sullen look; blurting out negative statement toward teacher	▪ Stimulus control: Move Luke's seat to front of classroom so he doesn't see student's reaction to teacher. ▪ Classical counterconditioning: Teacher gently places her hand on Luke's shoulders when she is upset at another student.
Parents arguing	Sullen look; throwing things	▪ Stimulus control: Parents are to find a private space to argue, out of Luke's sight. ▪ Reinforcing new behavior: If he acts out, parents hug Luke instead of sending him to his room. ▪ Reinforcement/token economy: Family is to place a marble in a jar every time someone says something nice to each other. What is "nice" is determined by the person who receives the reinforcer. After the marbles reach a specific height in the jar, the whole family goes out to eat at their favorite restaurant (which has been determined to be motivating for all four family members). It is hoped that this will help, over time, to change the "mood" of the family. ▪ Stimulus control (reduction): Marital counseling to lessen the arguing of parents. ▪ Stimulus control (reduction): Individual counseling to reduce the irritability and depression of each parent and ultimately lessen the arguing.

teachers to participate, and listening to their ideas and feedback. Lia hopes that during their next meeting together, they can all agree on a new way of working with Luke that will reinforce positive behavior.

For You to Consider

1. Given what you know from your reading, what do you think the school counselor's role will be in assuring the intervention is effective? What cautionary notes will she need to give to Luke's teacher?

2. If you were Luke's counselor, are there other behavioral interventions that you think would have been useful?

3. Why do you think "modeling" was not used as one of the behavioral intervention techniques? Is there a way in which it could have been introduced?

4. From a behavioral perspective, if changes in Luke's behavior are not demonstrated, what should the counselor do?

5. Do you think a behavioral approach would be as effective for the parents as well as the children? Or for adults in general? Why or why not?

6. Compared to some of the other approaches you have looked at, do you think a behavioral approach would take a longer or shorter amount of time?

7. How important do you think it is for the behaviorist to use skills, such as empathy and team-building, to ensure that there is a good relationship between the therapist and the client? Can a behavioral intervention be effective without a "warm" relationship?

8. How important do you think it is for the behaviorist to have good consultation skills when working with teachers, parents, or other stakeholders?

9. Even if you are not a "pure behaviorist," do you think there might be times when you would want to integrate some behavioral techniques into your repertoire of techniques?

10. Think about your own culture and personality. How does the behavioral approach fit with your developing counseling style? What aspects of this approach would you find challenging? What aspects do you find attractive?

JAKE SEES AN REBT THERAPIST

Initially, when the flyer passed his desk, Jake had not given much thought to it: a workshop about dealing with anxiety seemed, well, a little hokey. Still, he had not been able to get himself to throw the flyer out and, ultimately, when the workshop began, he found himself sitting in the back of the room listening to the speaker, Paula Kim, explain rational emotive behavior therapy. On the following Wednesday morning, Jake makes an appointment with Dr. Kim.

Dr. Kim's office is decorated in beige and a gray that reminds Jake of cool, wet river stones. Jake notices the contrast between the aged feel of the hardwood floors and the modern look of the large whiteboard that spans one wall of the office. "So, Jake, can you tell me what has brought you here today?" A cascade of ebony hair falls just above her shoulders and frames Dr. Kim's shining black eyes.

"Well, sure, um," Jake begins cautiously. "I used to have a lot of trouble with panic attacks, but I haven't had one in months. Lately, though, when I'm at work, I sometimes get so anxious that I feel a wave of panic—not a panic attack, though." Aware of his initial awkwardness, he adds, "Um, I was at your workshop last week and I thought maybe you could help." Jake explains, "I'm starting to feel really stressed out by this new project at work. I was excited about it at first; it seemed to be going really well, but there is a new project manager, Nadia, and she's pushed up the time line and introduced some aspects that are really not in my area of expertise, if you know what I mean. The way she talks to me with her pushing and demanding is giving me those same old panic feelings."

"Even though this project has some exciting aspects to it, working with your project manager is getting to be harder and harder to deal with, especially when she starts to push and make demands," Dr. Kim offers. "Even though you've got the panic attacks under control, the worry that you might have another one is so distracting that it adds to the stress you already feel at work."

In the opening of the first session, Dr. Kim begins to gain some insight into Jake's beliefs about his work environment and some of the triggers and irrational beliefs that seem to be leading to Jake's anxiety. She believes it is important to convey her understanding of Jake's situation and to demonstrate empathy. However, Dr. Kim believes that Jake, like others, struggles with emotions not so much because of the challenging people and situations that make up his day but because of his irrational thinking about people and work. Dr. Kim would like to help Jake identify and challenge the counterproductive beliefs and replace them with new more rational ones.

"You're right, Dr. Kim. I am so worried that I'll have another panic attack. It would be—well, it would be humiliating if that happened at work. I just don't think that I could stand that," Jake says, eyes wide.

"I can see your concern written all over your face. Help me understand better what is frightening you about the possibility of having a panic attack at work," Dr. Kim probes.

"It's a couple of things, really. I don't know if you have ever had a panic attack, but when it happens, you feel like you are going to die! For me, I feel like I'm having a heart attack—I can't breathe, and I just want to get the hell out of wherever I am and get to a hospital," Jake says, his volume climbing a bit.

"That sounds terrifying, Jake," Dr. Kim replies. "You said there were a couple of things," she prompts.

"Yeah, the other thing is just that Nadia and the people at work would think I was some kind of nut job! I'd lose the little bit of credibility I have with her, and it would be a constant battle to get her to listen to anything I had to say," Jake replies, visibly upset. "I'm not sure how you can help me, Dr. Kim. It seems like my project manager is the one who needs to be here! If she'd get off my back, I'd be fine and I could get my work done."

"Maybe it would be a good idea for us to go over some of what I talked about at the workshop and see if we can figure out together how this applies to your situation at work," Dr. Kim says as she walks over to the whiteboard and begins to write. "You probably remember from the workshop that it isn't the specific events in our lives that pester us and cause us to suffer." Dr. Kim jots down the words *A = Activating Event* as she continues, "it is the way that we *think* about those events that lead to how we feel and act." She writes *B = Belief about Event* and *C = Consequential Feeling or Behavior* and then connects the three with an arrow, illustrating their connection. "Does that make sense so far?"

"I remember that part, but I'm still not sure how that fits with the situation at work," Jake confesses.

"Well, let's take a look." Dr. Kim begins. "When something happens, Jake, like when Nadia starts to ride you at work, that is an *activating event*." Dr. Kim jots her example on the whiteboard. "So, 'A,' in this case, is your project manager criticizing some aspect of your work. Here, 'B' is the belief you have about that event, and 'C' are your feelings, in this case, panic. Ultimately, it is your *beliefs* that you really can't handle your project manager's bad temperament and that because you can't handle Nadia you will inevitably have a panic attack that will lead everyone, without exception, to think you have lost your mind. It seems to me that your panic feelings are a response to all those concerning and distracting beliefs rather than your project manager's tone of voice."

"Well, I guess, I can see that," Jake concedes. "But to be honest, it really does feel pretty intolerable when this woman starts in on me—you should hear her!"

"Jake, I believe you. She sounds really difficult to deal with, but my focus is on you. Let's get your thoughts and reactions figured out so that you can deal with her—she's probably not going to change. I have some homework for you. In the coming week, I'd like you to note the self-critical and catastrophic thoughts that come to mind when Nadia is pressuring you. If you can, try writing some alternative thoughts that might be more productive. We'll talk about them the next time we meet."

Dr. Kim is pleased with her first session with Jake. They have been able to uncover some of Jake's beliefs and fears that seem to be feeding the anxiety he feels when he is working with his project manager. They have gone over the ABC theory and clarified connections between the theory and Jake's situation at work. Jake has agreed to document his thoughts and to make an effort to create alternative thoughts to challenge the counterproductive way he talks to himself.

Jake enters Dr. Kim's office for his second session looking a bit tired, eyes red, and his sleeves rolled up to the elbow, collar open and his tie askew. "This was not a good day," Jake says. "I had a hard time sleeping last night thinking about a meeting we were having at work today and wondering what Nadia was going to think about the new time line I've drawn up. I knew she was going to flip out on me and humiliate me in front of everyone at work. I kept imagining myself having a panic attack, an ambulance coming, and an EMT guy announcing it was all in my head. My heart was racing all night," Jake explains. "I was exhausted by the time I got to work."

"So what happened?" Dr. Kim prompts.

"Well, the meeting started off okay. Everyone presented their stuff. Of course, Nadia tore into the budget guy when his figures didn't match the initial projections, and she blasted the intern about the Web page. By the time I was supposed to go, I was feeling pretty nauseated, and I was sweating," Jake explains, wiping his brow.

"It sounds a little like lining up in front of the firing squad," Dr. Kim comments.

"Yeah, that sounds about right. I was starting to panic, so I excused myself. I felt like an ass, but I had to get myself together before I went back into the conference room. So I went into the bathroom and washed my face and took some deep breaths. After about ten minutes, I went back in and showed my time line. Then I told Nadia I wasn't feeling well. She said we could talk later about the time line and she let us go," Jake replies.

"Sounds grisly," Dr. Kim says. "What happened after the meeting?"

"As I was getting my stuff together, I overheard a couple of people in the office next to mine saying how much they hated these meetings. The lady from advertising poked her head in my office and said she was sorry I was sick but really glad that Nadia had ended the meeting early. She volunteered to be sick next time," Jake says, "I guess I'm not alone—lots of people seem to feel the same way I do about her."

"You lost a lot of sleep worrying that you would have a panic attack and that your colleagues would think that you were crazy," Dr. Kim points out. "Sounds like that didn't quite happen. You were right that Nadia, true to form, was pretty critical of everyone's work, but you managed through it and it sounds like your colleagues sympathized with everyone there."

"I was thinking about that on my way over here. I have been writing down some of the thoughts I've been having this week, like you asked, and I noticed that about half the time the thing I was afraid of never really happens, and the other half of the time, it wasn't nearly as bad as I thought it would be," Jake offers.

"What did you make of that, Jake?"

"Well, I was remembering what you were saying about beliefs causing emotional reactions, not the event. It seems like that is kinda true because I get myself all worked up to match my belief about what is going to happen, and it seems like it is way out of proportion to the actual event," Jake replies.

"Sounds like you are making some real sense of the ABC theory." Dr. Kim smiles. "I wonder if you remember the handout I gave at the workshop about the three core irrational beliefs? I've got a clean copy of it here for you," she says, handing a sheet to Jake. "Most irrational thoughts can be traced to one of these three ideas. I've adapted them to fit your situation."

(1) "I *absolutely must* under all conditions be sure my projects are perfect and that I have absolute approval from my boss and everyone else, or else I am an inadequate and unlovable person!"

(2) "My kids, Angela, my boss, and everyone I encounter *absolutely must* under all conditions treat me fairly and justly, and recognize my expertise, or else they are rotten, damnable, and intolerable persons!"

(3) "Conditions under which I live and work *absolutely must* always be the way I want them to be, give me almost immediate gratification, and not require me to work too hard to change or improve them, or else it is *awful, I can't stand* them, and it is impossible for me to be happy *at all!*"

After reading through the sheet, Jake laughs. "I guess I do think like this sometimes. It looks pretty silly on paper."

"Let's see if we can make some connections between some of the thoughts you wrote down this week and these three core ideas," Dr. Kim prompts.

Jake pulls his crumpled list from his pocket. "Well, the first one I had was, 'If this time line isn't perfect, Nadia is going to freak out on me and I will have a panic attack. Everyone will think I'm crazy and I will be a laughingstock.' That one really bothers me."

"So, what irrational beliefs do you see in there?" Dr. Kim prompts.

"I definitely see number one in there. I did feel like the project had to be perfect and that I needed everyone's approval. I didn't think about how if that didn't happen, I'm not a good person, but I do think that is at the core of this whole thing." Jake pauses. "I think if I'm really honest with myself there is a little of number three in there, too. I hadn't really thought about it in such extreme terms, but I guess I am insisting that things at work have to be just the way I want them to be in order for me to be happy. I hope that isn't true, because, like you said, Nadia probably isn't going to change."

"Jake, what do you think would be a more productive and maybe more rational way to think about the time line and the meeting with Nadia and your co-workers—instead of what you've written down?" Dr. Kim asks.

"Hmmm—well—maybe, 'Nadia may not like this time line, but it's the best projection I can make with the information we have. She might flip out but that doesn't mean I have to.' I guess another more rational thought might be that 'people at work might think I'm crazy, but I can't control them or their thoughts,'" Jake replies.

"What feelings come up for you when you use the alternative thoughts?" Dr. Kim asks.

"I feel relief, to be honest, and a little foolish, too, for letting myself get too caught up in these ideas that are more like fantasies than fact," Jake says.

Looking over her session notes, Dr. Kim considers where she and Jake might take their next sessions. Dr. Kim begins to draft homework assignments for the coming weeks. She would like Jake to read more about REBT so that he has a deeper understanding of the philosophy. She believes that Jake would benefit from understanding that we are born fallible and are not perfect, and that we are not bound by our past. Through reading and reflection, Jake may more fully accept himself as fallible and stop berating himself when mistakes are made. By becoming aware of his absolutist thinking, he has the power to combat it and ultimately to affect the feelings that result from these beliefs.

Dr. Kim would also like to teach Jake some basic coping skills for managing anxiety when it arises. She believes that in addition to rational thoughts, Jake can make use of controlled breathing and imagery to help ward off an influx of panic. She would like to suggest that Jake consider starting an exercise program, since regular exercise seems to reduce stress and anxiety. Another practical step that Jake might take would be to reduce the amount of caffeine he drinks— Dr. Kim has watched Jake drain a large coffee nearly every session since he began coming to the office.

During their last session together, Jake sits looking out of the large window in Dr. Kim's office, noticing how the season has changed since their first meeting. The yellow and red leaves that lie like a carpet on the narrow patch of lawn edging the sidewalk signal the passage of time. "I guess I've made a lot of progress with these irrational thoughts. I noticed this morning that I hadn't felt any really strong anxiety in weeks," Jake says, as if to no one in particular. Then, turning to Dr. Kim, "Nadia announced yesterday that she is leaving; she didn't say why, but she said that I should apply for her position. She said she thought I'd do a really good job."

"There is some sadness in your voice, Jake. What are you feeling?" Dr. Kim asks.

"Well, I guess I'm kinda left feeling confused and, yeah, I guess, sad. I mean, for months I was just miserable, and to hear Nadia talk now, it seems like she likes the work I do. I don't get it. It seems like such a waste. It makes me mad at her. I mean, why act that way if she didn't hate my work? But more importantly, why didn't I trust myself? I knew I was knocking myself out to do the best work I could do—so why did I do that to myself?"

"I think I understand how you feel. For several months there, you were absolutely miserable, and for what?" Dr. Kim replies. "Sounds like from now on you'll be using your own measuring stick to judge your work and using rational thinking to manage challenging projects and prickly people."

"I guess that about captures it. I can't do anything about what the people at work do or think, but I have got control of myself. I don't really have to feel like that again if I don't want to. I have you to thank for that, Dr. Kim," Jake offers with a shy smile.

"You did it, Jake—I just provided the ideas," Dr. Kim says, returning the smile.

For You to Consider

1. Dr. Kim believes the thoughts that are related to Jake's anxiety and negative feelings are irrational. Do you agree with her?

2. Jake has struggled with anxiety about his children and their safety. What irrational thoughts do you think might underlie these fears? Can you create a chart depicting Jake's anxiety at home using the ABC theory?

3. As with Jake, many of the irrational beliefs that we develop are born in early experiences. What experiences do you think helped to form Jake's irrational thoughts?

4. What irrational beliefs do you think Celia and Luke might be developing as they struggle with their own difficulties in school and at home?

5. Do you think REBT can be applied to children like Celia and Luke? What changes might you make in such an approach when working with children?

6. What cultural considerations might you encounter using an REBT approach with Angela, who identifies with two different cultures, Nigerian and American?

7. Do you believe that a rational approach, like REBT, might be more appealing when working with one gender as opposed to the other? Why?

8. Relative to some of the other theories you have studied, how comfortable are you with the more directive and didactic approach taken in REBT?

9. Dr. Kim frames Jake's reactions to his program manager as based in irrational expectations that she would always treat him fairly and that she must appreciate his work. How might you think about Jake's reactions to Nadia using another theoretical perspective?

10. Some people struggle with the words "rational" and "irrational" in REBT. What are your thoughts on their usage?

11. Think about your own developing counseling style and beliefs about human nature. What challenges might you experience if you were asked to use an REBT approach?

12. By examining the three core irrational beliefs, can you identify any of them as your own? In what situations might they affect your well-being?

13. If you identified any core irrational beliefs of your own, are there any self-management techniques that you can develop to challenge those beliefs? Would you be willing to see an REBT therapist to work on challenging those beliefs?

ANN MEETS WITH A COGNITIVE-BEHAVIORAL THERAPIST

Ann sits in the lobby arranging and rearranging the items in her bag. She has completed an intake form and a short questionnaire about her feelings of depression and anxiety, and considers thumbing through one of the parenting magazines on the coffee table as she waits for the counselor Jake had recommended, Carol Allen, to emerge from her office. Ann looks at the family sitting stiffly on the couch directly across from her and offers a weak smile. Carol, a round-faced woman with graying hair and soft wrinkles around her eyes, smiles at Ann and invites her into her office. Ann is already crying before Carol is able to shut the door.

"I don't know where to start, so I'm going to start in the middle, or maybe at the end, I don't know. Two months ago I had my sixty-fifth birthday. It has hit me like a ton of bricks. It just got me thinking about my life." Ann pauses a moment, reaching inside her purse and then, thinking better of it, sets her purse aside. "There was a birthday party. My husband, Ted, and my children, Jake and Justine, were there. Jake's wife Angela and my grandchildren, Luke and Celia, were there, too, of course. Evangeline and Dexter, Angela's parents, helped Tom set up the whole thing. A lot of my old friends came, too, and even some of my piano students from way back and then—this is what got me I, think—Justine brought a boyfriend."

"Your daughter, she brought a man with her. What was it about Justine's date that troubled you?" Carol asks.

"Well, Justine moved out of the house last year and into a group home. She had an accident as a child that left her with—I can never quite get this out—she's retarded. This man she was with, Carl, he lives in the group home, too. He has Down syndrome," Ann explains. "That wasn't what bothered me, though. It was just seeing all my friends and catching up on their lives and watching Jake with his kids and Justine with Carl. I should have been happy for everyone, but to tell the truth, I just felt really cheated. Here I am, 65 years old, and I was robbed of my children's childhood, robbed of a career, and now I'm just left behind. Everyone has their lives, their families and careers, and I—I have nothing to show for my life! Even Justine has a life of her own now, after years and years of having only me." Ann wipes the tears from her cheeks.

"Ann, when you saw your daughter at the party with Carl, can you remember the first thing that popped into your mind?"

"Yes, I thought, 'This is not how it's supposed to be.'" I know how selfish that sounds." Ann pauses and adds, "I have always felt it was unfair that my friends' children grew up without the kinds of troubles that Justine had. And I spent so much time tending to Justine after the accident that my relationship with Jake fell apart. We were so close before, but there's been a distance ever since the accident. Also, I just never could move on with my career. You know, I had been a piano teacher, and I was hoping to eventually go back to that—and maybe start a music school. But Justine just took up so much of my time!"

"Have you noticed what kinds of feelings you experience when those thoughts of things not being the way they should be move across your mind?" Carol asks Ann, handing her a box of tissues.

"Sadness, then sometimes anger and regret." Ann wipes her wet cheeks and blows her nose. "I get so depressed that things didn't work out the way that they were supposed to."

"I felt that from you, Ann, a lot of sadness, regret, and anger, and it sounded like there were feelings of being helpless, too, like you were just pushed around by the tide of events and left standing on the shoreline alone." Carol allows some silence before continuing. "Ann, how often do you think that you have thoughts of how things should have been different?"

"A lot. It was one of the first things I thought about after the doctor told us that Justine had a brain injury and that she wasn't going to recover from it. I remember Ted and I drove home after that consultation with the doctor and the streets were crowded with cars, children in the neighborhood were running round outdoors, and people were playing tennis at the tennis court. It was like nothing had happened. Our world was crumbling and the rest of the world seemed completely untouched. I remember thinking, *this is so unfair.*" Ann pauses a moment. "I find myself thinking about how unfair life is a lot."

"You and Ted and your children have been dealt a rough hand, that's for sure. There is a part of me that agrees with you—what happened in that accident wasn't fair; it was a tragedy. But it seems to have cast a shadow over your whole life. What I would like to do today is talk about how those thoughts you have—I call them your 'automatic thoughts'—affect so much of your life and cause you to feel the way you do. But, before we go on to talk some more about automatic thoughts, I'd like to switch gears for a moment. If it's all right with you, I'd like to take some time going over your intake form and together try to get a sense of where you are right now and hopefully end with some goals for our coming sessions."

After covering more of Ann's history and evaluating her functioning, Carol ends the session by educating Ann about automatic thoughts and their connection to the feelings and behaviors that trouble most people. Carol and Ann explore the feelings Ann experienced when the thoughts of the world being unfair came to mind. Ann agrees to be mindful of the times when these thoughts arise in her mind and to make a note about it. Together, Ann and Carol agree that in their next session they will work on ways to replace Ann's automatic thoughts with thoughts that are more productive for her and less distressing. Carol also provides Ann with readings about automatic thoughts and thought-stopping strategies.

When Carol and Ann meet for their next session, Carol notices a difference in Ann. "Your eyes look brighter than they did last week, Ann. How did your week go?"

"It was better than the week before; I was busy with some projects at church, so I was distracted. I did my homework, though." Ann reaches into her purse and produces a small notebook, which she passes to Carol along with the mood questionnaire form she was asked to fill out as she waited for the session to begin. "I took notes on the reading that you gave me and I kept a little log of my thoughts."

"Oh, this is great, Ann," Carol says as she flips through the notebook. "And according to your questionnaire, your mood seems to have improved some since last week. It seems that something about our last session was helpful to you. Can you tell me what that was?" Carol asks, creating a bridge between their first session and this one.

"I think it helped a lot to just get some of those feelings out. I just don't think I could say those things to Ted or to any of my friends. But talking about those automatic thoughts was a 'light bulb' moment for me. I have been carrying those thoughts around with me for 30 years, and they really do influence my feelings. When I was writing my log I noticed that when I have those thoughts and then start to feel angry, I really take it out on Ted. I didn't realize how much time I spend criticizing him, but I do," Ann confides. "Other times, I just get depressed."

As the session continues, Carol begins to connect Ann's automatic thoughts to a number of cognitive distortions, which she describes to Ann. Some of them include catastrophisizing, discounting the positive, tunnel vision, and overgeneralization. Then, she gives her some homework techniques to use to combat some of her automatic thoughts.

Over the next few sessions, Ann and Carol work on combating her automatic thoughts, and then Carol starts to teach Ann about the connection between her automatic thoughts, her intermediate thoughts, and her core beliefs. At one point, Carol begins to chart the relationships among Ann's core beliefs, intermediate beliefs, automatic thoughts, and reactions (see Figure B.1). Although Ann receives a fair amount of relief from working on her automatic thoughts, the long-term changes for Ann are going to take place after she begins to focus on her core beliefs and concomitant behavioral changes. Although this will take some amount of time, Carol expects Ann to be able to make some major changes in her life fairly quickly.

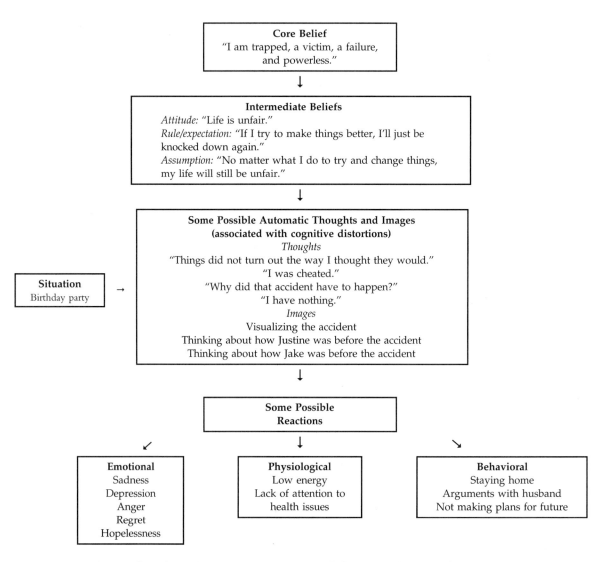

FIGURE B.1 The Relationships Among Ann's Core Beliefs, Intermediate Beliefs, Automatic Thoughts, and Reactions

For You to Consider

1. This therapist spent some time using basic attending skills to listen to Ann. How important do you think those skills are in cognitive therapy?

2. Even though some basic attending skills were used by Carol, at one point, she somewhat abruptly shifts gears to make sure that the information in the assessment is covered. Do you think this kind of shifting gears is appropriate? How else could Carol have handled this?

3. How easy do you believe it is for most clients to "catch" their automatic thoughts?

4. In this example, some possible cognitive distortions were identified that may be associated with Ann's automatic thoughts. Can you explain how those cognitive distortions feed into Ann's automatic thoughts?

5. Do you think other cognitive distortions may have also been involved in Ann's thinking processes? If yes, which ones?

6. Ann seems pretty amenable to looking at the cognitive model that Carol is identifying (e.g., automatic thoughts, intermediate thoughts, core beliefs, etc.). Do you think most clients would so readily agree with this process? Why or why not?

7. Using cognitive therapy, how might you address Ann's insight that she takes her anger out on her husband? Do you think you might have suggested creating a goal from this problem? What might this goal look like?

8. Ann was eager to do the homework that Carol assigned. If you were Ann's counselor, how do you think you would work with Ann if she had chosen not to do her homework?

9. How long do you think it will take Ann to work on changing her core beliefs? Explain.

10. Given endless resources (which often is not a reality!), do you believe that once Ann understands the cognitive therapy process she can do most of the work on her own, or would it be better for her to continue in therapy with her therapist for an extended period of time? Explain.

11. Some of Ann's concerns seemed to have an existential ring to them. How might an existential therapist work differently with Ann? Which approach would you be more apt to use with Ann? Why?

12. Can you identify any cognitive distortions, intermediate beliefs, or core beliefs of yours that you can work on? How might you go about changing them?

MARKUS MEETS A REALITY THERAPIST

Angela knocks loudly on the door, and finally lets herself in. "Markus! Markus! It's me, Angela! Are you up?" Angela makes her way past stacks of newspaper, dozens of books, plates with shriveled pizza, and several discarded beer bottles.

A stale smell hangs in the air, and dust seems to be dancing in the light streaming in beneath the tightly drawn shades. "Hey, Markus, come on, it's me." Angela finds Markus lying on his bed, staring at the ceiling. "Come on, Markus, we have an appointment."

Once in the car, Markus asks, "Where are we going? I don't remember having an appointment." Angela watches the light change and pulls into the intersection. "We are going to see a counselor. His name is Mike Watkins. I know you liked Dr. Bertram, but she is on some kind of sabbatical or something, and you need someone right now." Angela makes another right and slows the car. "We are looking for 307 Second Street, Markus. Keep your eyes peeled."

Mike Watkins's office is a cramped space in a belowground office. A vaguely musty smell reminds Angela of Markus's apartment. Mike offers Markus a seat and indicates that Angela should wait in the lobby.

"Mike—right?" Markus begins. "I didn't know Angela was bringing me here until we pulled into the parking lot. I don't really know what to say."

Sitting back in his chair, Mike waits a moment for Markus to continue.

"My partner, Rob, left a month ago. I don't mean he left for good, just that his company got him working in the Middle East on a government project and he won't be back for five months. I asked him not to go, but he's sure it will be good for his career."

"So help me understand why you are here, or why you think Angela brought you," Mike probes.

"I guess she's worried. After Rob left, something just clicked, or maybe unclicked, and now I can't seem to focus on anything. Sometimes I feel like I can't move or even think. Angela's worried about my comps." Mike looks confused, and Markus continues, "I'm working on my Ph.D., and I have a series of papers to write for my comps. To be honest, I don't know how I'll get myself together in time to submit to my committee. I spent the whole morning staring at the ceiling, and I'd probably still be there if Angela hadn't dragged me out of bed." Markus throws his hands up in frustration. "I have one task to do—write those papers. It's not a big thing. I'm worthless! I'm asked to do one thing and I can't do anything but sit on my butt."

"That's a lot of pressure, Markus—comps on one hand and wondering what Rob is thinking about your relationship on the other. No wonder you've been thrown off-kilter. It seems to tap into two basic human needs: the need to love and be able to count on love from others, and the need to feel like you're succeeding at something worthwhile—in this case, your comps." Mike scratches his head, considering the problem. "It makes sense to me that you've been struggling lately."

"That's about the size of it. It sounds like an old country song, but that's how it's been," Markus says, relaxing into his chair.

"Markus, as you've been going over these concerns about Rob and with your comps, have you given much thought to the image of how your life would look if everything was ideal? What would your *quality world* look like?" Mike asks, curious to understand Markus a little bit better.

"Well, Rob would be here. He wouldn't have left in the first place, because our relationship would be more important than his damn career! He knew I was in the middle of preparing for my comps. I don't know why he felt like he had to leave now. How am I supposed to think straight with him halfway across the world? That's the part that keeps going through my mind. I wonder if he's just going to pack up and leave any time something comes up at work. Is our relationship always going to be second for him? I think about that a lot."

"And how would it be if your relationship was not second and things were just as you'd like them to be?"

"We'd have a house with kids. I would have a job teaching at a university, like my dad did. I guess that is what I'm looking for. My dad had a good life, happy family, and a solid career teaching, and time to take trips to Nigeria in the summer. I want that for us, too. Not Nigeria necessarily, but our own life that is ours outside of work. Does that make sense?"

As Mike reflects on his first session with Markus, he considers what he has learned about his new client. A reality therapist, Mike is interested in the basic needs that Markus is working to fulfill in his life. Mike notes that Markus uses language that portrays how he feels controlled by others and outside events, such as his belief that he can't think straight while Rob is away. Mike hopes that in the upcoming sessions, he can help Markus choose behaviors and language that will help him satisfy his needs in his quality world in effective ways. Mike notes in Markus's chart that he has given Markus some material to read that describes five basic needs: survival, love and belongingness, power, freedom, and fun. He has also given Markus some reading about total behavior and the role of behavior in making productive choices to meet our basic needs.

When Markus arrives for their second session, Mike shakes his hand and gestures to a chair. "No Angela today?" he comments.

"No, I thought I could get myself here this morning, though she did call last night and this morning to remind me. Angela has this caretaker thing going on." Markus and Mike laugh as Markus settles into a tattered chair beneath the ground-level window. "I read the material you gave me, and I was thinking a lot about those basic needs. I never thought of my work on my comps as meeting power needs but I guess that is what that is, right? If I pass the comps, I have a sense of achievement—and I guess I feel powerful. But, Mike, I'm at a place right now where it will be a miracle if I can get my comps written before the deadline; I have five weeks to finish all three topics. If I fail my comps … I'll feel completely worthless."

"That puts some pretty high stakes on turning this thing around." Mike leans forward in his chair. "Did you read anything in that packet I gave you that might help?"

"I've been thinking on and off about the idea that control comes from within and not outside us, but I can tell you that is a lot easier to talk about than to do. I think about the way that Rob being gone has me so depressed and how hard it is for me to do anything, and I just don't know how I'm supposed to control that."

"Markus, maybe part of having control starts with how you think about your obstacles, and next with how you talk about them." Mike notices Markus's confused look and continues. "You've said *Rob being gone has me so depressed it is hard for me to do anything.* Maybe you can take back some of your control by thinking of it like this: *I've chosen to depress myself and to do little else than think about Rob being gone.*"

"When you say it like that, Mike, I feel like you are saying that I am to blame for being so depressed. I don't like the way that feels. I love Rob, and it is really hard to have him gone when I need him so much right now."

"What if it wasn't about blame? For instance, how do you hear these two things differently?" Mike asks. "*I have writer's block* compared to *I'm choosing not to write, right now.*"

"Well, the first one, the one about writer's block, makes it sound like this thing called 'writer's block' is stopping me from writing, but that second statement makes it sound like I'm the one who's stopping me from writing. I guess, in a way, the second one sounds more hopeful, because if I am the one in charge, not this thing called 'writer's block,' then I choose whether or not I write."

"Then you see my point. If you take a look at the problem from the standpoint of something happening to you, like writer's block, you have little power over it—you have to wait for it to go away. But, if you decide to look at it from a perspective of something happening within you, a choice in the way you approach your struggle, then you have your control back. I call that 'internal control' because you are the one who is in the driver's seat. Internal control means that if you choose to, you could pick up your pencil and write, right now—right here."

"What, here? Right now?" Markus laughs.

Mike shrugs, reaching into his desk, taking out a pad and pencil, and handing it to Markus. "Why not? The consequences for not writing—what are they? You have time to think about your relationship with Rob, but your comps are due in five weeks. From where I'm sitting, you have a couple of choices: you can write or not write, but only one of those choices is going to get you any closer to your dream of teaching at a university."

Mike is certainly surprised when Markus takes the last 20 minutes of their session to write an outline for his first paper. Markus seems to respond well to prompts from others; he came to counseling with his sister's prompting and was able to write given a little prompting. Mike would like to help Markus gain a sense of his own efficacy, to see solutions as arising from within, out of his own efforts and not from Rob, Angela, or his counselor.

As the session comes to an end, Mike begins to teach Markus about the WDEP system. He has given Markus some reading materials, and tells Markus they will begin their next session by discussing Markus's quality world, his wants, the direction he is going in, what he is doing to get there, and evaluating what he is doing. He hopes to encourage Markus to evaluate how his behavior has worked toward and against his dreams. Ultimately, Mike would like to help Markus create a plan of action that will help to bring his wants to fruition.

As the next session begins, Mike says, "I was hoping that we could spend some more time talking about what it is you want for yourself, Markus, and some about the direction you are taking to make those wants a reality. Did you have a chance to read the materials I gave you?"

"I did, and it got me thinking some. Not just about me and my relationship with Rob, but also about my relationship with my sister, Angela, and my parents. Sometimes I feel like no matter how old I am, I am still the kid brother, you know? Every relationship I have has some element of somebody helping me in some way, prodding me along. I thought about that for a long time, and I know that when people take care of me, that's when I feel loved," Markus begins.

"It helps to meet your need for love and belongingness," Mike adds.

"Yep. But there is this other side to it. When other people help get me through a rough spot and I accomplish something thanks to their help—I don't know, it doesn't feel right. It is like it isn't mine anymore. Does that make sense?" Markus asks.

"You mean like that need to feel like you accomplished something gets diminished somehow?"

"Yes, like it isn't my accomplishment anymore. Now if I get through my comps it will be because Angela brought me here and because you handed me that pad of paper. Don't get me wrong, it helped to have that little push, but I want to stand on my own two feet. I can't go through life waiting for Rob and Angela, or even you to get me going." Markus explains.

"Well, Markus, when you look at the doing and direction part that was described in the literature I gave you, did you think of anything that you are doing that is contributing to this experience?" Mike asks.

"I think I know that Angela is my safety net. If I start to fall, she will be there to catch me, just like she did a couple of weeks ago. Something about Angela, well, taking care of others, that's important to her. But Rob … it bugs him. I feel like I may have driven him away by leaning on him for all my direction and answers. In fact, it seems like the very thing I do—act all dependent on Rob—is the very thing that drives him away. And it's the very thing that makes me not feel accomplished, because I often feel like others are doing for me and I'm not doing for myself." Markus thinks a moment and adds, "I feel good about getting myself here this week, though. Angela didn't have to come by and get me. I've done this on my own, at least today. And last night, I set the timer on the stove and told myself to write until the timer went off. It worked pretty well, so I feel good about that."

"The way you've described it, Markus, you've evaluated your direction and doing for yourself, you've decided what is working, monitoring yourself with a timer, for example, and things that haven't worked so well, like leaning too heavily on Rob and Angela for motivation and direction." Mike pauses briefly. "I suspect that somehow you learned in the past that you could meet your need for love and belonging by being dependent on others. However, in the long run, being dependent on others hasn't really gotten you what you want—which is a more mature sense of love and belonging with your partner and a sense of accomplishment for yourself. I wondered if you had any thoughts about how you might shape your behavior in the coming weeks to get you through your comps and to help you navigate your relationship with Rob and your family."

"Well, right now, my focus needs to be on completing my comps. I want to feel like this was my accomplishment when I graduate. I think that by making a writing schedule, using my timer to pace myself, and really sticking to it, I know I can finish. The relationships, though, that is the harder part. I think I could use your help to understand that better before I make a plan for what to do differently," Markus offers.

"I agree, Markus; spending some time understanding those relationships better would really help you understand yourself better and might even help you imagine more clearly what it is that you want from them and how you can get it."

As Mike begins his session notes, he is feeling hopeful for Markus. Markus is beginning to understand internal control language and has a beginning sense of the relationship between his wants, the direction he has been moving toward, and the manner in which he has attempted to fulfill his needs.

For You to Consider

1. What techniques do you think are most important in building a relationship with Markus while helping him to understand the basic principles of reality therapy?

2. How important do you think it is to explore Markus's past, especially how it relates to his ability to have his need for love and belonging met?

3. Do you believe Markus can move forward and work on his issues with little or no discussion of his past?

4. Since reality therapists believe that just about all emotional problems are self-made, if Markus came in extremely depressed and suicidal, can a reality therapist justify referring Markus for medication to help relieve the depression?

5. If Markus continues not to take responsibility for his feelings, how far should a reality therapist go in confronting his lack of taking responsibility for his emotional state?

6. Do you believe that Markus's depression is only of his doing, or do you think that outside circumstances have had some affect on how he feels? What would a reality therapist believe?

7. If you were to continue as Markus's reality therapist, how might you use the WDEP system to support him in exploring and creating a plan to strengthen his relationships?

8. What multicultural issues does Markus's counselor need to attend to?

9. If Markus becomes more independent, how might his relationship with Angela change? How might Angela experience these changes?

10. If Markus becomes more independent, how might his relationship with Rob change? How might Rob experience these changes?

CELIA MEETS WITH A NARRATIVE THERAPIST

One afternoon, as Angela is finishing some of her work in her home studio, the phone rings. She eyes the telephone suspiciously. School only started a week ago, and she has already had two calls from the school nurse. Though Celia seemed relaxed and happy over the summer, her anxiety seems to be a problem for her again.

Angela recognizes the school counselor's voice almost immediately. "Hello, Ms. Miller. I am calling about Celia ..." Once Angela and the school counselor finish talking, Angela decides it is time to take Celia to see a counselor in the community, someone who can help Celia deal more effectively with her fears.

Celia holds her mother's hand tightly as they enter the lobby of the counseling office. It is within walking distance of their home and situated in a large, Victorian-style house that has been converted into office space. The large front porch with porch swing and flower pots give the building a welcoming and homey kind of feeling that Angela likes but that doesn't seem to soothe Celia's nervousness. Claudette Mendoza, Celia's new counselor, is tall and slender, with a bright smile, warm, sandy-colored skin, and long, dark curls that frame her face and fall down her back.

Claudette and Angela had talked briefly on the phone about Celia's anxiety. Claudette, a narrative therapist, hopes that in their first few meetings, she will get to know Celia and understand her story and how she has made sense of her fears. Claudette believes that the first step in helping clients, the joining phase, is to learn how clients perceive their worlds and understand their problems. Claudette will be listening for language that suggests that Celia might be crystallizing negative beliefs about herself, and listening for ways that she might be internalizing her difficulties.

Claudette enters the lobby and introduces herself. "You must be Angela and Celia. I'm Claudette. It's nice to meet you," she says, extending her hand. "Celia, I thought we could go into my office and get to know each other a little better. Do you think your mom will be okay out here while we visit?" Celia reluctantly follows Claudette down a bright hallway and into her corner office. Celia smiles and walks over to the tall bookshelves that frame a large, open window that looks out over a small, private garden. The bookshelves are lined with books and a number of small figurines Claudette has collected from around the world. Claudette notices that Celia seems interested in the small bronze statue of the dancing Shiva that she picked up in Delhi. "You can pick that up if you like," Claudette offers. "It is heavy and won't break. That is Shiva, the destroyer of obstacles. Shiva is the bravest of all the Hindu gods."

Celia lifts the statue, carries it to a small armchair opposite Claudette, and begins examining the small figurine in her hands. "Celia," Claudette begins, "can you tell me a little about why your mom brought you to see me?"

Celia makes eye contact and then returns her gaze to the Shiva cradled in her hands. "I get nervous at school," Celia replies. "Sometimes, my stomach hurts so much the nurse calls my mom and I have to go home. I think my teacher is mad at me. I don't think she believes me about my stomach."

"You don't think your teacher sees how much the worry hurts your stomach. How about your mom and your dad? Do they believe you?" Claudette asks.

"Dad says that Luke, he's my brother, is just like Aunt Justine. Luke will try anything. He just wants to have fun all the time. Aunt Justine used to be like that, too, but she got herself hurt really bad playing in Granddaddy's car and she got most of her sense conked out of her—that's what Luke said. Daddy says I am more like him. He used to get stomachaches a lot, too. Sometimes, Daddy gets so scared he feels like he's getting a heart attack! One time, when we were playing in the car, Luke and me, it rolled in the street. When Daddy saw that, he fell right down in the grass and the ambulance had to come. The ambulance man said Daddy didn't really have a heart attack; it was just all in his head. Luke says I'm just like Daddy; I have problems with my head," Celia explains, a note of sadness punctuating her words.

In their second session, Claudette and Celia sit on the floor in front of the coffee table. Claudette places a piece of paper in front of Celia, along with some crayons and markers. The paper depicts a silhouette of a girl that Claudette has drawn for her. "Celia, think about a time when you felt really anxious at school," Claudette prompts.

"You mean like in the lunch room last week?" Celia asks.

Claudette nods. "Can you remember how that felt when you first started to feel anxious in the lunch room? What color was that?"

Celia looks over the crayons and, after a moment, holds up a yellow-green crayon. "It is like this, kind of a sick-to-my-stomach green."

Claudette nods and prompts, pointing to the silhouette, "Where does the sick-to-your–stomach-green feeling start? Can you show me?"

Celia chooses a spot and begins coloring a bit of green in the center of the silhouette. "Right here in the bottom of my stomach."

"Then what happens?" Claudette prompts.

"Well, it starts to get bigger and bigger. It starts to fill up my whole insides, like this." Celia's delicate silhouette becomes overwhelmed with green as she colors furiously on the page.

Claudette leans forward, scratches her head. "Well, this helps to explain things, doesn't it? Worried stomach can be tricky and can make you believe that the worry has filled up your stomach and your whole body with more worry than will really fit."

"Can we make the worried stomach go away?" Celia asks sincerely.

"Absolutely," Claudette replies, "without a doubt."

Claudette is satisfied with how the last few sessions have gone. She's gotten a good feel for how Celia understands her anxiety, the role her family takes in constructing her vision of herself, and her difficulty with anxiety, and together they have given it a name, *a worried stomach*, and externalized it. Claudette and Celia won't focus on what is or is not in Celia's head; they will focus on the strengths Celia has that are different from the fearful and somewhat helpless character that she and her family seem to believe her to be. Together, they will draw on these exceptions to her storied understanding of herself and use them to help her to master the tricky nature of the worried stomach. Claudette believes that Celia is ready for phase two of narrative therapy: challenging patterns.

Claudette would like Celia to examine her time at school and search for exceptions to the times when she feels overwhelmed by anxiety. As a narrative therapist, Claudette believes that Celia is building a story in which she envisions herself almost like a cartoon character, embodying a single personality trait: anxiousness. She would like Celia to see that there are many aspects of her personality that she can draw upon. She decides to investigate with Celia the times when she is different, those times when she has been brave.

Celia sits cross-legged in the armchair across from Claudette, her shoes left behind beneath the coffee table, the Shiva figurine from Claudette's bookshelf in her lap; Celia is smiling broadly. "You look like the cat who just swallowed the canary," Claudette comments. "What are you up to?"

"I turned 8 on Saturday, and guess what? I walked here by myself! I told Mom that I knew I could do it and that I would be really careful about the cars. I'm not a baby."

"So how was it?" Claudette asks.

"I liked it. I felt brave like her." Celia holds up the Shiva figurine.

Claudette smiles to herself. It is easy to see why Celia might think Shiva is a woman, with his slender waist, the fire behind him that looks something like her mother's braids flying in the wind as he dances above the earth. "Celia, tell me about other times when you have felt brave like her," Claudette prompts, indicating the figurine. "Tell me about a time at school."

"Hmm, that's hard." Celia pauses thoughtfully. "Well, I felt brave on Monday. It was that dumb Simon. He is one of the big kids that is always making fun of me and pushing me around."

Claudette prompts, "What happened?"

"He pinched me right here," Celia replies, pointing to a dark bruise on her cinnamon-colored skin. "He said I should take a bath and then some of the dirt might come off," Celia says angrily. "I yelled at him and told him he better stop or I would tell Miss Blake."

"That was incredibly brave, Celia. You remind me of David in the story of David and Goliath! How did you find the courage to stand up to that big kid like that?" Claudette asks, leaning forward.

"I don't know, it just made me so mad for him to say that to me," Celia replies.

"Does that happen a lot at school?" Claudette probes.

"Mmhmm, especially with Simon. He pulls my hair, pinches me, and makes fun of my brown skin. I get a worried stomach just thinking about him," Celia explains, turning the Shiva in her hands. "Last year, my teacher wanted me to sit next to Simon on the bus all the way to the zoo! It was a field trip. I got so worried—" Celia pauses "—that I wet my pants. I had to go home, but I was glad."

"I guess your worried stomach kind of protected you from Simon that day," Claudette offers. "Maybe your worried stomach has been trying to tell everyone something that you haven't been ready to tell until now."

"You mean about Simon?" Celia asks.

"Maybe it was trying to tell us that sometimes you don't feel safe at school," Claudette offers.

Claudette has been able to help Celia identify times when she has been brave and has begun to help Celia begin work on phase three of their time together, re-authoring. She has helped Celia to reframe or redefine Celia's worried stomach from a *problem with her head* to a kind of warning system. Claudette hopes that Celia will begin to see herself as both brave and capable as they work together to identify her moments of strength and explore the results of her courage. Claudette also recognizes that Celia is experiencing some very real bullying and racism at school. As a social activist, Claudette would like to get Celia's permission to talk with her mother and to contact the school counselor to see what measures can be taken to stop the bullying and address the racism that seems to be fueling it.

In the following weeks, Claudette and Celia revisit different phases of their work together. Claudette helps Celia recognize the many different ways in which she has been able to stand up to others on her own behalf and on the behalf of some of the younger children on the playground, despite the worry she sometimes feels in the pit of her stomach. Celia has become proud of her ability to stand up to her brother Luke when he comes up with an idea that might get them hurt or in trouble—or both. As Celia begins to see herself in a new light, she finds herself more willing to take risks, which has reduced the arguments between her and Luke and generally changed the way the two of them talk to each other.

One afternoon, Celia announces, "I think today is going to be my last day. I guess I don't have very much trouble with worried stomach any more. Simon finally quit being such a jerk, and I am not scared of him anymore anyway." Claudette has been noticing the difference in Celia and is ready to approach the subject of termination as part of the fourth phase, moving on. Celia seems much more confident in herself and in her ability to advocate for herself, and has a new vision of herself that Claudette hopes she will use as the foundation for a lifelong story of empowerment and strengthened sense of self.

For You to Consider

1. How have the family stories influenced the way in which Celia initially made sense of her experience of anxiety?

2. Do you think that Celia's anxiety can be partly due to her temperament—something inherent in her that gives her a tendency to have an anxiety disorder? Can a belief in a "temperament" and an "anxiety disorder" fit into the view of human nature of a narrative therapist?

3. Do you think focusing on Celia's anxiety being "in her head," as Luke suggests, could have been helpful in any way? Why or why not?

4. Claudette uses a concrete avenue (coloring the silhouette) to help Celia find a name for her difficulty and externalize her problem. How might you have worked to externalize the anxiety if Celia were 3 or even 5 years older?

5. Claudette makes use of cultural stories to help Celia reframe her story of herself (David and Goliath, and Shiva). What other stories might Claudette have been able to draw upon to help Celia envision herself differently?

6. Do you think offering Celia some concrete ways of dealing with her anxiety (e.g., cognitive disputing, exercising, medication, etc.) could have been helpful?

7. Do you believe that Celia has conquered her anxiety? Why or why not?

8. In this vignette, Claudette decides to take on an advocacy role with Celia by talking with her mother and school counselor. Do you believe it was appropriate for Claudette to go outside of the relationship to help the change process? When do you think such advocacy roles are important for counselors and therapists?

9. How might you work with Jake, Angela, or Luke using a narrative approach? What benefit do you see in this approach for each?

10. Think about a pattern in your own life, a way of responding to difficulties that you would like to change. Can you think of exceptions or times that you responded differently and with better results? What do you think this means?

ANGELA'S EXPERIENCE WITH A SOLUTION-FOCUSED BRIEF THERAPIST

Angela reaches for her robe and slowly rolls out of bed. "Can't sleep?" Jake asks, only half-awake. Angela finds her slippers in the darkness of the early morning and slips down the hall. She checks on Luke and then on Celia, and then rechecks the front and back doors. This pattern has become a week's-long routine in which Angela wakes sometime close to 1:00 A.M. and often is not able to get back to sleep. Her exhaustion is starting to show; she is losing her focus at work and hasn't been painting. She's lost her temper with Jake and the kids often enough that her crankiness is more the rule than an exception.

By the time the workday has begun, Angela is exhausted. Picking up the phone, she knows she has to get some help if she is ever going to sleep well again. The phone rings a number of times, and Angela is about to hang up when she hears a voice at the other end of the line. "Hello, this is Lou Thomas."

"Hi." Angela is suddenly self-conscious. "Um, my name is Angela and I was calling to see if you could help me with a problem I've been having for about a month and a half." She paused and then finished in a single breath, "It started when I had gone to a dinner party with some friends of mine. It was a big party for a guy who was running for city council. Anyway, there were a lot of people there and I was mingling. Sometime during the party, someone stole my purse. Whoever it was got my wallet, my I.D., my phone with my calendar, the keys to my car and to the house ..." Angela can feel a wave of panic coming over her; tears begin to stream down her face.

"Angela, I'm really sorry to hear about that. I can't imagine how frightening that must have been for you," Lou says, responding to the anxiety in her voice.

"Well, that's why I'm calling. I know it's crazy, but I just don't feel safe. That creep is out there somewhere, and he knows where I live. He knows where I am supposed to be better than I do—after all, he has my calendar! I haven't been able to sleep, even though my husband has changed all the locks. I feel sick to my stomach just thinking about it," Angela explains. "I really think I need to see someone and get a grip on myself."

"I see," Lou begins. "If you like, I can meet with you on Thursday at 11:00 and we can talk together about a solution to this difficulty. You know, Angela, sometimes just making a call can be the start of some small but important improvements in a problem that seems overwhelming. I wonder if you would keep track of any improvements you notice between now and when we meet."

"Well, yes, I'll try," Angela agrees. "Thursday at 11:00; I'll see you then."

It seems like forever before Thursday comes, but here it is. Angela climbs the narrow steps to Lou's office. She feels herself wanting to look behind her, aware of this feeling of being followed, of being unsafe. She takes a deep breath and opens the door to Lou's office. She is surprised to see how tall Lou is; his voice had been so gentle and understanding, she hadn't expected him to be so imposing in his height. Lou's eyes are reassuring and warm as he invites her inside.

Angela begins to explain how difficult it has become for her to sleep or concentrate since her purse was stolen. She admits to Lou that she had been nervous leaving the house to come to her meeting with him. "I am at my wits' end! Part of me feels that this is just really silly. People get their purses stolen all the time, don't they? Jake and I have done everything we can to secure the house, so why am I still so afraid?"

Lou, a solution-focused therapist, wants to help Angela shift her focus from her problem and onto her resiliency and strength and how she will use these characteristics to find a solution to her fears. "Angela, I am frankly amazed that you have been able to continue to get to work and even to come to my office when you have been so frightened. How do you think you have been able to do that?"

"Gosh, I don't know. I guess I've just been pushing myself to get through the day for Jake and the kids. To tell you the truth, I just wish I could crawl in bed and never come out. I know that sounds extreme. It doesn't make sense even to me, but that is really how I feel."

"It sounds like part of what you've been able to do is to notice and acknowledge how afraid you have been, and yet at the same time, you've been able to reach inside and find a well of courage that you've drawn from to get out of bed and carry on. Where are you getting all this courage?"

"Well, it sounds a lot better when you say it; I feel like a coward." Angela smiles at Lou. "I don't know how I do that. I think I just realize that I don't want to live like a prisoner."

"Help me understand a little more clearly what it will look like when you are not living like a prisoner," Lou begins probing.

"I wouldn't be afraid all the time. I wouldn't be so worried that there was someone out there ready to hurt me or my family!" Angela replies.

"That makes a lot of sense. It sounds like you'll know our time together has been successful when you are feeling confident again about your safety. Angela, can you tell me about a time since your purse was stolen when you have *not* felt really terrified or very distracted?"

"Well, things actually improved a lot after Jake changed the locks on the house, and then they got a little better again when we contacted a person who specializes in identity theft and she worked with us to monitor our credit. But I think it is the unknown part that is still so frightening to me. You know, the idea that this guy is out there somewhere, and he could find me and hurt me or my family."

"If you were to think about the feelings that you have been experiencing, say on a scale from 0 to 10, where 0 is the most frightened that you can imagine being and 10 is a feeling of safety and comfort both at home and in the community, where would you say that you are right now?" Lou asks.

"Hmmm, well, that's a good question." Angela considers Lou's question. "There was a time once when I was more afraid than I am now, when I was a child and I was separated from my parents in an airport in Germany. I was afraid for weeks after that … I would say I'm at about a 4."

"I see; so you can remember being more frightened than you are now, and this feels more like a 4. If we were to make just one small step toward your goal, to, say, a 5 or 6, what would have to change?" Lou asks, now very curious about how Angela will begin to construct a solution.

"I think a 5 would be if I felt safe at home. I know I am safe there and feeling safe would be a step in the right direction." Angela considers a moment. "But to get there I think I need to trust myself—and Jake, too—that we have done everything we can to make sure the house is secure. That's all anybody can do."

Lou looks at his watch, surprised how quickly the time has passed. "Angela, as we are coming to a close, I have one last question: What changes have you noticed since you called to make your appointment?"

"Well, I did notice that last night I didn't wake up until 3:00; that was a welcome change. It has been exhausting waking up so early. This time, I just reached out and touched Jake instead of getting out of bed to check on the kids. It took a while, but I did get back to sleep."

"That sounds like a pretty important difference to me—you had said the sleeplessness was really getting to you. It sounds like you are already on your way to finding a solution to this problem," Lou points out.

Lou conceptualizes his counseling in seven stages: Stage 0, pre-session change; Stage 1, forming a collaborative relationship; Stage 2, describing the problem; Stage 3, establishing a preferred outcome; Stage 4, problem-to-solution focus; Stage 5, reaching a preferred outcome; and Stage 6, ending therapy. Lou believes therapy should be brief and that as soon as Angela is able to put effective strategies into action, they should be ready to end therapy.

Lou is happy with his first session with Angela. In Stage 0, after Angela's initial call, she was able to notice small but meaningful changes that helped her to enter their first session with a sense of hope in finding a solution to her feelings of fear and vulnerability. He has formed a solid collaborative relationship with Angela, and her resiliencies and strengths have been highlighted (Stage 1). Lou now understands the problem as Angela sees it (Stage 2), and has made use of a scaling technique in order to frame where she is now with her concern and where she hopes to be when she is ready to end therapy (Stage 3). On the whole, Lou feels that his first session with Angela has been a success. As he prepares for their second meeting, Lou hopes to help Angela begin to let go of her problem-saturated talk and to focus on solutions. Though this process is underway, Angela's thoughts still seem to drift to "problem thinking."

"This was a rough week; it seemed like some things were a little better, but still I felt upset and even a little depressed all week. I just decided to skip the farmers' market with the kids Saturday, and I could tell they were disappointed. Getting sweet kettle corn at Mr. Shank's stand is one of our favorite things to do on the weekend, but I just didn't want to be around all those people," Angela begins.

"Angela, I was thinking as you were talking—I wonder how things would be for you if this problem was no longer there?" Lou muses.

"That's a really interesting question!" Angela says, looking Lou in the eye for the first time in that session.

"How about you imagine this? You can close your eyes to help you imagine, if you wish. The evening winds down, pretty much the same way it does every other evening; you climb into bed and eventually drop off to sleep. But as you are sleeping, a miracle happens. Somehow, your problem is just lifted from you and it is completely gone. As you wake up in the morning, you have a sense that something has changed. All the familiar feelings of dread and fear are simply gone." Lou's voice is soft and calming, giving Angela a chance to become involved in the image. "Angela, what is the first thing you notice is different as you are waking up?"

"The first thing I would notice is that I would have slept past the sunrise. Maybe Jake would already be up making coffee and I would have the whole bed to myself."

Lou prompts, "What would you notice next?"

"I would get out of bed and feel relaxed. I wouldn't be racing to the kids' rooms to check on them; instead, I would go take a long shower and then join Jake for coffee," Angela replies.

"It sounds like you would be taking more time for yourself, especially on the basic kinds of self-care stuff," Lou offers.

"Yeah, I think so. The next thing I would do differently is that I would go out on the patio next to the garden and read the paper. I haven't felt comfortable being out there in the open like that, but if this problem were gone, I could enjoy the patio and the garden again; it is one of my favorite places," Angela explains. "I'm realizing that this fear isn't so much about scary, difficult things like panic attacks—Jake struggles with those now and again—for me, it is more the loss of all the little things that added up to be the pleasures of my life. I feel like those have been taken from me."

"So, put like that, is there one small step that you could take tomorrow morning to begin to take back some of the pleasure in your life?" Lou asks.

"Well, I guess I could do some of those things I enjoy even when I feel anxious or blue; at least I would have that back," Angela says.

As Lou begins to write his session notes, he reflects on Angela's gradual shift from problem-saturated talk to a focus on solutions. He is encouraged that she is able to come up with small steps that have the potential to really turn things around for her, which is essential if she is going to make the transition from Stage 4, problem-to-solution focus, into Stage 5, reaching a preferred outcome.

At the opening of their third session, Lou notices that Angela seems to have something she wants to tell him. "I've been so distracted lately, I had forgotten my birthday was coming. After I left your office, I went home and found the kids had packages for me on the hearth and Jake had made me a cake—it looked like a train wreck, but it was delicious. We had such a nice afternoon I just kind of forgot about my purse and that whole mess." Angela seems to be enjoying telling Lou about her surprise party; Lou hasn't ever seen her so animated. "The big surprise was that Jake had gotten tickets for a concert at the local stadium. I didn't think we would be able to go—I thought it would just be too expensive. Anyway, I don't want to tell you how much I wanted to get out of that. When we heard about the concert four or five months ago, I was really excited about it, but when Jake showed me the tickets, I thought I was going to be sick—the thought of all those people … But when I looked at Jake, I knew I couldn't tell him."

"Wow, you were in between a rock and a hard place; what did you decide to do?" Lou asks.

"While I was getting ready, I kept thinking about how I didn't want to go, and then I remembered that idea I had last week—that maybe I could just enjoy some things for me. I wasn't sure exactly how I was supposed to do that—enjoy something I was afraid of—but it dawned on me that I didn't want that guy to take my birthday present from us, too. I got it in my head that I was going to have fun, and that was that!'

"And how was it?" Lou prompts.

"It was a lot of fun. I was so exhausted I slept through the night and past dawn, just as if there really was a miracle."

"I imagine it does feel like a miracle, but it seems to me that your own efforts made the evening what it was. You really paid attention to how you were feeling and the thoughts going through your head. Somehow, you settled on the idea that you were going to take back your birthday and enjoy this time with your husband and put the theft behind you. I really applaud you," Lou points out.

"Well, I guess you are right about that. You know, I have felt almost like my old self again. It really is such a relief." Angela beams.

Angela and Lou are reaching the end of her therapy, Stage 6. Angela is beginning to implement the solutions she has developed with Lou, and she is finding her difficulties have been easier to overcome than she had expected. Her therapy has been very brief, only three sessions, helped along by the fact that her fears were spurred by a specific event and not a longstanding pattern of anxiety. Lou believes that solution-focused therapy was a good choice for Angela. Not only did she find a solution to a problem that was beginning to become entrenched, she also learned a strategy for looking for solutions on her own. She also gained confidence in her ability to solve problems, even those that seem irrational or overwhelming.

For You to Consider

1. In what ways do you think Angela's anxiety and Jake's anxiety were different? How were they similar? Do you think Jake would have responded as well to solution-focused therapy as Angela seems to have?

2. Angela's therapy was very brief. How comfortable are you with the brevity of her therapy? Why?

3. In this case, do you believe that brief therapy will have long-lasting effects?

4. Do you think that there are instances when brief therapy will not have long-lasting effects? Explain.

5. Lou used a scaling technique and asked Angela to scale her feelings of fear. Can you think of anything else Lou could have chosen to scale that might have been as effective for Angela?

6. Can you come up with other ways in which Angela could have made herself feel safer?

7. Do you think a solution-focused therapist should offer other ways for a person to feel safe? For instance, what if Lou suggested that Angela bought some pepper spray, or learned to use a handgun and carried one around with her? Is it the place of the solution-focused therapist to make such suggestions?

8. Do you think it would be legitimate if a therapist, who was not solution-focused, spent months examining deep-rooted reasons (e.g., a person's not feeling safe due to lack of attachment to parents early in life) as to why Angela may be "holding on" to her anxiety about the stealing of her purse?

9. Sometimes clients are uncomfortable with the miracle question and are reluctant to use their imaginations in session. What other tools did Lou have at his disposal had Angela not responded to the miracle question?

10. Can you think of a problem in your life that you would like to be rid of? How would you use scaling to build a solution of your own? How about the miracle question?

THE MILLERS IN STRUCTURAL FAMILY THERAPY

Individual counseling seems to have helped the Millers. Jake has gained some mastery over his anxiety and found a new interest in working for child safety, and he is beginning to get excited about the shift in his work to this area. Angela has begun to use her artistic talents in a way that is meaningful for her and is learning more about herself in the process. Luke seems to be thriving at school; his behavior problems are few and far between—pretty typical, actually, for his age. And Celia has made friends in her classroom and seems to have a newfound confidence to accompany her cautious approach to the world. However, the past few months have been eventful ones for the Millers. Recently, the family was excited to find that Angela was expecting a baby. Initially, the family greeted the news as a sign of new beginnings, a new life to go with the growth each of them had experienced. Then, things seem to slide downhill.

Unfortunately, Angela's pregnancy isn't going smoothly. She has developed dangerously high blood pressure and is eventually diagnosed with preeclampsia. Her obstetrician insisted that she stay in bed for the remaining 3 months of her pregnancy. With Jake's additional work and projects that seemed to need additional attention, he and Angela decided to ask Jake's mother to help with Luke and Celia. Ann moved in two and a half months ago, and while initially things seemed to be going well, Jake and Angela are bickering again, and Luke has become downright ornery. Celia seems to be holding her own for the time being. The family's old patterns seem to have found their way back into their lives. Individual counseling has worked for each of the Millers, and when a friend mentioned she had seen a family counselor, Danni Finch, the Millers thought they would give her a call.

Jake's mother, Ann, sits, looking sullen, on the far side of the long, sleek leather couch in Danni's sun-filled office. Celia sits close to her grandmother, resting her head on Ann's shoulder. Next to Celia, Luke has his arms crossed and looks like he might slide off the couch, and his father is making an attempt to get him to sit up. "Oh, for heaven's sake, Jake," Ann snaps, "why don't you let him be? He doesn't want to be here anymore than the rest of us do!"

Angela, wedged between Luke and Jake, looking uncomfortable and tired, leans forward to make eye contact with Ann. "Ann, we are all making an effort to be here because it is important—Luke, *please sit up*—so can we just give this a try?"

"Angela, you were told to stay in bed, are you sure you need to be dragging yourself all the way to the other side of town to talk with a stranger about your parenting problems?" Ann snaps back.

Angela makes eye contact with Danni and Jake and then rubs her temples. "Luke, honestly, sit up!"

Jake interrupts, "Either sit up, or sit in the car until we are done!"

Celia, interested now, leans forward, saying, "Daddy, you said we couldn't be in the car without an adult. Is Grammy going to the car with Luke? If Grammy and Luke sit in the car, I want to go, too!" Angela leans back into the couch, looking defeated.

Danni sits listening to the family reenact the patterns that she believes are getting in the way at home. As a strategic family therapist, Danni believes that families begin to have difficulties when appropriate boundaries between family subsystems are breached. As she had hoped, her first session with the family is beginning to reveal some of the boundary concerns in the family. As the session continues, Danni begins to mentally map out the boundaries in the Miller family. In this session, of course, there are three generations represented. Ann, Jake's mother, who sometimes takes on a parenting role; the parent and spousal systems comprised of Jake and Angela; and the sibling system comprised of Luke and his younger sister Celia. From what Danni can tell, Ann seems to have crossed the parental boundary by allying with her grandchildren against Angela and Jake, going as far as to contradict Jake's attempts to discipline Luke and all but blaming the tensions in the family on Angela and her "parenting problems." Ann's actions seem to be amplifying boundary problems. Luke's actions, meanwhile, seem to draw attention away from adult conflict. Jake's threat to send Luke to the car diverts attention away from spousal issues and onto something that feels safer.

Danni is interested to know what it is that the adults in the house see as the problem, and once the family is settled in, Danni puts that question to Ann. "Well, it's about time somebody asked me about something—after all, I raised two adult children. I think I know what I am doing," Ann replies. "Part of the problem is that Jake is just too hard on the children. He doesn't seem to understand that children are *children*, and if you just let them be, they will grow up just fine. He seems to think he has to get in the middle of everything they do." Ann takes a deep breath and glances at Angela. "I don't blame her for not really knowing how to raise children—after all, she isn't really *American*. I mean, not 100 percent, and so I don't know how she is supposed to know how to raise children here."

Danni looks at Ann and says, "So, as you see it, Jake's parenting stresses a lot more oversight than what you think is needed. But, I'm afraid I'm a little lost, though—you said that Angela is not really American. What did you mean?" Danni asks, looking from one family member to another and gauging their reactions.

"She means that Angela's father is Nigerian and her mother is American," Jake interrupts, and turning to Ann, continues, "We've been over this, Mom, Angela is just as American as you are. She was born here and she is a citizen just like you."

Danni, turning to Ann, asks, "Is that what you meant, Ann? Instead of telling me, why don't you go ahead and talk directly to Jake and Angela?"

"Well, actually, Jake, that *isn't* what I meant." Ann pauses before continuing. "Angela, didn't you spend a lot of your childhood in Nigeria? I think you've got your ideas about how to run a proper household all mixed up with whatever it is that they do in Africa."

"Let me see if I understand this," Danni reflects to Ann. "There are some differences in how you would approach Celia and Luke and the way that Angela handles situations, and you feel like those differences are cultural, but at the same time you aren't really sure what cultural beliefs Angela might have about parenting or how they might complement the beliefs she has from her life in America. Angela, what do you think—"

"I don't think it helps any that Mom doesn't seem to trust Angela's parenting," Jake interrupts suddenly. "This stuff about Angela not really being American is just crazy talk; it always gets me mad, but it sends Angela through the roof and we end up having a fight about it. She expects me to be able to do something to change Mom, but you are a counselor, so you and I both know you can't change other people. Besides, she's my mother; I get a little tired of hearing a litany of complaints about her the minute we are alone."

"I'm not really asking you to do anything, Jake," Angela responds. "All I really want is for you to listen; have a little empathy! I'm home with her alone all day while the kids are in school and you are at work." Angela's voice rises and softens again as she looks over at Ann's crestfallen expression. "Ann, I'm sorry, but I feel like you are constantly criticizing me. It isn't really fair, and it is hard to listen to for hours on end."

Almost out of nowhere, Luke leans over and delivers a stinging slap to his wide-eyed younger sister. "Dad!" Celia yelps, "Luke hit me!"

"It seems that when there is a chance that there might be some serious disagreement, the conversation is somehow interrupted by someone in the family," Danni offers directly. "It's almost as if you have a rule: *no disagreement allowed.*"

As Danni sits down with her session notes at the close of the first session, she first notes that the Miller family stress could be described as transitional, as they prepare to add a new life and personality to their nuclear family, as well as idiosyncratic, in that Angela's unexpected illness has shifted the normal family routines and has made it necessary to ask for help to support the family until the baby is born. Additionally, Danni notes that Ann's lack of understanding about Angela's ethnic background has introduced some hurt and tension between Jake and Angela. Danni notes that Jake has a tendency to interrupt and speak for both his mother and his wife, though given the chance, both women seem willing to speak for themselves. Jake also makes attempts to get Danni to side with him (triangulation) against Angela and her venting about her mother-in-law. Also important, Danni notes that Luke plays a pivotal role in ensuring that conflict between the adults does not escalate by drawing attention to himself. The Millers seem to have an idiosyncratic rule that conflict between adults is not allowed. Jake's interrupting (which is allowed by Angela and Ann) and Luke's acting out seem to serve the function of putting a lid on conflict before it can be fully understood or resolved.

Ann's use of the word "stranger" to describe Danni and the counseling session tells Danni that she will have to give special attention to how she joins with the family. It will be important to gain the family's confidence if she is going to be able to help them to restructure their counterproductive dynamics. She considers her own biases and how important it will be to avoid siding with Angela, allowing herself to become triangulated in the conflict between Jake and Angela, or unwittingly colluding with Ann to treat Angela as an incompetent or as a child.

As session two opens, Danni hopes to accomplish two primary goals: the first to successfully complete the joining process by cementing her relationship with the family, and the second to help the adults in the family realign themselves in a healthy and supportive hierarchical structure. Danni also hopes that by opening the conversation in a nonthreatening way, she might be able to help Ann let go of some of her misconceptions about Angela's heritage by emphasizing goals that the two share in parenting. Danni realizes that she knows little about Nigeria and even less about Nigerian parenting practices, and decides to consult with her supervisor about where she might get some good information.

As session two begins, Danni asks a question that she hopes will bring the family together to focus on a single goal and will give Jake and Angela an opportunity to take the lead. Danni will work to help shape and restructure the family boundaries. "Last week, when we met for the first time, we talked together about some of the challenges that had emerged for each of you since starting the transition to welcoming a new baby into the family. I thought today we could start by talking together about your goals for the family. I wondered if you would start, Jake," Danni prompts.

"I think the first thing that needs to happen is that the kids need to get back to where they were about four or five months ago. Celia and Luke were doing great at school and they were really pretty good about not fighting with each other. And I think Mom and Angela need to come to some kind of understanding about how to handle the kids while I am at work. At least I think so; what do you think, Angela?"

"Well, Jake, I think it would be helpful if we *all* got on the same page about the kids, not just when you are at work, but all day. You make it sound like your mom and I are at the bottom of all the conflict and chaos, but you are part of this, too. Remember when we were here last week and you threatened to send Luke to the car? I thought we agreed not to send Luke out of the room when he gets angry. That seemed to be working," Angela says, her expression revealing her frustration.

"Ann, you look like you want to say something," Danni prompts, noticing that Ann seems irritated.

"For once, I think I agree with Angela. Good grief, Jake. You act like you are going to ride in here on a white horse and straighten us out. I've kinda been thinking the same way Angela does about Luke. It's not really such a big disaster if he gets mad, is it?"

"It seems like the divide that you imagined between your grandparenting style and Angela's parenting style might not be as wide as you imagined, Ann," Danni offers. Danni is beginning to reshape some of the alliances between family members that are undermining important structure and boundaries. By helping Ann and Angela find common ground, Danni begins to disrupt the counterproductive pattern in which Angela expects Jake to remedy her frustration with Ann. She has also planted the notion that Angela and Ann may share key ideas in how to raise the children, lessening the divide Ann has been imagining. She has also been careful to frame Ann's role as "grandparenting," something she hopes they can talk more about in their next session. Finally, before this session ends, she decides to give one task to Angela and Ann. She looks at them both and says, "I was wondering if you can do something for me before our next session." The two of them nod in agreement. "Can you two sit down? Angela, can you share with Ann what it was like spending some time in Nigeria as a child? Also, can you tell Ann what the parenting style you grew up with was like? Then, can the two of you make a list of things you both like about the parenting styles that each of you experienced growing up?"

"Sure," they say simultaneously. Danni is hoping that this will do a number of things, including build a stronger bond between the two of them, diffuse the "Nigerian issue," and find some common parenting ground.

Danni believes that the Millers have the basic structural strength for restoring peace to their family, but she believes there is more to do before Jake and Angela are working closely as a parenting unit and communicating well with Ann and the children. She also has lingering concerns about Ann's negative attitude toward Angela's heritage. Ideally, Ann will come to better understand and appreciate Angela and her family's culture; at the minimum, however, Danni would like to help the family establish new and more positive ways of including this part of what is not only Angela's heritage, but the children's, too.

For You to Consider

1. Joining is a technique in which the family therapist works to align herself with the family. What opportunities do you see for joining with the Millers and creating a strong therapeutic alliance?

2. Given all that you have read about the Millers, how would you describe the Miller family's boundaries with the community? And with each other?

3. Soon after meeting with the Miller family, Danni sees that they have a rule against direct conflict. Can you identify another of the Miller family rules? Do you feel this rule is productive for the family? Why or why not?

4. Ann's perceptions of Angela as not fully American and somehow "backward" causes tension among the adults in the family. What effect might Ann's attitudes have on Celia and Luke? How might you address this concern with the family?

5. Relative to the Millers, what do you believe Danni needs to know about Angela's unique experiences in Nigeria? How comfortable are you with working with families with cultural backgrounds different from your own?

6. Sometimes, family counselors can find themselves siding with a single family member or with family members against a single member (triangulation). Is such siding always harmful? Can you think of any time when it might be helpful?

7. Sometimes, our own issues result in liking one or more family members more than others. How might this affect the role of the therapist? What should the therapist do to assure that he or she is working effectively despite these feelings?

8. In session one, Ann criticizes Jake's tendency to "get in the middle of everything" the children do, and suggests he should "just let them be." Jake is protective of the kids and feels strongly about careful oversight of the kids. What unresolved conflict might be behind Jake and Ann's tension on this aspect of parenting?

9. As a budding family therapist, is your inclination to avoid any unresolved conflict between Jake and Ann for now or to explore it? Should you decide to explore this issue, what would be your goal? How might you approach it?

10. Using what you know about structural family therapy and what you know about the Millers, construct a structural map of the family.

Index